'TERRIERS' IN INDIA

War and Military Culture in South Asia, 1757–1947

www.helion.co.uk/warandmilitarycultureinsouthasia

Series Editors
Professor Emeritus Raymond Callahan, University of Delaware
Alan Jeffreys, Imperial War Museum
Professor Daniel Marston, Australian National University

Editorial Advisory Board
Squadron Leader (Retired) Rana Chhina, Centre of Armed Forces Historical Research, United Service Institution of India
Dr Anirudh Deshpande, University of Delhi
Professor Ashley Jackson, King's College London
Dr Robert Johnson, Oxford University
Lieutenant Commander Dr Kalesh Mohanan, Naval History Division, Ministry of Defence, India
Dr Tim Moreman
George Morton-Jack
Dr David Omissi, University of Hull
Professor Peter Stanley, University of New South Wales, Canberra
Dr Erica Wald, Goldsmiths, University of London

Submissions
The publishers would be pleased to receive submissions for this series. Please contact us via email (info@helion.co.uk), or in writing to Helion & Company Limited, Unit 8 Amherst Business Centre, Budbrooke Road, Warwick, CV34 5WE

Titles

No 1 *'Swords Trembling In Their Scabbards'. The Changing Status of Indian Officers in the Indian Army 1757–1947* Michael Creese (ISBN 978-1-909982-81-9)

No 2 *'Discipline, System and Style'. The Sixteenth Lancers and British Soldiering in India 1822-1846* John H. Rumsby (ISBN 978-1-909982-91-8)

No 3 *Die in Battle, Do not Despair. The Indians on Gallipoli, 1915* Peter Stanley (ISBN 978-1-910294-67-3)

No 4 *Brave as a Lion. The Life and Times of Field Marshal Hugh Gough, 1st Viscount Gough* Christopher Brice (ISBN 978-1-910294-61-1)

No 5 *Approach to Battle. Training the Indian Army during the Second World War* Alan Jeffreys (ISBN 978-1-911096-51-1)

No 6 *The Indian Army in The First World War: New Perspectives* Edited by Alan Jeffreys (ISBN 978-1-911512-78-3)

No 7 *War without Pity in the South Indian Peninsula 1798–1813: The Letter Book of Lieutenant-Colonel Valentine Blacker* Edited and with introductory notes by David Howell (ISBN 978-1-912390-86-1)

No 8 *Of Islands, Ports and Sea Lanes: Africa and the Indian Ocean in the Second World War* Ashley Jackson (ISBN 978-1-912390-74-8)

No 9 *Ceylon at War 1939-45* Ashley Jackson (ISBN 978-1-912390-65-6)

No 10 *For The Honour of My House: The Contribution of the Indian Princely States to the First World War* Tony McClenaghan (ISBN 978-1-912390-87-8)

No 11 *'Terriers in India: British Territorials, 1914–1919* Peter Stanley (ISBN 978-1-912390-82-3)

'Terriers' in India

British Territorials, 1914-19

War and Military Culture in South Asia, 1757–1947 No. 11

Peter Stanley

> – a year he was to India's plains assigned
> Nor heard the spite of rifles, nor the rage
> Of guns; yet pondered oft on what the mind
> Experiences in war …
>
> 'LP' [Laura Palmer]
> *Letters from Mesopotamia*

Helion & Company

Helion & Company Limited
Unit 8 Amherst Business Centre
Budbrooke Road
Warwick
CV34 5WE
England
Tel. 01926 499 619
Email: info@helion.co.uk
Website: www.helion.co.uk
Twitter: @helionbooks
Visit our blog http://blog.helion.co.uk/

Published by Helion & Company 2019. Reprinted in paperback 2022
Designed and typeset by Mach 3 Solutions Ltd (www.mach3solutions.co.uk)
Cover designed by Paul Hewitt, Battlefield Design (www.battlefield-design.co.uk)

Text © Peter Stanley 2018
Images © as individually credited
Maps drawn by George Anderson © Helion & Company 2018

Every reasonable effort has been made to trace copyright holders and to obtain their permission for the use of copyright material. The author and publisher apologize for any errors or omissions in this work, and would be grateful if notified of any corrections that should be incorporated in future reprints or editions of this book.

ISBN 978-1-804510-51-3

British Library Cataloguing-in-Publication Data.
A catalogue record for this book is available from the British Library.

All rights reserved. No part of this publication may be reproduced, stored in a retrieval system, or transmitted, in any form, or by any means, electronic, mechanical, photocopying, recording or otherwise, without the express written consent of Helion & Company Limited.

For details of other military history titles published by Helion & Company Limited contact the above address, or visit our website: http://www.helion.co.uk.

We always welcome receiving book proposals from prospective authors.

Contents

List of Photographs		vi
List of Maps		ix
Series Editor's Preface		x
Acknowledgments		xii
Prologue		xv
Introduction: 'Without anything very special to chronicle'		xvii
Notes		xx
1	Imperial Service	25
2	Passages to India	45
3	A Soldier's Life in India, 1915	57
4	Kitchener's Test	70
5	Encountering India	89
6	Terriers abroad	107
7	Body, mind and soul	117
8	Defeat in Aden; disaster in Mesopotamia	134
9	A Soldier's Life in India, 1916	150
10	Terriers and Indians	168
11	Terriers and Britons	181
12	Stalemate in Aden; victory in Mesopotamia	196
13	A Soldier's Life in India, 1917	207
14	Internal security	225
15	Terriers on the Frontier	238
16	Beyond Mesopotamia, 1918-19	253
17	Armistice, 'flu and Siberia	266
18	Demobilisation and Amritsar, 1919	277
19	War with Afghanistan and repatriation	295
20	Territorials after India	305
Epilogue		322
Appendices		
I	Territorial units in India, 1914-19	326
II	Glossary	329
Bibliography		331
Index		350

List of Photographs

Joe Cox as a sergeant of the 1/5th West Surrey in his room in India, probably in Lucknow in 1915. (Surrey History Centre) — xv

Tent-mates belonging to No. 4 Section, C Company of the 6th East Surrey Regiment during the battalion's annual camp, 1910. (Surrey Heritage Centre) — 27

Territorial units included many brothers and even some fathers and sons. (Rifles Berkshire and Wiltshire Museum) — 31

A group of signallers of the 4th Wilts at ease in camp at Bovington in the opening weeks of the war. (Rifles Berkshire and Wiltshire Museum) — 35

Territorials of the East Surrey Regiment leaving Canterbury in October 1914 (Surrey History Centre) — 46

A scene on the dockside at Bombay when the 2/4th Wilts arrived in January 1915. (Rifles Berkshire and Wiltshire Museum) — 50

The 1/6th Hants marching into Dinapore cantonment soon after their arrival in India. (Royal Hampshire Regiment Museum) — 53

A dhobi-wallah pounding clothes, an image appearing in many Territorials' albums. (Maidstone Museum) — 61

A Kent Territorial is about to step into a fruit stall to buy bananas. (Maidstone Museum). — 64

A page of Alan Swift's diary showing the precautions taken to secure rifles against 'loosewallahs', and a five-rupee note. (Surrey History Centre) — 67

East Surrey Territorials undergoing Kitchener's Test, in a trench near Fyzabad, March 1915. (Surrey History Centre) — 71

Kitchener's Test, as depicted by 'X.Y.Z.' in the popular annual *Indian Ink*, 1915. — 73

The posterior belongs to Private Allen of the Middlesex Regiment, one of hundreds of Territorials detached as drivers. (*The Raiders of the Sarhad*) — 76

A 'punkah boy' pulling a rope to fan the air within a bungalow. (Surrey History Centre) — 81

Somerset Territorials and a Hindu fakir at Benares. (Somerset Heritage Centre) — 91

'The Morning Prayer', an artistic rendering of a scene at the Golden Temple, Amritsar. (Surrey History Centre) — 94

A cartoon published in *Indian Ink* that played on the Territorials' growing grasp of Hindustani. — 98

List of Photographs   vii

Wilts Territorials display the bodies of animals they have shot on 'shikar'. (Rifles Berkshire and Wiltshire Museum)	102
Hants men in a train in which they travelled 2500 miles across India. (Royal Hampshire Regiment Museum)	104
A platoon of the 1/4th Border Regiment parading at the Ottoman prisoner-of-war camp at Thayetmyo in Burma. (Cumbria's Museum of Military Life)	109
Aberdeen settlement in the Andaman Islands. (Somerset Heritage Centre)	114
Four East Surrey sergeants playing tennis. (Maidstone Museum)	119
Some of Arthur Bell's drawings. (Surrey History Centre)	124
The 1/7th Hants 'Costume Concert Party'. (Royal Hampshire Regiment Museum)	128
The Arab town of Lahej. (Imperial War Museum)	136
Esme Bowker on the way to India. (Royal Hampshire Regiment Museum)	138
Territorial volunteers of a reinforcement draft arriving in Basra in 1915. (Australian War Memorial)	140
Company officers of the 2/5th Hants training at Chasma Tangi camp, Baluchistan. (Royal Hampshire Regiment Museum)	151
Percy Wilkinson and his mates. (Royal Hampshire Regiment Museum)	154
Arthur Copeland's exasperated drawing, showing the exact arrangement of hose-top and puttee. (Hampshire Record Office)	160
'T, for the Tommy', exposing the Territorials' initial ignorance of the Indian Army. (*The Indian Army A.B.C.*)	173
The battalion orderly room staff of the 1/4th Cornwall. (Cornwall's Regimental Museum)	176
Men of the 1/1st Kent Battalion in the sudder bazaar at Dalhousie. (Maidstone Museum)	179
East Surrey Territorials and North Staffordshire Regulars at Murree. (Surrey History Centre)	187
East Surrey men in a punkah-festooned bungalow displaying embroidery and crocheting skills they had learned from Regulars. (Surrey History Centre)	189
'Greetings from Mhow', a postcard sent by 'Jack' to his mother in Wales. (Regimental Museum of the Royal Welsh)	193
Territorial gunners of the 2/1st Devon Battery at Aden. (Imperial War Museum)	198
East Surrey skirmishers seeking cover from Ottoman snipers in the front line at Aden. (Surrey History Centre)	199
Men of the 1/4th Hants rehearsing for the crossing of the Tigris at the Shumran Bend in February 1917. (Imperial War Museum)	202
A group of East Surrey men taking a break in a train journey. (Surrey History Centre)	208
A barrack room of the 1/1st Kent Battalion. (Maidstone Museum)	215
The funeral of a Brecknock Territorial at Mhow. (Regimental Museum of the Royal Welsh)	221
East Surrey troops making a 'flag march' through Fyzabad in 1915. (Surrey History Centre)	227

A 'mobile column' on parade at Malappuram in 1915. (Somerset Heritage Centre)	229
A newly-arrived private fails to grasp the importance of his colonel. (*Indian Ink*)	235
Badges of British regiments that had served on the frontier. (Surrey History Centre)	239
'Looking towards the frontier', from Fred Wignall's album. (Cumbria's Museum of Military Life)	241
Men of the 1/1st Kent Battalion on active service on the frontier. (Maidstone Museum)	245
The 'Joys of the Waziristan Stunt' depicted in the battalion magazine of the 2/6th Royal Sussex. (*Royal Sussex Herald*)	247
Two men, probably of the 2/4th Somerset, ticking off another of the wonders of the world before beginning the arduous campaign in Palestine. (Somerset Heritage Centre)	255
Survivors of the Western Front, a party of the 2/4th Somerset Light Infantry march with the battalion colours through Bath in June 1919. (Somerset Heritage Centre)	258
A column of Ford cars. (Australian War Memorial)	263
Men of the 1/1st Kent in 1918. (Maidstone Museum)	267
The 1/9th Hants leaving Vladivostok for Omsk, 1918, dressed in Canadian fur hats against the Siberian cold. (Royal Hampshire Regiment Museum)	275
Ridgewell's final cartoon in *Indian Ink* offers a rueful comment on the Territorials' state of mind as they impatiently awaited repatriation in 1919.	279
A British soldier stands by while a sepoy or policemen flogs an Indian civilian, an image published by Benjamin Horniman. (*Amritsar and Our Duty to India*)	287
A section of the 2/4th Border Regiment on active service on the Baluchistan frontier during the third Anglo-Afghan war of 1919. (Cumbria's Museum of Military Life)	296
Lorries entering the Khyber Pass, showing how by 1919 motor transport was supplanting the camel caravans. (Cumbria's Museum of Military Life)	297
A platoon of the 2/4th Border Regiment photographed in a blockhouse on the Mohmand Blockhouse Line. (Cumbria's Museum of Military Life)	303
Family members greet a man of the 1/9th Hants on the battalion's return to Portsmouth on 5 December 1919 after its three-year absence. (Royal Hampshire Regiment Museum)	308
Mrs Fanny Say laying flowers at Trowbridge's new war memorial in memory of her son John. (Rifles Berkshire and Wiltshire Museum)	309
Ridgewell anticipates one of the difficulties returning Territorials might face. (*Indian Ink*)	314
Joe Cox towards the end of his life.	324

List of Maps

1	The 'Indian' Territorials' counties and towns	a
2	British India 1914	b
3	India: Army Commands and Divisional Areas	c
4	Agra Cantonment	d
5	Mesopotamia	e
6	Aden	f
7	Asia	g
8	The North-West Frontier	h

War and Military Culture in South Asia, 1757–1947
Series Editor's Preface

The aim of this academic historical series is to produce well-researched monographs on the wars and armed forces of South Asia, concentrating mainly on the East India Company and the Indian armed forces from 1757 until 1947. Books in the series will examine the military history of the period as well as social, cultural, political and economic factors, although inevitably the armies of the East India Company and the Indian Army will dominate the series. In addition, edited volumes of conference papers, memoirs and campaign histories will also be published. It is hoped this series will be of interest to both serious historians and the general military history reader.

The resurgence of interest in the history of warfare in South Asia has been very apparent in the growing historiography of the colonial period, particularly in the era of the World Wars. For example in the field of Second World War studies and the period until Partition, Daniel Marston and Tim Moreman have spearheaded this historical research with their volumes: the prize-winning *Phoenix from the Ashes: The Indian Army in the Burma Campaign* (2003), *The Indian Army and the End of the Raj* (2014) and *The Jungle, the Japanese and the Commonwealth Armies at War* (2005) respectively. These are complemented by Raymond Callahan's *Churchill and His Generals* (2007), a seminal work published in the United States that deserves better attention in the United Kingdom, and Steven Wilkinson's *Army and Nation: The Military and Indian Democracy since Independence* (2015). In addition, are the important wider studies of Christopher Bayly and Tim Harper, *Forgotten Armies: The Fall of British Asia, 1941-1945* (2004) and Ashley Jackson on *The British Empire and the Second World War* (2006). The most recent publications include *Approach to Battle: Training the Indian Army during the Second World War* (2017) published in this series, as well as Tarak Barkawi's *Soldiers of Empire: Indian and British Armies in World War II* (2017) and Raymond Callahan's *Triumph at Imphal-Kohima: How the Indian Army Finally Stopped the Japanese Juggernaut* (2017). Furthermore the Indian home front has been covered in Yasmin Khan's social history of the period entitled *The Raj at War: A People's History of India's Second World War* (2015).

The aforementioned rise in interest has been mirrored in India as eight volumes of the official histories of the Indian Armed Forces during the Second World War were reprinted in India in 2012 and another four in 2014 (they were originally published between 1954 and 1960). As Squadron Leader Rana Chhina stated at the launch of the reprints: 'As a resurgent India seeks to be a major player on the world stage, it behoves it to discard its narrow post-colonial world view to step up to reclaim the role that its armed forces played out on a global scale' during the Second World War. This resurgence is amply demonstrated by the publication of Srinath

Raghavan's excellent overview *India's Wars : The Making of Modern South Asia* (2016), alongside the Kaushik Roy's *India and World II: War, Armed Forces, and Society, 1939-45* (2016) snd Anirudh Deshpande's *Hope and Despair: Mutiny, Rebellion and Death in India, 1946* (2016). However, even in this crowded arena, there is still much research and work to be published on both war and military culture in South Asia during the Second World War.

The series editors, members of the editorial advisory board and our publisher, Duncan Rogers of Helion, are all delighted to be involved in this series, most of the volumes of which are also being published in India under the Primus imprint. We hope it will be of interest in the UK, India but also globally.

Alan Jeffreys

Acknowledgments

Duncan Rogers, Helion's publisher, has been a steadfast and patient supporter of this venture, and I dedicate this book to him in recognition of his work through Helion in documenting and interpreting the history of the old Indian Army and of Britain's long relationship with India.

I am grateful to the Rector of UNSW Canberra, Prof. Michael Frater, whose Rector's Start-Up Award in 2015 enabled me to spend a month touring the regimental museums and county archives of southern England gathering the essential primary sources on which this book is based. I appreciate the support of successive Heads of the School of Humanities and Social Sciences at UNSW Canberra, Prof. David Lovell and Prof. Shirley Scott, while the School's Director of Research, Prof. Toni Erskine, who supported additional funds for a 2018 research trip to India. Many colleagues in the School of Humanities and Social Sciences at UNSW Canberra took an interest in my research.

I have drawn on the work of several research assistants. Jane Bryan-Brown worked in the British Library. Adil Rana Chhina tenaciously hunted down sources in New Delhi, as did Satarupa Lahiri in St James's, Delhi. Above all, Emily Gibbs worked, mostly voluntarily, for more than a year, reading her way through the massive quantity of Terriers' letters and diaries and alerting me to evidence which appears in these pages.

In Australia, librarians at several libraries, notably the National Library of Australia, Canberra, at the State Library of Victoria, Melbourne. I am grateful to the staff of the Australian Defence Force Academy Library, and especially to Hayward Maberley, who found both the first and the final inter-library loan sources I used. Tasmania-based Simon Parker Galbraith's website devoted to the 1/25th London http://www.25thlondon.com/ has been especially valuable.

In India, Squadron Leader Rana Chhina (Retd) of the United Service Institution of India has been a firm friend, while Dr Radhike Singha of JNU repeatedly provided suggestions for sources I would not otherwise have known of. I acknowledge the assistance of the staff of the National Archives of India, New Delhi, the National Library of India, Kolkata and the Library staff of the Connemara Library in Chennai, the libraries of the University of Mumbai and the University of Madras, Asiatic Society branches in Kolkata and Mumbai, in the latter especially Dr Maya Avisia, Ms Helna Korgaonkar and Mr Shankar Thombre. I am also grateful to Prof. Kaushik Roy and through him to Arka Choudhury, Moumita Choudhury, Priyanjana Gupta, and Satarupa Lahiri. At Bhowanipore Commonwealth War Graves Cemetery, Kolkata, I was assisted by Rajindraram; at the New Delhi cemetery by Ravi Singh, and at Ferozepore cantonment cemetery by Rohit William and Rev. Mahseh William. Dr Amit Pathak kindly accompanied me to the Meerut cantonment cemetery. I am grateful to Rev. Longjam Bipin Angomcha of Danapur cantonment for facilitating my visit to Danapur's

St Luke's Church and its cemeteries. I am especially grateful to Rachael and Abraham of the Ootacamund Club.

A number of relatives of Indian Territorials responded to appeals made in the British provincial newspapers in 2017. I acknowledge the assistance of Tony Ball, Fred Brown, George Chilcott, Jane Dendle, Karen Dunford, Clare Flanagan, Liz Hocking, John Husband, John Joliff, Mike Kipling, Keith Solomon and Colin South.

On several British research trips I depended on many librarians, archivists, curators and researchers: at the Maidstone Museum, Steve Finiss and Samantha Harris (where Christopher Jupp and Tony Miles generously shared their research into the 1/1st Kent); at the Kent History and Archives Centre (Maidstone): Debora Saunders; at the Surrey History Centre (Woking): Gillian Walsh, Rhona Elston, Miriam Farr, Margaret Griffiths, Laurence Spring and Jane Lewis; at the West Sussex Records Office (Chichester): Frances Lansley and Rhodri Lewis; at the Hampshire Record Office (Winchester): Caroline Edwards; at the Royal Hampshire Regiment Museum, (Winchester): Colin Bulleid and Rachael Holmes; at Cornwall's Regimental Museum (Bodmin): Hugo White and Verity Anthony; at the Keep Museum (Dorchester): Peter Turner, John Murphy and Helen Jones; at the Dorset History Centre, (Dorchester): Moira Priestley and Sarah Downton; at the National Army Museum (London and Stevenage), Sarah Hume, Ben Fellowes, Fiona Jenkins and Alastair Massie; at the Rifles Berkshire and Wiltshire Museum, Alistair Riggs; at the Shropshire Archives (Shrewsbury): Karen Young and Sarah Davis; at the Shropshire Regiment Museum (Shrewsbury): Christine Barnarth and John Taylor; at the Swindon and Wiltshire History Centre (Chippenham): Joy Bloomfield, Margaret Moles and Gill Neal; at Cumbria's Museum of Military Life (Carlisle): Stuart Eastwood and Matt Lund; at the Museum of the Royal Regiment of Wales (Brecon) Richard Davies and Sylvia Davies.

Ms Angela Fooks-Bale at Aginhills Farmhouse B&B, Taunton, kindly shared her family copy of the 5th Somerset Light Infantry's *Book of Remembrance*. I am grateful to John Ellis, whose book *Newton Abbott's Great War* was among the earliest sources I read. Ms Kate Holliday of the Kendal Local Studies Library, Kendal, Cumbria. Dr Jane Howells of the British Association for Local History, who kindly published an appeal in the Association's bulletin. In Singapore, Duckworth Chen of the National Library of Singapore, and in Hong Kong the staff of the Hong Kong Central Library were helpful. Prof. Mark Connelly, Director of Gateways to the First World War, promptly and generously provided a copy of his hard-to-find article on the British campaign in Aden. I also appreciated Prof. Ian Nish, CBE, responding to my appeal in *The Historian* to recall the experience of sleeping under a punkah in Napier Barracks, Lahore in the Second World War, and the help of Dr Peter Friedlander of ANU with Hindi translation.

The Rector and congregation of All Saints, Corston, and Gathorne Girdlestone and the extended Bartelt family extended a welcome to Ms Claudia Hyles, who attended the peal of bells and service marking the centenary of the dedication of the bells commemorating Captain Fritz Bartelt. I am also grateful to the Verger at All Saints, Fulham, which commemorates the 1/25th London and who generously showed me the memorials.

Participants at various conferences at which I discussed this project, notably the Myriad Faces of War conference sponsored by Massey University in Wellington, New Zealand, in April 2017, and the 'First World War: Indian Context' symposium held at St Aloysius College, Mangalore, Karnatika, in January 2018. At that conference I met Dr S. Narender Prasad of JSS College for Women (Autonomous), Saraswathipuram, Karnataka, who kindly provided entrée to Mysorean sources.

At Helion, I am hugely grateful to Kim McSweeney and George Anderson, who were responsive and patient in setting and designing the text and the maps respectively as well as Vicky Powell, who has been a great help throughout the preparation of this book. Helion's reputation for quality partly depends on their professionalism and creativity.

My most profound thanks are due to Claire, who has shared my interest in Territorials in churches and cemeteries in Britain and India. Notwithstanding all the assistance I have drawn on, responsibility for any errors is mine.

Prologue

In 1914 Joe Cox was working as a wheelwright in Alton, a few miles inside the Hampshire county border, the next village to Jane Austen's home at Chawton. Joe was unmarried, though he had a long-term understanding with Edie, in domestic service in one of the district's houses. Joe was a very social man. He was a member of the Church Army and the Ancient Order of Foresters, and a chorister and bell-ringer in his local parish church. And Joe was a member of a battalion of the Territorial Force, though living as he did on the doorstep of the next county it was more convenient for him to serve in the West Surrey rather than his own county's regiment. Joe had served in the Territorials since its formation in 1908, like many long-serving men transferring from the Volunteer units that had constituted Britain's force of citizen soldiers for the past sixty-odd years.

Though not having been formally apprenticed as a wheelwright, Joe was a skilful and experienced worker, proud of his ability to select, cut, shape and build in wood. He had made wheels for huge tree-cradles used to transport great oaks cut from Hampshire's forests, tiny wheels for dog-carts, and every kind of agricultural wagon or domestic carriage in between. He especially took pleasure in making and repairing the big farm carts drawn by strong shire horses that local farmers had used for decades. One of the last carts he repaired before he went off to the Territorials' annual summer camp in July 1914 was a farm cart first built exactly a century before, and Joe admired the craftsmanship of his forebears, doing his best work to refurbish and paint it so it could last for decades to come. Motor cars and tractors were still rare on Hampshire's dusty country lanes: few could anticipate the immense changes the war would herald, in the demise of farm wagons and much else in Joe Cox's world.

Recollections of the golden summer of 1914 – the last weeks of peace that Britain and Europe would enjoy – have become a familiar strain in memoirs and histories. Joe, writing *An Ordinary Working Man's Life Story* in hospital at Alton a

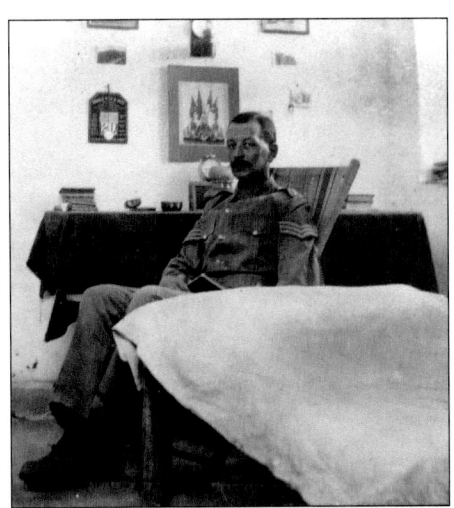

Joe Cox as a sergeant of the 1/5th West Surrey in his room in India, probably in Lucknow in 1915. While sharing a room with another sergeant, they enjoyed more space, privacy and servants than men in their barrack-rooms. (QRWS/30/CRAV/2, Surrey History Centre)

few months before his death in 1967, looked back nostalgically on those weeks as the European crisis made Britain's entry into the coming war increasingly likely. He remembered riding his bicycle to work along the lanes around Alton, several times stopping on the crests of familiar gentle rises, drawn to gaze out on the lovely sight of the fields and vales of Hampshire clothed in green and gold, recalling 'how beautiful the countryside was'. Reaching Alton, he went into a pub to buy a simple dinner of a pint of beer, a cob of bread and a lump of cheese – tuppence apiece. Joe remembered thinking about the peaceful rural scene he was a part of and feeling that 'the old country was worth fighting for' – the newspapers were already full of rumours of war. As it turned out, Joe was not to do much fighting, but the war would also take him far from the quiet lanes and green fields of Alton.

A literate, skilled country worker, 37 years-old, unmarried, an Anglican and a 'joiner', in two senses, Joe Cox embodied many of the Territorial soldiers who before the year was out would be serving the empire in India. Unlike the great majority of them, Joe recorded his memories of his Indian service. Thanks to his memoir, and the letters, diaries, reminiscences and photograph albums of dozens of other Territorials, men and officers, we can recapture their experience of India during the Great War, when a war of empires took them away from the villages and towns of southern England.

Introduction: 'Without anything very special to chronicle'

This book takes us back a century to an England barely out of memory: I knew people who grew up in this time; the period explored by Paul Thompson in his pioneering oral history *The Edwardians*. And yet it now seems impossibly remote, a world of long working days; horses in village streets; heavy manual labour and skillful craftsmanship; of seaside holidays, with whelks and pierrots; of music halls and silent cinemas, of suffragettes and trades unionists (and, indeed, Unionists), of things made to last of wood, metal and leather, of tuberculosis and blood-poisoning, of kippers and fish-and-chip suppers, of charabancs, trams and steam trains; of a time when Britain had an empire, and a navy, both the world's largest.

The Great War profoundly changed life in Britain and Europe and in some ways the world. It broke empires (and enlarged others, including Britain's) and created new nations. It brought suffering and grief to millions. The war gave many caught up in it experiences they could never have anticipated in August 1914. It took millions of people across the world – citizen soldiers from distant colonies and dominions to fight in Europe, Africa and the Middle East; men from China, Indo-China, India and Africa to serve as labourers; and it created refugees who made new lives in new countries. The people to whom war showed the world included the 50,000 British men who went to India as members of Territorial units.

Very little of the Terriers' years in India was recorded in print, not even by the histories their regiments published in the years between the wars. Christopher Atkinson, chronicler of the Hampshire and other regiments, observed that 'the battalions in India' – and the Hampshires had no fewer than eight, more than any other – 'meanwhile carried on their routine of duties without having anything very special to chronicle'.[1] A handful of published memoirs and a couple of compilations of correspondence have since described their war experience, but with one partial exception, not one secondary book exclusively about their experience in India has ever been published.

And yet the Territorials' encounter with India occurred in the midst of a titanic struggle that affected practically every protagonist or participant the world over. It certainly changed the destiny of India: the sub-continent accepted the King Emperor's declaration of war but its end saw the atrocity of the Amritsar massacre (in which Territorials played a supporting role) and after the war British India would change forever. It seems extraordinary that a century on, when British military historians have explored, documented and celebrated seemingly every aspect of the Great War, that the experience of 50,000 Territorials has remained neglected, but it is so. It

---

1 Atkinson, *The Royal Hampshire Regiment*, Vol. II, p. 126

seems even more extraordinary that an Australian historian should be the first to explore how men from Kent, Surrey, Somerset, Shropshire and Devon served in Agra, Bangalore, Rangoon, Fyzabad and Kamptee a century ago.

That this book has been possible at all is due to Britain's remarkable array of museums, archives and county history centres. The British Army's celebrated regimental system ensured that its constituent regiments established morale-building museums, housing their artefacts and archives; now in peril from the twin threats of the army's inevitable contraction and the Defence Ministry's parsimony.[2] County archives, record offices and their modern incarnations, history centres, have also collected and documented their people's and regiments' service in war and peace, often taking over and preserving their county regiments' historical collections. Their holdings, in the case of the Territorial units that served in India, are located across nine southern counties and three other counties, as well as several national collecting institutions. As a result, by aggregating the material held in all of these places it has been possible to gain both a broad overview of the service of Territorial units in India, and to understand the experiences through accounts written by some of their members.

Unlike most 'war history' books, this one relies relatively little on official records such as war diaries (that is, the report of a unit's doings recorded daily and submitted monthly), because units in India were not usually on 'active service' and therefore were not obliged to maintain such records. Accordingly, 'private' or unofficial records have been much more prominent in research; indeed, as Christopher Mills (one of the handful to have published on the Territorials' Indian experience, but only of several men of the Somerset Light Infantry) wrote, 'first-hand accounts … remain the most complete records of those units available to us'.[3] This has meant, inevitably, that some individuals have become more conspicuous. These men appear as broadly representative of Territorials; or at least Territorials who left evidence of their time in India.

The Territorials proved to be poor chroniclers of their own experience in print. During the war, only some of Robert Palmer's letters were published, posthumously by his parents. While some battalions published lively magazines, few published anything after 1919. In 1922 General Nigel Woodyatt (who had commanded Territorials in India) published his memoirs of Indian service (*Under Ten Viceroys*) and later that year delivered a lecture on Territorials in India at the Royal United Services Institution in London. In the same year the Hampshire Territorial officer, Alban Bacon, published his *The Wanderings of a Temporary Warrior*. Their regimental histories understandably devoted little space to the doings of battalions which saw either no active service or little, and that in distant 'sideshows' such as Aden and Mesopotamia; and in any case they were Territorials, who, despite belonging to the same regiments and fighting well, were still dismissed by Regulars. Accordingly, except for an informal history of the 2/4th Wilts by George Blick and a commemorative chronicle on the 1/5th and 2/5th Somerset, all that appeared in print about the Territorials' experience of India were a handful of memoirs,

---

2   Under 'reforms' imposed in 2017 regimental museums, which documented the history of historical regiments successively amalgamated since the 1870s, have again been obliged to merge, though without necessarily gaining commensurate funding. Large, far-sighted or well-connected regimental museums may well survive, particularly those which anticipated the crisis and transferred their collections to county archives and museums decades ago. Others will inevitably fail, putting irreplaceable community and military heritage at risk.
3   Mills, *A Strange War*, p. 4

transcribed journals or a book of correspondence. While up to twenty unpublished memoirs were donated to regimental and county collections, published memoirs were few. In 1935 Joseph Gale (a printer from Marlborough) published *With the 2/4th Wilts to India* and in 1967, just before his death, Joe Cox described his war service in *An Ordinary Working Man's Life Story*. (Both were privately published in limited editions, and both authors come across as the most likeable of men.) In 1988 Chris Mills published *A Strange War*, based on memoirs and an interview with several men of the 2/5th Somerset, including his grandfather. In 1999 John Mackie edited the letters of his uncle Captain Jim Mackie of the 2/4th Somerset (published as *Answering the Call*) and Ann Noyes edited the letters of Captain Stanley Goodland of the 1/5th Somerset (published as *Engaged in War*). In 2011 The Rifles Museum in Salisbury published Ken Mundy and Mary Waylen's transcription of Fred Mundy's *Journal* of his service in the 1/4th Wilts. Remarkably, apart from that, the service of over 50,000 British citizen soldiers in a war that has attracted unprecedented attention over the past twenty-odd years especially, has gone virtually unrecognised.

The Territorials' experience is so unrecognised that even on the British Army's unofficial 'Rumour Service' website a contributor responded to my appeal for family stories (which included a brief account of the Terriers' Indian service) by remarking 'Blimey – that would be astonishing, if true'. This book at least demonstrates that the story is indeed true, but I think it is indeed also astonishing.

Ootacamund Club
Tamil Nadu
India
15 January 2018

Notes

Unit titles

British regimental titles are venerable, arcane (with many parenthetical honorifics) and easy to get wrong. In lists, they are usually recorded in order of precedence, based on the date of the earliest formation of one of their components, using a numerical sequence for 'regiments of foot' – infantry – that the army had actually stopped using in 1881, rather than, say, alphabetically. (And to complicate matters, Territorial units often preferred a different order to that of the Regular army, one based on the raising of the volunteer units from which they were descended.) The full titles of the Territorial battalions that served in India 1914-19 appear below. For readers' ease, short titles will be used (with units listed in the army's order of precedence):

The Queen's (Royal West Surrey) Regiment	West Surrey
The Buffs (East Kent Regiment)	The Buffs
The Devonshire Regiment	Devon
Prince Albert's (Somerset Light Infantry)	Somerset[1]
The Brecknockshire Battalion, South Wales Borderers	Brecknock
The Duke of Cornwall's Light Infantry	Cornwall
The Border Regiment	Border
The Royal Sussex Regiment	Royal Sussex
The East Surrey Regiment	East Surrey
The Hampshire Regiment	Hants[2]
The Dorsetshire Regiment	Dorset
The Queen's Own (Royal West Kent Regiment)	West Kent
The King's Shropshire Light Infantry	Shropshire
The Duke of Cambridge's Own (Middlesex Regiment)	Middlesex
The Wiltshire Regiment (Duke of Edinburgh's)	Wilts
The London Regiment	London

1. Regimental titles underwent periodic and often subtle changes. The very word 'Regiment', for example, was rendered both within and outside parentheses; distinctions cherished by their members. The full title adopted by the Somerset Light Infantry in 1912 explains why Somerset newspapers referred to men as members of 'the P.A.S.L.I.'. I have simplified this by calling it 'Somerset'.
2. Hampshire men and units invariably shortened the name of their county to 'Hants'; likewise Wiltshire to 'Wilts'.

I feel that I should apologise for not using some of the forms familiar to or expected by military enthusiasts, but this book is aimed at a wider readership than just 'buffs'. For example, I will use 'West Surrey' rather than 'the Queen's' and 'Cornwall' rather than 'Duke of Cornwall's Light Infantry' or 'DCLI'.

Each battalion bore a number, such as '1/4th' or '2/5th'. The second number indicates that Territorial battalions followed the parent regiment's Regular or Special Reserve battalions (usually the 1st, 2nd and 3rd, respectively); so most Territorial battalions that served in India were the 4th or 5th battalions of their parent regiments, though the Hampshire went up to 1/9th.

The '1/' or '2/' in the units' titles are a result of the army's expansion from 1914, when Territorial units were 'doubled' – so that 4th battalions spawned a duplicate, soon after numbered 2/4th (and called 'first line' and 'second line'), though there was little in quality to distinguish them.

Place names

In the 75-odd years after Independence many place-names in India, Burma and Pakistan have changed. I have chosen to use place names as they were in 1914, so Mirat is Meerut, Pune is Poona, Hinthada is Henzada, Yangon is Rangoon, Mumbai is Bombay and Kolkata is Calcutta, and so on. To use one style in quotations and another in the text seemed absurd, so I have retained the names of a century ago, taking the *Imperial Gazetteer of India* as the authority.

Measurements

The Britons whom this book is about thought, spoke and calculated in feet, inches and miles, and in pounds, shillings and pence in Britain and in rupees, annas and pice in India. Twelve pennies equalled a shilling and twenty shillings a pound (£). In India men used rupees, annas, pice and pie: 1 rupee = 16 annas; one anna = four pice; 1 pice = 3 pie. Prices paid by troops were: post-card 1 pice; letter to Britain: 1 anna per ounce. A rupee was worth about one shilling and four-pence (making about 15 rupees to the pound), though the purchasing power of the two was very different.

Abbreviations

I have long sought to eliminate abbreviations from writing about military history, which confuse and alienate lay readers, and have largely succeeded in this book. I have declined to use common military abbreviations, such as 'CO', 'NCO', 'HQ' or 'Bn' except in quotations, and have decided not to refer to units by familiar military acronyms (such as QORWK – Queen's Own Royal West Kent).

Abbreviations for libraries, archives and journals do, however, appear in footnotes:

BL	British Library (London)
CMML	Cumbria Museum of Military Life (Carlisle)
CRM	Cornwall's Regimental Museum (Bodmin)
DMM	Dorset Military Museum (Dorchester)
DRO	Dorset Records Office (Dorchester)
HCA	Hampshire County Archives (Winchester)
IWM	Imperial War Museum (London)
JRUSI	*Journal of the Royal United Services Institution*
JSAHR	*Journal of the Society for Army Historical Research*
JUSII	*Journal of the United Services Institution of India*
KH&AC	Kent History and Archives Centre (Maidstone)
LHCMA	Liddell Hart Centre for Military Archives (London)
MM	Maidstone Museum (Maidstone)
NAI	National Archives of India (New Delhi)
NAM	National Army Museum (London)
NAUK	National Archives, UK (London)
NLA	National Library of Australia (Canberra)
RHRM	Royal Hampshire Regiment Museum (Winchester)
RBWM	Rifles Berkshire and Wiltshire Museum (Salisbury)
RMRW	Regimental Museum of The Royal Welsh (Brecon)
SA	Shropshire Archives (Shrewsbury)
SHC, Woking	Surrey History Centre, (Woking)
SHC, Taunton	Somerset Heritage Centre (Taunton)
S&WHC	Swindon and Wiltshire Heritage Centre (Chippenham)
WCL	Wiltshire County Library (Salisbury)
WSRO	West Sussex Record Office (Chichester)

References

The sources of all direct quotations are given in footnotes, using short titles or abbreviated details of archival sources, full details of which are given in the Bibliography.

Individuals

Due to the dearth of official sources, and the abundance and richness of private records, much of this first history of 'Indian' Territorials relies on the letters, diaries and memoirs of over a hundred individuals. Their words build a picture of men, all citizen soldiers, who may never have dreamed that they would be regarded as so valuable a century on. Their names and indeed characters will become familiar in these pages. They include:

- Private Reg Bailey of the 1/4th Buffs, who arrived in India, reluctantly, in 1916 and whose detailed letters to his sweetheart, Hilda, describe many aspects of cantonment life.

- Sergeant William Bisset, 2/4th Hants, whose diary and memoir show how fully Territorials became a part of the administrative machinery of the Army in India.
- Major Gerald Bonham-Carter, a South African war veteran who at 50 dutifully went to India with the West Kent and endured long months of tedium in the big infantry depot at Bangalore, from where he wrote insightful letters to his sister Joan.
- Lieutenant-Colonel Francis Bowker of the 1/4th Hants, who proudly took his battalion to war as the first Indian Territorials to see action, and he and they paid the price.
- Private Harry Canham of the 2/4th Border, a later arrival, a cotton mill clerk from Blackburn, Lancashire, whose candid letters provide a cynical commentary from the barrack-room.
- Captain Olaf Caroe, a young architect from Liverpool who served in India with the 1/5th East Surrey and, falling in love with the country and its people, devoted the rest of his life as an administrator in the Punjab.
- Private Hugh Creek of the 1/4th Devon, whose letters to his parents in Penzance reveal soldiers' lives and his own feelings.
- Private Oswald Early, a Hants signaller who returned from Mesopotamia and whose detailed diary records the crisis the Army in India faced in 1919.
- Private Herbert Ewing, a teenaged member of the 1/5th Somerset, whose diary is observant and perceptive.
- Company Quartermaster Sergeant Joseph Gale, a 31-year-old printer from Marlborough, whose memoir of his four years with the 2/4th Wilts is one of the most evocative accounts of the Territorials' service.
- Sergeant Thomas Heard of the 1/4th Cornwall, a tailor and devout Wesleyan, whose now elderly daughter still worships at the chapel where he returned to play the organ.
- Lance-Corporal Henry Rawstone Lamplugh, whose literary and musical endeavours while a member of the 1/1st Kent embodies the Territorials' cultural life.
- Captain Jim Mackie, a young Somerset student whose chatty letters to his family in Frome describe aspects of how junior officers experienced Indian service.
- Sergeant Victor Manley, 2/4th Hants, the author of a massive diary, who fell in love with Baluchistan especially and whose drawings and water-colours embody the Territorials' curiosity about India and its people.
- Sergeant Fred Mundy, a Salisbury school-teacher, whose journal illuminates the interior life of the 1/4th Wilts as a battalion.
- Captain Hon. Robert Palmer, 1/6th Hants, the witty, intelligent and humane son of the Earl of Selborne, whose letters to his family powerfully depict the pathos of his loss; the Territorials' representative of the Lost Generation.
- Sergeant Ted Rice, 1/5th West Surrey, whose memoir suggests how Territorials responded to the opportunities offered by service in India, and beyond. His diary records aspects omitted by others — he is the only one to describe a cantonment brothel.
- Private Owen Smith, 2/4th Hants, a Portsmouth retail pharmacy shop assistant, both a diligent Anglican and a devoted attender of 'gaffs', who volunteered for Mesopotamia, who wrote long, detailed letters to his sister.
- Private Allan Swift of the 1/6th East Surrey, who kept a detailed, perceptive and candid diary.

This book is dedicated to the memory of these men, and all those Territorials who served in India a century ago.

1

Imperial Service

The Territorial Force, formed just six years before the outbreak of the Great War, represented a reservoir of military power which was to offer a vital resource just when the empire most needed it. Despite their supposed commitment to home defence, in 1914 Territorials found themselves volunteering for overseas service, on the understanding that they would return to fight Germany.

'A real national army': citizen soldiers

In the decade before the Great War Britain's citizen soldiers proudly claimed a lineage, imaginatively reaching back to the Anglo-Saxon fyrd and successive manifestations of part-time military forces. They saw themselves as the descendants of the London Trained Bands of the Civil War, the Volunteers and Militia of the Revolutionary and Napoleonic wars, the Rifle Volunteers of the 1850s and the local and county Volunteer units gradually absorbed into the army's structure during the late nineteenth century. This lineage was complex, even then largely of interest only to the county gentry who comprised its officers, and now virtually forgotten, known only to a small band of collectors of esoteric military badges. But the Territorials' origins as local citizen soldiers gave them their distinctive character.

In Surrey, for example, disparate volunteer rifle companies formed during the war scare with France in 1859 were a decade later brought together as the Surrey Rifle Volunteers, and in the early 1880s associated with the 2nd or Queen's Regiment of Foot, itself newly married to Surrey under the Childers reforms as the Queen's Royal West Surrey Regiment. With the formation of the Territorial Force in 1908 the county's rifle volunteers lost their green uniforms and 'rifle' nomenclature and adopted red uniforms as the 4th and 5th Battalions of the Queen's. (Most Territorials believed they were special in some way: the 4th West Surrey claimed to have been the first Territorial unit to have received colours – that is, their distinctive regimental flags, while Devon and Middlesex citizen soldiers pressed claims based on the formation of distant precursors to be the oldest Territorial units, regardless of the seniority of their parent regiments.) In the last years of Edward VII's reign a Scottish Liberal layer and MP transformed Britain's citizen soldiers into what became in 1908 the Territorial Force.

Richard Haldane, MP for East Lothian, had been a Liberal Imperialist during the Anglo-Boer war of 1899-1902, during which he had developed an interest in the perennial pursuit of the 'Army Reform' that had preoccupied politicians for a century. As Secretary of State for War Haldane drove through the establishment of a 'General Staff', the creation of the basis for an Expeditionary Force, the Officers' Training Corps that produced generations of subalterns in time to die in Flanders and, not least, the reorganisation of auxiliary forces. Haldane intended to unite and rationalise three voluntary forces – the old Volunteer force, the Militia and the Yeomanry (cavalry). In a characteristically British fashion these forces had been allowed to co-exist though diverse in terms and conditions of service, uniform, equipment, and role in defending Britain in time of war. Haldane's intent was both revolutionary (in 'recasting ... the entire military system') but also conservative (in its 'adaptation of established institutions to modern military requirements'.)[1]

Volunteer units, most dating from various war scares in the mid-nineteenth century, reflected a great variety of uniform, energy and efficiency. Their members now feared a loss of autonomy and identity. The Militia had become virtually moribund, a source of men considering a military career or seeking pay for attending its annual camps. The Yeomanry cavalry, largely independent and sustained by county gentry and their retainers, objected to being subordinated into a system of units. Haldane planned essentially to turn the Militia into depot units for the Regulars (re-casting them as the 'Special Reserve', usually forming a 3rd Battalion for most regiments) while the Volunteers became the infantry and the Yeomanry the cavalry of a new force ostensibly intended for home defence. Though often represented as a force for the defence of Britain, Haldane saw the Territorial Force, as Peter Dennis put it, as 'the second-line behind the Regular Army component of the Expeditionary Force'.[2] In several memoranda he envisaged an auxiliary force that would create 'a real national army', one embodying the civic virtue of a democratic nation meeting its responsibilities for what he called, for Parliamentary tactical purposes, 'Home Defence'.[3]

Haldane's master-stroke was to devolve the administration of the new force to some 92 county 'Associations'– the Cromwellian connotation was deliberate. They supported between 66 (Nairn) and 27,000 (London County) volunteer troops.[4] Most associations were run by their familiar local power-brokers. By leaving uniform, equipment and management in the hands of committees of local worthies under the chairmanship of the lords lieutenants, he acknowledged Edwardian Britain's ingrained hostility to central government. While local, usually long-serving volunteer or militia officers commanded its units, command of the new force's formations lay in the hands of Regular officers. Haldane's genius was to 'create a solidarity of feeling between the community and its part-time army'.[5] However, the new force did not forge a solidarity of feeling with the Regular army, many of whose officers remained suspicious that the new amateur force would compete for weapons, facilities and funds. Major-General Edward

---

1 Baker, *The Territorial Force*, p. 1
2 Dennis, *The Territorial Army 1906-1940*, p. 19
3 Beckett, 'The Nation in Arms' in Beckett & Simpson, (eds), *A Nation in Arms*, p. 6; Spiers, *Haldane: an Army Reformer*, p. 112
4 *Statement showing the Financial Position of Territorial Force County Associations on 31 March 1914*, PP, 1914-16, Vol. 39 (Cmd 7678). Inexplicably, Hampshire does not appear in this paper.
5 Sellwood, *The Saturday Night Soldiers*, p. 15

Tent-mates belonging to No. 4 Section, C Company of the 6th East Surrey Regiment during the battalion's annual camp near Lewes, on the South Downs in Sussex, 1910. Seaside camps were one of the main attractions for working men to join the Territorial Force. (ESR/25/BOWE/1, Surrey Heritage Centre)

Bethune, the Director-General of the Territorial Force at the war's outbreak, later explained that 'the old Army was a very close craft Trades Union and it did not like diluted labour'.[6]

Skillfully steering his 'little Bill' through Parliament, Haldane overcame the suspicion of his fellow Liberals, helped by the populist *Daily Mail*, an invasion scare and King Edward VII, as well as a healthy Parliamentary majority.[7] Even so, it took the king's active lobbying of the lords lieutenants before all counties formed associations. The *Territorial and Reserve Forces Act* received royal assent on 2 August 1907 (the first legislation passed by Henry Campbell-Bannerman's Liberal government) and the new force came into existence on 1 April 1908, the Territorials' 'birthday'.

'Perhaps no military body in the whole wide world', one of its officers wrote, 'has ever been so much criticized as has the Territorial Force'.[8] One of its premier historians, Bill Mitchinson, frankly acknowledged that before 1914 the force had been 'openly ridiculed' (especially by those favouring a conscripted army).[9] It attracted derisory nicknames: 'Dog Shooters', 'Featherbed

---

6 Comment by Lieutenant-General Sir Edward Bethune in Woodyatt, 'The Territorials (Infantry) in India', *JRUSI*, 1922 p. 735
7 Haldane, *An Autobiography*, p. 194
8 Webster, *Britain's Territorials in Peace and War*, p. 1
9 Mitchinson, *The Territorial Force at War*, p. 2

Heroes' and, of course 'Saturday Night Soldiers'.[10] Victor Manley, a Hampshire student who joined the Territorials as soon as he could (his father had been a Volunteer) expressed his resentment at the 'taunts and jeers' he encountered in the streets.[11] Nor were its critics necessarily anti-militarist. Regular officers largely disregarded the Territorials as 'a military irrelevance whose officers were social climbers'.[12] Proponents of compulsory service denigrated the Territorials from the outset.

Establishing Territorial artillery had been one of Haldane's greatest successes. Opposition to 'amateur artillerists' had been powerful, uniting radical MPs and Lord Roberts, who had himself entered the Bengal Artillery in 1851. Roberts, already a VC in the Indian Mutiny, had become the darling of the empire as Kipling's 'Our Bobs' after his daring march from Kabul to Kandahar in 1879 and had served as the army's last Commander-in-Chief. Roberts had derided the suggestion that Territorials could possibly serve effectively in war,

> by reason of their unsatisfactory composition, the want of proper organisation, and their lack of anything approaching sufficient training … would not … be the slightest use in the field … a positive danger.[13]

The size, composition and equipment of its artillery had been one of the fiercest aspects of the debates that preceded the Territorial Force's creation. One of Charles à Court Repington's most trenchant essays in its support was on 'Artillery and its Critics', who alleged that part-time artillery would be 'not only useless but dangerous', and Haldane and his supporters spent much ink and energy arguing that citizen gunners could be useful and safe.[14] Paradoxically, many Royal Artillery officers supported Haldane, rightly seeing in the increase in gunners an accession of strength, despite their being equipped with obsolete weapons hastily developed for service in South Africa.

Each county association's president was its lord lieutenant, with several large committee of local grandees, magnates and notable retired officers, with a smattering of commercial and professional gentlemen. The associations were responsible for recruiting, clothing, equipping and running a county's units, including establishing and maintaining drill halls and rifle ranges and supplying horses. The War Office paid grants for expenses based on standard rates – £100 for an infantry company, for example, with the costs of training camps carefully divided between it and associations, though both civil servants and association secretaries often wrangled over who had paid or was owed what. The larger associations, such as Middlesex, controlled thousands of pounds' worth of real estate (Hampshire's Association built over £50,000 worth of new buildings between 1908 and 1914), while associations in less populated counties had to take over or even build many smaller halls and ranges.[15]

---

10   Sellwood, *The Saturday Night Soldiers*, p. 10
11   Victor Manley, 'A Khaki Diary', 49M91W/Q3/6, HRO
12   Keith Simpson, 'The Officers', in Beckett & Simpson, (eds), *A Nation in Arms*, p. 68
13   Sellwood, *The Saturday Night Soldiers*, p. 66
14   Repington, *The Foundations of Reform*, p. 344. Repington was military correspondent of *The Times*.
15   *History of the Hampshire Territorial Force Association*, p. 15

Haldane and his supporters promoted the new force energetically – an officer who attended a dinner intended to encourage local supporters recalled that he would 'boom it hard'.[16] Haldane largely succeeded in grafting the Territorials onto the existing stock of local military endeavour. Despite derision, abuse, resistance and apathy the force grew. On 1 June 1909, as it reached a strength of almost 269,000 men (and several hundred Territorial nurses) King Edward VII presented colours to 108 new Territorial units at Windsor Castle. By 1914 the force comprised 55 regiments of yeomanry, 123 batteries of field artillery and 207 battalions of infantry, including thirteen cyclist battalions. Many of the artillery, engineer, medical, veterinary and transport units numbered in multiples of seven – the force formed fourteen infantry divisions and fourteen mounted brigades. The Territorial divisions most relevant to this story were the Home Counties and the Wessex divisions (and the '2nd Wessex' when the latter was duplicated late in 1914). Territorial divisions were numbered consecutively only in July 1915, beginning with the East Lancashire, which as the first to go overseas in 1914 (to Egypt) became the 42nd, while the three 'Indian' Territorial divisions later became the 43rd (Wessex), 44th (Home Counties) and 45th (2nd Wessex). The numbering was notional because by then, of course, they no longer existed as divisions.

Many Regular officers still had to be won over, though retired officers became stalwarts of county associations (such as Sir Thomas Sturmy-Cave in Hampshire, whom Joe Cox knew and admired). While the idea had been that Territorials would imbibe the all-important regimental identity from their parent regiments, the Regulars were often less than welcoming. Regimental journals did not always report the doings of their Territorial battalions, and Regular officers forbade Territorials using embellishments to which they felt they were not entitled. The Somerset Light Infantry's badge, for example, featured the battle honour 'Jellalabad' (won in Afghanistan in 1842) but Territorials were denied it, accorded only a spray of leaves on its version of the badge. Conversely, some Territorial battalions declined to accept the parent regiments' badges. Several Hants battalions, for instance, retained their own badges: the 1/7th's depicted a mediaeval 'dog gauge' used to police dogs intruding into the New Forest, the part of Hampshire where it recruited. But Territorials also identified with their parent regiments, celebrating regimental anniversaries such as Minden Day (in Hampshire battalions, 1 August) Albuhera Day (the Middlesex, 16 May) or Arroyo dos Molinos Day (Border, 28 October). The Brecknock Battalion naturally marked St David's Day by pinning leeks to their caps.

Its own Director-General, Sir Edward Bethune, admitted that the force was 'rather despised'.[17] It was under-strength, in September 1913 fielding only 78% of its establishment of 312,000.[18] Territorials used obsolete equipment, the 'long' Lee-Enfield rifle, leather rather than the new webbing belts, while its artillery comprised the obsolescent 15-pounder gun, though in simple numbers the Territorials just out-numbered the Regulars.

The force was ostensibly intended for home defence. Its officers faced the prospect of fighting an enemy – increasingly identified as German – in their own fields and woods. A London Territorial officer helpfully published *Promotion While You Wait* to assist other aspiring subalterns. He gave examples of various tactical problems, such as 'The Reds have landed a party of unknown strength at SOUTHEND', and requiring them to propose solutions. (The answer 'it

---

16 Woodyatt, 'The Territorials (Infantry) in India', *JRUSI*, 1922, p. 718
17 Woodyatt, 'The Territorials (Infantry) in India', *JRUSI*, 1922, p. 717
18 Edward Spiers, 'The Regular Army', in Beckett & Simpson, (eds), *A Nation in Arms*, p. 57

is impossible that such a force could land there …' was not acceptable.)[19] But, as befitted a part-time force, many Territorial officers brought initiative and flair to training. In the early summer of 1914, for example, Kent Territorial adjutants and colonels organised 'tactical exercises without troops' through the county for the prices of tickets on slow Sunday trains. Annual camps, though (Fred Mundy recalled) were 'looked upon muchly as a holiday'.[20] At first (according to one of the Territorials' supporters) 'haphazard to a degree', camps gradually became more organised and standardised.[21] Territorials were expected to attend forty hour-long drills and a week or two of annual camp in his first year, and thereafter ten drills and the annual camp. Still, as Ted Rice, a Surrey apprentice bookbinder later admitted, 'all we were really doing was playing soldiers'.[22] That changed in mid-1914.

'Somewhat feudal': Territorial units

Who were the Territorials? What was the nature of this new element which would soon comprise the largest single component of the British force in India? The pre-eminent historian of the Victorian and Edwardian army, Ian Beckett, argued (in his 'The Nation in Arms') that the Territorials were 'more genuinely representative of society at large than the regulars'.[23] But who were these men? Is it possible to form a picture of them? The sources seem unpromising. Few rolls or registers have survived in regimental and country collections that enable us to calculate, say, the average age of particular groups of Territorials at various points in their service (which anyway extended over more than five years). It is hard to work out what percentage were married, or even what proportion had joined the Territorial Force before the war rather than after its outbreak. It is almost impossible to give any empirical basis for a calculation of the trades or occupations men had followed before enlistment, or to establish with certainty exactly the class composition of their officers.

Territorial officers were drawn from the provincial middle class, from towns and businesses as well as estates and manors. Territorial officers were, naturally, highly local. A pre-war list of the 'town' and 'country' addresses of the 33 officers of the 5th East Surrey shows that all but eight hailed from Surrey, and seven others lived or worked in nearby London. One gave his 'country address' as 'Gold Coast Colony', but eight men lived within a radius of five miles, between Epsom and Leatherhead.[24] Though often leaders of their communities they lacked the skills of Regular officers – or so Regular officers told them. Ian Hamilton, even as he praised the quality of the volunteers who flocked to join the force in August 1914, expressed concern that the 'weak point of the show still lies in the Officers, and their lack of self-confidence'.[25] Regular officers criticised Territorial units for failing for enforce the rigid distinctions between officers and men.

19 'A Territorial Officer', *Promotion While You Wait*, pp. 64; 114
20 Mundy, *A Journal of the 1/4th Battalion Wiltshire Regiment*, p. 267
21 Webster, *Britain's Territorials in Peace and War*, p. 67
22 Ted Rice, 'All for a Shilling a Day', QRWS/30/RICE/1, SHC, Woking
23 Beckett, 'The Nation in Arms' in Beckett & Simpson, (eds), *A Nation in Arms*, p. 6
24 List of officers of 5th East Surrey, c. 1913, 1984-11-114-12, NAM
25 Letter, 17 October 1914, Hamilton papers, 6/1, LHCMA

The spirit of a pre-war Territorial battalion (in this case the 4th Wilts) was, an officer admitted, 'somewhat feudal'.[26] When he turned 21 in 1917 Lieutenant Viscount Folkestone treated his entire battalion (the 1/4th Wilts) to dinner. While some officers were county gentry, and even nobility (the 1/4th Wilts's colonel was Jacob Pleydell-Bouverie, 6th Earl of Radnor) most were either the sons of landowners or the provincial professional and commercial classes. Most battalions included at least one titled officer. The Hon. Robert Palmer, son of the Earl of Selborne, also represented the best of aristocratic youth. He looked askance on some men of the 'commercial' class who also became officers in the 1/5th Hants. One, Palmer told his father, had been 'brought up to be the boss of a Portsmouth firm of govt grain contractors & his ideas on … the treatment of employees & women, are a depressing eye-opener as to middle-class standards'.[27] For country gentlemen, voluntary soldiering 'filled in the interval between the last meet of the [fox-hunting] season and the opening of partridge shooting'.[28] Gerald Bonham-Carter was perhaps representative of the county gentry who provided many of the Territorials' officers. Except that he was 49 in 1914, he was typical, as a landowner and having served in the Hampshire Yeomanry in South Africa. His family was representative of the upper-middle class commitment to politics and empire (one brother was an Indian civil servant) and to military service – four of ten brothers served and one of his them died in the war.

Territorial units included many brothers and even some fathers and sons. Here, ex-Regular George Andrews, a lock-keeper on the Kennet and Avon Canal, poses with his 17-year-old son Harry, who volunteered for Mesopotamia, was captured at Kut and died in Baghdad a month later. (SBYRW36888, Rifles Berkshire and Wiltshire Museum)

Territorials appear on the whole to have been young men, naturally, though with exceptions and qualifications. Territorials often behaved like boys, with pillow fights in barracks. When the 1/5th moved to Lucknow early in 1915 Surrey Territorials played leap-frog on the station platform, to the amusement of watching Indian civilians. But Territorial units, both pre-war and 1914-raised, also tended to include large proportions of older men, who provided a steadying

26 Blick, *The 1/4th Wiltshire Regiment*, p. 11
27 Letter, 24 March 1915, Robert Palmer, 1/5th Hants, 19M75/F/C19, HRO
28 Atkinson, *The Dorsetshire Regiment*, Vol. II, p. 112

influence. A sample of cemetery registers revels not only a few underage youths (one young man of just 16, who should never have been allowed to embark) but also men over 40, including a private of the Buffs who died on the eve of Armistice Day aged 51.[29]

Most southern Territorials came from predominantly rural counties, though Hampshire units came from the big cities of Southampton and Portsmouth, and London men joined the East and West Surrey, West Kent and Middlesex regiments. Several battalions played up their rural character, and it seems that they were genuinely representative of the communities that sustained them. Indeed, there is abundant evidence that Territorial units usually manifest a distinct local character. The 1/5th Hants was 'Southampton's Own'; the 1/7th Hants identifying with the New Forest, the 1/4th 'recruited from Winchester and the towns and villages in that part of Hampshire'.[30] The history of the Hampshire Association even claimed that 'local patriotism' – a man's feelings for 'his own County, Town, Village or Hamlet' – was stronger than 'Imperial or National patriotism'.[31] At the outset, and until mid-way through the war, units retained their regional character – only 5% of the 2/4th Border's 767 men hailed from outside Westmoreland or Cumberland.[32]

With drill halls spread about the county, Territorial units were highly localised, their men able to meet for training because of the reach of Britain's railway network. Comrades were often neighbours or work-mates. 'F' Company of the 1/25th London comprised 'practically all men from Harrods'.[33] None of the towns and villages across the 4th Dorset's area were more than 28 miles distant from the mock-medieval (but actually mid-Victorian) stone 'Keep' at the top of the high street in Dorchester, and most were under twenty. A Terrier with a bicycle was within easy reach of either his local drill hall or a railway station able to take him there. (Indeed, the 4th Dorset included a cyclist company, so keen were young men on bicycling, and the county association had built six new drill halls since 1909, so that units could parade close to men's homes.) Some units maintained the practice of describing their companies not only by their letters but also by their place of origin, so Roger Haslewood's company of the 1/4th Shropshire was 'E Company (Shifnal)'. Territorial artillery was also raised locally. The 2nd Home Counties field artillery brigade's three batteries belonged to Eastbourne, Bexhill and Pevensey, all within a twelve mile stretch of Sussex coast, all linked by the Southern Railway. These units had their own characters, known to their members. Joe Cox's D Company of the 1/5th West Surrey was known to be 'an excellent shooting company'. His battalion was known to look after its men in camp, erecting mess tents, for example, while the neighbouring Hampshire battalions preferred to camp under 'active service conditions' supposedly to accustom their men to hardship, though it was also cheaper.[34]

Units attracted friends, relatives and workmates. So many men of the 1/1st Wiltshire Battery worked at the Great Western Railway workshops at Swindon that its pre-arranged mobilisation signal was the sounding of the works hooter. Great Chart, a village close to Ashford in Kent,

---

29   Based on a survey of Imperial (later Commonwealth) War Graves Commission cemetery registers available at https://www.cwgc.org/. About a third of cemetery registers include men's ages.
30   Clipping in Esme Bowker papers, M1539, RHRM
31   *History of the Hampshire Territorial Force Association*, p. 25
32   MacGlasson, (ed.), *Diary of the 2/4th Battalion The Border Regiment*, p. 33
33   Letter, 12 November 1978, Reg Howgego, 1/25th London, Mss Eur C340/2, BL
34   Cox, *An Ordinary Working Man's Life*, p. 29

supported a Soldiers and Sailors Fund. The sixty names on its Roll of Honour included four Brungers, two Mannerings (brothers), three Skinners and five Hugheses. The 1/4th's Hants' thirty officers included three Burrells. At the war's end the 1/9th Hants included *at least* twenty pairs (or even trios) of brothers, and possibly more, men who had been lost to the battalion in the course of the war. At first, sub-units were exceptionally local. In Malappuram early in 1915, Jim Mackie took over 'a platoon of Radstock miners whom no one has ever been able to manage properly' (though after a 'rather stormy' time they had 'given in at last'). The following month he was surprised to find among them men from men from Paulton – four miles distant in their native Somerset.[35]

A witness to Somerset Territorials training in drill halls recalled the kind of instruction imparted, in the process capturing their distinct regional complexion:

> Now I want you chaps to understand theas thing is caw'd a rifle. But as all o'ee caw'n a gun, I be gwaine t'do the zame 'zo'z thee c'n understand I better … when I tell thee to "zlope arms". Chuck 'n up thee zide like this; catch howld o'n wi' theas hand round the narrey part there 't'other 'and up there. Then thee put'n on the opposite shoulder, like zo, and be careful t'kip thee girt heads still …'[36]

As this vignette suggests, southern English soldiers have been described as 'stolid'. Alban Bacon, himself of Winchester, found frustrating the 'slow-going Hampshire men' he trained in 1914.[37]

The social composition of forty battalions makes generalisation hazardous. Several battalions, mainly urban, included companies of a distinctly 'superior' social complexion, including university undergraduates, clerks or civil servants. Most Territorial battalions, Walter Saunders, a former Middlesex Terrier explained in transcribing his wartime diary, 'were of a very mixed class'. His own battalion included two companies almost entirely drawn from students at two Anglican teachers' colleges, St John's Battersea and St Mark's Chelsea, while the other six companies comprised a mixture of clerks, tradesmen and members of north-west London's labourers. In 1915 Middlesex men held an 'Old Boys' dinner for former members of one of its old 'single' companies. Held at the Savoy Hotel, Calcutta, the function was organised by a committee mostly comprising privates, but giving every evidence of a respectable middle-class event (though the main course comprised the plebeian-sounding 'Veal Cutlets, Green Peas and Chips').[38]

The Territorial Force's character – its social mixture, local composition, patriotic zeal and the composition of units – would influence both its members' experience of India and their contribution to the empire's war in and beyond India. The War Office's returns show that by the first quarter of 1915 over 33,000 Territorials would be serving in India, a larger number then than anywhere at that time outside Britain.[39] Many more Territorials would soon see action, in France and on Gallipoli, and their experience would essentially resemble that of their Regular,

---

35 Letters, 10 February and 2 March 1915, Jim Mackie, 2/4th Somerset, Mackie, *Answering the Call*, pp. 35; 38
36 Fisher, *The History of Somerset Yeomanry, Volunteer and Territorial Units*, p. 115
37 Bacon, *The Wanderings of a Temporary Warrior*, p. 12
38 Henry Iggulden, 1/10th Middlesex, 2010-12-8-9, NAM. 'Single' as opposed to 'double' companies.
39 'Returns of the Territorial Force Serving Abroad', WO114/52, NAUK

Reservist and New Army comrades. But in India the Territorials' experience was dominant and distinctive. Extraordinarily, that experience has never been explored in the century since the last Territorial left India. That deficiency is now rectified.

'Mobilize': August 1914

The international crisis preceding the war's outbreak coincided with the Territorial Force's annual summer camps. Territorial brigades were camped around the training grounds of Salisbury Plain and Aldershot: the Surrey brigade at Borden, the South-Western brigade at Sling Plantation, the Kent Brigade at Longmoor and the Middlesex brigade at Larkhill. Some Territorials had finished their camps and had dispersed to their depots and homes – the 4th King's Shropshire Light Infantry had returned to Shrewsbury from Aberystwyth on Sunday 2 August, though the headlines kept the drill hall crowded with men awaiting news. On Salisbury Plain, where the 4th Wilts were encamped at Sling Plantation, men eagerly read the Sunday newspapers, though a member of the nearby 10th Middlesex recalled that no one took any notice of the newspapers (or if they did it was the crisis in Ulster they discussed, not the Balkans).

Since 1908 each district headquarters had kept stocks of forms and envelopes ready to post to call up Territorials in the event of 'mobilization'. On Tuesday 4 August 1914 the War Office distributed a Special Army Order in which the Regulars and reservists were mobilised and the Territorial Force was 'embodied'. The envelopes were taken to post offices, handed to designated postal officials and delivered to men in the area. When the expected notices arrived most men were still in uniform or were returning from the annual camp. They had time to return home 'heave a sigh of relief, kiss the missus and kids and make for headquarters'.[40]

At the Territorial Association office in Taunton, Somerset, 4 August 1914 was 'a day of waiting, waiting'. Eventually, at 5.15 that afternoon, the expected telegram arrived: 'Mobilize'.[41] Units assembled as planned. Within ten hours of men receiving individual mobilisation instructions 95% of the 6th East Surrey were at the depot.[42] Ted Holter of the 2nd Home Counties artillery recalled how within hours of receiving mobilisation orders his unit's members paraded at the drill hall 'all dressed up in our uniforms, with kits packed, ready to take on the German Army … Only it didn't work out quite like that'.[43]

Britain immediately mobilised the six Regular divisions – about 160,000 men – of the Expeditionary Force, which proceeded to embark for France, where in due course it was practically destroyed at Mons, and at Ypres, losing half its strength in killed and wounded by the year's end. Mobilisation also entailed the 'embodiment' of the Territorial Force. Under Haldane's plan embodiment did not, however, mean 'mobilization for war', but for 'war training' – the Territorials were not expected to be fully trained and were not intended to see service except in the case of raids or invasion.[44]

---

40   Webster, *Britain's Territorials in Peace and War*, p. 144
41   Fisher, *The History of Somerset Yeomanry, Volunteer and Territorial Units*, p. 154
42   'The East Surrey Regiment in India 1914-19', ESR/10/14/3/1, SHC, Woking
43   Ted Holter, 'A Terrier in World War I', Doc 4545, 81/9/1, IWM
44   Baker, *The Territorial Force*, pp. 88-89

A group of signallers of the 4th Wilts at ease in camp at Bovington in the opening weeks of the war. Note that of the fifteen men, four are smoking pipes and five cigarettes; probably a representative proportion of smokers. (SBYRW 17252d, Rifles Berkshire and Wiltshire Museum)

On 5 August instructions directed colonels and adjutants to open the 'sealed orders' prepared in advance and kept in every unit. It was 'an awkward moment': most Territorial formations were holding their annual camps, while the country as a whole enjoyed glorious summer weather of the August Bank Holiday.[45] As they marched to railway stations Territorials saw that the condescension and disdain they had often suffered had melted away. Walter Saunders, of the 10th Middlesex, noticed the changed demeanour, with crowds 'beginning to regard anybody in uniform as a hero'.[46]

Units immediately moved to the 'war stations' assigned to them, following complex railway plans devised in anticipation of just such an emergency. Some units had mobilised 'Special Service' sections on 28 July, parties allocated to guard cable or wireless stations, bridges or naval installations. Enthusiastic Hampshire Territorials took it upon themselves to guard 'a lonely bridge, on the Hampshire North Downs', before being reprimanded by the railway company for 'butting in'.[47] Their formal mobilisation orders advised them to 'proceed to war stations' to guard installations more substantial than country railway bridges. Watchful Territorials were alert for spies, saboteurs and submarines, displaying an excess of zeal verging on panic. A subaltern of

---

45 Wyrall, *The Die-Hards in the Great War*, Vol. I, p. 67
46 Transcript of diary and letters, Walter Saunders, 1/10th Middlesex, Doc. 6571, 79/15/1, IWM
47 Bacon, *The Wanderings of a Temporary Warrior*, p. 9

the 4th Dorset raided a house allegedly concealing a wireless at Devonport, rousing out young women in 'night attire' while his men searched for 'incriminating evidence' – unsuccessfully.[48]

Mobilisation, and especially its scale, called the entire basis of the Territorial Force into question. The Kent Association's secretary, writing a month after the war's outbreak pessimistically reported that 'the Association ceased to administer the Territorial Force on the first day of mobilization' and now, 'the men having gone from us, the presumption is that our administrative grants automatically cease'.[49] Without funds to manage, what purpose did the county associations serve? The Kent secretary was unduly gloomy. Despite the distrust Lord Kitchener (the Secretary of State for War) nursed against Territorials (and his attempt to create an entirely separate 'New Army', in fact the Associations were needed to recruit and equip the huge numbers of men – over 1.1 million by the year's end – who were swelling the queues outside their depot gates.[50] Even so, Kitchener's prejudice against the Territorials meant that 'everything was done for the new Armies, to the neglect of the Territorial Force', as the Hampshire Association's history bemoaned.[51] Still, Association staffs continued to expand, not least because they remained responsible for Territorials' pay, and the 'separation allowances' paid to men's families.

Battalions moved to their initial war stations reasonably smoothly. The 4th Shropshire went from Shrewsbury to Barry and Newport in Wales – followed five days later by its blankets, kettles and kit. Its men supervised the internment of German ships' crews, as one of their officers, Roger Haslewood told his mother, 'with orders to shoot if there was the slightest attempt to escape'. (Already, Haslewood, a solicitor from Bridgnorth, was calling Germans 'swine'.[52]) Gradually the Territorial divisions concentrated for intensified training; the Wessex on Salisbury Plain, the Home Counties in Kent. The 9th Middlesex went to Sheerness, then Sittingbourne 'eagerly awaiting orders to embark … to France'.[53]

At first clad in an assortment of uniforms and civilian clothes (volunteers in Cornwall even wore chocolate-coloured overalls) the newly formed or enlarged battalions began training and learning how units worked as best they could, schooled by 'old soldiers' and often by scarce and sometimes 'dug-out' retired officers. Senior officers inspected units repeatedly: their brigade and divisional commanders, by General Sir Ian Hamilton, who commanded the Home Forces responsible for meeting raids or even invasion (before being given command of the Dardanelles invasion force), by Edward Bethune, their nominal commander; by Lord Kitchener, even the King himself. At first, even officers such as Hamilton echoed Kitchener in deprecating Territorials. As commander of Central Force, the huge reserve force held in Britain in the war's opening months as Territorial and New Army formations trained, Hamilton snidely companioned to Edward Bethune, the Director-General of the Territorial Force how he had seen Terriers

---

48 [Dorsetshire Regiment] Regimental History Committee, *History of the Dorsetshire Regiment*, Part II, p. 9
49 Kent Territorial Force Association, General Purpose Committee, 28 August 1914, MD/TA, KA&HC
50 'General Annual Reports on the British Army (including the Territorial Force…) for the Period from 1st October, 1913, to 30th September, 1919, Parliamentary Papers, 1921, Vol. 20, Cmd 1193
51 *History of the Hampshire Territorial Force Association*, p. 22
52 Letter, 7 August 1914, Roger Haslewood, 4th Shropshire, 3614/2/142-161, SA
53 Wyrall, *The Die-Hards in the Great War*, Vol. I, p. 69

creating 'a bad impression by loafing about with their hats on the back of their heads'.[54] Within weeks, though, greater contact with Territorials brought Ian Hamilton to change his mind. By October he found that they had '"come on" with a wonderful rush', were 'quite different from the old Territorial Force', with volunteers 'replaced by new men of a new class; four inches taller … and keen as mustard' and even – improbably – 'indistinguishable from Regulars'.[55]

'Not the ordinary run of Tommy': volunteers in 1914

While the Territorial Force had often struggled to meet its establishment before 1914, the patriotic fervour so much a part of the war's opening months saw queues of volunteers form at depots, intensifying the force's local character. At Wye, five miles from Ashford, 44 students of the town's College enlisted in the 4th Buffs on one day. The Duke of Cornwall's Light Infantry depot at Bodmin was typical, with reservists and volunteers sleeping in the gymnasium, the married quarters and even the detention cells. Many of the Territorial volunteers were of what Edwardian England would have regarded as of a distinctly superior type. While many were of working class families, every battalion included a strong leaven of the sons of tradesmen, shopkeepers, small farmers and skilled workers, with (as would become evident in India) enough men with secondary education to give the entire force a distinctly cultured character. A letter sent to a Hampshire officer in India from the Borough Treasurer at Portsmouth suggests the social complexion of Territorial privates. He had just farewelled a young junior member of his staff, a clerical worker had volunteered for the Territorials – in this case the 1/6th Hants. The official wrote to an officer of his acquaintance asking him to keep 'a fatherly eye upon him'. 'He is quite a superior boy … with excellent manners and comes from a superior home … not the ordinary run of Tommy'.[56] It was an epitaph that could be applied to the Territorial force as a whole.

Wartime Territorials reflected the social mix characteristic of the Pals' battalions. 'The 'average "Terrier"', Arthur Copeland wrote home from the Red Sea to his parents near Southampton, was 'rather a rough and rather vulgar person'. But was Arthur himself typical? He was 22, single, a naval architect and a pre-war Terrier. Though of typical age and marital standing, as a skilled technician he was much better educated and qualified than his comrades. But their 'grumbling and grousing', Arthur thought, was 'generally good humoured'.[57] While even Regular recruits were far from comprising only uneducated or unskilled working-class youths, Territorial volunteers, especially in wartime, reflected a broader and generally higher social complexion. George MacMunn, a Royal Artillery officer, was in many ways a classic Anglo-Indian (he thought that nationalist protest in 1919 stemmed from 'the cloven hoof of babu English'), but he noticed the differences between Territorials and the Regulars they replaced. He described them as coming from 'a more educated class of citizen, differed in culture and in manners from the hearty lads from field and workshop who usually took the King's shilling'.[58]

---

54 Letter, 22 August 1914, Hamilton papers, 6/4, LHCMA
55 Letter, 17 October 1914, Hamilton papers, 6/1, LHCMA
56 Letter, 20 November 1915, Reginald Welch, 1/6th Hants, M1446, RHRM
57 Letter, 31 October 1914, Arthur Copeland, 1/5th Hants, 128A08/1-4, HRO
58 MacMunn, *Turmoil and Tragedy in India*, pp. 73-74. 'Anglo-Indian' was in a state of transition. In 1911 the Government of India began using it to mean 'Eurasians', but it still connoted 'British-Indian'.

The swelling of volunteering in the war's first months imparted a strong stamp of idealism upon the Territorials, and gave them a character similar to Kitchener battalions in that they reflected a great diversity in social composition. Unlike New Army units, which suffered such horrific losses, on the Somme especially, decisively altering its character, many 'Indian' Territorial units retained their characteristic composition for much of the war. Ted Rice's platoon in Lucknow early in 1915 would still comprise 'a wonderful cross-section of British manhood', including the sons of businessmen, bank clerks, journalists and teachers as well as labourers, tradesmen, newspaper sellers and (like him) apprentice book-binders.[59]

Though the formation of Kitchener's 'New Army' worked against them, many Territorial units attracted strong enlistments, probably because they represented a familiar, uniformed, local presence. Second Lieutenant Stanley Goodland of the 5th Somerset visited Minehead at the end of August and returned with 80 volunteers, twice as many as he had expected.[60] Soon many units were over-establishment.

Verses, sung to the tune of 'It's a Long Way to Tipperary', composed in India by a man of the 1/7th Hants, suggests both the strongly regional character and the social cohesion of Territorial battalions:

> Our Colonel was Lord Montague
> He shook us each by hand
> And told us all how pleased he was
> The Battalion to command
> Our Captain's name was Stanley
> He came from Totten way
> He was a real good sort to us
> So all our company say[61]

In this the Territorials manifest the sort of local comradeship traditionally celebrated among Kitchener's 'Pals' battalions.

Kitchener envisaged a long war: the insight explained his raising of what became known as Kitchener's or the New Army. It also explained the decision to duplicate the existing Territorial formations, most of which within a month had greatly exceeded their establishments (the 4th Buffs was 1,300 strong by the end of August).[62] County associations were authorised to form what were at first called 'reserve' units, consisting of men opting for home service, including the thousands of civilian volunteers who were enlisting in Territorial units rather than in the New Army. Territorials who had 'failed to volunteer' for foreign service were transferred to what became a '2/' battalion (so men of the 4th Buffs reluctant to go overseas formed the basis of what

---

59 Ted Rice, 'All for a Shilling a Day', QRWS/30/RICE/1, SHC, Woking
60 Messenger, *Call to Arms*, p. 72
61 'It's a Long Way to Dear Old England', Alexander papers, M2564, RHRM. The papers of John Douglas-Scott-Montagu, 2nd Baron Montagu of Beaulieu (in LHCMA), are a key source. An Etonian, Montagu (not 'Montague') had worked in a railway workshop as an engineer and became devoted to mechanisation – he funded the magazine *The Car*. Returning to India with his mistress, Eleanor Thornton (the model for the Rolls Royce bonnet figure), she died in the torpedoing of the SS *Persia* in the Mediterranean on 30 December 1915.
62 Moody, *Historical Records of the Buffs*, p. 66

became the '2/4th Buffs').⁶³ The 4th and 5th Somerset Light Infantry, for example, spawned the 2/4th and 2/5th Battalions which accordingly formed part of the 2nd Wessex Division. Some of the wartime volunteers had been in uniform a matter of weeks before embarking – William Bisset was attested in the 2/4th Hants and boarded the transport *Caledonian* within a week.⁶⁴ Called, logically if somewhat disparagingly 'second line' divisions, as they were 'reserve' formations comprising mostly wartime volunteers, their units were particularly poorly equipped. Many of their infantry had 'the very old non-charger loading long rifles' which were practically unserviceable, and its artillery was obsolete and ineffective.⁶⁵

'I wish to go on Foreign Service': volunteering for Imperial Service

Lord Kitchener, as historian Peter Dennis put it, 'had nothing but contempt' for Territorials, a prejudice dating from witnessing how badly French volunteer troops who happened to share the name had performed in 1870.⁶⁶ His friend Haldane admitted that he had been 'unable to prevail upon him to adopt, or even make much real use of' the force Haldane had created.⁶⁷ This prejudice seems to have persuaded Kitchener to raise the 'New Armies' from scratch rather than, as Winston Churchill wrote, forming the new volunteers upon the Territorial Force as cadres to be 'duplicated or quadruplicated in successive stages'.⁶⁸ Kitchener's perversity left Britain with three major wartime forces, the Regulars, Territorials and New Army troops. As the newspapers of the empire reported in 1914, Kitchener was 'Preparing for [a] Long War'. He had already called for an additional half-million men to supplement the Regulars, reservists and Territorials, and would raise an entirely 'New Army' for a conflict that he intuitively understood would not be over soon. Part of his grand plan depended upon the Territorial Force being 'able and willing to go abroad'.⁶⁹ Not all were. As Sergeant Fred Mundy recalled of his Wilts comrades at Plymouth in the war's first weeks, 'very few were willing at first'.⁷⁰ (Scepticism over imperial service was expressed as soon as the prospect arose. When Herbert Ewing told his father that the 1/5th Somerset would go to India, Mr Ewing replied dismissively 'humbug!'⁷¹)

The 1907 Act establishing the Territorial Force quaintly stipulated that 'no part of the Territorial Force shall be carried or ordered to go out of the United Kingdom'.⁷² Its members,

---

63 This caused confusion at the time as well: a contributor to the 2/4th Hants *The Tiger's* 'Battalion Notes' complained that his unit, which had only existed for four months, had been called 'Reserve-Home Service', 1st Reserve – Second-Fourth' and now (as it remained) '2/4th' Hants. This also demonstrates the pronunciation – '2/4th' was spoken as 'second-fourth'.
64 Diary, 7-12 December 1914, William Bisset, 'Dum Spiro Spero', p. 1, M1834, RHRM
65 For clarity, from this point, battalions will be called 1/ or 2/, even though the form did not become fixed until early 1915.
66 Dennis, *The Territorial Army 1906-1940*, p. 30
67 Haldane, *An Autobiography*, pp. 278-79
68 Churchill *The World Crisis 1911-1914*, p. 236
69 *Sydney Morning Herald*, 2 October 1914, p. 8 (quoting *The Times* of 11 August)
70 Mundy, *A Journal of the 1/4th Battalion Wiltshire Regiment*, p. 6
71 Memoir, Herbert Ewing, 1/5th Somerset, Doc.15428, 07/8/1, IWM
72 *Territorial and Reserve Forces Act* 1907

however, could volunteer for what was termed 'Imperial Service', and their units would be accepted if more than sixty percent of their men agreed to the proposal. Few had done so before 1914: only five battalions in total out of more than two hundred in the force as a whole, though they included the 6th East Surrey. Typically, officers had opted for imperial service – every officer the 4th and 5th West Kent, for example. Men who had elected for 'Imperial Service' wore a small rectangular silver badge on their right breasts, bearing those words under a crown. Extraordinarily, no one but retired generals had considered how India's British garrison might be affected by a great European war. In a pamphlet published in 1914 a Hampshire general had suggested that India's 'first reinforcements should come from Australia, New Zealand and South Africa' and urged the War Office to 'consider how the necessary troops to reinforce India and our Colonies adjacent' might be found; though no one had suggested the Territorial Force.[73]

Within a week of the war's outbreak Kitchener had asked Edward Bethune whether any battalions were available for service abroad. Within a month, 69 Territorial battalions were reported to have volunteered. Some colonels called for volunteers and gained a 'very satisfactory' response; sufficient to embolden Kitchener to set aside his prejudice against Territorials and to consider them for a role greater than the defence of Britain against attack or invasion.[74] Challenging the shibboleth of home service required tactful enquiries. Bethune sounded out selected Territorial officers in order to convey to Kitchener the men's feeling. He summoned to London Major Arthur Garrett of the 4th King's Shropshire Light Infantry, apparently because he regarded it as 'a typical County battalion'. Garrett told Bethune that his men expected to be sent to France but were 'ready to go to any part of the world'. Bethune then left Garrett and spoke to Kitchener, who was waiting in an adjoining room.[75]

The War Office decided that if two-thirds of a battalion declared for imperial service then the battalion would be accepted for service overseas, with unwilling men transferred to hastily formed 'reserve' battalions. Among Shropshire Territorials 85% soon declared for voluntary service, despite the rat-ridden billets they occupied in Kent. Battalion commanding officers were urged to persuade men to volunteer. 'They presented it more or less as a Cook's Tour at Government expense', Alban Bacon recalled, though his own company commander advised him against volunteering, because he was 35.[76]

Charles Clinker, who would maintain a prosaic diary of departures and arrivals from 1914 to 1919, preserved a postcard addressed to his company commander at the 6th Hants' depot in Portsmouth informing him simply that 'I wish to go on Foreign Service'.[77] Why, he did not say; like most men. Ted Holter recalled that a senior officer had explained that by agreeing to serve overseas they would be releasing Regulars to go to France. (His mother was upset that he would be leaving home, but when she realised that he was going 'somewhere where there was no fighting she seemed quite pleased'.[78]) Men's actions did not always conform to the expected

---

73   Chapman, *Reinforcements for India, Ceylon, and the Straits Settlements and Hong Kong, in Time of Need*, np
74   Wylly, *History of the Queen's Royal Regiment*, Vol. VII, p. 139
75   de Wood, *The History of the King's Shropshire Light Infantry in the Great War*, p. 96
76   Bacon, *The Wanderings of a Temporary Warrior*, p. 13
77   Undated postcard, September 1914, Charles Clinker album, M3538, RHRM
78   Ted Holter, 'A Terrier in World War I', Doc 4545, 81/9/1, IWM

class response. In the 10th Middlesex the 'non-college' companies volunteered immediately and almost unanimously. The students of A and B companies, though, hesitated. While patriotic, many knew that their families had sacrificed themselves to see them enter teachers' college, and they needed to go home to confer with their parents.

Many Middlesex men volunteered for overseas service thinking that it would mean France. 'The most imaginative man in the battalion', one of the 9th Middlesex's officers recalled, had no notion that they would go much further than France.[79] The first volunteers naturally hoped to get to France. Private Allan Swift, a London businessman who had joined the 6th East Surrey specifically because it was one of the few battalions already willing to serve overseas, had 'great hopes of seeing active service amongst the first draft of Territorials to be sent across to France'.[80] When Devon Territorials realised that they were to not go to France they actually telegraphed the King. He reassured them, telegraphing back that they would be 'helping him and his Kingdom as much' by going to India.[81]

While Territorials were willing to go to India the military authorities in India were less willing to have them. Their hasty expansion, lack of training and poor equipment partly explains why British Indian officials were particularly scathing of Territorials. The Commander-in-Chief in India, General Sir Beauchamp Duff described its members as 'immature'. Lord Hardinge, the Viceroy, dismissed them as having 'very small military value'.[82] Proposals to supplement them with equally untrained New Army divisions failed – Kitchener wanted to retain all the new formations for the long struggle he rightly foresaw on the Western Front, and wartime volunteers, however patriotic, did not meet the need for trained Regulars.[83] While Hardinge accepted the need to release Regular battalions, he and his staff disagreed about what they could afford to lose. On Duff's advice, Hardinge wanted to retain at least nine Regular battalions, to form the British component of the three most active divisions 'since the danger zone is Afghanistan and the tribes against whom we must always be fully prepared'.[84] In the end Duff and Hardinge released all but eight Regular battalions.

The Government of India's military advisors particularly deprecated the replacement of Regular by Territorial artillery. The quality and presence of artillery became after 1857 one of the premier guarantors of British power — except for twelve mountain batteries all artillery in India was exclusively manned by British soldiers. Duff had to be persuaded forcibly by Kitchener to accept Territorial gunners and especially their obsolescent 15-pounder guns. Duff saw them as 'a limit beyond which risk becomes a serious danger'. 'You hardly seem to realise the seriousness of our position on the Continent', Kitchener replied testily the week after the first Marne battle, 'I cannot understand your refusal to accept the 15-pdr'. Hardinge tried to persuade Duff

---

79 Wyrall, *The Die-Hards in the Great War*, p. 68
80 Diary, 17 August 1914, Allan Swift, 1/6th East Surrey, ESR/25/SWIF/1, SHC, Woking
81 Aggett, *The Bloody Eleventh*, p. 4
82 Telegram 6 May 1915, Tel H-4714, Viceroy (Army Department) to Secretary of State, and 15 May 1915, S-10101, Commander-in-Chief to Secretary, War Office, WWI/147/II, War diary, Army Headquarters, India, Vol. 17 Part I, 1-31 May 1915, NAI; Telegram [Hardinge to Crewe], 1 February 1915, Kitchener papers, PRO30/57/69, NAUK
83 Letter, 1 February 1915, [Crewe to Kitchener], *Ibid*
84 Telegram 21 September 1914, Tel 1018, Viceroy (Army Department) to Secretary of State, WWI/286/H, War diary, Army Headquarters, India, IEF 'E', Vol. 1, NAI

but failed, and a week later was still writing 'an angry message in reply', but eventually both acceded to Kitchener's firm telegrams.[85]

The creation of the Territorial Force had been soured by deep dissension, and many Regular officers remained sceptical that its members could possibly meet the demands of a modern war against what was called in the jargon of the time a 'first-class enemy'. Even demi-official propagandists, such as the popular writer Edgar Wallace (author of *Sanders of the River* and, in time, *King Kong*) conceded that 'splendid as our Territorials were, they could not compare with these seasoned battalions', moreover, Regulars 'kicking their heels in far-away corners of the globe'.[86] But Territorials represented a huge reservoir of military strength. The British Expeditionary Force despatched to France in August included 60 infantry battalions: India's Regular British garrison numbered 52 battalions. Where were the troops to replace them to come from? One possible source was the 'white' dominions of Australia, Canada and New Zealand. At the war's outset the Melbourne *Argus* was already urging that 'contingents from the dominions can be sent to India to set free the British regulars'.[87] The Territorials, which were at least partly trained, offered a reservoir of 'white' troops. Indeed, those sent to India were not the first Territorials to go overseas — East Lancashire Territorials went to Egypt on 10 September, and two battalions of the Middlesex Brigade went to Gibraltar (which explained why Shropshire, Border or Welsh battalions came to be included among Indian Territorials). Why the Home Counties and Wessex divisions were selected is not clear. Hamilton had inspected brigades of the Home Counties Division. He told Charles Repington, *The Times's* influential military correspondent, that they were 'not in the front rank, but still … not so bad either' – hardly a ringing endorsement. Several days later he added that they 'produced a much more splendid impression' than even Regulars at Aldershot, hardly convincingly.[88]

To encourage men to volunteer for imperial service Kitchener and the King inspected the divisions, not altogether successfully. The Surrey Brigade waited for three hours in drizzling rain for them, and when they at last drove by, Ted Rice recalled, 'they both looked as fed up as we were'.[89] At least Kitchener arrived: Fred Mundy, the 4th Wilts and the entire Wessex Division paraded at Bustard Camp only for Kitchener to be called away. Despite these rebuffs they remained keen and confident. Edward Ewens's memoir, 'A Cook's Tour in Burma and India', written by a former member of the 2/5th Somerset in the later 1920s, expresses perfectly the idealistic, naïve and trusting character of the Territorials answering Kitchener's call:

> We are only terriers called up at our Country's need, amateur soldiers, not soldiers by profession, but still keen on doing our best, and with as much esprit de corps as any regular battalion that ever left England.[90]

---

85 *Report of the Commission appointed by Act of Parliament to enquire into the Operation of War in Mesopotamia*, Parliamentary Papers, 1917-18, Vol. 16 [hereafter Mesopotamia Commission], p. 124
86 Wallace, *Kitchener's Army and the Territorial Forces*, p. 164
87 *Argus* (Melbourne), 4 August 1914, p. 8
88 Letters, 24 and 26 October 1914, Hamilton papers, 6/12, LHCMA
89 Ted Rice, 'All for a Shilling a Day', QRWS/30/RICE/1, SHC, Woking
90 Edward Ewens, 'A Cook's Tour in Burma and India', DD\SLI/17/1/62, SHC, Taunton

Ewens affirmed that he and his comrades were 'intent on doing our bit ... and so uphold the name of Somerset'. Few of those who volunteered asked about the material consequences of their decision. Rates of pay for Territorial infantry embodied for war service were supposedly the same as Regulars; that is a shilling a day for privates (a rate unchanged for decades, though 'stoppages' for rations or clothing had largely ended) rising to 1/8 for corporals, 2/4 for sergeants, 4/- for company sergeants-major and 5/- for regimental sergeants-major. County associations undertook to pay 'separation allowances' to families, but enlistment cost many men a serious cut in family income which was to bring hardship to many. No statistics exist establishing exactly how many Territorials were married, but figures for the two Middlesex battalions in India suggest that between a quarter and a fifth of the initial battalions' members were married, and the two Middlesex battalions' men had near 500 children between them.[91]

'In France you'll fight': Kitchener's promise

On Salisbury Plain, Major-General Colin Donald received a telegram commanding him to visit the War Office the following day. Entering Kitchener's office, he 'got a little bit of a shock' when Kitchener asked (as was his wont, without any preliminary small-talk), 'I want you to take your Division to India; will they go?' Donald replied that he didn't think that anyone had thought about it, but that if Kitchener wanted them to 'they will go there right enough'. Kitchener told him to parade his troops and 'to tell them from me that ... by going to India they will be performing a great Imperial duty'. He explained that he was bringing British troops home and needed 'white troops' to replace them. He then told Donald that 'at the end of six months' he 'intend[ed] to bring them home ... they will share in all the honours of the War just as if they had gone to France'.[92] Edward Bethune later added that he had been summoned immediately after (their cars crossed paths on the way to the War Office) and Kitchener both sought Bethune's advice and offered the same undertaking. Bethune lamented that it had seemed necessary to induce men to volunteer for overseas service by giving them an undertaking which reflection must have demonstrated would be impossible to fulfil. 'It was not necessary to "kid"' the Territorial soldier, Bethune thought, 'not necessary to humbug him'.[93] By September Territorials were enthusiastic. Fred Mundy's fellow Wiltshire Territorials, who had been so unwilling at Plymouth, now 'all shouted for joy ... "India" was the talk of the camp'.[94] Stanley Goodland told his fiancée Elsie that much as he dreaded the idea of a long sea voyage 'next to going to France' Indian service was 'the greatest honour the War Office can bestow'.[95]

Given the British army's emphasis on regimental history and tradition – a heritage emphasised in badges, mottos, colours and uniform distinctions – every man under embarkation orders would have known of his regiment's connections with the military history of British India. The Regular battalions of every one of the fourteen regiments arriving in 1914-15 had served in

---

91 Minutes, 28 June 1915, Middlesex Territorial Association, 0994/002, LMA
92 Comment by Major-General Colin Donald in Woodyatt, 'The Territorials (Infantry) in India', *JRUSI*, 1922 p. 730
93 Comment by Major-General Edward Bethune in *Ibid*, p. 727
94 Mundy, *A Journal of the 1/4th Battalion Wiltshire Regiment*, p. 8
95 Letter, 24 September 1914, Stanley Goodland, 1/5th Somerset, Noyes, (ed.), *Engaged in War*, p. 8

India at some time in the succeeding 150-odd years, some for long periods. The Hampshires wore a tiger on their cap badges to mark the 21 years which the 37th Foot had served in India from 1805; Somerset Light Infantry Regulars (though not its Territorials) bore the battle honour 'Jellalabad' on theirs. Men could recite the 'battle honours' adorning their regiments' colours – six of which bore those for 'Afghanistan', five for the 'Indian Mutiny' and six for the two Anglo-Sikh wars, with others – Seringapatam (1799), Gwalior (1843), Burma (both 1824-26 and 1885-87), and campaigns on the north-west frontier; Chitral (1895), Dargai (1897) and Tirah (1897-98). Territorials were to remember their parent regiments' Indian wars. The 2/6th Royal Sussex would march from Bangalore to Mysore and back in mid-1916, camping at Seringapatam, the men marvelling at the prowess of their forebears who besieged and took the fortress twice in the late eighteenth century.[96] In Delhi the 1/4th Wilts would hold annual Ferozeshah Dances to mark the 61st Foot's 1845 battle against the Sikhs. When the 1/4th Cornwall arrived in Lucknow in 1914 its men laid wreaths at the memorial (of Cornish granite) to the men of the 32nd Cornwall Light Infantry who died in the siege in 1857.

In any case, orders for India did not, they understood, mean that they would remain there. 'At the end of six months', Kitchener had assured Donald, 'the Division would be replaced in India by other troops, and would then go direct to serve on the Western Front'.[97] 'Kitchener's Promise', as it became widely known, was repeated and recorded in many diaries and letters. It is the first of the grievances expressed by the epic doggerel, 'A Territorial's Life in India' composed by a Somerset Territorial in 1916:

> "Now come with me," our Colonel cried,
> "To India so bright,
> And I'll guarantee that in 4 months
> In France you'll be to fight …"[98]

Not all Territorial officers were happy to go to India rather than to France. One told Christopher Atkinson, the historian of several regiments, that they considered being sent to India 'a poor form of service', but they complied nevertheless, accepting the undertaking that they would be back before 1915 was out.[99]

---

96 'Bangalore to Mysore City and Back by Road', *The Royal Sussex Herald*, 12 August 1916, pp. 182-83
97 [Dorsetshire Regiment] Regimental History Committee, *History of the Dorsetshire Regiment 1914-1919*, Part II, p. 11
98 'A Territorial in India', Mackie, *Answering the Call*, p. 211
99 Atkinson, *The Queen's Own Royal West Kent Regiment 1914-1919*, p. 69

2

Passages to India

Accepting the invitation to serve overseas soon saw the equivalent of three Territorial divisions embark for India. Their voyages opened them to the wider world, but also revealed the Territorials' relationship to military authority and to the sub-continent they had come to hold for the empire.

'They disappeared into the night': embarkation orders

From 9 and 30 October the infantry and artillery of the Home Counties and Wessex divisions embarked from Southampton in convoys of eleven and eight ships. The second Wessex Division (the 'reserve' or '2/' battalions) left in seven ships on 12 December, all three convoys bound mainly for Bombay. In the end, 41 Territorial battalions were to go India: 36 in 1914, one in 1915 and four in 1916.[1] All came from southern English counties with the exception of the 1/1st Brecknock, 1/4th Shropshire and two battalions of the Border Regiment. These battalions were 'Army' units for the Welsh and Lancashire districts, un-allotted to brigades and therefore available. Curiously, the four Territorial Royal Sussex or Hampshire 'Army' battalions allotted to the two divisions did not accompany them to India but were shifted elsewhere, a sign of the improvisation necessary in the crisis of the British army's expansion early in the war.[2]

Departing troops had little notice – the 1/6th East Surrey had twelve days between notification and embarkation and most battalions granted men 48 hours leave to farewell their families, manage business, estate and family affairs and to sort out matters that could not wait. Battalions were ordered to transfer men surplus to a fixed establishment and to entrain for Southampton on

---

1   Nigel Woodyatt, in the only article on the Territorials in India, published in 1922, mentioned 45 battalions, but he was counting several battalions of the Rifle Brigade as Territorial. While these Rifle Brigade battalions may have been *called* 'Territorial', the Rifle Brigade had no Territorials before 1914, and all their members had joined after the outbreak of war. I have not counted them.
2   Kitchener had seemingly intended to send the Welsh Division to India, a proposal scuppered by Lloyd George, who dreamed of (and intrigued for) a Welsh Army Corps, without success. The Brecknock was a Territorial battalion of the South Wales Borderers. Though it recruited in Monmouthshire, Herefordshire and Brecknockshire, the 1/1st's men mostly hailed from Brecknockshire.

Territorials of the East Surrey Regiment leaving Canterbury in October 1914, complete with tropical sun helmets. (ESR 25/BOEW/1, Surrey History Centre)

a rigid schedule involving the co-ordination of dozens of trains and convoys of merchant ships and naval escorts. Did they know where they were going? Some units (such as the 1/4th Wilts) were told before departure, some guessed after being issued with sun helmets, while others were ignorant even when boarding. Bert Rendall of the 1/5th Somerset had no idea of the *Ionian's* destination, though the rumour of Burma spread as the ship passed Malta.

So early in the war, few who knew troubled to keep their destination secret. When a group of Hampshire Territorials met an elderly patriot in a pub in Wiltshire before leaving, he asked them whether they were off to 'the Front'. '" … we're going to India first', they replied, 'and after a few months we are to return to the Front"', reflecting what the Territorial divisions had been told by their officers.[3] Captain Roger Haslewood of the 1/4th Shropshire sent a telegram to his mother: 'Sailing tonight on Desado' and then, a month later, 'All well Bombay'.[4] Many civilians farewelling relatives and friends knew and joked about their destination. Somerset Territorials leaving Wells were asked by well-wishers for 'Indian trophies', including a parrot (a man replied that he was sorry but he'd already promised to return with five elephants 'so he said'). They marched to the station behind the Wells City Band, joined by the Glastonbury Half-Company,

---

3   'A Territorial in India', *Punch*, 27 January 1915, p. 69
4   Telegrams, Roger Haslewood, 1/4th Shropshire, 3614/2/142-161, SA

which 'added additional excitement'.⁵ When the 2/5th Somerset left Taunton by train some men's families were able to farewell them. Bert Rendall's parents saw him off at the station. His father, a former soldier, turned to his mother and said 'You won't see him no more, Hannah, for five years' – an accurate prediction.⁶ The Territorials' departure essentially severed their links with home administratively as well as emotionally. General Edward Bethune, the Director-General of the Territorial Force, recalled in introducing a lecture (the *only* lecture) about their Indian service that 'I saw them off at Southampton and they disappeared into the night'.⁷

'Going the wrong way': the voyages

Territorials' diaries and memoirs naturally devote disproportionate space to their voyage to India. It was most men's first time out of Britain, it was an encounter with the unfamiliar and the exotic, and they had time to fill. They shared the experience with other large contingents of citizen soldiers from around the empire – Australians, Canadians and New Zealanders – who at exactly the same moment were also voyaging to war, part of an epic such as none had previously experienced. Like Anzacs and Canadians, they were all volunteers (for this war and for overseas service), they were making a sacrifice: and they were anticipating an adventure, the like of which none of them could have anticipated.

The ships 'taken up from trade' by the Admiralty, were a mixed bag. Whether men enjoyed the voyage depended upon the ship to which their unit had been allocated. Allan Swift, aboard the overcrowded *Grantully Castle*, along with 1600 other East and West Surrey men, as well as three batteries of artillery, found the 'meals uneatable, accommodation insufficient … voyage unenjoyable'.⁸ To their indignation they learned that the rest of the 1/6th East Surrey had gone in the *Almara*, which was much better. The 1/9th Middlesex was also divided in two, half going in the *Dilwara*, the rest in the *Dongola*. The *Dilwara* was a smelly, over-crowded tub. Its coal bunkers caught fire and it had to put into Gibraltar, to be greeted by the Middlesex Territorials forming its garrison. Aboard the *Kenilworth Castle* was General Colin Donald (who accompanied his division to India), the 1/4th Wilts, the 1/7th Hants and artillery batteries from both counties. Stanley Goodland told Elsie that it seemed 'like a swagger hotel' – the more so because he was among the party of 1/5th Somerset officers transferred from the *Alnwick Castle* because it lacked sufficient cabins considered suitable for officers.⁹ Fred Mundy thought that his comrades were lucky to have the largest and fastest of the transports. Others were less fortunate: Victor Manley's 2/4th Hants in the *Caledonia* had just six wash-basins for 2,400 passengers, while Arthur Copeland caught lice in the *Cawdor Castle*.

A blow struck at the Territorials' efficiency was that literally half-an-hour before some cast off, all the battalions' Regular adjutants were withdrawn. The first two Territorial divisions left soon after casualty returns arrived from the first battle of the Aisne, in which the Regulars of the British Expeditionary Force suffered so heavily. The Territorials offered a ready source

---

5   *Wells Journal*, 2 October 1914, p. 15
6   Interview with Bert Rendall, Mills, *A Strange War*, p. 9
7   Woodyatt, 'The Territorials (Infantry) in India', *RUSJ*, 1922, p. 717
8   Diary, 11 November 1914, Allan Swift, 1/6th East Surrey, ESR/25/SWIF/1, SHC, Woking
9   Letter, 14 October 1914, Stanley Goodland, 1/5th Somerset, Noyes, (ed.), *Engaged in War*, p. 10

from which to replenish losses among trained officers. The 10th Middlesex's adjutant, Captain Arthur Docker, was whisked off the ship as it left Southampton, cheered by the men he had trained since 1912, and he reported to France, where he was killed within days of reaching the trenches. Territorial officers took over the crucial jobs as adjutants.

Beyond the stormy Bay of Biscay the weather cleared, and the convoy steamed through brilliant sunshine, over a sparkling blue sea under an azure sky. In the Mediterranean men were excited to see porpoises and sharks, and the exotic sights of Gibraltar, Malta and Port Said. Gerald Gibbs, a Kingston Grammar boy in the 1/5th East Surrey aboard the *Alaunia*, would never forget 'the first thrill of the big ship, the open sea, the foreign places and the land smell coming off the coast of North Africa and Egypt by night'.[10] He thought that it made such an impression because he was just seventeen (having put his age up on volunteering), but judging by their diaries, letters and memoirs the voyage affected many men regardless of their ages. Early in November ships wireless operators received news eventually passed to the troops which was to be portentous for many: 'we have just got a wireless through to say that Turkey has declared war'.[11] Perhaps a thousand of the Territorials aboard the ships would lose their lives directly as a result of that decision.

At Gibraltar the convoys broke up, with ships proceeding independently at their best speeds and all made for the Suez Canal. There, Territorials' diaries often mention passing troopships carrying east the Regular battalions from India used to improvise the 8th, 27th, 28th and 29th Divisions. In 1915 they would lose heavily, in France or (for the 29th Division) on Gallipoli. As the canal was narrow enough for passengers on passing ships to communicate, naturally the Regulars chaffed the Territorials: diary after diary refers to it. Arthur Copeland described how they called out 'You are going the wrong way'.[12] 'The conversation between us was always the same', another Hants man wrote, 'Hi! You are going the wrong way!'[13] (Regulars who had served in Burma caused the 2/5th Somerset consternation when they replied 'God help you' to Territorials calling out their destination.) When the *Royal George* met French civilians in Tewfik its 'Sinjuns' (Middlesex men of St John's Battersea) sang the Marseillaise in French – 'the ladies nearly went mad with excitement', Walter Saunders wrote, a further sign that they were hardly 'ordinary Tommies'.[14]

The voyage gave hints of the Territorials' temper. Not all accepted inoculation (often re-using the same needle), the Territorials' privilege to refuse. On the *Ionian*, carrying the 2/5th Somerset, 2/4th Devon and the 2/4th Dorset, the ship's promenade deck (taking up much of the open space) was reserved for the 100 officers aboard. The 2000 'other ranks' were squeezed into a much smaller area, with 'nothing to do and no room to do it in'.[15] The men 'packed in like beasts in Taunton Market', Edward Ewens recalled, almost staged a mutiny. 'Older hands' – both non-commissioned officers and men – talked the restive men out of protesting.[16] But Devon men objected to the quantity of food served on the *Ionian* (the crew had stolen flour and sold

10 Gibbs, *Survivor's Story*, pp. 12-13
11 Diary, 5 November 1914, Cyril Burgess, 1/5th Buffs, Doc.6711, 91/26/1, IWM
12 Letter, 24 October 1914, Arthur Copeland, 1/5th Hants, 128A08/1-4, HRO
13 Clipping, Stokes-Roberts papers, M2185, RHRM
14 Transcript of diary and letters, Walter Saunders, 1/10th Middlesex, Doc. 6571, 79/15/1, IWM
15 Edward Ewens, 'A Cook's Tour in Burma and India', DD\SLI/17/1/62, SHC, Taunton
16 Mills, *A Strange War*, p. 15

hungry soldiers buns). They marched about the deck singing 'We want grub' to the hymn tune 'Lead kindly light'.[17] Protests over scanty food also emerged among Shropshire men on their onward voyage from Calcutta to Rangoon. During the four-day train journey from Bombay to Calcutta men had gone thirteen hours without food on the first day, and at breakfast next day received 'half a pint of tea and no food'. Once aboard the *City of Marseille*, men 'became troublesome and began to shout', and the next morning 'they gave us a better lot of food'.[18] The Shropshires' experience suggests both the forbearance Territorials often showed, but also that it had limits. The voyages exposed the class divide between officers and men. At a concert aboard the *Kenilworth Castle* Old Etonian officers rendered 'The Eton Boating Song', while Lord Radnor sang 'Forty Years on', the Harrow school song. 'The troops', an officer recalled, 'remained unmoved'.[19] Though citizen soldiers learned to accept military discipline in India, that assertive demeanour would again emerge at the war's end.

'Pride and perspiration': arriving

Most ships arrived at Bombay; a few, carrying units destined for the Punjab and Baluchistan, docked at Karachi. 'Travellers who have not been in the east before', Murray's 1913 guide had promised, 'will be struck by the picturesqueness of the scene on landing in Bombay'. Indeed, Terriers' letters and diaries echo its evocation of the scenes it described: 'the crowds of people dressed in the most brilliant and varied costumes; the Hindus of different castes … the gaily-painted bullock carts; and other sights of equal novelty combine to make a lasting impression on the stranger's mind.'[20]

The day the 1/5th Hants arrived in Bombay was a day 'of pride and perspiration' though the anonymous writer, who supplied a series of facetious but informative articles to *Punch*, mistakenly believed that his battalion landed first.[21] India figured in the regimental histories of the regiments represented by the Territorials arriving at Bombay. The Dorset Regiment, which as the 39th Foot had fought under Clive at Plassey in 1757, proudly wore on its cap badge the motto 'Primus in Indis' – it had been the first 'royal' regiment (as opposed to European mercenaries of the East India Company) to serve there. When Major-General Colin Donald had addressed the Wessex Division at Durrington he turned to the 4th Dorset and said,

> You men of the Dorset Regiment – your Regiment bears the proud motto, "Primus in Indis". You shall be the first of the Territorials to set foot in India.[22]

It was a matter of pride – and of unusually canny management on the part of the War Office – that the Dorset should be the first Territorials to disembark: and they did. On 10 November

---

17 Memoir, A.E. Serle, 1/4th Devon, Doc.7350, 76/154/1, IWM
18 Diary, 3–8 December 1914, Ben Nicholas, 1/4th Shropshire, Private collection
19 Blick, *The 1/4th Battalion The Wiltshire Regiment*, p. 22
20 Anon, *A Handbook for Travellers*, p. 6
21 'A Territorial in India', *Punch*, 20 January 1915, p. 53
22 [Dorsetshire Regiment] Regimental History Committee, *History of the Dorsetshire Regiment 1914-1919*, Part II, p. 11

Captain John Roper of the 1/4th Dorset was 'first off the *Assaye* ... so we were Primus in Indis' again'.²³ Within days of their arrival they were guarding compliant German civilian internees in a large camp at Ahmednagar, 150 miles east of Bombay. The Dorsets were greeted by three military bands, including the Ox and Bucks Light Infantry, which played the newcomers into the cantonment and promptly left to serve in Mesopotamia. When it arrived in January 1915 the 2/4th Dorset also went to Ahmednagar, with a detachment at a camp at Poona. One of these men inflicted the Territorials' first casualty on the enemy. A Dorset patrolling the barbed wire surrounding the Poona camp warned an internee apparently trying to escape, and then bayonetted him. Because the man died the next day civil authorities wanted to charge the Dorset man with manslaughter (Nigel Woodyatt rewarded his 'zeal' by having him promoted to lance-corporal.²⁴) Curiously, one of the Germans interned at Ahmednagar was a former member of the 1/5th Hants found to have been born in Germany.²⁵

A scene on the dockside at Bombay when the 2/4th Wilts arrived in January 1915. The snapshot, over-exposed and out of focus, suggests the Territorials' disorientation as they first encountered India. (SBYRW32075, Rifles Berkshire and Wiltshire Museum)

A versifier in the *Times of India* celebrated the Territorials' arrival:

> From Eastshire and Westshire,
>   From country and from town,
> From Northshire and Southshire,
>   From coast and rolling down;
> From counter, workshop, office,
>   (With your pay by much decreased)
> You left the old familiar haunts
>   To seek the shiny East²⁶

'A closed book': British India in 1914

What did the Territorials know of India when they arrived? Alexander Sturt's booklet, *Our Indian Empire*, offered 'some hints for the use of soldiers proceeding to India', distributed on

---

23 Diary, 10 November 1914, John Roper, 1/4th Dorset, 1971-71, DMM
24 Woodyatt, 'The Territorials (Infantry) in India', *RUSIJ*, 1922, p. 721
25 Anon, *History of the Hampshire Territorial Force Association*, p. 139
26 Sheppard, *Territorials in India*, p. 3. Regulars spoke of India thus; often just as the 'The Shiny'.

troopships.[27] Much of what novices would know of India would have been gleaned, Sturt accepted, from 'school books and cheap fiction', to which might be added cigarette cards and illustrated magazines. Few possessed more than this superficial knowledge. 'India remains a closed book to ninety-nine percent even of educated Englishmen', a British-Indian author had written in 1914.[28] Few understood, for example, the import of the 'Morley-Minto reforms of 1909, which heralded modest political changes. But surely most saw India as 'the 'jewel' of the empire. The great cricketer Ranjitsinhji had captained Sussex, a legend as a batsman in the youth of many of those now facing Indian service. Many Territorials could have known retired Anglo-Indian civilians. Historian David Gilmour found that the most popular counties for Indian officials to retire to were 'Surrey and Devonshire, followed by Sussex and Hampshire' – counties from which hailed seventeen Territorial battalions.[29]

'A certain section in India', a tiny minority of Indians, mostly educated in English and politically active, 'looked forward to a measure of self-government', the Secretary of State for India, the Marquess of Crewe, had acknowledged in the House of Lords in 1912. Crewe saw 'no future for India on these lines'.[30] Influential and representative Indians had responded willingly to the empire's crisis in 1914. The rulers of princely states had offered money and men unstintingly and spontaneously. India's moderate nationalist congress had also loyally expressed its support for the war against Germany. For four years the Viceroy had been Charles, Lord Hardinge, grandson of the Governor-General who had presided over the first Anglo-Sikh war in the 1840s. Hardinge's term saw the raj grapple with what its officials called 'sedition' and 'terrorism', the manifestations of frustrated nationalist aspiration, and the creation of Delhi as a new imperial capital. The architect of the new Delhi, later called New Delhi, Edwin Lutyens, began work under Hardinge, tormented by Hardinge's desire for both speed and economy. One of the first buildings completed for the new scheme, the Secretariat Building, a long, low, white-washed building in the syncretic Indo-Saracenic style New Delhi made its own, was to become part of the Territorials' sojourn in India. The 1/4th Wilts was to use its offices as barrack rooms for up to six men each, its larger rooms for a regimental institute, and was to hold concerts in the council room (now the chamber of the Delhi Legislative Assembly).

Sir George Barrow, Military Secretary at the India Office (and therefore India's most influential soldier, second only to the Commander-in-Chief) dismissed the Territorials as 'indifferently armed and only partially trained' in 1914. But he, like Duff, had been obliged to accept them, because the empire's actual need in Europe trumped India's potential need for Regulars. Barrow himself conceded that in August 1914 India enjoyed 'profound peace. The Frontier was tranquil … not a cloud on the horizon'.[31] That calm would not last long, and its end would affect the Territorials.

27 Sturt, *Our Indian Empire*, title page. The medical officer of the 1/5th West Kent thought that too few copies were made available for it to have much influence.
28 Archer, *India and the Future*, p. xxiii
29 Gilmour, *The Ruling Caste*, p. 313
30 Archer, *India and the Future*, p. 4
31 'Military situation in India consequent on the war', 17 June 1915, CAB37/129/16, NAUK. Barrow was at the time serving in France, so his view must have been based on advice from India.

'Fred Karno's Ragtime Army on Tour': their first stations

The movement orders handed to Territorial adjutants when they reached the docks at Bombay dictated their initial experience of India. Most battalions went to stations in northern India. Even Murray's tourist Handbook noted that 'six of the nine Army Divisions ... are in the corner of India, N.W. of Lucknow'.[32] At first, some battalions seemed to be posted close to others from the same brigade, so the four Surrey battalions went to Allahabad, Lucknow, Cawnpore and Fyzabad, and the three Devon battalions went to the Punjab. But the 1/5th, 1/6th and 1/7th battalions in the 1st Wessex Division's Hants brigade were immediately separated, going to Poona, Dinapore and Bombay respectively, barely seeing each other for the rest of the war. Among the last of the Territorial units to reach India was the 2/4th Border, one of the 'Army' battalions drafted in to make up the numbers, which arrived in Poona on 1 April 1915. By then the exchange between India's exclusively Regular and mainly Territorial garrison was complete.

The Territorials' troop trains left Bombay on journeys commonly taking several days, their first sight of India exciting great interest. 'Their curiosity', commented a reporter in *The Indiaman*, 'was insatiable'.... As the long slow trains crawled across the plains the windows sprouted "topis"' – sun helmets – as men gazed at the novel country and its people.[33] Surprisingly in wartime, perhaps, their destinations were well publicised both in newspapers in India and in men's local papers – the *Kent Messenger* published accounts that listed where all the Buffs and West Kent battalions had been stationed, and the three Kent batteries. Somerset and Wiltshire newspapers also gave details of the movements and stations of their various battalions.

Several of these locations were almost immediately changed, with battalions and batteries making the first of many changes of station, the perpetual condition of British units in India. Almost all units changed stations at least twice a year, the exceptions that the 2/4th Hants were to remain in Quetta for two years, the 2/4th Wilts in Poona for two-and-a-half, and the 1/1st Brecknock at Mhow from its arrival from Aden in August 1915 to August 1919. (At Mhow, the Brecknocks' adjutant, Molyneux Thomas wrote, 'one day is much the same as the other'.[34] Mhow, Murray's *Handbook* admitted, had 'no special interest for a traveller'.[35])

Territorials arriving in their first cantonments often received hearty greetings. At Secunderabad practically the entire population of the station, European and Indian, turned out to welcome the 1/5th West Surrey. At Ferozepore the cantonment was en fête, with firecrackers let off at the railway station, all the Indian pleaders (and 'respectable bankers') greeting the 1/4th Devon, and school-children dragooned into flag-waving.[36] In remote Baluchistan 'the whole of Quetta' turned out, but what they saw was, Alban Bacon of the 2/4th Hants admitted, 'a bedraggled, travel-worn battalion, many of whom had palpably handled rifles for the first time on the boat', their unfamiliar topees clumsily bound with pagris in a myriad of fantastic shapes. 'Everything conspired', Bacon admitted, 'to give Quetta a poor impression of the first

---

32   Anon, *A Handbook for Travellers*, p. 293. A tenth Division occupied Burma.
33   Sheppard, *Territorials in India*, p. 4
34   Letter, 5 December 1916, Brecknock Battalion, South Wales Borderers 1911-1939, 2013-58, Box 17, RMRW
35   Anon, *A Handbook for Travellers*, p. 112
36   *Bulletin* (Lahore), 16 November 1914, Ex2384-9, DMM; Diary, 1914, Charles Gibson, 1/4th Devon, 2007-1474, DMM

The 1/6th Hants marching into Dinapore cantonment soon after their arrival in India, late in 1914, a postcard sent by Owen Smith to his sister. (M766, Royal Hampshire Regiment Museum)

Territorials to arrive in that desert land'.[37] Edward Ewens admitted that his comrades' attempts to don the new webbing belts were laughable and men of the 2/5th Somerset joked that they were 'Fred Karno's Ragtime Army on Tour'.[38] At Jubbulpore the 1/5th Somerset created a poor impression when the welcoming band played at 120 rather than the Somersets' accustomed light infantry 140 paces a minute.

As 'griffins' – newcomers to India – the arriving Territorials encountered many of the novel features of India that Britons had been dealing with for three centuries, what the 2/4th Hants history called 'the interior economy peculiar to that Country'.[39] Regimental histories often paid tribute to the 'conducting parties' detailed from the departing Regular battalions who were to instruct the newcomers to the ways of India, its bazaars and cantonments and often of the army – at least half of the first contingents of Territorials were practically civilians, and the proportion of later units was even higher. The conducting parties seem to have done their work diligently. The 2/5th Hants at Secunderabad described the help of 1st Royal Sussex men as 'simply invaluable', finding that they 'completely identified' with the novices.[40]

'The new arrival', a booklet issued to Territorials advised, 'cannot do better than follow the example of those who have learnt by experience'.[41] This was certainly true and necessary when

37 Bacon, *The Wanderings of a Temporary Warrior*, p. 18
38 Mills, *A Strange War*, p. 12. Fred Karno was a popular music-hall slapstick comedian, supposedly the inventor of the pie-in-the-face routine.
39 Anon, *History of the Hampshire Territorial Force Association*, p. 125
40 'History of the Second Fifth', *Regimental Journal, 2/5th Hampshire Battalion*, August 1916, p. 14, RHRM
41 Sturt, *Our Indian Empire*, p. 24

it came to the precautions to be taken with India's sun, insects and microbes. The Regulars also passed on their way of dealing with the country's inhabitants, that shouting, cuffs and abuse worked with servants or bazaar shop-keepers. 'We are getting more like the regulars every day', Herbert Ewing wrote approvingly in his diary a month after arriving in Ambala.[42] The Regulars obliged to stay in India, and especially their officers, were still 'deeply cursing their fate', not yet realising the magnitude of the casualties among the British Expeditionary Force at Ypres.[43]

Men of the 2nd Wessex particularly were new both to military life as well as to India. The second-line units struck observers as 'distinctly raw'. Soon after a wing of the 2/4th Dorset arrived at Kirkee in January 1915 an officer and sergeant doing the rounds of sentries at the arsenal found one sitting down reading a newspaper. When reprimanded the sentry said 'he could do the job "sat down" as well as he could do it "stood up"'.[44] Territorials repeatedly expressed their 'civilian' character – when the 1/5th Hants was taking its Kitchener Test companies on the march were required to turn in a half circle, and naturally men began to sing 'Here we go round the Mulberry Bush'.[45] Tyro units repeatedly demonstrated their inexperience, in military procedures and in coping with India. When the 1/4th Wilts marched up to the hills during its first hot weather, platoons followed each other too closely, and so ate the dust of the platoon in front. The next day they set off at longer intervals, but then made the mistake of marching in step across a suspension bridge over the River Jumna when the rhythmic march-step set the bridge swaying.

Arrival often heralded disillusionment. Geoffrey Coombs of the 1/4th Buffs wrote to a former Dover school-friend from Bareilly describing how 'all my pre-formed notions of the mystic East were soon dispelled' by a closer acquaintance with Indian towns. Coombs recalled his revulsion at 'the filth of the bazaars, the indescribable squalor of the native inhabitants' and 'the servitude of the women'.[46] Within weeks of their arrival indications appeared of Territorials realising the implications of their blithe decision to opt for 'Imperial Service'. *The Statesman* of Calcutta published a letter from Lord Esher, Chairman of the County of London Territorial Association (which had not actually provided units for India, though Londoners were common in Middlesex, Surrey and East Kent units). Esher rebuked those who declined to volunteer for overseas service unless it meant going to France. 'It is just as high an honour to be sent to India, Aden or Malta', he wrote, 'The honour is in obedience to Lord Kitchener'.[47]

'A big risk': the armies of British India

As men of the Territorial battalions and batteries stretched their weary limbs after their long rail journeys they became part of Britain's military epic in India. The East Surrey found themselves in Kandahar Barracks, Fyzabad, named for Field Marshal Sir Frederick Roberts's triumph in 1879, and then at Roberts Barracks, Rawalpindi, named for 'Bobs' himself, who had died almost exactly as they arrived in India at his home in Surrey. The army the Territorials were joining

---

42   Diary, 9 December 1914, Herbert Ewing, 1/5th Somerset, Doc.15428, 07/8/1, IWM
43   Bacon, *The Wanderings of a Temporary Warrior*, p. 16
44   Regimental History Committee, *History of the Dorsetshire Regiment 1914-1919*, Part II, p. 71
45   Clipping, Hinton Harris, 1/5th Hants, M1543.2, RHRM
46   Letter, 21 March 1916, Geoffrey Coombs, 1/4th Buffs, EK/U127/2 KA&HC
47   *The Statesman*, 20 January 1915

was surely one of the most remarkable military forces in history. It comprised two components, the Indian Army (its formal title for less than a decade) and the British 'Army in India'. In 1914, as its name suggested, the Indian Army comprised soldiers of India, mainly 'natives' but commanded by British officers, comprising 39 regiments of cavalry and 138 battalions of infantry. The Army in India constituted British soldiers, about 75,000 men and officers, serving tours of ten years or more. They included nine regiments of British cavalry, 52 battalions of British infantry and 56 batteries of field or horse artillery.[48]

Kitchener had wanted all but three Regular battalions to go to war, though by the year's end they numbered just eight battalions, two cavalry regiments and thirteen batteries. For several weeks, until the Territorials arrived, Lord Hardinge recalled, the total British garrison amounted to no more than 15,000 men: 'a big risk'.[49] Despite acceding to Kitchener's plan, Indian officials remained sceptical. Crewe, the Secretary of State for India (advised by Hardinge and reflecting his doubts), in a letter to Kitchener decried the Territorials as 'half-baked', fearful of the British garrison 'getting into very low water'.[50]

India had been for almost a century the British Army's second home: Corelli Barnet in his *Britain and Her Army* even suggested 'perhaps its first'.[51] After what they called the 1857 Mutiny British troops had served alongside the sepoys and sowars of the native armies of Bengal, Madras and Bombay, a ratio of about 1:2, the Indian Army used and lauded, but not entirely trusted. Indians paid for this force through the misleadingly named 'Home Charges'. (Shashi Tharoor not unreasonably pointed out in his acerbic *Inglorious Empire* that 'Indians literally paid for their own oppression'.[52])

In the decade before the Great War Kitchener had challenged this composite force. While reforming its organisation, distribution and governance, he had confronted the Viceroy, Lord Curzon and bested him. Curzon had condemned the army's 'absurd and uncontrolled expenditure … lack of method and system … slackness and jobbery [and] a want of fibre and tone'.[53] Though it had been partially overhauled in the 1890s (when the old 'presidency' armies had been abolished, though their ghosts lived on in the army's order of battle, still listed in the order of Bengal, Madras and Bombay) the army remained unprepared for all but frontier warfare. Kitchener succeeded in bringing the entire army, including its logistic services, under the control of the Commander-in-Chief, reversing a venerable and (for previous commanders-in-chief) vexatious separation of authority.

By 1914 the army's purpose in India was three-fold. It was now charged with protecting India from external threat, with safeguarding it from internal subversion and with supporting the empire by making available its massive military strength for campaigns beyond India. Allowing a generous proportion to what were coming to be called 'internal security' duties, the Indian Army formed ten infantry divisions and five cavalry brigades, though their actual composition changed as units were posted around the country. From 1907, when rivalry with Russia subsided

---

48 'Estimate of the maximum number of Men on the Establishment of the Army', Army Estimates, 1921-22, Parliamentary Papers, 1921, Vol 20, p. 3
49 Hardinge, *My Indian Years*, p. 102
50 Letter, 30 January 1915, Kitchener papers, PRO30/57/69, NAUK
51 Barnet, *Britain and Her Army*, p. 278
52 Tharoor, *Inglorious Empire*, p. 20
53 Curzon to Kitchener, 31 March 1901, quoted in Heathcote, *The Military in British India*, p. 183

after the formation of what became the Entente Cordiale, the Indian Army's field forces passed to the disposal of the empire. Even so, it was organised, trained, equipped and supplied essentially to fight limited campaigns on the North-West frontier, not an array of enemies in a major war. For now, the partially trained Territorial battalions formed the bulk of the Army in India's strength.

3

A Soldier's Life in India, 1915

New to India and military service, Territorials became acquainted both with the demands both made upon them, the physical surroundings they inhabited and the people who served them and lived off them. They discovered that their decision to accept Kitchener's offer came with unanticipated costs in the course of 'A Soldier's Life in India', as Archie Brewer headed a section of his diary.[1]

'Greybacks' and 'knicks': on duty

Installed in stations across India, Territorials shed the sweat-stained serge uniforms in which they had travelled and donned the clothing which would identify them thereafter. Their clothing and kit reflected a century of experience in coping with India's climate and understandings (and misunderstandings) of its effects. On duty they invariably wore long 'bush' cotton shorts (which they called 'knicks' – knickerbockers), a 'greyback' collarless flannel shirt, woollen puttees, socks and heavy boots. They wore 'sola' topees (made from the pith of the sola tree, nothing to do with 'solar' protection), often with a cotton flap to protect the neck from exposure to the sun. Typically, they at first wore outmoded leather belts, unlike the webbing worn in France. Sometimes, drivers and men on active service would be issued with green-tinted 'glare-glasses', but mostly men simply squinted to keep out the sun. Obedient to doctors' advice, many wore a quilted woollen 'spine pad' because, as Harry Canham explained, 'the spine is a very vulnerable part of the anatomy'.[2] In winter, long trousers, cardigans and even woollen 'cap-comforters' were sometimes necessary. Dressed and equipped thus the Territorials immediately commenced their duties, even though only the 'first-line' units were partially trained, and both 'first' and 'second line' units included large numbers of men with no military training at all.

Much of their duties were both harassing and monotonous. Every cantonment included buildings (such as treasuries or arsenals) or other installations (such as bridges or wireless stations) that were deemed worthy of 'guarding', so many spent days on sentry and nights on guard, or

---

1 Diary, nd, Archie Brewer, 1/9th Hants, M4243, RHRM
2 Letter, 12 July 1917, Harry Canham, 2/4th Border, CMML

sleeping in uniform and kit. At Poona, the 2/4th Wilts had to provide over a hundred men daily to guard the Kirkee arsenal and other installations, meaning that often men had only two nights in bed each week, fewer than the supposed minimum.[3] The Regulars' departure left those remaining attempting to cover the same range of duties. In Rangoon, for example, two Somerset companies performed duties previously undertaken by a full battalion of Regulars. But guard duty was dull. In Jubbulpore Herbert Ewing, a 17-year-old member of the 1/5th Somerset, discovered how dull. He was posted beside a tiny oil lamp outside the cantonment's gun-carriage works, feeling alone and 'very eerie', jumping at the noise of 'visiting rounds' (the sergeant checking on the guards). A few days later he wrote 'tired of these guards', but neither for him nor for Territorials would there be any relief from routine duties.[4] Douglas MacMillan described the routine of guard duty with the 1/4th Somerset at Madras, but it was exactly the same all over:

> The orders were to challenge anyone seen loitering … thus: Who comes there? If they reply: A friend, you answer Advance one [pace] friend & give the countersign … one of them advances & gives the pass word in lowered tones so that if anyone was hanging about they would not overhear it …[5]

And so on, over and over, for years. As early as March 1915 a Wilts Territorial at Delhi was telling his family (in a letter published in *The Wiltshire Times*) that 'without exception we are all "fed up"', eager to 'turn our backs on India … while we get back to Blighty' (the Hindustani word for Britain, a sign of how they were adapting).[6] In the meantime, they settled in to living in cantonments.

Barracks and bungalows: cantonment life

Cantonments occupied huge areas close to but separate from 'native' cities. All under the army's direct control, they were often landscaped, in more lush regions looking, as Fyzabad did to Allan Swift, 'like an English park'.[7] (Other cantonments were less enticing. Jim Mackie described Lahore cantonment, dusty, bare and open to the sun's glare in the hot weather, as 'beastly … rather depressing'.[8]) Their barrack blocks – known as 'bungalows' no matter how large (and even though often two-or-three stories high) – were set far apart, to allow ventilation, held to be vital for health. On the plains, most barrack blocks were immense, accommodating a company or more; in hill stations they might be wooden chalets. At Wellington, high in the Nilgiri Hills, the huge Victorian barrack ranges were identical to barracks in Britain. Regardless of location, they were often uncomfortable. Dalhousie Barracks, in Fort William, Calcutta, was one of the largest barrack-blocks in the empire. From outside it looked like a palace, but from within it was

---

3   Bavin, *Swindon's War Record*, pp. 284-85
4   Diary, 19 25 November 1914, Herbert Ewing, 1/5th Somerset, DD\SLI/17/1/61, SHC, Taunton
5   Douglas MacMillan, '1/4th Somerset Light Infantry in India', DD\SLI/17/1/87, SHC, Taunton
6   *The Wiltshire Times*, 10 April 1915
7   Diary, Allan Swift, 1/6th East Surrey, ESR/25/SWIF/1, SHC
8   Letter, 25 May 1917, Jim Mackie, 2/4th Somerset, Mackie, *Answering the Call*, p. 211

cheerless: like 'a bare stone Church'.⁹ While most cantonment buildings reflected the energetic building program of late-Victorian British India still visible in India today, some of the bungalows and barracks in which Territorials lived were a century old, and bore the signs of the many monsoons and summers through which they had passed. (And the insects that often infested them: on an inspection tour in Bombay, Lord Montagu of Bailllieu, who had arrived in 1914 as colonel of the 2/7th Hants, to his disgust killed two bed bugs on the walls of a bungalow.) Almost all were lit by lamps, often too dim for reading. Cooling them depended upon their high ceilings, thick walls, their placement relative to prevailing winds, and flapping ceiling curtains called 'punkahs', which 'punkah wallahs' pulled for up to sixteen hours a day in summer, ceasing only when the cool of the early morning permitted fitful sleep.

All except the smallest hill stations had a large, usually dusty maidan or parade ground. Most large stations were situated close to a railway line (explaining the many 'Canntt' stations across India) and while most were sited a discreet distance from the nearest 'native city', each also had a 'sudder bazaar' close by, whose merchants provided all the troops' requisites. Almost all had at least an Anglican cantonment church, and often a Wesleyan chapel and a Catholic church, and all had at least one cemetery, with separate plots for various denominations. Most had a regimental institute with its 'wet' or 'dry' canteens, coffee shop, billiard and reading rooms, and a YMCA or a Soldiers' Home, offering recreation and spiritual sustenance, an officers' mess (often several) and bungalows for officers and their families. As the army's technical capacity grew, cantonments acquired more specialised buildings, such as warehouses ('go-downs' in Anglo-Indian jargon) for supplies, transport sheds and workshops.

The military day and week had their own rhythms. Men rose early – at 'gunfire', traditionally 5.30 am, often wakened by barrack servants proffering tea or even shaving them as they slept. After drill in the morning cool they ate breakfast, with further drill only in the cooler months. Tiffin came at what at home the troops called 'dinner'. Thursday was 'banyan day' – the Indian Army's holiday – and Sundays meant church parade.¹⁰

A bungalow became a little community all of its own, temporary for its British inhabitants, semi-permanent for the Indians who lived off it. Besides the vendors and servants who depended upon it economically, cantonment communities also encompassed Indian civilians. At Ambala Owen Smith's bungalow had a resident beggar, 'Old Blind Charlie', who would come around asking for 'Any old Rhoti [bread] couple or one pice Any old sock any old shirt for old blind Charlie' – a chant perhaps taught him by Regulars long gone. The beggar learned soldiers' names and if any of them gave him anything he would sing a little verse, bringing in the soldier's name: 'Private Jones Sab gentlemen today'. 'He does pretty well', Smith concluded.¹¹

Officers, of course, lived better. Their bungalows might house several subalterns, or even one individual captain or major – colonels occupied large bungalows, often in their own compounds. Jim Mackie described those at Bangalore as 'absolute little palaces, beautifully furnished and fitted out'. All enjoyed the services of up to a dozen servants apiece. Even many middle-class officers had not had body servants at home, and some struggled with their more personal ministrations. Jim Mackie found himself rebuked for pulling off his own boots by a bearer who would

---

9 Walter Saunders, 1/10th Middlesex, Doc. 6571, 79/15/1, IWM
10 Why Thursdays? Jim Mackie was told that it was because Queen Victoria had been proclaimed Empress of India on a Thursday, but 1 January 1877 had been a Monday.
11 Letter, 2 September 1916, Owen Smith, 1/6th Hants, M766, RHRM

'much against my will … proceed to dress you'. Jim sent them off on errands so he could dress himself.[12]

It was very easy for men to feel miserable in cantonments, especially in hot weather, with 'nothing to do & nowhere to go'. Geoffrey Coombs confessed that the hours between dusk and 'lights out' were 'the most miserable of all'.[13] Not that all Territorials could be accommodated in cantonments. The Indian Army's voluminous indexes to its Departmental Proceedings are full of references in 1914-15 to 'Accommodation – Territorials', which was plainly deficient. The 1/4th Wilts could not be housed anywhere in Delhi but in tents (at the dusty Kingsway camp, the scene of the great Durbar of 1911). Then, as the weather warmed up, they were accommodated in improvised quarters in offices vacated by civil servants' in the new Secretariat Building, and even in the Army Headquarters buildings (whose usual occupants had left for the cool of Simla).

Secure within their cantonments' park-like settings, men could avoid encountering India at all if they chose. When they did, its crowds, noises, smells, sights and sensations often confused and exhausted them. Allan Swift, who served as a regimental policeman and so came to know the bazaar at Fyzabad intimately, would retreat to the gardens beside the officers' mess to find solitude and quiet.

A cantonment's 'sudder', or main, bazaar, was usually the only 'native' area which soldiers were allowed to enter but was often disappointing. At Maymyo it comprised 'nothing much besides a street which nearly knocks you down with the smell'. The local stall-holders, however, 'seem to crack on us': soldiers and what could be got out of them formed the mainstay of a cantonment's economy.[14] Regimental police patrolled cantonments and their associated bazaars, checking licensed hawkers' chits and warning off those trying to move in on the lucrative trade with soldiers. British soldiers, especially at first, were unused to bargaining, but soon realised that they needed to haggle if they were not to be done down. Some soldiers never got the hang of India's ways. Allan Swift often saw men frustrated with bargaining throw the goods down and storm off.[15] Others learned: Ted Rice bought a silk shawl. The shopkeeper asked Rs15; Ted twice walked away and got it for 5 – his wife was to wear it for thirty years.[16]

Wallahs: followers, servants and vendors

One of the greatest surprises of India was 'the luxury of menial service', as an Anglo-Indian journalist observed.[17] Every battalion included a contingent of 'followers' – about 40 'public' followers, comprising cooks, grooms, sanitary coolies, and servants, as well as 'private' followers, who worked either for individual officers or for various battalion messes. 'Followers' often received army numbers, identification discs and a rudimentary uniform sometimes including an arm band proclaiming the unit they belonged to. In some battalions they paraded under

---

12   Letter, 13 January 1915, Jim Mackie, 2/4th Somerset, Mackie, *Answering the Call*, p. 25
13   Letter, 21 March 1916, Geoffrey Coombs, 1/4th Buffs, EK/U127/2, KH&AC
14   Clipping, Lawrence Hoggarth, 1/4th Border, Album 35 Acc. Nos 3024-3345, CMML
15   Diary, c. 1915, Allan Swift, 1/6th East Surrey, ESR/25/SWIF/1, SHC, Woking
16   Ted Rice, 'All for a Shilling a Day', QRWS/30/RICE/1, SHC, Woking
17   Sheppard, *Territorials in India*, p. 4

A dhobi-wallah pounding clothes, an image appearing in many Territorials' albums. Men invariably complained that the thrashing their clothes received damaged buttons and wore out fabric. (Album 5, NMERM: 881, Maidstone Museum)

the provost sergeant, travelling with it on active service, receiving no extra pay and not always a pension if wounded, though their names would be listed on memorials if they were killed. A British artillery battery included in its establishment over a hundred 'public' followers, mainly *syces* (grooms) and grass-cutters, as well as 'private' followers serving the officers' and sergeants' messes. Because they actually worked with British other ranks in caring for the unit's horses, it is more likely that relations between the two were closer than in infantry units.

Every barrack-room was served by a select group of approved barrack servants, distinguished by the badges that allowed them into men's bungalows. Newly-arrived soldiers were surprised and delighted to find that Indians did 'all what a servant would do in England' (as Herbert Peake later wrote) and that even barrack fatigues such as emptying latrine buckets, cleaning the room and kit (buttons and boots but not their rifles or eating utensils) would be done for them, for a small monthly fee.[18] 'All we had to do was to get on parade', Fred Mundy wrote.[19] Thomas Heard, a pre-war Territorial and probably a tailor in civil life, was amazed at the life of ease soldiers were living. 'We don't do any work ourselves', he wrote, 'I have a servant who does everything for me ... don't even carry a bag myself'.[20] This astonishment at the availability

18 Diary, nd, 1915, Henry Peake, 1/5th West Surrey, QRWS/30/PEAK/1, SHC, Woking
19 Mundy, *A Journal of the 1/4th Battalion Wiltshire Regiment*, p. 21
20 Diary, 14 November 1914, Thomas Heard, 1/4th Cornwall, CRM

of servants – soon taken for granted – is found in practically every source dating from the Territorials' arrival.

Soldiers soon learned to distinguish between servants. They found that each performed only one kind of task. 'To ask a bearer to sweep the bungalow out', Allan Swift explained, 'would be met by a refusal', one that many soldiers would ascribe to 'laziness' and meet with 'a few kicks'. Swift, having troubled to 'gather some information as to their different customs' understood that it reflected the rigidity of caste. His bearer explained that if he were to clean a toilet 'caste break it, Sahib'.[21] Some units (such as the 1/9th Hants, which arrived only in 1916) had a reputation for 'kind treatment' toward servants, which, as Archie Brewer wrote. 'I am sorry to say is not the case with all troops'.[22] At Ahmednagar, Captain John Roper of the 1/4th Dorset decided within weeks of arriving that he had been unduly lenient with his bearer and sacked him. 'I have hardened my heart', he wrote, 'and shall now adopt the usual way of the country which is nearly always right, and that is to beat them like a good dog … they don't understand anything else'.[23] Men soon became used to evading almost all cleaning tasks by paying a few annas a week. Even on the sporting field soldiers had servants. When East Surrey men kicked their ball over the edge of the *khud* on Kuldana's tiny parade-ground-cum-football field, they sent 'coolies' to fetch it from hundreds of feet below.

Many men respected their servants, some, perhaps, developing as close to friendships as was possible when relationships were so constrained by convention. Joe Cox wrote of 'my own servant', Lam Sal, as 'such a trustworthy fellow'.[24] Many soldiers recorded 'their' servants' names and took photographs of them. They were universally addressed as 'boy', but as Douglas MacMillan recalled of his servant, 'Sambo', in Madras, 'it seems absurd to call him boy, for he was 55 years old.'[25] Owen Smith described his comrades' servants and sent a photograph of them home. They included Sirati 'very superior & speaks English well', Chotern 'very merry & bright always laughing', but Owen was unsure of how to spell their names – 'the native who told me their names could not even spell his own'.[26] Officers, of course, had several individual bearers, and they duly appeared in their employers' photograph albums. Stanley Goodland sent his fiancée Elsie a photograph of his, taken at Christmas 1914, when they insisted on presenting him with sugar cakes and garlands as a mark of their loyalty. His 'dressing boy', 'Tiger', shrewdly addressed Goodland as 'My Lord'.[27]

Among the servants most visible in letters and photograph albums were nappi-wallahs – barbers – and dhobi-wallahs – launderers. Nappi-wallahs were renowned for sometimes performing the trick of shaving men as they slept, though medical officers warned against skin infections from shared razors and brushes.[28] Dhobis also often featured in diaries and albums, because their services were essential and frequent – men often tried to accumulate enough shirts and underclothing so they could change at least daily, while dhobis washed the sweat out of

---

21   Diary, nd, Allan Swift, 1/6th East Surrey, ESR/25/SWIF/1, SHC, Woking
22   Diary, nd, Archie Brewer, 1/9th Hants, M4243, RHM
23   Diary, 2 December 1914, John Roper, 1/4th Dorset, 1971-71, DMM
24   Cox, *An Ordinary Working Man's Life*, p. 40
25   Douglas MacMillan, '1/4th Somerset Light Infantry in India', DD\SLI/17/1/87, SHC, Taunton
26   Letter, 6 October 1915, Owen Smith, 1/6th Hants, M766, RHRM
27   Letter, 2 February 1915, Stanley Goodland, 1/5th Somerset, Noyes, (ed.), *Engaged in War*, p. 23
28   Jefferiss, 'Suggestions for removing the difficulties encountered by British units …', *JUSII*, 1917, p. 166

sodden garments. Men typically paid 14 annas a month, though items needing to be cleaned quickly were washed by 'flying dhobis' at a small extra cost. Dhobis' methods, however, also explain their prominence in memoirs and letters. They would flog the dirt out of garments, often smashing buttons. Harry Canham complained that dhobis cleaned his socks by filling them with sand or gravel, obliging him to buy new socks or darn torn ones. A Hants man complained that durzies [tailors] and dhobies seemed to be in cahoots, obliging men to repair or replace damaged clothing.[29]

When units shifted station some servants followed the battalion, but most remained, to await the arrival of another, which was sure to need, food, shaving, milk, clothing and sex. When the 1/6th East Surrey left Fyzabad, Allan Swift wrote, their route to the cantonment railway station was lined with 'natives' – servants, shopkeepers and residents, all muttering 'teek' ('tiga' – signifying agreement or appreciation). Swift thought that they were grateful 'because we had dealt more leniently with them than the regular battalions' before them.[30] Working far from their homes, servants might be stranded if they were dismissed. 'Param', a bearer employed by an officer of Swift's battalion, complained that he was being left unemployed in Muttra (near Agra) and his family were in Nowshera. In a letter probably written by a scribe, Param wondered 'How now I can go back [to] my home to Nowshera from this foreign country?' He asked his former employer to 'be pleased [to] have pity toward me' and asked for 'a railway fair expence' in recognition of his 'work & honesty'. What happened we do not know, but the voice of a servant, so rarely heard directly, comes out of a letter the officer preserved.[31]

Beyond barrack servants, a community of vendors – collectively known as '-wallahs' – sustained every bungalow, providing services to the successive occupants of cantonments. Wallahs were forbidden from entering barrack rooms, often confined to trading on defined 'pitches' between buildings. They had usually leased the right to trade in particular barrack blocks or parts of cantonments, paying a commission or a bribe to a bazaar contractor or perhaps cantonment board staff or even British quartermaster sergeants. The vendors included the 'sweet-wallah', who traditionally chanted 'Jimmy Kelly good for belly, taste and try, after buy', though 'one wonders how they are made', Herbert Ewing asked.[32] Then there were the 'nail cut it'-wallah, the 'socks mend it'-wallah and of course the char-wallah – 'they come round the bungalows & call out like newsboys', Owen Smith explained.[33] Indeed, newly arrived men discovered that, as Smith found in Dinapore, 'natives constantly have something for you to buy', and many men found that these small amounts added up.[34] Wallahs generally allowed men to buy on credit, settling up on pay days. Even when men gave the illiterate hawkers false names ('Harry Cantpay', 'Lord Kitchener') the vendors knew who owed what.[35] Wallahs' calls conjure up the sounds of a bungalow. Herbert Ewing recorded the chants of the various wallahs whose calls

---

29 'Indian Impressions', *Regimental Journal, 2/5th Hampshire Battalion*, August 1916, p. 6, RHRM
30 Diary, nd, Allan Swift, 1/6th East Surrey, ESR/25/SWIF/1, SHC, Woking
31 Param to Edward Orr, 1/5 East Surrey, ESR/25/ORR/6, SHC, Woking. Gerald Bonham-Carter discharged a bearer who contracted scabies, but paid his railway fare home.
32 Diary, 15 February 1915, Herbert Ewing, 1/5th Somerset, Doc.15428, 07/8/1, IWM
33 Letter, 26 April 1916, Owen Smith, 1/6th Hants, M766, RHRM
34 Letter, c. 20 November 1914, *Ibid*
35 Ted Rice, 'All for a Shilling a Day', QRWS/30/RICE/1, SHC, Woking

'Anna Sahib!' A Kent Territorial is about to step into a fruit stall to buy bananas, a drawing by Ernest Cross published in the battalion magazine, *The Invicta*. (Maidstone Museum)

broke the tedium of afternoons in hot weather: 'cake-wallah!', 'monkey-nut wallah!', 'dude-wallah!' 'char-wallah!', 'fruit wallah!'[36]

Veterans offered contradictory advice. Alexander Sturt, the author of *Our Indian Empire*, enjoined men to be 'ordinarily polite'.[37] Old sweats of the conducting parties, however, proposed a more robust attitude. It is clear from passing remarks even in battalion magazines that soldiers offered servants violence. Punkah wallahs, for example, who slacked would draw calls to 'Markaro him … chuck your boot at him'.[38] Had not Kipling endorsed striking the *bhisti* (water-carrier), Gunga Din? ('You put some *juldi* in it or I'll *marrow* you this minute'.) Charles Gibson, a decent man judging by his diary, recorded throwing his boots to keep his punkah wallah working. When Allan Swift wrote that finding outdoor servants inside barracks 'we kick them out', he probably meant it literally.[39]

Lizards and loosewallahs: hazards of Indian service

Cantonment life was often physically unpleasant, and its hazards and dangers dominated many men's letters home, especially at first. Henry Brain copied into his notebook a poem, 'The Torments of India', presumably written by a comrade at Fyzabad:

> Fleas nibbling at my body
> Bugs around my head will crawl
> From the guard room thatch above me
> Lizards on my face will fall …[40]

Regular conducting parties wasted no time in putting the wind up novices with stories of India's many natural hazards, and the Terriers themselves generated their own. Snakes, and especially cobras, figured prominently in anecdotes. 'Snakes are very plentiful', Charles Byford told his fellow villagers in Kent – he had seen many on the rifles ranges at Kamptee.[41] Douglas Skinner assured them that it was 'nothing to see a snake about 6 to 7 feet in length'.[42] Dorset men told how one had 'felt' a snake on his leg – but it turned out to be a loose putty. On the other hand, another told his disbelieving comrades one night that he had just killed a snake with his entrenching tool handle. The next morning they were shocked to find a dead cobra under his bed.[43]

Despite the prominence of snakes in recollections and stories, medical statistics disclosed that a minute percentage of men were bitten by snakes, in contrast to the thousands of Indians who, lacking stout ammunition boots, were bitten and invariably died. As is often the case, dramatic

---

36 Diary, 16 April & 29 May 1915, Herbert Ewing, 1/5th Somerset, Doc.15428, 07/8/1, IWM. By 'dude' he meant '*dudh*' – milk.
37 Sturt, *Our Indian Empire*, p. 64
38 *The Invicta*, Vol. III, No. 4, 1919, p. 46
39 Diary, nd, Allan Swift, 1/6th East Surrey, ESR/25/SWIF/1, SHC, Woking
40 Memoir, Henry Brain, 1/6th East Surrey, ESR/25/BRAIN/2, SHC, Woking
41 Letter, 9 July 1915, Charles Byford, 1/5th Buffs, Great Chart Fund, Book 5, KA&HC
42 Letter, 12 August 1915, Douglas Skinner, 1/5th Buffs, *Ibid*
43 [Dorsetshire Regiment] Regimental History Committee, *History of the Dorsetshire Regiment 1914-1919*, Part II, p. 16

cases of snake-bite attracted undue attention. In 1914-15 there were no cases of snake-bite, but 51 admissions to hospital due to eating 'off' tinned beef.[44] In 1918, only two British soldiers were admitted to hospital with snake-bite: though they both died.[45]

The most troublesome animal hazards, however, were the smallest: flies and mosquitos. Joseph Gale's memoir devotes pages to 'all manner of creeping and crawling things' he encountered – beetles, flies, ants and bugs, including the loathsome 'Spanish' flies which left painful blisters when squashed against the skin.[46] Few bungalows had insect screens, and while Indian authorities devoted energy to 'conservancy' – to collecting and disposing of 'filth', clearing drains and draining ponds – India's climate brought insect life indoors. Hugh Creek described flies 'infesting' the bungalows at Ferozepore in March and a few weeks later at Dalhousie it was 'bugs in the barracks. Millions of them'.[47] Bert Rendall recalled sixty-odd years later the irritation and the horror of the trouble he faced from mosquitos in Burma. For him mosquitos were 'one of the biggest pests on God's earth', despite mosquito nets …

> They would wake you up if they were in the nets; like a bugle. The noise really gets on your nerves … When you went to catch the mosquito it had gone, you'd get nice and drowsy again and back it would be around your head and ears …[48]

For the Territorials' first six months in India they were expected to obtain and pay for their own mosquito nets. While orders could be promulgated directing that mosquito nets be issued, the Indian army's customary inertia often interposed. (Insects also interfered with other aspects of military life. The funeral of Sir Alexander Pinhey, the British Resident of Hyderabad, who died of enteric fever in 1916, was disrupted when bees attacked mourners and the guard of honour. Officers and the Regimental Sergeant-Major of the 2/5th Hants were badly stung when the noise of a harmonium disturbed bees nesting in the roof of the portico.)

A human hazard, especially in the north-west, were 'loosewallahs' – rifle thieves, Regulars warned. Rifles were valuable on the frontier, and to lose one stolen was a serious offence. Loosewallahs were supposed to try all sorts of expedients, such as smearing their bodies with oil to evade seizure. So serious was the risk that rifles were secured through elaborate combinations of racks, padlocks, lamps, rifle orderlies and sentries, though Allan Swift was sceptical of the Regulars' tales. Even so, the entire cantonment of Peshawar was protected by a barbed-wire perimeter. Elsewhere, troops would be ordered to sleep with rifles under their mattresses. 'How much truth there is in this I don't know', a doubtful Herbert Ewing wrote in his diary, 'but it makes a good story to keep Territorials alert when they are on guard'.[49] But loosewallahs were a real hazard. In May 1915, on the march to the hill station of Kuldana, a three-day march from Rawalpindi, the 1/6th East Surrey nervously watched Pathans waiting for a chance to seize rifles from men who fell out of the column. Several months later, on the way back from the hills,

---

44 *Report on Sanitary Measures in India in 1914-1915*, Parliamentary Papers, 1916, Vol. 7
45 *Annual Report of the Sanitary Commissioner with the Government of India for 1918*, European Army, p. 22
46 Gale, *With the 2/4th Wilts to India*, pp. 36, 59, 75, 86-87
47 Letters, 26 March & 19 April 1915, Hugh Creek, 1/4th Devon, EX2543, DMM
48 Interview with Bert Rendall, Mills, *A Strange War*, p. 55
49 Diary, 18 March 1915, Herbert Ewing, 1/5th Somerset, Doc.15428, 07/8/1, IWM

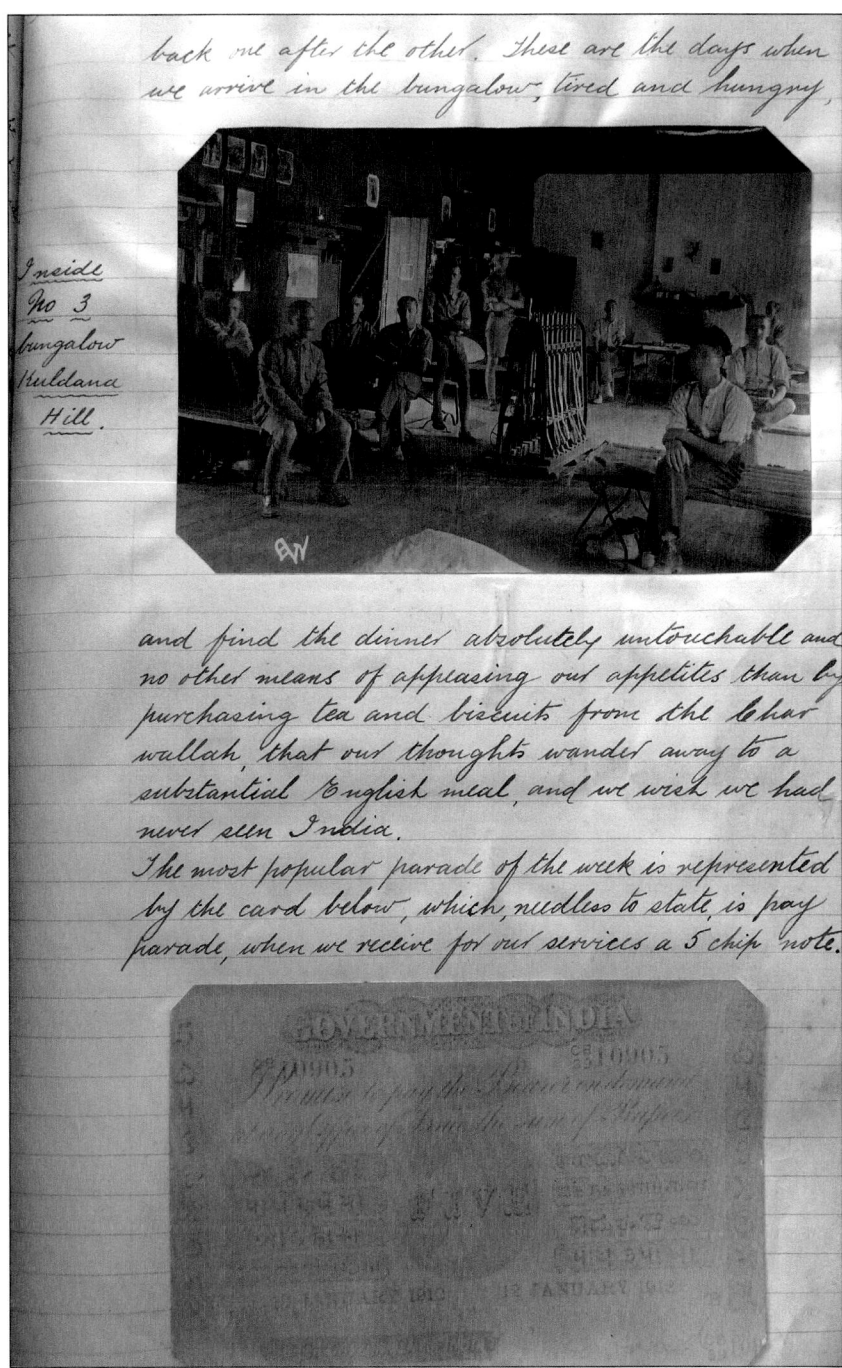

A page of Alan Swift's diary showing the precautions taken to secure rifles against 'loosewallahs', and a five-rupee note, often all that was paid to men of the 1/6th East Surrey in 1915. In between is Swift's complaint about the quality of the rations he received. (ESR/25/SWIF/1, Surrey History Centre)

two men of the battalion actually were ambushed and robbed, one killed and another wounded in the struggle over their rifles.

One unforeseen hazard was isolation. Half-trained battalions were often broken into smaller detachments, moved without explanation. The 1/5th Hants sent two companies off from Allahabad to Cawnpore immediately on arrival in India in November 1914 and except for a few weeks in Fyzabad in 1916 'was never together again in one station' until it left India in October 1919.[50] In 1915 the 1/6th Hants was distributed between Allahabad, Cawnpore and Benares, a distance of over 200 miles along the Ganges valley. The 2/5th Somerset served for two-and-a-half years in Burma distributed in four detachments up to 750 miles apart.[51] Some battalions sent companies to remote stations. Jim Mackie's was among several companies of the 2/4th Somerset sent to Malappuram, on the Malabar coast 200 miles from headquarters at Bangalore, where Jim was one of just five European civil or military officers. Like infantry battalions, the Territorial artillery brigades were also immediately split up. Five Hants batteries were distributed between Peshawar, Lahore and Lucknow; the three Devon batteries between Allahabad, Dinapore and Barrackpore, with the Dorset battery at Bareilly and the Wiltshires at Delhi – from Peshawar to Barrackpore is 1300 miles. Paradoxically, though separated, batteries often remained intact longer than infantry counterparts.

'Why British troops are in India': Proclamation Day 1915

The Territorials upheld their first Indian Christmas as well as they could in the unfamiliar and even alien surroundings of their cantonments. Newly embodied units enthusiastically took up military customs (such as men being served dinner by their sergeants) and colonels made suitably hearty speeches as all toasted absent friends at home. Men of the 1/4th Buffs at Mhow ate 'English fare', and played football – Margate v Folkestone – taking no notice of 'lights out' and playing furious pillow fights in the barrack rooms.[52] Once they recovered from their potations they faced their first major ceremonial duty in India.

It was traditional on New Year's Day for the entire garrison of British India to take part in large and impressive parades, on station maidans. Almost every surviving Territorial diary or memoir refers to the ceremony, differing only in the identity of the troops present. The parade commemorated the proclamation of Queen Victoria's accession as Empress of India on 1 January 1877. Troops, British and Indian, marched in review while bands played and the Union Jack was hoisted. It was the Territorials' first experience of ceremonial in India, and they were both proud and apprehensive to be a part of such an imperial gala. The Territorial artillery batteries in particular played an important part, firing salutes in honour of the King-Emperor. All over India, civilians (both British and Indian) watched curiously to see how the newly-arrived Territorials would perform. In Delhi, Lord Hardinge's prejudice against Territorials seemed fulfilled when he sniffed that it was 'remarkable' how many Territorial officers 'could not manage their horses' (and they were officers of the 1/4th Wilts, noticeably more 'county' than

---

50 Anon, *History of the Hampshire Territorial Force Association*, p. 137
51 Anon, *The Book of Remembrance*, p. 87
52 *Kent Messenger*, 30 January 1915

most).⁵³ On Calcutta's Maidan while all appreciated the Territorials' bearing, the appearance of the local volunteer units excited the greatest admiration, particularly the newly-formed Calcutta Scottish, a mark of partiality particularly apparent in *The Statesmen's* reporting of military affairs in the city.⁵⁴ At Fyzabad, Allan Swift wrote in his diary 'the whole scene was very impressive and must have conveyed to the onlookers the reason why British troops are in India'.⁵⁵ That was indeed the reason.

---

53   Hardinge, *My Indian Years*, p. 108
54   *The Statesman*, 2 January 1915
55   Diary, nd, Allan Swift, 1/6th East Surrey, ESR/25/SWIF/1, SHC, Woking

4

Kitchener's Test

India had already confronted newly-arrived Territorials with many challenges, but as the cooler weather ended early in 1915, they faced their first formal trial as soldiers, in the 'Kitchener's Tests' devised by the man who had sent them to India when he had reformed the Army in India as Commander-in-Chief, 1902-09.

'Three very strenuous days': Kitchener's Tests

Training had begun almost immediately after arrival, as soon as troops received the necessary uniforms and kit. Not only were they rusty after their long, inactive voyage, but many men were practically untrained, having only drilled in Britain before embarkation, especially in newly-raised 'second-line' units. Preparing for the tests imposed exacting training just as the weather in north India turned from pleasantly warm to uncomfortably and dangerously hot. Arthur Copeland described how men of the 1/5th Hants fared at Allahabad, in one of the hottest stations in the Ganges valley. 'Fancy route marches with the temperature about 100°!' he wrote to his parents in balmy Southampton:

> We go out without tunics on, but wearing belt, pouches, bayonet and with rifles and after about ten minutes march everyone is practically wet through with perspiration – dripping off the end of one's nose, chin, ears, eyebrows and knees …[1]

After returning to barracks amid 'good-humoured swearing and cursing' Copeland and his mates had three showers (which Arthur Cornell, unfamiliar with them, called 'rain baths') and often a plunge bath daily, though usually cold.[2] (It is possible that tropical service gave a fillip to the British working class's acceptance of showers, unknown in Britain hitherto, and that advice to 'always wash your hands before touching food and on leaving the latrine or urinal' helped to disseminate ideas of hygiene.[3])

---

1   Letter, 29 April 1915, Arthur Copeland, 1/5th Hants, 128A08/1-4, HRO
2   Arthur Cornell, 'A short account of our life and duties at Meerut', DD\SLI\17/1/84, SHC, Taunton
3   'Health Maxims for Men', Bennett Young, 1/4th Dorset, 1983-05-91, NAM

Territorials embraced the training enthusiastically. They had accepted their despatch to India on the basis of what they saw as an understanding. They were 'buoyed up', Nigel Woodyatt later wrote, 'by promises at home that it was only a temporary duty', and that they would return when their training had been 'fully completed'.[4] Units followed a standard training syllabus, beginning with drill and proficiency with individual weapons and moving on to basic tactics based on ideas of 'fire and movement' enshrined in recent manuals and on unfamiliar weapons, such as machine-guns. A dozen Territorial battalions sent officers to train at a machine-gun school near Poona in January 1915, to be instructed how to impart the skills to the men of the machine-gun sections they each commanded. (For battalions in distant cantonments, this involved journeys back across India within weeks of arriving at their new stations – for the machine-gun officers of the 1/4th Border and 1/4th Shropshire, in Burma, it meant a week's journey by train and ship each way.)

East Surrey Territorials undergoing Kitchener's Test, in a trench near Fyzabad, March 1915. (ESR/6/9/5, Surrey History Centre)

Not all the Territorial battalions could train. Least able were the newly-raised units of the '2nd Wessex' Division, which had embarked within weeks of being raised and were then scattered across India, often split up into detachments. A March 1915 report from Army Headquarters described the division's units in February 1915 as 'unsatisfactory'.[5] The two Dorset battalions guarding the big internment camp at Ahmednagar, for example, found the duties so harassing that they were unready for their test. Many of the 2nd Wessex battalions were too poorly equipped to undertake all aspects of it. The 2/5th Hants could do virtually no musketry training at all until mid-1915, and only then because they inherited obsolete 'long' rifles discarded by the 1/5th Hants.[6] They underwent their Kitchener's Test only in December 1915.

In the United Provinces, Nigel Woodyatt, commanding the Bareilly district, tested three battalions, the 1/4th Wilts at Delhi, the 1/6th Hants at Agra and the 2/4th Cornwall at Bareilly. The hot weather was upon them, and he had to test them in turn, each over 'three very strenuous days'. Woodyatt cut down the duration of the test and started the long route march at 4 a.m. to evade the worst of the sun. All passed, the 1/6th Hants even though it had been split up in detachments and hardly able to train as a unit, the 2/4th Cornwall even though it comprised

---

4   Woodyatt, *Under Ten Viceroys*, p. 256
5   'Correspondence regarding the deficiency of troops in India, February 1915', L/MIL/17/5/2386, BL
6   Anon, *History of the Hampshire Territorial Force Association*, p. 146

mostly young soldiers who were badly affected by having to make a mock attack in the heat.[7] At Kamptee the 1/5th Buffs made 'two very stiff attacks', finishing with tunics wet through from sweat. A participant thought it 'a bit thick' making men attack in the heat.[8] The 1/4th Border referred to 'the battles of Battery Ridge and Camp Valley'.[9]

Preparation for the tests wrought a great change in Territorials' bodies and minds. Arthur Copeland remarked on the 'improvement in discipline, physical fitness, marching drill work and field work' which he thought 'simply wonderful'.[10] His officers were less convinced – Robert Palmer described his company's musketry performance as 'rotten': 40 out of his 68 men failed to qualify.[11] Two months later more than half of his company scored less than half the maximum: ('Not good, but not quite so bad as it sounds, as the conditions were very difficult …').[12] Palmer's company took part of its Kitchener's Test within a few hundred yards of the Taj Mahal. They confronted Territorials with strenuous challenges. The 1/5th Somerset at Ambala practised realistically for several weeks, conducting field days involving 'running about all morning, lying down, skirmishing, attacking and so on'. Under the eye of an inspecting general the battalion marched 15 miles, 'skirmished up a wadi firing ball [i.e. live] ammunition' and then bivouacked in blanket shelters. The next day men sparred with a Sikh battalion, in warm weather and then more rain. After a further 20-mile route back to Ambala, skirmishing half the distance, Herbert Ewing felt 'none the worse for the liveliest and hardest day so far'. His comrades expected to be sent to the Persian Gulf.[13]

Military training mattered more than the inhabitants of the areas chosen for the tests. Hugh Creek wondered how outraged the farmers in his native Cornwall would be if troops were to trample their crops as the Devons did near Ferozepore, with wheat, barley, oats and corn, all 'in ear'.[14] At Kamptee the 1/5th Buffs attacked a village with fixed bayonets, sending villagers fleeing in terror. The 1/9th Middlesex underwent its test in March 1915 near the village of Anandpur on the River Sone in Bihar. Police cleared the villagers out for the duration, because the troops fired live ammunition. (The test, an officer thought, 'resembles the real thing as nearly as possible'.) They made a night march and had a sham-fight with the 89th Punjabis as the enemy, though in March, with the hot weather beginning, officers felt that 'hard work in the open was no longer possible for white troops'.[15] Those who went on to serve on the frontier, in Mesopotamia and Palestine would find that that the war would challenge that assumption.

Terriers themselves believed that by the time they had passed Kitchener's Tests they were ready for whatever the war would bring. *Punch's* Hampshire clerk affirmed a simple syllogism:

---

7   Woodyatt, 'The Territorials (Infantry) in India', *RUSIJ*, 1922, pp. 723-24
8   *Kent Messenger*, 17 April 1915
9   *1/4th Border Gazette*, No. 4, 1915, Lawrence Hoggarth, 1/4th Border, Album 35 Acc. Nos 3024-3345, CMML
10 Letter, 10 February 1915, Arthur Copeland, 1/5th Hants, 128A08/1-4, HRO
11 Letter, 7 January 1915, Robert Palmer, 1/5th Hants, 19M75/F/C19, HRO
12 Letter, 11 March 1915, Robert Palmer, 1/5th Hants, *Ibid*
13 Diary, 1-12 March 1915, Herbert Ewing, 1/5th Somerset, Doc.15428, 07/8/1, IWM
14 Letter, 7 February 1915, Hugh Creek, 1/4th Devon, EX2543, DMM
15 Wyrall, *The Die-Hards in the Great War*, Vol. II, p. 334

Kitchener's Test, as depicted by 'X.Y.Z.' in the popular annual *Indian Ink*, 1915, one way in which Territorials impinged on the awareness of Anglo-Indian society.

> The best British troops are those trained in India:
> We are trained in India:
> [therefore] we are the best British troops …[16]

Already some were concerned at reports from home that they had 'come to avoid active service'. Protesting that 'it was no fault of ours' and that tropical service was 'not all honey' seemed unavailing. A Bournemouth man replied in the local newspaper, pointing out (correctly) that Indian Territorials were 'more fit than the greater part of Kitchener's army'.[17] By the end of 1915 almost all battalions had convinced inspecting officers that they were ready to go to war. But would they?

'Unhasting dignity': Indian Army bureaucracy

In the meantime, Territorials (about half of whom as 1914 volunteers were new to military and not just to overseas service) became accustomed to army life, and to life in India. A target of soldiers' annoyance was the futility, inefficiency and absurdity of much of military routine and practice. As the weather grew warmer in 1915 Jim Mackie, in a bungalow in Calicut, applied himself to 'master the ten volumes of Indian Army Regulations'.[18] He hardly exaggerated. Military management in the Indian Army had always been bound in red tape. While India's notorious official inertia reflected a century of bureaucratic sloth in a generally enervating climate, it had arguably been intensified by Kitchener's supposed 'reforms', which centralised decision-making even more. As staff officers acknowledged, the Commander-in-Chief dealt directly with the commanders of divisions and even independent brigades and which included no machinery for managing mobilisation or for sustained warfare, shortcomings that were to bear rotten fruit in Mesopotamia.[19]

Novices to the Indian Army's ways found its bureaucracy a source of astonishment and exasperation. *Punch's* Territorial correspondent, a clerk in civil life, was soon ordered to report to a divisional headquarters. As he discovered, clerking in India differed from clerical work at home not just because it was performed in shirtsleeves and shorts, but because all transactions were more detailed, protracted and tedious. He described the process for despatching a telegram, one worth quoting at length to convey how ponderous were the army's procedures:

> A document comes out of the Records Department three days old, having been duly headed, numbered, summarised and indexed. The clerk to whom it is handed thinks it advisable to wire a reply, so he writes at the foot, "Wire So-and-so telling him this-and-that?" initials it and sends it to the Chief. The Chief writes "Yes, please" initials it and sends it back. The clerk then drafts the actual telegram, initials the draft and sends it to the Chief, who, if he approves, initials it and sends it back. The draft is then handed to a second clerk, who, after due consideration, types two copies and initials them. These are then taken to the Chief,

---

16 'A Territorial in India', *Punch*, 22 December 1915, p. 506
17 Clipping, Stokes-Roberts papers, M2185, RHRM
18 Letter, 17 March 1915, Jim Mackie, 2/4th Somerset, Mackie, *Answering the Call*, p. 43
19 General Staff Branch, *The Army in India and its Evolution*, p. 33

who signs them and sends them back. One copy is filed and the other goes to a third clerk who enters it *verbatim* into a book and has the book initialed by clerk No. 1, after checking. Then it goes to a fourth clerk, who numbers it, makes a *précis* in another book, and hands it, with explanations, to a *patti wallah*, who takes it outside to an orderly, who conveys it (with unhasting dignity) to the post-office.[20]

Those obliged to work within this system often found it frustrating. Harry Canham, who spent several years as a headquarters clerk in the north-west, objected that 'India absolutely stinks with military etiquette … the stress laid on the most trivial detail ... is most harassing and humiliating at times'.[21] When an officer of the 1/4th Wilts disposed of a machine-gun mule that had arrived at Delhi dead (selling the beast for its hide to save the bother of having to transport and bury the corpse) his neat solution was pursued by 'babu' auditors for the next fifteen months.[22]

Some of the Territorials' grievances stemmed from their own officers' unfamiliarity with army procedures. The 'weakest point', an officer who commanded and inspected them pronounced, was 'their lack of knowledge of "administration" and especially of Indian regulations'.[23] But Territorial officers came to suspect that a slavish adherence to procedure was itself one of the Indian Army's weaknesses. Montagu of Beaulieu felt that Regular officers, and especially those he encountered in departmental offices in Simla and Delhi, regarded his interest in motor transport as that of 'an inconvenient enthusiast'. His energy seemed to them as bad form – he had struck, he reported, 'constant obstruction'. Montagu had toured the frontier fourteen times in three years, reconnoitring and reporting on routes, but only once met a senior departmental officer in the field.[24] This was the opposite of the direct, personal leadership characteristic of Territorial units. They became familiar with the Indian Army's bureaucracy because they were increasingly drawn from their units and posted to specialist jobs across India and beyond.

'Every other kind of specialist': Territorials transferred

From their first weeks in India in 1914 Territorial battalions lost men possessing useful skills. The Indian Army's need for clerks, typists, telegraphists and telephone operators culled dozens, perhaps hundreds within months. Headquarters called for lists of the trade backgrounds of their men, and soon there began a steady dribble of men transferred as supervisors, mechanics, drivers, signallers, machine-gunners, artificers, 'and every other kind of specialist and workman'.[25] The losses of men were serious – the 1/4th West Surrey was mobilised to go to Mesopotamia in January 1916, orders cancelled when Army Headquarters realised that transfers left it only 600 strong.[26] The loss of men to 'employments' remained a 'substantial drain', the Hampshires'

---

20 'A Territorial in India', *Punch*, 20 January 1915, p. 53. Sadly for historians, only a tiny fraction of this immense amount of documentation has survived. A patti wallah wore a belt as a badge showing he worked as an office menial.
21 Letter, 11 April 1918, Harry Canham, 2/4th Border, CMML
22 Blick, *The 1/4th Battalion The Wiltshire Regiment*, p. 44
23 Woodyatt, 'The Territorials (Infantry) in India', *JRUSI*, 1922, p. 721
24 'Army Administration in India', Montagu papers, 7/52, LHCMA
25 Woodyatt, *Under Ten Viceroys*, p. 258
26 Wylly, *History of the Queen's Royal Regiment*, Vol. VII, p. 140

The posterior belongs to Private Allen of the Middlesex Regiment, one of hundreds of Territorials detached as drivers, who drove the car of the charismatic but ultimately disastrously impulsive Brigadier Rex Dyer all the way to Seistan and back. (*The Raiders of the Sarhad*)

history complained.[27] It was also essentially a permanent loss, with men returned to their units only if incompetent. Once men found a 'cushy billet', as it was called, they were in no hurry to give it up. Even Harry Canham, among the most moral of soldiers, accepted a job in the station quartermaster's office at Peshawar and resolved to make himself 'as indispensable as possible'; in which aim he succeeded.[28]

Because they came from all walks of life, the Territorials brought to the army in India skills that it could have otherwise acquired with difficulty. In April 1915 Montagu of Baillieu went to Army Headquarters as its first Director of Mechanical Transport, and began to urge the Indian Army to use motor transport and to repair roads neglected through the reliance on railways. Montagu led the introduction of lorries, cars and motor-cycles to an army that away from railways had moved at the speed of men on foot. The benefits his drive brought would become apparent on the North-West frontier later in the war; in the meantime the new vehicles needed drivers and mechanics: found from Territorials.

Montagu explored the feasibility of routes across practically roadless terrain in Baluchistan, sponsoring an expedition in December 1915 that saw ten Territorial drivers and mechanics (protected by a dozen Indian pioneers) take three Fiat lorries and an Austin car three hundred miles from Nushki (90 miles west of Quetta) to Robat, in Seistan on the India's western-most frontier with Persia. Travelling at an average of three miles an hour, when they were able to move, the vehicles' passengers suffered motion sickness as they clung to the top of loads of food, fuel and spare parts, and spent Christmas Day 1915 digging their Austin out of a deep sand

---

27 Atkinson, *The Royal Hampshire Regiment*, Vol. II, p. 17
28 Letter, 15 March 1917, Harry Canham, 2/4th Border, CMML

drift.²⁹ The expedition strengthened Montagu's conviction that motor vehicles could go where railways cost time and money. (Army headquarters seem to have accepted the venture because it bolstered military opposition to the construction of a railway to Seistan: a railway that could support invaders as well as defenders.)

Territorials became drivers for most senior officers. Nigel Woodyatt's chauffer was a Wilts Territorial, probably recommended by his friend, Lord Radnor. The man, a private named Moore, remained with Woodyatt for over two years, 'and got on remarkably well with all classes of Indians, whether native baboos, Mahommedan servants, Sikh and Gurkha orderlies, or frontier Pathans'.³⁰ Reginald Dyer's driver, a Middlesex Territorial named Allan, drove him across the desert from Nushki to the Seistan frontier, the most remote corner of British India. Dyer depended on Allan's imperturbable competence. At one point Allan fitted a spare axle when his car broke down in the dune country.

Most transfers at first came from the infantry battalions rather than the artillery batteries, but the loss of technically trained men left many batteries up to twenty men fewer by the end of 1915. It is impossible to compare the reasons for the decline in numbers in units (men left on drafts to the Gulf as well as on transfer) but some battalion commanders evidently resisted the departure of skilled men, while others accepted the loss for the common good. By the end of 1915 the War Office strength returns reveal marked differences between units. Having arrived with a similar strength, within a year the 2/4th Wilts reported 799 all ranks, the 2/4th Dorset exactly a hundred men fewer.³¹

'Teeming with complaints': Territorials' grievances

Early in the war, both Territorials in India and their families and friends in Britain regarded that the hardships imposed on them included, as the Marquess of Crewe put it, 'for the time being lost their chance of serving at the Front'.³² As north India's summer began, in about March 1915, Territorials in India expressed other, more substantial, grievances over pay, food and unforeseen consequences of their decision to volunteer for Imperial Service. Kentish Territorials who wrote to the Great Chart Soldiers and Sailors Fund appreciated the gifts they had received. But men used their bread-and-butter letters to express grievances. John Mannering of the 1/5th Buffs wrote from Kamptee in July 1915 explaining that they were 'not having such a grand time as some people think'.³³

Territorials had been assured that 'pay and conditions of service will be exactly as for Regulars', but that seemed not to be so in India.³⁴ Although prices seemed to be low – many men described buying a hand of bananas for less than a penny, they noticed that – paradoxically – 'a shilling in England will go much further than a rupee … here', as six Shepton Mallet men complained in

---

29 *Report on Seistan Motor Transport Reconnaissance*, Simla, 1916, Montagu papers, 7/18, LHCMA
30 Woodyatt, 'The Territorials (Infantry) in India', *JRUSI*, 1922, p. 728
31 'Returns of the Territorial Force Serving Abroad', WO114/52, December 1915, NAUK
32 Marquess of Crewe, House of Lords, *Hansard*, 5 May 1915
33 Letter, 1 July 1915, John Mannering, 1/5th Buffs, Great Chart Fund, Book 5, KA&HC
34 *The Territorial Year Book*, p. 27

a letter to their local newspaper.³⁵ It was a common complaint. As novices they were of course over-charged. Accustomed to being in regular work and mostly enjoying reasonable pay (as clerks, tradesmen and so on) Territorials were taken aback to discover the financial penalties that their patriotism imposed. A 'Pathetic War Ballad', a parody of the hymn 'We are but little children weak' circulated among Hants battalions in 1915. It enjoyed 'a great vogue' and became 'a popular marching song':

> We are but little Terriers weak,
> We only get five chips a week,
> The more we do the more we may,
> It makes no difference to our pay.³⁶

Many married men's families reported not receiving their correct separation allowances. This appeared to be a result of the War Office expecting Territorial Associations to take up the responsibility without sufficient instruction or resources. But well into 1915 no agency seemed to be responsible for ensuring that Territorials' families received their allowances, and when the associations formally accepted the responsibility they had to compete with other departments for clerical staff. Women clerks typically filled the gap, a sign of the profound social changes the war would impose on Britain.

Although all Territorials attempted the intensive musketry training regarded as the foundation of their military skill, many realised that unlike Regulars they would not be eligible for the three-pence per day proficiency pay awarded to Regulars qualifying as 'first class shots'. 'We have not been in the Army long enough', an anonymous man of the Buffs explained a man to his father in Malling, Kent.³⁷ He continued, complaining (in a letter published in a newspaper read widely in Kent) that he expected to be 'done out of' a quarterly kit allowance, and that he and his mates expected to receive 'about half the pay of the Regular, and worse food'. They suspected that the Indian government was profiting from allowances withheld and 'doing jolly well out of the "Terriers"'.³⁸ Because musketry proficiency was rewarded in arrears, even when Territorials qualified none of them were paid until after the 1916 tests. Captain Geoffrey Burrell of the 1/4th Hants was still agitating for his men to receive proficiency pay at the end of 1916, arguing that as they had been on active service in Mesopotamia for that time they deserved it.³⁹

Inadequate rations incensed many men. The Hampshires' 'Pathetic War Ballad' complained of receiving 'One pound of bread and meat a day, / And Irish stews we cannot eat;/ We have to "tick up" all the week'.⁴⁰ On the voyage to Mesopotamia Len Bithell, a boxer, sold medallions he had won to buy food.

---

35 *Shepton Mallet Journal*, 23 April 1915, p. 3
36 Clipping, Owen Smith, 1/6th Hants, M766, RHRM. A 'chip', an accompanying note explained, was a rupee.
37 *Kent Messenger*, 17 April 1915
38 *Ibid*
39 Godfrey Burrell, 'The Diary of a Company Commander', p. 8, M1838, RHRM
40 Clipping, Owen Smith, 1/6th Hants, M766, RHRM. To 'tick up', an accompanying note explained, was to seek credit.

As well as grumbling, to each other and families at home, some men acted. At Fyzabad, where men of the 1/6th East Surrey also felt unhappy at their 'scanty and inferior' food, 'several companies refused to parade' in protest.[41] Aware of their men's feelings, officers mobilised influential friends at home – an orderly room clerk of the 1/4th Devon recalled his colonel dictating letters to a cousin who was a senior civil servant.[42]

Word of the Territorials' grievances became public in Britain within four months of their arrival. 'The county', the Earl of Selborne said in Parliament of Hampshire, 'was now teeming with complaints' as men realised how badly off they had become, had written home, where parents had written to local newspapers, to MPs or local figures. Men were asking their families for money to buy boots, clothing and food. Others claimed men had sold their accoutrements for money.[43] Parliamentarians raised a rash of questions about their constituents' sons (indeed, given volunteers' ages, some had voted for them) being disadvantaged relative to either Regulars or absolutely. Eventually Crewe had to concede that 'on certain points … the Territorial does not come off so well as the Regular'.[44]

The situation differed between provinces, divisions and cantonments, and indeed units, with pay sergeants, new to India and its idiosyncratic currency, puzzling over the various deductions recorded in every man's pay book. Items provided in one place were charged to men individually elsewhere. The difference in stoppages between cantonments could be as high as Rs7/6 or as little as Rs1/5.[45] Men may have been surprised to find that shirts and shorts – the Territorials' typical dress – were 'not authorised articles of clothing', and that men were dunned for items that were compulsory but not issued (at a cost of Rs2 for shorts and Rs1/12/- for shirts, several of each being required because men came off duty bathed in sweat). In all stations men had to pay monthly subscriptions for messing, cooking, washing, haircutting, a library and for 'barrack damages' (the latter a venerable ploy by the army to charge men for the maintenance of their barracks). In many stations men were asked to pay for sporting club subscriptions regardless of whether they played, for Royal Army Temperance Association fees even if they drank, and some gunners had to pay the syces who cleaned their harness.[46] One of the most oppressive facts of cantonment routine was that soldiers were obliged to pay individually for services which in Britain would have been provided by the army. Men had to pay to transport baggage when changing stations, for laundry (which men could not do themselves), or for shaving (which custom demanded be performed by nappi-wallahs).

These deductions were based on the assumption that men were paid as Regulars, but as the Malling man explained, Territorials' pay was lower than their Regular counterparts. Fewer Territorials were old soldiers, so they received nothing based on seniority (such as good conduct pay). Territorials were ineligible for proficiency pay (amounts added to the pay of, say, machine-gunners, bandsmen, stretcher-bearers or signallers). New to India, Territorials paid more for goods and services, both individually (if they were inexperienced in bargaining) or collectively

---

41 Diary, nd, Allan Swift, 1/6th East Surrey, ESR/25/SWIF/1, SHC, Woking
42 Annotations to memoir, A.E. Serle, 1/4th Devon, Doc.7350, 76/154/1, IWM
43 *The Times*, 17 March 1915, p. 12
44 Marquess of Crewe, House of Lords, *Hansard*, 16 March 1915
45 'Territorial grievances. Information called for by Secretary of State regarding –', No. 16115-25, Army Department, War Branch 1914-15, NAI
46 Telegram P., H-4604, 1 May 1915, Viceroy to Secretary of State for India, WWI/147/H, NAI

(when merchants colluded to raise prices between Regulars leaving a station and Territorials arriving). Most importantly, because Territorials were more likely to be supporting wives and children, or aged parents, the allotments many men paid left them more severely out of pocket than their Regular comrades. John Mannering reported that many of his mates were finding it hard to remit even sixpence a day to their parents in Kent. (As single workers, many had supplemented their parents' income.) All in all, John Mannering wrote, 'I don't think some of the 5th Buffs have been treated as they ought to have been'.[47] The authorities remained, critics alleged 'extremely niggardly and paltry'. Men still paid allowances to families – seventy percent of the Somerset battalions' men according to an aristocratic supporter (a former Conservative MP in Somerset).[48]

The War Council briefly noticed Territorials' 'complaints' on 19 March. Haldane, now Lord High Chancellor (and presumably feeling some responsibility for the men of the force he had created), reported 'some grumbling', with Crewe explaining that were especially concerned at their rations. Kitchener acknowledged that 'he had noticed a tendency among Territorial troops to think that they had been overlooked'. He brusquely asserted 'that the authorities must employ them in whichever place was best ... They would learn this', he loftily concluded, 'when they had been longer with the Colours'.[49]

Despite Kitchener's customary lordly ruling, in mid-1915 the Government of India at last recognised the discrepancies between the Territorials and Regulars' pay. It increased the daily pay of privates by 3d and reimbursed the difference since their arrival. Soldiers' letters into 1917, however, continue to complain that men were short of money, unable to save and asking families for remittances.

'Kincho, punkah-wallah!': the first summer

As the Regulars had grimly warned the 'griffish' Territorials, the hot weather would be their ultimate test. The Allahabad *Pioneer* published temperature figures recording north India's transformation into a baking hell for those unaccustomed to its heat.

Those unlucky enough to remain in the plains – the majority – were, as Hugh Creek explained to his parents, 'doomed to be burned to cinders ... in the broiling heat all the summer' – though he was writing in March, well before it had started.[50] Once the summer began in earnest (around the middle of April at Agra) all that could be done, Ted Holter remembered, was 'shut all the doors, get the Punka Wallah on the job and settle down and sweat it out'.[51] Across the subcontinent, from Burma to Baluchistan, men realised what Indian service entailed. 'We are sweltering inside the walls of our Fort like twopenny loaves in a baker's oven ... the heat as we step outside seems to leap up from the ground and hit us with a bang in the face'.[52] In Mandalay in April men walked about the barracks at night, unable to sleep, dreading dawn and the heat and

47 Letter, 1 July 1915, John Mannering, 1/5th Buffs, Great Chart Fund, Book 5, KA&HC
48 Lord Harris and Lord St Audries, House of Lords, 16 June 1915, *Hansard*
49 War Council notes, 19 March 1915, CAB42/2/14, NAUK
50 Letter, 26 March 1915, Hugh Creek 1/4th Devon, EX2543, DMM
51 Ted Holter, 'A Terrier in World War I', Doc 4545, 81/9/1, IWM
52 'A Territorial in India', *Punch*, 2 June 1915, p. 438

A 'punkah boy' – in this case actually a child – pulling a rope to fan the air within a bungalow. If conditions inside the barrack room were unpleasant, the temperature for the punkah wallah outside must have been unbearable. (ESR/6/9/8, Surrey History Centre)

humidity. Men would urge punkah-wallahs to pull (or pull harder) with oaths and injunctions such as 'juldi' ('faster'). Joseph Gale described how the shout of 'kincho [pull], punkah-wallah!' would be heard through the hot weather.[53]

Old India hands warned that in Lucknow, 'even being in the sun for a short time, such as running over to a cook house may be sufficient time to give a sunstroke, and anyhow a bad headache'.[54] The weather alone led many Territorials to regret their decision to volunteer for imperial service: 'I would fifty times rather be at the front', wrote Hugh Creek to his parents near Penzance.[55] A man sweltering in Baluchistan wrote nostalgically of 'June in Hampshire', imagining how when 'on the fields at twilight/ All softly falls the rain/ We shall come home again …' As a parody verse adjacent to the poem of nostalgic longing quipped, it was indeed, 'a long, long way to go to Quetta'.[56]

Army headquarters (itself shifting from Delhi to Simla in April to avoid the heat) accepted that with so many Territorials all arriving more-or-less simultaneously it would be prudent to 'allow Territorials more latitude than is usual with regulars'. Battalions and batteries were directed to send parties to hill stations, with those left behind on the plains being allowed to

53 Gale, *With the 2/4th Wilts to India*, p. 82
54 'A Few Hints to Territorial Officers', QRWS/30/WIGA/17, SHC, Woking
55 Letter, 26 March 1915, Hugh Creek, 1/4th Devon, EX2543, DMM
56 *The Tiger*, May 1915, p. 48

swap later in the season. Some 5000 men began moving to a dozen hill stations.[57] Who should go? Acting on the advice of experienced officers of the Indian Medical Service, colonels and adjutants pored over rolls with company commanders and regimental medical officers to select men who would be better off away from the plains. In this way, the outspoken John Mannering of the 1/5th Buffs decided, the 'oldest and the youngest were pinched out and sent up to the hills'.[58] In some battalions men were selected individually, in others men under twenty and over forty sent off. These men were fortunate, as were the 5000-odd who replaced them in a couple of months, but over 20,000 men remained in cantonments in the plains to face the heat of an Indian summer: more Territorials suffered through their first hot weather than escaped it. Their letters and diaries are full of attempts to convey just how unpleasant they found it.

Confined in their stuffy bungalows for ten hours a day, men slept, read, played cards and quarrelled. (Alban Bacon found that his men of the 2/4th Hants at Quetta became 'more nearly insubordinate than they ever were before, or since' in summer.[59]) To kill time, Territorials took up the barrack crafts taught by Regulars. Herbert Ewing described Somerset men during long, hot days at Ambala knitting cholera belts or embroidering flag designs on canvas 'quite gay and effective'.[60] In photographs Territorials can be seen knitting or embroidering, and Fred Wignall's collection, in Cumbria's Museum of Military Life, includes large two embroidered badges (of the Border Regiment's badge) which he made while 'taking it easy' (as he captioned one of his photographs of barrack life).[61] There were limits to crafts, however, when Bernard Searle, a former tailor, became too popular with his mates, fashioning cloth hold-alls for letters and personal effects, a durzi working for his battalion complained and his company commander forbade him from competing.[62] Enduring their first hot weather left many men exhausted but proud of having withstood an ordeal which practically defined the British soldier's experience of India.

While Territorials in India suffered, the force's creator, Richard Haldane, underwent a trial of his own. It was already arguable that while the creation of Kitchener's 'New Army' was a magnificent achievement, Kitchener would have done better to have heeded Haldane's advice and based the army's expansion on the successive enlargement of the Territorial organisation. No New Army formations saw action until August 1915 (on Gallipoli), by which time even second-line Territorial divisions were in action. Territorials became, Haldane's first biographer wrote, 'the Cinderella of the Army'.[63] In the meantime, Haldane had lived in an 'atmosphere of poison gas', the subject of wild allegations that he had treated with the Germans in 1912 and had weakened the army's artillery (when in fact his reforms had greatly strengthened it) and in 1915 he was hounded from office. A contributor to the *1/4th Border Gazette* in Burma lauded how

---

57 Telegram P., No. H-5690, Viceroy to Secretary of State for India, 6 May 1915, WWI/147/H, NAI
58 Letter, 1 July 1915, John Mannering, 1/5th Buffs, Great Chart Fund, Book 5, KA&HC
59 Bacon, *The Wanderings of a Temporary Warrior*, p. 19
60 Diary, 29 March 1915, Herbert Ewing, 1/5th Somerset, Doc.15428, 07/8/1, IWM and the photograph SBYRW32097, showing a group of men of the 1/4th Wilts embroidering on a veranda at Chaubattia in 1916; RBWM. For other examples of embroidery, see the entry on Charles Davis of the 1/25th London, IND15 in the Liddle Collection at the University of Leeds: http://www.25thlondon.com/cjd.htm
61 Pte Frederick Wignall, 2/4th Border, E94/2016, CMML
62 'My Journey Home', Bernard Searle, 1/1st Kent, NMERM 2008-1640, MM
63 Maurice, *Haldane 1856-1915*, Vol. I, p. 361

Haldane had been reported to have sung an old Border marching song in the House of Lords, moved by Kitchener's report of the services of the regiment (with Regular battalions in France and Gallipoli, two Territorial battalions in India and several New Army battalions training).[64] But others wondered at the aspersions cast on Haldane's loyalty. Even Victor Manley, who had been a wholehearted peacetime Territorial, wondered in his memoir whether Haldane – a 'great friend of the Kaiser' had tried to damage the Regular army.[65] As the hot weather began in earnest, at home, Asquith's Liberals formed a national Government with Andrew Bonar Law's Conservatives. One of Bonar Law's conditions was that Haldane was not a part of it. He never again held public office. Whether many Territorials in India noticed the departure from politics of the creator of their force is unknown. They lay in a torment of heat, literally confined to their barracks for as long as the Indian sun burned, allowed out only early in the morning and in the evening.

'More like a Celestial …': the hills

Those lucky enough to go to the hills enjoyed the cooler air and vistas of a score of hill stations created by the British over the previous century as a refuge from summer heat. Ranging in altitude between 4700 and 7500 feet, they included, from north-west to east Murree, Mussoorie, Dalhousie, Simla (and its satellites, including Jutogh, Solon and Dagshai), Dehra Dun, Naini Tal and Darjeeling (for officers, with nearby Jalaphar and Lebong for other ranks). In Madras, Ootacamund ('Ooty') was also for officers only, with Wellington for other ranks. In Bombay Mahabaleshwar and Mount Abu served at various seasons, with a host of other minor stations. Chakrata, for example, the station for troops from Agra, was so elevated (at 6950 feet) that a Hampshire colonel, Frederick 'Jumbo' Playfair, quipped that he felt 'more like a Celestial than a Territorial'.[66] Getting to the hills often entailed a railway journey and a stiff climb over several days. On reaching the hills the climbing did not stop. Most stations were built over ridges and valleys so men were forever climbing up or down the 'khud' (hillsides) to get to bazaars, drill, meals or church.

Once there, Territorials who had seen nothing higher than Leith Hill or the Quantocks confronted the spectacle of the Himalayas or the Nilgiris. Many men responded ecstatically to the hills. Ted Rice soon saw the rising sun illuminate Kanchenjunga. 'Nothing can compare with that first dawn', he remembered, describing the view from Tiger Hill. Looking out at the imposing snow-covered peaks, he 'formed the first real impression of space and the great plan of the universe'.[67] Joseph Gale did not see the hills until sent to Darjeeling in the summer of 1917. When he did he too rhapsodised about the view of Kanchenjunga and the Himalayas from Tiger Hill:

---

64 *1/4th Border Gazette* [No. 4, 1915], Captain Lawrence Hoggarth, 1/4th Border, Album 35 Acc. Nos 3024-3345, CMML
65 Victor Manley, 'A Khaki Diary', 49M91W/Q3/6, HRO
66 Letter, 26 August 1915, Francis Bowker, 1/4th Hants, Doc. 8094, 99/15/1, IWM
67 Ted Rice, 'All for a Shilling a Day', QRWS/30/RICE/1, SHC, Woking

> Dawn was just breaking as we reached the top, and away to the east the sky became shot with wonderful tints of rose-pink and orange, pearly blue and gold ... I shall never forget the indescribable beauty ... suddenly the drifting clouds parted like a curtain and in between them appeared Mount Everest, etched like a sugar-cone of purest white ...[68]

Each hill station had a particular character; some sedate, some 'fast'; some attracting officials, others 'box wallahs' (that is, commercial folk): all firmly repelling Indians unless they were servants, or wealthy princes. Owen Smith, a devout Anglican inclined to be censorious, visited Kasauli from Solon and found it full of Europeans 'very smart & dressy, very uppish ... rather fast and the ladies smoke cigarettes quite openly' – a sure sign of depravity for him. Tellingly (compared to the civilians he had known in Agra) 'they won't look at soldiers'.[69] One of the attractions of hill stations, other than an equable climate, was that they attracted 'many fair visitors', and gymkhanas, patriotic fairs and even church services gave Territorials a chance to see if not speak to European women.[70] Not that hill stations were necessarily resorts. Robert Palmer was at Naini Tal when he received orders to go to Mesopotamia and described the hotel he stayed in as 'about the worst in the world ... though there are two in Naini reputed to be worse'. The views provided compensation. Palmer rode early one August morning to see 'a most glorious view of the snows, one of the finest I have ever seen'. He marvelled at 'four or five ranges ... their valleys filled with shining seas of rolling sunlit cloud', and above all Nanda Devi 'the highest mountain in the Empire'.[71]

The Territorials' claims to superior social standing resulted in some gaining entrée to civil society in the hills. In the summer of 1915 Herbert Ewing, a private in the 1/5th Somerset, received an invitation transmitted via a clergyman he knew in Somerset to stay in Simla with the family of Everard Coates. There he met 'Mrs. Coates', 'the leading woman novelist in India' – the Canadian Sara Jeanette Duncan – and enjoyed tea and toast in bed and the delights of Simla, including its charming Gaiety Theatre. Sight-seeing at the gates of Vice-Regal Lodge, he gave the Viceroy, Lord Hardinge 'a terrific salute' as his carriage swept out. 'I hope he was impressed with his Terriers', Ewing wrote, 'he probably didn't even see us'. Best of all, Ewing met and was able to dine with 'Queenie', a girl he had met briefly at Ambala.[72] But officers soon monopolised her – 'no opportunity to speak', he recorded glumly.[73] Whether 'other ranks' encountered 'white women' depended upon the collective tone of the civilians of the station. For every man who bemoaned never seeing white women, there was a man like Owen Smith, who relished meeting what he called '"toff" ladies' at church and philanthropic functions. At a Red Cross Sale of Work he met 'several smart ladies' including the racy Mrs. Fergusson, the Magistrate's wife '(who smoked a cigarette)'.[74] But it was up to the ladies to acknowledge the soldiers; anything else would have been impermissible.

---

68 Gale, *With the 2/4th Wilts to India*, p. 74
69 Letter, 7 June 1916, Owen Smith, 1/6th Hants, M766, RHRM
70 'Dagshai', *The Braganza*, 1 June 1918, p. 11
71 Palmer, *Letters from Mesopotamia*, pp. 8-9 (Mt Everest is of course in Nepal and China.)
72 Diary, 13-22 May 1915, Herbert Ewing, 1/5th Somerset, Doc.15428, 07/8/1, IWM
73 Diary, 14 March 1915, Herbert Ewing, 1/5th Somerset, *Ibid*
74 Letters, 8 & 16 December 1915, Owen Smith, 1/6th Hants, M766, RHRM

Officers could be accommodated into the structures and rituals of the hill station, its church and club. Jim Mackie's description of Kasauli (in the Simla Hills) represented many. 'The ladies have absolutely nothing to do', he told his parents, 'they just sit and discuss one another', all going to the club, (along with the church) the focus of their insular communal life.[75] Soldiers – that is, 'other ranks' – did not always find these little communities congenial, and the feeling was often mutual. In any case, most had to return to the heat of the plains. Fred Mundy, who had enjoyed the summer at Kailana, tossed a coin with another sergeant, and lost. He left for Delhi, feeling the damp, monsoon heat and humidity rise as he descended to the plains.[76] Soon he was marching for two miles daily in the heat supervising guards around Delhi, waiting expectantly for the monsoon to break.

Living in the smaller hill stations allowed soldiers opportunities to encounter Indians away from the formality of big cantonments. While spending the summer of 1916 at Solon Owen Smith rambled about the Simla Hills with three companions, enjoying 'a most delightful khud climb'. They found 'a very interesting "Indian" thing', – a bullock working a threshing machine, which the farmer explained, miming to them as they sat on corn sacks on a little plateau high on a ridge. They later walked to Dyers Brewery (owned by the brother of Brigadier Rex Dyer: see later), saw lizards basking in the sun, tasted wild strawberries and gave an anna to an old beggar ('*very* profuse in his thanks, of course we did not know what he said'). The days were enjoyable, even though at the brewery, having been shown over the works, 'we did not get a sample!' As he described his time to his sister Anna he could hear 'Tum Tum' drums and 'ramsamying'.[77] It was a side of India he had not seen in the big cantonments at Agra and Ambala, and he now admitted that he enjoyed his time in Solon.

'Blindingly vivid and absolutely marvellous': the first monsoon

Thomas Heard was at Bareilly's Wesleyan chapel when the monsoon of 1915 broke, as a sudden fierce wind blew open doors and windows and the clouds burst. Heard and the other Territorials faced their first monsoon. As the north Indian plains baked in June the first signs of rain could be detected. Huge clouds built up, the air heavy and still. Electrical storms flashed and at last the skies opened and the rain fell in torrents. Sheltered by their verandas, men watched in awe as massive electrical storms exploded over Rawalpindi, soaking the area with rain so heavy that speech was impossible.[78] At Allahabad, Arthur Copeland described the power of his first tropical lightning storm: 'blindingly vivid and absolutely marvellous'.[79] There the maidan was flooded two-feet deep and water rushed away down big monsoon drains, but in a few hours the ground was dry again. Standing guard in monsoon rain often subjected men to either a drenching or – if they wore heavy greatcoats – to the dangers of heat exhaustion. Copeland

---

75 Letter, 26 July 1917, Jim Mackie, 2/4th Somerset, Mackie, *Answering the Call*, p. 271
76 Mundy, *A Journal of the 1/4th Battalion Wiltshire Regiment*, pp. 45-46
77 Letter, 3 May 1916, Owen Smith, 1/6th Hants, M766, RHRM
78 Gale, *With the 2/4th Wilts to India*, pp. 46-47
79 Letter, 9 April 1915, Arthur Copeland, 1/5th Hants, 128A08/1-4, HRO

mildly but truthfully observed that 'well, even the best and mildest of fellows are apt to break out into bad language then'.[80]

Those troops in the hills (no more than half and often a quarter of a battalion's strength) often lived within clouds, and often amid fierce thunderstorms. In some hill stations men had the eerie sensation of hearing thunder in the cloud-filled valleys *below* them. As the storms cleared men could often see far across the plains of north India for what seemed like hundreds of miles (something no longer possible now that vehicle emissions have so much limited visibility). The humidity that followed confronted them with new challenges. As Joseph Gale wrote, 'bayonets become rusty and brass buttons turn green in a night; boots grow a crop of mildew in a couple of days: the beds have a frowsy smell ...'

The monsoon brought an increase in 'fevers' – mostly mosquito-borne malaria. Medical officers were able to prevent infection by enforcing orders to sleep under mosquito nets, and to suppress the symptoms of malaria by administering bitter-tasting quinine, masked with fruit drops, which they eagerly requested from home. Many men believed old soldiers' tales about malaria. Harry Canham, sleeping in a barrack room at the hill station of Cherat, near Nowshera, recorded that most men slept with their heads to the centre of the room, enabling them to evade the 'mist ... which creeps up the walls & spreads its deadly embrace round anything near the wall'.[81] (This old soldier's tale was current nearly twenty years after Robert Ross identified the anopheles mosquito as malaria's actual carrier.)

By the first anniversary of the war's outbreak, having experienced the 'cool weather', summer and monsoon, Territorials began to come to terms with their presence in India, even if they would rather be elsewhere. (The winner of the 2/6th Hants speech-making competition held to mark the war's first anniversary supposedly gave a short but eloquent address that attracted resounding cheers:

> 'India – er – um India,' he began nervously, ' ... well, India is a hell of a place and I shall be thundering glad to get out of it.'[82]

But with the equivalent of three divisions of Territorials in India and, as Kitchener must have known, no easy way to replace them, the question remained: what were they actually to do?

'Springing like the dragon's teeth': what were Territorials for?

Senior officers in India and at home agreed that Territorials were not available to fight the King-Emperor's enemies. Despite their enthusiasm, many of the newly-raised 'second-line' battalions were unready for anything more demanding than guard duties for perhaps a year after their arrival. Even the regimental history of the 2/4th Border conceded that it was capable only of 'simple company schemes' as late as December 1915.[83] Despite letters from Somerset men, published in local newspapers, boasting that the 1/4th Somerset had become 'the first

---

80 Letter, 1 July 1915, Arthur Copeland, 1/5th Hants, *Ibid*
81 Letter, December 1917, Harry Canham, 2/4th Border, CMML
82 'A Territorial in India', *Punch*, 15 September 1915, p. 226
83 MacGlasson, (ed.), *Diary of the 2/4th Battalion The Border Regiment*, p. 11

Territorial regiment ... to be sent to the frontier', the one thing that Territorials would not be used for, it seemed, was to join experienced Regular and Indian units in responding to unrest on the frontier. A more sober assessment came from a Widcombe man, who had told his mother that she may 'hear some yarns ... that we have been fighting the Afghans, but ... I don't think that's likely to happen'.[84] (The first Territorial battalion to be sent to Rawalpindi had actually been the 1/4th Hants, by this time in Mesopotamia.)

Instead, Territorials spent much of their time performing exacting but unexciting guard duties. Many photographs in their albums depict them, their creases sharp, webbing freshly blanco'd, weapons shined, boots polished; kit arranged just so. Guard duty was both tedious and demanding. Optimistic soldiers such as Arthur Copeland could find interest while on Main Gate guard at Allahabad fort – 'plenty to do on that guard' – paying complements to officers, regulating the traffic in and out, sounding the time gong – 'the time passes fairly well ...'[85] But Territorials were not merely passing the time. On them the security of British India now depended. A correspondent to *The Indiaman* in 1915, quoted approvingly in another colonial possession, observed that the Territorials arrival 'duly impressed the Indian population – delighting the loyal majority by showing the might of the British Sirkar [government] ... springing like the dragon's teeth from the soil of Great Britain'.[86]

That military power rested above all on the exclusive possession of artillery, and now most of the guns and gunners were from Home Counties and Wessex batteries. Ted Holter of the 2nd Home Counties brigade described how his battery settled in to Ambala cantonment under the tutelage of gunners of the Royal Horse Artillery's 'A' Battery. The Regular gunners, Holter remembered, 'were tough and they tried to make us tough too'. They were introduced to the routine of 'riding school, gun drill, driving drill, foot drill, fatigues, guards [and] pickets, day in, day out', and at the Regular troops' standards, more exacting than the Territorials'.[87] Largely because of their many horses, gunners worked practically every day – even on Christmas Day 1917, Reuben Rusbridge recorded at Delhi, came parade at 7, exercising the gun teams, rubbing them down and feeding them.[88]

Territorial units had generally been issued with obsolete weapons and the artillery's 15-pounders – 'no better than gas pipes', the Viceroy declared, surely echoing the words of antagonistic Regulars.[89] The brigades arrived not only without their ammunition columns (the supply unit that enabled them to serve in the field) but also without any spare parts, at least for the 2nd Wessex Division's units. Indian authorities begged for drawings and tools so they could fabricate missing or scarce gear. Not until mid-1916 did Territorial batteries receive the 18-pounder guns that had been the standard weapon of Regular field artillery units since 1904.

British India's leaders were in no doubt that the Territorial artillery began further behind and took much longer than their infantry comrades to become efficient. Lord Hardinge claimed in his memoirs that their artillery pieces could not be fired, 'as the breech blocks, instead of having fittings of asbestos, had wood painted to look like asbestos'. Their ammunition, he said, had

---

84 *Shepton Mallet Journal*, 24 September 1915, p 2
85 Letter, 22 April 1915, Arthur Copeland, 1/5th Hants, 128A08/1-4, HRO
86 'Territorials in India', *Singapore Free Press and Mercantile Advertiser*, 15 March 1915, p. 8
87 Ted Holter, 'A Terrier in World War I', Doc 4545, 81/9/1, IWM
88 Diary, 25 December 1917, Reuben Rusbridge, Surrey Battery, Doc. 13388, 05/7/1, IWM
89 Hardinge, *My Indian Years*, p. 106

been marked 'Dangerous and not to be used for practice'.[90] The Territorial gunners' disadvantages and deficiencies would sooner or later be rectified. Lord Hardinge conceded that within six months they became 'very smart and efficient', and he snobbishly ensured that the Wiltshire battery commanded by Major Henry Molyneux Paget Howard, 19th Earl of Suffolk and 12th Earl of Berkshire (known as Lord Suffolk) served in Delhi (along with Lord Radnor's 1/4th Wilts). For the time being Territorials had to accept that the one place they would not go was to fight Germans on the Western Front.

---

90 Hardinge, *My Indian Years*, p. 107

5

Encountering India

Though never having expected to see India, many Territorials responded to it with curiosity and enthusiasm. They took an interest in its people, their religions and culture, travelled over it, and returned with images of it, and with trophies.

'To drink deep of its history': the anthropological eye

'I wish someone would give us a talk on this great country', Herbert Ewing wrote, and later that very day he attended a lecture on Alexander's campaign in the Punjab.[1] Men's curiosity could have been sparked by their proximity to India's cultural heritage, even to a retail pharmacy assistant from Portsmouth. Soon after he arrived at Agra Fort (in which a company of British troops was always stationed) Owen Smith of the 1/6th Hants sent his family a postcard of its Pearl Mosque. It gave 'but a slight idea' of its magnificence – and, Owen added, 'this is only 50 yards from our Bungalow'.[2]

Many Territorials took an active interest in the people and culture among which they found themselves. Olaf Caroe, a young architect and a subaltern in the 1/5th East Surrey, and among the most articulate of Territorial memoir-writers, wrote of how he 'rejoiced' to arrive in a place he had read about and imagined. 'I longed to see India', he later wrote, 'its diverse and fascinating people, cultures and climates, and to drink deep of its history and splendour'.[3] Less eloquent men expressed their amazement at what they saw. Within weeks men were writing that they had seen snake-charmers and their cobras, a mongoose just like the one Kipling wrote about, fakirs and any number of people in turbans and sarees. Somerset men had sung 'The Road to Mandalay' on their ship on the way to India, and then actually served there.

Alban Bacon grew to find in Baluchistan 'a fascination about the country due it its very bareness' with 'practically no trees, nothing but broken rocks … tortured into strange shapes … of every conceivable shade of red, brown, grey, and white'.[4] In a region of extremes, he learned to

1 Diary, 13 January 1915, Herbert Ewing, 1/5th Somerset, DD\SLI/17/1/61, SHC, Taunton
2 Postcard, December 1914, Owen Smith, 1/6th Hants, M766, RHRM
3 Caroe, 'The Flames of Enchantment', p. iv-5, PP/MCR/207, IWM
4 Bacon, *The Wanderings of a Temporary Warrior*, p. 26

wear simultaneously a fleece-lined greatcoat for warmth and a topee to avoid sunstroke. The dry heat of Baluchistan differed from the damp heat of central India – Bacon saw his first punkah only in 1916 when he went to Mhow on a staff course. (India often defied easy generalisation: Fred Mundy did not see an elephant until reaching Bareilly in April 1916.)

Most Territorials who noticed India and its people did so out of casual interest, often recording bafflement or distaste. Charles Albery described to his sister Dolly a 'Ram-Sammee' – the troops' word for any Indian religious festival – he saw at Chaubattia in May 1915. He described how 'the people dress up in their best gaudy clothes' and dance around 'a contraption on a pole' to the beat of a 'tom-tom'. To Charles it was 'an infernal row' and 'as good as going to the pictures' (and cheaper).[5] Many men, such as John Syddall, who wrote long accounts of Burma to his former pupils in Westmoreland, took an interest in local culture but like many retreated baffled. He attended a fair held at a pagoda in Maymyo, describing all he saw with much verve but little condescension. But when watching a temple 'dancing girl' he could not understand her attraction for the numerous spectators.

> What their interest or pleasure consists in, I am at a loss to conceive There was no attempt at dancing as we understand it, but the girl attired in the tightest of skirts (lungyi) simply paraded backwards and forwards for a space of about ten yards, with … an occasional lifting of one foot from the ground … although the performance was interesting at first, the novelty soon wore off

He concluded that 'the natives appreciated the performance so it mattered little what we thought of it'.[6] Other men viewed India, its people and customs with distaste – Hugh Creek, who was also a school-teacher, dismissed Hindu cremation as 'too gruesome to describe' (though he sought it out to see).[7] Victor Manley, whose diary is full of drawings and paintings of agricultural implements, artefacts and folk-life in Baluchistan, also described the people he encountered around cantonments on the plains as 'miserable, dissipated and indolent … scarcely worth considering as human'.[8] Significantly, Manley disparaged Hindu barrack servants, having decided in Baluchistan, like many British observers, that he regarded Muslims as superior in their 'simplicity'. (Manley was not the only Territorial to warm to Muslims. A lance corporal of the 1/5th Somerset at Ambala, a former schoolmaster, gave a series of lectures at St Paul's church on 'Mahomadism', all without notes; 'a most clever man'.[9])

But others were able to regard Indian life with what can only be described as an anthropological eye. Allan Swift noted the 'devotion and humility shown by the Indians whilst at worship', often observing ceremonies at temples and mosques and took care to step aside to avoid polluting food.[10] When a party of 'daftar wallahs' – the battalion's British clerks – from the 1/25th London visited the Golden Temple in Amritsar they good-humouredly accepted the

---

5   Letter, 20 August 1916, Charles Alberry, 1/4th Wilts, SBYRW 4259, RBWM
6   Clipping, Lawrence Hoggarth, 1/4th Border, Album 35 Acc. Nos 3024-3345, CMML
7   Letter, 26 March 1915, Hugh Creek, 1/4th Devon, EX2543, DMM
8   Preface, Victor Manley, 'A Khaki Diary', 49M91W/Q3/6, HRO
9   Letter, 27 February 1916, Owen Smith, 1/6th Hants, M766, RHRM
10 Diary, nd, Allan Swift, 1/6th East Surrey, ESR/25/SWIF/1, SHC, Woking

Somerset Territorials and a Hindu fakir at Benares, demonstrating the curiosity about India and its religions characteristic of them. (DD\SLI/15/7/84, Somerset Heritage Centre)

necessity to remove their boots and hand over tobacco (smoking being anathema to Sikhs).[11] Among many possible episodes is Joe Cox's reaction to a visit he made to Benares, taking advantage of its proximity to the location of the West Surreys' Kitchener's Test in 1915. (Typically, enough men were interested in India's culture for the visit to be popular – 'half the battalion going one week and half the next'.) Joe saw sacred cows in the streets, a large 'Nandi' bull statue, sexually explicit carvings and witnessed cremations at the burning ghats. Of the cremations he observed that they were 'very much like our English service'.[12] For an active Anglican who believed in the literal truth of the Bible, Joe's tolerance was remarkable.

Indian service turned many men into amateur anthropologists, and many articles in battalion magazines testify to their curiosity to record, explain, speculate and judge the people among whom they served. A Surrey man spending time at Lebong, near Darjeeling, took an interest in the hill tribespeople he met in the bazaar, trying to distinguish Bhootias from 'Sikimese' and Tibetans from Lepchas using Sir Joseph Hooker's *Tibetan Journals* and other texts from the local library. Kent men investigated the religious customs and traditional music of south India while at Bangalore, publishing articles ('A few words about [the Hindu festival of] Dasara') and on the music of Mysore in the battalion magazine.[13]

---

11 *The Londoner*, May-June 1918, p. 1. A group of Hampshires visited a mosque as part of its 'Adventures in Lahore', reluctant to take off their footwear but willing to put cloth coverings over them – only to find that their 'ammunition boots' were too big for those provided. The incident suggests that British soldiers – Regulars – had never visited before.
12 Cox, *An Ordinary Working Man's Life Story*, p. 39
13 *The Invicta*, November 1916, pp. 62; 69-70

India's history and culture fascinated enough Territorials to make their curiosity a distinctive aspect of their experience of the country. Philip Gosse, a Territorial medical officer who spent much of his time in India collecting specimens of animal skins for British museums, deplored that the 'uninquisitive type of Englishmen is all too common'.[14] By contrast, many fellow Territorials remained curious. Senior officers, especially those familiar with the limited horizons and particular appetites of Regulars, noticed how many Territorials took an interest in India and its people; what they often called, as did Henry Brain, 'Native Life'.[15] Brain described in his memoir the shops and villages he passed through, making many astute observations of a life and people utterly unfamiliar, and to him fascinating. Nor was he alone.

Many took a deeper interest, learning from guides and guidebooks, looking more closely and describing what they saw more carefully. Joseph Gale, of the 2/4th Wilts, often described Indian customs with an observant eye, describing the explosion of paint at Holi (not usually thrown at Europeans) as having 'quite a Futuristic effect' on white garments in Poona.[16] At Allahabad fort Arthur Copeland saw a huge *mela*, 'one of the most wonderful sights in the world'.[17] Soldiers watched tens of thousands of Hindu pilgrims stream through the gates to worship at an underground temple in the middle of the fort. Arthur and his friends would stroll down to the river bank or hire a boatman to take them past the vast encampment, which Arthur tried to photograph. Joseph Gale also not only saw a mela from the ramparts of Allahabad fort but walked among the hundreds of thousands of Hindu pilgrims, frankly curious at the sadhus, fakirs, elephants, and those bathing in the holy Ganga, but not in the least judgmental.[18] Their proximity to cantonment servants brought Terriers close to the religious rituals that punctuated and governed their lives. Late in 1916 Sussex men in Bangalore found themselves becoming part of a Hindu festival (probably marking the end of Dussehra), in which a man's 'boy', named 'Sam, blessed his rifle, painting it with red and white spots and garlanding it with flowers – decoration which the armourer sergeant would not have approved. 'Sam' assured the Territorial that he would now be quite safe, which the Sussex man took to mean that he would remain in India until the war's end.[19]

An awareness of the complexity of religions so different to the Christianity with which they had grown up troubled a few men. George Owers, who had felt a calling for the Primitive Methodist ministry in his native Sussex, was shaken by the experience of visiting temples and learning something of Hinduism: 'in India I had grave doubts as to the truths of the Christian faith', he later confessed.[20] Improbably for a man from the green fields and forests of Hampshire, Victor Manley also fell in love with Baluchistan. At first he thought the country 'the most abrupt, sterile, and inhospitable I ever beheld', with the nearby mountains 'as repulsive in appearance as they are barren in reality'.[21] Through 1915, Manley grew to find Baluchistan's austere and arid landscape more appealing, not least because he also became acquainted with its inhabitants. He

---

14 Gosse, *Memoirs of a Camp-Follower*, p. 194
15 Memoir, Henry Brain, 1/6th East Surrey, ESR/25/BRAIN/2, SHC, Woking
16 Gale, *With the 2/4th Wilts to India*, p. 37
17 Letter, 16 January 1915, Arthur Copeland, 1/5th Hants, 128A08/1-4, HRO
18 Gale, *With the 2/4th Wilts to India*, p. 80
19 *West Sussex Gazette*, 7 December 1916, p. 9
20 Memoir, George Owers, Sussex Battery, Doc.11927, 02/5/1, IWM
21 Diary, 11 January 1915 [sic], Victor Manley, 'A Khaki Diary', 49M91W/Q3/6, HRO

found it 'a fit setting for an Elijah or John the Baptist', describing the battalion's training camp at Chasma Tangi as 'awe-inspiring' and relishing the 'serenity' of its wilderness. Increasingly admiring its Muslim people (their simple roadside shrines were 'far more soul-raising than a musty, enclosed village church') he claimed to find similarities in the arrangement of their cemeteries and the stone circles of Stonehenge and Avebury.[22] Manley's stay at Chasma Tangi seems to have brought a profound change in his attitude to life, let alone India, where 'I learned there to hate civilisation with all its transitory values, and to meet God amid his temples reared by rugged nature'.[23]

Like Manley, a few men responded to Indian life with notable sensitivity. Their diaries and letters repeatedly comment on talks, conversations or lectures they enjoyed or quote guidebooks or articles they had read about India, its people, their religions and culture. A Middlesex man who spent time in villages near Nowshera admitted that it was 'not often that the British soldier in India is allowed to acquire any intimate information about the village life of the N.-W.F.P.'.[24] He lived in a hotel in the cantonment and visited villages each day, but even that was an achievement. Pre-eminent among them was Victor Manley, whose diary-cum-scrapbook of the two-and-half years he spent in Baluchistan resembles the field notebook of an amateur ethnographer. Manley made detailed drawings and water-colours of women's clothes (including the patterns of their embroidery), camel furnishings and agricultural technology. He described the Muslim religious festivals he witnessed, and not just one representative event, but every occasion, year-by-year, his observations becoming sharper and more informed as his knowledge grew. He watched plays in 'Hindustani', walking miles to visit new villages to record folk tales (possibly verbatim – his language skills must have improved; possibly from books). He would eat and chat with villagers, making notes on 'Village Life', all described in pages and pages in his diary; all virtually unread to this day. Manley's diary is unrewarding for anyone seeking details of the duties of sanitary orderly or battalion police sergeant, but his hundreds of pages demonstrate that a few Territorials were profoundly affected by their experience of India, and sought to record it.

'What I saw in India' Territorial photographers

The Territorials' fascination with India is apparent as nowhere else in the thousands of photographs they took. 'India abounds in glorious pictures', Fred Burton assured prospective 'pictorialists', members of the 1/1st Kent's Invicta Camera Club.[25] They were among the many Territorials who recorded India using small, portable cameras. Photography was a response distinctive to Territorials – judging by collections likely to hold photographs taken by Regulars, very few used cameras, certainly not 'other ranks'.

Officers were at first more likely to take photographs – Jim Mackie bought a camera before his battalion, the 2/4th Somerset, left Bath in December 1914. His ambition was modest: 'I hope to be able to illustrate our voyage with a few photographs', a sign that embarkation for

22 Diary, June-September 1915, Victor Manley, 'A Khaki Diary', 49M91W/Q3/6, HRO
23 Victor Manley, 'A Khaki Diary', p. 161, *Ibid*
24 *Middlesex Regiment Magazine*, 1 March 1917, p. 84. The North-West Frontier Province.
25 'Pictorial photography', *The Invicta*, January 1917, p. 127

'The Morning Prayer', an artistic rendering of a scene at the Golden Temple, Amritsar. The Territorial photographer, Edward Orr of the East Surrey, must have been inconspicuous enough to capture such a moment, within a few hundred feet of the most holy Sikh shrine. (ESR/25/ORR/4-6, Surrey History Centre)

war service could resemble a holiday trip.[26] Many Territorials created a photographic record not just of their journeys but of practically all aspects of the war service. Their albums, preserved in regimental and county archives, document their experience almost as thoroughly as do their equally abundant written records.

Harry Canham, noticing that 'most of the men here [in Peshawar] have some sort of hobby to occupy their spare time' decided to follow many others and take up photography.[27] Harry and two mates chipped in to buy a second-hand Box Brownie. Harry found he had a knack, and within a few months was selling prints to comrades – including at least a hundred copies of photographs of the Mohmand blockhouse line (see page 303). Harry's mates' interest in photography soon waned, but he traded up to a Brownie folding automatic camera. Nor was he alone. 'Bought a camera between us' is a typical line in a diary – in this case of William Bisset at Quetta early in 1915.[28] Thereafter photography (and the developing and printing of images) figures often in his diary, and he too seems to have acquired sole rights over the camera. In 1918 he invested in a vest pocket Kodak of his own for Rs30. So much were cameras and the business of developing, printing, cropping and tinting part of the everyday conversation of the barrack room that the 1/9th Hants concert party, 'The Queries', could confidently stage a skit or monologue called 'Photography' at a concert at Ambala in 1918, sure that the audience would appreciate the humour.

Soon after arriving in Cawnpore, Arthur Copeland asked his parents to send him a camera. As a member of the 1/5th Hants 'sanitary police', Arthur had licence to roam all over the cantonment. He explained that 'there are so many strange things one sees that almost every time one goes out of Barracks one wishes for a camera'.[29] Copeland also became a keen photographer, processing and printing his own photographs despite the obstacles India put in his way.

26   Letter, c. 14 December 1914, Jim Mackie, 2/4th Somerset, Mackie, *Answering the Call*, p. 12
27   Letter, 21 September 1916, Harry Canham, 2/4th Border, CMML
28   Diary, 27 February 1915, William Bisset, 2/4th Hants, M1834, RHRM
29   Letter, 16 January 1915, Arthur Copeland, 1/5th Hants, 128A08/1-4, HRO

He struggled when the weather was too hot for developing, or too humid for printing, wrestling with faulty viewfinders, film spoilt by local studios, poor quality paper and over-exposure from his unfamiliarity with India's harsh light. Arthur included over 300 photographs, most of which he had taken himself, in the thousand pages of diary-cum-memoir he later transcribed.[30] A man of the 1/25th London even took and tinted over sixty colour photographs of scenes, including of Amritsar during the 'Punjab disturbances' in 1919.

Some battalions went to special trouble to collect photographic records of their service. The routine orders of the 2/4th Somerset in February 1916 requested that:

> With a view to compiling a photographic record of the travels of the battalion and its members – will any Officers, NCOs or men who have taken photos please send a copy to the PRI [President of the Regimental Institute] who will be pleased to defray cost.

The order reminded donors that the 'name of scene [was to] to be written on back of photo in pencil'. The appeal suggests why the Somerset Heritage Centre, Taunton, has such a comprehensive photographic record of the Somerset battalions' service.[31] The Kents' camera club, which ceased meeting when the battalion went on operations in 1917, was re-formed, its members (officers and men) asked by staff officers to make a record of their service on the frontier. Unit photographers also proved their worth in that they were able to photograph the graves of men buried in cantonment cemeteries, and to illustrate battalion magazines, and sometimes to provide images for presentations or Christmas cards, though that business seemed to remain with the commercial photographers who lived off the occupants of stations.

It was not even necessary to own a camera to become a collector of photographs. The album of Charles Clinker of the 1/6th Hants includes an album of views of *Picturesque Bangalore*, which begins with a photograph of Doveton's studio (in Infantry Road). It shows that Doveton, a 'photographic artist' occupied a bungalow in the cantonment, the portico of which displayed panels bearing over thirty views he had taken, which soldiers could buy as prints to send home to relatives curious about their life in India. Doveton's advertised that it sold 'the largest and finest selection of photographs of Indian Temples, Views and Characters on Post Cards', and many men posted images home.[32]

Accordingly, many men became dealers in and collectors of images they had not themselves taken. Bert Rendall recorded how in his motor transport company the sergeants and corporals 'went into Rawalpindi and bought all the different cameras they could find'. But Bert himself was 'no photographer', so he simply bought prints of others' photographs. In this way he soon accumulated over 700 photographs of the North-West Frontier as a whole and another 100 of the Khyber Pass.[33] It is notable that many men illustrated their diaries with snapshots either they took or which they obtained from comrades. Oswald Early, for example, kept a diary and compiled an album including photographs of many places his diary does not record him visiting. A brisk trade developed in many battalions or cantonments as men sought 'snaps' of local sights

---

30 Diary, Arthur Copeland, 1/5th Hants, *Ibid*
31 Part 1 orders, 2/4th Somerset Light Infantry, February 1916, DD\SLI/6/36, SHC, Taunton. (NCO stood for 'non-commissioned officer' – sergeants or corporals.)
32 Advertisement in issues of *The Royal Sussex Herald*, 1916-17
33 Recollection of Bert Rendall, Mills, *A Strange War*, p. 98

to send home. (Though India was not necessarily cheap: 1/5th Buffs found that in Kamptee's sudder bazaar half a dozen photographs cost nearly three times the going rate in Ashford or Maidstone.³⁴)

Men's albums are also full of picture postcards, though in investigating their subjects it becomes clear that not all men could have actually visited every place their cards depict. Fred Wignall of the 2/4th Border included in his albums postcards of over a dozen places, from the boats on Dal Lake, in Kashmir, to Coonoor in the extreme south, and palaces in Rajputana, all of which he could not possibly have visited. They included 'The Famous Gun "Zam Zama"' in Lahore, the Elephant Falls in Shillong, Assam, and scenes in Hyderabad, Bangalore, Agra, Delhi and Calcutta.³⁵ Owen Smith was at least honest. He sent his family a postcard of 'Coolies Sheds Calcutta' but admitted 'I have not seen *this* place absolutely but it might be anywhere round here'.³⁶

Reg Howgego's album, 'What I saw in India 1916-1919', now in the British Library, contains an example of practically every visual trope in Terriers' photographs. He both took and bought or swapped prints, for example, ordering forty of a record of 'cloud effects' at Murree.³⁷ Assuming that he recouped his costs and added a bit, owning a Box Brownie could make a canny photographer enough to pay for film or even developing supplies. The photographs in Howgego's and dozens of other Territorials remain scattered, largely uncatalogued and slowly deteriorating in collections all over Britain, a precious but virtually unused source.³⁸

'A slight knowledge of Hindustani': lingo

At the outset, one of the Territorials' disadvantages was that hardly any of them (except their few 'old sweats') could speak any Indian language. One of Archie Brewer's 'First Impressions of India' was the 'strange lingo … we could not understand a single word'.³⁹ This was not in itself disastrous. Barrack servants and bazaar shop-keepers perforce spoke and understood English after a fashion, and the newcomers soon acquired a working grasp of barrack-room Hindustani, at least sufficient for asking for (or demanding) what they wanted. As Owen Smith's letter to his mother demonstrated, within a week of arriving at Dinapore he had begun to pick up useful words:

> England is "Blightie" [;] come here is pronounced "Hithera" [;] presently or bye & bye is "Peachy" [;] make haste; do it now is "Jelly" that is the pronounciation … [sic; or mispronunciation, in his case]⁴⁰

---

34 *Kent Messenger*, 13 March 1915
35 Pte Frederick Wignall, 2/4th Border, E94/2016, CMML
36 Postcard, nd, Owen Smith, 1/6th Hants, M766, RHRM
37 Letter, 11 September 1917, Reg Howgego, 1/25th London, Album C340/9, Mss.Eur.C340/2, BL
38 The notable exceptions to 'uncatalogued' include the Rifles Museum, Salisbury, the Somerset Heritage Centre, Taunton, and the National Army Museum, London.
39 Diary, nd [1916], Archie Brewer, 1/9th Hants, M4243, RHRM
40 Letter, 22 November 1914, Owen Smith, 1/6th Hants, M766, RHRM

But lack of language frustrated Territorials wanting to communicate with Indians, as many did. Later in the war Reuben Rusbridge and a fellow Surrey gunner walked from Roorkee cantonment

> through native village … natives very shy, tried to get into conversation with them but not many of them could understand English and of course, we could not understand what little they said.[41]

Many men enrolled in language courses, either to do their jobs better, to pass the time, or for the modest allowance qualifying commanded. They included Hugh Creek (though his munshi absconded with the fee Hugh had paid, and he failed the Pushtu exam). Harry Canham also studied Pushtu under a munshi at Peshawar. Passing the Lower Standard would gain him 80 rupees – no small sum; about £5 – but passing the higher standard would garner 800 rupees. But 'only one so far as I know has successfully tackled the higher standard … a schoolmaster and rather a smart chap'.[42] Charles Ellis, newly commissioned in the Middlesex, learned Persian and Urdu to counter the boredom of garrison life in Lucknow. YMCA officials often organised cheap or free Hindustani classes, popular because men trusted the organisation. At Bangalore in 1916 so many men signed up that the number of twice-weekly classes was doubled, though the lessons may have been of doubtful use 'judging by the experiments the members have been trying on the native servants in the Barracks'.[43] Regardless of formal classes, after they had been in India for a year men found, as did Owen Smith, that 'there are lots of little words … which we now use quite in ordinary conversation'.[44]

By 1915 cartoons (such as those appearing in *Indian Ink*, an annual published by and for Anglo-Indian civilians) were playing on the Territorials' grasp of Indian languages. In a cartoon by 'Jo Hookm', a Territorial falls into a tank or pond, ignored by three Indians smoking a hookah on its bank. After he struggles ashore he berates them in pidgin Hindi: 'You dekos me in the peni kapani. Yer ears me bolo and yer kutchperwannis!'[45] (Owen Smith of the 1/6th Hants at Agra liked *Indian Ink* enough to send a copy home as a Christmas present.) Three years later, *Indian Ink* was publishing cartoons, 'From a Hindustani Manual', possibly by a Territorial, which satirised cantonment life and whose jokes actually depended upon a grasp of barrack-room Hindustani.

Routine orders often stressed 'the importance of a slight knowledge of Hindustani in Northern India', and manuals such as *Ready Aid to the Pushtu Language* were made available when serving in the north-west. The phrases offered in a guide for troops suggested the tone of soldiers' dealings with barrack servants at least:

> 'Make haste … Clean this properly … Hold your tongue … Take off my boots … You are a fool'[46]

---

41 Diary, Reuben Rusbridge, Surrey Battery, 12 January 1918, Doc. 13388, 05/7/1, IWM
42 Letter, 16 May 1918, Harry Canham, 2/4th Border, CMML
43 'Y.M.C.A.', *The Royal Sussex Herald*, 15 April 1916, p. 23
44 Letter, 20 December 1915, Owen Smith, 1/6th Hants, M766, RHRM
45 'The Bat', Digby, *Indian Ink* [1915], np 'You saw me in the water. You heard me shout and you did nothing!'
46 *Britishers Indian Handbook*, p. 53, Bernard Searle, 1/1st Kent, NMERM 2008-1640-6, MM

A cartoon published in *Indian Ink* that played on the Territorials' growing grasp of Hindustani. The irate Territorial berates the 'natives' for ignoring his cried for help after he had fallen into the 'tank'.

If anything, though, like western visitors to India (who make far more use of please and thank you than do Indians), Territorials tended to speak more politely than was customary, another contrast to Regulars. In Indian languages, William Archer reminded his readers, there were 'formulas of servility and adulation' but 'no forms of politeness … no "please" or "thank you," or "I beg your pardon"'.[47]

Clearly some men possessed more than merely barrack-room Hindustani. Francis Solomon of the 1/4th Cornwall worked in Quartermasters stores in Bareilly and other places, and from dealings with local merchants and their employees 'became quite fluent in Hindi' – or rather the patois known as 'Bazaar bat'.[48] Victor Manley's excursions to local villages to take photographs led to him to encounter Baluchis and Pathans in their own environment. He essayed a mixture

47 Archer, *India and the Future*, p. 112
48 email from Mr Keith Solomon, 30 May 2017

of Pushtu and Hindustani, and claimed to have enjoyed intimate and friendly conversations, in which his hosts displayed both traditional 'Eastern' hospitality toward a guest and the respect Manley deserved as 'his master, the Englishmen'.[49] Equipped with a smattering of Hindustani, some Territorials were ready to leave their cantonments and see more of India.

'Tommy on leave': Territorials as tourists

For much of their time in India troops serving in India were manifestly not at war, and as they became more familiar with India many obtained leave seeking, as a correspondent to the *Pioneer* put it, 'to see a little of the country'.[50] Not surprisingly, one of Fred Wignall's three photograph albums is labelled 'My Holiday'.[51]

As the chronicler of Anglo-Indian life, Charles Allen, observed, 'it required considerable initiative on his part to break out of the barracks and see the "real" India'.[52] Sergeants and corporals could readily obtain furloughs, as could privates with good conduct records and sufficient funds. Men could travel cheaply on railway warrants and stay at YMCA dormitories, in Soldiers' Homes or in the bungalows of units in nearby cantonments – almost every routine order detailed men of other regiments passing through stations. Sometimes groups of men travelled as excursion parties, such as when Kent men visited Benares to view priests performing Hindu rites by the Ganges, and Calcutta, where local British civilians gave them a 'glorious' time.[53] Large groups of men (up to 60 from the 1/4th Devon) went from Amritsar to Lucknow, Benares and Cawnpore at Christmas 1915, and men were able to add to that itinerary – Hugh Creek and three Devon pals went on to Agra and Delhi.

With 'the Mutiny' among the most memorable of the military epics of British India, sites associated with 1857 acquired a special place in Territorials' travels. The longest single section of Murray's 1913 guide to India dealt with 'The Mutiny of 1857'. Mutiny sites abound in Terriers' photograph albums: the Kashmir Gate and Mutiny Memorial at Delhi, the Residency at Lucknow and above all, the 'Massacre Ghat' at Cawnpore. The most compelling Mutiny sacred site was the well at Cawnpore, with its vivid white angelic statuary, photographs and postcards of which appear in many Terriers' albums.

In September 1915 Sergeant Fred Mundy obtained almost a month's furlough, when he and a friend left from Delhi to visit Cawnpore, Benares and Calcutta. Mundy's account, one of the most detailed of any Territorial tourist, suggests the variety of his and others' interests. Cawnpore's main attractions were the infamous 'Massacre Ghat', the 'Memorial Well' and the church commemorating the European victims of 1857. Around the same time Ted Rice explored the ruins of the Residency in which a British garrison had withstood the siege in 1857, imagining he heard the sound of bagpipes as he toured its peaceful gardens (like Jessie Brown, who despite the celebrated poem had also only fancied she heard the relieving force's pipes). Jim Mackie found the Residency ruins 'awfully picturesque' (as they still are) and guides

---

49 Diary, 29 August 1915, Victor Manley, 'A Khaki Diary', 49M91W/Q3/6, HRO
50 *Pioneer*, 26 March 1916
51 Pte Frederick Wignall, 2/4th Border, E94/2016, CMML
52 Allen, *Raj: a Scrapbook of British India*, p. 108
53 *The Invicta*, Vol. III, No. 4, 1919, p. 35

also showed him where Jessie had supposedly heard the Highlanders' pipes.[54] But even India's imperial attractions did not move all Territorials. A disgruntled Wiltshire man wrote to his family gloomily expecting 'another year or 18 months in what he called 'this d____d country of niggers, mosquitoes and sun'. He had not been persuaded by his encounter with the epic of the race: 'if the Natives wanted India in 1857 it's a pity they didn't get it', he moaned.[55]

Beyond sites of significance to Britons in India, many Territorials became curious to know more about the varied and complex peoples among whom they served. They recorded visiting municipal museums and parks, while tombs, temples and palaces became popular jaunts on leave, at least once. Allan Swift visited tombs around Fyzabad, and even visited 'Ayhudya' (Ayodhya, in the United Provinces), 'one of the centres of the Hindu religion'. Though he also noted that had been warned it was 'not safe' to do so, he spoke to pilgrims and devotees, enquiring about caste marks and, having visited during Holi, became covered in red fluid thrown by excited devotees.[56] In fact, while Mutiny sites remained important in Territorials' tourist itineraries, they visited many more than them, as accounts of several of the many reports in diaries, letters and memoirs attest.

When Fred Mundy and his friends had left Cawnpore, they moved on to Benares, where the focus of their interest became Hinduism – the 'Monkey Temple' (and the city's 'mass of Hindoo Temples'), including the cremation ghats. Like tourists in Varanasi today they hired a boat and saw the 'magnificent sight' of the city's 'domes and pinnacles pointing to the sky' from the Ganges. Though repulsed by the 'scores of cripples, blind and sick' around the Nepalese temple, they saw 'a most wonderful and beautiful sight in the sunset as they left. Despite the 'nasty kind of damp heat', Fred and his friend enjoyed a 'good, easy time' in Calcutta. They stayed for three weeks, travelling mostly by tram, admiring the grand buildings around Dalhousie Square and visiting the zoo, the botanical gardens, the celebrated Jain temple, the collection which would be displayed in the new Victoria Memorial (then under construction) and spending two whole days in the Indian Museum. On the way back to Delhi they stopped for a week at Lucknow, taking in both the palaces of the rulers of Oudh and the sites of the 1857 siege. Fred had been interested in seeing something of Hindu India, and in its civic and industrial development under the British, as well as in the imperial epic of the Mutiny.[57]

Judging by their accounts of their journeys, and the albums of photographs they created, other soldier tourists took similar interests in India. In December 1915, for example, Victor Manley and a comrade took a month's furlough to travel from Quetta to Delhi, Agra, Amritsar and Lahore. Characteristically, Manley recorded his impressions of 'glowing scarlet mountains', drew diagrams of irrigation systems and made notes on the geology of the country. They also witnessed a cremation, paid nautch girls to dance and visited temples and tombs (though not the Taj by moonlight, an omission Manley bitterly regretted). At Delhi he too reflected on 1857 sites, but recorded his interest both in the Mughal emperors and the British hero of John Nicholson.[58] Unusually, Manley, who respected Muslim places of worship especially, worried that he was disturbing sacred sites by his visiting as a mere sightseer.

---

54   Letter, 10 March 1916, Jim Mackie, 2/4th Somerset, Mackie, *Answering the Call*, p. 154
55   Letter, 10 August 1916, Jack Welch, 1/4th Wilts, SBYRW 26535-6, RBWM
56   Diary, nd, Allan Swift, 1/6th East Surrey, ESR/25/SWIFT/1, SHC, Woking
57   Mundy, *A Journal of the 1/4th Battalion Wiltshire Regiment*, pp. 52-58
58   Diary, December 1915, Victor Manley, 'A Khaki Diary', 49M91W/Q3/6, HRO

The greatest Indian attraction, then as now, was of course the Taj Mahal at Agra. Many men took the opportunity to visit Agra specifically to see the famous tomb, and it appears in many Territorials' photograph albums. Even Captain Godfrey Burrell, who confessed that he was 'not gifted with a fervor for sightseeing' was glad that he had been able to see the Taj Mahal ('the most beautiful building that exists') on the way from Poona to Rawalpindi in January 1915.[59] They visited alone, in pairs and in groups, even as entire battalions – the 1/9th Hants visited the Taj while en route from Bangalore to Burhan in December 1916. When Fred Mundy and three comrades travelled from Delhi to Agra in February 1917 they seemed no mere sensation-seekers, first visiting Akbar's tomb at nearby Sikandra and the tomb of Itimad-ad-Daula before crossing the Jumna to see the Taj. Mundy, a school-teacher in Wiltshire, enthused over it ('this is a most marvellous building and rightly classed as one of the marvels of the world'). The next day, after visiting the fort and the Jama Masjid ('not to be compared with the one at Delhi') he returned to the Taj to see it by moonlight. Mundy and his comrades were able to compare the sights of Agra with those of Delhi because they had often stood guard in Delhi fort and were 'very interested in all the historical buildings as they were built by the same Moghul Kings' [sic].[60] Even so, few British soldiers recorded being moved by any of the three great religions of India. While Olaf Caroe admitted that 'the religious element' 'goes far to explain its attraction for me', he disclaimed that it was 'not something specifically Hindu', but that India had a universal appeal.[61]

Some more adventurous men went further afield – Harry Canham spent a furlough in the Swat valley early in 1919. Charles Gibson, who had been an engine inspector in Devon, made a point of visiting stations and workshops all over northern India, travelling to Simla to see the Kalka-Simla Railway as much for the pleasures of the resort. Among the most adventurous expeditions was that undertaken by a Sergeant E.V. Williams of the 2/6th Royal Sussex, who with two companions made an eight-day trek north from Simla on the Hindustan-Tibet road, staying in dak bungalows, their baggage carried by coolies, walking 145 miles but at a cost of only six rupees a day.[62] In 1918 and 1919 William Bisset and his friends, Territorial clerks at Army Headquarters, would walk all over the same area, trekking up to thirty miles a day in the spectacular mountainous country of the Simla Hills. Compared to India's now vast tourism industry, soldiers' destinations were limited, with a standard itinerary running from Delhi, through Benares, Cawnpore, Lucknow, Agra and Delhi, with side trips to hill stations and, occasionally, to Lahore or Kashmir. Tourism to, say, Rajasthan (then Rajputana), caves such as Ajanta, temple sites such as Hampi or Kerala's backwaters did not exist; indeed, large parts of east and south India and most 'natives states' saw no British soldiers at all.

'Shikar': collecting and hunting

Like the curious Territorial medical officer Philip Gosse, newcomers to India responded to its natural history as well as its human cultures. An officer of the 1/4th Wilts at Kuldana began

---

59 Godfrey Burrell, 'The Diary of a Company Commander', p. 7, M1838, RHRM
60 Mundy, *A Journal of the 1/4th Battalion Wiltshire Regiment*, pp. 103-04
61 Caroe, 'The Flames of Enchantment', p. 10, PP/MCR/207, IWM
62 'From Simla to the Sutlej', *The Royal Sussex Herald*, 2 November 1918, pp. 209-11

Wilts Territorials display the bodies of animals they have shot on 'shikar' – a black buck and a leopard. (SBYRW32076, Rifles Berkshire and Wiltshire Museum)

a 'Natural History Collection' and a sergeant of the 2/4th Hants, a spiritual descendant of Hampshire naturalist Gilbert White, published an article advising his comrades how to collect the creatures such as scorpions, centipedes, locusts and crickets which, to their revulsion, abounded around Quetta.[63] Many soldiers took to collecting butterflies or other insects, and not just as adornments or to pass the time. Though disgusted with both India and the army, Hugh Creek of the 1/4th Devon started a butterfly collection at Dalhousie, inspired by a retired Eurasian doctor he had met. Also at Dalhousie, a man of the 1/5th East Surrey proposed the formation of a Regimental Natural History Society and started 'the latest craze', for butterfly hunting.[64] Other Territorials took an interest in India's botany: 'one of the greatest glories of India', Joseph Gale thought, was 'its trees', describing the 'Flame of the Forest' tree in rapturous terms.[65]

Other Territorials took an interest in India's wildlife in order to hunt and kill it. Many officers had doubtless read in their Murray's Guide of the scope for 'sport'. When the 1/10th Middlesex arrived in Calcutta in November 1914 staff officers were astounded to see that its officers brought such an 'assortment of fishing rods and gun-cases' that Howrah station reminded one of Euston in early August.[66] Officers accustomed to the hunting and shooting pursuits of the county gentry looked forward to India's prospects for sport. When Stanley Goodland heard in October 1914 that the 1/5th Somerset was destined for Jhansi all he knew of it was that it was 'very hot and full of snakes but a fine sporting centre so we should have a good time'.[67] India was 'a land where Game Laws are practically non-existent'.[68] White men could hunt almost anywhere, restrained only by what peasants were willing to allow. Officers at virtually all stations had unlimited entrée to field sports: what Anglo-Indians called shikar: hunting.

63 *The Tiger*, May 1915, pp. 46-47
64 *5th East Surrey Magazine*, 1 July 1915, pp. 8-9
65 Gale, *With the 2/4th Wilts to India*, p. 41
66 Woodyatt, 'The Territorials (Infantry) in India, 1914-1920', *JRUSI*, 1922, p. 720. The grouse-shooting season traditionally opened on 12 August.
67 Letter 5 October 1914, Stanley Goodland, 1/5th Somerset, Noyes, (ed.), *Engaged in War*, p. 9
68 'Territorials in India', *Singapore Free Press and Mercantile Advertiser*, 15 March 1915, p. 8

References to hunting recur in officers' letters, diaries and memoirs. Robert Palmer detailed his 'bag' in letters to his father in Hampshire (15 hares, 11 quail, three partridges …). The Rajah of Bhurtpur invited him to shoot in the wetlands which are now one of India's most significant bird sanctuaries.[69] Alban Bacon of the 2/4th Hants was among the most enthusiastic hunters. The only Territorial infantry officer to publish a memoir of his time in India, he sub-titled it a 'Narrative of Service (and Sport) in Three Continents'. In Baluchistan he enjoyed shooting chikor (partridge) and, in Sind, duck, quail and snipe – 339 animals, including a wild pig and (unforgivably) a pelican. At Lahore a Hampshire officer of the 1/1st Wessex artillery became its Master of the Hounds. In northern Burma Somerset officers shot everything from waterfowl to elephants, while Border officers hunted bears in the jungle around Maymyo. At Christmas 1917, in a hierarchy characteristic of that army and that country at that time, the Hants officers enjoyed partridges, its sergeants hares and grouse and privates pork from wild pigs.[70]

Officers naturally pursued field sports, whether out of familiarity and enjoyment or at the invitation of sporting civilians or fellow officers. But many 'other ranks' also hunted. Except that the country around large cantonments was often 'shot out', most were close to good hunting country – even in Delhi Wilts men shot boar. A West Kent company training in jungle near Jubbulpore early in 1916 flushed out a wild boar, which bowled a man over and bent the bayonet of another who tried to kill it.[71] Thomas Heard and a friend went hunting for three days in the jungle around Bareilly, shooting buck, hare and peafowl startled by a field firing exercise. (Sometimes shikar found them – two of Herbert Chapple's comrades came face-to-face with a cheetah when out in the jungle near Calicut.) 'Other ranks' had more difficulty hunting, not least by lacking leave, guns and the means to hire shikari servants. Men of the 1/1st Wilts Battery, however, used their horses to run a pack of hounds at Meerut in 1916, chasing jackals and silver foxes and even, with the encouragement of their aristocratic officer commanding, indulging in pig-sticking ('a sport generally reserved for officers').[72]

Shikar brought officers and men into contact with villagers, though it is not clear what either made much of the encounter: 'Villagers are very suspicious of strangers and find it difficult to understand any European except the officers of their own district', a civil servant warned.[73] Both made their modest contribution to the devastation of India's wildlife.

'The Troop Train Tragedy': railways

The Territorials' first real experience of India (after they had seen Bombay from the decks of their transports or the docks) was of the railway. Britain's quintessential bequest to India, railways dominated the troops' experience and consequently their records of it, in letters, diaries, memoirs and photograph albums. Troops not only first saw India from between the slats of

---

69　Letter, 7 January 1915, Robert Palmer, 1/5th Hants, 19M75/F/C19, HRO
70　Anon, *History of the Hampshire Territorial Force Association*, p. 117
71　*The Queen's Own Gazette*, Vol. XXXV, No. 2, February 1916, p. 3455
72　Bavin, *Swindon's War Record*, p. 251
73　'Lecture delivered to territorial officers in various cantonments in February 1916', Hinton Harris, Hampshire Regiment, M1542, RHRM. Parts of this book were written sitting beneath hunting trophies displayed on the walls of the Ootacamund Club.

Hants men in a train in which they travelled 2500 miles across India, the, glare, heat and discomfort of the journey fully apparent. (M4236, Royal Hampshire Regiment Museum)

railway carriage windows, but repeatedly used railways to travel between stations, on changes of cantonment, or to travel for courses or on leave. 'Travelling', a Middlesex man wrote in his battalion magazine, 'is the most natural thing in the world in India, and is not confined to the few'.[74] Indeed, it was on railway journeys, on platforms if not in carriages, that Territorials most directly encountered India and Indians.

The railways' principal purposes were strategic. Their ability to move large numbers of troops long distances quickly justified their construction: economic considerations were secondary. Except for many stations in the hills, cantonments were connected to the rail network extending across the sub-continent. It enabled battalions and detachments to be shifted long distances when needed, as they were many times during the war. British units moved frequently. The 1/5th Hants history records that its battalion headquarters moved eleven times between late 1914 and late 1919 – about twice a year – with eight other stations occupied by detachments.[75] Units moved epic distances by British standards – 43 hours from Karachi to Quetta, 63hours from Bombay to Bangalore; four days from Madras to Jullunder.

Troops travelled by a variety of types of trains, often 'built more for utility than comfort', as a private of the 1/4th Border ruefully wrote to a Carlisle newspaper soon after arrival in 1914.[76] Often they occupied carriages fitted out to carry troops, with seats able to convert to bunks for sleeping. But as often they were allocated carriages marked as suitable for 'natives', which merely

---

74 'Records and impressions of the Battalion …', *Magazine of the 9th Battalion The Middlesex Regiment*, 1 February 1917, p. 40
75 Anon, *History of the Hampshire Territorial Force Association*, p. 145
76 Clipping, Lawrence Hoggarth, 1/4th Border, Album 35 Acc. Nos 3024-3345, CMML

emphasised how even British troops occupied a lowly position in the hierarchy of British India. As a West Surrey man put it, fed up after a long journey from Lucknow to Lebong,

> Sixteen men in a railway train
> (Yo, ho, ho, and a mugful of tea),
> None of 'em anxious to do it again,
> Fairly fed-up *and* without a rupee.[77]

Railway journeys were popular occasions for photographs, both of scenes from trains and of trains and their passengers. Percy Harrison's photographs include a shot of twelve men of his 2/4th Border, in a small compartment with bare wooden benches, the sun glaring in the windows.

The appalling experience of a draft of a thousand reinforcements, mostly Territorials, on a railway journey in 1916 became a telling event, even for men without any connection with it. They arrived at Karachi on the transport *Ballarat* early in June 1916 (unusually: drafts traditionally arrived in the 'cold' weather, but the war disrupted accustomed patterns). The troops were immediately put onto a troop train running north through Sind, at the very hottest part of the year. Railway transport staff at Karachi organised the train on the cold-weather scale, in crowded third-class carriages with corrugated iron roofs, and with insufficient medical stores – almost no ice remained by the second day. The men aboard the train were new to India and some exposed their bare heads to the sun, an act regarded as fatal.

By the time the train reached Rohri, 300 miles north, men were being carried off in distress and taken to hospital. Over 130 men were left in hospitals en route – in cantonments among the hottest in India. On a train soon after, Alban Bacon met a doctor in whose house 'several Territorials had been taken to die, about a week before'. The doctor answered Bacon's questions about the incident with 'a placid, "I don't know!"'[78] If officials in India were indifferent, Territorials (who had all experienced the discomforts of rail travel) were outraged: 'whoever was responsible for it ought to be hung', Joseph Gale wrote after hearing of it in Poona.[79]

Rumours of the deaths reached Britain in mid-July. A former Indian official asked in *The Times* whether 'their lives have not been thrown away through somebody's thoughtlessness'.[80] Waldorf Astor (Liberal MP for Plymouth and husband of Nancy Astor) sought details from Austen Chamberlain, who released telegrams from Simla disclosing that 136 men had been hospitalized, with 15 deaths (later amended to 19), and that the affair was being investigated.[81] An enquiry ordered by Simla disclosed the facts, which were released in Parliament as over the next four months the affair was raised in both houses on nine occasions.

MPs' questions gradually disclosed a terrible combination of inexperience, ineptitude and blind adherence to regulation (the Indian Army's inherent defect). Contrary to denials issued at first, the train had been over-crowded, it had been drawn by under-powered locomotives, and so travelled unusually slowly, and the weather had been exceptionally hot. No emergency

---

77 'Lebong', *The Braganza*, 1 March 1917, p. 16
78 Alban Bacon, *The Wanderings of a Temporary Warrior*, p. 37
79 Gale, *With the 2/4th Wilts to India*, p. 58
80 *The Times*, 18 July 1916, p. 7
81 Waldorf Astor, House of Commons, *Hansard*, 17 July 1916; *The Times*, 21 July 1916, p. 7

justified moving troops through the Sind desert, rather than sending them to cooler stations in the Deccan until the monsoon broke. 'Somebody has blundered', Viscount Midleton declared in the House of Lords: but who?[82] Several officers were dismissed, including Major-General David Shaw, the officer commanding the Karachi Brigade (who, reprehensibly, had been responsible for the debacle of the march to Lahej in Aden, which resulted in the deaths of Brecknocks; see Chapter 8). Lord Ampthill, a former Governor of Madras, defended Shaw, pointing out that nearly forty men died of heatstroke on a hospital ship in the Persian Gulf a week later and claiming that he had been a scapegoat.[83] While officers in India certainly had blundered, officers at home, who had despatched a ship scheduled to arrive at the height of the hot weather, went un-reprimanded, while the actions or omissions of officers of Army Headquarters, which ordered the enquiry, went unexamined. Henry Forster, the Financial Under-Secretary to the War Office in one of the matter's final Parliamentary outings simply affirmed that 'the men were urgently wanted ... we cannot observe the ordinary rules of peace time'.[84]

Territorial other ranks – as the most likely to be affected by travel in the hot weather – took an interest in newspaper accounts of the investigation – Victor Manley pasted clippings about it, including reports of its mentions in Parliament, into his scrapbook-cum-diary. As simply 'the Troop Train Tragedy' it reverberated throughout the Territorials' service. It certainly alerted transport staff officers to the hazards of travelling in the heat. In July 1916 (just six weeks later) the Quartermaster General issued *Rules to be Observed by British Troops Travelling in India during the Summer Months by Rail*. It advised 'soldiers arriving in India for the first time' of the dangers of hot-weather travel, offering counsel such as 'don't put your head out of the window'.[85] When the 2/4th Wilts at last left Poona in April 1917 they were supplied with ice, soda water and fans.[86] About the same time the 2/4th Hants were given 'ice enough to freeze a polar bear'.[87] After the Sind debacle all troop trains carried medical officers (a regulation that allowed Philip Gosse and other curious officers to see a great deal of India). When Reg Bailey's reinforcement draft of Buffs travelled from Bombay to Bareilly in March 1917 he described 'the very latest kind of troop train; there was not a complaint'.[88]

Not all railway transport officers heeded the findings of the enquiry, and the many photographs of trains in albums suggest that troops continued to board unsuitable, or at least uncomfortable, trains. When the 1/4th Wilts at last left Delhi in the spring of 1917 its men entered 'filthy third class native compartments', with others infested with vermin: 'far from being nice'. This was unexpected after 'the great scandal' of the Sind tragedy.[89] Territorials would continue to travel around India by rail, and would travel far beyond, but by ship.

---

82 Viscount Midleton, House of Lords, *Hansard*, 25 July 1916. Midleton was formerly Sir John Brodrick, who had served as Secretary of State for War and for India a decade before.
83 Ampthill, 'Fiat Justitia: The Case of a Scapegoat', *National Review*, April 1920, pp. 205-10
84 Henry Forster, House of Commons, *Hansard*, 15 August 1916
85 *Rules to be Observed by British Troops Travelling in India during the Summer Months by Rail*, William Evans, M906, RHRM
86 Gale, *With the 2/4th Wilts to India*, p. 64
87 Bacon, *The Wanderings of a Temporary Warrior*, p. 58
88 Letter, 15 March 1917, Reg Bailey, 1/4th Buffs, 2011-12-3, NAM
89 Mundy, *A Journal of the 1/4th Battalion Wilshire Regiment*, p. 106

6

Terriers abroad

Towards the end of his first six months in India, Gerald Gibbs of the 1/5th East Surrey, while marching to church parade one Sunday in Cawnpore 'suddenly realized that we were beginning to look like, and in fact were, a real force'.[1] Ignorant of the authorities' doubts about their capabilities, having passed their Kitchener's Tests the Territorials considered that they had qualified for war. 'We are always wondering when we shall again embark', one wrote home, considering that Kitchener's undertaking might be in some way binding.[2] Terriers did embark from India, however, for Burma, Singapore, Hong Kong, the Andaman Islands, and even Australia.

'Really out of it': Burma

Burma, acquired by Britain in three wars over the preceding 90 years, was part of the Indian empire, though ethnically, geographically and climatically distinct. The first Territorials (the 1/4th Shropshire, 2/4th Somerset and 1/4th Border) arrived during the cooler season, but still found the heat 'unendurable', as John Syddall of the 1/4th Border wrote to the pupils of his former school, at Kendal Green. (Syddall's travelogues are among the Terriers' most vivid accounts, full of acute observation and colourful detail: 'Monkeys abound ... There is one playing about within a few yards of me as I write'.[3]) The first Territorials to arrive were greeted in Rangoon early in December 1914 by civilians distributing cheroots and flowers.

The final British conquest of Burma had occurred only thirty years before, and Burmese resistance – regarded by the occupiers as *dacoity* (outlawry) – demanded a strong garrison. British troops were stationed around the country, at Myitkyina, Shewbo, Prome, Moulmein and Mandalay (of course – though both mentioned in Kipling's celebrated poem they were over 200 miles apart) and Burma's capital, Rangoon. Sale Barracks in Rangoon, as John Syddall explained in a letter printed in Kendal's *Westmoreland Gazette*, was 'right beside' the great Shwe Dagon pagoda, symbol of Burmese Buddhism, and 'one of the Seven Wonders of the World'. Sheathed

---

1 Gibbs, *Survivor's Story*, p. 13
2 Letter, 8 November 1915, James Nickalls, 1/10th Middlesex, Great Chart Fund, KA&HC
3 Clipping [*Westmoreland Gazette*], Lawrence Hoggarth, 1/4th Border, Album 35 Acc. Nos 3024-3345, CMML,

in gold leaf, 'it is grand when the sun shines upon it'. The pagoda was 'one of the finest sights in the world', Murray's guide enthused – a reminder of how volunteering for imperial service brought unexpected rewards.[4] Troops at Thayetmayo and Shwebo also guarded Turkish prisoners of war captured in Mesopotamia. Captain Lawrence Hoggarth's photograph album documents Border men guarding the camp at Thayetmayo, evidently former go-downs and bungalows wired off. Providing rosters of guards, and of the unrelenting vigilance required, imposed hardships on the company on duty at the camp. While Rangoon seemed metropolitan, more isolated cantonments could feel very remote from the great events that had brought them to India. 'We had little news of the war', Bert Rendall recalled, even 'in Rangoon we felt really out of it'.[5]

Burma had its own hazards as well as its particular history and culture. Bert Rendall remembered encountering its scorpions, and was painfully bitten or stung by a large and loathsome black beetle on guard outside the lieutenant-governor's bungalow in Rangoon. Fortunately, the lieutenant-governor's own doctor treated him immediately, and he was excused duties for a week, but 65 years after still had a lump from the bite. In Burma, as in India proper, newcomers learned their way about from old hands. The Somersets became 'extremely friendly with the European sergeants of the Rangoon Police', as Ed Ewens explained.[6] As self-conscious (not to say self-important) white men there was little chance that they would allow 'natives' to take liberties. But, especially in the smaller up-country stations, opportunities to speak to 'natives' were more frequent. John Syddall told the pupils of his old school that at Maymyo many 'understand English quite well and make a good attempt to speak it'. Territorials were less willing to master local languages, 'though common phrases are easily acquired'.[7]

The 2/5th Somerset was split between Rangoon and Shwebo and even smaller places, such as Bhamo ('right up near the Chinese border') from its arrival in Burma in 1914 to May 1917, when it went to India.[8] When Sir John Nixon, Commander of the Southern Army, inspected the 1/4th Border in Maymyo in January 1915 he reassured them that the Territorials had taken the place of the regiment's 1st Battalion as the 'guardians of the Chinese frontier'. Border men regarded this as 'some compensation for their disappointment in not being sent to the front'. Soon after, a wing of the battalion was despatched to 'restore order' among the Kachins and later the Shans, the men happy to 'have a good slap at them'.[9] The following year a company of the 2/5th Somerset also marched through the Kachin Hills (their baggage carried by elephants), supposedly dispelling the popular belief that the war had destroyed British military power, by marching through bazaars with bayonets fixed.[10]

Several battalions' time in Burma is adequately documented, though mostly by scrapbooks and memoirs rather than official records. Other battalions in Burma were less well served. The history of the 1/5th Hants published by the county association devoted just one paragraph to the nine months it spent at Maymyo in 1918. The 1/4th Border was to remain in Burma until 1917, but their Shropshire counterparts soon moved on.

4   Anon, *A Handbook for Travellers*, p. 570
5   Interview with Bert Randall, Mills, *A Strange War*, p. 39
6   Mills, *A Strange War*, p. 42
7   Clipping, Lawrence Hoggarth, 1/4th Border, Album 35 Acc. Nos 3024-3345, CMML
8   Interview with Bert Rendall, Mills, *A Strange War*, p. 49
9   Clipping, Lawrence Hoggarth, 1/4th Border, Album 35 Acc. Nos 3024-3345, CMML
10 Anon, *The Book of Remembrance*, pp. 86-87

A platoon of the 1/4th Border Regiment parading at the Ottoman prisoner-of-war camp at Thayetmyo in Burma, a reminder of the routine duties that occupied Territorials, day-in, day-out. (Album 68, Acc. Nos. 6973-6991, Cumbria's Museum of Military Life)

'A Jehad feeling: the Singapore mutiny

The 1/4th Shropshire almost immediately faced the ultimate purpose of British India's military garrison. On the evening of 21 January 1915 reports reached Burma's acting Lieutenant-Governor, Sir George Shaw, that the 130th Baluchis in Rangoon was on the verge of mutiny – the most potent word in the lexicon of empire. The garrison was swiftly and discreetly roused and by 5.30 the next morning the Indian troops had been disarmed and the would-be mutineers foiled. Captain Roger Haslewood described the 'pathetic sight' of bemused sepoys in irons: the 'faithful' in the battalion would be sent to East Africa.[11]

Two weeks later the Shropshires sent two companies on an 18-day march through the In Sein district (today within the area of greater Yangon; then a tract of riverine jungle). The campaign sought to intimidate the 'dacoits' operating in the still imperfectly pacified area. While the column was still underway Burma's lieutenant-governor received an urgent telegram from Delhi, on the evening of 16 February. Word of mutiny in Singapore sent the Shropshires to embark on the transport *Edavana* and leave within twenty-four hours.

Monday, 15 February 1915 had been a public holiday in Singapore, in honour of the Chinese lunar new year, and the streets had been full of the bangs of fireworks. That afternoon, men of the 5th Light Infantry, which was on the point of leaving Singapore, broke into a violent mutiny. The troops committed 'a number of dastardly murders', killing at least 17 Europeans and

---

11   Letter, 27 January 1915, Roger Haslewood, 4th Shropshire, 3614/2/142-161, SA

sparking panic, retribution and the hasty summoning of the 1/4th Shropshire from Rangoon.[12] Most of the Shropshires arrived in Singapore's Keppel Harbour after a swift 72-hour voyage from Rangoon. The Governor, Sir George Young, greeted the ship and briefed the officers. The battalion reached Tanglin barracks on the late afternoon of 21 February, six days after the outbreak, finding bungalows in disarray still, their walls stained with blood.

While most of the men of the 5th Light Infantry remained in barracks, 'like children [awaiting] the coming punishment', a few mutineers dispersed into the interior of Singapore island, still largely covered with dense jungle.[13] A mixed force of police, Malay States Guides, British, French, Russian and Japanese sailors scoured the island seeking out and rounding up groups of Indians, many confused about the outbreak in which they had been caught up. Shropshire light infantrymen immediately joined the search, transported around the island in private cars loaned by civilians anxious to eliminate the last mutineers, sleeping in plantation sheds and in the cars. They searched rubber and pineapple plantations, swamps and the jungle, literally plunged into tropical campaigning. It seems that they killed some mutineers – it was said that mutineers preferred to surrender to native police (mainly Indians) rather than white soldiers, who may have summarily executed them. Roger Haslewood told his mother that 'we are simply dying to get a shot at … the swine'.[14]

Those taken into custody were tried and on 23 February the Shropshires paraded when the first of 47 mutineers were executed – by firing squads of Singapore Volunteers, many the friends and neighbours of those killed on 15 February. Sergeant Ben Nicholas recorded that he 'had the pleasure of escorting two of the 5th L.I. out to be shot'. He expressed no regret when their bodies were brought in and he saw 'great holes had been blown out of their backs by the bullets'.[15] Troops were still rounding up mutineers in the first days of March. The 'Singapore riots', as the mutiny was misleadingly called officially, affected troops thousands of miles away, when jumpy commanders placed units as far away as Delhi on alert. This suggested the latent uncertainty with which the Raj thought of its security. The Marquess of Crewe, the Secretary of State for India represented the outbreak as merely 'a regimental riot' arising from bad feeling between ethnic groups over jealousies over promotion, and not 'what is known as a Jehad feeling'.[16] British response to the outbreak, and their sensitivity to Muslim feeling in India especially, gave the lie to that claim. The mutiny was only one (but the most serious) internal disturbance among Muslim troops in 1915, one of the markers of the Indian empire's vulnerability to Muslim pressure on or within the frontier with Afghanistan.

'That welcome shade': the Kelantan expedition

In April 1915, only weeks after the shock of the mutiny of the 5th Light Infantry at Singapore, 'another call was made for us', a man of the 1/4th Shropshire recalled, to meet rebellion in the

---

12 Colonial Reports – Straits Settlements, Parliamentary Papers, 1916, Vol. 19, pp. 26-42
13 *Ibid*, p. 37
14 Letter, 25 February 1915, Roger Haslewood, 4th Shropshire, 3614/2/142-161, SA
15 Diary, 5 April 1915, Ben Nicholas, 1/4th Shropshire, Private collection
16 Marquess of Crewe, House of Lords, *Hansard*, 2 March 1915

Malay state of Kelantan.[17] Though historians of colonial Malaya debate the details, new taxes introduced in Kelantan induced the peasants – *bumiputera* – to protest. Instigated by a shadowy figure known as Tok Janggut (or 'the Old Long Beard'), mobs killed policemen and looted police stations. British officials despatched reinforcements to Pasir Puteh, a kampong about 25 miles south of Kota Bharu, just south of the Siamese border. A force, comprising 163 men of the 1/4th Shropshire, 50 Royal Garrison Artillery gunners and 21 men of the Singapore Volunteer Infantry, was shipped from Singapore in a British sloop. A large crowd watching them land 'seemed scared' because 'white troops had never been there before' – the state had become part of British Malaya only in 1909, taken over from Siam.[18]

The force slept in a corrugated iron picture-theatre at Kota Bharu (after watching the film-show) before marching south for Pasir Puteh in intense heat. They saw burned villages, and were warned not to abandon their wounded, for fear they would be mutilated. That 'made us think we were going to see something real', one remembered.[19] They encountered 'swarms' of bumiputera armed with spears and parangs but wearing red armbands, indicating their supposed loyalty to the British administration; or to the Sultan of Kelantan: no one was sure. After two days the troops reached the Sultan's palace, sustained by coconut milk – the novice campaigners' preparations were inadequate, and men overcome with heat-stroke returned in bullock carts tailing the column. 'Do you remember the march we made?' a man later asked, 'heaven be thanked for that welcome shade'. One of the Shropshire officers abused his dilatory men, deriding them as 'a disgrace to the British Army' and accusing them of having 'not bad feet but bad hearts'.[20] Despite the heat, their unfitness and the rebels' knowledge of the terrain, the British force succeeded in driving them over the border into Siam.

Large numbers of Malays wearing red arm-bands followed the force about. When British troops failed to find any rebels, some Territorials began to suspect that they were actually rebels shamming loyalty. Before the Europeans could find the rebellious peasants they were relieved by Indian troops of the Malay States Guides, who attacked the rebel leader's band and killed him. Later that year the Malay States Guides were despatched to, of all places, Aden, where they remained until November 1919.[21] The two-week-long expedition ended with the Shropshire men camping on a beach on the South China Sea, living on ducks and chickens bought from local farmers; a relief from bully beef in the tropical heat. For them the brief episode gave them insights into the exotic life of the *tuans* of Malaya:

> Do you remember that place Kelantan
> On the borders of Siam?
> Our rations were bully, and biscuits and jam
> Under the coconut tree.[22]

---

17   Anon, *The Coconut Tree – and After*, p. 15
18   Diary, 3 May 1915, Ben Nicholas, 1/4th Shropshire, Private collection
19   Anon, *The Coconut Tree – and After*, p. 15
20   Diary, 6 May 1915, Ben Nicholas, 1/4th Shropshire, private collection
21   Bagoo, 'The Origin and Development of the Malay States Guides', *Journal of the Malayan Branch of the Royal Asiatic Society*, pp. 75-76
22   Anon, *The Coconut Tree – and After*, p. 5

The 1/4th Shropshire was not to serve as a battalion for two-and-a-half years after its disembarkation in Rangoon. A detachment had gone to the Andaman Islands, and it was split between Singapore and Hong Kong, which had been defended by local forces since Regulars left in 1914.

For two years the battalion remained divided between Singapore and Hong Kong. In both the troops enjoyed generally better pay and rations than in India, though their barracks were less comfortable (and the climate of both colonies was trying and without the relief of hill stations). As the Hong Kong dollar fell in value their pay declined in purchasing power. The colony's governor, Sir Francis May, claimed that he had a 'more intimate acquaintance' than had been usual with Regular battalions (possibly because some lived beside his residence at the Peak). Judging by the paucity of mentions in the *South China Morning Post*, however, the troops kept their distance from local British civilians (possibly physically in that they occupied barracks in the New Territories and at Stanley, on the island's south coast). Except for burying one man in the cemetery at Happy Valley (in an 'enclosure … reserved exclusively for the graves of soldiers who have died in Hong Kong'), the Shropshires left few reminders of their sojourn.[23] Arthur Garrett (now Lieutenant-Colonel) lobbied the commander in Singapore, Major-General Sir Dudley Ridout, arguing that on the basis of Kitchener's undertaking his men should be allowed to return to fight in France. Ridout promised Garrett that if he could train his battalion to 'battle standard' he would do what he could. He reported that the 1/4th Shropshire was efficient and in due course it was relieved by a Kitchener battalion, the 25th Middlesex.[24] The *Straits Times* acknowledged that its men had 'had a hard time here financially'. A fund opened under the patronage of Singapore's governor soon gathered over 2000 Straits Dollars to give the Shropshires 'a hearty send off'.[25] The battalion had arrived in Hong Kong on 7 April 1915 and left exactly two years later. Sir Francis farewelled them, jocularly commenting that seven was a lucky number: he could not have been more wrong, as the battalion would discover in France.

'On the Empire's business': Territorials in Australia

Small parties of Territorials made journeys from India. In June 1915, for example, a platoon of the 2/4th Border travelled to Mesopotamia and East Africa and back, escorting a shipment of explosives from the Kirkee arsenal. At least three contingents travelled to Australia, in 1915 and 1916.

The first, under Bridgnorth solicitor Captain Roger Haslewood, took him, a subaltern and 28 men of the 1/4th Shropshire from Singapore to Adelaide, escorting a group of 58 German internees. In April 1915 they travelled on the *Uganda*, 'jolly glad of the chance of seeing so much'. Handing over their charges to Australian gunners, Haslewood's party immediately boarded a train for Brisbane, travelling 1500 miles over four days. There they boarded the *Montoro* to return to Singapore, completing a month in constant motion. 'I am about fed up with travelling', Haslewood wrote to his mother on the return voyage.[26]

---

23 The grave of L/Cpl John Rowley, who died on 1 January 1917 is in section 3 of Hong Kong's 'colonial cemetery', which I visited in August 2017.
24 Comment by Major-General Sir Dudley Ridout, in Woodyatt, 'The Territorials (Infantry) in India', *JRUSI*, 1922, p. 733
25 *The Straits Times*, 2 April 1917, p. 8
26 Letters, 17 April & 11 May 1915, Roger Haslewood, 1/4th Shropshire, 3614/2/142-161, SA

In November 1915 a party of 1/4th Devon escorted a party of Germans who had been interned in Ceylon. They were housed in the Sydney showgrounds and were given Australian uniforms to supplement their light khaki tunics and shorts, which were unequal to the chilly weather they had encountered on the voyage. They were taken on trips to the country by train, embarrassed by the effusive attention directed at them.[27]

Early in 1916 another party men of the 1/4th Shropshire arrived in Sydney, escorting German internees from Hong Kong bound for the huge 'German Concentration Camp' near Liverpool, south-west of the city. While 'in Sydney on the Empire's business' the Shropshire men not only paraded with Australian troops, but remained in Victoria Barracks on alert when on Valentine's Day 1916 thousands of volunteers training for the Australian Imperial Force rioted in the city's streets because their training hours had been increased without being paid more.[28]

Correspondents to the local newspapers appealed to Sydney-siders to offer them hospitality, as Britons were welcoming Australian soldiers arriving in Britain at that very time. The Territorials were at first accommodated in agricultural pavilions at the Sydney showground, given what a migrant ex-Grenadier Guards sergeant described as 'dirty sacks' to sleep on.[29] Like the Devons, the Shropshire men went on excursions, including to the nearby Blue Mountains. One of their officers wrote to thank the Premier, William Holman, for the kindness shown to his men, revealing one of the strains of service in what they called 'the East'. 'You can, perhaps, hardly realise', he wrote, 'how great a treat it is' after 18 months in India, Burma, Singapore and Hong Kong, 'to come to a country where the people are so essentially British'.[30]

'That fever-stricken land': Somersets in the Andamans

The East India Company had claimed the Andaman and Nicobar archipelago in the late eighteenth century and British India, now ruled by the Crown, had developed as a penal settlement at Port Blair after the 1857 mutiny-rebellion. By 1914 it held about 15,000 long-term convicts, mostly criminals from all over British India, but with a small number of political prisoners, effectively exiled for life. A small military garrison provided a guarantor of order but did not directly supervise the convicts; that was left to ex-convicts relying on bullying, petty tyrannies and exploitation and who, according to a former 'political' inmate, regarded their charges as 'working machines'.[31] The 2/4th Somerset arrived from Madras early in 1915, in response to reports – or rather rumours – that German raiders planned to descend on the islands and liberate its convicts. While, as the Somersets' history recorded, 'the remainder of the year passed by and nothing happened more alarming', just before Christmas officers slept in the orderly room 'on a war footing' while naval vessels cruised off-shore.[32] Though the troops did not realise it, and

---

27 *Evening News* (Sydney), 22 November 1915, p. 4
28 *Sunday Times* (Sydney), 20 February 1916, p. 9. For an account of the 'Liverpool riots', see Stanley, *Bad Characters*, pp. 59-61
29 *Singleton Argus*, 19 February 1916, p. 2
30 *Farmer and Settler* (Sydney), 22 February 1916, p. 2
31 Banerjee, *Memoirs of a Revolutionary*, p. 119
32 Fisher, *The History of Somerset Yeomanry, Volunteers and Territorials*, p. 216; '2/4th Battalion P.A. Somerset Light Infantry', DD\SLI/1/12, SHC, Taunton

Aberdeen settlement in the Andaman Islands, where Somerset Territorials were garrisoned in 1915, one of their most remote and uncomfortable stations. (DD\SLI/15/7/84, Somerset Heritage Centre)

their officers were unable to disclose until the following year, for several months in 1915 the garrison had been on alert against a reported German-inspired plot to descend upon the island to liberate the prisoners.[33] The convicts noticed the extra troops posted to the Andamans and took heart, excited by the possibility that a German submarine or Dreadnought might appear to set them free. The garrison, they felt, was 'not sufficient to guard the place', as Vinayak Savarkar, a Hindu nationalist serving a 50-year sentence, recalled.[34] The reports came to nothing but the possibility at least justified the Territorials' Indian service.

The Somersets' six-month sojourn in the remote equatorial penal settlement was cramped and uncomfortable. Ross, a tiny island off Andaman where the barracks was located, was too small for troops to drill, and they trained on the main island. Men fell ill with 'Rangoon fever' – an infection spread by scratching prickly heat with dirty finger-nails. The battalion's routine orders show a marked increase in sickness, and the vigorous steps ordered to suppress mosquitos and to preserve men's health. Men lived on two or three rupees a week – as in India they had to pay for their own suppers, barrack servants, tobacco and other requisites. The troops felt that they were 'very much looked down upon' by the islands' civilian officials.[35] They took an interest in the more sensational political prisoners. 'The Tommies had no means of amusement and recreation', Vinayak Savarkar recalled, and 'invented all sorts of stories about ... my former revolutionary activities.[36]

33 Routine orders, 20 December 1915, 2/4th Somerset, DD\SLI/6/29, SHC, Taunton
34 Sarvarkar, *The Story of My Transportation for Life*, pp. 358-59
35 Letters, 29 April & 19 May 1915, Jim Mackie, 2/4th Somerset, Mackie, *Answering the Call*, pp. 60-69
36 Sarvarkar, *The Story of My Transportation for Life*, p. 363

One of the Somersets' versifiers expressed the troops' antipathy to their posting in heartfelt verse:

> 'From Bangalore we travelled
> To the Andamans so grand,
> And was very sorry when we reached
> That fever-stricken land.'[37]

Early in 1916 the 2/4th Somerset were relieved by the 18th Battalion of the Rifle Brigade, nominally Territorial but actually composed of relatively elderly National Defence volunteers. ('I feel quite sorry for them', Jim Mackie wrote on Christmas Day, able to convey details of military movements in India without fear of censorship.[38]) The Somerset battalion moved to Bengal (to Dinapore, Dum Dum and Barrackpore), relieving the 1/9th Middlesex in the continual minuet of postings that occurred several times a year.

'Not without anxiety': forebodings for 1916

As their experiences in stations out of India but connected with its interests had demonstrated, the Territorials had become part of the military resources of empire, and those resources came increasingly under strain. Through 1915 the Cabinet periodically reviewed 'the Military Situation in India', considering reports from Hardinge that revealed that he was 'not without anxiety' in September.[39] By the year's end the officers responsible for India's security were certainly worried. In late November General Sir George Barrow, the India Office's chief military advisor, explained the reasons for Hardinge's anxiety, stressing that 'on the defence of that frontier largely depends the internal peace of India'. Six months before he had foreseen 'mutterings of "jehad"' though 'the "blaze" has not yet come'. Now, he feared 'the whole frontier may be in a blaze' – already 'Ministers may be surprised to learn' the force employed in mobile columns (that is, the units earmarked for local internal security) amounted to the equivalent of over two divisions. 'We shall be able to hold our own', he reassured them, 'but the "if" is fraught with such tremendous issues'.[40] With defeat on Gallipoli and disaster in Mesopotamia, the foreboding of those responsible was to deepen in 1916.

Barrow's minute showed that the available British force in India totalled only 50,000 troops, a third fewer than in 1914, comprising eight Regular and 32 Territorial battalions, supported by 13 Regular and 27 Territorial batteries. But the number of units was not the only worry. Few reinforcement drafts had arrived in 1915, while staff officers calculated that over 1700 Territorials and 350 Regulars would be discharged as 'time-expired' over the 1915-16 trooping season. Barrow foresaw a need for 10,000 reinforcements – the equivalent of the infantry of another complete division. In response, four more Territorial battalions would arrive in 1916.

---

37 'A Territorial's Life in India', Mackie, *Answering the Call*, p. 211
38 Letter, 25 December 1915, Jim Mackie, 2/4th Somerset, Mackie, *Answering the Call*, p. 121
39 'The Military Situation in India', 7 December 1915, CAB42/6/5, NAUK
40 'The Military Situation in India and the Middle East', by General Sir George Barrow, Military Secretary at India Office, CAB42/5/21, NAUK

In 1916 the Territorials in India took their part in the security of Britain's Indian empire and, if they were allowed, the wider empire's war. As they grew accustomed to the country, its climate and especially its people, a change came over them. As an Anglo-Indian civilian perceived in a tribute sponsored by Bombay's British community, their Indian experience had changed them. 'In a few short months', he wrote, 'the Territorial, … is half transformed into the typical Anglo-Indian of the corresponding class'. The newcomers, he thought had learned both 'the habit of command and its correlative habit of decision … so instructive to the sahib and … so impressive to the stranger'.[41] Two years was the period E.M. Forster judged that it took to turn 'quite a nice boy' into a sahib.[42]

---

41   Sheppard, *Territorials in India*, p. 11
42   Forster, *A Passage to India*, p. 9

7

Body, mind and soul

Territorial battalions often resembled the provincial communities from which its men hailed. They too supported a range of sporting and cultural clubs and societies, with their athletic, football, choral, chess, camera, and mutual improvement societies or Literary and Scientific institutes. Except that cantonment life was not conducive to the formation of pigeon-fancying, gardening or rabbit-breeding clubs, Territorial battalions in many ways re-created the communal relationships their members had sustained at home, in sport, creativity and in religion.

'Developing the highest fighting qualities': sport

When climate and military duties permitted, men played sport, often lots of it. To readers of the *Kent Messenger*, in which men from Ashford and Tunbridge Wells described football and hockey matches, Territorial correspondents acknowledged that 'it may seem a little out of place' to concentrate on games 'while thousands of our countrymen are engaged in the greatest war of all', but explained it as being 'essential to health'.[1] Senior officers valued and encouraged sport, and not merely as a means of passing the time. Sporting competition fostered a healthy rivalry between men and units. The *Memorandum on Army Training in India, 1916-1917* emphasised that 'games … can be a means of developing the highest fighting qualities, moral and physical'. It discouraged units 'specialising' in one sport and banned money prizes.[2] With the great majority of Territorials young men, most in their twenties and with energy to spend, many took to sport with enthusiasm. Participation was quasi-official, though most battalions emphasised it. Sport was played almost year round, either in the afternoons in the cooler weather, or on hot weather evenings, impossible only at the height of summer and during monsoon downpours.

Sport brought men and officers together. Many battalions' games committees included both, and they met each other on the sporting field as well. In the 1/4th Wilts, for example, the cross country teams in 1915 mixed privates and lieutenants, and officers and men played each other at billiards, tennis and cricket. In most units a Regimental Sporting Committee, usually chaired

---

1 *Kent Messenger*, 22 May 1915
2 *Memorandum on Army Training in India, 1916-1917*, pp. 9-10

by an officer but including men of all ranks, organised the various sports; always football, but also cricket, hockey, boxing, and occasionally running or even 'amusements' such as billiards or even chess.

Competitive sport provided an outlet denied to units fulfilling sedentary roles. The 2/5th Somerset, which saw no active service (except on internal security duties) through the war, proudly recorded in its history its successes in winning the Burma Cup in polo in 1916, the prestigious Calcutta Cup (the premier prize in army rugby) in 1918 and in 1919, and in reaching the semi-finals of the All India Cup in football.[3] Some battalions were known to be football-mad – in the 1/4th Wilts members of the battalion team had no other duties – it may have prompted official criticism of specialism, serving as it had in proximity to Army Headquarters in Delhi. But the Wilts' policy paid off – the team lost only 8 out of 58 matches, and scored three times as many goals as it conceded.

Indeed, football was by far the most popular game, played and followed at every level from intra-platoon leagues within battalions, matches against neighbouring units and the Indian Football Challenge Shield competition, which drew battalion teams across the sub-continent to play each other and 'native' civilian teams in front of huge crowds of both European and Indian spectators. Whenever units halted for more than a day or so out came 'the inevitable football … without which no regiment could possibly be happy'.[4] Many Territorial players had been members of municipal or even league clubs before volunteering, ensuring that the game was played to a high standard even in friendly matches. (But even older men could take part in 'walking matches', in which players were fined for running.)

Football on hard, often baked earth cantonment pitches required different skills to games played on grass and mud at home. Hampshire men playing in virtually rainless Baluchistan discovered that 'speediness and dash are more requisite in Quetta football than in English'.[5] At Kuldana the 'hill tribe' of the 1/4th Wilts (that is, men posted to the hills in summer) played Gurkhas at football – Gurkhas were more willing to mix with British troops than other Indian troops. Territorials played against 'native' teams and discovered that while generally lacking boots they possessed dash, speed and stamina. But vigorous games could be risky in India's climate. In July 1915 the 1/4th Cornwall football team played in Calcutta. Two of its men were knocked out and one of them died; 24-year-old Albert Facey of Callington.

Cricket was less popular than might be supposed, because heat limited the season and prevented long games. Boxing was more popular, and could be arranged indoors, even after dark and during the monsoon. Officers and men could come together on a level in the ring. Olaf Caroe, who had found that his East Surrey men regarded him as 'priggish' (fresh as he was from Magdalen College, Oxford), discovered that his skill in boxing and cross-country running gave him a 'road to the soldier's heart'.[6] In boxing, sporting challenges and successes could be individual, in several senses. In 1916 a man of the 1st Garrison Battalion of the Ox & Bucks Light Infantry challenged four named men of other regiments (including Albert Falkenstein, of Dallington, Sussex), a challenge published in the Royal Sussex's magazine.[7] Falkenstein led

3   Anon, *The Book of Remembrance*, p. 107
4   *The Queen's Own Gazette*, Vol. XXXV, No. 2, February 1916, p. 3455
5   *The Tiger*, March 1915, p. 3
6   Caroe, 'The Flames of Enchantment', p. iv-3, PP/MCR/207, IWM
7   'A Challenge', *The Royal Sussex Herald*, 29 July 1916, p. 176

Four East Surrey sergeants playing tennis, for many Territorials an unfamiliar new sport, but also a sign of the force's social composition. (Album 4, NERM: 825, Maidstone Museum)

a Sussex team to Simla in September 1916 to box in the All-India tournament, meeting men from Regular, Territorial and other units. In boxing, generally tougher Regular opponents were successful.[8] (That four 'other ranks' were trusted to travel from Bangalore to Simla and back under only a corporal said much for the Territorials' ethos – Regulars were invariably not trusted with such initiative – and about Falkenstein himself, who was soon after commissioned.)

Indian service introduced men to unfamiliar sports, such as hockey, cross-country running and even tennis (traditionally a middle-class game, judging by photograph albums it was embraced by sergeants, with enough players for one battalion to build three new courts). Hockey, generally neither familiar nor popular, caught on in some units and in some stations, passed on by Indian troops, among whom it was widespread. The 1/4th Devon organised about twenty games a week in the cooler weather; the 2/4th Somerset played it all year. At Lebong, 'a wave of enthusiasm for Rink Hockey' – that is, played on rollers skates – swept 1/5th East Surrey men in the Hills for the summer of 1915, playing teams of soldiers and civilians.[9]

Some battalions, reflecting the influence of enthusiastic officers, encouraged cross-country running – it had been prominent in the 1912 Olympic games in Stockholm. At Ross in the Andamans Jim Mackie took his men on cross-country runs, leaving before dawn and returning

8   'Our Visit to Simla', *Ibid*, 4 November 1916, p. 72
9   'Lebong', *5th East Surrey Magazine*, 1 August 1915, p. 13

covered in mud. A hot bath left them feeling 'very much fitter' – Jim believed that the exertion helped to deter fever.[10] Some took up running peculiar to India, when Royal Sussex men in the hills went 'khud running' (traditionally a Gurkha sport, both demanding and dangerous). Running depended upon the weather, but was possible in the monsoon. Many units in the Hills took up less demanding 'Dog and Stick walks' – in essence orienteering over a fixed course, a favourite in the early morning in summer.[11] Others encouraged walking races or walks, carrying long 'khud' sticks (like Scottish cromachs, priced at one anna; more with a regimental badge included).

While many stations had plunge pools in which men could cool off, few had swimming pools as such. Two battalions, the 1/25th London and the 1/10th Middlesex, travelled to Calcutta and entered the All India Swimming Championships in 1916. They trained in the tank adjacent to Calcutta University and competed against both Anglo-Indian and Indian teams in the pool of the Calcutta Swimming Club. (Significantly, the two Territorial units that competed came from London, with its plethora of municipal swimming baths.)

Few Territorial officers played the archetypal Indian game of polo, though officers of the 2/5th Somerset (who may have been more horsey than most) once carried off the Burma Cup. It fielded a team of officers of one company and with the opposition, a Burma Police team riding ponies the Somerset had sold them because they were just about to leave Burma for India.[12] Officers mainly played rugby (and other ranks who had played it at school, though presumably it was also popular among the Brecknocks), but the season was short because grounds were too hard for vigorous tackling – reports of injuries often accompanied accounts of rugby matches.

Sport provided the mainstay of reports in battalion magazines, and was an important route by which Territorials met and became known to Anglo-Indian civilians, Regulars and other Territorials. The detailed records of matches and games in contemporary records do not, however, necessitate a corresponding quantum of attention in retrospect.

'To unearth any hidden talent': mind

Territorials often sought to reproduce in barracks the intellectual and cultural bodies so much a part of provincial society at home. Their ranks encompassed a great variety of conditions of men. They included men who were illiterate and unskilled, who left few traces in their units' abundant records. But they also included a noticeable leaven of men of education and culture, who brought to their units what one contributor to *The Invicta* characterised as 'M.A.L.D.' – Music, Art, Literature and Drama – 'the four arts'.[13] Some men excelled in all spheres – Percy Ellis of the 1/25th London learned Urdu, Italian and French in India, played the oboe, flute, clarinet and piccolo, and made watercolour and ink sketches. Lance-Corporal Henry Rawstone Lamplugh of the 1/1st Kent wrote poetry, edited the battalion magazine and conducted its choir. Harry Canham, a teetotal Wesleyan, played the piano and tennis and joined the 2/4th Border's debating society.

10   Letter, 8 September 1915, Jim Mackie, 2/4th Somerset, Mackie, *Answering the Call*, p. 105
11   Diary, 8 June 1915, Herbert Ewing, 1/5th Somerset, DD\SLI/17/1/61, SHC, Taunton
12   Anon, *The Book of Remembrance*, p. 107
13   *The Invicta*, Vol. III, No. 4, 1919, p. 55

Confined indoors for the daylight hours for several months of the year as they were, reading became one of the Territorials' most popular pastimes. Finding books was always difficult – they were expensive, and hard to obtain. Hugh Creek felt frustrated that Amritsar's only bookshop was out of bounds in the 'native city'. (As 'other ranks' Territorials were often excluded from club libraries, and few battalions had the libraries that many Regular units had created.) Having obtained books, lack of light – most barracks had only dim oil lamps – made reading on long 'cold' weather evenings difficult. Owen Smith, a great reader, was frustrated by the rules of the Ambala station library that prevented him changing his books more often. In the heat of August 1916 he complained that 'I have *nothing to read* till I change my book tomorrow, & *nothing to do* ... there is so much spare time in the Hot season'.[14] The arrival of month-old newspapers from home was naturally welcome.

Many Territorials surmounted the problem of what to read by writing themselves, for an extraordinary range of battalion magazines. Their magazines represent a rich and complex body of amateur literary endeavour. Much of their contributions comprised banal reportage, conventional and derivative light humour and sporting reports, but across the range of a dozen or so magazines we can discern writing of notable talent and even emotional power. Many battalions produced 'demi-official' magazines which gave men opportunities to exercise their creative impulses as well as record sporting achievements. The editors of *The Braganza*, the magazine of the West Surrey, reminded their readers of their objectives in publishing:

> ... to let our people at home know of our doings ... to unearth any hidden talent we may have among us; to air any legitimate grievances ...[15]

But only 'legitimate' grievances: Territorials' unofficial efforts brought trouble. Two privates at Bangalore in early 1916 were prosecuted for publishing *John Blount*, presumably a satirical magazine, condemned by officials as 'full of bad feeling' but which has not survived.[16]

Encouraged by officers but entirely funded by subscribers and dependent upon voluntary creative labour, magazines performed several useful functions, then and later. They helped to generate the collective identity on which effective military units drew, enabled men to pass their time productively, and provided their officers with useful measures of men's feelings. Men often sent copies home, with their company's sporting triumph against another circled. Some anticipated the need to record their service: 'what better memorial ... of your old battalion and the memorable years of the war?', asked the editor of *The Tiger* in its inaugural issue.[17] As this book shows, battalion magazines constitute a valuable source of evidence on the Territorials' service.

Many units contained men adept at light verse, often used to express grievances or common views subtly. In the 2/4th Hants a Private Lucas published poems in *The Tiger* that perhaps spoke for many. In 'Barabbas' (the thief crucified with Christ, a reference every Sunday-school-going Terrier would know) he wrote playfully, but perhaps with a point, about the exactions of barrack servants:

---

14 Letter, 30 August 1916, Owen Smith, 1/6th Hants, M766, RHRM
15 *The Braganza*, 1 June 1918, p. 2
16 *Pioneer*, 25 May 1916
17 *The Tiger*, March 1915, p. 1

> Truly oriental, full of craft and guile,
> Alas! he is symbolical of every eastern wile.
> He comes round in the morning with an early cup of tea,
> His statement of accounts and mine by chance do agree …[18]

Some magazines, such as the 2/4th Hants *The Tiger*, were mostly chatty chronicles of interbattalion sport and leg-pulls directed as comrades' foibles or droll sayings, but others strove for a standard of culture. *The Royal Sussex Herald* was among the most high-minded, publishing poetry, art of real talent (mostly by Oswald Barrett) and earnest articles such as 'The Function of Art', by Rawstone Lamplugh, which prompted a reply by Barrett. Often they were written and published by subalterns and echo the school magazines they would have known, written for and read just a few years before. But most magazines' contributors were, like their readers, other ranks.

The tone of the more self-consciously literary articles can be seen in, say, an anonymous article in the *Middlesex Regiment Magazine* in 1917 on 'Three impressions of Delhi … the Art of Aristocracies', which represented the higher end of the spectrum:

> The fort of Delhi brought to being under the fiery radiance of the potent India sun is an art of power, and their art like the sun is strong and dangerous …[19]

Their tenor was often that of a Literary and Philosophical Society or Mechanics' Institute, of the the kind found in county cities and provincial towns. Authors mused on India's ignorance and superstition ('once the main population can read and write, think and learn for themselves, the old order of things will crumble and fall').[20] A Kent man stationed at Ferozepore contributed an extraordinary Wellesian article to *The Invicta* in 1918. He imagined 'The Newer Ferozepore', a city of boulevards and parks, 'greater than Calcutta', with electric 'autocars' and paraffin-powered buses, with a daily air service to Europe. The old cantonments would be preserved in a park as a memorial. Since 'East and West combined', the anonymous author felt, 'nothing has been impossible'. It was a vision few others shared – particularly since the first pioneer flight from Britain to India was a year away.[21]

Battalion magazines reveal how men thought about India, as two examples from some of the most literary magazines suggest. 'Bookworm', in *The Royal Sussex Herald*, argued that fiction set in India (by popular novelists such as Ethel M. Dell or Maud Diver – though he did not mention Kipling) had 'created a false idea' of India, one portraying its 'mystery and romance'. Encountering 'the India of fact', however, Bookworm claimed that men had learned to loathe the country out of the very disappointment' of realising the discrepancy.[22] Perhaps the most extraordinary creative response was a parody of a 'Book of the Month' column published in *The Londoner*, the magazine of the 1/25th London in 1916. Ostensibly a review of *Gannaway Junior*

---

18 *The Tiger*, September 1915, pp. 86-87
19 *Middlesex Regiment Magazine*, 1 March 1917, p. 82
20 'When the Sleeper awakes', *The Royal Sussex Herald*, Vol. I, No. 3, p. 59 (the title drawing on H.G. Wells's 1910 novel)
21 *The Invicta*, Vol. III, No. 4, 1919, pp. 31-33
22 'Fiction and India', *The Royal Sussex Herald*, 19 October 1918, p. 193

by 'Miss Jane Caroline Platt', a novel that 'might very well bear the sub-title "The Experiences of a Territorial in India", it was in fact a very clever spoof; the essence of a literary in-joke. There is no such book, not one published by 'Stodder and Houghton', but the anonymous reviewer used it as a way to satirise the Territorials' situation and express their grievances. He described the novel as being set in 'Bangapet' – obviously Bangalore – 'in which 'no detail escapes her', from the serving of chota hazri to night, when 'each man's native "boy" rushes up to relieve him of his rifle and equipment'.

> How daring, and yet how true, is the scene in which young Gannaway reproves the slack subaltern for proposing to dismiss his platoon a quarter of an hour too early … The contemptible subaltern crawls away abashed and subsequently takes to drink.

The reviewer praises 'Platt' for 'her contention that our luxurious tiffins and eight course dinners tend to render us slack and effeminate'. And, of course, the novel ends with the Territorials returning home; five years after the war's end.[23]

Notebooks and albums reflect how individually some men responded to India by reaching for pens and brushes. Many men made sketches or paintings in their diaries or memoirs, striving to convey the sights they had seen and the experiences they had had, to record them for themselves and to pass them on to those at home. Victor Manley's water-colours of the country and people of Baluchistan reveal his infatuation with them. Manley's 'pet hobby' – 'one of my favourite uncharted excursions of discovery', as he characteristically termed it – was to 'wander around odd corners of mud villages where no white man either dared to go or dreamed of going', taking photographs and sketching. He acknowledged the risks – 'of getting one's throat slit by some fanatic' – but judged it worth the reward of 'meeting with some agreeable experience of which one would not read of the like in books'.[24] His extraordinary vivid diary, with its dozens of illustrations, is proof of his curiosity. Likewise, Ernest Head, of the 1/6th East Surrey, had not practised art before (it seems) but as a member of the battalion's scout section he was introduced to military sketching. That may explain why his memoir of service in India and Aden (written in 1918) includes drawings of the barracks at Rawalpindi and sketches of Aden.

The example of Arthur Bell of the 1/6th East Surrey offers one of the most remarkable examples of how service in India could change a man's life. The son of a piano maker who grew up in extreme poverty and neglect on the Old Kent Road, Arthur Bell had been conscripted in 1917 and reached India after a long, poorly organised and uncomfortable voyage (his draft seems to have gone for weeks without a change of clothes). Sent to the hill station of Chaubattia he responded to both the discipline imposed by the battalion's formidable sergeant-major and the beauty of its scenery. Arthur was to find in India inspiration and opportunity to begin to draw and paint, for which he had a flair. Encouraged by sympathetic officers, he even attended Lucknow Art School at the war's end. He was, he later reflected, 'a very lucky young man to have this opportunity'.[25] His delicate water-colours of barrack scenes and Indian life are the

---

23 *The Londoner*, November 1916, pp. 29-30
24 Diary, 29 August 1915, Victor Manley, 'A Khaki Diary', 49M91W/Q3/6, HRO
25 "RF & MP', 'Scenes of India during the First World War', *Queen's Royal Surrey Regiment Newsletter*, SHC, Woking

Some of Arthur Bell's drawings, of his comrades sleeping in bungalows in 110-degree heat, and of part of the Pearl Mosque at Agra. (ESR/25/BELA/1, Surrey History Centre)

most skilful and evocative works produced by Territorials, and formed the basis of Arthur's long career as an artist and teacher.

The minority of cultured Territorials may be contrasted to Anglo-Indian 'club' society, which, as E.M. Forster found, 'left literature alone … their ignorance of the arts was notable'.[26]

'A concert out of the usual': Territorial music-making

Art was essentially individual and private, but music was very much a communal affair, much more significant in the battalions' lives. While a few units fostered drama, virtually all encouraged music. Evening entertainment was largely in men's own hands. While larger cantonments boasted cinemas (the Electric Theatre was 'Bangalore's Premier Place of Amusement'), and Soldiers' Homes would often organise impromptu concerts and sing-alongs, for much of the time men had to make their own amusement after dark. Senior officers naturally worried that their men would drink, with all the consequences that entailed, and accordingly encouraged the formation of concert parties, a distinctive response among Territorials in India in their scale and skill.

Territorials came of a culture comfortable with music-making. *Punch's* Hampshire Territorial observed a sight in barrack rooms that would never have been seen among Regulars. Watching men rehearsing their drill movements at night (early in their service; later they became jaded) he noticed that as well as counting as they performed various movements ('*one* and *two* and *three* and *four* …') some men remembered the rhythm by mnemonics such as Latin declensions – 'Mensa, mensa, men*sam* – mensae, mensae, men*sam* …' – or adapting verses, of the popular children's hymn:

> There is a happy *land*
> Far, far *away*,
> Where soldiers don't have *stew*
> Three times a *day*[27]

Their units brimmed with musical talent: when the 'Old Boys' of the former D Company of the 1/10th Middlesex held a dinner at the Savoy Hotel in Calcutta in 1915, organised by a committee of privates, it featured a concert of twenty musical items offered by men of just one company of about a hundred strong.[28] Musical performances were important at a time when little recorded music could be heard outside clubs and officers' messes. Most battalions formed at least a bugle and drum band, even war-raised second-line units. The men of the 2/5th Hants felt that forming a band justified every man subscribing a rupee to purchase instruments – the talent to play them already resided in the ranks, notably in Lieutenant Peter Latham, a piano-playing subaltern.[29] Some formed string orchestras, such as the 1/4th Devon and 1/6th East Surrey,

---

26 Forster, *A Passage to India*, p. 37
27 'A Territorial in India', *Punch*, 22 December 1915, p. 506. Curiously, the usual tune for the hymn was a 'Hindustani Melody' to which it had been set in 1850.
28 Programme, Henry Iggulden, 1/10th Middlesex, 2010-12-8-9, NAM
29 *The Hampshire Regimental Journal*, October 1915, p. 337

which entertained their comrades on the voyage to India. A Dorset battery – fewer than 150 strong – also formed its own string band. The 1/6th East Surrey sent its string band to Kuldana during the hot weather in 1915, where it accompanied church services in the hill station's little church. Its concerts featured a mix of medium and lowbrow music, with Tchaikovsky's '1812' overture, local civilians playing Bohm's 'Ensemble', songs ('Mountain Lovers'), sentimental favourites ('When Irish eyes are smiling') and as a finale 'When the Midnight Choo Choo', with 'humorous effects'.[30] More musical groups were proposed than survived. 'Music lovers' in the 2/4th Border in mid-1918 suggested forming a Glee Club, but it 'never survived its infancy', though a 'Gaff party' – an informal concert party – did.[31] (In the Army', Owen Smith explained to his mother from Agra, 'the word "Gaff" signifies any concert or entertainment or theatre show'.[32])

The colonel's attitude was, of course, crucial, and the officers' mess provided audience, patronage and even performers. The 1/1st Kent's colonel, William Gale Moore, himself sang Schuman at a concert in the Assembly Rooms at Dalhousie, at which the battalion's string orchestra played Verdi, Private Oswald Barrett played the slow movement of Mendelsohn's violin concerto and the battalion choir sang (naturally) Gounod's Soldiers' Chorus. The choir's conductor, a school organist, Lance-Corporal Lamplugh, wrote that it was 'a concert out of the usual for India': except that it actually was not.[33] Lamplugh was unusual, however, in his dedication to musical endeavour – at Easter 1916 he mobilised choral and orchestral resources (including persuading several officers to take solo parts) to stage Sir John Stainer's 1887 oratorio *The Crucifixion* in St Mark's Cathedral, Bangalore, but he was only one manifestation of the Territorials' drive to express culture in Indian cantonments.

A few Territorials played music seriously, such as oboist Percy Ellis, or Charles Ellis (no relation), an Australian orchestral violinist and oboist who, having survived the Western Front though thrice wounded, arrived in the 1/10th Middlesex in 1917. At least one Territorial musician also composed: Peter Latham, a former Balliol man who had been commissioned in the 2/5th Hants. While in India he wrote a dozen pieces, either works for violin and piano or songs in Edwardian aesthetic manner, such as 'With rue my heart is laden: from a Shropshire lad'.[34]

Men like Latham contributed to a distinctively cultured ethos in Territorial units. Percy Ellis, who played oboe in the 1/25th London band, recorded a program of performances in 1918. In just over six months in Jutogh and Simla he and his fellow performers played at sixteen 'troop concerts', at the officers' mess once or twice a week, at officers and sergeants' tennis-at-homes, at the colonel's dinner party, at a local hospital, other sergeants' events, twelve 'Grand Concerts' at a hotel in Simla, and at 'Miss Lister's wedding'. The pieces played (usually eight, plus encores) comprised pieces such as a Haydn symphony, Elgar's Salut d'Amour, von Suppé overtures, and the anthems of the various allies, by then no longer including imperial Russia's stately hymn to the Czar.

30 Clipping in ESR/10/10/2/7, SHC, Woking
31 Letters, 20 June; 6 October 1918, Harry Canham, 2/4th Border, CMML
32 Letter, 2 December 1915, Owen Smith, 1/6th Hants, M766, RHRM
33 *The Invicta*, Vol. III, No. 1, June 1918, p. 34
34 Communication from Christopher Latham, 16 November 2017

'Brixham Jim Ding-Dong and Stiffy': concert parties

Much musical energy in Territorial battalions went into the many concert parties they formed, so much so that it deserves a separate treatment. The troupes they formed from early 1915 included the 'Tryards' (1/6th East Surrey), 'The Warbling Wallahs' (1/5th East Surrey), 'Sharps and Flats' (2/6th Royal Sussex), 'Terriers' (1/9th Middlesex), 'the Brown Bs' (1/6th Hants) and the 'Jolly Boys and their Jester' (1/4th Buffs, which Owen Smith thought 'splendid' – as good as a professional party in Britain.[35]). The 1/9th Hants even formed platoon concert parties – 'The Queries' (No. 4) and 'Ye Merrie Buzers' (No. 5). The troupes reflected the character of their units. The 1/4th Wilts, for example, formed 'The Moonrakers' (the Wiltshire Regiment's nickname, based on a story playing on the stupidity of country yokels). It emphasised the self-deprecating humour by wearing farm labourers' smocks and singing songs such as 'he can't take a rise out of Oi'.[36]

Not all flourished or survived, but among the best documented battalion concert party (and arguably wartime India's best) was the 1/7th Hants 'Costume Concert Party', the records of which are preserved in the papers of its pianist, Bertram 'Little Willie' Gotobed, in the excellent Royal Hampshire Regiment Museum. As its name suggested, the Costume Concert Party's performances were notably more elaborately costumed, appearing 'Italiano', in 'a Spanish stunt' and as the more usual Pierrots (in costumes of black and yellow, the Hampshire Regiment's traditional colours). Its performances were also more original than most, with pieces composed by Gotobed and a subaltern who championed the party, who at times improvised words and music in response to suggestions from the audience. They were also conspicuously more facetious than most. Items from a program at Delhi in November 1915 included:

> 'How to dance the "Tiddle-y-pom" by the Party … Reggie Rose will annoy you … P.G. Fraser will yell you about "Sammy the Dashing Dragoon" … J. Colborne will sing "Until" (he is stopped) …

Talented Territorials 'would have done credit to many a London theatre', a Dorset officer recorded.[37]

The *Indian Daily Telegraph* judged that while Delhi had seen 'many Territorial concert parties' it had never had such enjoyable entertainment. The *Telegraph's* reviewer applauded the party's 'varied range of talent', the 'perfect understanding' between its artists and concluded that 'there was not a dull moment'.[38] The party's many other reviews of other programs, preserved as clippings in Bertram Gotobed's papers, were as positive, as was Owen Smith's account after the 1/7th's party played for the 1/6th at the Ambala Regimental Theatre. The party toured all over north India from Calcutta to Rawalpindi, including many hill stations (and in mid-1917 four nights in Simla's celebrated Gaiety Theatre) and went as far as Mesopotamia and Aden. It raised over Rs14,000 for twenty (mostly Anglo-Indian) charities between 1915 and 1918, including the Catholic memorial fund at Ambala, the Subathu Leper Asylum and Lady Willingdon's Bombay

---

35   Letter, 7 June 1916, Owen Smith, 1/6th Hants, M766, RHRM
36   *The Wiltshire Times*, 3 February 1917
37   Regimental History Committee, *History of the Dorsetshire Regiment 1914-1919*, Part II, p. 72
38   Clipping from *Indian Daily Telegraph*, 3 December 1915, Bertram Gotobed, M2338, RHRM

The 1/7th Hants 'Costume Concert Party' with its pianist and musical director, Bertram Gotobed, at the piano, an image capturing the zaniness of the Territorials' concert troupes. The man banging the drum wears a cap referring to the Royal Army Temperance Association, a reference all soldiers would comprehend. (M916/89, Royal Hampshire Regiment Museum)

War and Relief Fund.[39] The pity of Gotobed's papers is that they preserve the facts of the battalion concert party's existence without ever capturing the spirit of their lively performances.

Newspaper readers in Kendal could read a long account of a typical battalion gaff offered by men of the 1/4th Border at the Barrack Theatre in Maymyo in mid-1915. It opened with a rendition of the Border march, 'John Peel', and featured a 'humorous' song recounting the battalion's travels since mobilisation. The program featured both old music hall favourites (such as 'My Old Kentucky Home' and 'Gilbert the Filbert') and wartime songs such as 'Sister Susie's Sewing Shirts for Soldiers'. The 35-strong Border party performed as a minstrel show, with men blacked-up playing stock characters such as 'Bones', 'Remus', 'Massa Tambo' and 'Sambo'.[40] In 1916 the 1/4th formed the 'Border Minstrels', smart in tropical mess jackets complete with two female impersonators (or 'charming flappers', as a battalion magazine put it).[41]

39 Bertram Gotobed, 1/7th Hants, M2338, RHRM
40 *1/4th Border Gazette* [No. 4, 1915], Lawrence Hoggarth, 1/4th Border, Album 35 Acc. Nos 3024-3345, CMML
41 *The Invicta*, Vol. III, No. 4, 1919, p. 53

Territorials offered entertainment to British-Indian communities jaded at the company of the insular circles at the station club or assembly room. East Surrey Territorials contributed 'the lion's share of entertaining' at Fyzabad in the war's first winter, putting 'new heart into everyone'.[42] The 1/9th Middlesex's 'Original Terriers' concert party spent four months performing in desolate camps in Mesopotamia to huge audiences – up to 13,000 men in three performances at Abu Shitab on the Tigris. They played virtually in the front line, less than a mile from Turkish lines at Sanna-i-yat and viewing Kut from the foremost British lines at Sinn. The Middlesex players gave their comrades in India an insight into what they would encounter in Mesopotamia the following year when they reported how 'thousands of flies came into our tent and worried us terribly' at Arab Village and how a mounted policeman was so covered by flies that 'he looked as if he was wearing a black uniform'.[43]

Except for set-piece songs using published tunes, much of what the concert parties performed has gone the way of all ephemera. Whatever the 1/9th Hants party meant by this note in a program for its platoon party, 'The Queries' is now long lost:

> P.C. PARKER assisted by Longboat, Brixham Jim Ding-Dong and Stiffy in a side-splitting race entitled "WORKING HIS TICKET"

While much of the humour visible from the concert programmes is heavy-handed, rich in weak puns and ponderous levity, the concert parties' programmes at times suggest the vigour of the communities of young men whose creative energies were channelled into their performances. The 'Scarlet Serenaders' – sergeants of the 1/9th Hants – included several pages of drollery in an undated program from 1918 in which they urged their audience not to 'Give the "Glad eye" to their "Girls" – female impersonators, advertised 'found ... a ladies purse containing three pin curls, one child's balloon (deflated) and a return ticket to Pokesdown ...' and 'During the asparagus season, gentlemen are requested not to use the umbrella stand'.[44] These snippets suggest the anarchic humour that in the following generation (during a second world war) would flower in what became the Goons. The phenomenon remains one of the most remarkable of the Terriers' experience in India.

'Polite pagans': religion

The Territorials reflected the religious complexion of contemporary England. The great majority of men were nominally Anglican, though with strong pockets of Methodists in West Country and especially Cornish battalions, and Catholics a distinct minority. While many were conventionally religious, a few men were notably devout. Men of the 1/5th West Surrey formed a 'Territorial Christian Association' aboard the *Grantully Castle* in the Red Sea, inspired by their proximity to Biblical lands. (Others speculated on Moses's crossing of the Red Sea as they passed through it.) Men of the 1/4th Dorset petitioned the captain to read Divine Service

---

42 *Pioneer*, 4 February 1915
43 'The "Original Terriers" on Service', *Magazine of the 9th Battalion The Middlesex Regiment*, 1 April 1917, pp. 133-36
44 Programme, Bertram Gotobed, 1/7th Hants, M916/89, RHRM

twice on Sunday on the transport *Assaye*. On the voyage out the 2/4th Hants' voluntary services attracted 200 communicants, and the battalion was said to provide 80% of Quetta's Anglican congregation.[45]

Clergymen and the familiar and consoling rituals they alone commanded were most appreciated at times of crisis, in illness or in the imminence or fact of death. In India, no Territorials were buried without their ministrations. In cantonments, ministers often co-operated more than would their civilian counterparts, often acting as informal welfare officers, conscious that they shared a battle against the abuse of alcohol and prostitutes. In the smaller hill stations churches were often un-consecrated, allowing Catholic chaplains to use them as well. Territorials, especially those from strongly non-conformist counties, were arguably more religious than were Anglo-Indian civilians: 'churchgoing is not an Anglo-Indian habit', as Robert Palmer observed at Naini Tal.[46] But many men did attend services voluntarily. Walter Gosling of the 1/1st Kent described the large St Mark's Cathedral, Bangalore, as 'packed full' for an evening service, most soldiers – but the station held over 4000 troops, meaning that only the most committed Christians attended church again, though the several hundred soldiers represented a sizeable minority.[47]

Organised religion was a part of army life, with 'Parade Services' mandated in *King's Regulations*. Unless men specifically sought exemption they were expected to attend 'church parades', usually weekly. It seems that Territorial battalions embarked without seeking padres (the army's term for uniformed ministers of religion) on their strengths. They relied upon station chaplains, missioners and even devout lay preachers in the ranks. Men often detested church parades, though not (a clergyman hastily claimed) because of the services, but because of the need to clean, prepare and lay out kit before-hand. Even so, experienced army padres suggested that services be 'abbreviated' and that the sermon (no more than ten minutes) should 'have a point ... and one only'.[48] Because church parades were generally compulsory, they offer no fair test of religious practice. But as a result, 'some of the men have been to church more during the past nine months than the whole of their previous life', as Herbert Ewing observed.[49] Some men objected – in 1916 two dozen Devon men were awarded pack-drill for failing to go to church parade, whether for principled or other reasons.[50] Units did not necessarily take religious obligations seriously. (Walter Gosling described the perfunctory 15-minute church parade (taken by his colonel) in Waziristan in March 1917 as 'a farce'.[51])

Church parades reminded men of the fragility of British rule, just as '*geraja*', as Hindustani speakers called churches, reminded Indians of the alien faith of their rulers. Men often attended cantonment churches (usually large and often ugly tin-roofed edifices capable of holding hundreds of worshippers) armed, carrying rifles and ammunition. The rifles they fixed into recesses especially cut in the pews in front of them (which they might rattle gently as a subtle signal of dissatisfaction if sermons tried to make more than one point). The reason for this

---

45 *The Tiger*, March 1915, p. 8
46 Palmer, *Letters from Mesopotamia*, p. 10
47 Diary, 13 August 1916, Walter Gosling, 1/1st Kent, 1985-12-29, NAM
48 Wright, *Priest and Parish in India*, p. 126
49 Diary, 19 September 1915, Herbert Ewing, 1/5th Somerset, Doc.15428, 07/8/1, IWM
50 Aggett, *The Bloody Eleventh*, p. 33
51 Diary, 18 March 1917, Walter Gosling, 1/1st Kent, 1985-12-29, NAM

was, it was widely believed, because the 1857 mutiny-rebellion had broken out while troops were unarmed and at church in Meerut – practically every correspondent and memoir-writer mentions the 'fact'. (Ironically, while the outbreak at Meerut in 1857 had occurred when troops were at evensong, at that voluntary service troops were not required to carry arms, and the premier historian of the outbreak regarded the coincidence as 'mere legend'.[52])

Church-going, of course, also offered cultural and recreational opportunities, with music a joy regardless of faith. It was probably not piety that moved Herbert Peake to join the garrison church choir at Lebong: a few months later he got out of church parade 'I wasn't having any. *I did not go.*'[53] Because the army turned worship into a parade, effectively compulsory for men who had invariably declared a religious affiliation on enlisting, many men heard more sermons and sang more hymns as soldiers than they had since giving up Sunday school. Indeed, because churches provided important social, recreational and philanthropic institutions, men routinely encountered them more in uniform than at home. Churchmen ran the Church of England Soldiers' Institute, Wesleyan Soldiers' Homes, the YMCA centres, the Royal Army Temperance Association (actually operated by soldiers and ex-soldiers but strongly supported by chaplains and local ministers). Soldiers' Institutes tended to be run by local Anglican ministers, Soldiers' Homes usually by pairs of matronly missionaries and YMs by muscular Christians who often sought out opportunities to go on active service. Troops became adept at sizing up the mettle of the Christians they encountered. Missioners in 'Soldiers' Homes' evangelised, working hard at the uphill business of bringing drunken Regulars to Christ. Miss Elsie Fisk, a missioner in Miss Sandes's Home in Quetta through the war, found that the presence of Territorials made their task easier, a sign that they were more religious than hard-bitten Regulars. Not that attendance at church necessarily made all soldiers believers, or still less practitioners of a Christian life. Bert Rendall mentioned visiting the dancing-girl prostitutes of Rangoon on the same page as he described joining the Rangoon cathedral choir (a free feed and being excused guard duties may have been an incentive in the latter case).

Bert's ability to balance his inclinations aside, in this Territorials differed markedly from Regulars. Services, prayer, Bible study and hymn-singing provided a comfort to young men far from home. 'It would surprise you to see what a lot of chaps go to services', a man of the 1/7th Hants wrote to his parents from Bombay, after the battalion's choir sang in a service in the imposing 'Afghan' church in Colaba.[54] Individual sources show that many devout men sought out church services. Herbert Chapple of the 1/4th Devon walked two miles from Wellington to Coonoor to attend a Wesleyan service to his taste, Thomas Heard held open-air prayer meetings with half-a-dozen other Cornwall men in Aden, and William Fox attended four-men prayer meetings in Lucknow. Albert Bray reported 'good congregations' among the 1/4th Cornwall (evenly divided between Anglicans and Methodists), for voluntary services conducted by local or station clergy, but also by Methodist lay preachers in the battalion.

The YMCA proved to be one of the most assiduous supporters of soldiers generally, and Territorials in particular. Its officers operated in most cantonments and even in the tented camps Territorials occupied – at Delhi and Hebbal, near Bangalore. (At Kingsway camp the YMCA tent held 500 men, where 'many ladies' served meals and drinks to Territorials in the

---

52 Palmer, *The Mutiny Outbreak at Meerut*, p. 56
53 Diary, 31 October 1915, Henry Peake, 1/5th West Surrey, QRWS/30/PEAK/1, SHC, Woking
54 Clippings, Stokes-Roberts papers, M2185, RHRM

unexpectedly early hot weather.[55] Bangalore's extensive YMCA program operated from its large headquarters, carrying one of the major responsibilities for soldiers' welfare in one of India's biggest cantonments. At the express wish of its officers, Albert Bray's account of the 1/4th Cornwall specifically mentioned the 'hearty and cordial fellowship' its men had enjoyed at Red Triangle huts and rooms across India.[56]

As might be expected from men of the English Edwardian working and lower middle-class, many Territorials brought with them profound Christian convictions, and many attempted to live their beliefs despite the temptations of army life. Every battalion had a small group of devout Christians, though the total (across all denominations) might add up to perhaps ten percent of its strength. In Peshawar in 1918 Harry Canham attended the station's Wesleyan chapel on Sunday evenings, with fewer than two dozen others, seeking 'an antidote for the profane atmosphere of the barrack room'.[57] An Anglican bishop claimed that Territorials were 'an extremely God-fearing lot of men' and men's letters and diaries reveal that many un-self-consciously sought out spiritual support.[58] When late in 1914 Thomas Heard found himself in hospital at Bareilly he had a long chat with the station chaplain and they decided to hold Bible class and prayer meetings in the battalion. It is certainly clear that attendances at non-compulsory church parades and voluntary gatherings remained healthy. In India, in 1915 the *Kent Messenger* reported that the 37 men of the 5th Buffs' prayer circle had only two Bibles between them, relaying their request for donations.[59] Still, that represented only about 5% of the battalion's strength. Many men were not so much hostile to organised religion as indifferent to it – the anonymous bishop then conceded that the most common attitude was one of 'polite paganism'.

Soldiers rarely became part of civil congregations. Anglo-Indian civilians were known to ask soldiers to 'undertake to behave properly' before allowing them to attend church in smaller hill station churches, a mark of their assumptions about Regulars.[60] In Bangalore, so Oswald Early believed, civilians actually wrote to the vicar of St Mark's complaining that soldiers were 'flooding' their church. The vicar apparently tackled the objection openly in church, telling his disgruntled parishioners that 'he would rather preach to us … and told them if they didn't like it there were other churches to which they could go'.[61] Owen Smith continued to attend church services voluntarily and regularly, as well as Bible classes and hymn-singing at the Soldiers' Homes at Agra and Ambala and, though he did 'take a drink', as they said, also attended Army Temperance meetings. In India, as in Edwardian England, religion, the nuances of belief and practice were complex.

While convalescent, recovering from enteric fever he caught in Mesopotamia, Joe Cox read the Bible through, at three chapters a day taking three months. In Mesopotamia, he had passed the site of what was called the Garden of Eden, whose present desolation did not undermine his literal understanding of the Old Testament.[62] Joe held to an uncomplicated faith, like his

---

55 *Pioneer*, 20 March 1916
56 Albert Bray, 'Brief notes on service', p. 6, B.4289, CRM
57 Letter, 1 September 1918, Harry Canham, 2/4th Border, CMML
58 Clipping, Owen Smith, 1/6th Hants, M766, RHRM
59 *Kent Messenger*, 16 October 1915
60 Letter, 25 April 1915, Hugh Creek, 1/4th Devon, EX2543, DMM
61 Diary, 29 October 1916, Oswald Early, 1/9th Hants, M4236, RHRM
62 Cox, *An Ordinary Working Man's Life Story*, pp. 51; 37; 43-44

patriotism, whose assumptions he shared with many others. The demonstrable faith of a small but seemingly significant proportion of Territorials in India not only testifies to the spirituality of the England from which they came, but provides a counterweight to the excesses of some of their fellows, which will become apparent in due course. But the anonymous bishop was surely truthful (depressingly for him) in observing that the deeper consolations of Christianity played little part in most Territorials' lives, in India or elsewhere.

8

Defeat in Aden; disaster in Mesopotamia

Among the campaigns sustained by British India the operations in Aden were, despite an initial set-back crucially involving Welsh Territorials, among the least prepossessing, conclusive or costly. By contrast, the campaign in Mesopotamia, which began so negligently and with grossly grandiose if vague aims, became the Indian Army's most significant and costly, and one with implications that reverberate in the Middle East a century on. The two campaigns are linked in that despite Indian commanders' misgivings, Territorials took part in both.

'1 degree cooler than hell': Aden

Aden, a British-Indian possession since 1839 at the south-western tip of Arabia, was a much disliked posting: as the Buffs' historian gravely commented, 'not a white man's station'; though British units served there (notoriously when Curzon exiled the 1st West Kent there as punishment for men and officers conniving to conceal evidence of the rape of a Burmese woman).[1] A coaling station on the route from the Suez Canal to India, it was 'a narrow isthmus of flat ground, three-quarters of a mile wide … barren and black, dreary and waterless, destitute of every natural gift except the possession of a fine harbour'.[2] Many of the transports carrying Territorials to India in 1914 had stopped at Aden. Kent men had been told, and dutifully reported home, that Aden had 'a very bad reputation as about the worst British foreign station'.[3] Except for sandfly fever, Aden was regarded as 'a very healthy station for troops' though 'the climate is very enervating'. The most trying seasons were May-June and September-October, when 'heat apoplexy' was a danger. In the monsoon months between, breezes eased the stifling combination of heat and humidity.[4] Aden in summer, Henry Peake was told, was '1 degree cooler than hell'.[5] Murray's guide described it as 'hot but healthy'; not that it attracted tourists.[6]

---

1   Moody, *Historical Records of the Buffs*, p. 118
2   MacDonnell, *The Outlines of Military Geography*, p. 205
3   *Kent Messenger*, 2 January 1915
4   *Military Report on the Aden Protectorate*, 1915
5   Diary, 23 November 1914, Henry Peake, 1/5th West Surrey, QRWS/30/PEAK/1, SHC, Woking
6   Anon, *A Handbook for Travellers*, p. liii

Technically, an Ottoman force 'invested' the territory; that is, it held a ring of positions around the neck of the peninsula on which the settlement sat. The forces involved were modest. In 1915 the Ottomans mobilised 2500 troops and 1500 Arab levies, with about twenty guns. The British Aden Field Force was larger, three of its four battalions comprising Indian troops (and the Malay States Guides, sent to Aden after the mutiny of the 5th Light Infantry in Singapore). While its British battalion – always composed of Territorials – took its turn in the front line, British troops mainly lived in the city, acting as a reserve and guarding vulnerable points such as the garrison's searchlights, the passes, cable station, and the all-important condensers providing the defenders' drinking water.

Hardinge reported to Crewe in February 1915 that the 'situation at Aden is also unsatisfactory', complaining that the force there could do little but defend the port, not the hinterland and tribes ostensibly under British protection.[7]

'Our milk boy was also dead': defeat at Lahej

The 1/1st Brecknock Battalion arrived in Aden November 1914, relieving the 1st Lancashire Fusiliers, which went on to be slaughtered in the invasion of Gallipoli while the survivors died on the Somme. The Welshmen's arrival had been aggravated by to-ing and fro-ing. The ship carrying them from Britain had called at Aden and then carried them on to Bombay. Then, after four days at anchor it had steamed back to Aden. The answer (provided in Parliament) was that accommodation at Aden was unavailable until the Regular regiment had left, but some Brecon Territorials complained to the Earl of Selborne, whose son Robert was a subaltern in the 1/6th Hants. The Welshmen, under a former Grenadier Guardsman, Lord Glanusk, spent their first months becoming accustomed to Aden's trying climate but like their counterparts in India, unprepared for active service. In early July offensive moves by the Ottoman Yemen Army Corps (actually no larger than a weak division) prompted Major-General David Shaw to order his Aden Moveable Column to sally out of the port and occupy the town of Lahej, 25 miles inland, to support its pro-British sultan. The Brecknocks formed the largest single part of a 1000-strong British-Indian column which, followed by an improvised gaggle of baggage camels, set off across the desert in the hottest month of the year. The first two heat-stroke casualties fell within a few miles of Sheik Othman, at the very neck of the peninsula on which Aden sits, 'both, as it happens, particularly strong and athletic fellows', the regiment's historian wrote.[8]

The next day the column started at three a.m. on 4 July, losing more men to heat-stroke and straggling into the mud-walled town by late afternoon. That night the Indian and Welsh infantry fought off assaults by Ottoman regulars and their Arab levies

Glanusk commanded only about a quarter of his 400 men, firing from a walled garden. Meanwhile, the baggage camels stampeded, uncontrolled by their panicked civilian cameliers, and the column lost its reserve ammunition, food supplies and much of its water. At dawn it became clear that the British had to withdraw. Fortunately the Ottoman force was also prostrate

---

7 Telegram, 16 February 1915, Kitchener papers, PRO30/57/69, NAUK
8 Atkinson, *The History of the South Wales Borderers*, p. 132

The Arab town of Lahej, which the Brecknocks defended on the evening of 4 July 1915 before retreating across the desert to Aden. (Q13093, Imperial War Museum)

with heat and did not pursue the increasingly disordered British as they plodded back through soft sand.

Soldiers' letters published in *The Brecon County Times* revealed details of the disaster of the kind that military censors soon succeeded in concealing. Gilbert Hawkes, formerly a printer on the paper, wrote a graphic description of the deaths of 'Brecon and Talgarth men', naming them and even recording their last words. He described how 'poor Ernie Green' had died, laughing hysterically as comrades poured their last water over him. Gilbert went in search of an ambulance but by the time he returned Ernie was dead. He learned that William Lloyd had also died, disclosing how local a Territorial unit could be. He was with:

> Edwards and Smith, the butchers, at one time, and was a cousin to the one that was at the Queen's Head. Then, again, someone passing told me that Rees Williams, [of] the Forge, our milk boy, was also dead, and I began to wonder if all the men would go, because I knew that heaps of men were ill.[9]

They eventually reached the safety of Aden – abandoning The Tanks, its water supplies at Sheik Othman – retreating to the port and its immediate defences. The battalion lost eleven men as a result of the sortie to, mostly of 'heat apoplexy', with another dying a week later in the station hospital at Aden, the first Indian Territorials to lose their lives in action. One Brecknock man, Henry Povey, formerly employed by a retired general of Crickhowell, was posted 'missing'.

The Ottomans briefly occupied Aden's water supply at Sheikh Othman, though reinforcements hastily called from Egypt regained it within the month. The two sides faced then each other across a wide no man's land. The expedition to Lahej remained notorious to troops of the garrison even in 1919 and the campaign was to continue to the war's end. In the meantime, the tragedy, not to say scandal, of Mesopotamia would bring profound consequences, not least for the Territorials drawn into it.

---

9   *The Brecon County Times*, 29 July 1915, p. 5. Two men named Lloyd died in the retreat from Lahej. This one was 'Lloyd who used to work for Edwards Butcher': Letter 8 July 1915, George Thorogood, 1/1st Brecknock, Brecknock Battalion, South Wales Borderers 1911-1939, 2005.83, Box 17, RMRW

The failure at Lahej – because it was clearly a defeat, inflicted on a nominally superior British force – had little impact beyond the shocked and sun-struck men of the Brecknock Battalion. The officer primarily responsible for the disaster, Major-General David Shaw, was relieved in Aden and given command of the Karachi Brigade, where the following year his negligence resulted in the deaths of more Territorials. New of the failed sally to Lahej was not, of course, reported in closely censored newspapers in Britain, and in any case the continuing tragedy of the Western Front dwarfed its losses.

'The country of the Arabian nights': Mesopotamia

The force despatched from India in October 1914 to Basra and the Shatt-el-Arab in southern Mesopotamia would in time consume a larger force – and more lives – than all of other forces combined. At first comprising one division (the 6th Indian) by 1918 'Force D' would grow to become a major army, including Indian and British troops, and men of the Indian Territorial battalions. Mesopotamia, the Ottoman empire's most south-easterly province, had been part of the Government of India's accepted sphere of influence, and its troops were sent to Basra at first to secure the Anglo-Persian Oil Company's refinery at Abadan (on the Shatt-el-Arab but actually in Persia). Gradually, by inertia, ambition, muddy thinking and carelessness, the British-Indian force advanced up the Tigris River, drawn by the illusion of easily capturing Baghdad.

The heart of the 'fertile crescent' of antiquity, Mesopotamia – the land between the river Tigris and Euphrates – had stagnated since the Mongols had devastated the region in the 13th century, destroying the irrigation works on which its fertility depended. As the campaign began at the head of the Persian Gulf it was at first known as 'the P.G.' and later 'Mespot' or 'Mesup', the latter a justifiable pun. As in the Dardanelles, British officers repeatedly under-estimated the skill and tenacity of their Ottoman opponents, and the Turkish troops and Arab auxiliaries delayed the British-Indian advance. As Stanley Goodland foresaw in a letter to his fiancé, Elsie, 1915 was 'going to be a devil of a year'.[10]

Soon, losses from battle, but overwhelmingly from disease and heatstroke, created a need for reinforcements. But if more Indian troops were to be despatched to the front, then British battalions also had to be found. Under the convention that the Indian Army had observed from before the 1857 mutiny-rebellion, an 'Indian' brigade usually included a British battalion. While some Indian brigades served without a British unit (the 29th Indian Infantry Brigade on Gallipoli a notable and highly successful example) the pressing need to send more Indian brigades to Mesopotamia entailed the selection of Territorial battalions for active service. When reinforcements were first needed, early in 1915, Territorial battalions had not yet faced their first Kitchener's Tests, but pressure mounted, with Crewe (the Secretary of State for India) asking in March 1915 that a brigade of two Territorial and two Indian battalions be sent. In the event only the 1/4th Hants went (along with the 1/5th Hampshire battery, despite its obsolete and defective guns), arriving in Basra in March and moving to Qurna a month later.

Exactly why Francis Bowker's 1/4th Hants was selected, even before it had undergone its Kitchener Test, is unclear. (A sister battalion, the 1/5th Hants, believed that the movement

---

10   Letter, 2 February 1915, Stanley Goodland, 1/5th Somerset, Noyes, (ed.), *Engaged in War*, p. 22

order was intended for it and a typo resulted in the 1/4th going.[11]) Especially considering the low opinion in which senior officers held of Territorials, the choice was, however, a considerable tribute. Geoffrey Burrell, one of its company commanders, thought that the fact that the battalion had done a 21-mile route march around Peshawar without a man falling out might have influenced the decision. Though the mobilisation order arrived at three a.m. on a Sunday, the battalion was ready to depart on the Tuesday night. It had to borrow machine-guns from the neighbouring 114th Mahrattas, and had not received up-to-date rifles.[12]

Bowker wrote to his wife, Esme (in Winchester) as the battalion entered the Persian Gulf that they looked forward to seeing 'the country of the Arabian Nights, Haroun-al-Rashid & old Sinbad the Sailor'.[13] The reality was less romantic. Troops faced a climate of baking hot summers and freezing, wet winters, with the country either a flat, dry, dusty plain or a morass of slimy mud from the rivers' annual flooding. Within weeks of reaching Basra Bowker's men were enduring a 'daily round of digging and heavy fatigues' with 'dust, dirt, flies as usual' and 'very hot days'.[14] Within three months more than half of the battalion was sick and most men under 20 and over 40 were sent back to India (but not Bowker, though he was 47).[15] Of all the Indian Territorial battalions, the 1/4th Hants saw the most severe service. It was to serve in Mesopotamia for the entire war, losing a company in the fall of Kut, enduring four of the theatre's notorious summers and (as we will see) remaining in the region long after the war's end.

In May 1915, moving in great heat, Bowker's battalion became part of 'Townshend's Regatta', when a flotilla of assorted boats pursued the retreating Ottomans as they withdrew up the Tigris, the 1/4th Hants' machine-gunners using the guns they had begged from the Mahrattas. The battalion followed the advance up-river,

Esme Bowker on the way to India, where, sadly, she would not manage to see her husband before he was killed in the fighting to relieve the siege of Kut in January 1916. (M1360, Royal Hampshire Regiment Museum)

---

11   The *History of the Hampshire Territorial Force Association*, pp. 137-138, alleged that the original telegrams ordered the 1/5th Hants battalion and the 1/4th Hants Battery to Mesopotamia, but that in the end the 1/4th Battalion and the 1/5th Battery went.
12   '1/4th (T) Battalion Notes', *The Hampshire Regimental Journal*, May 1915, p. 151
13   Letter, 16 March 1915, Francis Bowker, 1/4th Hants, Doc. 8094, 99/15/1, IWM
14   Letter, 14 May 1915, Francis Bowker, 1/4th Hants, *Ibid*
15   Letters, 16 & 21 June 1915, Francis Bowker, 1/4th Hants, *Ibid*

passing over the battlefield of Shaiba days after the fight, its men shocked at the sight of dead and wounded still lying about, with 'heaps of horses' burning. 'The sight and smell was awful' wrote an anonymous Hampshire Territorial.[16] His company continued up-river, camping at nameless places in the desert, overwhelmed by sandstorms and drinking slimy river water fouled by animals and corpses. Without changes of uniform they passed through torrential rain, extreme heat and humidity. By June fewer than 250 men were fit for duty, and the anonymous Territorial himself was evacuated to India ill, by August recuperating at Subathu, in the Simla Hills. His colonel, Francis Bowker, was twenty miles away and several thousand feet higher, convalescing at Simla from a wound inflicted by a Turkish bullet passing through his binocular strap, forearm and chest.

Simply serving in Mesopotamia cost men's health. By mid-June, ten weeks after arriving, the 1/4th Hants had 180 men on the sick list, with 84 men evacuated to India seriously ill and some men dead: half of the battalion ineffective. When the advance resumed it had just 300 men available, all afflicted by sores and boils – the result of a poor diet. A month later it numbered just 150, and in August it was sent back to Nasiriya on one barge. 'Too weak for employment', its headquarters and a company went up the Tigris to join Townshend's force as it advanced toward its nemesis at Ctesiphon and then Kut.[17] Troops endured flies, mosquitos and sandflies. A card drawn for the 1/4th Hants' first Christmas in Mesopotamia included a facetious coat of arms for Force D that included 'Mosquito couchant', 'Eight fleas doing squad drill', 'two sand flies in bivouac' and a thermometer reading 130°.[18]

'Draft for the Gulf': volunteers for Mesopotamia

Casualties in the agonising advance up the Tigris were so severe that in the hot weather of 1915 Territorial units across India sent drafts of up to fifty men to replace losses among the five Regular battalions in Force D. These drafts invariably comprised volunteers, eager to see active service. When the 1/5th West Surrey called for fifty volunteers for Mesopotamia practically the entire battalion stepped forward, and many men's diaries record the same response. Its men showed 'tremendous enthusiasm … We couldn't wait', Private Peacock recalled.[19] So many men volunteered that adjutants had to devise novel ways to select men. The 1/6th East Surrey took only men of four to five years' service (most of whom were killed, wounded or captured with the 2nd Norfolk). The 1/4th Devon accepted volunteers only from what its officers described as 'pure Devonshire men' – Hugh Creek, though serving in a Devon battalion, hailed from Cornwall and so missed out.[20] Some men refused. The denial of proficiency pay moved some men to argue that as they did not receive proficiency pay they were clearly not proficient, and so refused to volunteer: 'if we are not yet good enough to get that 6d a day we are not good enough to fight', William Jupp reasoned.[21]

---

16 Diary of an anonymous Hampshire Territorial, 1915, Misc123, item 1916, IWM
17 Atkinson, *The Royal Hampshire Regiment*, Vol. II, pp. 124-126
18 Clipping, Esme Bowker papers, M1539, RHRM
19 A. [probably Alfred or Arthur] Peacock, 1/5th West Surrey, QRWS/30/PEAC/3, SHC, Woking
20 Letter, 25 April 1915, Hugh Creek, 1/4th Devon, EX2543, DMM
21 Letter, 10 August 1915, William Jupp, 1/5th West Kent, Doc.17422, 10/3/1, IWM. But all the same he did go to Mesopotamia, in 1916, dying of fever at Basra as a lance corporal aged 22.

A 'Draft for the Gulf', as a photograph caption read, often came as a welcome break once the novelty of India had begun to pall. Lieutenant Robert Palmer of the 1/6th Hants told his mother that 'after all these months of hanging about' he welcomed the order to take a draft to the 1/4th Hants because a friend claimed that 'the Hampshires are dying like flies at Basra', and he wanted the opportunity to prevent men getting sick or being killed.[22] Six months later, when the 2/4th Somerset sent a draft of 100 men to Mesopotamia, its colonel still felt obliged to insert a paragraph in battalion orders that

> ... whilst fully appreciating the spirit of those who have volunteered for active service drafts, [he] regrets that he has had to adjust the lists ... by the inclusion of some specialists. Opportunity will doubtless arise later for those now excluded to see active service.[23]

Territorial volunteers of a reinforcement draft arriving in Basra in 1915. Most of these men will be killed, wounded or captured at Kut. (A02267, Australian War Memorial)

The drafts were critical to the British units' capacity to continue. 'What the state of these battalions would have been had they not been supplied with drafts from Territorial Regiments in India', the Mesopotamia Commission later noted, 'may well be imagined'.[24] Drafts came from all over – two-thirds of the men captured while serving with the 1/4th Hants came from five other Hampshire battalions in India.[25] Seven battalions whose drafts were recorded in detail totalled over 500 men in as many months. When Robert Palmer took his draft of Hampshires to Basra in August 1915, with them on the overcrowded SS *Varsova* were men from forty-one other units, including 28 Territorial battalions.[26] By the year's end at least a thousand Territorials had volunteered to go to Mesopotamia, on whom fell the burden of the disastrous campaign of 1915.[27] Losses among the drafts were severe. Of a draft of thirty the 1/5th Somerset sent to the 2nd Dorset in May 1915 only nine survived

---

22 Palmer, *Letters from Mesopotamia*, p. 7
23 Part 1 orders, 2/4th Somerset Light Infantry, March 1916, DD\SLI/6/36, SHC, Taunton
24 Mesopotamia Commission, p. 40
25 'Presumed Prisoners of War', Esme Bowker papers, M1830, RHRM
26 Palmer, *Letters from Mesopotamia*, p. 24
27 A relic of the British regimental system was that until 1916 men could not be compelled to be transferred between regiments, but had to volunteer.

to go into captivity at Kut, and of them only two survived; the rest were killed, wounded or evacuated sick.[28]

Some men knew how unpleasant Mesopotamia would be – Hugh Creek, writing on 25 April 1915, thought that 'the Dardanelles would suit me better'.[29] Men were in no doubt about what volunteering for 'the Gulf' could entail. Within months of the departure of drafts for the 1/4th Hants in Mesopotamia the 2/4th's magazine published a casualty list detailing the names of men killed and wounded there.[30] Men volunteered even as they learned more of its discomforts and dangers. (Fred Mundy met convalescents Hampshires in the hills in 1915 whose tales were 'none too jolly of that place'.[31])

'A disaster in Mesopotamia': Kut

None of the contending empires in the Middle East, Arabia or central Asia were able to make good their strategic desires. British troops were able to occupy Basra and advance up the Tigris, but they could not overcome either the Ottoman defenders or the obstacles of Mesopotamia's climate and terrain. The Ottomans could not expel the invaders. The Germans, though devoting much energy and cash to fomenting intrigue and unrest among the populations of Arabia, Persia and Afghanistan, could not get rebellion to spark. The result was costly fighting in inhospitable terrain and an uncomfortable, indeed, unbearable, climate, for gains which were hardly worth the cost. The British, having arrived to protect their oil supplies, found themselves advancing up-river for no rational reason, toward what became defeat and humiliation.

Mesopotamia's was the Government and Army of India's own debacle. Everything needed – including every stick of firewood – came from India, though much that was needed did not arrive, or if it arrived could not get to the foremost troops. Francis Bowker gave his wife Esme an instance of Anglo-Indian apathy toward its support of troops in Mesopotamia. In March 1915 he ordered smoked glasses for his men from a British Bombay agency – a commercial firm. The order had arrived on 14 May, but the clerks wrote asking him to complete a customs declaration on 21 May, and posted the letter a week later. He was finally able to distribute the glasses in mid-June.[32] Despite the Indian Army's expertise in supporting frontier expeditions, the management of a complex, distant, riverine campaign was beyond its slow-moving administrative procedures, and it was far bigger than any one charismatic individual could influence, given that the individuals mainly responsible, Hardinge, Duff and senior officers (Sir John Nixon from April 1915 and Sir Percy Lake from January 1916), did not possess the necessary qualities. This would be revealed, but only after much suffering and disastrous failure.

In mid-1915, now commanded by the incompetent and arrogant Major-General Sir Charles Townsend, Tigris Corps resumed the advance up-river, with the vague intention of capturing Baghdad (on the assumption that its seizure would bolster British prestige in the Moslem world). The desire to assert British prestige came at the expense of prudence. The

---

28　Anon, *The Book of Remembrance*, p. 32
29　Letter, 25 April 1915, Hugh Creek, 1/4th Devon, EX2543, DMM
30　*The Tiger*, September 1915, p. 89
31　Mundy, *A Journal of the 1/4th Battalion Wiltshire Regiment*, p. 47
32　Letter, 12 June 1915, Francis Bowker, 1/4th Hants, Doc. 8094, 99/15/1, IWM

advance was improvised, not always happily. Troops used hundreds of unwieldy local boats, *bellums* or *mahailas*, with guns transported on clumsy rafts, carried and supplied by too few river steamers. In October, for example, the 1/5th Hampshire howitzer battery formed part of a column despatched from Kut-el-Amara to Aziza ('a small village of mud huts in the bare desert') to join the advance grinding up the Tigris toward Ctesiphon. The column marched far from the river in hot weather, many of the men already suffering from beri-beri.[33] The force lacked adequate artillery, engineering, supply and above all medical supplies. A month later the Hants gunners formed part of Townshend's force that fought in the shadow of the great brick arch of Ctesiphon, ten miles from Baghdad, the high-water mark of the first, misguided British attempt to seize Baghdad. Indian authorities remained unduly confident of the outcome of the campaign – in November 1915, shortly before the disastrous reverse at Ctesiphon, Hardinge had wired Austen Chamberlain blithely explaining his plans to announce the anticipated triumph 'as soon as Baghdad is actually occupied …'[34]

Instead, defeated at Ctesiphon and reluctantly accepting the necessity of retreat, Townshend withdrew down the Tigris. His many wounded and even more numerous sick were crowded onto steamers to be transported laboriously down-river. Among the sick lying in their own excrement on the notorious 'hospital ships' were Territorials who barely a year before had been civilians. Hardinge and Duff belatedly realised that Mesopotamia needed more formations. One of the 1/4th Hants's companies accompanied a convoy of river-boats carrying wounded, marching beside the river to keep off marauding Arabs – Joe Cox's most compelling memories of Mesopotamia in 1916 involved sizeable skirmishes against Arab tribesmen. An 'Emergency Force' hastily formed in India and despatched early in December 1915 included Territorial infantry (the 1/5th West Surrey and the 1/5th Buffs), but also the entire 1st Home Counties Field Artillery Brigade with its three Sussex batteries. Soon after Christmas 1915 it was spread between Qurna, and Nasiriya, almost immediately plunged into action by advancing on Butaniya in a failed attempt to divert Turkish pressure from Kut.

In anxiously debating the risk of accepting Territorials in exchange for Regulars, in February 1915 Hardinge had foreseen the 'inevitable' consequences of 'a disaster in Mesopotamia' – conflict with Persia, Afghanistan and the frontier tribes.[35] Disasters certainly occurred: the campaign became a by-word for bungling of Crimean dimensions. Territorials sent to Mesopotamia became victims and witnesses of the pervasive incompetence. Robert Palmer relieved his feelings by describing how on reaching Basra his men disembarked into open barges at mid-day, then waited 22 hours for food, and loading and unloading their baggage while hungry. 'Nobody could complain if we'd been defending Lucknow …' he wrote, 'but …'. He described the authorities as 'criminal … scatter-brained nincompoops' when three of his men came down with heatstroke.[36] One of Palmer's men, William Bisset, detailed to help carry wounded men from barges and steamers felt profoundly depressed: 'everything seems to look so black just now and when one sees all this suffering it makes one wonder whether it is worth the huge sacrifice we are making'.[37] Hideous though it was to be wounded in Mesopotamia, especially in the advance to

33 Moberly, *The Campaign in Mesopotamia*, Vol. II, p. 37
34 Telegram, 10 November 1915, 'Confidential Telegrams, 1914-15', IOR R/20/A/4108, BL
35 Telegram, 16 February 1915, [Hardinge to Crewe], Kitchener papers, PRO30/57/69, NAUK
36 Palmer, *Letters from Mesopotamia*, pp. 29-30
37 Diary, 10 January 1916, William Bisset, 2/4th Hants (attached to 1/4th Hants), M1834, RHRM

Ctesiphon in late 1915, being wounded could be a ticket to survive. Of the fifty men the 1/9th Middlesex sent to the 2nd Norfolk in 1915 thirty returned, most only because they had been wounded. Of the twenty who were captured at Kut, all perished.

Senior figures in Britain told constituents and newspaper readers that the campaign was being conducted responsibly but officers on the spot gave a more accurate account. After Austen Chamberlain assured members in the Commons that 'ice and fans are installed wherever possible', in Mesopotamia Robert Palmer commented to a friend in Britain '*i.e.* nowhere beyond Basra.'[38] In India, though, Territorials often learned of the reality of the campaign by meeting convalescents recovering from wounds or illness in transit, in hospital or on leave. Men of the 2/4th Border, for instance, met men of the 1/5th Buffs who were waiting to return to Mesopotamia when the Buffs' depot was established in the fort at Sitabaldi (at Nagpur), which was garrisoned by a Border company. It would be possible for Territorials to not learn of the mismanagement in the Gulf only if they were stationed in cantonments through which men did not pass, such as in Baluchistan, Burma or the Andamans.

An Ottoman force under Nureddin Pasha invested Townsend's garrison in Kut on 8 December, though, confident of relief, the besieged force remained on full rations until Christmas. They suffered from dysentery and pneumonia (it was now bitterly cold, and wet) and after a hard year on active service many troops developed deficiency conditions such as beri-beri. Soon after the siege began, news of the final humiliating evacuation of Gallipoli arrived. Their victory released Ottoman troops for other fronts and depressed the spirits of troops facing hardships of fighting a determined, tough and skilful enemy in a dreadful climate and inhospitable terrain – now as wet and muddy as it had been dry and dusty in the hot season.

The siege of Kut became the compelling, climactic drama of the first years of the Mesopotamian campaign. Although only a Hampshire battery and a company were formally part of Townsend's besieged force, hundreds more Territorials were among the besieged, having joined other British units as volunteers. The defenders' artillery included the howitzers of the 1/5th Hampshire Battery, whose four guns formed a tenth of Townshend's artillery. The gunners worked 'incessantly' to strengthen the town's defences, building emplacements near the 'brick kilns' practically at the centre of the bend in the Tigris on which Kut sits.[39] The guns were just over a mile from the initial Turkish lines, though later floods forced their trenches one or two miles further away. But the Ottoman besiegers were not going to take Kut by storm: the garrison was starved into surrender. Rations were cut and cut again until after months of privation all were weak and ill.

The humiliation of Kut's capitulation on 29 April 1916, on top of the revelations of medical mismanagement, intensified questions about the campaign. Even before the surrender, Aubrey Herbert, a Conservative MP and Ottoman expert, reflected on its 'chaos'. He damned the use of Indian troops against a Muslim power, the lack of transport and the shortcomings of 'Indian Generals who looked on the expedition as a frontier campaign'.[40] Further revelations and wider questioning led to the establishment of a Mesopotamia Commission in August 1916.

Within days of Townsend's surrender men in India had heard the news, many, like Owen Smith, concerned both at the fate of their comrades who had been drafted to the Gulf ('some of

38 Palmer, *Letters from Mesopotamia*, p. 39
39 Moberly, *The Campaign in Mesopotamia*, Vol. II, p. 166
40 Herbert, *Mons, Anzac and Kut*, p. 227

the 6th Hants are with him') and at its effects ('likely to prolong the war').[41] In the same week news broke of the Easter rising in Dublin.

'A slow march to our deaths': fighting to relieve Kut

Many more Territorials served in the relieving force which assembled, slowly and amid great hardship and confusion over Christmas and New Year 1915-16. Under the direction of Sir Percy Lake it made repeated but futile efforts to raise the siege, losing in casualties (about 25,000) many more than were besieged in Kut (about 8000). By early January Ottoman troops had blocked the Tigris at Sheikh Sa'ad, a village on a bend of the river about thirty miles east of Kut. British and Indian troops under General Sir Fenton Aylmer began to probe for their positions on both banks of the river. In January he made three costly and ineffective attacks on Ottoman entrenchments on the left or northern bank of the Tigris blocking the relief force's route to Kut.

The reinforcements included the 14th Indian Division, with its three British battalions, the 1/5th Buffs, 1/4th Devon and 1/6th Devon. They stolidly accepted the fate that had sent them to one of the most unpleasant and unhealthy climates in which British troops served in the war. (When Aubrey Herbert asked some of the newly arrived 1/6th Devon about the safety of a route up-river, they replied '"We be strangers here, zur," as if they were Exeter men in Taunton'.[42]) Southern English troops acquired a reputation for uncomplainingly accepting the atrocious climate, poor rations and the prospect of wounds or illness if not death.

The attack on Sheikh Sa'ad in the first week of January, delayed by mist in the morning and mirages at noon, ran into determined Ottoman fire, often coming from trenches British-Indian officers could not even see, and in flat desert that gave no cover. The 1/4th Hants, one company of which was in Kut, were part of the advance. The glare prevented the Sussex gunners from even finding the Ottoman trenches. The attacking infantry, British and Indian, endured murderous rifle fire – heavier than on the Western Front, observers thought – and, as so often in Mesopotamia, witnessing the sufferings of the wounded, which neither they nor over-worked medical units could do much to relieve. Aylmer regarded the several days of fighting at Sheikh Sa'ad as a success, but in truth his losses – around 4000 killed, wounded and sick – did little to distract or defeat the besiegers of Kut. Russell Braddon recorded an incident contained in a letter from a Hants captain who survived, who described how one of his men had been wounded in the leg. As he lay in no man's land and Turkish bullets fell about him, he scraped a mud rampart around himself, 'a sort of mud coffin … the water inside it getting deeper with the rain and redder with his blood'. Eventually two stretcher bearers found him and carried him back for three hours to the ambulance point. He was put aboard a boat which reached Basra a week after he had been wounded. 'All my friends in the regiment are gone', he wrote, though he was lucky – he eventually reached Bombay.[43]

Relief operations continued in the attack on The Wadi a week later, including the 1/5th Buffs and 1/1st Sussex gunners, while the 1/4th Hants, by this time of only three weaker companies, held the old bridgehead at Sheikh Sa'ad. Taking The Wadi, which inched the relief columns

41 Letter, 3 May 1916, Owen Smith, 1/6th Hants, M766, RHRM
42 Herbert, *Mons, Anzac and Kut*, p. 230
43 Braddon, *The Siege*, p. 170

fractionally closer to Kut, cost 6000 British-Indian casualties, again overburdening the medical units. It is perhaps no coincidence that in these operations the attacking force's few Territorial battalions were mainly held in reserve. It seems that the prejudice against Territorial units took time to overcome among British Indian officers, and the only acceptable proof to the contrary was the lives of their men.

Amid driving rain, strong winds and cold, Aylmer reassured Townshend that relief was on the way, and prepared for a further attempt. The Mesopotamia Commission detailed the sufferings of the wounded, confirming, to the embarrassment of British-India's medical establishment, that the steamers carrying wounded down-river lacked sweepers, orderlies, bandages, medical comforts, blankets, bedpans, urine bottles, cutlery and crockery'.[44] Many wounded arrived at Basra with their field dressings caked with mud, blood, pus and excreta – their own and others'.

For a third time, on 21 January, Aylmer's force, supplemented by reinforcements but depleted by heavy losses, attacked strong Turkish entrenchments at Hanna, a couple of miles further west from The Wadi. Again the 1/5th Buffs, alongside the Indian 97th Infantry (the entire '35th Brigade') went over the top, running toward Ottoman trenches barely touched by the supporting artillery. Alongside them the 1/4th Hants attacked, joining the Buffs in holding the first Turkish line but unable to get further. In soaking, chilling rain, the ground turning to mud, with telephone lines between brigade and divisional headquarters broken down, amid confusion and acrimony among British commanders, the attempt ended. Aylmer lost nearly 3000 casualties, and the wounded again suffered severely: it was so cold that the marsh actually froze. Among the dead was Francis Bowker, mortally wounded as he led the 1/4th into fire on dead level ground facing strong loop-holed Ottoman trenches protected by barbed wire.

A fellow officer described the attack at Hanna as 'pure slaughter', in which the Territorials attacked across bare, wet, muddy ground into heavy machine-gun fire. A Hants private wrote that 'we never made a rush, and just walked slowly through the rain. A slow march to our deaths …'. Eye-witnesses described the wretched scene, as the 1/4th got into shell-holes and Turkish trenches, where after dark, in the terrible phrase, 'medical arrangements broke down'. The dead also included the sensitive, witty, curious, verse-writing Captain the Hon. Robert Palmer, whom a footballing injury had prevented from going to Kut with one company of the 1/4th Hants, but was killed anyway. Palmer's parents read that Robert had died of wounds as a prisoner. Not until Aubrey Herbert spoke to Ottoman officers in May was he able to confirm that Robert had died of a chest wound after several hours in Turkish hands.[45]

So depleted were the Hants and Buffs battalions that for six months they were temporarily merged, naturally called the 'Huffs'. Reinforcement drafts arrived from all over – no fewer than 21 regiments (not battalions, but regiments) – a sign of the strain under which the Tigris force was operating.[46] Over the summer of 1916 little stirred on the Tigris front, though the troops continued to suffer from the mismanagement of the campaign and the climate. Ted Rice, whose 1/5th West Surrey arrived with the 12th Brigade in August, found 'no canteen, no Y.M.[CA], no recreation tent, no beer', and even 'no tea'.[47] Indian Territorials knew of this. Owen Smith,

---

44 Mesopotamia Commission, pp. 67-68
45 Palmer, *Letters from Mesopotamia*, pp. 124-29
46 Anon, *History of the Hampshire Territorial Force Association*, p. 114
47 Ted Rice, 'All for a Shilling a Day', QRWS/30/RICE/1, SHC, Woking

who had recently commented on Robert Palmer's death, spoke to a Hampshire man who had been evacuated wounded 'he had a very rough time there', he tactfully told his family.[48]

Within a month of leaving Nowshera, in the shadow of the mountains, in late January 1916 the 1/4th Somerset was marching across flat, featureless desert in the night attack on the Dujaila redoubt as part of the fighting to relieve Kut. Assembling at the Pools of Siloam (utterly prosaic places often boasted Biblical names) the 1/4th Somerset led a column, moving silently across the level desert. A participant described the sensation, of 'walking in a dream with thousands of others who seemed asleep', greeting their comrades at dawn 'as though they had just wakened'. Having made a flawless night advance, its officers adhered too closely to their orders not to occupy the undefended redoubt until other positions had been taken, and when it at last attacked the redoubt had been reinforced. Nearly seventy men were killed and wounded out of a battalion already reduced to 500. The battalion acted as rearguard, covering the retreat back to El Orah, their wounded jolting along in unsprung carts, in conditions little changed from a century before.[49] A month later the 1/4th Somerset again attacked through waist-deep marshes, taking nameless Ottoman trenches in the futile and failed relief operations.

The Indian Territorials had expected to see war amid the rolling green hills of their native southern England. Here they served in flat, mud-brown plains, relieved only by palm groves, and amid dust storms in summer and acres of clinging mud whenever it rained. The novelty of the Biblical landscape – steamers on the Tigris tied up at the Tree of the Knowledge of Good and Evil and units bivouacked in what was said to have been the Garden of Eden – palled in the reality of 'Mespot's' climate and terrain. There were moments of beauty – Dorset men recalled an evening concert beside the Tigris, illuminated by the lights of a ship and a full moon over the river. But for the most part Mesopotamia was at best uncomfortable and at worst horrific. Edmund Candler, the official 'eyewitness' who had the unenviable task of chronicling the terrible defeats of 1915-16 described how in 1916 'each day we attacked a new ditch and each ditch became the grave of the inheritors of the green fields of England' and admitted 'one could not keep depression at arm's length …'[50] A 1914 man described the experience of serving in Mesopotamia as 'a long nightmare of heat, sweat, filth, typhoid and sleepless nights'.[51]

Other Indian Territorial units in Aylmer's force faced similar ordeals. The 1/6th Devon's adjutant opened his battalion's war diary the moment he received mobilisation orders in Lahore. The last entry before the battalion's transport reached Basra in December 1915 read, 'commenced sharpening bayonets'.[52] The men's first task was to bury men killed five months before. They re-buried bodies up-rooted by wild dogs, identifying men posted 'missing' and collecting keepsakes to send home. Depleted by battle and illness (typhus and scurvy) the 1/6th numbered 180 other ranks. Word of the sufferings of the wounded and sick in Mesopotamia spread by word-of-mouth and uncensored letters sent to comrades all over India. 'Their story of endurance is most horrible', William Hughes wrote of the men of the 1/5th Buffs who had returned wounded.[53]

48   Letter, 15 February 1916, Owen Smith, 1/6th Hants, M766, RHRM
49   Fisher, *The History of Somerset Yeomanry, Volunteers and Territorials*, pp. 211-12
50   Candler, *The Long Road to Baghdad*, p. 31
51   'Efack' in *Bombay Chronicle*, 13 March 1919
52   War diary, 1/6th Devon, December 1915, WO95/5177, NAUK
53   Letter, 4 February 1916, William Hughes, 1/5th Buffs, Great Chart Fund, KA&HC

As we have seen, suggestions that Territorials could go to war had been not just disregarded but were derided. One of the several arguments Hardinge and Duff used against Kitchener's request that they accept Territorials in place of Regulars was that 'we could not send Territorial Infantry and Artillery against the Turks', as Hardinge wrote, six weeks before the Ottoman empire actually entered the war.[54] Their forebodings proved to be unfounded. The 1/5th West Surrey, which had joined the Tigris Corps in December 1915, brigaded with three Indian battalions of the 34th Brigade, was commended for its 'very steady fire control ... discipline excellent'.[55]

'Kut' came to encompass a universe of suffering, both for the unfortunate troops locked within the bend of the river, and for the much larger force that for four desperate months struggled to break the siege at a cost in casualties several times larger than the besieged force. Conditions were no better for the Ottoman troops and their Arab and Kurdish auxiliaries besieging the town and holding off the relieving force. The sun beat down on all equally, and the microbes that brought dysentery afflicted guts regardless of origin. Ottoman medical arrangements were even more primitive than those of the British, but Tigris Force's medical outrages became the most notorious in British military history. Even before Kut's fall pressure had been mounting to investigate the conduct of the Mesopotamian campaign. Lord Charles Beresford, a retired admiral, described in the House of Lords successive British commanders in Mesopotamia as acting like losing gamblers – 'a plunger – when he loses one game, he tries another to win'.[56]

'Never since heard of': prisoners of war after Kut

Starved out, Kut fell after a siege of 146 days, the emaciated survivors of its garrison staggering out to face greater hardship and brutality than any British troops in history besides those enslaved by the Japanese a quarter-century later. The accounts gathered by the Parliamentary committee investigating the ordeal of prisoners of Kut managed to obtain what Lord Justice Younger described as 'a portion of the truth'.[57] It was a partial account, because British officers did not disclose how Khalil Pasha, Nureddin's superior, had at least attempted to exchange the survivors. The suffering and deaths of the Kut prisoners is therefore not only attributable to Ottoman mismanagement, incapacity, indifference and the active persecution by guards and their officers, but also because the British commanders who condemned them to battle and siege also failed to effect their exchange. However, some 1300 of the wounded of Kut were immediately exchanged, and another 345 a few months later. They included a Hampshire man who was discovered – but not recognised – by his brother.

The survivors were ordered to assembled at a 'camp' beside the Tigris – no more than a patch of bare river flat – and given nothing but hard, coarse Turkish biscuits. These some mashed in river water, and soon the first men died of gastro-enteritis (described as cholera). Turkish troops looted them of boots, clothes, food and valuables, which British officers could not prevent as they were soon separated, to be transported away in carts. Beginning on 5 May, their men

---

54 Mesopotamia Commission, p. 124
55 Wylly, *History of the Queen's Royal Regiment*, Vol. VII, p. 182
56 Lord Charles Beresford, House of Lords, *Hansard*, 30 March 1916
57 House of Commons, *Report on the Treatment of British Prisoners of War in Turkey*, No. 24, 1918, p. 3

had to march across the desert into captivity, to Baghdad and on to Mosul, Ras-al'Ain and Aleppo (steamers were unavailable, being used for Ottoman operations).[58] Soon, survivors of A Company of the 1/4th Hants became separated, 'scattered through the length and breadth of Asia Minor'.[59]

British officers assumed that the Ottoman Turks would be 'considerate', and that the Germans, the senior partners in the alliance, would be brutal. It was unlikely, a correspondent writing to the Allahabad *Pioneer* thought upon learning of the scale of the capitulation of Kut, 'that they will allow the Germans … to interfere and impose their brutal methods'.[60] In fact the prisoners' guards, many Kurdish or Arab, treated them abominably. At Ras al'Ain many were herded aboard railway trucks, though the journey on foot over the Amanus mountains was described as 'the worst of all'.[61] Of the 2600 British rank and file captured at Kut about two-thirds died, many before they reached prison camps in distant Anatolia. Many survived only through the aid of German and Austrians encountered on the road and the intervention of American diplomatic staff. They suffered along with the people of Anatolia the rigors of its climate and from the waves of epidemics that swept across the country.

A previously unpublished account by an American missionary who treated British prisoners who reached Tarsus, near Anatolia's southern coast, late in 1916, includes horrific testimony of the prisoners' condition on their journey to the camps in northern Anatolia. William Nute's report describes the arrival of 250 sick and starving men, treated 'worse than cattle, … cared for less than beasts', 120 of whom died soon after. Perhaps the most horrific paragraph in his 16-page report described their burials 'most crude … bodies were thrown into … holes' and then, to his distress, dug up and eaten by dogs.[62]

Captured officers were transported by carts and steamers. Though treated poorly they were spared the brutality, starvation and execution that became their men's lot. None (except Townshend) were treated as the 'honoured guests' of Ottoman rhetoric, but instead endured an ordeal unlike any previous British prisoners of war.[63] A British report on the treatment of prisoners of war noted 'violent inconsistencies'. At Afion officers were 'ruled with a cow-hide whip' while those at Broussa enjoyed 'practically hotel life'.[64] Officers were at times treated with 'almost theatrical politeness and consideration', while at other times with 'indifference and inertia … simple neglect and incompetence' often 'ruled by nothing but mere chance'.[65]

Very few managed to escape. One man of the 1/5th Hants battery escaped from a railway construction camp in northern Syria. After a strenuous month-long journey he reached the

---

58   Even those who condemned Ottoman 'barbarity', such as Dorina Neave, conceded that British commanders 'knew' that 'the Turks did not possess enough tents to make a camp for the garrison, nor had they sufficient transports to send them to Baghdad, and the men in their starved condition were far too weak to march out of Kut': Neave, *Remembering Kut*, p. 87
59   Anon, 'War-time Wanderings of the 1/4th Battalion, Hampshire Regiment', p. 32, M3910, RHRM
60   *Pioneer*, 5 May 1916
61   House of Commons, *Report on the Treatment of British Prisoners of War in Turkey*, No. 24, 1918, p. 10
62   'The Story of 3000 English and 10,000 East Indians …', P1282, Christie Family papers, Minnesota Historical Society Archives. I am grateful to Vicken Babkenian for alerting me to Nute's account.
63   Johnston & Yersley, *Four-Fifty Miles to Freedom*, p. 11
64   *Report on the Treatment of British Prisoners of War in Turkey*, House of Commons, No. 24, 1918, pp. 12; 14
65   Moberly, *The Campaign in Mesopotamia*, Vol. II, p. 460

British outpost line in northern Mesopotamia in October 1917 with long hair and a beard, looking like one of the emaciated Armenian refuges with whom he had travelled.[66] In August 1918 Lieutenant Frederick Ellis of the 1/4th Cornwall and Captain 'Perce' Harris of the 1/4th Hants were among a group of eight British officers to escape from Yozgad camp. They walked south over 300 miles of Anatolia in 36 days, stealing a boat to reach Cyprus. An account by two Regular officers implied that Ellis, the Cornish amateur, had been something of a nuisance: a noisy sleeper, losing kit; dislodging boulders that narrowly missed his comrades in the Taurus Mountains. But it was Ellis who found edible carob beans and scavenged food in deserted villages.[67]

The battalions which men had left as drafts of volunteers maintained an interest in those captured. In Aden the 1/4th Cornwall recorded a list of 19 of its men who had been captured at Kut (as members of the 2nd Dorset), the only document in its time in Aden important enough to be typed.[68] After her husband had died in the failed operations to relieve Kut, Esme Bowker dedicated herself to maintaining contact with the families of the 150-odd men of her husband's battalion who had gone into captivity. Her papers in the Hampshire Regiment's museum includes a sad list of men 'presumed to have been captured at Kut, but never since heard of', with names crossed out as she learned of their fate.[69] Details of a few men's fates slowly filtered to Winchester. In May 1919, Henry Forster, representing the War Office, gravely told the House of Commons that 155 Kut prisoners remained unaccounted for. They included Private Reginald Piper of the 1/4th Wilts, whose fate was raised in Parliament by Brigadier-General George Palmer, a Wiltshire Territorial now MP for Westbury in Wiltshire, Reginald's home town. He had volunteered to go to the Persian Gulf in 1915, posted to the 2nd Dorset.[70] Captured at Kut at the end of April 1916, he had, it seems, simply disappeared. It was perhaps some comfort to his family that Reginald's grave was later discovered in Mosul, where he had died on the last day of 1916. Captured Territorials' graves today lie as far from India as the lovely Haidar Pasha cemetery in Istanbul, far from Kut, but also from Westbury, Wiltshire.

---

66 *History of the Hampshire Territorial Force Association*, pp. 77-83
67 Johnston & Yersley, *Four-Fifty Miles to Freedom*, pp. 178, 190, 193, 194, 235
68 War diary, 1/4th Cornwall, June 1916, WO95/5438, NAUK
69 Prisoners of War notebook, Esme Bowker, M1830, RHRM
70 George Palmer; Henry Forster, House of Commons, *Hansard*, 29 May 1919

9

A Soldier's Life in India, 1916

If 1915 had been a year of becoming accustomed to India, in 1916 Territorials saw changes, not least in political and military command. They faced their second Kitchener's Test, their second summer and the consequences of changes in their status as soldiers of an empire at war.

'A high state of efficiency': Kitchener's Test again

Early in 1916 British battalions again faced Kitchener's Test, more exacting than the year before since it had become clear that if the demands on the frontier were to be met then Territorials might have to supplement the too few Regular battalions. The 1/9th Middlesex, now at Rawalpindi, marched to Nowshera, across the Indus and 90 miles closer to the frontier, over four hot, dusty days at the start of the hot weather. (In the 1/5th Hants, however, a cholera outbreak disrupted the tests.) Kitchener's Tests were taken seriously. When Owen Smith's 1/6th Hants took its 1916 test, near Ambala, they performed a mock attack on neighbouring Somersets, in the process getting (as he told his sister) 'tired & filthy dirty, dust in the Rifles & everywhere, it gets right into your boots, &c., you have no idea how dusty & dirty we get'.[1] The 1/6th East Surrey's report was again favourable:

> This battalion has reached a high state of efficiency under a capable commandant [sic]. The men are strong and active, quick movers in the fields [sic], well taught and well led.[2]

Owen Smith, who wrote long, chatty letters to his family, summed up his feelings about India in a letter marking the first anniversary of his arrival. He detailed his doings in the previous week – a smoke social in his corporals' mess, a battalion gaff, a film show, inter-company football, a Bible class, and a gymkhana at the Soldiers' Home. 'India is quite alright now', he concluded. '… there is a sort of nice feeling … plenty to do, plenty of fun …' now that the 'long, hot summer' had ended.[3] (Five months later, his mood had changed. Writing from the isolated

---

1 Letter, 27 February 1916, Owen Smith, 1/6th Hants, M766, RHRM
2 'The East Surrey Regiment in India 1914-19', ESR/10/14/3/1, SHC, Woking
3 Letter, 2 December 1915, Owen Smith, 1/6th Hants, M766, RHRM

A Soldier's Life in India, 1916   151

Company officers of the 2/5th Hants training at Chasma Tangi camp, Baluchistan. It was on these men that the efficiency and discipline of Territorial battalions principally depended. (M1535.1, Royal Hampshire Regiment Museum)

hill station of Solon, which had been left unoccupied for several years and was full of insects, he told his sister that 'I shall be thankfull when we return to England. I have had quite enough of Indian Soldiering' [sic]. It proved to be a temporary attack of homesickness, what he called 'the "Hump"'.[4]) As ever, the great fact of cantonment life was boredom. Leslie Nickalls described his time at Lucknow as 'monotonous ... nothing exciting or even interesting having occurred for many a day'.[5] Pay remained a grievance. In March 1916 the Bugle Major of the 2/5th Somerset composed a bugle march cheekily entitled 'We're hard up'.[6]

One sign of the Terriers' familiarity with India was that within months of arrival men began to acquire pets. They included monkeys and parrots, but at Fyzabad East Surrey men kept a crocodile in a bathtub – for a while. At Ambala the gunners of the 4th Sussex battery went through a craze of buying parakeets, and then puppies (until their major got wind of it). Men of the 1/4th Devon returned to Ferozepore at the end of their first hot weather in Pathankote and Dalhousie with a menagerie including half a dozen dogs, a bear, a civet and a monkey (which would ride around on the dogs' backs). The Brecknocks acquired a goat mascot (named Taffy of

4   Letters, 16 April and 12 May 1916, Owen Smith, 1/6th Hants, *Ibid*
5   Letter, 9 October 1916, Leslie Nickalls, 1/10th Middlesex, Great Chart Fund, Book 5, KA&HC
6   'Bugle marches by T.H. Hughes, Bugle Major, 2/5th Somerset, DD\SLI/19/6/5, SHC, Taunton

course), and a monkey called Jennie, while in Siberia the 1/9th Hants would adopt a bear named Chin, who ended up in a zoo in London.

The most popular animals were dogs. They became a fashion accessory when in 1915 Territorials, especially in hill stations, took to 'Dog and Stick walks' for exercise. But dogs could also be used to intimidate Indians, who (rightly) feared rabies: Reg Bailey's dog, Hector, 'simply delights in frightening the niggers', he told his family.[7] While fear of endemic rabies led to periodic purges, the popularity of pets overwhelmed even the strictures of *Standing Orders* – in the 2/4th Hants, the clause stipulating that animals not be allowed to sleep under verandas was eventually crossed out as unworkable. Numerous group photographs include dogs on knees or at feet. 'Our mascot' of the 1/4th Somerset, Bobby, adorns this book's cover.[8]

'Fine spirit of patriotism': Captain to Viceroy

1916 brought political change, though not the sort that Congress desired. While his term had been extended, Lord Hardinge had enjoyed mixed success as Viceroy. Surviving a nationalist assassination attempt (by a bomb in 1912) he had mobilised princely India in the war but had less success in charming educated nationalist opinion. He had endured personal tragedy when his wife died under a routine operation in 1914 and his son of wounds before the next Christmas. Of greater relevance to the Territorials was his failure to impose his will on the Commander-in-Chief, Sir Beauchamp Duff and presiding over the mismanagement and unnecessary enlargement of the growing Mesopotamian debacle. When he left Delhi at the end of March 1916 a guard of honour of Wiltshire Territorials lined Flagstaff Road. (Hardinge told the proud Wilts that they 'did as well as any regular soldiers', despite his misgivings in 1914.[9])

Hardinge's successor was Frederick Thesiger, Viscount Chelmsford; or Captain Chelmsford as he was addressed by his men in the 1/4th Devon. Anglo-Indian opinion praised his 'fine spirit of patriotism' for serving in such a junior rank.[10] Chelmsford's elevation to Viceroy in March 1916 was marked by parades and salutes all over India. Promotion from Territorial captain to the Viceroyalty says more about Chelmsford's social standing than it does for the political interest and influence of Territorial officers. The chronicler of Viceroys, Mark Bence-Jones, dismissed him as 'little more than a nonentity', but he took office at a crucial period in the history of British India.[11] He tended to the indecisive, relying too much on better informed subordinates (a legacy of his time in Australia, which had effective elected state governments). When he visited a remount depot to select horses in 1914 the foreman asked him if he knew anything about 'Walers' – horses imported from New South Wales. Chelmsford said he did, having spent five years in Australia. 'I never came across you,' the man replied, 'what was your job?' 'Governor', Chelmsford replied; a story that makes him sound much more wry than he was.[12]

---

7   Letter, 19 September 1918, Reg Bailey, 1/4th Buffs, 2011-12-3, NAM
8   Album 'India 1915-16', DD\SLI/15/7/83, SHC, Taunton
9   Mundy, *A Journal of the 1/4th Battalion Wiltshire Regiment*, p. 66
10 *Pioneer*, 22 January 1916
11 Bence-Jones, *The Viceroys of India*, p. 221
12 *Age* (Melbourne), 4 March 1916, p. 13

Chelmsford took office at a critical time in British India's political evolution, though he had little sympathy for Indian nationalists, even of the moderate Congress variety, taking for granted their support for the war. He defended press censorship (little more serious in wartime than in 1914) because a free press would 'play upon the weaknesses of impressionable boys' and he refused to countenance any relaxation for fear of 'a gradual increase of violence', though terrorist incidents declined during the war, from fewer than a dozen to a handful annually.[13] He sought to strengthen British India's relationship with the Indian princes, who had responded loyally to the empire's challenge in war, aware that they needed Britain as much as it needed them.

Though he had arrived in India as a Territorial, Chelmsford made little reference to his former comrades in his long and uninspiring speeches, but he knew the character of the force he had left. He recalled, with some exaggeration, that 'every one of those Territorials had someone at home to whom he had no scruples in writing if conditions were not ... up to the mark'. Chairing a lecture in London in 1928, Chelmsford recalled that in 1916 – before he became Viceroy – he heard that Army Headquarters planned to cut pay, a proposition he knew 'would have roused the very devil' among his men. Capitalising on his family connections, he wrote to the Commander-in-Chief (Beauchamp Duff) and told him 'if the order were not cancelled there would be trouble'. He heard a week later that the order had been issued 'by mistake'. His audience laughed knowingly.[14]

'There's a rankling in me heart': Terriers not at the front

Even early in 1915 Territorials realised that they might have unwittingly committed themselves to a long exile: a 2/5th Hants man published in *The Tiger* a sarcastic account of his battalion's return to Winchester in 1930, after 16 years absence in India, 'walking slowly & apparently in rag-time up Jewry Street amid the thunderous applause of its grand-children'.[15] Constantly referring to Kitchener's undertaking that they would return to fight the Germans once trained, men wasted no opportunity to remind the authorities. The program for a concert offered by men of the 1/5th Buffs at Kamptee early in 1915 included a mock advertisement:

> 'Ready for immediate use in Europe. Over 900 superbly trained and equipped men. Apply O.C. Troops, Kamptee.'[16]

Some twenty Territorial battalions were on the Western Front by December 1914, with the first Territorial divisions taking the brunt of the Loos offensive in September 1915, but no Territorials left India for France. Territorials wrote home informing MPs of Kitchener's undertaking, which was already being denied. In March 1915 when asked about 'any assurance or undertaking' being given to the 1/4th Wilts that it would be relieved once trained, the Under-Secretary for War simply denied that any undertaking had been given.[17]

---

13 Das, *India from Curzon to Nehru & after*, p. 58
14 *The Times*, 15 November 1928, p. 9
15 *Ibid*, March 1915, p. 9
16 *Kent Messenger*, 27 March 1915
17 Mr Harold Tennant, House of Commons, *Hansard*, 16 March 1915,

Men in India grappled with the fact that despite its hazards Indian service was nowhere as dangerous than fighting elsewhere. A Border man contributed a 'lament' to the *Border Gazette* in Maymyo in 1915. He began admitting that 'the Lakeland hills are calling' as were 'me missus and me kids', but regretted that 'I'm out in fuzzy Burma sweltering'. But though he enjoyed the exotic sights and the comradeship of his mates:

> Still behind it all there's a rankling in me heart a grievous sore,
> Why the Hades' when there's war on don't they send us to the war.
> For more men are wanted badly, and out here it's hard to tell
> Whether I'm really quite as useful as a snowball entering Hell …

Percy Wilkinson (pouring the beer) and his mates, a reminder of the robust male comradeship that the Territorials offered. (M830, Royal Hampshire Regiment Museum)

He protested that 'T'ain't that I'm a slacker really'.[18] It was a feeling shared by many Territorials, and most apparent from the clutch of letters written by men from Great Chart serving in the 1/5th Buffs in mid-1915, who repeatedly expressed their concern that they were not facing danger. 'We are certainly better off than the chaps at the front', Ernest Harding wrote home.[19] His brother, William, voiced 'our great desire' to go to the front, and explained that 'we are given to understand that our labours here are as useful as any'.[20] 'When we feel most like grumbling', William Brunger wrote from Kamptee to former neighbours, 'we have to think of our less fortunate comrades maimed and broken in the trenches'. 'We often wish we could stand shoulder to shoulder with them', Sergeant Brunger wrote.[21] Territorials received news of casualties at 'the front' in letters from families, newspapers posted from home and in regimental magazines. The Great Chart men had read the Buffs' magazine, *The War Dragon*, which published many pages in small type giving news of men from Kent who had been killed and wounded, mainly in France. The papers of a man of the regiment include clippings and in memoriam notices for men whom he knew who had been killed in France. The collection also includes letters from men in France commenting that the Buffs' were 'having a simply great time in India'.[22]

18 Clipping, Captain Lawrence Hoggarth, 1/4th Border, Album 35 Acc. Nos 3024-3345, CMML
19 Letter, [mid-1915] Ernest Harding, 1/5th Buffs, Great Chart Fund, Book 5, KA&HC
20 Letter, 5 August 1915, William Harding, 1/5th Buffs, *Ibid*
21 Letter, 8 July 1915, William Brunger, 1/5th Buffs, *Ibid*
22 H.B. Watson, 1/6th Buffs, Doc.13205, 13/8/1, IWM

Many Territorials came to realise how fortunate they had been, especially perhaps the junior officers on whom the cost of the war fell so disproportionately. Olaf Caroe, 22 in 1914, reflected how 'most of my friends and contemporaries fell on the Somme, around Ypres, or in Gallipoli or Mesopotamia, and some who did not fall lost their balance and equanimity'.[23] The Western Front, the theatre in which its outcome would be decided, was far away. The same communiqués and reports appeared in British Indian newspapers as at home – also heavily censored and always positively slanted – but the war seemed remote.

Territorials gradually realised that their faith in what they thought of as 'Kitchener's promise' might have been misplaced. 'Our chances may come', William Mannering wrote, to take 'a more active part in this titanic struggle … though it seems doubtful'.[24] When the 1/4th Border arrived in Maymyo, Burma – the most distant station to which Territorials were at first sent, they were inspected by Burma's lieutenant-governor. He welcomed them to Burma, commended their patriotism and said that he hoped that they would reach the front 'if the war lasted long enough'.[25] It was perhaps their first inkling that they might not see action against Germans. Indeed, the 1/4th Border never would. One part of Kitchener's promise was fulfilled. He had assured Colin Donald that he would be allowed to return from India after he had visited every unit. Donald spent five months and 20,000 miles travelling around India by the time he had visited them all.

Territorials continued to hope that Kitchener would honour what most saw as a bargain and allow them, or 'some of us at any rate', as Francis Bowker wrote to his wife, Esme, 'to get a show in the Big Business before the war is over'. He and other Territorial colonels lobbied to have 'some of K's latest raised Battalions' replace them.[26] Meeting senior officers and officials while recuperating in Poona, Bowker learned that 'there is *no* intention of sending any Territorials home'.[27]

Kitchener never had the chance to make good his undertaking. On 5 June 1916 he died when the cruiser, HMS *Hampshire*, taking him to Russia, hit a mine off the Orkney Islands. At Solon, Owen Smith and some friends, waiting for a dance to begin at the sergeants' mess, watched a man hoisting a union flag. They speculated that it boded good news – 'Peace proclaimed, perhaps' – but it was hoisted and then lowered to half mast. The dance was cancelled.[28] Territorial units all over India held parades to mark the passing of the man whose orders had caused them to be in India in the first place and whose promise was, as one who arrived in 1914 and served in Mesopotamia ruefully realised was 'rash', but also undeniably effective.[29] (Ironically, while Kitchener never fulfilled his celebrated 'pledge' he 'never tired' – so an admiring biographer claimed – of extolling the Territorials' 'splendid response' in volunteering for India.[30])

---

23 Caroe, 'The Flames of Enchantment', p. 6, PP/MCR/207, IWM
24 Letter, 23 July 1915, William Mannering, 1/5th Buffs, Great Chart Fund, Book 5, KA&HC
25 Clipping, Lawrence Hoggarth, 1/4th Border, Album 35 Acc. Nos 3024-3345, CMML
26 Letters, 2 April & 21 June 1915, Francis Bowker, 1/4th Hants, Doc. 8094, 99/15/1, IWM
27 Letter, 21 August 1915, Francis Bowker, 1/4th Hants, *Ibid*
28 Letter, 12 June 1916, Owen Smith, 1/6th Hants, M766, RHRM
29 'Efack' in *Bombay Chronicle*, 13 March 1919
30 Arthur, *Life of Lord Kitchener*, Vol. III, p. 310

'A new driver': Monro as Commander-in-Chief

One of the greatest changes, from October 1916, was that a new Commander-in-Chief arrived. Sir Charles Monro had already retrieved one imperial debacle by presiding over the evacuation of Gallipoli and was now to invigorate the army in India. A former West Surrey officer, he had served competently in India (on the north-west frontier in 1897-98), and in South Africa. He had commanded the Territorial 2nd London Division before the war and on the Western Front demonstrated the required tenacity in divisional, corps and army command. Monro reluctantly accepted Haig's direction to go to India his latest biographer described it as 'a severe personal blow' he had nursed hopes of higher command in the theatre that mattered.[31] Monro offered a profound contrast to his predecessor, Duff. Soon after his arrival officers at least realised that 'a different driver … was handling the reins'.[32] The first sign was that officers at Army Headquarters, still at Simla for the summer, were required to wear khaki service dress Duff had allowed peacetime blue patrol dress and mess dress to continue. Duff, though extended in his command by several months, could not escape the opprobrium of the Mesopotamian debacle. Summoned to London to testify at the inquiry into the extent and cause of the command failings, he was replaced. The commission revealed his inadequacies as Commander-in-Chief; he fell into alcoholism and in January 1918 he killed himself.

Monro displayed a notable energy in managing the immense responsibility of the Indian command. His black memoranda books are filled with hundreds of firm demands, requests, instructions and desiderata, almost all with the annotation (in red or blue pencil) 'This has been done' or 'Dealt with' in his appalling hand-writing – 762 of them for the first year of his command, another 1400 for the rest of the war. Monro's style was direct, but, almost inevitably given the centralising nature of Indian command, unduly personal and far too specific: 'it must be decided what Barracks at Rawal Pindi should be selected as Hospital in case of necessity'. Monro, far more than Duff, got out to visit his troops, British and Indian. He recorded chats in hospitals with soldiers from Winchester and Hythe, both almost certainly Territorials. One of Monro's innovations was to sponsor 'Monro Canteens' at railway stations all over India, and especially in the north-west. Staffed by volunteer memsahibs (uniformed, strictly disciplined and charged for the food they ate) the canteens served a range of hearty meals (almost entirely British, with only 'curry, rice and dhal' for any with a taste for Indian food) at no more than four annas apiece.[33]

As they gained in experience Territorials began to gauge the personalities of senior officers whom they either never saw or saw only briefly at inspections. While he was noted for getting out among the troops, the 1/4th Wilts only saw Monro at formal parades in Delhi and later at Kirkee, and was then unpopular because of 'his everlasting fads re dressing, saluting and walking out'.[34] Later in 1916, though, Monro spoke to newly-arrived men of the 1/9th Hants, creating a favourable impression, even though disappointing their hopes of seeing active service overseas or on the frontier. Inspections, however, were frequent, especially in the cooler weather – the 1/5th Hants was inspected three times, by the Commander-in-Chief, the commander of the Northern Army and the divisional commander, at Agra during Christmas week 1917.

---

31   Crowley, *Loyal to the Empire*, p. 252
32   Barrow, *The Life of General Sir Charles Carmichael Monro*, pp. 123-24
33   Monro Canteens regulations and price lists, Monro papers, Mss.Eur.D783/9, BL
34   Mundy, *A Journal of the 1/4th Battalion Wilshire Regiment*, p. 113

Having commanded a London Territorial division before the war, Monro especially welcomed the 1/25th London to his house at Simla.

Monro had absorbed the lessons the war had imposed. The *Memorandum on Army Training in India, 1916-1917* reflected his desire that the Army in India implement the changes forced upon British forces so painfully in the war's first three years. It laid down changes to individual and collective training, stressing the need to adapt traditional syllibi to the technological and tactical changes the war had brought. Monro saw the Army in India as part of an imperial war.

'Draft wallahs': the 1916 Military Service Act

For the first two years of war Territorials retained their pre-war conditions of service. Men who had joined the Territorial Force before 1911 faced the profound question of whether to re-enlist. In the 2/6th Devon, one of the few units for which a complete accounting survives, about 95 men went home as time expired between May 1915 and November 1916; a tenth of the battalion. In other units, time-expired men chose to remain with their comrades. By the time the Territorials had been in India for about a year perhaps 1500 men – the equivalent of two battalions – had been lost because men insisted on taking their discharges in the war's first years.[35] Some of these men returned to India. Wiltshire men farewelled as time-expired in April 1916 were seen returning in August, having been called up again and posted to India as members of the 2/4th Dorset.[36]

Despite his disaffection with his officers and his dislike of India, Hugh Creek actually signed on again, explaining to his no doubt perplexed parents, who had been anguished by his pessimistic letters home, that he felt it 'only right that everyone should give government the least trouble … and sacrifice private ambitions for public welfare'.[37] But other men made different decisions. By late 1915, Leslie Nickalls told his erstwhile neighbours in Great Chart, 'a fair number of our men have sailed for home' as what was called 'TX' – time-expired.[38] In order to halt this drain Indian military authorities reached an arrangement with the War Office allowing Territorials re-engaging for the duration to serve 'at home or in France' – but only 'as soon as he can be spared'.[39]

For as long as voluntary enlistment remained possible (until early 1916) British men faced the decision whether to enlist. Territorial Associations and units competed for volunteers with Kitchener units and Regular recruiting parties. One of the means used to induce men to enlist was posters, plastered on walls and hoardings. In Shropshire recruiters appealed to men using large, colourful posters, asking questions many found hard to answer:

> What will you lack when your mate goes by with a girl that cuts you dead?
>   What would men tell their children, they asked: 'Where will you look when they give you a glance that tells you they know you FUNKED?[40]

---

35 Telegram, 7 November 1915, Tel H-8990, Viceroy (Army Department) to Secretary of State, WWI/153/H, War diary, Army Headquarters, India, Vol. 22, NAI
36 Gale, *With the 2/4th Wilts to India*, pp. 56; 59
37 Letter, 15 September 1915, Hugh Creek, 1/4th Devon, EX2543, DMM
38 Letter, 8 November 1915, Leslie Nickalls, 1/10th Middlesex, Great Chart Fund, Book 5, KA&HC
39 Part 1 orders, 2/4th Somerset Light Infantry, March 1916, DD\SLI/6/36, SHC, Taunton
40 King's Shropshire Light Infantry recruiting poster, 1915, 3614/2/166, SA

The 1916 *Military Service Act* changed that, obliging Territorials to serve for the duration. It also meant that thereafter few reinforcements arrived in India voluntarily. Under the Derby scheme (introduced early in 1916, essentially stopping just short of compulsion) 'Derby men' reached India from mid-year. While many hailed from the same county as the Territorial units they joined, they often came from different recruiting areas within the county. (So the 1/4th West Kent received men from the 1/5th's.[41]) Jim Mackie found the Derby men arriving in the 2/4th Somerset 'perfectly hopeless … volunteers in name but they certainly act as if they were conscripts'.[42] They lacked the earlier Territorials' keenness, reluctantly playing games.

Continual losses (as drafts to 'Mespot', men leaving as 'specialists', as 'time-expired', to be commissioned, going sick or – a few – dead) left all battalions under-strength. The 1/7th Hants provided an accounting of the 769 men – just over half of those who had passed through the battalion in the four years it had served in India by January 1918:

Drafts to the Persian Gulf	213
To Machine Gun Corps	38
To Garrison Battalion (Bedfords)	42
NCOs and men granted commissions	30
Remained at Depot, Ambala	266
To Signal Service	66
To Supply and Transport Corps	24
Died, Discharged, Time-expired Despatch Riders, Searchlight Company, Telegraphists, RAF, Hospital orderlies, etc.	90[43]

Reinforcements for the troops in India continued to arrive, though infrequently, and in large drafts. Threatened by German submarines, they travelled on troopships and transports either escorted through the Mediterranean or sailing on the longer but safer route around Africa. The largest single contingents to arrive in 1916 were the four former cyclist battalions (their only bicycles the ones on their cap badges). They travelled from Bombay to Bangalore and during the long journey (three days and two nights) 'our eyes and mouths opening wider and wider with astonishment'. Harry Oke, drum major of the 1/25th London, told his parents that 'India is just as I had pictured it', quoting Kipling.[44]

In 1914 the Territorial force included thirteen cyclist battalions, the embodiment of Haldane's plan for what even his opponents sought: 'an efficient Army for Home Defence'.[45] That was exactly the cyclist battalions' task for the first two years of the war, even though the 1/1st Kent Cyclists had volunteered for overseas service in September 1914. Cyclist battalions patrolled stretches of the south and east coasts, vigilant against raids which were never going to come – the 1/9th Hants in Sussex, the 2/6th Royal Sussex in East Anglia. At last, it became clear that

---

41 *The Queen's Own Gazette*, Vol. XXXV, No. 8, August 1916, p. 3533
42 Letter, 20 October 1916, Jim Mackie, 2/4th Somerset, Mackie, *Answering the Call*, pp. 207-08
43 *History of the Hampshire Territorial Force Association*, p. 163
44 Letter, 1916, Harry Oke, 1/25th London, 2004-05-43, NAM
45 Spiers, *Haldane: an Army Reformer*, p. 168

they could be used overseas and in November 1915 they lost their cycles. The cyclists had been considered (and even equipped) for East Africa, Egypt or France, but in February 1916 the four battalions (the 1/9th Hants, 1/1st Kent, 2/6th Royal Sussex and 1/25th London) became the last four Territorial battalions to reach India.

As the transport *Berrima* travelled across the Indian Ocean in April 1916 its passengers doubtless anticipated their arrival in the east, mounting a performance of 'Aladdin and the Magic Lamp', inspired by tales of the Arabian Nights. Within a year some would actually be in Baghdad. They were certainly as closely packed as Ali Baba's men in the oil jars in the celebrated story – the ship had been built to carry 600 passengers but 1800 soldiers were crammed in. These men often manifest lower physical standards. Len Bithel, who reached the 2/4th Wilts in March 1917, admitted that he had expected to go to France but was found 'unfit after three examinations', and so was posted to India.[46] Jim Mackie reported that the 2/4th Somerset received drafts in 1916 including boys as young as fifteen, though it is hard to credit it. Though 'keen as mustard' they naturally found the climate trying and many succumbed to heatstroke.[47] Some of these men fell victim to the Sind Troop Train Tragedy.

'On the absence of crime': discipline

British soldiers meant two things when they talked of 'discipline'. First, they meant bearing: whether a man, or his unit, was 'smart'; neat, clean and correct in uniform, precise in marching and drill, punctilious in 'rendering compliments' (saluting) and deferential to all superiors, from lance-corporals to lieutenant-generals: in short, whether they behaved in 'soldier-like' manner.[48] This standard Territorials achieved variably. While many officers and sergeants took Regulars as their model and instruction manuals and drill books as their texts, not all Territorials attempted or achieved 'Regular' standards of dress and turn-out. This did not prevent battalion orders or sergeants-major insisting on it. Arthur Copeland reflected on how 'luck has a great deal to do with not getting "run" for trivial offences. He instanced a recent order to wear stocking tops with a double-fold to a depth of four inches, a matter of smartness rather than comfort or utility.[49]

'Discipline' also meant the way they observed, or did not observe, the complex and exacting standards of behaviour expected of British soldiers, and it could be measured, if the evidence were preserved, by the number of men placed on charges or convicted of military offences. (Note that statistics of offences and had no necessary relation to morality: many offences under military law had no counterparts in civil life – insolence, for example, or failure to attend church parade reflected men's subordination, not their ethics.) The evidence is also largely lacking, both absolutely and comparatively.

---

46 Diary, 6 January 1917, Lionel Bithel, 2/4th Wilts, SBYRW 1999 RBWM
47 Letter, 26 May 1916, Jim Mackie, 2/4th Somerset, Mackie, *Answering the Call*, p. 174
48 A paragraph on saluting (number 258) from the *Standing Orders of The Brecknockshire Battalion* makes the point: 'When riding a Bicycle the handlebars will not be released [but] the head and eyes will be turned towards the Officer and the rider will free wheel'.
49 Diary, 25 January 1917, Arthur Copeland, 1/5th Hants, 128A08/1-4, HRO

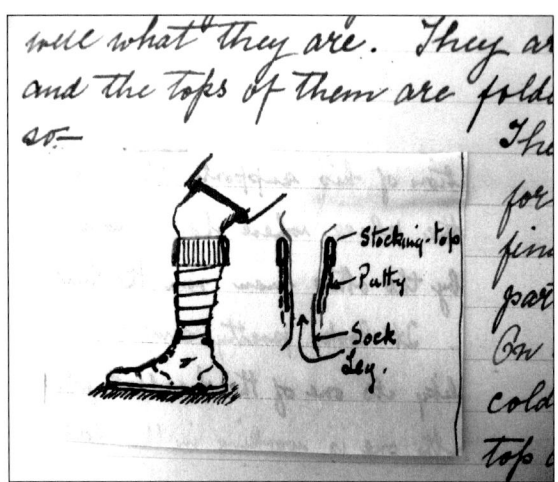

Arthur Copeland's exasperated drawing, showing the exact arrangement of hose-top and puttee as stipulated in the 1/5th Hants. (128A08, Hampshire Record Office)

Military discipline had been unexacting for Territorials in peacetime, largely a matter of enforcing uniform regulations and policing men's attendance at drills and camps. In wartime, an East Surrey officer claimed, 'after the first few weeks they all realised what strict military discipline entailed', but Territorials' discipline was never as rigorous as Regulars', or even as Kitchener units trained by Regular officers and sergeants.[50] Military discipline was often petty and harassing – Herbert Peake received three days 'CB' – confined to barracks – for a 'dirty' bayonet scabbard (and 'dirty' was a comparative term, meaning 'not clean enough'). In India the army's expectations became sharper, exposing men to the direction of sergeants and officers who were often no more experienced in administering discipline than they were in obeying it. The processes of military justice deterred – and was intended to deter – men from protesting against their superiors' decisions, something that Territorials, still influenced by civilian notions of negotiation, at first did. At Kamptee Private 'Pym' Vyner of the 1/5th Buffs found himself on a charge of missing a parade. He was marched 'as a prisoner' before his company commander. He successfully contested the charge, arguing that as he had been on duty as an orderly he was excused parades. His boldness excused six other men facing the same charge, 'so I am quite the hero', he told his family in Maidstone.[51]

Soldiers were always subject to scrutiny. For example, conscious of the need to demonstrate regimental identity, every unit adopted a 'flash' – a coloured cloth badge, as many units had during the South African war. Usually worn on the left side of the sun helmet, it might include the regiment's badge, symbol, name or initials (for example, the West Kent displayed the regiment's white horse on a black lozenge, with 'KENT' in red below it, the Wiltshire a large green cloth cross, a stylized version of its cap badge) and attracted an 'intensity of feeling … an unsoldierlike civilian cannot be expected to appreciate'.[52] But the disciplinary aspect of this device was that a man caught 'out of bounds', say, but clad only in 'greyback' shirt and shorts could still be identified as belonging to a particular unit by his helmet flash. Like any community, soldiers largely policed themselves. Bungalows and platoons were often effectively regulated by their own members, often older men, whether sergeants or corporals or not. Don Stevenson described the men of his platoon of the 1/5th Hants as 'quite a decent lot' and while 'there are of course

50 'The East Surrey Regiment in India 1914-19', ESR/10/14/3/1, SHC, Woking
51 *Kent Messenger*, 17 April 1915
52 Victor Manley, 'A Khaki Diary', p. 442, 49M91W/Q3/6, HRO. See the photographs of George and Harry Andrews on page 31, of men of the 1/4th Border on page 109 and of the 1/4th Cornwall orderly room staff on page 176 for examples of flashes.

always rotters in every platoon', he explained to his father, he only had one or two, and they were 'sat on by the rest of the platoon'.[53]

It is important to stress is how rare crime actually was in Territorial battalions. The 1/4th Wilts is said to have held not one court martial in its entire time in India.[54] Likewise, despite being posted back and forth in 1917 the 2/4th Dorset recorded not a single case of indiscipline or even drunkenness while in Bombay in April-May. The General Officer Commanding praised its 'exemplary conduct in a city like Bombay', with troops more open to temptation that an isolated cantonment.[55] Several substantial runs of routine orders (from the 2/6th Royal Sussex, 2/4th Border and 1/6th and 2/6th Devon) offer indications that Territorial battalions manifest little 'crime', even in the particular way the army defined it. (The figures are slippery: even an unusually strict battalion, as the 2/6th Royal Sussex seems to have been, did not mean it was necessarily more badly behaved than a battalion with a less exacting standards.)

These routine orders suggest some tentative conclusions. In ten months in 1915 the 1/6th Devon saw only eighteen offences worth recording in battalion routine orders (minor offences coming before company commanders went unrecorded). They all attracted periods of detention, averaging three-and-a-half days, and the most common offences were for defying authority (insubordination, insolence, refusing to obey an order).[56] The 2/6th Devon imposed a harsher disciplinary regime. In eleven months in 1916 it saw 19 regimental sentences (most comprising both days of detention and days of pay forfeited) but also sent two men to District Courts Martial. Defiance figured only in half a dozen charges, and most involved men going absent, breaking out of barracks or neglect of duty. The heaviest sentences in the 2/6th (84 days detention and heavy 'stoppages' to make good kit lost) were for attempted desertion, which seem not to have been serious attempts to actually desert.[57] In the 2/6th Royal Sussex the largest group of offences related to what the army called 'insubordination'. Samples of its battalion orders disclose that it often saw an unusually large number of such offences: 'non-compliance with an order', 'improper language to an NCO', 'insolence' (to both NCOs and officers), not complying with an order'. These offences, which each gained an average of about a week's detention, suggest that even after several years some Territorial soldiers continued to answer back, tell officers or sergeants what they thought and generally resist the army's demand for subordination.

Drinking, which traditionally contributed to indiscipline, was rarely a problem. Officers who knew Regulars were often pleasantly surprised by how temperate Territorial units were. Officers of the 2/4th Dorset agreed that it was 'a noteworthy fact that the Territorial Army in India was not addicted to drunkenness'.[58] But the judgment varied between battalions, and depending upon a man's conception of what constituted drunkenness. Harry Canham, a Wesleyan teetotaller, thought that it was 'rife' in the 2/4th Border.[59] Other battalions certainly gained a reputation for temperance. At a New Year's 'smoking concert' at Quetta 'a great number were

---

53 Letter, 22 October 1915, Don Stevenson, 1/5th Hants, Doc. 1383, 87/18/1, IWM
54 Sanders, *Trowbridge Roll of Honour*, p. 22
55 Regimental History Committee, *History of the Dorsetshire Regiment 1914-1919*, Part II, p. 73
56 Routine orders, 1/6th Devon, 1915, EX1219, DMM
57 Routine orders, 2/6th Devon, 1916, EX1213, DMM
58 Regimental History Committee, *History of the Dorsetshire Regiment 1914-1919*, Part II, p. 73
59 Letter, 4 January 1917, Harry Canham, 2/4th Border, CMML

abstainers' from the beer (and cigarettes) available free.[60] Indeed, the 2/4th Hants appear to have had the largest proportion of men join the Royal Army Temperance Association – over 400; about half its strength, 'and more are joining every day'.[61] Most units and stations had a Temperance Association branch, which regimental and staff officers recognised did much to help keep men from the consequences of over-indulgence. Though some branches only accepted teetotallers: moderate drinkers could join as 'full' members (the irony unintended). The Temperance Association offered coffee shops and recreation rooms, venues which took men away from wet canteens, but not as earnestly evangelical as Soldiers' Homes, even awarding medallions charting the duration of men's sobriety.

Some men certainly tried their officers' patience. In the 2/6th Devon 2439 Private Brown seems to have had an unusually poor record. In the first six months of 1916 he was charged four times, for 'disrespectful language', attempting to desert (selling his kit to gain money to do so), refusing to salute an officer and then 'wilful defiance'. He spent over 130 days in detention over the six months. But Private Brown was unusual.

While Regular officers may have deprecated the 'amateurs'' shortcomings, everyone agreed that generally Territorials' transgressions were relatively benign – occasional 'drunkenness', 'neglect of duty', absence from a parade or urinating outside the wet canteen, but few of them. More serious offences such as rape were almost unknown: where sex was so cheap sexual assault was effectively commercialised. Other battalions' routine orders confirm this impression: that offences were relatively rare (fewer than twenty for units totalling over 750 men over the course of a year) and minor, such as 'men have been seen throwing stones at ... young mangoes'.[62] As a quip in *The Tiger* put it, 'he put in his thumb and pulled out a plumb and said – see Battalion Order on the absence of crime'.[63]

'The most moral set of young men': Sex

Cantonment society was overwhelmingly male. Territorials particularly missed the company of what they called 'white ladies' – Geoffrey Coombs told his former school-mate, Lillian, that he had spoken to only two in two years (though for one of those years the 1/4th Buffs had been in Aden).[64] Several Territorials' letters lament never seeing European women. A subaltern of the 2/4th Border on the Mohmand blockade line in 1918 complained that 'I haven't seen a girl (i.e. a white girl) for 3 years', followed by no fewer than eleven exclamation marks.[65] What a Surrey man described as the 'lamentable absence of ladies' led to the widespread jocular phenomenon of female impersonation, documented in many photograph albums. In their Punjab fort on the first anniversary of the war's outbreak, for example, after a football match, singing and

60 *The Tiger*, March 1915, p. 4
61 *The Tiger*, March 1915, p. 12
62 Routine orders, 2/4th Somerset, 17 April 1916, DD\SLI/6/36, SHC, Taunton. The routine orders for the 2/6th Royal Sussex substantiate the impression, with 8 out of 22 in 1916 for defiance of one kind or another: RSR/MSS/ 6/9, WSRO.
63 *The Tiger*, September 1915, p. 1
64 Letter, 21 March 1916, Geoffrey Coombs, 1/4th Buffs, EK/U127/2, KH&AC
65 Letter, 28 November 1918, H.S. Priestley, 2/4th Border, Doc 16482, 08/96/1, IWM

speech-making competitions, the detachment of the 1/5th Hants held a 'beauty competition'. The winner was a private 'made up as an English flapper', wearing a skirt made from a bed-sheet, his wig a coir mat. 'Anything remotely resembling an English girl now knocks us clean off our balance', *Punch's* Hampshire clerk admitted.[66]

'Women' meant for most troops Indians or Eurasians, but guidebooks, their officers, medical officers and chaplains all warned them 'Don't talk to the black women'.[67] But most 'native women, subject universally to patriarchal traditional societies, had neither desire nor opportunity to mingle with British soldiers. Henry Brain noted in his memoir how women would run in fear from soldiers, whether justified or not. Literally unapproachable, as men's photographs attest, they exerted an exotic attraction.

Soldiers in India, a clergyman who knew them observed, led 'an unnatural and, in a sense, unhealthy life'. They were 'separated from all decent women of their own class, without home life and without privacy'.[68] The anonymous author of *Our Indian Empire* counselled, elliptically and probably unavailingly, that lust would damage men's health, without specifying exactly how. 'The man who runs after women is not,' he warned '… the sort who goes out for sport'.[69] But 'the sort' was common. Sir Cuthbert Sprawson (who had had medical charge of a brothel for British troops at Jhansi around 1905) expressed the conventional wisdom, that 'when a body of healthy young men are … far away from their homes and from refined feminine influence, the care of their sexual morality, particularly in a warm country, is always a difficult matter'.[70]

British evangelical organisations in India strove against what the YMCA called the 'fearful and fiery temptations of the different moral atmosphere of the East'.[71] Temptation and opportunity lay in every sudder bazaar. India was a country where women could literally be bought, and it was assumed that British soldiers would want to use Indian women for sex. When William Bisset asked a gharry driver to take him to Karachi's 'big bazaar' the man either misheard him or assumed he meant the 'Bibbie Bazaar' and took him to the brothel quarter.[72] When Joe Cox paid a man to allow him to photograph a naked 'young girl' near the Taj Mahal ('posing perfectly innocently') the girl 'thought we had bought her'.[73] While station commanders claimed that men contacted infection while on leave elsewhere, practically every cantonment had a 'tolerated brothel', run by Indian contractors whose employees were registered and inspected in an attempt to reduce rates of infection.

Every city and cantonment had its brothel quarter, in which hundreds if not thousands of Territorials lost their virginity. Presumably the conducting parties of Regulars told Territorials about, for example, Rangoon's streets of brothels, many with Japanese prostitutes notable for their cleanliness. One of Rangoon's several cinemas also offered a playhouse in which, Bert Rendall remembered, 'Burmese girls would come and dance, stark naked'. 'For a little bit extra you could go out the back when the show was over'. In Shwebo Rendall actually encountered a

66 'A Territorial in India', *Punch*, 15 September 1915, p. 226
67 Herbert Jones, 7th North Stafford, Doc 7306, 76/111-112/1, IWM
68 Wright, *Priest and Parish in India*, p. 119
69 Sturt, *Our Indian Empire*, pp. 77; 128
70 Cuthbert Sprawson '37 Years in the I.M.S.', pp. 45-46, LHCMA
71 *Age* (Melbourne), 7 January 1916, p. 7
72 Diary, 15 October 1915, William Bisset, 2/4th Hants, M1834, RHRM
73 Cox, *An Ordinary Working Man's Life Story*, p. 38

Burmese prostitute who propositioned him by quoting a line from Kipling's 'Road to Mandalay' ('Come ye back ye British soldier ...'[74]) As a result, Burmese stations regularly made up a third of the fifteen with the highest rates of VD.[75]

Ted Rice described a brothel in the sudder bazaar at Fyzabad, a mud-walled building with tiny windows and half-a-dozen cubicles lit by paraffin lamps, in of which stood a charpoy. Women smelling strongly of coconut oil could be had for 6 annas a time – the price of three pints of local beer or a meal. A West Surrey medical officer advised men to use the women in the brothel because he regularly inspected them. 'If you must indulge,' he said, 'use the proper place' known to the troops as the Bull Ring.[76] A brothel (or 'chakla') might have twenty to thirty women under several older women, themselves former prostitutes, living in a compound in the station's sudder bazaar, along with their children. Prostitutes in some large stations were not only Indian, but (at Ambala in 1916, for example,) included Japanese, Armenians and 'Jewesses'.[77] Large cities, such as Madras or Bombay, had recognised brothel quarters – off Mount Road and Grant Road respectively. (Madras's police had supposedly evicted European prostitutes just before the war, but they probably remained, receiving officers surreptitiously in several hotels.[78]) Policing chaklas as station or unit police (identified by an arm band and armed only with a wooden truncheon), as did Ted Holter at Dalhousie, was 'the worst duty of the lot', and he managed to get out of it after a fortnight.[79] The teenaged Edward Read of the 1/6th had a similar duty as a battalion policeman at Agra in 1915 – 'what a job!' he wrote, unhelpfully ambiguous.[80]

Territorials did not necessarily behave as their Regular counterparts had and did. As the Wessex and Home Counties Territorials embarked for India Sir Ian Hamilton, having inspected their units and read reports on them, told the Adjutant-General that Territorials were 'probably the most moral set of young men who have ever been collected together in large numbers in this Kingdom'.[81] Ministers and welfare workers tried to ensure that they that they would remain so. They put their efforts into exhortation – sermons encouraging men to remain 'pure' – and into what the YMCA called 'prevention by preoccupation' – games, entertainment and recreation facilities in the hope of defeating the boredom that often led men to the wet canteen and the sudder bazaar.[82] Despite this, there was always, as Gerald Bonham-Carter wrote of Bangalore to his sister, 'much degrading temptation'.[83]

As their rates of venereal infection show, Terriers certainly visited brothels. The first issue of *The Border Gazette*, a chirpy newsletter produced by energetic subalterns of the 1/4th Border in Maymyo, contained a 'Things we want to know' column, full of in-jokes about the battalion's personalities and incidents. It includes the line: 'Whether anyone has got any souvenirs of Grant

---

74 Interview with Bert Rendall, Mills, *A Strange War*, pp. 43-44; 48
75 'General Report and Statistics of Venereal Diseases Amongst British Troops in India' [1919], p. 26, L/MIL/7/13393, BL
76 Ted Rice, 'All for a Shilling a Day', QRWS/30/RICE/1, SHC, Woking
77 Wood, *Milestones of Memory*, p. 137
78 Raj, 'Studies in the History of Prostitution in Tamilnadu', PhD, pp. 126; 160-68
79 Ted Holter, 'A Terrier in World War I', Doc 4545, 81/9/1, IWM
80 Edward Read, 'Hampshire to the Himalayas', p. 2, M1798, RHRM
81 Letter, 4 November 1914, Hamilton papers, 6/4, LHCMA
82 *Age* (Melbourne), 7 January 1916, p. 7
83 Letter, 14 April 1918, Gerald Bonham-Carter, 1/5th West Kent, 94M72/F305, HRO

Street [sic]'.[84] The battalion had spent a day in Bombay before beginning its long journey to Burma. Whether any man had the initiative or opportunity to visit a brothel on his first day in India seems unlikely, but it hints at the perennial connection between soldiers and prostitutes, and that Territorials were no exception. The Territorials' rates of infection were at first, however, much lower than the Regulars' had been. Before the Territorials' arrival the average rate of infection had been 5.5%; in 1915 2.9%, a fall ascribed to Territorials being 'of higher social standing and education', with more married men.[85] Each year during the war, however, the rate rose – to 5.2% in 1917 and 8.7 in 1919.[86]

Medical officers and clergymen attempted either to deter men from visiting brothels, or to deal with the medical consequences. They contested deeply entrenched notions. Many soldiers (and officers and medical officers) believed, for example, that

> If you want to be thoroughly fit you must go with women …
> … every man must expect to have venereal disease at some time
> … a man's desires were given to him to be satisfied whenever he likes
> … venereal disease may do a man no real harm.[87]

In fact, venereal diseases did great harm. The prevailing treatment, intravenous injections of the newly devised synthetic drug Salvarsan (Arsphenamine) or intra-muscular injections of mercury, suppressed symptoms but did not necessarily cure the condition, and many men returned home to infect their wives and children, leading to blindness and other complications years later.

Stations cinemas became part of the campaign against VD. The Napier Cinema in Poona screened *The Warfare of the Flesh*, a Dutch film reminding men of the perils of sex; though its veiled eroticism may have exacerbated the problem medical officers and ministers sought to solve.[88] Those who devised and maintained the system reasoned, realistically, that men would have sex with prostitutes, and that ensuring that they were 'clean' was preferable to men using 'sand rats', or uncontrolled women. Many stations had prophylactic stations at which men could wash their genitals after sex – Joe Cox described how the cantonment at Cannanore, like practically all large stations, had an 'ablutions room'. It was usually contrary to *Standing Orders* to either conceal, not report or self-medicate any infectious disease. Clerical opponents of this approach argued that even offering prophylaxis signalled to a man that 'he was expected to sin and might do so with impunity'.[89]

The highest admissions relative to strength came from the big port cities (Bombay, Karachi and Calcutta) which, the authorities admitted, were 'out of control'.[90] The most heavily infected

---

84 Clipping, Lawrence Hoggarth, 1/4th Border, Album 35 Acc. Nos 3024-3345, CMML
85 'Note by the Medical Adviser', [Sir Richard Havelock Charles, 1921], L/MIL/7/13393, BL
86 'General Report and Statistics of Venereal Diseases Amongst British Troops in India' [1919], p. 1, L/MIL/7/13393, BL
87 Wright, *Priest and Parish in India*, p. 119
88 Advertisement, Napier Cinema, 2-3 January 1919, Herbert Jones, 7th North Stafford, Doc 7306, 76/111-112/1, IWM
89 Wright, *Priest and Parish in India*, p. 137
90 'Venereal Disease in India. Report for the year 1918', L/MIL/7/13393, BL

cluster of cantonments was throughout the war the Poona Division, which included Bombay.[91] Its higher rates probably reflected men on leave from Mesopotamia. (Prostitution was almost unknown in Mesopotamia: Cuthbert Sprawson, who worked in hospitals in Basra, commented that 'a more continent army than ours can never previously have invaded the East'.[92]) The lowest incidences were at Mhow (1/4th Buffs and the 1/1st Brecknock) and Quetta (2/4th Hants) where the rate of infection was about a third that among Somerset Territorials in Rangoon. In Burma, where Territorials replaced Regulars almost entirely, the VD rate fell from 10.3 percent to 4.4 percent in 1915 (though higher than in India proper, and rising through the war). At Aden, where abstemious Brecknock Territorials replaced lascivious Regulars, the rate fell from 5.1 to .97%.[93] Confidential reports submitted to London (only six copies) revealed that the most infected Territorial units in the entire war were the 1/1st Dorset Battery, in Bareilly, with a VD rate of 10% and the 2/5th Somerset in Burma with a rate of 12.3 percent.[94]

These figures suggest that the difference was attributable either to the diligence of the medical officers responsible for policing the women in the bazaar brothels, or to the character of the members of the units. (That battalions of the same regiment could have vast differences in infection rates – the 1/5th East Surrey at 7.2 percent and the 1/6th at 2.4 percent – suggests how crucial medical officers were.) The pragmatic policy of tolerating and inspecting brothels achieved its aim. 'We never had any cases of VD reported … at Fyzabad,' Ted Rice recalled of the brothel there, 'and I think it was used quite a bit'.[95] Men were warned off seeking sex anywhere else. Among the 'Health Maxims for Men' which Bennett Young copied out was a stern and explicit warning to '*avoid intercourse with bazaar women … many are infected with venereal disease*'.[96] While cantonment bazaars were both well patronised and policed, the evidence suggests that in 1918 VD rates in Ahmednagar rose because 'wayside prostitution' was one of the few means village women suffering in the prevailing famine could obtain money.[97]

Church-men and -women in India and Britain had campaigned for decades to eliminate tolerated brothels, not recognising the hazards of uncontrolled sex for both users and used. In 1917 a clergyman, George Wright, and his wife, travelled all over India at the instigation of the YMCA, inspecting cantonment brothels. George interviewed customers and Mrs. Wright spoke to the women they used. They returned with an overwhelming amount of evidence that showed, they argued, that tolerated brothels were bad for both men and women. They argued that though sanctioned brothels attempted to keep both men and women free of disease, they represented 'a direct inducement to sin', accurately analysing that they directly fostered a 'black

---

91 *Annual Report of the Sanitary Commissioner with the Government of India for 1918*, European Army, p. 18
92 Sir Cuthbert Sprawson '37 Years in the I.M.S.', p. 121, LHCMA
93 *Report on Sanitary Measures in India in 1915-1916*, Parliamentary Papers, 1917-18, Vol. 10, Cmd 8873, p. 31. Later in the war, after it moved to Mhow, its rate rose to 6.2% in 1918.
94 'General Report and Statistics of Venereal Diseases Amongst British Troops in India' [1919], p. 27, L/MIL/7/13393, BL
95 Ted Rice, 'All for a Shilling a Day', QRWS/30/RICE/1, SHC, Woking. Official figures confirm Rice's impression, though inevitably there were cases, with condoms unavailable and medical inspections irregular.
96 Bennett Young, 2/4th Dorset, 1983-05-91, NAM
97 *Annual Report of the Sanitary Commissioner with the Government of India for 1918*, European Army, p. 19

slave traffic'. Their report persuaded the Commander-in-Chief, Sir Charles Monro, who was firmly 'against this particular vice', as he wrote in endorsing a bishop's tract.[98] In August 1917 he formally outlawed brothels on cantonment land (in India, though not in Burma). Colonels were still allowed 'a great deal of latitude', and many brothel owners simply moved premises, while medical officers, who tended to take a more pragmatic view of the issue, continued to police women's health.[99] The result, the India Office's medical adviser concluded, was that there was 'no question whatsoever that the closing of the brothels in the cantonments was coincident with the rising incidence of Venereal Disease'. His repeated recommendation to follow 'the sensible policy advocated by the Australian Army' in France (which had recognised that men would seek out prostitutes and so sought to prevent infection, treating it as a medical rather than a moral matter) was ignored. Charles judged that 'moral teachings' had 'failed utterly to check the ravages of this scourge', and men returning from India, and their wives and children, were to pay the price in the years after the war.[100]

---

98 Monro's foreword to *A Last Message from the late Bishop of Calcutta*, [1919] p. 4, Monro papers, Mss. Eur.D783/9, f.44, BL
99 Wright, *Priest and Parish in India*, p. 136
100 [Richard Havelock Charles], 'Venereal Disease in India. Report for the Year 1916', L/MIL/7/13393, BL

10

Terriers and Indians

On the dockside at Bombay newly-arrived Territorials encountered beggar children calling 'Buckshee's, Sahib!' ('alms, sir') 'whatever that was', remarked Ted Rice's comrades. 'We were soon to find out'.[1] During their five years in India Territorials developed close, complex and changing relationships with India and its people, both soldiers and civilians.

'Why, these men are all *sahibs*!': the Territorials' reception

The Territorials' arrival had 'puzzled' the 'ordinary natives' of India, wrote Nigel Woodyatt, a charismatic but not always effective Indian brigadier. They were clearly different to the Regulars whom Indians had seen (at least in major cities and cantonments). They behaved differently: they drank less, they spent more. A shopkeeper in Multan asked 'Who are these new soldiers who have cheque books?'[2] Woodyatt noticed how compared to Regulars

> … they treated the Indians with much more civility, they appeared greatly interested in all they saw, they never got drunk, and they never hammered the natives.[3]

Jim Mackie noticed that his Somersets had 'made a very good impression' on Indians in Malabar. 'The natives at once found out the difference between Territorials & Regulars & in the bazaars are known as the Gentlemen soldiers'.[4] From Allahabad a Hampshire Territorial confirmed that 'the natives call us gentlemen … because we are free with our money'.[5] The belief was widespread – Wessex gunners learned that 'natives' believed Territorials to be 'full of money' and 'sahibs, playing at being soldiers'.[6] General George MacMunn, often a reliable witness only in unwittingly exposing Anglo-Indian prejudice, claimed that Indians remarked of newly-arrived

---

1   Ted Rice, 'All for a Shilling a Day', QRWS/30/RICE/1, SHC, Woking
2   Woodyatt, *Under Ten Viceroys*, p. 257. They were probably men of the 1/5th Devon.
3   Woodyatt, 'The Territorials (Infantry) in India, 1914-1920', *JRUSI*, Vol. 67, No. 468, p. 728
4   Letter, 27 January 1915, Jim Mackie, 2/4th Somerset, Mackie, *Answering the Call*, p. 31
5   *Pioneer*, 25 January 1915, p. 8c-d
6   *History of the Hampshire Territorial Force Association*, p. 59

Terriers, 'Why, these men are all *sahibs*!' – his own surprise revealing the caste gradations within India's 'white' community.[7]

What might the consequences be for Britain's relationship with India and its people of the arrival of so many citizen soldiers? The direct evidence of the effects is sketchy. Writing from Singapore, a leader writer reflected early in 1915 that the war, and specifically the Territorials' service in India, would 'confer a mutual benefit on the future relations between Great Britain and India', quoting the newspaper *Indiaman*.[8] One sign of the Territorials' initial lack of racial prejudice is that they recorded meeting their Indian counterparts. Thomas Heard, a tailor in his native Cornwall, took an interest in the work of Indian durzis, commenting on fabrics and styles and visiting 'native tailors' at work, even seeking out local tailors in Aden, with whom he discussed the finer points of sewing machines. As agricultural workers, Territorials took an interest in farming methods and techniques, albeit often condescendingly. A ploughman of the Brecknocks had himself photographed trying out the team of his counterpart near Mhow.

The Territorials arrived at a propitious time for relations between Indians and Britons. Politically aware Indians mostly approved of Britain's war and visibly supported the imperial war effort, and while Britons had no concept of racial equality, influential authors observed that 'bad manners are no longer good form' and that notions of racial superiority were being supplanted by 'respect for the human rights of the Indian'.[9] In that Territorials thought and behaved towards Indians differently was potentially propitious for relations between rulers and ruled.

What effect the Territorials' arrival had on Indians remains obscure. English-language and vernacular newspapers, and personal papers held in the Nehru Memorial Library and other repositories defy any one researcher's ability to comprehend them, but hints can be found. In his *The Autobiography of an Unknown Indian*, Nirad Chaudhuri in 1914-15 a student boarding at the Oxford Mission hostel in Calcutta, described his first sight of Territorials. He began to notice in the Eden Gardens and on the Maidan (close to Fort William) British soldiers of what he called 'a new and very attractive type'. They wore a different shade of khaki compared to the Regulars who had previously garrisoned Calcutta, looking 'very much younger and more refined' than the Regulars. These men, whom he soon learned were Territorials, volunteers and formerly civilians, represented to him 'the best of the youthful generation of England'. 'These boyish soldiers', Chauhuri wrote forty years later, 'made an immense appeal to me'. He met some of them at social occasions hosted by earnest Anglo-Catholics. Chaudhuri recalled their 'dreamy unworldliness' remembering how it was 'so natural and so easy to idealize' these men.[10] Evidence of the reactions Terriers excited among other Calcuttans is sparse, partly because of the logistic and linguistic challenges of researching the question. Chaudhuri, an archetypal member of Bengal's English-educated *bhadralok* or middle class, worked for a time as an Indian Army clerk before turning to journalism, and must have been aware of the differences between Regulars and Territorials.

7   MacMunn, *Turmoil and Tragedy in India*, p. 73
8   *Singapore Free Press and Mercantile Advertiser*, 15 March 1915, p. 8
9   Archer, *India and the Future*, p. 19
10 Chaudhuri, *The Autobiography of an Unknown Indian*, pp. 316-17

'Hopes and desires': nationalist politics

Even newspaper-reading citizen soldiers could not be expected to have a detailed understanding of the political changes which India was experiencing, not least because Anglo-Indian newspapers either ignored or could not comprehend the mood of the nationalist movement. For the time being moderate, respectful and constitutional, its leaders pondered how they should respond to the challenge and opportunity of war. Territorials could have no idea of this turmoil. The handbook, *Our Indian Empire*, issued to Territorials on the ships in which they travelled to India, told them frankly that 'India is not yet a nation'.[11]

Living as they did in cantonments, Territorials were largely insulated from the political currents of Indian life – none of them had any idea of the vernacular press, and reports in British newspapers such as the *Statesman* or the *Pioneer* gave a distinctly one-sided view. They saw some of the consequences of the Government of India's response to what it regarded as sedition and terrorism. In Ambala in September 1915 men of the 1/4th Devon guarded the prison and then witnessed the executions of twelve men hanged in public on the maidan as an example. The Raj's police reacted vigorously to extremism – the Marquess of Crewe, Secretary of State for India 1910-15, bluntly affirmed that he was 'not ... at all particular about the liberty of the subject' in wartime.[12]

Officers doubtless talked Indian politics with civilians and box wallahs in the club but few Territorials' letters reveal much interest in Indian politics. (As the membership records of the Ootacamund Club reveal, Territorial officers joined and visited clubs as guests – the Royal Bombay Yacht Club made visiting Territorial officers honorary membership at its eclectic Venetian-Gothic-Tudor-Saracenic building on the waterfront beside the Taj Hotel.[13]) One of the few to record a detailed opinion was Robert Palmer, whose letters to his father, the Earl of Selborne, provide a commentary on nationalist affairs ('the death of Gokhale is felt to be a great disaster ...')[14] Palmer devised and sent to his father (who was President of the Board of Agriculture and a respected figure in Asquith's government) a comprehensive scheme for the co-ordination of India's technical education and its agricultural needs. On the eve of his departure for Mesopotamia he wrote an analysis in which he rightly foresaw that 'the moment the war stops unprecedented clamours will begin', and he anticipated India's needs to justify 'self-government within the Empire'. Sadly, Palmer did not live to see either the war's end or India's self-government. But even he, whose vision encompassed 'India's welfare, not British interests' as the basis of his plan for Indian development, emphasised that he would 'deal very firmly with all forms of disorder'.[15]

For British India, 1915 became 'a year of exceptional anxiety'.[16] Nationalist unrest continued – the *Ghadr* movement in the Punjab, 'conspiracy' cases in Delhi and Lahore; repeated 'terrorist' outrages in Bengal, shadowed by the suspicion that German provocation sustained nationalist agitation. Hardinge regarded activism as 'anarchistic rather than revolutionary' but conceded

---

11   Sturt, *Our Indian Empire*, p. 74
12   Telegram, 6 March 1915, quoted in Rumbold, *Watershed in India*, p. 33
13   Members Register Ootacamund Club, c. 1914-18, Ootacamund Club
14   Letter, 24 February 1915, Robert Palmer, 1/5th Hants, 19M75/F/C19, HRO
15   Palmer, *Letters from Mesopotamia*, pp. 14-15
16   Hardinge, *My Indian Years*, p. 131

to a journalist that it was still 'dangerous'.¹⁷ Melodramatically, the 2/5th Somerset ate their Christmas dinners at Rangoon sitting with their rifles between their knees, because of the fear of a German-led rising.¹⁸

But the threat did not come from leaders of Congress, who sought moderate, progressive change. Whatever they felt privately, publicly Congress leaders tended to avoid even acknowledging the military basis of British power. In two dozen speeches in a book respectfully entitled *How India Can Save the Empire* only Bal Gangadhar Tilak referred to how India was 'kept under military subjection'.¹⁹ Few Indians distinguished between Territorials and Regulars. A survey of the papers of contemporary nationalist activists in the Nehru Memorial Library, and published sources, suggests that Indian nationalist politicians paid little attention to the Territorials' arrival specifically: the composition of British military occupation made little difference to its imposition. British officials scrutinising the pages of 'native' newspapers did pick up some concern. The *Dipak* newspaper in Lahore, an official reported in January 1915,

> … wants to know who will pay for the maintenance of the Territorials … India is bearing the expenses of her army … she should not be required to meet the expenses of the newly arrived troops.²⁰

Old India hands believed as an article of faith that, as one of their senior Pharisees, George MacMunn, put it, 'India, or at any rate cantonmental India, does not change'.²¹ More observant commentators recognised that the war was bringing tensions, in the demands made by the British of India, and of Britain by Indians seeking to use the war as a lever for change. Whether they were interested or not, military officers responsible for maintaining order needed to understand the system they defended, and Territorial officers were offered lectures on Indian government. The Secretary of the Board of Revenue in the United Provinces, for example, delivered a talk on 'The Machinery of British Administration' to Territorial officers in various cantonments' in February 1916, sadly, a lecture that would hardly have inspired them.²²

Occasionally lecturers spoke to gatherings of soldiers, through the YMCA and other church bodies, and the 2/6th Royal Sussex seemed especially interested in fostering an awareness of Indian politics. An Indian professor at Fergusson College, Poona, published an article at the request of the editor of *The Royal Sussex Herald*, earnestly urging 'mutual understanding' between Indian and Englishmen. After establishing his own love of cricket the professor suggested that while 'our customs and manners differ from those of the British … in no way do they betoken an inferior civilization'.²³ A few weeks later a YMCA speaker addressed men on 'Hopes and Desires of India', who spoke of 'the desire to see India stand alone, independent … great in her adolescent glory'.²⁴

---

17   Anon, *Loyal India*, pp. 8-9
18   Anon, *The Book of Remembrance*, p. 85
19   Anon, *How India Can Save the Empire*, p. 61
20   *Dipak*, 5 January 1915, Reports of Native Newspapers, Punjab, Microfilm accession 1856, NAI
21   MacMunn, *Behind the Scenes in Many Wars*, p. 6
22   'Lecture delivered to territorial officers in various cantonments in February 1916', Hinton Harris, Hampshire Regiment, M1542, RHRM
23   'Mutual Understanding', *The Royal Sussex Herald*, 24 June 1916, p. 123
24   'India's Ambition', *Ibid*, 29 July 1916, p. 168

The war would transform India's politics. While British repression suppressed extremists, compliant moderates gained confidence, co-operating with British authorities in growing expectation that their reward might be greater self-determination if not the 'home rule' demanded by Mrs. Annie Besant.

'Just the same as you and me': Terriers and sepoys

Territorials arrived with firm images of the reputation and image of Indian soldiers, familiar with Bengal lancers, Sikhs and Gurkhas from magazines, cigarette cards and the illustrations of artists such as R. Caton Woodville. They encountered Indian soldiers soon after arrival. Arthur Copeland saw Indian cavalry in an adjoining train, 'splendidly fit and keen'.[25] Victor Manley's 2/4th Hants shared a voyage to Karachi with Indian troops after reaching Bombay. He was taken with their 'height, fine features under a bronzed complexion, and innocent good nature'.[26] Like many British and dominion citizen volunteers, Terriers were impressed by the bearing, turnout, discipline and professionalism of India's Regular troops, especially those serving in 1914.

Alexander Sturt, author of *Our Indian Empire*, evidently an 'old India hand' declared that there existed a 'mutual trust' between Indian and British troops, and much of the booklet was devoted to explaining the differences between India's 'martial' ethnic groups in uniform, diet and behaviour and the etiquette of dealing with them respectfully. But even he conceded that when working with Supply and Transport Corps drivers 'the British soldier sometimes treats the driver with little respect'.[27] (Routine orders indeed confirm that Territorials 'abused and ill-treated' cart drivers.[28]) Territorials gradually learned to distinguish between both types of Indian troops – to tell Mahrattas from Sikhs, say, though both wore the turban (or pagri, as it was properly called) and to tell sepoys from non-commissioned officers (naiks and havildars) and even to respect Indian officers. (The cartoon compilation, *The Indian Army A.B.C.*, directed sarcastic scorn at the novice 'Tommy' who 'much to his joy … refers to the subedar major as "Boy"'.[29] The subedar major in question was depicted as literally squirming in frustration.)

Territorials witnessed several of the mutinies that afflicted the Indian Army in the war's first year; in the Punjab, Burma and Singapore. Other Territorial units guarded prisons in the Punjab after *Ghadr* activists tried to suborn Indian troops, leading to a series of 'conspiracy trials', though they actually had little success. In Delhi early in 1916 the 1/4th Wilts paraded when two men of the 7th Rajputs were sentenced (to death and transportation to the Andamans) for their part in planning an outrage. (The Wilts had guarded the prisoners in Delhi fort, and had in fact allowed one man to escape for a short time.) Herbert Ewing and his comrades guarded the mutinous Sikhs of the 21st Cavalry in the military prison at Dagshai ('fine strapping big fellows'), and some escorted them to Ambala ('a miserable and sad affair') and were present at

---

25 Letter, 11 November 1914, Arthur Copeland, 1/5th Hants, 128A08/1-4, HRO
26 Diary, 6 January 1915, Victor Manley, 'A Khaki Diary', 49M91W/Q3/6, HRO
27 Sturt, *Our Indian Empire*, pp. 5; 23
28 Routine orders, 23 June 1916, 2/6th Royal Sussex, RSR/MSS 6/9, WSRO
29 Anon, *The Indian Army A.B.C.*, np ('T, for the Tommy')

'T, for the Tommy', exposing the Territorials' initial ignorance of the Indian Army. (*The Indian Army A.B.C.*, courtesy of Rana Chhina)

their executions ('a rather gruesome business').[30] Two sowars of the 8th Cavalry murdered a captain of the 1/5th West Kent, along with five other British soldiers, 'running amok' at Jhansi in June 1915, apparently aggrieved over being split up, but it was not a political crime.[31]

Territorials gradually came into contact with 'native' troops and gained clearer understandings of their skills, strengths and capabilities. When from 1915 Territorial battalions began to be combined into administrative if not operational brigades they began to encounter Indian units and their members. They saw the professionalism of Indian Regulars at field days and Kitchener Tests (when Indian troops often acted as adversaries) and sometimes went on joint route marches. Robert Palmer found Eurasian assistant surgeons 'far more competent than British R.A.M.C. officers'.[32] At Mountain Warfare schools it was Gurkha and Nepalese troops who impressed lessons on inexperienced Territorials. They had a universally favourable view of Gurkhas, Oswald Early remarking that they were 'three times as good as the average Indian'

---

30 Diary, 30 July – 5 September 1915, Herbert Ewing, 1/5th Somerset, Doc.15428, 07/8/1, IWM
31 *The Queen's Own Gazette*, Vol. XXXIV, No. 9, September 1915, p. 3381
32 Palmer, *Letters from Mesopotamia*, p. 17. RAMC stands for Royal Army Medical Corps.

soldier.³³ After watching a Gurkha football team draw with a British team Henry Broad of the 1/5th Hants thought that they were 'the only native on an equal footing to us'.³⁴

The Indian Army's officers tended not to notice Territorials. When Ted Berryman, a Garhwal Rifles officer, attended a concert given by men of the 1/4th Wilts in Delhi in 1916 he told his mother that he had found it 'quite a good show' and their sports day 'quite amusing', but the memoirs and correspondence of Regular Indian Army officers are notable for how little they referred to Territorials.³⁵

Private Lucas, one of the versifiers of the 2/4th Hants, ended 'Barrabas', his diatribe against rapacious barrack vendors, with a reminder of other Indians:

> But in our fighting forces there are Indians you know,
> As good as any men you'll find where're you chance to go
> This rhyme does not apply to them, they're soldier men you see,
> They are soldiers of the Empire just the same as you and me.³⁶

On campaign, in Aden, Palestine, Persia and overwhelmingly in Mesopotamia, Territorials often served in the British battalion in 'Indian' brigades. Coming into close contact with Indian troops enhanced their respect for their characteristic patience, endurance and devotion.

'There are natives everywhere': attitudes

Even as they alighted from the trains carrying them from Bombay, Territorials had been warned to be wary of 'natives'. A private of the 4th West Kent from Maidstone wrote home (a letter his family passed to the local paper) describing how:

> There are natives everywhere, and we have been advised as to the way we should treat them, because apparently they avail themselves of any opportunity of taking advantage of people who do not understand the customs of the country …³⁷

At first untouched by the particular prejudices of British India, Territorials often simply dealt with Indians as they found them. Men recorded meeting Indians apart from barrack servants and vendors especially early in their time in India. At Quetta William Bisset 'spent the afternoon underneath the trees … talking with a group of natives'.³⁸ In Burma John Marsh agreed to have a young English-educated Burman share his train compartment: 'we had a very interesting chat on Burmese customs and religions … his talk on reincarnation was very convincing'.³⁹ When soldiers were able to speak with 'natives' they recorded encounters unimaginable in, say,

---

33 Diary, 27 February 1917, Oswald Early, 1/9th Hants, M4236, RHRM
34 Diary, 19 November 1914, Henry Broad, 1/5th Hants, Doc. 14551, 67/164/1, IWM
35 Letter, 30 December 1916, Nesham, *Socks, Cigarettes and Shipwrecks*, p. 166
36 *The Tiger*, September 1915, pp. 86-87
37 *Kent Messenger*, 4 March 1915
38 Diary, 27 June 1915, William Bisset, 2/4th Hants, M1834, RHRM
39 John Marsh, 'My Service in India', M757, RHRM

Reuben Rusbridge's native Surrey. At Christmas 1917 in Delhi a 'native boy' invited Rusbridge and his mates to go to the cantonment servants' quarters to see a nativity scene they had made. The 'boy' turned out to be a 43-year-old Christian Indian Army veteran with nine children. He invited the soldiers to watch a 'Native Dance ... fun, fast and furious' which made its way around Kingsway camp for a couple of hours.[40]

Old India hands soon put them straight. The Regimental Sergeant Major of the 2/6th Royal Sussex, who had served in India in the 1880s with the West Surrey Regiment, told his Territorial charges directly: 'keep natives at arm's length, though with kindness and civility'.[41] The suspicion of 'natives" motives, imparted initially by Regulars, appears in many other letters, diaries and memoirs. It coloured the Territorials' attitude to and experience of India. Soon after Oswald Early arrived in Bangalore in 1916 he took a stroll to one of the villages near the cantonment, now swallowed up by the city's growth. As was usual, he described it as 'filthy', but it was the villagers' reactions to his presence that struck him. Women simply ran away, but men 'look at us as savage as they can, as if they would like to hit us over the head'. Oswald carried a stick and a revolver.[42] 'You would be surprised how afraid they are of us', a 'Sheptonian' wrote in a story published in his native town, Shepton Mallet in Somerset.[43] Even if Indians made friendly overtures they could be rebuffed. When villagers in Bihar travelled six miles to greet a party of Somerset troops and offered them fish they had caught, the detachment's medical officer 'promptly disposed of them'; the fish that is.[44]

For many men 'India' often – usually – meant the cantonment and its immediate environs – the sudder bazaar servicing their needs. Many men went nowhere else. In some stations it was unsafe and often prohibited to try. At Rawalpindi in 1915 men were advised that villages less than three miles from the cantonment were 'not safe'.[45] Routine orders constantly directed troops to keep to 'bounds' – within the limits of their cantonments – and to be wary when moving beyond them. A 2/4th Somerset routine order in Dinapore reminded officers and sergeants that 'when any party exceeding 50 in number leaves barracks it will always throw out advanced and rear guards'.[46] In larger, cities, men sought 'Permanent Passes' in order to be free of living 'in bounds'. In 1916 Henry Iggulden of the 1/10th Middlesex was allowed a pass allowing him to leave Fort William from four p.m. to 12.30 a.m. – but not in a long list of districts or even individual addresses (Kerr's Lane, No. 4) where, if found, he would be disciplined. The 'out of bounds' list included 'all native houses'.[47]

It was possible but unusual for Territorials and Indians to mix. Ted Rice struck up a friendship with a wealthy Hindu merchant at Fyzabad and was invited to attend a family wedding, amazed at watching nautch dancers (until the battalion provost sergeant arrived). Henry Iggulden, who as a private had been forbidden from entering 'native houses' in Calcutta in 1916 was by 1918 (now a sergeant) invited by an Indian lawyer to attend a garden party to farewell Syed Iftikhar

---

40 Diary, 25 December 1917, Reuben Rusbridge, Surrey Battery, Doc.13388, 05/7/1, IWM
41 'Our Veterans No. 1', *The Royal Sussex Herald*, 26 August 1916, p. 212
42 Diary, 17 March 1916, Oswald Early, 1/9th Hants, M4236, RHRM
43 *Shepton Mallet Journal*, 18 December 1914, p 3
44 Letter, 1 February 1917, Jim Mackie, 2/4th Somerset, Mackie, *Answering the Call*, p. 231
45 Diary, nd, Allan Swift, 1/6th East Surrey, ESR/25/SWIF/1, SHC, Woking
46 Routine orders, 2/4th Somerset, 11 February 1916, DD\SLI/6/32, SHC, Taunton
47 Henry Iggulden, 1/10th Middlesex, 2010-11-2-1, NAM

The battalion orderly room staff of the 1/4th Cornwall, including two chuprassis (uniformed messengers, with their large badges of office), showing how Indians and Britons worked together on duty. (B.1824, Cornwall's Regimental Museum)

Husain Saheb, an Indian deputy collector in Lucknow. When Harry Canham worked under a 'Tehilsdar' (an Indian civil official) in Waziristan in 1917, the man called him 'Mr Border' and said that 'he likes the Territorials much better than the Regulars' – presumably because Harry treated the man decently. Harry had 'several hot discussions on the subject' with Regulars working in his headquarters.[48]

British soldiers were allowed an extraordinary licence. Soon after arriving in Calcutta in 1917 Edward Ewens was one of several Somerset sergeants being shown around the city by a Hants sergeant. In Dhurrumtollah Street their taxi collided with a man carrying a huge bundle of hay. Though the coolie later died of his injuries Ewens 'heard nothing further'.[49] Battalion routine orders, however, disclose that men charged with 'striking a native' could receive between five and seven days detention, with lance-corporals losing their stripe, but also that the offence was rarely recorded.[50]

48   Letter, 31 May 1917, Harry Canham, 2/4th Border, CMML
49   Edward Ewens, 'A Cook's Tour in Burma and India', DD\SLI/17/1/62, SHC, Taunton
50   Routine orders, 1/6th and 2/6th Devon, 1915 and 1916, EX1213 and EX1219, DMM

Map 1 The 'Indian' Territorials' counties and towns

The Territorial battalions sent to India hailed from thirteen counties, and London, most from southern England; the Home Counties (Kent, Surrey, Sussex and Middlesex) and Wessex (Hampshire, Wiltshire, Dorset, Somerset, Devon and Cornwall). The recruiting area of the South Wales Borderers comprised the counties of Hereford and Monmouth (in England) and Brecknockshire, in Wales, though Territorials of the 1/1st Brecknockshire Battalion mostly came from that county.

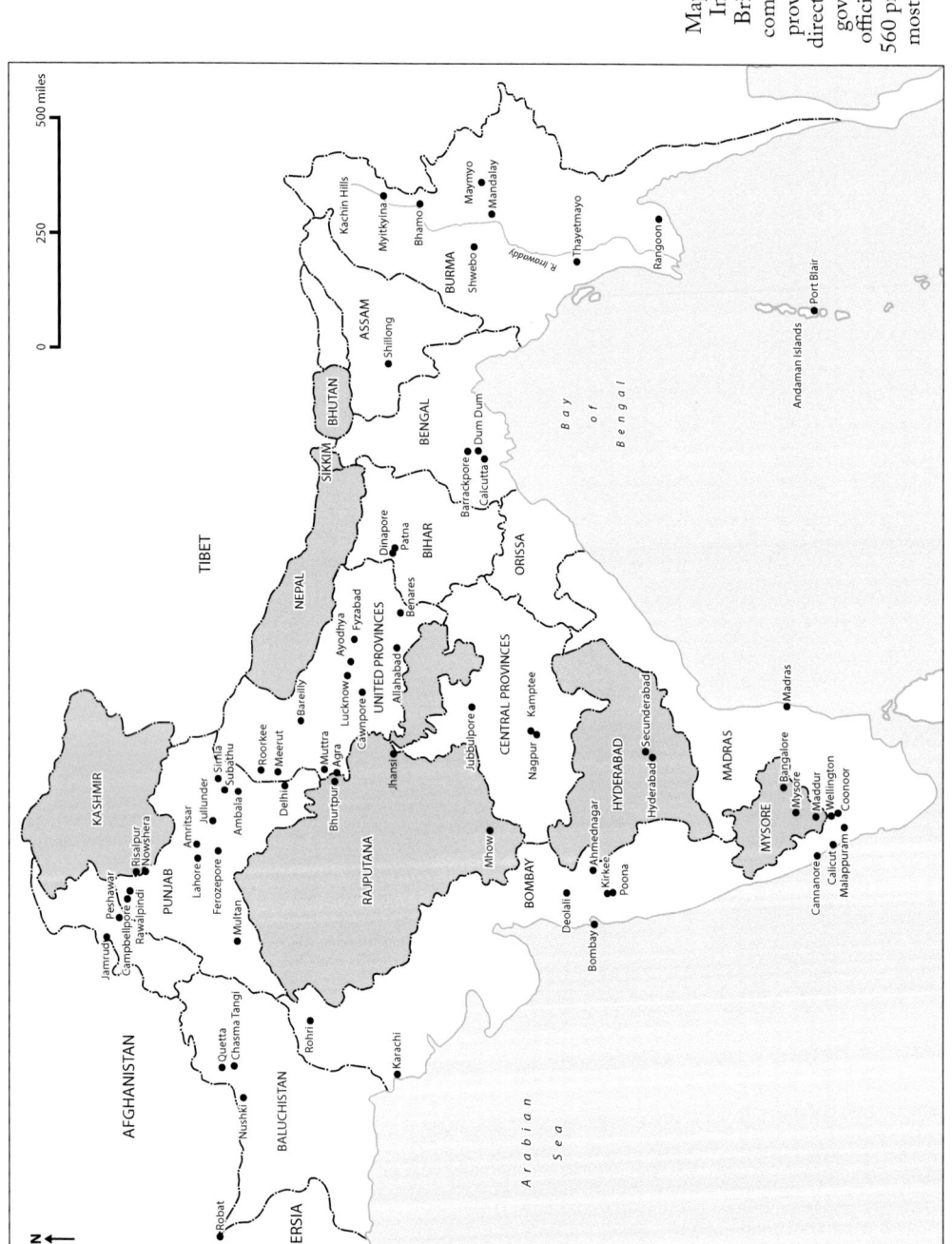

Map 2 British India 1914
British India comprised both provinces ruled directly by British governors and officials and over 560 princely states, most small, a few large.

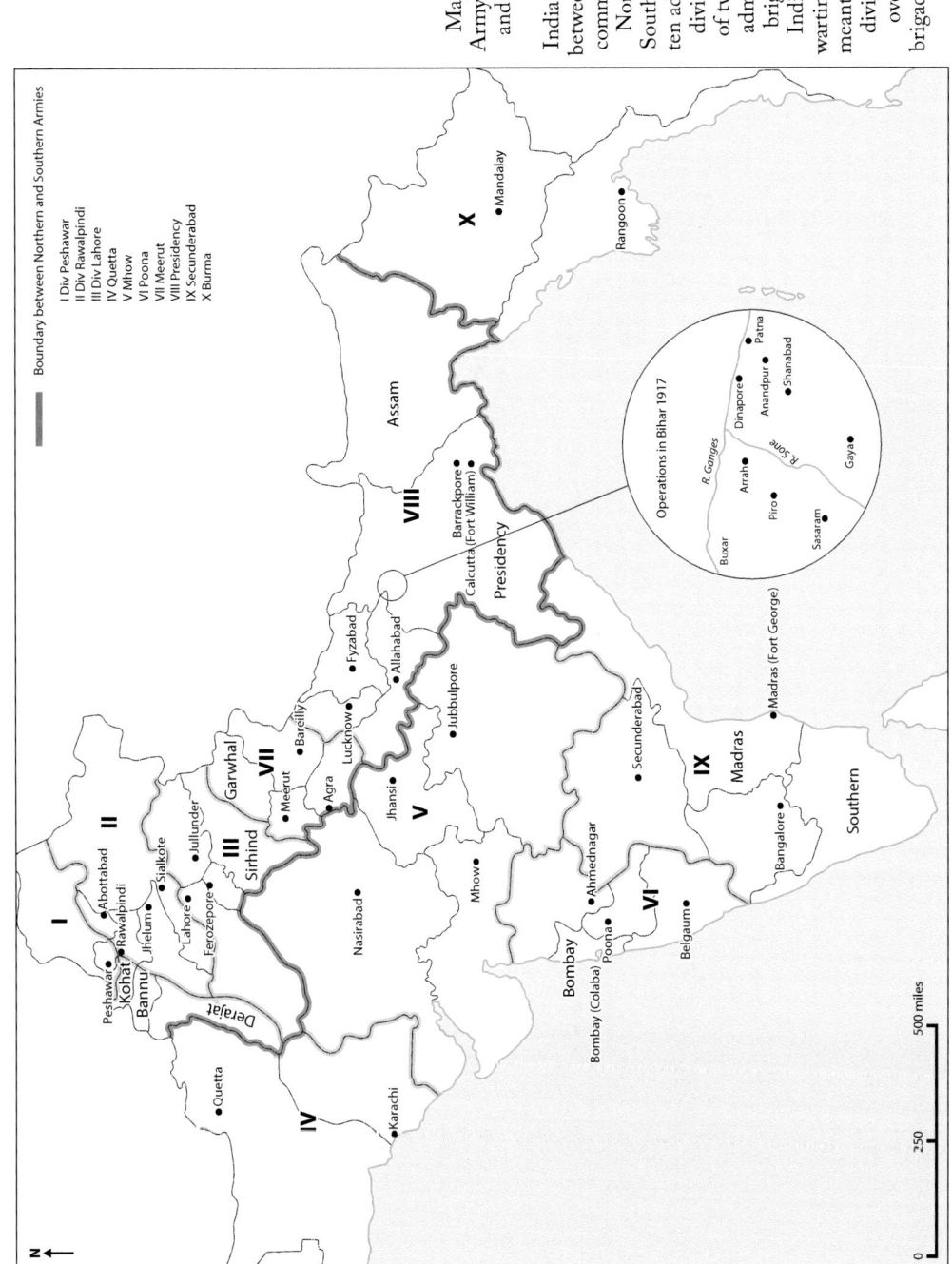

Map 3 India: Army Commands and Divisional Areas
India was divided between two major commands — the Northern and Southern Armies, ten administrative divisions, each of two or more administrative brigades. The Indian Army's wartime expansion meant that though divisions went overseas the brigades remained intact.

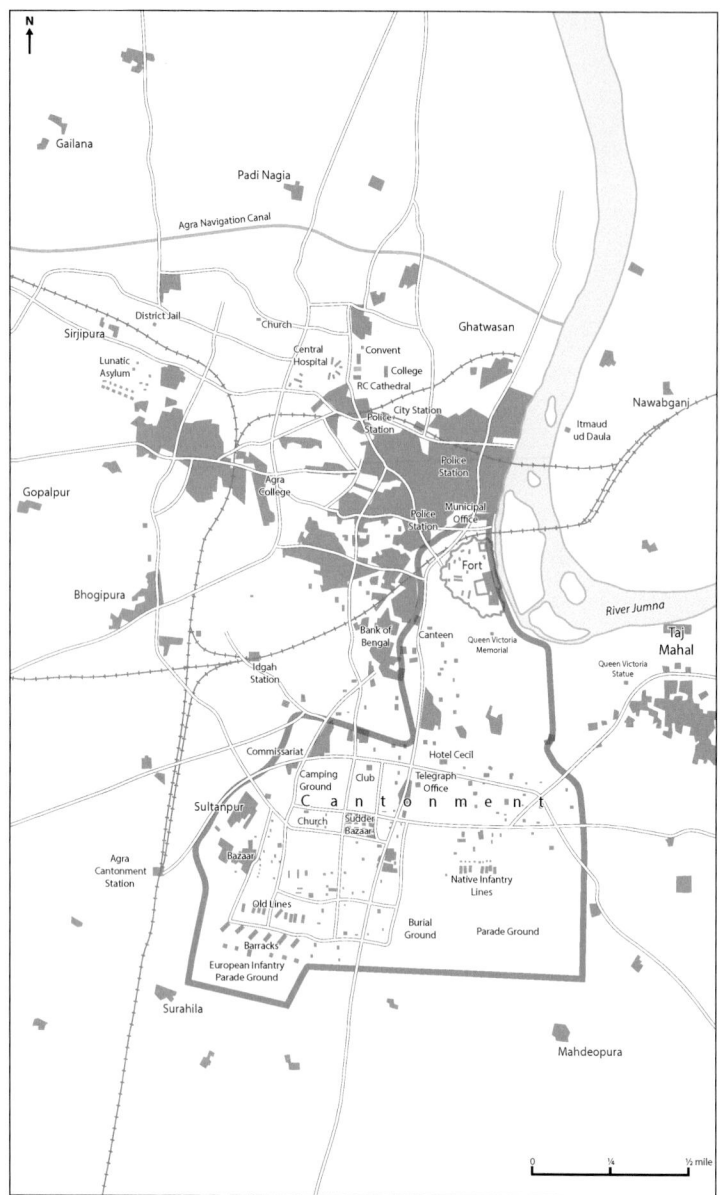

Map 4 Agra Cantonment

British India's military force occupied about a hundred cantonments across the sub-continent. This major cantonment, Agra, on the River Jumna in the eastern United Provinces, displays most of the significant features of cantonments. The cantonment occupied a large area, created on what had been agricultural land south of and adjacent to the old city, surrounded by villages. Several railway lines led north, south, east and west. The cantonment, clearly delineated, comprised large areas of park-like bungalows, churches, clubs, banks, commissariat go-downs, a post office, slaughterhouse, magazine, hospital, race course and parade grounds, with rows of large barracks for British soldiers and separate 'lines' for 'native' troops. Agra was unusual in including both a huge Mughal fort and (to the city's east) the Taj Mahal beside the Jumna.
(From Murray's *Handbook for Travellers in India Burma and Ceylon, 1913*)

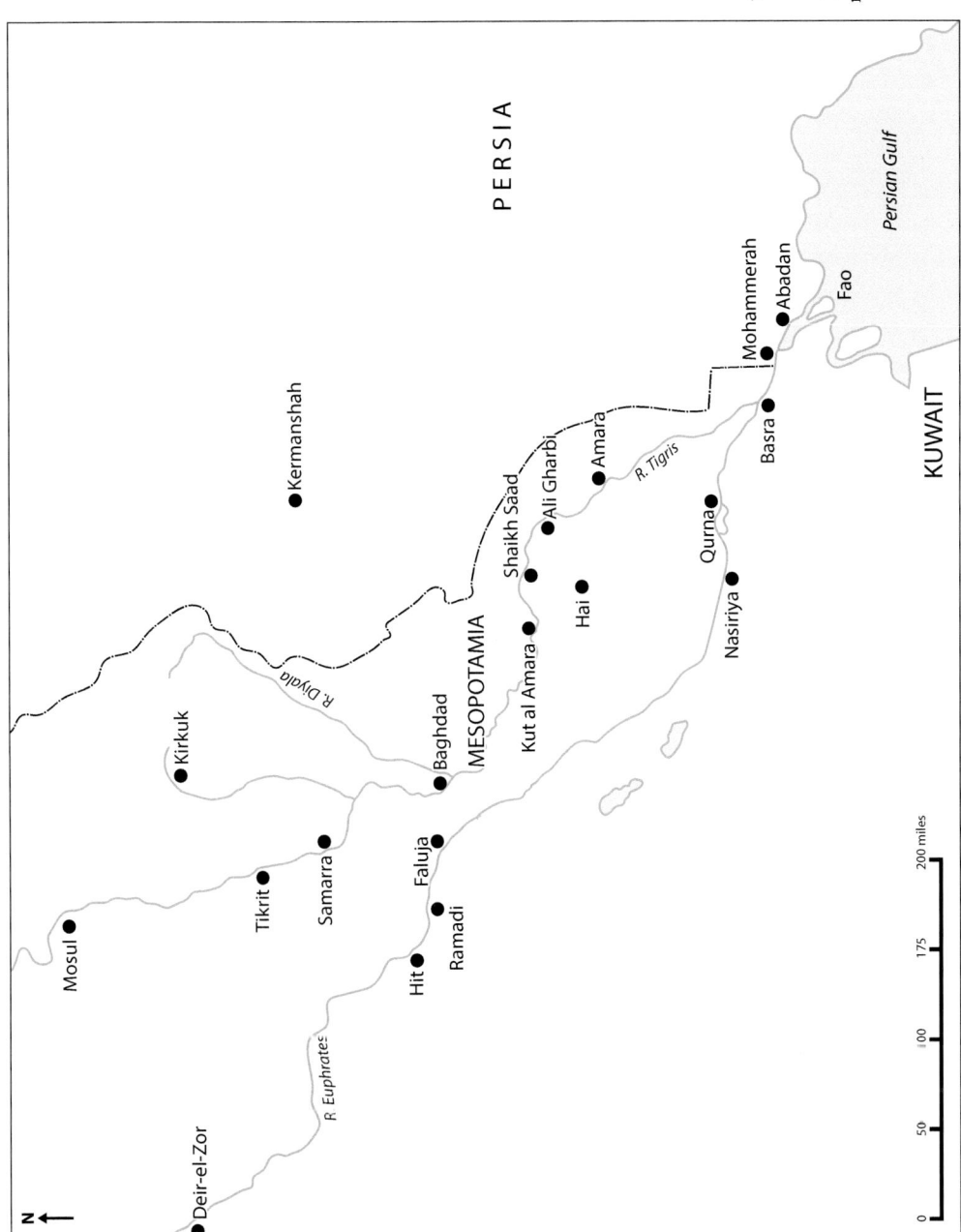

Map 5 Mesopotamia The campaign in Mesopotamia occurred essentially along narrow corridors following the major rivers, the Euphrates and especially the Tigris and its tributaries. With the collapse of the Russian empire late in 1917 the British war effort moved northwards to northern Persia and into Transcaspia and even Turkestan.

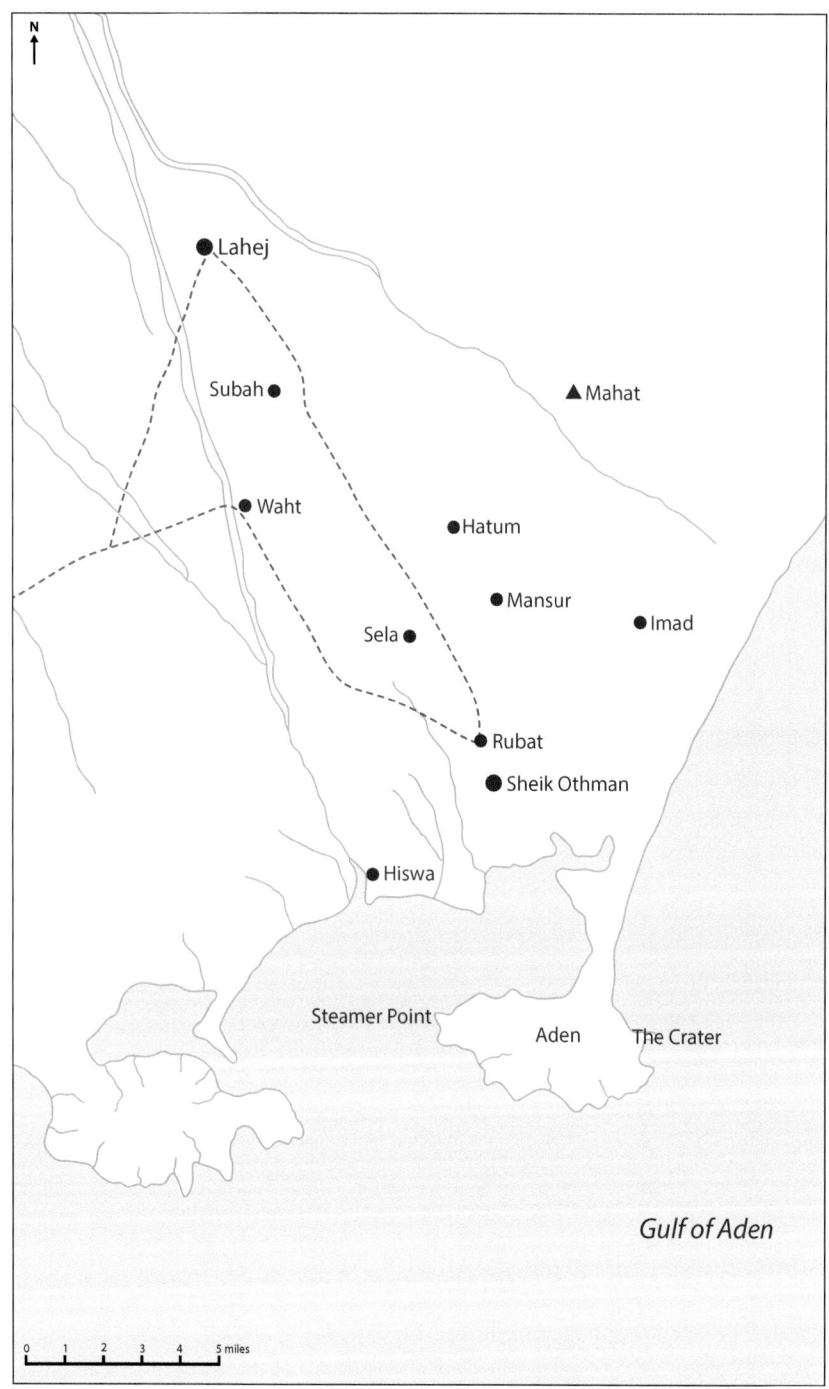

Map 6 Aden
The theatre of operations in the Aden protectorate was tiny it was just over twenty miles from the centre of Aden town to Lahej and for most of the war the front lines, several miles apart, barely moved.

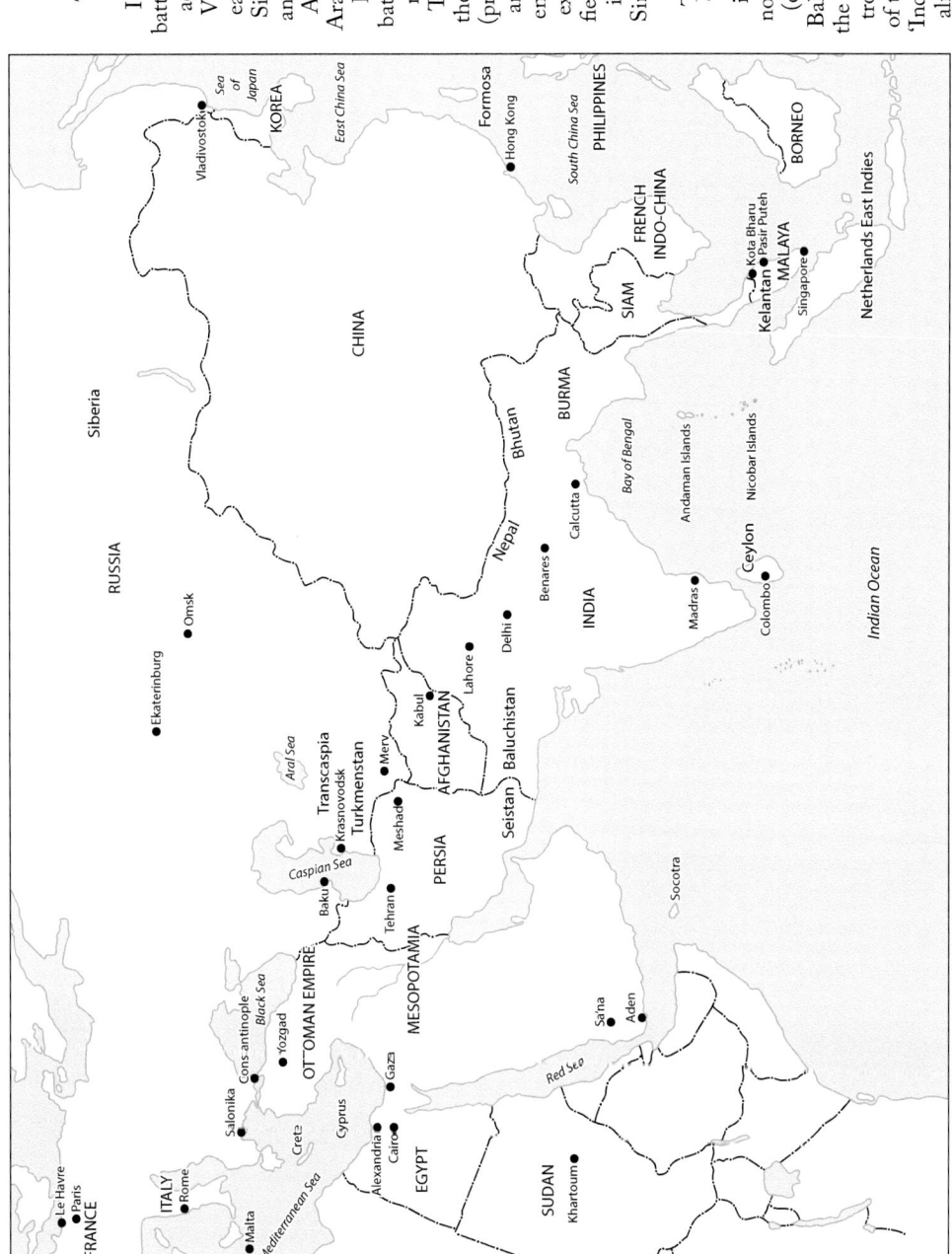

Map 7 Asia
Though at first despatched to India, Territorial battalions later served across Asia, from Vladivostok in far eastern Siberia, in Singapore, Malaya and Hong Kong to Aden in southern Arabia and Palestine. Eventually four battalions eventually reached France. The war between the Entente powers (principally Britain) and the Ottoman empire saw British expeditionary and field forces fighting in Aden, Egypt, Sinai and Palestine, Mesopotamia, Transcaspia and Turkestan, and in Persia, in the north-west, Seistan (on the border of Baluchistan), and on the Gulf coast. Indian troops served in all of these theatres and 'Indian' Territorials in almost all of them.

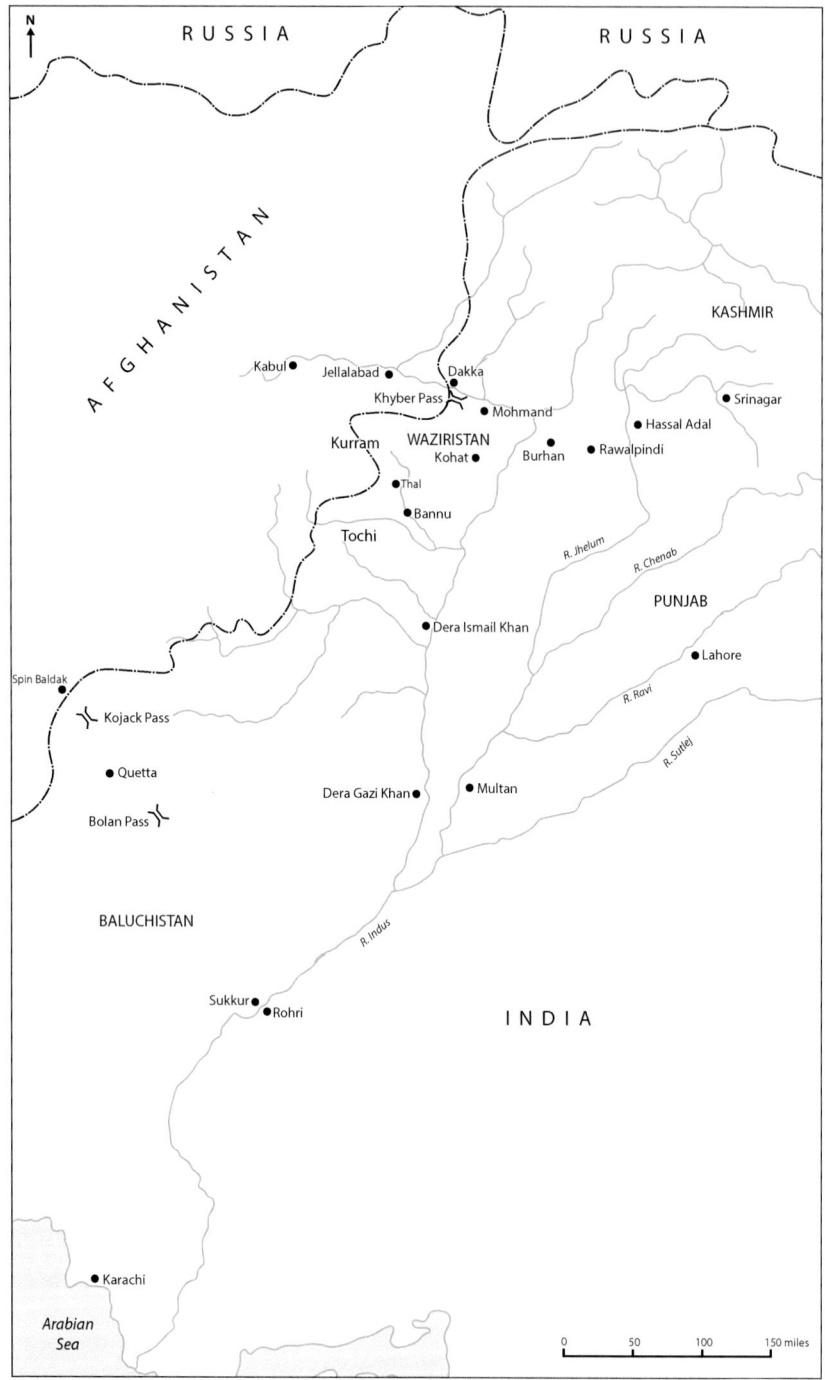

Map 8 The North-West frontier
By 1917 Territorial units were serving on the North-West frontier, from north of Peshawar south-west to Baluchistan.

While British soldiers had little opportunity to mix socially with Indian civilians, they worked with many. In cantonment 'dufters' (offices), they encountered 'babus' – Indian clerks, whose devotion to official procedure became legendary. (In the Indian Army A.B.C. 'B is the babuji – don't let him start. Or he'll spout you the whole of Vol. 2 off by heart'.[51]) A photograph of the quarter-master's staff of the 2/4th Border at Poona in 1917 includes ten men; six British – the battalion quartermaster, his quartermaster sergeants and clerks – and four Indians, at least two of whom were old soldiers, one a havildar. These men worked together to keep the battalion supplied with the goods its men needed.[52] Every battalion's establishment included numbers of Indians working as personal or mess servants, labourers or 'coolies' doing manual labour of shifting stores or equipment, or the dirty work of what the Indian Army called 'conservancy' – that is, waste removal, both human and natural, often working literally by hand. At the other end of the scale, a battalion's officers' mess employed over thirty bearers (typically dressed in white kurta with a colourful cummerbund and pagri, often with the regimental badge). Indeed, battalion routine orders name dozens of peons, drivers, sweepers, bhisties and other workers, one of the few English sources in which they appear as individuals. A Somerset man who employed four 'black people' in his cook-house, decided that 'Well, there are good and bad', he explained judiciously, 'they work very hard out here'.[53]

Though conscious of their standing as White Men and finding racial equality unconscionable, some Territorials retained the lack of prejudice with which many had arrived. In July 1916 the 2/6th Royal Sussex marched from Bangalore to Mysore (on which the former cyclists showed that they could march for sixteen days, Frank Johnson's way of demonstrating his battalion's superiority over other Territorials at Bangalore). The march had been possible only because of the 'unfailing courtesy and assistance' of the Maharaja of Mysore, Krishna Raja Wadiyar IV and his officials (as Johnson, reported).[54] On the way, the battalion football team accepted a challenge from the owner of a silk factory at Maddur to a match. The local side (the 'Raising Star') were all 'natives', playing presumably bare-footed, and on an uphill pitch with rocky outcrops actually on the field. Before a huge crowd of 'natives' the Sussex team won 5-1, despite the 'mountain warfare'. Perhaps the Sussex's account would have been less good-humoured had its team been beaten by 'natives'.[55]

As this suggests, sport brought the two together at times, such as when the 4th and 5th Buffs played 'Native Teams' at Jubbulpore and Kamptee in February 1915 ('wiry little chaps', who played in bare feet).[56] The 1/1st Kent played the boys of St Joseph's College (but only the 'B' team) at Bangalore in 1916, and the football-mad 1/4th Wilts played the Delhi 'Mughals' in 1917. As they became more secure as 'sahibs' contact with Indians declined. That Territorial teams played against 'natives' suggests that their passion for sport trumped the racial ideology associated with the Raj.

51 Anon, *The Indian Army A.B.C.*, np ('B is the Babuj')
52 RSM Percy Harrison, 2/4th Border, CMML
53 *Shepton Mallet Journal*, 14 May 1915, p. 5
54 Letter, 31 July 1916, Johnson to Headquarters, Territorial Brigade, GM1915, 561 of 15, No. B.215, *Mysore Administrative Papers*, Vol. IV, pp. 96-98
55 'Football Match at Maddur', *The Royal Sussex Herald*, 29 July 1916, p. 175
56 *Kent Messenger*, 4 & 13 March 1915

British soldiers invariably met Indian men – practically all barrack servants and vendors were men. Muslim women were largely hidden, and while 'the average Britisher' was 'shocked to see [Hindu] women going about … with bare arms and legs', they rarely got close to do more than ogle.[57] 'Whenever a white man passes they pull up the draping over their shoulders and arms', Harry Oke explained 'the modesty of the women' to his parents from Bangalore.[58] They could meet Indian Christians at church functions, often taking on the prejudices of Anglo-Indian society toward 'half-castes' or what they illogically called 'lower caste Christians'. One consequence of this separation was that men's photograph albums often featured images of Indian women, taken at a distance (unlike the close-up portraits Indian men were happy to sit for), anonymous and often salacious – some albums include snapshots of women bathing. Another consequence was that the only Indian women some men met were in cantonment brothels.

'A certain amount of brutality': relations with 'natives'

In a circular issued to units of the 1st Wessex Division on embarkation in October 1914 a senior staff officer warned its members that 'it must never be forgotten that the natives of India are a subject race, and therefore not to be bullied, but treated with kindness and consideration'.[59] Aboard the transport *Corsican* as the first convoy approached Bombay an old India hand of the Buffs gravely told Territorials 'not to take notice of the women' and to 'avoid having a row with the natives at all costs'.[60] Military authorities did all they could to prevent collisions. Even when they were not ordered to accept that villages and bazaars were 'out of bounds', British other ranks were discouraged from mingling with 'natives' when off duty. Very rarely did they seek to go beyond cantonment boundaries. Newcomers often had no compunction in speaking to 'natives' – Alfred Cornell freely engaged a 'native youth' in conversation while waiting at a railway station on the way to Meerut in 1916.[61] But experience, example and advice soon made men reluctant to chat. Within a few weeks Cornell was describing the people of Meerut as 'great thieves and very sly', the bazaars 'dirty', their inhabitants 'trying to rob anyone who is purchasing but our boys are too fly for them now'.[62]

But it was common for soldiers to insult or abuse 'natives', and few suffered any consequences. When 1/9th Hants men were travelling from Bangalore to the north-west in 1916 a man threw an egg at a well-dressed native, making a mess of his clothes. 'We all laughed', Oswald early recorded in his diary, as the train moved off.[63] Men routinely referred to Indians as 'niggers' (even Reg Bailey, who may have been a teacher, or at least a clerical worker). Miss Elsie Fisk of Miss Sandes's Soldiers' Home in Quetta noticed that 'when a man becomes a real Christian, his attitude to the people of India alters', the 'acid test' being that men no longer spoke of 'niggers'.[64]

57 'Indian Impressions', *Regimental Journal, 2/5th Hampshire Battalion*, August 1916, p. 6, RHRM
58 Letter, 1916, Harry Oke, 1/25th London, 2004-05-43, NAM
59 General Order, 4 October 1914, Francis Bowker papers, M1539, RHRM
60 Diary, 26 November 1914, Cyril Burgess, 1/5th Buffs, Doc.6711, 91/26/1, IWM
61 Diary, 4 May 1916, Arthur Cornell, 1/5th Somerset, DD\SLI/17/1/84, SHC, Taunton
62 Arthur Cornell, 'A short account of our life and duties at Meerut', DD\SLI/17/1/84, SHC, Taunton
63 Diary, 5 December 1916, Oswald Early, 1/9th Hants, M4236, RHRM
64 Fisk, *The Great Shikār in Quetta*, pp. 123-24

Men of the 1/1st Kent Battalion in the sudder bazaar at Dalhousie, with off-duty Territorials smartly attired and carrying the sticks that became a fashionable walking-out accessory. Soldiers and civilians are close but do not interact. (Album 5 MNERN: 881, Maidstone Museum)

Not surprisingly, violence often erupted. When Herbert Chapple and some of his mates visited a village close to Kateri camp (in the Nilgiris near Wellington), he found the villagers 'very frightened of us': imposing, uniformed men, red-faced, unable to speak their language, with the villagers perhaps with stories or memories of ill-treatment by soldiers years or even decades before.[65] Nor were Territorials exempt. When the 1/4th Hants passed through Karachi en route to Mesopotamia in March 1915 word spread of 'a native trying to cheat a man of the battalion'. Men of the man's company gathered and 'the stall goods and other things were smashed by the Rowdy ones'.[66] Occasionally, violence flowed the other way. Men were warned against being out of barracks alone at night, and some were attacked. Douglas Skinner told his fellow villagers in Great Chart how 'they do not like the English and some of them would very soon knife you if you got out to[o] far alone'.[67] A private of the 2/6th Royal Sussex was set upon by up to 40

---

65 Diary, 7 March 1915, Herbert Chapple, 1/4th Devon, DMM
66 Memoir, anonymous man, 1/4th Hants, Misc. 123, item 1916, IWM
67 Letter, 12 August 1915, Douglas Skinner, 1/5th Buffs, Great Chart Fund, Book 5, KA&HC

natives in Brigade Road, Bangalore, losing an eye. The assault was greeted with 'regret and indignation', though not retribution, this time.[68]

The Indians troops saw most of were their barrack and office servants, and with proximity easy racist generalisations faltered. Harry Canham, sweating over his typewriter in Peshawar in August humidity was honest about his treatment of the punkah wallah who worked the fan in his dufter: 'I threaten to take his life at least a dozen times a day'. But Harry also sympathised with their plight:

> … if sweated labour ever existed it is to be found in the punkah wallah … he sits on the verandah and pulls for 14 hours out of the 24 and receives the princely sum of 8 rupees a month! … One does not like to be too hard upon them …[69]

Percy Harrison, Harry's battalion sergeant-major, was also sympathetic, captioning his snapshot of a punkah wallah 'boy' (though he too was a grown man) 'the most monotonous job in existence'.[70] The Regulars who introduced Territorials to the intricacies of cantonment life, the use of mosquito nets and the niceties of bargaining in bazaars also taught them 'how to handle the natives'. Victor Manley, for all his engagement with India's religion and culture reflected that 'I have since learnt that … it is necessary to assume a certain amount of brutality towards the lower classes' – to display kindness was to invite them to be 'indecently familiar'.[71]

Olaf Caroe, among the most sensitive observers of an India he came to love, saw beyond his servants' raggedness and illiteracy. He recalled being impressed by the 'mingled courtesy, grace and dignity' of the servants allocated to him in Secunderabad in 1914. 'The memory of these remains close to the heart, and evokes an esteem and gratitude not always adequately expressed.'[72] Far from affecting an indifference to their Indian servants, Territorials' diaries and memoirs reveal that they tended to speak to them, a habit Regulars deprecated. For example, when the 1/1st Kents' servants sacrificed goats and chickens in the grounds of Baird Barracks, Bangalore, Walter Gosling asked the reason. They told him that they were giving thanks for being in employment – and perhaps too that their novice masters were so easy-going compared to previous employers.

---

68 'Battalion Notes', *The Royal Sussex Herald*, 9 September 1916, p. 226
69 Letter, 6 August 1918, Harry Canham, 2/4th Border, CMML
70 RSM Percy Harrison, 2/4th Border, CMML
71 Diary, 9 January 1915 [sic], Victor Manley, 'A Khaki Diary', 49M91W/Q3/6, HRO
72 Caroe, 'The Flames of Enchantment', p. iv-5, PP/MCR/207, IWM

11

Terriers and Britons

The evidence of Territorials' relations with Anglo-Indian civilians is frankly perplexing. At Delhi a 1/4th Wilts Territorial recorded that 'the English residents here are extremely kind to us'.[1] A man in the 2/4th Wilts, however, complained to the same newspaper that Anglo Indian civilians in Poona 'absolutely ignore the Tommy'.[2] Nigel Woodyatt loyally claimed that civilians encountering Territorials had been 'much struck with their patriotism' as *citizen* soldiers', but the evidence of their regard is at best mixed. It is true that clubs entertained Territorial officers and that throughout India their men were invited to tennis, musical parties, picnics, concerts and motor drives.[3] The testimony from Territorials supports this, but also qualifies it. The only way to reach some sort of conclusion is to the examine the evidence on both sides.

'Towards us are like ice': the case against

In 1914 the Russian consul in Calcutta reported to St Petersburg on the low quality of Territorials, dismissing them as 'only raw material … not suitable for military actions on the north-western border'.[4] How could he have reached this judgment? He was probably reflecting the dismissive views of Calcutta's official and commercial community, doubtless members or supporters of the auxiliary units such as the Calcutta Scottish, which certainly gained the lion's share of press coverage.

Jim Mackie expressed the common grievance toward Anglo-Indian civilians, that 'there are hundreds of men in Calcutta … of military age who are doing absolutely nothing but live a life of luxurious ease'.[5] One of Jim's men penned the epic 'A Territorial's Life in India' which included a couple of verses complaining about civilians:

---

1 *The Wiltshire Times*, 10 April 1915
2 *Ibid*, 11 September 1915
3 Woodyatt, 'The Territorials in India, 1914-1920', *RUSIJ*, 1922, p. 727
4 Letter, 18-31 December 1914, Chakravarty, *Anatomy of the Raj*, pp. 307
5 Letter, 7 December 1916, Jim Mackie, 2/4th Somerset, Mackie, *Answering the Call*, p. 217

The white folks of this country,
Towards us are like ice,
They do not seem to realise
How great our sacrifice.

We do not want ought of them,
But only what is right,
And that is their good manners,
To speak and be polite.[6]

Anglo-Indian civilians were at first inclined to regard Territorials as they had the Regulars they had been used to; that is, to practically ignore them. Philip Gosse found that as 'temporary gents' Territorials were 'of the untouchable caste'; 'chota [little] sahibs' in the eyes of the 'pucka sahibs' of Bombay.[7] An Anglo-Indian correspondent ascribed the lack of a 'hearty welcome' to the Territorials' 'reticence' in arriving to the supposedly 'involuntary coldness' of British-Indian civilians.[8] Many Territorials' diaries and letters mention this. When Herbert Ewing passed an Englishwoman while staying in Simla he noticed that 'she went out of her way to avoid passing me or looking at me'.[9] Civilians, Hugh Creek complained from Ferozepore, 'will hardly condescend to speak to one', even though 'they are glad enough to have his protection'.[10] British-Indian civilians were often, Geoffrey Coombes told his school-friend, Lillian, 'very distant to a Tommy'.[11] In Burma the 2/5th Somersets found that 'we had not been treated as though we were human beings … but rather as a nuisance'.[12]

Walter Saunders described how Middlesex Terriers were received in Calcutta's cafés in 1914-15. Though its British civilians 'treated us decently', and attended concerts the Territorials offered, men soon encountered the limits of their welcome. Off duty, men sought out Calcutta's cafés, reserved exclusively for Europeans. Saunders entered Castelazzo's café with a member of A Company (the Sinjuns – mostly middle class students). A civilian shouted 'Hi clear out' but they remained. The manager came to their table, apologising that 'I'm sorry gentlemen [acknowledging the Territorials' difference to Regulars] but I cannot serve you'. No order had been promulgated, but café managers knew that if they admitted soldiers they would lose the civilians' custom. Supporters in Britain and Calcutta took the matter up in the *Statesman*, Calcutta's newspaper, but despite 'quite a wordy warfare' the café's desire for exclusivity prevailed.[13] Oswald Early described a similar confrontation, apparently in Delhi at Christmas 1916, when 'English women' objected not to 'Indians' taking tea in the café but 'they wouldn't have their tea in the same place as soldiers'. 'These are the sort of women we have come 7000 miles to defend', Early wrote.[14]

6   'A Territorial's Life in India', *Ibid*, p. 211
7   Gosse, *Memoirs of a Camp-Follower*, pp. 200-216
8   'Territorials in India', *Singapore Free Press and Mercantile Advertiser*, 15 March 1915, p. 8
9   Diary, 25 May 1915, Herbert Ewing, 1/5th Somerset, Doc.15428, 07/8/1, IWM
10 Letter, 16 March 1915, Hugh Creek, 1/4th Devon, EX2543, DMM
11 Letter, 21 March 1916, Geoffrey Coombs, 1/4th Buffs, EK/U127/2, KH&AC
12 Edward Ewens, 'A Cook's Tour in Burma and India', DD\SLI/17/1/62, SHC, Taunton
13 Walter Saunders, 1/10th Middlesex, Transcript of diary and letters, Doc 6571, 79/15/1, IWM
14 Diary, 24 December 1916, Oswald Early, 1/9th Hants, M4236, RHRM

Allan Swift reflected on the irony that although soldiers protected 'the white population', the disdain showed by many civilians 'is felt keenly'. He claimed that notices on the gates of public gardens proclaimed 'Soldiers and dogs not admitted'. Whether this was literally true (and whether the notices also forbade the entry of 'natives', to which the Territorials did not object) it seems to have been widely believed. That Territorials were 'giving our services voluntarily' – and that many were of the same class as many Anglo-Indians – made their treatment all the more objectionable.[15] This disdain continued throughout the war. When Arthur Bell was studying at the Lucknow Art School in 1919 he met a young European woman working in a shop who was friendly when he was in mufti but when she saw he in uniform she cut him – 'not a sign of recognition … I was just a lance-corporal'.[16]

Army officers often found civilians, and especially women, indifferent to the wider conflict. 'They danced, played tennis and golf, flirted and generally carried on their usual peace time existence', Alban Bacon complained. Even when their husbands went to Mesopotamia, he claimed, 'they still managed to be fairly gay'.[17] In keeping with the ethos of the times, the war was not allowed to intrude. Philip Gosse, a Territorial medical officer who had served on the Somme before being posted to India, found that Anglo-Indian civilians 'played games, drank chota pegs and gossiped', but even those who had served at the front 'scarcely ever spoke of their experiences, even to one another'. The war was 'still too close and was deliberately ignored'.[18] Territorials were affronted by British Indian civilian men's refusal to contribute more directly to the war (even if officials were prevented from enlisting). When the Indian Army was greatly expanded in 1918 and Anglo-Indian men had to register for military service, Territorials were outraged at the suggestion that 'counter jumpers in European shops' might be commissioned, and were relieved to hear that 'intelligent 1914 Terriers' would be preferred.[19]

Territorials tended to believe that Anglo-Indian civilians were apathetic toward war charities and indeed the war. Gerald Wathen, who taught at Khalsa College, Amritsar (and who would play a notable part in helping to reduce tensions among his Sikh students in 1919) recorded an encounter he had with a British matron in the Amritsar Club early in 1916. Newly arrived in India, he cast about for conversational topics, asking if she made items for soldiers – she was making lace at the time. No, she replied, she 'really had no time to make things for soldiers', not with her lace-making, her dogs, and dinners at the club …[20] Territorials at Bangalore felt so strongly about 'European Social Ostracism towards the Territorial Forces' that its YMCA hosted a formal but one-sided 'debate' on the question, at which men of the former cyclist battalions spoke strongly against the treatment they had received, including 'personal slights'.[21] 'We have voluntarily given up good homes and positions in civil life', a Private Wheat of the Royal Sussex said, '"it therefore rather hurts us that we are treated with so much reserve by a certain section of the population who are our countrymen" (applause)'. It was significant that

---

15 Diary, nd, Allan Swift, 1/6th East Surrey, ESR/25/SWIF/1, SHC, Woking
16 'RF & MP', 'Scenes of India during the First World War', *Queen's Royal Surrey Regiment Newsletter*, SHC, Woking
17 Bacon, *The Wanderings of a Temporary Warrior*, p. 60
18 Gosse, *Memoirs of a Camp-Follower*, pp. 281-82
19 Letter, 19 August 1918, Ernest Twin, 1/9th Middlesex, Doc. 16077, 08/35/1, IWM
20 Trevelyan, *The Golden Oriole*, p. 476
21 'Renunciation?', *The Royal Sussex Herald*, 27 May 1916, p. 96

the Royal Sussex had arrived in 1916 from a country that had already endured two years of wartime social change (notably the blurring of class differences) of which Bangalore's civilians either were ignorant or, if they were not, perhaps deplored. Other Territorial speakers claimed that wounded Indian troops convalescing in Britain (most in Sussex) had found British people to be very different – that is, less haughty and more welcoming – than British civilians in India. Several Hampshire speakers said that 'the Brigade' – that is, the former Territorial cyclists – wanted 'recognition and civility' and not 'patronage and charity'. This seems to have expressed the nub of the Territorials' grievance. Anglo-Indian civilians were prepared to dispense largesse to citizen soldiers as a group, but not to befriend them as individuals. That the Territorials had met 'spontaneous hospitality' when visiting the commercial and industrial Britons living on the nearby Kola Gold Fields emphasised the stiffness of the condescension they had experienced at Bangalore.

Perhaps the most remarkable example of the disinclination of Anglo Indian civilians to acknowledge the Territorials' service was that the Bishop of Bombay (in whose diocese St Mary's, Aden, fell) declined to waive the Rs75 fee for the erection of a memorial plaque to the nineteen Brecknocks who died there in 1914-15.[22]

'Who never forgot us': the case for

While complaints by Territorial 'other ranks' that Anglo-Indian civilians ignored or despised them are common, there is – perplexingly – ample evidence that Anglo-Indian civilians took an interest in soldiers' welfare. In Calcutta, for example, where troops expressed grievances against civilians who supposedly wanted troops banned from European places of entertainment, the 'rich people of City' entertained 'all the thousand men of the Regiment stationed there' at least once a month, and in their homes.[23]

British Indian civilians (like most at home) tended to neglect Territorials in India in favour of those seeing a more active war, especially in Mesopotamia. Ted Rice's battalion received (and wrote to express thanks for) large red-and-white spotted handkerchiefs sent by 'the Ladies of Bombay', who 'never forgot us'.[24] The wives of senior officers led by example, commanding local war charities as their husbands did divisions and districts. Lady Flora Poore directed the Jhansi Comforts Fund (which sent most of its parcels to West Kent men in Mesopotamia), while in Simla Lady Mary Monro organised the 'Monster Lucky Bag' Red Cross drive in early 1917, which aggressively harnessed the philanthropy of both British officials and Indian princes, raising Rs50,000 by raffling over 1200 donated prizes including panther, lion and tiger cubs, a motor cycle, four peacocks, and a pot of quince jam.[25]

In more humble ways, the European community of Bangalore worked tirelessly to support the large European garrison and depot there, throughout the war. The diary-cum-commonplace book kept by Mrs. J.S. Tait, a Bangalore memsahib, details what a demanding effort that

---

22   Letter, 13 March 1916, Correspondence relating to the grave memorials in Aden and India during the Great War, Box 17a, RMRW
23   'The War Work of the Y.M.C.A.', *The Royal Sussex Herald*, 29 July 1916, p. 163
24   Ted Rice, 'All for a Shilling a Day', QRWS/30/RICE/1, SHC, Woking
25   Scrapbook, Lady Mary Monro, 1972-07-19, NAM

entailed. (Her journal also demonstrates that local British soldiers were only one of the calls on the community's time and money, which extended to supporting the British Red Cross, Belgian refugees, the Hospital Ship *Madras*, the Mysore Ladies' War Relief Fund, and charities for orphans, blinded and limbless soldiers, prisoners of war and various war loans.) Bangalore's Europeans, to whom before 1914 'the idea of entertaining private Soldiers was unknown' began hosting teas in 1915 for gunners of a Devon Territorial battery. This 'trickle' soon became 'a flood'. Before long, civilians were receiving requests from friends in Britain to look out for 'our very nice butcher's boy', 'the porter from the village station' or (tellingly in terms of the Territorials' class complexion) 'a young man from our Town'. Civilians also noticed groups of Territorials hanging about Bangalore and heard of them being cheated in the bazaars: 'something had to be done', Mrs. Tait recalled. Various church groups – Anglicans, Wesleyan and the YMCA – hosted teas entertaining up to 750 men at a time. Whist drives, concerts, excursions and dances followed. The redoubtable Mrs Tait affirmed that 'the idle memsahib of popular report did not exist in great numbers': the qualification is significant.

Mainly Christian groups – the Church of England Institute, the YMCA or the Wesleyans – responded, hosting events at which hundreds of men at a time were served tea and buns at the 'Blighty Tea Rooms'. The buns were incidental – the men wanted 'tea and conversation' with British women, even when the ladies were elderly. Working at such a pace for months the elderly volunteers neared 'cracking point'. One (Mrs. Coleman) 'went away for a rest from which she never returned' while another collapsed 'feeling the heat terribly ... the fag of the Soldiers' teas ... wearing her out'.[26] And teas were only part of the effort. The Church of England Institute had a thousand men to supper nightly, the Wesleyan Soldiers' Home 2-300 visitors daily among half a dozen voluntary bodies. The statistics for Bangalore's YMCA alone in 1918 are illuminating:

Concerts and sing-songs	58, with an aggregate attendance of 26,810
Lectures	77, attracting 20,013
Social dances	4 with 950 attending
Debates	13, with 2650 attending
Whist drives	50 with 5110 attending
Trips and outings	47 with 1582 attending

It seems that a station's size affected the civilians' hospitality. In large stations men met less personal contact; in smaller stations civilians were often glad of the company. In Calicut in south India, Herbert Chapple was welcomed into a clergyman's home, but also a judge's, something unlikely in Calcutta or Madras. Herbert Peake found Calcutta civilians staying at Darjeeling 'very nice to us' in the hot weather of 1915.[27] Rawalpindi, a large cantonment, was, it seems, notorious for its 'damn stinking snobbery', Bert Rendall claimed. There, lorry drivers were forbidden from passing through the civil lines – perhaps because of dust and noise – but 'the bloody tommy had to wipe his boots before he could even walk down the street'.[28] As

---

26 Diary, nd (1918), Mrs. J.S. Tait, Bangalore, Doc 9772, P394, IWM
27 Diary, 26 April 1915, Herbert Peake, 1/5th West Surrey, QRWS/30/PEAK/1, SHC, Woking
28 Recollection of Bert Rendall, Mills, *A Strange War*, p. 97

civilians came to know Territorials they began to realise that they were 'quite unlike the old regular troops', as one of the leaders of Bangalore's 'comforts' effort acknowledged.[29]

Territorials also found common ground with members of British-Indian volunteer units with whom they met socially. Both were, as Edward Ewens recalled, 'civilians like ourselves' – after serving in India for over three years he still did not consider himself a soldier – but there was also a distinct class dimension to Ewens's feeling of comradeship. The men of the Cossipore Artillery Volunteers who gave him 'a very fine evening' were 'fellows employed in the Jute Mills' around Calcutta.[30] They were 'jute wallahs', in trade; very different to the official civilians who predominated in up-country stations, who maintained a more stand-offish attitude to even wartime volunteer citizen soldiers.

The strain on philanthropic civilians continued long after comparable bodies in Britain reduced or ended their efforts, causing further tension between soldiers and civilians. Early in 1919 the *Bangalore Daily Post* published criticisms that civilians were neglecting troops' welfare, a classic Anglo-Indian spat that drew in the wives of the Bishops of Madras and even Calcutta. Soldiers who had enjoyed the ladies' attentions for months rallied to their defence, one thanking them for 'taking him out of himself' to combat his '"fed-upism" and sometimes depression bordering on melancholia'.[31]

'Fighting over a cap badge': relations between Terriers

As a function of their county and regimental identity, Territorial battalions manifested differences and rivalries, though hardly of much significance. Victor Manley of Hampshire decried men of the 4th Cornwall who shared the transport *Caledonia* in 1914 for their habit of indiscriminate spitting, while sporting competitions created temporary animosities. Rivalries arising from long-standing regimental jealousy were rarely serious – how much Territorials knew or were imbued with regimental ideology is uncertain. 'We saw some fights over cap badges … that was one thing you would stand up for', Bert Rendall recalled. What began as 'friendly banter' could sometimes lead to 'two damn fools fighting over a cap badge; there were some fools about …'[32] Young men spoiling for a fight might use insults over cap badges as a pretext. Not that units were necessarily at loggerheads – the 3rd Wessex field artillery brigade comprised three batteries – one each from Hampshire, Wiltshire and Dorset.

Diaries and letters contain evidence of rivalry between 'first line' and 'reserve' Territorial battalions. When Somerset men met the West Kent in Ambala in December 1914 Herbert Ewing dismissed them as 'a scraggy and untidy lot'.[33] 2/5th Somerset men were mystified why the 1/4th Border referred to themselves as 'First Line 4th Service Battalion of the Border Regiment … though they were only Terriers like us'.[34] The title might seem arcane and needs to

---

29 Diary, Mrs. J.S. Tait, p. 13, Doc 9772, P394, IWM
30 Edward Ewens, 'A Cook's Tour in Burma and India', DD\SLI\17/1/62, SHC, Taunton
31 *Bangalore Daily Post*, February 1919, quoted in Diary, Mrs. J.S. Tait, pp. 41-42, Doc 9772, P934, IWM
32 Recollections of Bert Rendall in Mills, *A Strange War*, p. 95
33 Diary, 4 December 1914, Herbert Ewing, 1/5th Somerset, DD\SLI\17/1/61, SH, T
34 Recollections of Edward Ewens in Mills, *A Strange War*, p. 60

East Surrey Territorials and North Staffordshire Regulars at Murree. The differences between them, invisible to the onlooker, were very real to both. (ESR/6/9/11, Surrey History Centre)

be parsed. 'First Line' was perhaps a dig at the 'second line' units formed late in 1914; 'Service' (a term usually applied to Kitchener battalions) implied, perhaps that it was ready for active service; 'of the Border Regiment' perhaps indicated a closer identification with the Regular regiment than was often the case. Indeed, contemporaries could detect subtle differences between battalions that in retrospect appear similar: of the East Surrey's two battalions, one based around Guildford was regarded as more snobbish than the 5th, from Croydon. The 5th's officers, Olaf Caroe found, had no snob values … mostly small professional men, with no pretentions to "county" status … not unlike a gathering of Rotarians', he explained (writing in the 1970s).[35]

County loyalty – encouraged by Territorial associations and units – seemed to be stronger in 1914 than it later became. When Somerset infantry challenged Devon gunners in boxing aboard the *Alnwick Castle* (a product of the ship's overcrowding) Herbert Ewing expressed it in county terms: 'too much swank these men of Devon'.[36] Sharing a county affiliation was no assurance of harmony – Reg Bailey found that while the Buffs got on with the Cameronians Garrison battalion at Bareilly 'it's the RW Kents that are not very sociable'.[37] The subtleties of inter-battalion politics, always obscure, are dimly discernible, warm or frosty. Hampshire battalions, the most numerous, enjoyed particularly close relations. At Chakrata in 1915 the

---

35 Olaf Caroe, 'The Flames of Enchantment', p. iv-2, PP/MCR/207, IWM
36 Diary, 5 November 1914, Herbert Ewing, 1/5th Somerset, Doc.15428, 07/8/1, IWM
37 Letter, 16 July 1917, Reg Bailey, 1/4th Buffs, 2011-12-3, NAM

1/6th and 1/7th happily shared the hill station's tiny parade ground on alternate days, and all the Hampshire units contributed to the county's patriotic fund.

The former cyclist battalions, however, which spent most of 1916 together at Bangalore, enjoyed an uneasy relationship. Adolphus Jupe of the 1/9th Hants resented how Frank Johnson, colonel of the 2/6th Royal Sussex, would waste no opportunity to emphasise his battalion was 'Royal', 'purposely to annoy us'. Even so, Jupe considered that the Hants battalion 'definitely surpassed them in sport, endurance, turnout and all the military arts'. The Hants men scored double or even treble the Royal Sussex's musketry scores, but when a Hants party passed a group of Sussex men the latter held their rifles in the air and directed 'rude and derisive jeering' at the Hants. The brigadier settled the bad feeling by selecting a platoon at random from each of his four battalion to fire a musketry card – and the Hants platoon scored more than the other three combined.[38] Men fell out over the final of the brigade football competition, when this time Sussex defeated Hampshire 1-0. When the Sussex's band exulted, playing by the Hants' lines, Oswald Early condemned them as 'the worst lot of sportsmen I've seen'.[39] However galling they seemed at the time, these squabbles seemed not to have any effect on the battalions' effectiveness in the active service they saw together the following year.

'Elder brothers' and 'Duration men': Territorials and Regulars

When the 1/4th Border was travelling through Burma towards Maymyo its train passed one travelling south to Rangoon carrying the Border Regiment's 1st Battalion. The two trains stopped, allowing the Territorials and Regulars to talk. 'God knows how many of them will return after they have been to France', a Kendal Territorial wrote soon after (a pessimistic but as it turned out realistic concern which was in due course published in a local newspaper).[40] The remaining Regular battalions introduced novice Territorials to cantonment life and they became familiar with 'old sweats' in cantonments and on courses. The 2/5th Hants reported hosting instructors from four of the eight Regular battalions left in India, and Territorials serving in the north-west, where the Regulars were concentrated, saw a great deal of them.

Battalions posted to frontier stations, such as the 1/4th Hants at Rawalpindi and the 2/4th Hants at Quetta considered that they were more fortunate, because they lived alongside Regular units able to school them more effectively. The Territorials heard enough stories told by Regulars to get an idea of what frontier warfare entailed. As a Widcombe man told his mother in Somerset:

> … people at home think the soldier in India has a holiday. Some do. But the soldier on the frontier (I mean the regulars), fighting the uncivilised Afghans and marching hundreds of miles in extreme heat over hilly country has a worse job than any soldier.[41]

Like the Territorials, 'they would rather be over in France, but someone has to do it', and for the time being that was the eight battalions of Regulars, and their more numerous Indian comrades.

---

38 Adolphus Jupe, 'Around the World with the "P.B.I."', pp. 11-12, RHRM
39 Diary, 28 August 1916, Oswald Early, 1/9th Hants, M4236, RHRM
40 Clipping, Lawrence Hoggarth, 1/4th Border, Album 35 Acc. Nos 3024-3345, CMML
41 *Shepton Mallet Journal*, 24 September 1915, p 2

East Surrey men in a punkah-festooned bungalow displaying embroidery and crocheting skills they had learned from Regulars. (ESR/6/9/11, Surrey History Centre)

Close acquaintance allowed judgments to be made. 'Their outlook on life was different to ours', Bernard Searle observed. At a signalling school in Poona Regulars 'didn't think much' of what the they called 'Duration men'. Searle's Territorial barrack-mates (drawn from various regiments) 'only cleaned enough to pass inspection by the Sergeant Major'. The Regulars, however, professed to be 'mighty proud of their Regiments and their Battle Honours' – the capitals reflect their regard – 'and spit and polish was the main object of their daily routine'.[42] Having observed 'the careerism of the mercenary army' in France, poet and Kitchener officer Richard Aldington damned its 'narrowness, its comparative idleness, its encouragement of unscrupulous emulation, its bullying, its monotony, its enforced respect for rank' and the feelings of 'rivalry, hatred, and bitterness' they fostered; all so different to the Territorials.[43] Frank Richards evoked the Regulars' cantonment life vividly in his memoir *Old Soldier Sahib*, with its descriptions of tough barrack-room culture, monthly visits to prostitutes in 'the Rag', drinking schools and using boots and fists to enforce natives' obedience. Above all, Regular units enforced a strict adherence to the hierarchy of rank, with privates and non-commissioned officers unable to mix socially, and men addressing officers only through sergeants as intermediaries. As a subaltern posted to the 2nd Royal Welsh Fusiliers in 1915, Robert Graves encountered a battalion recently returned from eighteen years in India (as it happened, the one Richards had served in). In *Goodbye to All*

---

42 Memoir, p. 16, Bernard Searle, 1/1st Kent, NMERM 2008-1640, MM
43 Aldington, *Roads to Glory*, p. 133

That he described how its men 'think … it's still in India. They treat the French civilians just like "niggers", kick them about [and] talk army Hindustani at them'.[44]

By contrast, as a Hampshire man explained in a report for his regimental journal, Territorials valued a 'feeling of unity and general "palliness"' in which 'everybody "mucks in" together, regardless of 'their relative positions in civil life'.[45] Territorials' letters and journals disclose many subtle differences between men of the two forces. Regulars, for example, could be simply ordered to undergo vaccination; Territorials (as the poem 'A Terrier's Growl' demonstrated) had to be persuaded to undergo inoculation for smallpox.[46] Fred Mundy recalled that 'after parade NCOs and privates mingled as they had always done at home. This behaviour was foreign to the regular', but was characteristic of Territorials.[47] Many Regulars had had no contact with Territorials, if they had not served at home before 1908. When the Territorials of the 4th Sussex Battery met fellow gunners, but Regulars at Rawalpindi in 1916 they found that the Regulars were 'dubious', but as fellow gunners made friends.[48] Some of the Territorials (Somersets and West Kents) came from regiments with Regular battalions obliged to remain in India. Their relations were cordial, but not close. When the 4th West Kent met the (Regular) 2nd West Kent at Nasirabad on the long rail journey to Jubbulpore, they reported that the Regulars passed on greetings, that the regulars 'wished to be remembered to all old townies', and the old sweats passed hints on Indian service – such as that Jubbulpore to them was simply 'Jubb'.[49] When serving in the same cantonments (and only a few Territorial battalions were able to) Regulars sought out the newcomers and were often condescending. At Rawalpindi in mid-1915 Regulars were 'anxious to make our acquaintance', Allan Swift wrote, and their stories of the frontier were 'thrilling and ghastly'.[50]

Territorials looked up to Regulars as 'elder brothers', as an East Surrey officer put it, with 'everyone keen to live up to the standard' they set.[51] At first condescending toward the newcomers, they found that in some aspects, such as fitness and sporting prowess, Territorials could readily compete. When the 1/4th Wilts played Regular teams at Kailana in the hills 'feelings ran very high' at their football matches, and the Wiltshire team won the local league cup 'greatly to the disgust of the Regulars'.[52] The 2/5th Somerset likewise found that when playing the Duke of Wellington's the Regulars 'suffered from swelled head a bit'.[53] Regulars dominated the All-India Boxing Tournament, widely reported in the British-Indian press. Surrey Territorial Gerald Gibbs thought that Regulars 'though brave men of good physique and endurance' seemed 'terribly narrow and set in their ways'.[54] Conversely, Regulars, Harry Canham thought 'look down on the "terriers" as soldiers', even as Territorials thought that Regulars were of 'a lower class of society than themselves'. They used 'lurid adjectives' too

---

44   Graves, *Goodbye to All That*, p. 168
45   *The Hampshire Regimental Journal*, October 1915, p. 339
46   *The Tiger*, April 1915, p. 27
47   Mundy, *A Journal of the 1/4th Battalion Wiltshire Regiment*, pp. 267-68
48   Ted Holter, 'A Terrier in World War I', Doc 4545, 81/9/1, IWM
49   *Kent Messenger*, 27 March 1915
50   Diary, nd, Allan Swift, ESR/25/SWIF/1, SHC, Woking
51   'The East Surrey Regiment in India 1914-19', ESR/10/14/3/1, SHC, Woking
52   Mundy, *A Journal of the 1/4th Battalion Wiltshire Regiment*, p. 45
53   Edward Ewens, 'A Cook's Tour in Burma and India', DD\SLI/17/1/62, SHC, Taunton
54   Gibbs, *Survivor's Story*, p. 13

freely, and he thought that one effect of the war would be 'a more extensive use of filthy language'.[55]

Later in the war, in a reversal of the situation in 1915, Regulars began to express dissatisfaction that Territorials were receiving allowances they did not enjoy (though it is possible that in fact the Territorials were merely catching up). Either way, Harry Canham thought, this 'has undoubtedly contributed towards the not too amicable relations which exist between the Regulars and Territorials'.[56] The comparison weighed particularly heavily upon Territorials. One of the consolations Francis Bowker felt while being evacuated from Mesopotamia to Bombay in July 1915 was that his battalion 'while in India & since out here ... the Regt has held its own with any of the Regular Battns'.[57] Men, and especially officers, of the eight Regular battalions left in India understandably resented missing out on the supreme professional challenge open to them. When William Villiers-Stuart inspected the 2nd North Stafford at Nowshera in 1918 he found them 'sulky', with inexperienced officers who had replaced those able to get away to war. Soon after he found the 2nd West Kent 'no good! ... below standard' – 'the only beastly inspection' he conducted, he thought because of its colonel's arrogance.[58]

Owen Smith (whose letters to his sister, Anna, explain much of the arcane details of troops' life) observed while enjoying tea one afternoon at Solon that 'Regular soldiers in India never have eatables for tea only a "Dixy of Chai" but we often have jam or butter'.[59] It was just one of the many distinctions that separated men of the two kinds of British soldier in India, differences that mattered. Territorials carried with them into military life the expectations and standards of their civilian lives. When the Hampshire clerk travelled back from his Christmas 1915 visit to relatives he travelled in a first-class carriage, though on the third-class ticket issued to British other ranks.

Territorials confounded many Anglo-Indian assumptions about who or what soldiers were. When Herbert Ewing, a middle-class man, spent a week at Simla as the guest of Everard Coats and his wife Sara Duncan his hosts expressed 'a great interest in our background, as if we were something new and strange to them dressed up in soldier uniform'. Ewing supposed that 'we are a bit quaint and perhaps puny compared to the smart rough and tough regular troops'.[60] Indeed, Territorials seemed not to exhibit the 'hardness' expected of Regulars. William Villiers-Stuart, one of the most experienced frontier soldiers (and during the war commandant of the Mountain Warfare School at Abbottabad), described how in 1916 his 1/5th Gurkha Rifles had been camped beside the 1/5th East Surrey. The Gurkhas were to break camp and leave very early in the morning and the Territorials' colonel, begged Villiers-Stuart not to wake his men. When the East Surrey eventually rose, at an hour acceptable to their solicitous colonel, they found that the entire Gurkha battalion had left without any of the Territorials realising.[61] Villiers-Stuart doubtless often told that story at the Surrey Territorials' expense.

55 Letter, 1 January 1917, Harry Canham, 2/4th Border, CMML
56 Letter, 20 December 1917, Harry Canham, 2/4th Border, *Ibid*
57 Letter, 30 July 1915, Francis Bowker, 1/4th Hants, Doc. 8094, 99/15/1, IWM
58 Maxwell, (ed.), *Villiers-Stuart goes to War*, pp. 215; 253
59 Letter, 26 April 1916, Owen Smith, 1/6th Hants, M766, RHRM
60 Diary, 25 May 1915, Herbert Ewing, 1/5th Somerset, Doc.15428, 07/8/1, IWM
61 Maxwell, *Villiers-Stuart on the Frontier*, p. 163

Condescending Territorials felt sorry for the Regulars, wondering (like Hugh Creek) 'how on earth fellows can stick the army in peacetime especially in a place like this, it isn't life … it's only a monotonous existence'.[62] 'I pity the poor regular who has seven years of this', Herbert Ewing wrote in his diary at the height of the hot weather.[63] Though photographs of them on parade might suggest that they were interchangeable, and while both might have seemed to be products of the Edwardian English working class, Territorials and Regulars came from different gradations of that culture, and its distinctions persisted.

'Salaams from India': keeping in touch with home

When a 13-year-old applied for a job in a boot workshop in Britain, the proprietor asked after his elder brothers, who had left the workplace to go to war. Two, Frank and Albert, were in France. What of the third brother, Lionel? Was he in France as well? The lad shook his head. 'e's mindin' India'.[64] What did the younger brother know of Lionel's life?

Naturally men wrote home, describing their voyages and the novelty of their situations, letters which many families passed on for publication in local newspapers free of censorship besides their editors' judgment. In the war's early months local newspapers published many articles and photographs – 'An Ashford Boy Abroad'; 'Axminster Territorials'. Reports of Border men's doings published in Westmoreland and Cumberland invariably included the towns from which men hailed – Appleby, Brampton, Windermere, Keswick and Kendal. Publishing soldiers' letters technically contravened *King's Regulations*, but was at first connived at because they were regarded as 'helpful to recruiting' and 'sustaining a genuine interest' in Territorials' service.[65] These letters provide vital evidence, but only until about mid-1915, when increasingly strict censorship ended their publication. Just before Easter (early in April) troops in India were 'warned against communication with the press' and cautioned that they would be held responsible for breaches by friends and family.[66] Once word percolated to Britain, detailed references to men in India practically dried up in local newspapers.

Accordingly, most County Associations lost touch with 'their' own units. Though still in being, the Associations had surrendered most of their functions to the War Office, and had little occasion to take a direct interest in their battalions in India. The Wiltshire Association minuted its quarterly (no longer monthly) meeting in 1918 that 'both the 1st and 2nd Line Units are still in India. There is nothing special to report'.[67] (In fact, the Association was seriously out of touch – by this time the 1/4th Wilts had been serving in Palestine for over a year, and in fact the colonel of the battalion had been mortally wounded – on the very last day it saw action.[68]) How complete was the ignorance in Britain of the Indian Territorials may be grasped from

---

62 Letter, 18 February 1915, Hugh Creek, 1/4th Devon, EX2543, DMM
63 Diary, 3 June 1915, Herbert Ewing, 1/5th Somerset, Doc.15428, 07/8/1, IWM
64 *Chronicle* (Adelaide) 13 February 1915, p. 55
65 Sir Harold Elverston, House of Commons, *Hansard*, 16 February 1915
66 Walter Saunders, 1/10th Middlesex, Transcript of diary and letters, Doc. 6571, 79/15/1, IWM
67 Wiltshire County Association (Territorial Force), Quarterly meeting, 19 September 1918, L1/100/3, W&SHC
68 Lt-Col Allan Armstrong was mortally wounded on 19 September 1918.

'Greetings from Mhow', a postcard sent by 'Jack' to his mother in Wales, though the local artist did not include Wales on the map of Britain at left. (1/1st Brecknockshire collection, Box 17, Regimental Museum of the Royal Welsh)

an exchange in the papers of Lord Chelmsford. Almost at the war's end Sir Harry Crichton, Chairman of the Hampshire Territorial Association, wrote to the Viceroy enquiring about the whereabouts and welfare of units from his county. Hampshire had sent eight battalions and nine batteries of artillery and 'I naturally take a very great interest in them, and especially in their Commanding Officers'. He had wanted to arrange for some recognition for their colonels, but the War Office had been unhelpful: 'being in India they can do nothing'.[69] Chelmsford replied, though not for a further three months, giving vague and brief details of their service, but naming only Francis Bowker, who had been killed, in Mesopotamia in January 1916, as Sir Harry surely already knew.[70] Neither example bespeaks the 'very great interest' professed, on either side.

While Territorial Associations had no role in recruiting or supplying 'their' units overseas, most took on the task of acting as an 'enquiry bureau', advising relatives about men's whereabouts and conditions of service such as pay, promotion and allowances. Otherwise, as the minute books of several associations reveal, they had almost nothing to do with their battalions serving in India.[71] On the outbreak of war higher commanders tended not to recognise the claims of the

---

69 Letter, 30 September 1918, Sir Harry Crichton to Chelmsford, No. 219a, Eur.Mss.E264/15, BL
70 Letter 13-14 January 1919, Chelmsford to Sir Harry Crichton, No. 162, *Ibid*
71 Kent Territorial Force Association, Minute books 1914-18, MD/TA, KH&AC; Middlesex Territorial Association Minute books, 0994/002, LMA

Territorial Force – the Territorial Force Advisory Council was abolished in 1914, and the Army Council made fewer references to Territorials as the war continued.[72]

Though regarded as part of the local community, establishing a presence within the county in the few years before the war, Territorials, and especially those in India, became merely a part of a vast war effort. As the fighting in France, Gallipoli or Palestine drew hundreds of thousands of volunteers, and later conscripts, into the forces, and cost many killed or wounded, the Territorials were understandably overlooked. While a few supporters enquired after Territorials' pay and conditions in 1916 (and the Troop Train Tragedy attracted Parliamentary scrutiny) as a whole the Territorials were largely forgotten by more pressing concerns – the shell crisis that ousted Asquith's government, Zeppelin raids, and the costly stagnation on the Western Front. Friends and even relatives lost contact. In mid-1916 Owen Smith was surprised to receive a letter from a former workmate at Timothy White's (the retail chemist's in Portsmouth) because 'they don't write so often as when I 1st came out here'.[73]

One of the best examples of how Territorials kept in touch with home comes through the letters compiled by the Great Chart Soldiers and Sailors Fund. In Great Chart, a village a few miles west of Ashford, Kent, Mrs. Elizabeth Strutts corresponded with villagers in uniform and created scrapbooks of their letters, which she made available to subscribers to a Great Chart Soldiers and Sailors Fund.[74] Mrs. Strutts circulated the books (but strictly 'among subscribers *Only*'), allowing them to hold them for just two days at a time. By the war's end she had created 22 volumes of correspondence, with Book 5 holding 'Letters received from men who are in India'; fourteen of them. 'Many a man', Sergeant William Brunger assured his friends in Great Chart, 'has been cheered to know that those … in his native village are constantly thinking of and praying for him'.[75] But it became clear that those at home were not thinking or praying constantly.

From late 1916 Indian Territorials attracted meagre attention, the subject of questions about electric fans in Barrackpore, 'where West of England regiments are stationed' (by a Devon MP), or a request that Territorial gunners be permitted to wear badges bearing the Royal Artillery motto 'Ubique' (they were not).[76] In 1917 MPs raised a handful of questions about them, concerning an obscure regulation about the relative precedence between Territorial and Regular officers, the cost of officers' quarters in Simla and the duty payable on tobacco sent to India (supposedly none, though , though when Newton Abbott's patriots sent Christmas puddings to the 1/6th Devon late in 1915 they were not delivered until they paid £4/10 in unpaid duty on tobacco sent earlier).[77] In 1918, MPs asked about awards to members of the Waziristan Field Force, the pay of Dorset Territorials in Bangalore and Territorials' eligibility for the 'Indian Frontier Medal' (they were not). Until Parliamentarians again became interested in

---

72 'Territorial Force Advisory Council', WO32/9698, NAUK; Index of the Decisions of … the Army Council … 1914-21, WO33/1021, NAUK
73 Letter, 1 August 1916, Owen Smith, 1/6th Hants, M766, RHRM
74 Great Chart Fund, Book 5, KA&HC
75 Letter, Sgt William Brunger, 1/5th Buffs, *Ibid*
76 George Lambert, House of Commons, *Hansard*, 25 October 1916; Henry Forster, House of Commons, *Hansard*, 2 November 1916. Territorial gunners wore an identical badge but without the motto 'Ubique', meaning 'everywhere'.
77 Ellis, *Newton Abbott's Great War*, pp. 31

their constituents' frustration at not being allowed to return home, Indian Territorials remained practically invisible.

Many units relied upon county charities (which naturally directed most of their effort to where most men served, on the Western Front) but some helped men of particular battalions. In Winchester, Esme Bowker formed a committee in Winchester in April 1915 for her husband's battalion, the 1/4th Hants. Within three months it had raised £778, sending to the battalion handkerchiefs, foot powder and 'vermin killer', in addition to spine pads and tinted glasses.[78] The '4th Buffs Comforts Fund' sought registration under the War Charities Act in December 1916. It collected £94 before the Army Council objected (on spurious 'security' grounds) to the use of a unit's identifying number. It became the Territorial Buffs Comforts Fund, but its fund-raising, now embracing more than just the 1/4th, seems to have remained modest, perhaps because the battalion was serving in India.[79] (Even so, its members, sent 992 shirts and 900 pairs of socks, made by 'village working parties' in east Kent, before it was subsumed by a larger organisation.[80])

A tiny portion of the letters, parcels and postcards that Territorials sent home from India has survived, and nothing but a handful of the even more numerous letters sent to them. We can only infer what 'Salaams from India' they sent – that phrase, written on a card sent by Cornelius Scarrott in Rawalpindi to friends in Small Dole, Sussex, survives only in a quotation in a letter to him from a friend.[81] Fanny Collins, a friend wrote to Cornelius, spending the hot weather of 1917 at Ranikhet, reminding him that 'your name is read out every Sunday evening in Beeding Church', a couple of miles down the River Adur.[82]

Two local rolls of honour offer opportunities to check a general impression against local evidence, from Trowbridge, Wiltshire (population 12,000) and Newton Abbott, Devon (population 14,000) with similar results. Trowbridge's detailed *Roll of Honour*, devotedly compiled by the Rev. Harry Sanders, shows that only two of Trowbridge's 300 dead actually died in India, with another eighteen serving in India before dying in Palestine or Mesopotamia.[83] Newton Abbott, in Devon, lost nearly 400 dead, but only four men died in India (three Territorials), with another sixteen in Mesopotamia.[84] The listing of Trowbrigians street-by-street suggests that the awareness of Indian service was much more general. No fewer than 54 of the town's 68 streets had families with Territorials in India, a total of 192 men (overwhelmingly members of the 1/4th and 2/4th Wilts, which in 1914 formed a company in Trowbridge, but including men of artillery units and other county Territorial battalions). This meant that families of Trowbridge men in India would have relatively easily been able to keep in touch with families in the same situation. Other locally-recruited units also sustained informal bonds. At Christmas 1916 the 2/4th Somerset received a sum of £55 from former volunteer officers in Bath 'to remind men that they are not quite forgotten by those at home'.[85]

---

78 Clipping in Esme Bowker papers, M1539, RHRM
79 '4th Buffs Comforts Fund', C/A 2/16/39, KA&HC
80 *The War Dragon*, November 1916, p. 9
81 Letter, 11 July 1917, Cornelius Scarrott, 1/5th West Kent, AM 719/1/4, WSRO
82 Ibid
83 Sanders, *Trowbridge Roll of Honour*, G15/229/4, S&WHC
84 Ellis, *Newton Abbott's Great War*, pp. 176-88
85 Part 1 orders, 2/4th Somerset Light Infantry, December 1916, DD\SLI/6/36, SHC, Taunton

12

Stalemate in Aden; victory in Mesopotamia

The Aden Field Force, now under a new, more prudent commander, Major-General James Stewart, resumed its watchful confrontation of the Ottoman force in Aden's hinterland. For the rest of the war, as an East Surrey manuscript history put it, 'no important changes took place in the Military situation'.[1] Stewart's force faced 'constant patrol skirmishes and small outpost actions', as Lord Curzon explained in the House of Lords in December 1917.[2] The campaign dragged on against an Ottoman force smaller than its British-Indian adversary and cut off from reinforcement or re-supply from Turkey. 'Is it not possible to drive out these Turks and get rid of them?', asked an MP (a retired colonel and a former Chief Commissioner in Baluchistan) in frustration in August 1918.[3] It seemed that it was not.

'A queer war': the 1/4th Buffs

The Brecknocks' losses in the disastrous foray to Lahej brought another Territorial battalion to Aden, the 1/4th Buffs, which relieved it in August 1915. (The 1/4th West Kent was at first warned for Aden, until the order was corrected and the 1/4th East Kent went. After 'a little rational reflection' the West Kents realised 'we had had a somewhat lucky escape'.[4])

The following month the Buffs sent out a column to Waht, the western anchor of the Ottoman line. It lost a man to Turkish fire ('the first of the battalion slain in the great cause of England'), but also a further seven men dead of sunstroke.[5] By November 93 men were in hospital, with another 120 attending daily. Aden was 'a waterless desert', Geoffrey Coombs wrote to a school-friend in Dover, 'we marched in places up to our knees in sand with the temperature over 120°

---

1 'The East Surrey Regiment in India 1914-19', ESR/10/14/3/1, SHC, Woking
2 Lord Curzon, House of Lords, *Hansard*, 4 December 1917
3 Charles Yate, House of Commons, *Hansard*, 7 August 1918
4 *The Queen's Own Gazette*, Vol. XXXIV, No. 8, August 1915, p. 3368
5 Moody, *Historical Records of the Buffs*, p. 119

in the shade'.[6] The most frequent entry in the Buffs' war diary is 'nothing to report' – on all but two days for November 1915.[7]

On much of the line and for much of the time the opposing front lines were far apart – up to six miles – so the trenches, redoubts and strong points were lightly manned, but the line remained stationary. Why did the British not launch an all-out attack and drive the Ottoman force off? Because the Ottomans and their local allies would probably have disappeared into the surrounding hills and waged a guerilla war, consuming a larger force in efforts to hunt them down. The British force, therefore, merely aimed to contain the existing front. It was, as a gunner officer explained, 'a queer war … really nothing more or less than field days with a real enemy'.[8]

'The desert is a weird looking place': the 1/4th Cornwall

The 1/4th Cornwall in turn relieved the Buffs in late January 1916 and distributed its four companies between the headquarters at the Crater and the port at Steamer Point. The Cornishmen formed an ammunition column to assist the British gunners of the Royal Garrison Artillery, and in March 1916 made ready a detachment of 350 men to go to Abyssinia until the orders were rescinded. Not until October did Cornishmen join the field force at Sheikh Othman. Thomas Heard recorded his first sight of the front line there. Rather than a continuous line of trenches (which rapidly filled with wind-blown sand) he found 'just a few outposts' and 'a lot of barbed wire entanglements laid all over the place'. But even to a man with Indian experience as he a Cornishman found 'the desert is a weird looking place' where 'sandstorms prevent one from seeing far ahead'. Heard, by this time a sergeant, described his experience of commanding a platoon in the firing line when his company fired on Ottoman troops on 7 December:

> We were fighting hard all the time … I took my section on to the firing line … and had a hot time from the Turks second line. I seemed to possess a charmed life and kept my men together all the time with shrapnel and rifle shots coming from every direction … [9]

The 1/4th Cornwall lost six dead and 13 wounded in this, its last action in Aden, a quarter of its 23 fatal casualties. In February 1917 the battalion left Aden, not to return to India, but to go to Egypt and on to Palestine.

Perhaps the most notable Territorial action at Aden in 1916, however, was near the village of Imad, on the far eastern side of the perimeter, on 16 March, when Territorial gunners of the 1/4th Hants howitzer battery took part in repelling an Ottoman incursion toward Sheik Othman. On the Turks' approach a 'flying column' set out to reinforce the defenders, while units of the 'General Reserve', mostly Indian infantry but including the Hants battery, were mobilised. The British-Indian force met and drove off the attack, by some 900 Ottoman regulars and 300 Arab irregulars, and as the Turks withdrew the supporting British mountain guns and the Territorials' howitzers did 'very heavy execution' on their columns, harrying them for

---

6   Letter, 21 March 1916, Geoffrey Coombs, 1/4th Buffs, EK/U127/2, KH&AC
7   War diary, 1/4th Buffs, November 1915, WO95/5438, NAUK
8   'One who was in it', 'A Queer War', *Journal of the Royal Artillery*, Vol. LIV, 1927-28, pp. 257-69
9   Diary, 7 December 1916, Thomas Heard, 1/4th Cornwall, CRM, Bodmin

Territorial gunners of the 2/1st Devon Battery, firing 4.5-inch howitzers at Sheik Othman in 1916. (Q13072, Imperial War Museum)

over a mile. The defenders lost just two dead and six wounded, but they estimated that over 350 Turks had become casualties. The howitzers fired about 350 rounds of Lyddite, high explosive shells (developed at Lydd in Kent), and the commander of the section of the Aden defences commended Major Archibald Hartnall, the battery's commanding officer, 'who handled his battery in an efficient manner and by accurate and well timed fire inflicted severe losses on the enemy'.[10] (Exactly a year later Hartnell, 42-years-old and from the Isle of Wight, was dead, dying, probably of illness, in Jubbulpore.) His battery's work was a sign that Territorials were ready to take their part in defending even the empire's most remote corners.

'Our first real scrap': 1/6th East Surrey

The 1/6th East Surrey duly relieved the 1/4th Duke of Cornwall's in February 1917. (Why particular battalions were ordered to Aden, war diaries and headquarters files do not record.) While recuperating at Chakrata, in the hills above Nowshera the following year, Sergeant Ernest Head, who had been a member of the East Surrey battalion scout section, wrote an account of the battalion's time in Aden. Ernest Head and his comrades left Karachi with 'very mixed feelings', though looking forward to active service, though neither they nor 'millions of English people' had heard of any fighting on 'such a small front … completely overshadowed by the European conflict'. Though accustomed to Indian heat, Ernest found Aden's climate 'very lowering'. Temperatures of more than 105°, its high humidity made it 'far more uncomfortable than an Indian heat wave'.[11] The airless Crater was exceptionally hot – Steamer Point barracks

---

10 'Action at Imad, 16 March 1916', WO106/565, NAUK
11 Ernest Head, 'Aden', Doc. 13306, 04/38/1, IWM

East Surrey skirmishers seeking cover from Ottoman snipers in the front line at Aden. (ESR/25/BURG/1, Surrey History Centre)

exposed to cooling sea breezes if also infested with vermin. Aden's climate compelled British troops to exceptional measures. East Surrey men received spine-pads, blue-tinted goggles, helmet shades, ankle puttees (and, for the scouts, white sandshoes), in addition to their sun helmets.

While it had arrived in February, the East Surrey entered the front line only in November. Rotating spells with Dogras, Rajputs and Punjabis, its men spent a week on the foremost picquets, a week in reserve and another as part of a 'flying column'. It too made raids on Ottoman posts, some up to 9 miles from the British lines. A line from the report on operations at Aden suggests their scale: 'East Surrey Scouts [including Ernest Head] had a skirmish with a Turkish party about 30 strong'.[12] Finding movement in soft sand trying, the East Surrey scout sergeant persuaded the authorities to allow his twenty scouts to mount mules (like French Foreign Legionnaires), making them the Territorials' only mounted riflemen; briefly – unruly mules and inexpert riders curtailed the experiment.

In mid-December the East Surrey had what Henry Brain called 'our first real scrap', losing two men killed and three wounded while covering an attack by Indian troops.[13] But two men gained recommendations for a Distinguished Conduct Medal and a Military Medal. A week later in another attack on Hatum ('undoubtedly the hardest fight we had'), it lost four killed and 27 wounded under heavy shelling, but soon after was ordered away from Aden.[14] To the men's 'great disappointment' it too returned to India rather than going on to Palestine.[15] On returning to Agra in the 'cold' weather, however, the East Surrey appreciated its 'lovely green trees and grass'.[16]

---

12 Operations of the Aden Field Force, 1 February-31 March 1917, WO106/566, NAUK
13 Memoir, Henry Brain, 1/6th East Surrey, ESR/25/BRAIN/2, SHC, Woking
14 'The East Surrey Regiment in India 1914-19', ESR/10/14/3/1, SHC, Woking
15 Pearse & Sloman, *History of the East Surrey Regiment*, p. 31
16 Memoir, Henry Brain, 1/6th East Surrey, ESR/25/BRAIN/2, SHC, Woking

Living conditions for some troops were more tolerable – the 1/6th East Surrey occupied the big pre-war, double-storied bungalows on the sea front rather than tents. Enjoying plenty of sport, the East Surreys were at their healthiest since leaving Britain. Head learned to play tennis at Aden, and troops at Steamer Point played football, and hockey, with golf 'reserved' for officers. Sport, Head wrote, 'made life worth living'.[17] Continuing the phenomenon of Territorials learning new skills, many learned to swim at Aden, in a pool safe from the sharks infesting its harbour.

Service in Aden demanded unremitting vigilance and stern discipline, evident from *Standing Orders* issued by the East Surrey during its tour. Men were warned, for instance, that 'no man must be allowed to empty his water bottle … just because it has become hot and unpalatable'.[18] General Stewart reported that his vigorous patrolling and harassment of the Turkish force occupying Aden's hinterland 'should facilitate decisive military action when the time comes'; but the time never came.[19]

'Nothing to report': 1/7th Hants

The 1/7th Hants arrived in January 1918, mostly remaining at Steamer Point and the Crater, though taking turns in the line at Sheikh Othman. The 1/7th had lost fewer 1914 men than most – 120 of its 500 other ranks had arrived in 1914, though only four of its 30 original officers remained. The battalion's war diary is replete with typed reports of very minor incidents, such as the account of a company which made a foray out of the line at Mansur in March 1918. Its officer's sense of frustration may be expressed in the conclusion that 'I had no casualties. No ammunition was expended', though two drums of Lewis gun ammunition was lost when a mule ran off.[20] Though more voluminous than the 'nothing to reports' that fill the war diaries of predecessors' war diaries, the Hants pages are equally uneventful.

The 1/7th Hants served on in Aden after the Armistice – the last Ottoman troops in Yemen only surrendered in March 1919. Then they watched drifting sand fill in the trenches on the outpost line. The Hants made the most of heavy-hanging time by finding and cleaning inscriptions (including regimental badges) created by Regular battalions serving in Aden before the war and maintaining the cemetery. The 1/7th's war diary includes on 31 January 1919 the note: 'strength … 24 officer 632 other ranks and 1 officer (R.A.M.C.) and 1 Pte (1st Brecknocks S.W.B.) attached'. This was Private Henry Povey, the man captured in July 1915 who had survived three and a half years of captivity in the isolated Ottoman camp in the Aden hinterland.[21]

---

17 Memoir, Ernest Head, 1/6th East Surrey, Doc. 13306, 04/38/1, IWM
18 *Standing Orders for field service, Aden*, ESR/10/6/1, SHC, Woking
19 'Operations of the Aden Field Force, 1917', WO106/567, NAUK
20 War diary, 1/7th Hants, March 1918, WO95/5438, NAUK
21 War diary, 1/7th Hants, January 1919, *Ibid*. Private Povey's family knew that he had been captured by October (*Brecon Radnor Express*, 7 October 1915), though parcels sent to him via Constantinople could not be delivered because the Ottoman force in Aden remained isolated. He seems to have remained a prisoner with British internees, looked after by the American consul either at Saana or nearby Manakhah, until the war's end: 'Letters sent to Prisoners of War', IOR, R/20/A/3965, BL

Just over half of the 80-odd British deaths in Aden were Territorials. A large number were Royal Artillery gunners (some of whom could have been Territorials), and some men who died in transit, often returning from India.[22]

'We shall win out here': Maude's offensive

The fall of Kut in April 1916 had left the troops holding the Tigris line demoralised and sick, with men suffering from dysentery and scurvy in the terrible shade-less summer heat, the air thick with flies in the day time and sand-flies at night. When the 15th Indian Division Territorials arrived, early in 1916, (comprising the 1/5th West Surrey – Ted Rice's battalion – the 1/4th Dorset and the 1/4th Somerset) they thought that conditions in the hospitals around Basra were 'distressing to a degree' and 'almost at their worst'.[23] In fact, the Mesopotamian Expeditionary Force's medical services had been overhauled after the appalling suffering of 1915.

General Sir Stanley Maude arrived to take over command in Mesopotamia in mid-1916. Building up his numbers and, even more importantly, re-organising and developing the British logistic system – docks and wharves at Basra, warehouses, roads, light railways, rest camps and hospitals – Maude decisively changed the mood and in time the fortunes of the British force. By the end of 1916 the 1/4th Hants was more-or-less back to strength, after large drafts from other Hampshire battalions in India; 'good men, well trained and fit', and for the rest of 1916 the battalion prepared for Maude's army to resume the offensive.[24] Sir Charles Monro, the incoming Commander-in-Chief, visited Mesopotamia in October on his way to assuming command in India. The War Office taking control in February, Maude's arrival in July and Monro taking command in November combined to reverse the campaign's fortunes.

Maude, a remote technocrat, unable to delegate and demanding of subordinates, devoted himself to reforming the Mesopotamian Expeditionary Force. From July to September 1916 he built up its strength and sought clarification of his mission. The reorganisation of Basra saw the introduction of dredgers, wharves, warehouses, a pilot service, and roads and railways to carry supplies up-country, as well as new steamers and river transport. Some Territorials found their way into the crews of river steamers, sardonically known as 'Kitchener's Bastards', while many others, who had been transferred to signals, transport and technical units took part in the campaign apart from the Territorial battalions forming about a tenth of Maude's force. Late in 1916 he shifted his headquarters from Basra to the front, a sign of his determination to re-open the offensive.

Reinforced in fighting units and sustained by a massively strengthened supply organisation, Maude's force renewed the attempt to advance up the Tigris, this time with Kut and Baghdad as its objectives. The attacks confronted the familiar challenge of Ottoman troops holding trenches anchored on the river, from which they enfiladed attackers on the opposite bank. Territorial battalions in the Indian brigades took a full part in these decisive operations. In October, the 1/5th Buffs and the 1/4th Devon were part of the force Maude directed as a feint against Turkish

---

22 Analysis of cemetery list, Maala War Cemetery, Aden, www.cwgc.org.uk
23 [Dorsetshire Regiment] Regimental History Committee, *History of the Dorsetshire Regiment 1914-1919*, Part II, p. 24
24 Atkinson, *The Royal Hampshire Regiment*, Vol. II, p. 167

Men of the 1/4th Hants rehearsing for the crossing of the Tigris at the Shumran Bend in February 1917. Half of those involved would be killed or wounded. (Q102859, Imperial War Museum)

lines above Kut. The next month the 1/6th Devon joined the assault on the main Ottoman line on the Shatt-el-Hai, joined soon after by the 1/4th Devon (and of course the Indian battalions of their brigades, which formed most of Maude's army). Despite astute British manoeuvering and dogged attacks, tenacious Ottoman defence forestalled Kut's re-capture until late February.

On the Shatt-el-Hai in February the 1/4th Devon attacked a warren of Ottoman trenches beside the 1/9th Gurkhas over ground on which the 36th and 45th Sikhs had been massacred the day before, just one episode in a twenty-day struggle to break out of the positions which both sides had held since the previous April. Next, Maude's infantry had to surmount the Shumran Bend, west of Kut. This entailed an attack over the river, with men of the 1/4th Hants poling pontoons across the swirling yellow flood to get Norfolks and Gurkhas across. The official history recognised that the Hants were 'among the heaviest sufferers'.[25] Almost half – 110 out of 230 – of the rowers were hit by the time the lodgement was secure, including 49 out of a draft of 100 men sent from the 2/7th to the 1/4th Hants a few months before.[26] After the crossing the 1/4th joined the frontal assault of the Ottoman entrenchments across the neck of the peninsula, in which it lost a further 182 men out of 450. Among the missing was Owen Smith, in whose last letter to his sister Anna he had told her that 'in my own mind I have not the slightest doubt that we shall win out here'.[27]

---

25 Moberly, *The Campaign in Mesopotamia*, Vol. III, p. 180n
26 *History of the Hampshire Territorial Force Association*, p. 167
27 Letter 22 February 1917, Owen Smith, 1/6th Hants (serving with 1/4th Hants) M766, RHRM

Maude's army advanced cautiously, conscious of the need to supply the foremost troops (and evacuate the wounded), but using the mobility conferred by the Tigris and its gunboat flotilla to panic the retreating Turks. At Charles Monro's urging, Maude made for Baghdad, the two armies circling around it, neither willing to fight in its warren of its streets. On 7 March the 1/5th Buffs landed by steamer to seize a bridgehead at Bawi, south of the city. Rather than contest Baghdad its Ottoman defenders abandoned the city and on the morning of 11 March the 1/5th Buffs marched in to raise the British flag on its Citadel.

The troops who had fought for so long to reach it regarded Baghdad as 'a bloody filthy hole', as Ted Rice of the 1/5th West Surrey wrote.[28] Arthur Foster, a signaller in the 1/4th Hants, entered Baghdad soon after its fall. He thought that 'the War in Mespot is about over now', recording how the battalion had returned to 'the old routine of clean clothes and spick and span guard mounting'. Men were expected to wear shiny boots – even if they had to use bacon fat as dubbing.[29] The battalion's war diary shows that despite losses from sickness especially it was continually refreshed by drafts from other Hampshire Territorial battalions still in India. And despite the victory men continued to die. Chelmsford's elder son, Frederick, a gunner second-lieutenant, died of wounds on 1 May 1917 and was buried in Baghdad.

By this time three Territorial field artillery brigades had been sent from India to Mesopotamia, totalling over a thousand gunners.[30] They included Ted Holter's 1/4th Sussex Battery, though like many men he was returned to India debilitated by the climate, though not sick enough to be sent home. Lord Suffolk's Wiltshire battery went to Mesopotamia early in 1917. Suffolk was killed – by shrapnel at Istabulat – in April 1917. Hardinge, the former Viceroy, lamented the death of 'the most perfect type of English gentlemen'.[31] In a sad postscript showing that rank and nobility provided no insulation from grief, Chelmsford wrote to Curzon that five months on Suffolk's widow, Marguerite, 'broods over her loss and will not put it behind her'. Thinking of his own dead gunner son, he and Lady Chelmsford, he wrote, simply had to get on with their duties.[32]

Territorial artillery in India had been re-organised and re-numbered, into ten new field artillery brigades, though two were soon disbanded. This was possible because regardless of their standing as Territorials (which after the passing of the *Military Service Act* of 1916 had little legal force) their members were part of the huge Royal Regiment of Artillery. The 1st, 2nd, 3rd and 4th Wessex brigades became the 215th, 216th, 217th and 218th respectively. The re-numbering made little difference to the dispersal of their constituent batteries, which by the war's end were distributed all over India, many with a purely notional strength, their members having been transferred to other artillery units, detached to other work or invalided home ill. *At least* 120 Territorial gunners died in India between 1915 and 1919, though it is almost impossible to trace men transferred to other Royal Artillery units (and indeed, Territorials who ended up in motor transport, machine-gun or other units).

28 Ted Rice, 'All for a Shilling a Day', QRWS/30/RICE/1, SHC, Woking
29 Diary, March 1917, Arthur Foster, 1/4th Hants, https://sites.google.com/site/ajcfosterhistory/home/4-diary
30 'Returns of the Territorial Force Serving Abroad', WO114/54, January 1917, NAUK
31 Hardinge, *My Indian Years*, p. 107
32 Letter, 7 September 1917, Chelmsford papers, Mss.Eur.E264/16, BL

'So much hushed up': the Mesopotamia Commission

While the War Office took over control of the Mesopotamian campaign, India remained its main logistical base, the destination of casualties evacuated to hospitals and men fortunate to be granted leave. ('Large leave parties' from the hard-worked 1/4th Hants spent the summer of 1917 in India.[33]) As well as receiving reinforcements direct from Britain, battalions in Mesopotamia continued to receive reinforcements from sister battalions in India. Not until 1917 did the first drafts of 'Derbyites' reach the battalion, and then many were still Hampshire men.[34]

The Mesopotamia Commission, which sat in secret in London, finally reported in May 1917. A majority report found the campaign, as a recent historian of the war in the Middle East summarised it, as

> necessary, but ill-run from the outset ... singling out the "untoward advance" on Baghdad in October 1915 as "... based on political and military miscalculations, ... attempted with tired and insufficient forces, and inadequate preparation".[35]

British Indian newspapers reported the Commission's disclosures. The Allahabad *Pioneer* described the 'complete breakdown of the medical arrangements' during the failed operations for Kut's relief – facts known to the many Territorials who had been evacuated sick or wounded to India. Harry Canham attended a YMCA lecture given by a padre who had served in Mesopotamia in 1916 who was openly scathing about the 'extraordinary incompetence' displayed by senior officers there.[36] All India knew of the 'serious censure' directed at the Government of India and the Indian Army for its mismanagement of the campaign's first two years.[37] The defeat on Gallipoli, set-backs in East Africa and Indian losses on the Western Front had shocked Indians who had accepted the superiority of British leaders. The fall of Kut and the disclosures of the Mesopotamia Commission further eroded the confidence of well-disposed Indian moderates. As well as embarrassing revelations of the ineptitude of British-India's strategy and appalling admissions about the treatment of the wounded and sick, the minority report of the Mesopotamia Commission in 1916-17 revealed evidence of the contempt in which Regular officers held Territorial units. Territorials in India read these disclosures. They of course already knew how badly the Mesopotamian campaign was being managed.

Stanley Goodland, a Somerset subaltern, reading the discreet reports in the press told his fiancée how 'the Mesopotamian enquiry sickens me – so many lies are told and so much hushed up'. He wished he could write to *The Times*.[38] The only consolation was that the scandals the Commission had exposed were now largely rectified and control of the campaign had been wrested from the Government of India and in February 1916 transferred to the War Office. India Office officials implausibly claimed that the Mesopotamian campaign had probably – somehow – averted a pan-Islamic movement spreading to inflame Persia, Afghanistan and the

---

33 Atkinson, *History of the Hampshire Regiment*, p. 283
34 *History of the Hampshire Territorial Force Association*, pp. 114; 117
35 Ford, *Eden to Armageddon*, p. 93
36 Letter, 20 June 1918, Harry Canham, 2/4th Border, CMML
37 *Pioneer*, 4 August 1917
38 Letter, 11 August 1916, Stanley Goodland, 1/5th Somerset, Noyes, (ed.), *Engaged in War*, p. 57

Frontier. They claimed that it was preferable 'to defend India on the Tigris than risk trouble on the Frontier', but it is hard to see that it was an economical solution to a hypothetical threat or, indeed, anything to do with the original aims of the campaign.[39]

While in the wake of the Mesopotamia Commission the worst faults of the campaign were addressed, the climate remained unpleasant. In winter the flooding of the Tigris and Euphrates banks evoked and explained the story of the Biblical flood, while men contracted 'Baghdad boils' – ulcers leaving life-long purple scars. Living in thatched huts in temperatures of up to 120°, men slept naked except for a towel around their waist (the 'old sweats' panacea, to prevent catching cholera'), tormented by flies in the daytime and mosquitoes at night. (Harry Canham attributed his freedom from cholera to having worn a 'body belt': even army medical officers endorsed what were effectively folk nostrums. With a quarter of the battalion on the sick list such remedies might have made sense.[40])

'We could not stop at Baghdad': Mesopotamia 1917

Mesopotamia is part of the story of the Indian Territorials not only because they formed about a quarter of Stanley Maude's British infantry, but also because as the campaign's major base so many men who were wounded or who fell ill there were evacuated to India to recuperate. Men like Charles Gibson, the train-mad sergeant of the 1/4th Devon, fell ill after three months in Mesopotamia and was returned to India (via Suez) and eventually, after running a transit camp at Kirkee, near Poona, returned to his regiment working in the orderly room. As losses from illness especially mounted, the Territorial battalions in Mesopotamia rapidly filled with drafts, many from India, which often included original Territorials. Men who had served in Mesopotamia for over a year were granted leave, to India or Ceylon for a month, and travelled about using free railway warrants, seeing even more of India than they had while stationed there.

Despite the widespread awareness of Mesopotamia's unpleasantness, there was never a shortage of volunteers for reinforcement drafts. In October 1916 the 2/4th Somerset Light Infantry was asked for a further draft of 40. Of the 304 men eligible (that is, who were over 20 and had served in India for more than six months) no fewer than 134 volunteered. A month later another 84 was requested, and the draft was still more than twice over-subscribed.[41] This willingness to face known hardship was the real measure of the keenness that the Territorials had manifest from 1914.

The Mesopotamian debacle had begun to defend the oil fields of south-east Persia, but through muddled thinking, misplaced ambition and mismanagement British and Indian troops had died in two advances up the Tigris. As the summer of 1917 began, Stanley Maude's army at last held Baghdad: but now was impelled to go further. 'We could not, of course, stop at Baghdad …' wrote the official 'eyewitness' to the campaign, Edmund Candler, in a line emblematic of the entire campaign.[42] Maude's formations slowly pushed northwards, facing weak and disorganised

---

39 Rumbold, *Watershed in India*, p. 26
40 Letter, 30 November 1916, Harry Canham, 2/4th Border, CMML
41 Part 1 orders, 2/4th Somerset Light Infantry, September & October 1916, DD\SLI/6/36, SHC, Taunton
42 Candler, *The Long Road to Baghdad*, p. 130

Ottoman forces, his subordinate commanders cautious, anxious not to replicate the mistakes and losses exposed by the Mesopotamian Commission. Without Russian support, which the developing revolution would soon erode, Maude was unable to advance to Mosul before the onset of the summer; an opportunity lost.

By late March 1917 the foremost British troops were approaching the southern extremity of the Jebel Hamrin, the long ridge barring the route to the north-west and the Russians, who for the time being confronted Ottoman forces on Russia's frontier. In untidy and confusing operations, British Indian forces faced uncoordinated Ottoman forces. The 14th Indian Division saw heavy fighting in the 'Battle of the Boot', the final action in the Samarra campaign that had begun when the Devons and Buffs had risen from their trenches on the Shatt-el-Hai five months before.

Soldiers' letters from Mesopotamia in 1917 give little indication that conditions had improved markedly from 1915 or 1916. Len Bithel, who arrived as a reinforcement draft in mid-1917, described drinking water from the Tigris 'full of maggots with small black heads but they taste all right'. Men were 'dying by the score' from dysentery and sand-fly fever. 'We never know who it will be next', he wrote, 'We will be talking to a mate and … ten minutes later he is dead'.[43] Maude himself died of cholera in November 1917.

By mid-1917 ten 'Indian' Territorial battalions were serving in Mesopotamia.[44] Several were merely 'details' – understrength remnants of units mauled in earlier fighting, but most were at or over-strength – the 1/5th West Surrey at 1187 all ranks the strongest. The system of using battalions in India as depots worked well, supplying drafts, no longer simply of volunteers but often from other battalions of the same regiment.

With much of the Tigris and Euphrates valleys now occupied by British empire forces, battalions were 'dropped off' to garrison key towns and locations. The 1/4th Somerset spent twelve uneventful months' in 1917-18 occupying Nasiriyeh on the Euphrates, inactive except for 'demonstrations' against hostile Arabs. Relieved in April 1918, it went to Nejef, a Shi'ite shrine, where it overawed a brief rebellion. In October 1918 it sent Lewis gun detachments out in Ford cars from Tikrit, co-operating with armoured cars to patrol and deter resistance. Service in Mesopotamia held few pleasures or compensations. (Only one battalion, the 1/9th Middlesex, brought its band instruments –in containers blandly marked 'regimental baggage'.)[45]

Late in 1917 the Mesopotamian army, now commanded by Sir William Marshall after Maude's death, returned to the offensive, if less dramatically than before. Massively outnumbering the thinly stretched Ottoman forces, it moved ponderously to extend the British occupation, actions in which the Territorials took a full part. In December 1917 the 14th Indian Division operated up the Diyala River north of Baghdad, while the 15th Indian Division took part in an advance up the Euphrates in March 1918. Marshall's troops increasingly drew upon mechanized support, including armoured cars and vast fleets of Ford vans, many driven or maintained by Territorials. By late October 1918 Marshall's leading troops had reached up the Tigris as far as Mosul. By then Marshall's troops, including Territorials, had penetrated far into Persia and Transcaspia.

---

43   Diary, 14 July 1917, Lionel Bithel, 2/4th Wilts, SBYRW 1999 RBWM
44   That is: 1/5th West Surrey, 1/5th Buffs, 1/4th Devon, 1/6th Devon, 1/4th Somerset, 2/7th Hants, 1/4th Dorset, and of course the long-suffering 1/4th Hants.
45   Wyrall, *The Die-Hards in the Great War*, Vol. II, p. 342

13

A Soldier's Life in India, 1917

Territorial units in India had become veterans of cantonment life. They understood the climate, could 'sling the bat', buy in the canteen and the bazaar, and deal with the hazards of Indian life: indeed, statistically all of them had endured several bouts of illness. While their units were continually refreshed by reinforcements, rather than relying on old sweats to pass on hints on living in India, now they could induct their own. India was now familiar: for many, too familiar. As Jim Mackie told his parents after returning to Lahore from the Simla hills in August 1917, 'for nearly three years we have been out here doing the same old things every day … the whole thing seems to be so futile'. Still, Jim was also 'very fond of India', one of many Territorials who found that the life of a sahib suited them.[1] By this mid-point in their Indian service it is possible to survey how it had affected and changed them.

'Straight Tips for Subs': officer candidates

Though many Anglo Indians remained unaware of its profound effects, the war changed forever British life, not least in disrupting the seeming verities of class. The Territorials' ethos set a premium upon promotion. Battalions depended upon encouraging a culture of modest ambition, so that capable privates in one year could become the corporals of the next. Not all men sought advancement. Arthur Bell, noticing how unpaid lance-corporals were 'at the beck and call of all higher ranks' refused promotion, but many men aspired at least to stripes, because promotion brought both higher pay and greater comfort as well as heavier responsibility.[2] And the war allowed men to become officers who would never otherwise have dreamed of such a change, not least among Territorials in India. Promotion to commissioned rank had never been very common in the British Army, not least because the social distance between even senior non-commissioned officers and officers left men commissioned (usually as quartermasters) uncomfortable socially and disadvantaged financially. The Great War would change that, as with many aspects of the army's pre-war expectations.

---

1 Letter, 9 August 1917, Jim Mackie, 2/4th Somerset, Mackie, *Answering the Call*, p. 211
2 *Queen's Royal Surrey Regiment Newsletter*, November 1999, SHC, Woking

208 'Terriers' in India

A group of East Surrey men taking a break in a train journey. These men are visibly veterans of Indian service. Note the monkey. (ESR/2/13/13 (10(3)), Surrey History Centre)

The war soon revealed two of the Indian army's most serious weaknesses, among both its Indian other ranks and its British officers. With a reinforcement system depending upon the recruitment of specific 'classes' of men from particular ethnic groups and districts, the disastrous losses of modern war could not be made up quickly or easily. Losses among British officers, who freely exposed themselves to death and wounds, soon outstripped the available supplies of young men possessing the mix of social background and linguistic skill considered necessary. Within weeks of the declaration of war – before Indian units had entered action – the Government of India identified a need for almost a thousand new officers, and during the war the need intensified. The losses the British Army suffered on the Western Front, on Gallipoli and on other fronts, left an even greater demand for men able to be turned into officers.

The Indian Army's expansion also imposed calls on the Territorials. When in 1917 large numbers of Indians were raised to form new units as well as to reinforce existing ones, to serve in Mesopotamia, Egypt and in India itself, the India Office officials' assumed that 'you will be able to draw many officers from Territorials' – that is, from men thought suitable for commissions serving as sergeants or even other ranks in Territorial battalions in India.[3] It turned out to be

---

3 'Provision of further troops to India', 28 March 1917, CAB24/9/17, NAUK

a reasonably safe presumption, provided men were acceptable even if they only had a grammar school, or even some secondary school, education, even if they could not ride, or did not own or had not worn a dinner jacket. Officer cadets selected to attend the Officers' Training School at Subathu, in the hills south of Simla, could be schooled in socially desirable as well as militarily necessary skills.

Officers usually approached likely candidates and encouraged them to apply to be selected for commissions. Early in the war, when virtually all Territorial units included middle class men in their ranks, identifying likely candidates was relatively easy. Herbert Ewing's company commander and colonel nominated him, and he was rejected only because (he was told) he was too young at just 18. Several months later they put his name forward again, and having had enough of a hot weather cantonment Ewing agreed, variously ecstatic or despairing as his application slowly made its way from the battalion through the machinery of the Adjutant-General's department. (Desperate to get away, he volunteered to go to Mesopotamia, but was not picked because he had an application for a commission pending. He was to survive three years on the Western Front.) Local newspapers sometimes proudly reported men selected for commissioning, and they suggest that regardless of rank men had some social advantage to justify it. An item in the *West Sussex Gazette* reported on three Brighton men – two had been teachers, the other a prominent Hampshire footballer.[4]

Finding officer candidates made a further drain on the Territorials' efficiency – the 1/4th West Surrey sent away three candidates a month for the second half of the war, and they were naturally men with leadership qualities.[5] On the other hand, a record of some 17 months of routine orders from the 2/4th Somerset discloses that only five other ranks gained commissions, and only five in the 2/6th Devon in 1915-16. If these records are complete they suggests that not all COs encouraged or allowed men to leave to take up commissions, though later in the war, as the need for subalterns grew, the numbers commissioned also increased. Courses for sergeants and corporals 'with a view to their receiving commissions' were held at Campbellpore (now Attock, Pakistan), with over 500 men passing through five courses between 1917 and 1919, though there is no indication how many proceeded.[6]

Gerald Bonham-Carter told his sister, Joan, how virtually all of his subalterns in 1918 had been promoted from the Territorials' ranks, and were 'not exactly gentlemen by birth or education'.[7] Individual biographies confirm Bonham-Carter's judgment: wartime promotions depended largely upon character and merit, and not social criteria. A Territorial sergeant in 1915 could end the war as a captain in a mountain battery, with a Military Cross and two mentions in despatches.[8] George Blick, a 'clothworker', was commissioned in February 1918 and went on to compile the 1/4th Wilts's history. James Bradfield joined the 2/4th Somerset as a private, was commissioned in India and served in Mesopotamia, After the armistice Bradfield joined the Arab Levies as a captain, and became caught up in the Iraq revolt of 1920. In command of a tiny outpost at Shrahraban north-west of Baghdad Bradfield's little party (of two British officers,

---

4   *West Sussex Gazette*, 31 August 1916, p. 4
5   Wylly, *History of the Queen's Royal Regiment*, Vol. VII, p. 146
6   *Principal measures taken in India during the War to Maintain Training at the Standard Required in Modern War*, p. 16
7   Letter, 7 April 1918, Gerald Bonham-Carter, 1/5th West Kent, 94M72/F305, HRO
8   C.R. Willis, 'Gunnery notes and other documents …', Doc.13809, 73/66/1, IWM

two British NCOs, including a sergeant-major of the 1/4th Dorset, and nine Arab Levies) fought off an Arab force for three days before they were overrun and massacred.[9] The depth of the reservoir that Indian Territorials represented especially is suggested by undated note in one of Monro's memorandum books, in which around late 1917 he recorded that 'we have still in India about 3000 men whom we could turn into officers'. 'Enquiry to be made', Monro characteristically noted.[10]

However, it is clear that many more men applied for commissions than were accepted, and that those who were overwhelmingly came from 'the right background' – essentially a grammar school education as a minimum. Harry Canham recorded that in his battalion, the 2/4th Border, several men applied each month but that very few were accepted. Even though 'there is a war on and an admitted shortage of officers', Harry complained in a letter to his sister, Florence, 'the authorities still cling to their prejudices with regard to "culture" and "education"'. A reluctant soldier at best, Harry had decided not even to try his luck.[11] Other, keener, men aimed to prepare themselves – Ernest Head's sergeant in Aden stood out by his initiative in leading the 1/6th Easy Surrey scout section, and while resting at Steamer Point set up map-based war games. Soon after he was commissioned.

Securing a commission exposed lower middle-class and some working class men to the challenge of making their way in an army structured on class lines and riddled with unwritten rules about how officers should conduct themselves. Ernest Atkinson, a pre-war Territorial (indeed, a Volunteer), a clerk with the London and South East Railway, he had arrived in India as a sergeant, a first-class shot. Commissioned into the Indian Army in January 1918, items in his papers suggest what a trial getting his pips would have been. He bought a pamphlet, *Straight Tips for Subs* [that is, subalterns – lieutenants]. It gave new officers (or those uncertain of mess etiquette) hints on what to do and not do. 'Be careful to call the Colonel, Majors or Adjutant, "Sir"', it advised, to approach the Colonel 'as you would treat a rich uncle of whom you have expectations' and if in doubt 'do as the other officers do'. As a junior subaltern, the newly-commissioned second-lieutenant was regarded as 'a blot on the earth', and should 'assume the attitude of a new boy at school'. The rules were as cryptic and confusing as those of a public school – which not all Territorial officers would have attended. Captains should not be addressed as 'Captain', but majors *should* be called 'Major'. The sergeant-major should be called 'Sir' by other ranks, but by officers 'Sergeant-Major'.[12]

Promotion entailed greater comfort, but also corresponding expense. A roneoed sheet, 'A Few Hints to Territorial Officers' advised new officers at Lucknow of the going rates for servants, and urged them to withstand requests to pay more.[13] A bearer could command Rs 15 a month, a syce (looking after his horse) Rs8, a dhobi Rs5 and a bhisti Rs3. But the expert local warned that 'Hindus will not do khitmagar's work … if a Hindu bearer is employed it is necessary to have a khitmagar in addition'. The demarcations were subtle: a bearer could fill a bath but not a kettle, a khitmagar the reverse. Newcomers had to be schooled on the niceties of servants'

---

9   Fisher, *The History of Somerset Yeomanry, Volunteers and Territorials*, pp. 222-23
10 Memorandum book of Sir Charles Monro, Commander-in-Chief India 1916-17, 7207-19-1, NAM
11 Letter, 21 February 1918, Harry Canham, 2/4th Border, CMML
12 *Straight Tips for Subs*, ESR/25/ATKI/9, SHC, Woking
13 'A Few Hints to Territorial Officers', QRWS/30, WIGA/17, SHC, Woking

demeanour. Mysteriously they were not to be allowed to wear the end of their turban hanging down, nor keep their shoes on indoors, nor enter a room bareheaded.

In October 1915 Herbert Ewing joined a group of officer cadets from various units, all travelling to board the *Caledonia* for officer training in Britain. 'There are not many people travelling', he wrote as the ship left Karachi 'but some of them give us very freezing glances', perplexed to see men ostensibly dressed as 'other ranks' travelling first class.[14] A proportion of those commissioned from the ranks were destined to serve on the Western Front. They travelled home in considerably better conditions than they had left. Some of the cadets had possibly travelled to India on the ship, which had carried Hampshire and Cornwall battalions in 1914. Gerald Gibbs recalled travelling first class on a P&O liner, dressed in a private's uniform but with a second lieutenant's pips, with seven pounds in gold for expenses. As subalterns destined for the Western Front, many would not have time to spend it.[15]

'The inevitable stew': food

On home service, in camp or in billets after mobilisation, the Territorials' diet had been stolidly English, that of the working and lower middle-class Englishmen they were. It was supposed to comprise bread, bacon and milky sweet tea for breakfast, a generous pound of meat with bread and vegetables (often just potato) for what was called dinner (with a pint of beer or, for teetotalers, mineral water), and for supper bread and sweet tea again, with a couple of ounces of cheese. The War Office recognised that this diet would not support men living and training in the open, so provided an allowance to buy extra food, either bought from unit contractors or canteens or supplied by the owners of the billets in which they lived. In India this diet was often neither possible nor palatable. European food in India was, Murray's Guide admitted, 'not very good'. Meat was 'lean and tough, the fowls are skinny, and the eggs ridiculously small'.[16] The official ration was both familiar and limited: filling, often tasty, but monotonous. Walter Saunders, like many better off Terriers, found the diet uninviting – a loaf, fresh cooked meat, cheese and fried bacon, but the same virtually every day, with jam and fruit available from 'dry canteens'.[17] Curiously, the stand-by of British troops elsewhere, 'bully beef' straight from the tin was rarely issued except on active service – William Bisset tasted 'bully and biscuit' for the first time on the voyage up the Tigris in October 1915, after being in uniform for ten months.[18]

Meals, prepared by experienced but virtually untrained company cooks, working with basic facilities (boiling or frying seemed to be the main options for preparation) produced simple meals able to be cooked in one pot and served on one plate. Often that meant what a Surrey man called 'the inevitable stew'.[19] A Territorial medical officer decried the cooking facilities he

---

14 Diary, 31 October 1915, Herbert Ewing, 1/5th Somerset, Doc.15428, 07/8/1, IWM
15 Gerald Gibbs went on to serve as a lieutenant with a Wiltshire battalion in Macedonia, and became an 'ace' with the Royal Flying Corps, eventually returning to India as the last British commander-in-chief of the Royal Indian Air Force.
16 Anon, *A Handbook for Travellers*, p xxvi
17 Walter Saunders, 1/10th Middlesex, Transcript of diary and letters, Doc. 6571, 79/15/1, IWM
18 William Bisset, 'Dum Spiro Spero', p. 39, M1834, RHRM
19 'Lebong', *The Braganza*, 1 March 1917, p. 16

had encountered as 'primitive', describing 'native' cooks producing meals in fly-blown kitchens and meals eaten by soldiers sitting on open verandas without even the means to wash their hands first.[20] During the hot weather men often could not stomach heavy meat meals – with the heat rising in Ferozepore Hugh Creek lived off puddings and bread, butter and jam. The 1/6th Hants mess corporals were more enterprising, providing 'very nice cold meat & salad, cucumber & onions for tea ... & today we are to have boiled eggs ... !!'[21] The exclamation marks suggest the rarity.

Among the most pressing of the Territorials' grievances was that they were left short of food. Across India men expressed dissatisfaction with the quantity and quality of their rations. The basic rations differed between cantonments. In Fort William the 1/10th Middlesex had a loaf of bread daily, with meat, a mixture of vegetables, tea, cheese and bacon, but the men needed their three-pence a day messing allowance to buy jam and fruit and provide an evening meal. In Rangoon most men of a company signed a 'round robin' of protest. Though they were put on defaulters' parade none suffered punishment. The men attributed their gaining an extra 3d daily messing allowance to the lobbying of the son of Lord St Audries, whose son was serving in Burma. He did indeed raise it in the House of Lords, but the grievance was so general that it is likely that his representations merely added to the protest. Another MP asked after the troops' rations 'in a country where the beef is bad and the mutton is miserable'.[22]

During the agitation over Territorials' grievances in 1915 Hugh Clutterbuck, colonel of the 2/4th Somerset, wrote to the *Shepton Mallet Journal*, the local newspaper of many of his men, to try to calm families' concern. He included a week's menu. It included a 'full breakfast' of boiled fish, parsley sauce and potatoes, haricot mutton stew or curried mutton stew, dinners of pea soup, boiled mutton and vegetables or beefsteak pie, rissoles, minced beef or shepherd's pie, often with a dessert such as jam roll or rice pudding. Men were served tea, bread and jam for tea, and beyond that had to buy their own. He explained that while diet scales in hot weather were lighter, for 'chota hazree' (the 'little breakfast served on rising at about 5.30 a.m.) men would receive two buns (and not merely a dry biscuit). Still, the quantities provided were not specified, and Clutterbuck was constrained to mention that men often bought eggs or more bread at the Soldiers' Home or the temperance rooms.[23]

Herbert Peake kept a record of the meals served to his mess-mates in the 1/5th West Surrey in Lucknow in March 1915. Soldiers effectively had only two meals a day: breakfast and dinner (served at midday) with a light 'tea', usually of bread and jam and tea each evening. Breakfast was meat (rissole or bacon) or porridge; sometimes with eggs, probably fried. Dinner: stew, potato cutlets (with rice), mince roll, potato patties and stew again. Owen Smith's descriptions of his time as 'Messing Corporal' at Agra tallies – except that the bobajis served 'spud cutlets' – meat and potato rissoles. Sometimes men pooled their funds to be able to cook familiar food. Hugh Creek and four Devon comrades invested in a frying pan and other utensils so they could cook what they liked for supper (which otherwise could have been just bread, jam and tea).

20   Jefferiss, 'Suggestions for removing the difficulties encountered by British units arriving in India ...', *JUSII*, 1917, p. 162
21   Letter, 30 August 1916, Owen Smith, 1/6th Hants, M766, RHRM
22   Sir J.D. Rees, House of Commons, *Hansard*, 3 March 1915
23   *Shepton Mallet Journal*, 10 September 1915, p. 2

These meals were accompanied by heroic quantities of tea (or '"char" as we now learned to call it').[24] Men drank it black. A bitter item in the Royal Sussex's Ten Commandments included 'VII – Though shalt not adulterate they platoon's tea by adding either milk or sugar or such other ingredients to make such tea drinkable'.[25]

Did British troops eat Indian food? The pass issued to Henry Iggulden in Calcutta specifically excluded him (and all British soldiers) from 'all eating houses' on Hogg Street and Market Street.[26] Lizzie Collingham in *Curry*, her survey of British-India's culinary legacies, shows that by the late nineteenth century Anglo-Indians had rejected the 'native' food their forebears had embraced for meals that resembled as far as possible British food. Indeed, among the many 'Health Maxims for Men' directed at British troops were firm and unambiguous warnings to *'avoid all food and drink* which does not come from your regimental messes, institutes or recognised Soldiers' Homes'.[27] Sometimes men would be served a 'curry' (as Owen Smith was after a communion service at Ambala in September 1916), but it was much more likely to have been stew made with a spoonful of Keen's Curry Powder than with the freshly ground ingredients the bobajis would use for their own meals. A curry in barracks invariably meant, as Douglas MacMillan recalled, 'either curried stew & rice or rice & curried stew'.[28]

Territorials' letters and diaries do mention local food. At Simla, William Bisset accepted 'weird sweetmeats' from his Muslim bearer at the end of Ramadan in 1918.[29] In Burma, John Syddall tried snacks of minced curried meat in the Maymyo bazaar, praising their makers as 'good cooks and some of their dishes are very palatable'. But he explained why he and presumably all other British soldiers avoided local food, that 'they will not make any attempt to keep either the tablecloth or the utensils clean'.[30] Imbued as he and all other troops were about the importance of cleanliness, he and they generally avoided the pleasures and the hazards of 'native food'. Lance-Corporal Burt wrote that army rations were 'very bad' but that 'after we got to know the ropes of the Indians we had better food' – perhaps meaning local dishes.[31] Significantly, none of the many menus of celebratory or farewell dinners preserved in private papers includes a 'native' dish.

The Territorials' accounts of their rations, and the menus of the various farewell and congratulatory dinners they attended, corroborate their reluctance to embrace Indian food. (Some battalions did make arrangements to serve 'local' dishes – the 1/4th Cornwall made sure to provide 'Pasties for Tiffin', the title of a song Thomas Heard made his party-piece at farewells and other festive events. But local meant specific to Cornwall, not Bareilly, its station at the time.) Regimental institutes and recreation rooms certainly offered pies and buns rather than samosas or iddlys.

The Territorials' greatest complain over rations in India was their scarcity. When Robert Palmer asked men of the 1/4th Hants why they preferred Mesopotamia to India they replied

24 Bacon, *The Wanderings of a Temporary Warrior*, p. 17
25 'The Ten Commandments', *The Royal Sussex Herald*, 27 May 1916, p. 96
26 Henry Iggulden, 1/10th Middlesex, 2010-12-1, NAM
27 Bennett Young, 2/4th Dorset, 1983-05-91, NAM
28 Douglas MacMillan, '1/4th Somerset Light Infantry in India', DD\SLI/17/1/87, SHC, Taunton
29 Diary, 11 July 1918, William Bisset, Army Headquarters, M1834, RHRM
30 Clipping, Lawrence Hoggarth, 1/4th Border, Album 35 Acc. Nos 3024-3345, CMML
31 H. Burt, 'Diary since 1914', B.6599, CMM

'Why, you gets a decent dinner here, Sir," a veiled dig at the shortages of food they had endured in India.[32] In India food so often led to ill-health.

'Strove to keep alive': health

Practically every soldier in India fell ill, statistically several times a year. References to stomach troubles appear often in diaries: 'feeling very seedy, diarrhoea and sickness …' is a typical entry.[33] To avoid common and endemic illness, India became for Britons 'a land of don'ts', a man who arrived in 1916 observed, listing some of the many prohibitions he had written down during lectures on board his troopship:

> Don't drink any of the native drinks
> Don't eat too much food made by the natives
> Don't stand with your back to the sun
> AND HUNDREDS MORE [34]

Experienced medical officers' advice found its way into the Standing Orders newly arrived units drafted and published. In the 1/1st Kent men were cautioned against eating under- or over-ripe fruit, or 'large quantities of any fruit'; were advised to seek medical aid if constipated or suffering diarrhoea, and warned against sleeping with their stomachs exposed for fear of catching fever or colic.[35]

The hazards of India demanded that battalions form sanitary sections assisting their medical officers' efforts to control supplies of water, the suppression of flies and the elimination of waste. In each battalion and in every cantonment an army of conservancy coolies who physically cleaned up waste to keep stations clean and men alive. Despite their disgusting work, British India's major cause of sickness remained gastro-intestinal diseases. As Henry Brain's depressing doggerel put it: 'Declining health from diarrhoea/ Numbers many with the dead/ And dysentery brings the soldier/ To his everlasting bed'.[36]

Malaria remained the major single threat to health – the admission rate remained at over 200 per thousand through the war.[37] Still, military public health had made dramatic progress in the decades before the war. Amoebic (though not bacillary) dysentery could be treated with ipecacuanha, and malaria (for only twenty years understood to be carried by anopheles mosquitos) with quinine, while advances in the application of germ theory greatly reduced infectious diseases such as typhoid fever. The 1/1st Kent was in India for five months before its first member died – of diphtheria.

32　Palmer, *Letters from Mesopotamia*, p. 48
33　Diary, 28 September 1915, William Bisset, 2/4th Hants, M1834, RHRM
34　Herbert Jones, 7th North Stafford, Doc 7306, 76/111-112/1, IWM. The maxims include 'Drink as little water as possible', surely leading to dangerous dehydration.
35　*1st Kent Regiment Provisional Standing Orders*, p. 14
36　Memoir, Henry Brain, 1/6th East Surrey, ESR/25/BRAIN/2, SHC, Woking
37　'Note by the Medical Adviser' [Sir Richard Havelock Charles, 1921], L/MIL/7/13393, BL

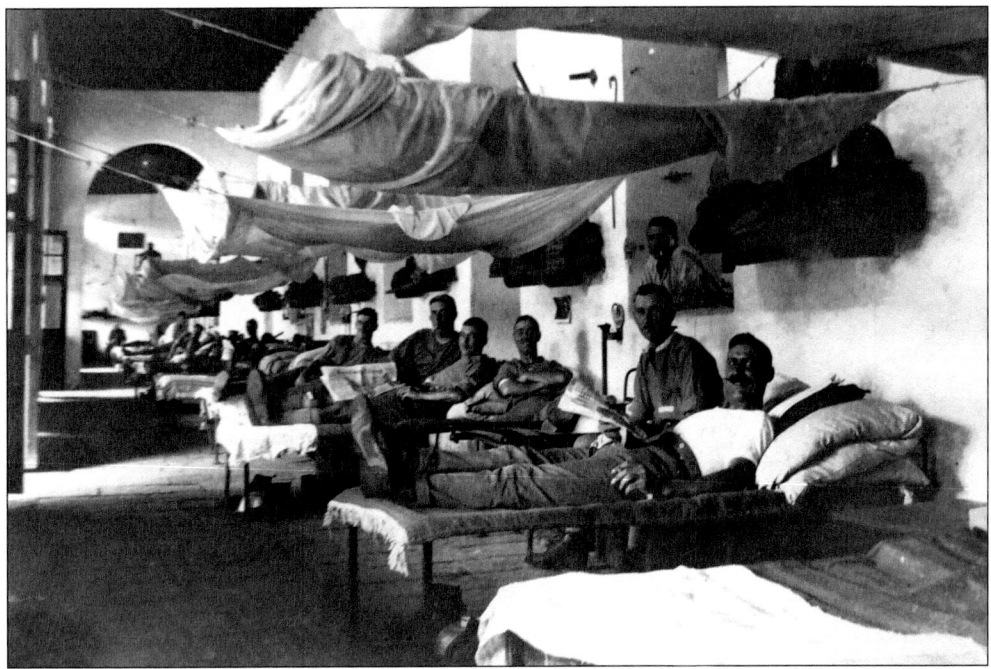

A barrack room of the 1/1st Kent Battalion, showing mosquito nets above men's charpoys. (Album 5 MNERN: 881, Maidstone Museum)

Malaria, of various strains, accounted for nearly 7000 admissions to hospital in 1915, though only 16 deaths. Infection rates for malaria increased through the war, because of relapses, but it was always worst among troops in the two divisions which saw the most action on the frontier, the Peshawar and Rawalpindi – two or three times worse than the Secunderabad Division in south central India. Cholera, though feared, caused very few deaths – 16 cases and eight deaths in 1915. Though fewer men contracted enteric fever than malaria, the death rate was higher – also only 16 deaths, but from only 83 admissions.[38] (Old sweats convinced novices that 'cholera belts' helped to prevent infection, and men knitted or otherwise fashioned them and sold them to comrades. It was 'said to be a good thing to keep the tummy covered up', a sceptical Herbert Ewing wrote.[39]) Ten men (six of them Territorials) were isolated as enteric carriers – literally isolated; kept in separate wards at Enteric Depots at Naini Tal and Wellington, fed separately with separate latrines, their stools and blood subjected to tests to determine whether they were infecting their comrades. In 1915, after months of tests, most suspected carriers were returned to their units, cleared of suspicion.

Old hands warned newcomers that among India's greatest dangers was the sun. They advised them to wear their topees whenever outside, and for most of the year, cautioning that to ignore the advice would literally be fatal. Alexander Sturt, author of *Our Indian Empire* described how he

---

38 *Report on Sanitary Measures in India in 1915-1916*, Parliamentary Papers, 1917-18, Vol. 10, pp. 2-9
39 Diary, 19 March 1915, Herbert Ewing, 1/5th Somerset, Doc.15428, 07/8/1, IWM

had once walked for thirty yards between buildings and had been struck down with sunstroke.⁴⁰ Robert Palmer (who saw his role as a subaltern as keeping his men alive by reminding them to 'boil their water and wear their helmets') recounted how one of his draft fell to heat stroke on the train from Agra to Bombay in August 1915, describing how the man experienced 'delirium, and red face and a hot dry skin'. He survived only because a railway official stopped the passing Punjab Mail, procured 22 pounds of ice for him and dropped him off at a hospital en route.⁴¹ Doctors distinguished between 'heatstroke' (172 cases and 33 deaths in 1915) and sunstroke (35 cases and no deaths). Jubbulpore, one of the healthiest stations for malaria, was the worst station for heatstroke.⁴² The worst stations for heatstroke generally were, however, not surprisingly in the north: Nowshera, Lahore, Ferozepore, Peshawar, Rawalpindi, Meerut, Ambala and Delhi.⁴³ Less dangerous but extremely uncomfortable was prickly heat, which Arthur Cornell described as 'very similar to nettle rash but more painful'.⁴⁴ Richard Cawsey told his mother in Portsmouth that it 'makes you feel as if you are lying on pins and needles and that an army of fleas are eating you away'.⁴⁵

As a result of these illnesses, a steady stream of men were invalided to Britain through the year (meaning that they often waited in hill stations, convalescent homes or transit camps until allowed to travel between October and about April). Territorials, who arrived in one large consignment as unacclimatised novices (rather than being introduced to India in yearly reinforcement drafts) suffered accordingly. Over 889 men were invalided in 1915, against 364 in 1914.⁴⁶ These were often men who developed medical conditions unrelated to service (such as cancer, diabetes or tuberculosis), sometimes men whose illnesses had not been detected in medical inspections before enlistment. Curiously, while the single most common cause of invaliding in 1913 and 1914 (among Regulars) had been 'diseases of the ear', from 1915 it became and remained heart conditions.⁴⁷

Some stations were dreaded because of their climate. Postings to the fort at Attock, guarding the crossing of the Indus west of Rawalpindi, was uncomfortable and unhealthy, with its heat, sandflies and mosquitoes (and it was notorious for snakes). After a few weeks there in the steamy heat of the late summer of 1915 three-quarters of an East Surrey company was on the sick-list. Other stations were regarded as healthy – the 2/4th Wilts at Poona went nine months before recording its first death, and then it was from a complication of appendicitis, not an endemic disease.

Despite the country's manifest hazards Indian authorities seemed dilatory. Only in April 1915, nearly six months after their arrival, did the Secretary of State for India confidently advise

---

40   Sturt, *Our Indian Empire*, p. 103. Coincidentally, Joseph Gale described how a man in the 2/4th Wilts died of sunstroke at Allahabad in May 1918 after walking thirty yards to the cook-house hatless: Gale, *With the 2/4th Wilts to India*, p. 82.
41   Palmer, *Letters from Mesopotamia*, pp. 12; 17-18
42   *Report on Sanitary Measures in India in 1915-1916*, Parliamentary Papers, 1917-18, Vol. 10, p. 30
43   *Annual Report of the Sanitary Commissioner with the Government of India for 1918*, European Army, p. 21
44   Arthur Cornell, 'A short account of our life and duties at Meerut', DD\SLI\17/1/84, SHC, Taunton
45   Letter, 22 August 1917, Richard Cawsey, 2/4th Hants, Doc. 12537, 02/55/1, IWM
46   *Report on Sanitary Measures in India in 1915-1916*, Parliamentary Papers, 1917-18, Vol. 10, p. 33
47   *Annual Report of the Sanitary Commissioner with the Government of India for 1918*, European Army, p. 23

the House of Commons that mosquito nets had been sanctioned for all Territorials who were to serve the hot season on the plains. The conclusion must be that they had been approved, not provided – and that many troops had been prey to mosquitos for months. In fact men had been able to buy them individually but nets were not issued freely until well into 1915.[48] Men's letters confirm that nets were not issued until the start of the hot weather of 1915 – by which time (as Hugh Creek's letters to his parents reveal) he had already suffered 'about 50 big red swellings' on his face and arms.[49] Later some cantonments engaged men of lower medical classification as 'mosquito killer'.

Territorials expressed their concern about India's many hazards to their health, and even their lives. *Punch's* Hampshire clerk published a mournful, not to say discouraging verse (which, surprisingly, was passed by the censor):

> Ten Territorials fancied India fine,
> Till one caught malaria, and then there were nine.
> Nine Territorials mourned his hapless fate;
> One found a cobra, and then there were eight.
> Eight Territorials hoped he'd rest in heaven;
> One took his topee off and then there were seven.
> Seven Territorials brooded on their fix;
> One picked up dysentery, and then there were six.
> Six Territorials strove to keep alive;
> One died from cholera, and then there were five.
> Five Territorials quaked more and more;
> One ate a little fruit, and then there were four.
> Four Territorials thought they'd better flee;
> One met a mad dog, and then there were three.
> Three Territorials felt extremely blue;
> One drank some water, and then there were two.
> Two Territorials wilted in the sun;
> One had a heat-stroke, and then there was one.
> One Territorial felt his day was done;
> He committed suicide, and then there were none.

'Yet, strangely enough,' the Hampshire Territorial wrote, 'we remain as a body fit and healthy'.[50]

---

48 Item 1290-1291, Army Proceedings, January 1915, Army Department Proceedings, January 1915, NAI
49 Letter, 29 March 1915, Hugh Creek, 1/4th Devon, EX2543, DMM
50 'A Territorial in India', *Punch*, 15 September 1915, p. 226. *The Tiger* published a similar parody, 'Ten little Hampshire boys' in April 1915. Presumably ditties like this circulated within and between battalions.

'Bad teeth no bar': dental health

Fatal illnesses were not, in fact the Territorials' most pressing health worries. Arthur Copeland's letters mentioned the irritating and debilitating illnesses which men in his company suffered: prickly heat, heat blisters, tropical boils, mosquito bites and 'dhobi itch', contacted from friction from imperfectly laundered underclothing. However, the most painful, if not fatal, health problem from which soldiers suffered was not malaria or dysentery but was bad teeth.

A Territorial cyclist recruiting poster before the war had promised 'Bad teeth no bar', but many men's diaries and letters demonstrate that many had been accepted despite them, and that they remained martyrs to poor dental health. Thomas Heard's diary records repeated trips to dentists. Charles Gibson's diary contains accounts of appalling procedures (such as '7 stumps drawn'), including extractions performed by friends.[51] When they did see dentist – an itinerant officer of the 1/6th Hants, a civilian dentist travelled around stations pulling teeth – they were often treated without anaesthesia (and outdoors, with a queue of waiting patients watching). And they usually had to pay for their own treatment – Thomas Heard's dental work in Aden cost him Rs41 – over £5. Even officers of the dentist's battalion exhibited poor dental health. When Robert Palmer was ordered to the 'P.G.' in August 1915 one of his first acts was to get two teeth filled. (He speculated that 'teeth decay extremely quickly out here.')[52] Jim Mackie, who had constant dental trouble, agreed. 'This is a very bad climate for teeth', he told his parents, visiting Lucknow from Dinapore to visit a dentist as well as the city's 'Mutiny' sites.[53]

In fact, the responsibility for the Terriers' generally poor dental health lay, of course, in the diet and standards of dental care in Edwardian Britain. A Eurasian doctor who extracted three of Arthur Copeland's teeth outdoors in Allahabad early in 1915 commented that 'the doctor who passed all you fellows with such teeth ought to be shot'.[54] The next week Arthur had another three teeth extracted and asked his parents to dip into his savings in order to buy dentures. Inadequate dental facilities meant not only that men suffered, but the force's efficiency was impaired. Dentists pulled the teeth of six otherwise fit men of the 1/4th Devon but as neither the army nor the Government of India could (or would) supply dentures, at length all six were invalided home. In 1916 28 men were invalided to Britain because of bad teeth.[55]

Territorials' dental problems even reached Parliament. Wiltshire Territorials (or their families) complained that while dental treatment of troops serving overseas elsewhere was at official expense, troops in India had to pay for their own. The Member for South Wiltshire, Captain Charles Bathurst, raised in Parliament poor dental health of the 1/4th Wilts, sending telegrams flying between the War Office and the Government of India.[56] One of the men concerned, Len Bithell, was told to have all his teeth pulled at Kirkee, relieved when the dentist decided against it, 'because [he admitted] I had got the wind up'.[57] Given the primitive state of contemporary

---

51   Diary, August 1915, Charles Gibson, 1/4th Devon, 2007-1474, DMM
52   Palmer, *Letters from Mesopotamia*, p. 8
53   Letter, 10 March 1916, Jim Mackie, 2/4th Somerset, Mackie, *Answering the Call*, p. 154
54   Letter, 26 March 1915, Arthur Copeland, 1/5th Hants, 128A08/1-4, HRO
55   *Annual Report of the Sanitary Commissioner with the Government of India for 1918*, Calcutta, p. 23
56   Captain Charles Bathurst, House of Commons, Hansard, 4 May 1916
57   Diary, 18 April 1917, Len Bithell, 2/4th Wilts, SBYRW 1999, RBWM

dentistry, Len's fear was not all in the mind; but the records make clear that many Territorials suffered from mental illness.

'Doolally': mental health

As *Punch's* Territorial's jocular verse acknowledged, in India, 'he committed suicide' was a conceivable fate. Mental illness had always been more prevalent among soldiers in India than elsewhere in the empire. In the 1880s, Cuthbert Sprawson, a distinguished medical officer, recalled, medical staff at Netley hospital in Hampshire could tell that a ship had arrived from India merely by examining the summary of its patients it carried, by the large number of 'insanes' on the manifest.[58]

Despite this experience, army medical authorities had a primitive or robust grasp of mental illness. Hugh Creek recorded that a man of his company had been hospitalised with rheumatism, but made little progress because of 'melancholia and home sickness', and he was eventually invalided home.[59] The number of men formally invalided due to 'insanity' each year was relatively low. In the year immediately preceding the Territorials' arrival 44 men had been invalided to Britain as 'Insanes'.[60] In 1915 only four men were sent home.[61] From 1916, however, numbers increased, to 42 in 1916, 103 in 1917 and 136 in 1918, presumably because separation from home exacerbated mental disturbances.[62] Asides in men's letters and diaries disclose the incidence of mental illness. Reg Bailey knew of men who 'went "potty" for a period', and was sent to escort a Wiltshire man 'who was a little mad' back to his battalion.[63] A verse composed by a Somerset Territorial reflected the troops' awareness of the possibility of mental illness:

> 'Now, boys, don't think this foolish,
> Or think it is all rot,
> For I'm sure if you were out here,
> It would drive you off your dot.'[64]

Hospital staff became familiar with the dangers of 'mental patients'. Marjorie Swynnerton, who worked as a voluntary nurse in hospitals in several cantonments, recalled in a memoir how senior nurses impressed on novices the need to police men remaining in bed. 'One night sister', she remembered, 'had failed to notice an "empty bed", and the occupant had been found in the wash-house with his throat cut'.[65] Such deaths were not always suicides – a man in the 1/5th Hants died after falling off a balcony while sleep-walking. (The nurses who cared for Territorials might sometimes have been fellow Territorials. Though the records are scanty, the

---

58 Sir Cuthbert Sprawson '37 Years in the I.M.S', p. 7, LHCMA
59 Letter, 3 March 1915, Hugh Creek, 1/4th Devon, EX2543, DMM
60 *Report on Sanitary Measures in India in 1913-14*, Parliamentary Papers, 1914-15, Vol. 49, p. 24
61 *Report on Sanitary Measures in India in 1915-1916*, Parliamentary Papers, 1917-18, Vol. 10, p. 32
62 *Annual Report of the Sanitary Commissioner with the Government of India for 1918*, p. 23
63 Letters, 16 July and 20 November 1917, Reg Bailey, 1/4th Buffs, 2011-12-3, NAM
64 'A Territorial's Life in India', Mackie, *Answering the Call*, p. 211
65 Marjorie Thomas, 'Child of the Empire', Doc 8236, 99/37/1, IWM

presence of a Territorial Force Nurse in the cemetery at Rawalpindi – Nurse Ruth Nodder, a 33-year-old rector's daughter from Derbyshire – suggests that Territorial Force Nursing Service sisters worked in India as part of a contingent sent during the war.)

Men's diaries and memoirs mention men who killed themselves, incidents generally only disclosed through men's letters and diaries. Soon after arriving at Dinapore in 1914 a Territorial gunner officer apparently shot himself, dying a lingering death, though the delay allowed the 1/6th Hants drummers to rehearse playing the Dead March.[66] One morning in Bangalore in 1916 Oswald Early of the 1/9th Hants heard a shot and rushed into an adjoining barrack room, finding a friend, Edward Craske, had blown off the top of his skull by placing his rifle in his mouth, apparently a victim of drink. He was buried later that day, with the battalion's colonel making a speech at the graveside. The grave register does not refer to suicide, and he was buried in consecrated ground.[67]

Mental illness was so commonplace that service in India bequeathed to English slang for a time a word, 'doolally' (sometimes 'doolally tap'), meaning 'slightly mentally disturbed': the 'tap' referring to the common sign of tapping the temple to indicate 'madness'. It derived from 'Deolali', the big (and unfortunately named) 'British Concentration Camp' 100 miles from Bombay, the depot for embarking drafts. The connotation was that long service in India disturbed men's minds but, as Edward Craske's death suggested, soldiers in India were also prey to the mental disturbances endemic to human society.

'Comrades Graves': death

The first Territorial to die in India was 22-year-old Private William Hodge of the 1/4th Cornwall, at Bareilly, probably of illness, on 24 November 1914, just a fortnight after arriving. When the secretary of the Great Chart Soldiers and Sailors Fund received news of a man's death she dutifully – and no doubt proudly – annotated the letters received from that man in the scrapbook in red ink with the word "Honour!"

Death came through illness and accident. Troops were often warned not to swim in rivers, to avoid crocodiles, parasites and illness contracted from water and accidental drowning, which were distressingly common. Readers of the *Shepton Mallet Journal* were sorry to read a description of how 17-year-old Fred Board, from the hamlet of Dowlish Wake, near Ilminster, stepped out of a boat on the Irrawaddy soon after arriving in Burma only to sink into quicksand and disappear.[68] His body was at last recovered and he was buried at Henzada, one of many isolated Territorial graves now lost.

Battalion orderly room staff often kept track of men who had died or been wounded in Mesopotamia, difficult when they had been drafted to other regiments. Men serving with other

---

66 Letter, 22 November 1914, Owen Smith, 1/6th Hants, M766, RHRM
67 Diary, 16 April 1916, Oswald Early, 1/9th Hants, M4236, RHRM. The man was Edward Craske, mistakenly called Graske in the published transcription of the diary (Early, *The Messenger*, p. 171). I looked for his grave in January 2018 but while over a dozen Territorial graves are visible, it was untraceable among hundreds of later burials.
68 *Wells Journal*, 12 March 1915, p. 3. Fred Board is now commemorated in Taukkyan War Cemetery in Myanmar.

The funeral of a Brecknock Territorial at Mhow. (1/1st Brecknockshire collection, Box 18, Regimental Museum of the Royal Welsh)

battalions of the same regiment could more readily be traced (because regimental numbers were allocated in blocks). In this way Brecknock men drafted to the 4th South Wales Borderers in Mesopotamia were be traced and the deaths of 11 men (with another 20 wounded) was announced in routine orders. (Many men must have learned of the deaths of friends from a casual perusal of a roneoed sheet pinned to a board.) Those at home often heard only months later. A Swansea family may have waited longer than necessary to learn of a man's death, killed in Mesopotamia, because his initial was misread and his officer, who probably would have written, had been killed as well.[69].

On active service, as millions of troops learned, death became almost prosaic. Newly arrived in Mesopotamia, Robert Palmer, serving with the 1/4th Hants at Amara, told his mother how 'a man in our Coy. died last night'. He described his shock at how routinely his fellow officers took the news:

> The Adjt. just looked in and said "who owns Pte. Taylor A." Harris said "I do: is he dead?"
> Adjt. "Yes: you must bury him to-morrow." Harris: "Right o."[70]

69   Comrades Grave Fund papers, Box 17a, MRRW
70   Palmer, *Letters from Mesopotamia*, p. 49. By coincidence, this was probably 'Perce' Harris, who was to be captured at Kut but who escaped from Yozgad camp.

A funeral in Mesopotamia – assuming a man received one – was prosaic: 'no ceremony – just the draped body on a mule cart and the small firing party behind', as a doctor recalled.[71] Men dying on the frontier could expect an unmarked grave as well. The Londons killed in Waziristan in 1917, Reg Howgego told his mother, 'had no cross or anything to mark the grave or the Mahsuds would disinter them'.[72] In India, however, men and units observed many of the decencies of Edwardian funerary practice. While death was more common than in civil life, it was never so common that the decencies of a formal funeral and the rituals of mourning were foregone. Many headstones bear the words 'erected by his comrades'.

It is of course sombre to contemplate the deaths of so many mostly young men in wartime. But at the time young men often failed to comprehend the fate they may also have faced, even at close quarters. When Marjorie Swynnerton served at the hospital at Naini Tal a firing party was summoned from the nearest cantonment, but arrived before the patient had actually died. The firing party found themselves at a loose end. 'They wandered round and round the hospital peering into his window', Marjorie recalled. 'An orderly tried to cheer him up by telling him … "Jacobs! Jacobs! Your firing squad's here, mate!"'[73]

Frequent and often sudden death had always been the inescapable condition of the British in India, and even though medical and sanitary advances had drastically reduced mortality, every unit suffered losses and left men in cantonment cemeteries – in the case of the Somerset Territorials, in sixteen cemeteries from Burma to the north-west frontier and from Dum Dum to Calicut.[74] Every cantonment and station, however small, had a cemetery. *Punch's* Hampshire clerk was delighted to find that in Indian Army file registries 'cemeteries' came under the heading of 'Accommodation for Troops'.[75] Equally unsurprisingly, cantonment cemeteries were governed by elaborate rules, whose 25 pages dictated, for example, the height of headstones and memorials (those under 3-feet high commemorating other ranks were exempt from fees and were maintained officially, but larger memorials attracted ground fees and maintenance costs, a problem for itinerant units).[76]

In every unit an officer (often the President of its Regimental Institute) administered the complex and expensive business of arranging for headstones or memorials. The most extensive records were left by the 1/1st Brecknock, the museum of which holds a large file of the arrangements for burying and commemorating the 50 Brecknock men who died, mostly in Mhow between its arrival from Aden in mid-1915 and 1919. The Brecknock's memorials became the special responsibility of Major Edward Cockcroft, who devotedly administered its 'Comrades Graves Fund'. Brecknock men began the fund by donating a day's pay and subscribed to it throughout their service individuals and groups to erect headstones. Later in the war the Indian government subsidised battalion funds by granting Rs80 per man for headstones.

71 Begg, *Surgery on Trestles*, p. 15
72 Letter, 11 September 1917, Reg Howgego, 1/25th London, Mss.Eur.C340/2, BL
73 Marjorie Thomas, 'Child of the Empire', Doc 8236, 99/37/1, IWM She changed the man's name.
74 [Extracts from Commonwealth War Graves cemetery registers relating to Somerset Light Infantry Territorial battalions], DD\SLI/20/6/7, SHC, Taunton
75 'A Territorial in India', *Punch*, 17 May 1916, p. 326
76 *Rules for the care and use of Government cemeteries throughout India, 1913*, Correspondence relating to the grave memorials in Aden and India during the Great War, Box 17a, RMRW

When individual headstones were impractical, units funded the erection of memorials – the Brecknocks' officers subscribed £57 to commemorate their 19 men who died in Aden, with the colonel beginning with £10, the majors £5, captains £2 and subalterns £1 or £2. Major Cockcroft not only administered the fund, but also oversaw the erection of headstones and ensured (often after the war) that the families of the dead received photographs of them.

Dead Europeans in India were if possible buried. The only known exception was Captain Freidrich (Fritz) Bartelt of the 2/4th Somerset, who died in Calcutta in September 1916, probably of food poisoning. Bartelt's case was exceptional, not just in that his colonel travelled to Calcutta for his funeral, but because his body was then cremated. This was an unusual enough practice in Britain at the time (cremation had only been legal since 1902) but for Europeans in India (in contrast to Hindus and Sikhs) it was almost unheard of. Bartelt, the son of a wealthy Bath soap manufacturing family, was commemorated by a plaque in St Luke's, Dinapore, and by a window and plaque in his parish church at Corston, Avon, where he had been a churchwarden.

While those close to men posted to India may have been spared the anxiety and all too often the grief that afflicted the families of those serving at the front, death in India was common enough that officers, chaplains and regimental office staff had well-established routines to follow in the event of death. Often families received word not by telegram (the usual practice with battlefield deaths) but by letter, sometimes in a blow softened by warning of illness. Just after Christmas 1918 the family of Lance-Corporal John Say in Trowbridge received a letter from Captain Neville Audrey, his company commander in the 2/4th Wilts. Audrey was writing to Asaph, John's father, to advise him that John was 'very seriously ill' with influenza and that he had now contracted enteric. John died of enteric on Boxing Day and soon after the Allahabad Garrison Chaplain wrote to assure his mother, Fanny, that 'everything possible was done for him'.[77] John was one of two Trowbridge Territorials who died in India.

News of distant deaths naturally distressed those at home. When his company commander wrote to Elizabeth, mother of Frank Woodward of Malmesbury, to tell her that Frank had died of malaria compounded by pneumonia, she died within days, of 'melancholia'.[78] Families notified of men's deaths sometimes wrote to seek details of the circumstances of deaths, and notices in battalion magazines asked men to respond to comfort grieving families. 'Notifications', however, elicited few responses, with families seemingly stoically accepting the news.

If families of 'other ranks' kept their grief to themselves, correspondence with the widow of the only Brecknocks officer to die suggests the anxieties common to bereaved families regardless of their social standing. Vivien Bailey was the widow of Captain the Hon. Lance Bailey of the Brecknocks, who died of smallpox in Mhow in October 1918. She 'simply long[ed] to go out & see it myself [and] perhaps I shall one day' – but she had the means to at least envisage doing so. Bailey had been the nephew of the Brecknocks' former colonel, Lord Glanusk, whose death Edward Cockcroft's file documents in detail.[79] 'It is so miserable being so far off, one feels so helpless ... just like a rudderless ship', Vivien told Mrs. Cockcroft, 'no one can realise

---

77 Letters, 17 December 1918 and 4 January 1919, SBYRW 25913, RBWM
78 Vernon, *Our Glorious Dead*, p. 122
79 Letter 'Tuesday' [September 1920], Correspondence relating to the grave memorials in Aden and India during the Great War, Box 17a, RMRW. Mrs. Bailey signed her letters 'Vivien' but for the inscription on Lance's grave she specified 'Vivienne'.

the loneliness and desolation till they have been through it'[80] Poor Vivien was living in lodgings, worrying over many matters, large and small, relying on an uncle to resolve problems for her, fretting most of all that Lance's grave was being neglected. In fact, Edward Cockcroft was visiting it often, ensuring it was kept tidy while the soil settled, but had failed to explain the delay to Vivien. At last, she chose a recumbent plain white marble cross. 'I will pay anything they ask, nothing will be too good for his memory' (though Cockcroft cautioned the masons that Bailey's widow was 'far from being well off').[81] Indeed, Vivien told Mrs. Cockcroft (whom she already knew), when she wrote to try to learn what was happening to her late husband's grave, that she was envisaging having to find work.

By the war's end Territorial graves could be found in 67 cemeteries in India proper, another six cemeteries in Burma, and in Vladivostok (seven Hampshire Territorials), Singapore, Aden, Hong Kong, in Persia and even in Ceylon (four Hants men who died of 'flu on the way to Russia). Nearly half of the Territorial dead were interred in ten major cantonment cemeteries, though 35 cemeteries, mostly in hill stations, hold fewer than five graves. The big cemeteries offer reminders of the cost of garrisoning India: Mhow has 24 Brecknock graves, Agra 20 East Surreys; Lahore 29 Royal Sussex, most victims of the 'flu epidemic (see Chapter 17).

Some battalions had commissioned memorial plaques in India. At the dedication of the plaque in St James's, Delhi, in September 1919 to the forty men of the 1/4th Cornwall who had died in India, Albert Bray noticed his colonel 'fraught with evident feeling' as he unveiled it. In the pews, 'tears could be seen on the faces of old friends of those who had fallen', even as men made 'a rigid effort at control'.[82] It records the names of 23 men who died in Delhi (mostly of 'flu) and seventeen who died in ten other places. Some of these memorials (including the Cornwalls' in Delhi) remain. For the time being at least, the Territorials' Indian dead are commemorated in durable stone.

---

80 Letter, 14 May 1919, Correspondence relating to the grave memorials in Aden and India during the Great War, Box 17a, RMRW
81 Letters, 24 August [1919] & 20 July 1919, Correspondence relating to the grave memorials in Aden and India during the Great War, Box 17a, RMRW
82 Albert Bray, 'Brief notes on service', p. 7, B.4289, CRM. I am grateful to Ms Satarupa Lahiri who visited and photographed the Cornwall memorial in St James's, Delhi.

14

Internal security

As the war continued '1914 men' admitted freely to feeling increasingly 'fed up'. Wilts men added a line to rhyme with the regimental bugle call: 'We are the boys who never go out to war'.[1] But while many Territorial battalions did not 'go out to war', they saw the 'internal security' duty, the Army in India's major responsibility after India's external defence.

'Markedly inferior': reinforcements

Reinforcements for Territorial units continued to arrive, though 'no one wants to read a description of a journey on a liner', wrote Philip Gosse, recalling his own voyage to India in 1917.[2] India was a low priority compared to the Western Front, but the introduction of conscription provided a flow of reinforcements. These men were different to pre-war Territorials or those who had volunteered in 1914. Harry Brown, a Yorkshire man, a conscript, married and a reluctant soldier, reached the 1/5th East Surrey in the middle of the hot weather in 1917. Harry met a fellow Yorkshireman who confessed that 'he would like to be out [that is, out of uniform], like all of us', but even Harry found his horizons widened by war service. On the voyage out, taking the long, submarine-free route via Sierra Leone and South Africa, he found himself enjoying a string orchestra on a pier at Cape Town, 'among the toffs', and when he reached his destination, Muttra, he visited nearby Agra. 'I would like you to see what I see', he wrote to his wife.[3]

Nevertheless, the drafts sent from the Wilts' depot were often men who had specifically joined the Territorials earlier in the war. When Fred Mundy took charge of a party of men of a draft at Chaubattia in 1916 he saw 'many faces I knew amongst them'.[4] The arrival of reinforcements and the return of convalescents from Mesopotamia continued to bolster the number of Territorials in India. By January 1917 War Office returns showed over 41,000 in India.[5] Indian

---

1 Mundy, *A Journal of the 1/4th Battalion Wiltshire Regiment*, p. 268
2 Gosse, *Memoirs of a Camp-Follower*, p. 193
3 Diary, Harry Brown, 1/5th East Surrey, ESR/25/BROW/1, SHC, Woking
4 Mundy, *A Journal of the 1/4th Battalion Wiltshire Regiment*, p. 77
5 'Returns of the Territorial Force Serving Abroad', WO114/54, January 1917, NAUK. They served in the Egyptian Expeditionary Force, in Salonika and in France and Belgium (91,000, 35,000 and

Territorials, however, comprised only about ten percent of the 400,000 Territorials serving overseas. Though rumours circulated that a yeomanry regiment would be sent to India to add to its Regular cavalry (by late 1917 the only British mounted regiment in India was the 21st Lancers) no more could be spared.[6] The only Territorials besides the infantry and artillery which arrived in 1916 were the four former cyclist battalions early in 1916 and two small sanitary companies (a total of 130 men) of London Territorials. Many of the reinforcements, mostly conscripts, were, Harry Canham thought, 'markedly inferior' physically, though they kept numbers up – the 2/4th Border in mid-1918 was still over a thousand strong, not counting a hundred men detached for various reasons.[7]

By this time the distribution of British troops had changed. Battalions were still distributed in cantonments, exchanging stations every six months or so and switching detachments with the hills in the hot weather. 1916 had seen an influx of Territorial reinforcements and especially the eighteen garrison battalions posted to India between November 1915 and March 1917. (Garrison battalions had been formed from mid-1915 from 'Category B' men considered able to serve overseas but not undertake active service. When they arrived Territorial battalions' bands greeted them at railway stations and Territorials, now wise in India's ways, provided 'conducting parties'.)

'Agitation': Indian politics

The years of the Great War saw a profound change in the political movements seeking the reform, and even the end of British rule. Popularly this wartime transformation is dated to the arrival in Bombay of Mohandas Karamchand Gandhi, the Indian-born lawyer, who returned to his home-land to inspire and eventually lead the nationalist struggle; what most Britons in India (and doubtless Territorials) thought of as 'agitation'.[8] A Surrey officer who attended the Punjab War Conference in Lahore in May 1918 'came away feeling that our rule in India was a very great and splendid affair'. He probably spoke for all Territorials in judging that maintaining the *'pax Britannica'* was worthwhile.[9]

British rule in the war's middle years seemed secure. Congress's leadership had declared its support for the King Emperor in 1914. Even Bal Gandaghar Tilak, the Maharashtran exiled to Burma for the 'sedition' of defending a bomb attack, on his return to Bombay sent George V a message of loyal support. But 'moderates' and 'extremists' drew apart. 1916 saw the formation of 'Home Rule' leagues, seeking self-government within the empire; more assertive than Congress, but still advocating boycotts rather than bombs. British officials remained vigilant. The Secretary of State for India summarised for the Mesopotamia Commission the way Hardinge

---

220,000 respectively), with small numbers in Mesopotamia (8,774, almost all from India), colonies (such as Malta and Gibraltar, 2400) and a handful in East Africa (348).
6   Private Ernest Hallum of the Hertfordshire Yeomanry – a Territorial – died at Muttra the day after the Armistice. How he came to be serving in India is a mystery. While men's entry into the army is almost invariably clear, postings, especially once they were serving overseas, were poorly documented and almost no British troops have surviving individual personnel files.
7   Letter, 4 July 1918, Harry Canham, 2/4th Border, CMML
8   *History of the Hampshire Territorial Force Association*, p. 153
9   'The Punjab War Conference', *The Braganza*, 1 June 1918, p. 12

East Surrey troops making a 'flag march' through Fyzabad in 1915, to remind its inhabitants of the potential power of India's British garrison. (ESR/6/9/11, Surrey History Centre)

and Duff especially were prone to 'colour the risks in India as darkly as possible'. Commander Josiah Wedgwood, whose minority report was even more damning than the Commission as a whole, expressed scepticism: 'There have been more than the usual number of dacoities [but] … curious semi-religious theories about the Germans … But there has been no armed rising, and the capture of 50 revolvers by revolutionaries is singled out as the most serious incident'.[10]

'Riot', an expert in 'Imperial Policing' declared, 'is at all times endemic in India'; but not at all places at all times.[11] Writing from Allahabad early in 1915, when he had realised that Indian service involved tedious guard duty in an uncomfortable climate, Arthur Copeland wrote to a brother in uniform in Britain that 'it's so tame out here that one almost wishes there would be a decent sized native rising!'[12] Stanley Goodland, writing a few days earlier from Ambala, hinted to Elsie of unrest he could not discuss but admitted that the garrison had 'been warned that we must be ready for any emergency' because 'you can't trust the natives one bit'.[13] Likewise, Owen Smith had told his family that during Mohurram troops were confined to barracks in Agra and that men were warned to be ready to go into the city in the event of communal disturbance, '& that is what we are now ready for'.[14]

10 Mesopotamia Commission, p. 130
11 Gwynn, *Imperial Policing*, p. 58
12 Letter, 4 March 1915, Arthur Copeland, 1/5th Hants, 128A08/1-4, HRO
13 Letter, 23 February 1915, Stanley Goodland, 1/5th Somerset, Noyes, (ed.), *Engaged in War*, p. 24
14 Letter, 17 November 1915, Owen Smith, 1/6th Hants, M766, RHRM

The troops had their own simple explanation for the strife they faced almost everywhere, potentially or actually: the cause of it is because of two religions, one the Mohamedans and the other Hindu, and they each think their religion is the best …', as a Somerset man explained from Amritsar.[15] In 1915, for example, detachments of the 1/6th Hants marched to Dehra Dun from Chakrata in case of communal unrest at Hardwar, where large numbers of Hindu pilgrims gathered. The great majority of such incidents were not anti-British protests, but were directed at other Indian communities. At Bareilly in July 1918, for example, Reg Bailey reported 'a big festival' which 'got to be a miniature battle' between Hindus and Muslims in which nine people were killed. One of the Buffs' companies stood to arms, but the local police dealt with the emergency.[16]

British troops could expect to be called out at any time. As routine orders show, all cantonments prepared contingency plans to protect vital features in their vicinity and to form 'moveable columns' in case of uprising. Early in 1915 at Malapuram in south India the 2/4th Somerset formed a column to support police suppressing a rising of the Muslim Moplahs. Shepton Mallet men described marching twice against unrest among the 'Moplars' early in 1915, and 'we do not know any moment we are to be called out again'.[17] In Burma, at Myitkyina the 1/4th Border were alerted against unrest in the district. There was 'no news of actual fighting' a newspaper conceded (in fact in either place) but 'the presence of the men is deemed necessary'.[18] At Dinapore, on the Ganges near Patna, the 1/9th Middlesex would have formed a column with the 2nd Devon Battery and the depot companies of the 89th Punjabis (whose parent battalion had served in Egypt, then briefly Gallipoli and later France and Mesopotamia). They prepared plans to move to secure the bridge over the River Sone, 20 miles to the west. Harry Canham hoped that armoured cars in Peshawar would 'put the "wind up" the niggers'.[19] But Indians did not need armoured cars to feel intimidated.

Even men who kept unreflective diaries might be moved to ponder the epic of which they had become a part. Herbert Chapple, a Devonshire man, pondered how he had had 'the opportunity of seeing some of our Empire. The more I see the more I marvel, to see millions of people governed by so few.'[20] Territorials certainly took an interest in the administration of the country in which they enforced order. In 1917 the magazine of the 1/9th Middlesex published a series of articles on 'How India is Governed', detailing the system of district officials up the Viceroy's Council. How did Territorials regard Indian nationalism? 'I was never much of a believer in the "little brown brother" idea', Captain Godfrey Burrell of the 1/4th Hants wrote at the time.[21] Few Territorials doubted the British mandate to rule. Jim Mackie, a 19-year-old subaltern, found himself acting as magistrate at Calicut: 'I deal out justice to the natives in the Cantonment', he wrote, just two months after arriving in India.[22] For all that Chelmsford was committed to the continuation of British rule, he wanted to grant a measure of self-government under that

---

15   *Shepton Mallet Journal*, 14 May 1915, p. 5
16   Letter, 12 July 1918, Reg Bailey, 1/4th Buffs, 2011-12-3, NAM
17   *Shepton Mallet Journal*, 23 April 1915, p. 3
18   Clipping, Lawrence Hoggarth, 1/4th Border, Album 35 Acc. Nos 3024-3345, CMML
19   Letter, 10 October 1918, Harry Canham, 2/4th Border, CMML
20   Diary, 31 December 1915, Herbert Chapple, 1/4th Devon, DMM
21   Godfrey Burrell, 'The Diary of a Company Commander', p. 4, M1838, RHRM
22   Letter, February 1915, Jim Mackie, 2/4th Somerset, Mackie, *Answering the Call*, p. 36

A 'mobile column', including men of the 2/4th Somerset, on parade at Malappuram in 1915, its bullock-drawn guns undermining confidence that it could respond to unrest rapidly. (DD\SLI/15/7/84, Somerset Heritage Centre)

framework. Following the 1917 announcement of the principle, Edwin Montagu, the Secretary of State for India, travelled to India in November 1917. Remaining for six months. Montagu, the more vigorous and, in effect, Chelmsford's superior, took the initiative in devising and framing the reforms. Chelmsford was dutiful, though his chilly personality did not inspire – an official observing him commented that he was too much of a machine to arouse admiration. Montagu's statement in the House of Commons, announced on 20 August 1917, that the 'increasing association of Indians in every branch of the administration' heralded 'the progressive realization of responsible government'. This promising vision would not long survive the war.

Chelmsford had become convinced, during the time he had spent in India before becoming Viceroy, that constitutional change was inevitable, once the war was over. As ever reluctant to move ahead of official opinion, he consulted his advisers and provincial heads. While some remained obdurate (Sir Harcourt Butler, lieutenant-governor of Burma, thought Britain would rule India 'for ever') the consensus was a vague acknowledgement that India should move towards a form of self-government as part of the empire, with the assumption that any vestige of parliamentary democracy lay in the far distant future.[23] Politicians in both Britain and in India realised that they were living through momentous times, with new notions abroad. As Lord Curzon advised the War Cabinet in June 1917 'in the course of the war forces have been let loose, ideas have found ventilated, aspirations have been formulated ... The Russian revolution has lent an immense momentum to this tide ... very likely more disturbing than the French revolution'.[24] The magnitude and implications of that change would become apparent at the war's end, and would affect the Territorials profoundly.

---

23 Rumbold, *Watershed in India*, pp. 54-59
24 Memo by Curzon, 27 June 1917, quoted in Rumbold, *Watershed in India*, p. 91

'They don't all love us': in aid of the civil power

Britain's tenure in India rested, ultimately on military power, and that meant the presence of reliable troops able to intimidate or coerce its people, and if necessary deter or suppress resistance. Contemporaries expressed it more delicately – the historian of the West Surrey wrote that 'the peace and integrity of India … rests … on a foundation of armed strength' – but no one doubted the British need for an army in India.[25] While Territorial units did represent Britain's military hold in its most literal and symbolic form, it is probably true that for the duration of the war more Indians did not see a British soldier than did. Troops were put on alert or called out at times of communal tension or (as occurred in 1919) active protest. More rarely they were ordered to use force.

Huge stretches of India neither contributed men as soldiers nor, seemingly, required troops to intimidate or police their populations. The provinces of Burma, Assam, Bengal, Bihar and Orissa required between them fewer than 5000 British soldiers.[26] No British troops served in north-east India or in most princely states, though Secunderabad was in the princely state of Hyderabad. The people of Mysore saw British soldiers only when Frank Johnson took his 2/6th Royal Sussex on a march from Bangalore to Mysore, where they were feted, something Regular troops had never done. (The Maharaja of Mysore entertained large numbers of the Royal Sussex, conducting them over his palace and its treasures. 'This', Woodyatt remarked, 'was a privilege never granted to British troops before or since' – Territorials were seen as different to Regulars.[27])

Instead, British troops were concentrated in the north and especially the north-west, with three of the army's ten divisions located in a tiny fraction of the country, around Peshawar and Rawalpindi. This was partly a legacy of the army's forward posture in the mid-19th century, when the Bengal Army had faced adversaries in the north-west, and a result of the railway network linking key cantonments, but it also reflected the historic fear that if invasion or internal rebellion were to occur, it would come in or out of the north-west.

British troops emerged from their cantonments to remind Indians that the Raj's power rested upon military force. Troops often went on 'flag marches' – route marches around cities and the surrounding country in order to none-too-subtly remind 'natives' of the latent power of British armed force. About once a month in 1915 the 1/5th West Surrey marched through Lucknow: 'we got no cheers', Ted Rice recalled.[28] George Owers marched through Ferozepore, 'Showing the Flag' as a member of a Sussex battery. He remembered the watching crowds as 'frightening … the whole attitude was of a hostility that could be felt'.[29] Men repeatedly recorded variations on this reaction. 'We don't get very kindly looks', wrote Herbert Ewing.[30] 'Some of them don't seem too friendly', wrote Alfred Groucher of the 1/4th Buffs from Bareilly in 1917.[31] An East Surrey officer who had begun to learn Urdu early in his stay in India thought at first that the shop-keepers and hawkers

---

25 Wylly, *History of the Queen's Royal Regiment*, Vol. VII, p. vi
26 'Proposal for raising Territorial units in India', 19 June 1916, CAB42/15/9, NAUK
27 Woodyatt, 'The Territorials (Infantry) in India', *JRUSI*, 1922, p. 727
28 Ted Rice, 'All for a Shilling a Day', QRWS/30/RICE/1, SHC, Woking
29 Memoir, George Owers, Sussex Battery, Doc.11927, 02/5/1, IWM
30 Diary, 26 February 1915, Herbert Ewing, 1/5th Somerset, Doc.15428, 07/8/1, IWM
31 Letter, 30 March 1917, Alfred Groucher, 1/4th Buffs, Great Chart Fund, Book 5, KA&HC

of Lucknow received his battalion's weekly 'flag march' 'reasonably well'. As his command of Urdu increased, though, he began to hear 'some taunts mingled with laughter' as the troops passed.[32]

If deterrence failed, troops – usually Indian – might be called out to deal with active rebellion, or with communal disturbance between ethnic or (more usually) religious communities. Even early in 1915 Territorials found that they were used to overawe protest – the 1/4th Devon was called out when rising food prices excited unrest in the Punjab. (Hugh Creek recorded that his company had been sent into the streets of Ferozepore with ten rounds and supposedly ordered to 'take no prisoners', but privates perhaps did not realise the careful procedures operating on troops called out 'in aid of the civil power' as such duty was termed.[33]) Reg Bailey, in trying to reassure his intended, Hilda, that he was better off in India than France, found himself admitting the possibilities of seeing internal security duty. 'There have been some nasty incidents that you don't hear about', he admitted, '& if anything did happen, we should have a very lively time, considering the number of the population … they don't all love us …'[34]

Given the British soldier's actual and iconic centrality to the suppression of challenges to British authority, it is ironic that Territorials were used on a large scale to suppress communal unrest rarely in India proper, notably in Bihar in 1917.

'All European troops available': Bihar 1917

Over the Muslim Bakr-Id festival in late September Hindus in Bihar attempted to prevent their Muslim neighbours from killing cows, offering to purchase goats for sacrifice instead. The arrangement broke down, and Muslims sacrificed cows, which large Hindu crowds tried to rescue. Within days the dispute had sparked Hindu mobs gathering to attack and loot the homes of Muslims. Shahabad, the district worst affected, was said (by Indian journalists) to be 'one of the most backward' in Bihar, its people 'ignorant and illiterate', entirely unaffected by nationalist politics.[35] Within ten days almost a hundred villages had been attacked and looted by large Hindu mobs, many of young boys. Muslim mobs retaliated, with mosques and temples being destroyed and defiled. As grain shops and money-lenders' premises were often ransacked, the disturbances linked Hindu fundamentalism with economic distress. The *Pioneer's* Patna correspondents described the cause of Hindu militancy as a 'widespread conspiracy to prevent cow sacrifice'.[36] Military police patrols fired on what they called 'rioters', killing several, while Hindu lawyers and community leaders attempted to disperse and dissuade mobs from attacking Muslim communities, with varied success.

The disturbed area eventually extended in a triangle from Gaya in the south-east about 120 miles north-west to Buxar on the Ganges and 70 miles eastward towards Patna, on both banks of the River Sone. The epicentre was Piru, a village on the right bank of the Sone, 60 miles south of Patna. The Commissioner at Patna requested military aid on 2 October, asking for 'all European troops available' to be sent to Arrah. Later that day a hundred Somersets boarded

---

32   Caroe, 'The Flames of Enchantment', pp. iv-7-8, PP/MCR/207, IWM
33   Letter, 24 February 1915, Hugh Creek, 1/4th Devon, EX2543, DMM
34   Letter, 14 October 1917, Reg Bailey, 1/4th Buffs, 2011-12-3, NAM
35   *Amrita Bazaar Patrika*, 20 October 1917, p. 6c
36   *Pioneer*, 24 October 1917

pony-drawn ekkas to go to the railway station at Dinapore to entrain for Arrah, about thirty miles and an hour away. The Magistrate at Arrah must have been concerned, asking for a further 50 Somersets later that evening. Mention of Arrah had a particular resonance for Britons. Many knew that it had been the setting of one of the minor epics of the Mutiny, when in mid-1857, some 18 civilians and 50 'native' police (mostly Sikhs) held off a larger force of sepoys for a week. The *Pioneer* noted that the area had 'won notoriety under the influence of Koar Singh during the Mutiny', a Rajput who had led the revolt in Bihar.[37] The 2/5th Somerset was the only British battalion in Bihar and Orissa, a province with a population of about thirty million people.

Divisional staff at Fort William responded to the civilians' request, despatching another 200 men of the 2/4th Wilts from Allahabad, alerted at tiffin and left before tea by train on 3 October. All the fit men of the 2/5th Somerset were summoned from Lebong, 300 miles away. By the first week in October just over 600 troops, two-thirds of them Somerset and Wiltshire Territorials, were distributed across the disturbed districts. Though the war years saw Home Rule activism blossom across India, newspapers supporting nationalism denied that the unrest arose from any political intent. The *Amrita Bazaar Patrika*, an English language 'native' newspaper published in Calcutta, reported the crisis in detail, seemingly confirming its communal and reactionary origins. But in their scale (over 50,000 Hindus gathered to avenge reports of slaughtered cows) the Bihar riots were 'more fierce and prolonged' than any under British rule, and apparently 'premeditated', a test by Hindu landlords who manipulated their tenants to probe the government's will to maintain order.[38] The rioters were 'operating on a definite plan', their targets selected; avoiding official buildings but attacking their Muslim neighbours. But 'snowball leaflets' urging Hindus to act included slogans such as 'British rule is gone', prophesying that troops would not fire for lack of ammunition.[39]

Military detachments were small and scattered. The 2/5th Somerset sent 130 men to five places south of Arrah, while the 2/4th Wilshire placed 269 men in seven detachments south of Buxar.[40] Later a further two hundred Somersets joined them. Curiously the most senior officer was a captain of the Wiltshires; all five of the Somersets' officers were lieutenants. Most commanded forces of fewer than 25 men, and some groups numbered under fifteen. They sent out 'patrols all over the country every day by motor car, motor boat (along the river) and on foot', sleeping in isolated court houses, railway halts and officials' compounds, assailed by mosquitoes at night.[41] While the Somersets were placed in villages in the north, between the Sone and Ganges, the Wiltshires were at railway stations, with the largest party at Sassaram, on the old Grand Trunk Road, and more importantly on the railway line running north-westwards through the disturbed area towards Benares. The Somersets' history described 'long forced marches over soft dusty roads', usually finding that rioters had decamped.[42] They learned that 'the Indians kept well clear of the troops', though once a small detachment faced and fired upon

---

37 *Pioneer*, 13 October 1917
38 Broomfield, 'The Bengal Muslims and September 1918', in Lowe, (ed.), *Soundings in Modern South Asian History*, p. 206
39 Lovett, *A History of the Indian Nationalist Movement*, p. 150
40 Enclosure to Dy. No. 68568, Arrah, 7 October 1917, WWI/405/H, War Diary, Army Headquarters, India, Miscellaneous, Vol. 33, 1-31 October 1917, NAI
41 Gale, *With the 2/4th Wilts to India*, p. 77
42 Anon, *The Book of Remembrance*, pp. 100-02

a crowd of 5000 Hindus.[43] In a 'turbulent and isolated country' the violence attracted neither concern nor censure.[44] The 2/5th Somerset lost one man killed, Ernest Binding of Watchet, who was accidentally shot by a comrade on 12 October.

The despatch of troops left Dinapore denuded of troops, with only 90 Europeans, including the staff of the artillery depot, and of its 989 Indian troops only 53 were trained. Brigadier Strange, commanding the Presidency Brigade, arrived from Calcutta to direct operations from Dinapore. On 4 October the magistrates reported 'most serious' rioting in Shahabad, fearing that the disorder could spread beyond the district. On the afternoon of 5 October the Commissioner at Arrah wired the commandant at Dinapore for more troops. By 10 October the force was occupying two dozen villages and towns across a swathe of Bihar, including detachments of three cavalry regiments (one British and two Indian) and three Indian infantry regiments (including Gurkhas and the 17th Infantry). They formed mobile columns, in which patrols in more than a dozen light cars accompanied by cavalry scoured the roads.[45] Wiltshires described 'scouting through the jungle, struggling through paddy-fields nearly up to the waist in mud and riding home again on borrowed elephants'.[46] Whether this effort was worthwhile remains debatable.

While the Somersets and Wiltshires' deployment to Bihar in the autumn of 1917 was the largest single commitment of Territorials to supporting civil authority – and while it might be regarded as effective since communal disorder petered out within weeks – it might also be seen as exposing weaknesses in the Territorials' part in maintaining internal security. That troops had to be summoned from Lebong, 300 miles away, suggests the scarcity of European troops. More significantly, the Territorials' actual contribution on the ground seems to have been limited, not least by mobility. The country in the months following the monsoon – rice paddies, jungle and swamps, with roads muddy – made infantry practically useless. Even the light cars, each holding four or five men, were unable to function effectively on rutted tracks. Only cavalry could keep pace with rioters who knew their way around the difficult terrain, and then several times charged large assemblies and even fired upon them. While the unrest occurred at a relatively benign time climatically, the 'native' journalists of the *Amrita Bazaar Patrika* noted that 'the infantry are always too late to stop looting and the European foot-soldiers … fade away very soon … in the heat of the sun.'[47] The Territorials remained in Bihar for over a month, until religious festivals likely to provoke both communities had passed, but Mohammedans, grateful for the troops' protection, often played the Wiltshires at football.

The arrival of the Garrison battalions enabled detachments to be returned to headquarters (so the 1/5th Hants was reunited – briefly – from five separate stations) and raised the possibility of more Territorials being sent on active service either to Mesopotamia or even to France. Delays due to the lack of shipping left units in a state of uncertainty; advised (officially or otherwise) that they were to move, but then shifted once or even twice for short periods. Jim Mackie described the 2/4th Somerset as 'absolutely fed up & depressed'. Officers and men were eager to

---

43 Edward Ewens, 'A Cook's Tour in Burma and India', DD\SLI\17/1/62, SHC, Taunton
44 Rumbold, *Watershed in India*, p. 103
45 WWI/405/H, War Diary, Army Headquarters, India, Miscellaneous, Vol. 33, 1–31 October 1917, pp. 92-95, NAI
46 Gale, *With the 2/4th Wilts to India*, p. 78
47 *Amrita Bazaar Patrika*, 9 October 1917

leave, though Jim recognised that by mid-1917 his parents would be glad that he was staying in India. But after nearly three years, he wrote, 'We deserve to get our chance'.[48]

This stagnation bred apathy and led energetic officers to try to get away, leading to complaints (familiar in India) that officers remaining were slothful or incompetent. Other officers were conscientious and competent. Gerard Bonham-Carter's letters, mostly to his sister, Joan, show him to have been dutiful. He spent much time studying manuals and regulations, and displayed patience on parade – when his West Kent Territorials botched parades he did not berate them but blamed himself. He paid his men promptly and made sure to record the details of all of his men who died and pursued contractors to ensure that their headstones were delivered and installed. He modestly reflected (in 1918, after four years of service and in his mid-fifties) how 'I generally manage pretty well but every now and then slip up and come a howler much to my mortification'.[49]

The Territorial battalions' composition gradually changed through the war. After the 2/5th Somerset shifted to Calcutta from Burma in May 1917 Edward Ewens thought that it was 'gradually losing its county and district character'. Though it had lost only eight men dead in Burma, it lost men in various ways, and gained men transferred from Garrison battalions, including 'a few rotters who caused us no end of trouble, having none of the usual esprit de corps manifested by the county men'.[50] (With the evident connivance of the Somersets' medical officer, some of these men were later put on a draft for Mesopotamia, though they were classified medically as B1.) This points to the importance of the battalions' colonels in determining their character and effectiveness.

'The best type of English gentleman': Territorial colonels

'The Colonel', as a parody of the Ten Commandments began, 'is thy only Boss; thou shalt have no other Colonels but him'.[51] The colonels of Territorial battalions were almost all county gentry or members of prominent commercial or professional families. The point is made, perhaps, by the name of the commanding officer of the 4th Duke of Cornwall's Light Infantry in 1914, Lieutenant-Colonel the Hon. John Hepburn-Stuart-Forbes-Trefusis. Because he was absent, travelling, he was temporarily replaced by a Major George Smith 'a fact that must have delighted the orderly room clerks', a regimental historian commented.[52] Some battalions, especially those that saw active service, saw a succession of officers in command – the 2/4th Somerset had six. A few battalions had one through the entire war, such as the 2/5th Somerset, which Lieutenant-Colonel James Paull commanded from October 1914 to February 1920.

The best colonels are easily found. Alfred Drayson, Arthur Bell remembered, 'was a good man and very considerate to his men'.[53] Drayson remained in command of the 1/6th East Surrey for the entire war. During its first Kitchener Test, when the battalion marched 24 miles, attacking

---

48 Letter, 16 May 1917, Jim Mackie, 2/4th Somerset, Mackie, *Answering the Call*, p. 211
49 Diary, 20 June 1918, Gerald Bonham-Carter, 1/5th West Kent, 94M72/F303-305, HRO
50 Edward Ewens, 'A Cook's Tour in Burma and India', DD\SLI\17/1/62, SHC, Taunton
51 'The Ten Commandments', *The Royal Sussex Herald*, 27 May 1916, p. 96
52 White, *One and All*, p. 215
53 Arthur Bell article, *Queen's Royal Surrey Regiment Newsletter*, 1999, SHC

A newly-arrived private fails to grasp the importance of his colonel. 'Don't you know I'm the Colonel?' the mufti-clad officer asks. ' … by gum tha will cop it, 't'sergeant's been looking for thee …' The man's dialect is that of the Border Regiment. (*Indian Ink*)

on the way, Drayson led an exhausted man (an old pre-1908 Surrey Volunteer) on his own horse, with another man's rifle strapped to the pommel. The battalion cheered Drayson on his arrival back at camp.[54] Gestures such as this endeared officers to their men. Perhaps the most exemplary colonel was Francis Bowker of the 1/4th Hants who, as we have seen, was both wounded in Mesopotamia, in 1915, and then killed there early in 1916. Obituaries praised him as a competent Regular officer, though he had retired as a major in 1905. In the following decade he distinguished himself as a leader of Longparish in Hampshire – a member of the District and Parish Councils, on the board of the County Hospital, and a founder of the local troop of the Boy Scouts, who sounded the Last Post at his memorial service. He was, as his obituary in a local newspaper put it, 'an example of the best type of English gentleman'.[55]

Nostalgia perhaps lent a rosy glow to memories of colonels in India, but a speech by Mitchell Banks, a former sergeant of the 1/5th East Surrey, in 1928 suggests one reason for the success of Territorial battalion commanders. He eulogised Lieutenant-Colonel Ralph Harvey because he had 'looked upon them as men and not merely as numbers … indeed, as his family'. The observation was greeted with 'loud and prolonged applause'; and not merely because Harvey was present.[56] Other battalion commanders aroused their men's curiosity, ire or worse. Lieutenant-Colonel John Waddy's routine orders regularly included quaint maxims ('a good soldier is never without his last round'; 'don't despise your enemy'; 'the bullet is a fool but the bayonet is a hero').[57] Lieutenant-Colonel Walter Naish of the 2/4th Hants, Victor Manley described as 'over-enthusiastic, martinet' who insisted on the insteps of boots being polished in Baluchistan's notorious dust. His men talked emptily about making 'as many holes in him as a colander whenever the opportunity should occur'.[58]

If any Territorial colonel could be regarded as representative it would be Lieutenant-Colonel Norman Cutler, who had served in the same West Surrey volunteer and Territorial battalion for his entire career (except for time in South Africa). He encouraged his battalion to volunteer to go to India, accepting the undertaking that they would soon return. He helped to shape the 1/4th West Surrey, imposing a necessary discipline, though 'irksome … to a conglomeration of civilians'.[59] When he returned to the battalion in Lucknow late in 1915 after undergoing medical treatment in Britain (and his returning was most unusual) his men not only cheered him at the railway station but pulled his carriage themselves to the cantonment. When he left them permanently at Jutogh in mid-1918, they again pulled his gharry to the station, drowning the battalion band playing Auld Lang Syne. It is possible that the battalion's collapse from sickness in Waziristan resulted in his departure, but his men appeared to not lose faith with him.

If colonels like these remained county or professional gentlemen, the war brought changes to the messes over which they presided. While men commissioned from Territorial battalions almost always went to other units (and, indeed, theatres), they received new officers from home who were no longer necessarily county gentry, but were, as the contemporary phrase had it,

---

54 Unidentified clipping, ESR/10/10/2/7, SHC
55 Clipping in Esme Bowker papers, M1539, RHRM
56 *The Herald* [Croydon?], 2 March 1928, in Press cuttings 5th East Surrey, 1984-11-110-2, NAM
57 Part 1 orders, 2/4th Somerset Light Infantry, April 1917, DD\SLI/6/36, SHC, Taunton
58 Victor Manley, 'A Khaki Diary', p. 139, 49M91W/Q3/6, HRO
59 *The Braganza*, 1 June 1918, pp. 2-3

'temporary gentlemen'. Alban Bacon thought (in 1917) that the 'average ... Territorial officer had never ridden before joining the Army', but had sat only on 'the office stool'.[60]

The Regular prejudice against 'amateurs' persisted. Territorial officers garnered few extra-regimental appointments, and even fewer of any prestige or value, which tended to be reserved for Regulars with career prospects. A Territorial officer complained in 1919 that 'they select a few Territorial Peers and MPs for good appointments for eye wash for the world at large, but there is not a Territorial Officer living, who does not feel that the Territorials have been badly treated all through'.[61] The 1/7th Hants sent only seven officers to staff positions in five years, and only one to Army Headquarters. The 2/4th Border carefully documented the extra-regimental jobs its officers secured, though in five years in India recorded only seven of its captains acting as (for example), 'Field Treasure Chest Officer' to the Peshawar Division during the third Anglo-Afghan war. Most officers, however, merely became 'GSO IIIs' – administrative staff officers or 'Station Staff Officer' dogsbodies; positions too mundane to give to scarce vernacular-speaking British Indian Army officers. One became the Post Commandant at Jamrud in the Khyber Pass, arguably the most romantically Kipling-esque position available in all India, and one which offers a reminder that Terriers served on British India's North-West frontier.

60 Bacon, *The Wanderings of a Temporary Warrior*, p. 70
61 Dennis, *The Territorial Army 1906-1940*, p. 53

15

Terriers on the Frontier

In 1914, Sir George Barrow recalled a year later, India had enjoyed 'profound peace'. That serenity did not long outlast the outbreak of the world war. By June 1915, with minor eruptions occurring along the north-west frontier, Barrow now feared war with Afghanistan or 'a frontier rising on the 1897 scale'.[1] The departures of trained troops, both British and Indian, in late 1914 had left India exposed, as an Army Headquarters report put it in February 1915 at the 'limit of risk'.[2] In 1915, as if insurgent tribes had known, a series of revolts and insurgencies placed the frontier divisions under pressure. The Mesopotamia Commission acknowledged (unconvincingly) that failure in Mesopotamia could be explained by the 'ever-present risk of invasion [by Afghanistan] … and the danger of simultaneous internal disturbance'. 'The preoccupation caused by this anxiety', it acknowledged, 'must not be forgotten in blaming the Indian Government for the inefficiency of the management of the Mesopotamian campaign'.[3] British India would later face both invasion and insurrection on the frontier.

'Fit for service': readiness for battle

In the cold weather of 1916-17 many Territorial battalions took part in brigade manoeuvres. The Delhi Brigade exercised for several days around the ruined Tughlakabad fort, including the 1/4th Wilts, 1/5th Somerset, 2/2nd Gurkhas and the Nepalese Mahindra Dal Regiment. Its brigadier, Lord Radnor, the 1/4th Wilts' former colonel, was not sceptical of the Territorials' prowess. He seems to have persuaded the commander of the 7th (Meerut) Division that they were ready for service. Nevertheless, the *Memorandum on Army Training in India* issued early in 1917 admitted that among some Territorial battalions 'work in the field is weak and requires attention'; a curiously candid admission to make in a training memorandum, and one that perhaps reflects the lingering prejudice among Army Headquarters officers against Territorials.[4]

---

1   'Military situation in India consequent on the war', 17 June 1915, CAB37/129/16, NAUK
2   'Correspondence regarding the deficiency of troops in India, February 1915', L/MIL/17/5/2386, BL
3   Mesopotamia Commission, p. 115
4   *Memorandum on Army Training in India, 1916-1917*, p. 69

Badges of British regiments that had served on the frontier in the previous several decades carved into a rock face at Cherat, a reminder to Territorials that they now shared the most critical burden of the British Army in India. (QRWS/1/16/13, Surrey History Centre)

Beyond the standard trials of the Kitchener Tests, units increasingly took part in more elaborate field days and the manoeuvres, then called 'field operations', in which brigade and divisional formations exercised over large swathes of country, from which its inhabitants had usually been temporarily evicted. These exercises demonstrated both commanders' and their units' fitness for active service, but also their shortcomings. Frank Johnson of the 2/6th Royal Sussex candidly detailed his battalion's errors in a report published in the battalion magazine. He described watching one of his subalterns lead his platoon to attack across 500 yards of open ground a force of two battalions dug-in with eight machine-guns and some guns, admiring their pluck but decrying the platoon commander's judgment. He admonished his junior officers for allowing an advance in 'artillery formation' (in which men and sub-units spread out to diminish losses) become a 'line of platoons in fours … a rather deadly formation'. Still, his divisional commander said that he was 'satisfied that we are now fit for active service' and that, Johnson acknowledged, 'is all that matters'.[5] Sure enough, before the year was out the Royal Sussex was indeed on active service, though against neither Germans nor Turks.

In arguing against Territorials in 1914 Duff had dismissed them as 'of course, quite unfit for frontier work'.[6] The process by which raw Territorial units became proficient is evident in a mosaic of anecdotal evidence, but it can be traced in the sequence of inspection reports for one battalion, the 2/4th Border, collated and published after the war. A succession of general officers inspected and commented on the battalion after periodic and often searching inspections, often conducted by men who were at first sceptical of the Territorials' fitness for active service. At first the main quality noticed was that men were merely 'cheerful'. By September 1915, a year after its formation, the battalion was 'satisfactory'. In February 1917 it was 'fit for war and well trained in all branches' – the judgment of Lionel Dunsterville, commander of the Peshawar Brigade, one of the Indian Army's most demanding commands. A year later, Dunsterville's successor judged that 'taking the pre-war standard of a Regular Battalion as 100, I fix the standard of this Battalion as 85', but still, 'fit for service'. In January 1919 another brigadier found the 2/4th 'a well-organised and efficient battalion … well-disciplined, keen, and anxious to do well'. The Inspector-General of Infantry (probably Nigel Woodyatt) had inspected it a few weeks before and decided that 'it would be difficult to find a battalion with a better spirit or more anxious to do well' – and that was after the 2/4th Border had spent some months split into penny-packets on the Mohmand blockade line.[7]

'Looking towards the frontier': trans-border warfare

Being passed as 'fit for active service', as the 1/6th East Surrey was in April 1915, enabled it to take its place as part of the Rawalpindi Brigade.[8] It comprised some of the most highly regarded British and Indian battalions, ready to embark on frontier service. They included the 1st Green Howards, 2nd North Stafford, 35th Sikhs and 84th Punjabis. This was a considerable complement to a battalion that had been in India less than six months, though it was not entrusted with anything more demanding than mounting guards around Rawalpindi cantonment. During one of the most severe years on the frontier, Territorials posted to Rawalpindi and Peshawar could only watch as Regulars marched off repeatedly, called out to respond to raids and depredations by Afrdis and Mahsuds.

The Regulars returned from these brief punitive expeditions full of stories to impress the novice Territorials. 'Keep a spare cartridge', they warned, in case of emergency', passing on venerable tales of the awful mutilation inflicted on wounded, stories that ensured men realised the necessary discipline of piquetting in the 'hill' or 'frontier' warfare.[9] (Some Territorials saw limited service, such as the 1/4th Somersets posted to Abezai, near Bannu, who because it was

---

5 'Divisional Field Operations', *The Royal Sussex Herald*, 12 August 1916, pp. 186-87
6 Mesopotamia Commission, p. 124
7 Diary, 2/4th Border, pp. 28-32
8 'The East Surrey Regiment in India 1914-19', ESR/10/14/3/1, SHC, Woking
9 Diary, nd, Allan Swift, 1/6th East Surrey, ESR/25/SWIF/1, SHC, Woking

'Looking towards the frontier', from Fred Wignall's album labelled 'My Holiday' (E94/2016, Cumbria's Museum of Military Life)

an active area qualified for a campaign medal, the 1914-15 Star, among the few Territorials to receive it.)

For almost the war's first two years Army Headquarters deprecated that the Territorials could possibly replace Regulars in the arena that mattered most – the frontier. In the exchange of increasingly terse telegrams between Kitchener and Hardinge in September 1914 over the possibility of the Territorials being sent to India Simla used the Territorials' inadequacy as a prime argument against their acceptance. 'We cannot regard Territorials as fit to cope in hill warfare with Pathans', Hardinge had written in 1914.[10] He and Duff persisted with their opposition in a succession of telegrams, published in the Mesopotamia Commission's minority report later in the war:

> Territorials are, of course, quite unfit for frontier work ... Second Line troops from home can hardly be regarded as suited for frontier defence ... It would be madness ...[11]

What the author of the minority report, Commander Josiah Wedgwood, deprecated as the 'resentment' of Territorials continued into 1916. As long as Duff remained Commander-in-Chief no Territorial battalion was trained for or sent to the frontier, the closest being battalions posted to the Rawalpindi and Peshawar garrisons.

In 1915 this had begun to change, informally. At Kailana in the hills in 1915 the 1/4th Wilts 'practised mountain warfare' – presumably on its officers' initiative.[12] At Dagshai, a Gurkha

10 Telegram 21 September 1914, Tel 1018, Viceroy (Army Department) to Secretary of State, WWI/286/H, War diary, Army Headquarters, India, IEF 'E', Vol. 1, 21 September-10 November 1914, NAI
11 Mesopotamia Commission, p. 124
12 Mundy, *A Journal of the 1/4th Battalion Wiltshire Regiment*, p. 44

colonel showed the 1/5th Somerset 'how to carry out frontier fighting … rather interesting' (the more so because though more comfortable in the hills, its men has done little but fatigues such as collecting used bullets off the ranges – 'convicts work', Herbert Ewing thought).[13] The 2/4th Hants had found that by the nature of the country in which it trained around Quetta 'we learned the uses of covering fire, and acquired some practice in picking up good defensive positions', assisted by manoevres against an enemy 'realistically represented by real Pathans in flowing white garments'.[14] In June 1915 – the height of summer – the battalion underwent a three-week course, learning the arcane business of hill-top picquetting, building sangars and moving rapidly across treacherous scree. These initiatives did not lead to mobilisation orders.

In 1916 officers of the 1/6th East Surrey, 1/5th West Kent and 1/4th West Surrey were included in a course of 'special training in hill fighting' at Nowshera in March.[15] Owen Smith also did a ten-day hill-fighting course at Solon in mid-1916. 'The principal idea as far as I can see,' he wrote to Anna, 'is to send a … Piquet up all the neighbouring hills to drive any enemy away while the troops pass below': it was a good start.[16] But even the prospect of seeing action did not impress some – some of Herbert Ewings's comrades saw mountain warfare training as a sign that they were to remain in India and approached the training 'not with any zest', though no sooner had they begun they were ordered to Mesopotamia.[17]

One of Fred Wignall's own photographs, evidently taken from Peshawar, depicts the hazy line of hills barely visible on the horizon. It is captioned, 'looking towards the frontier'.[18] From 1916 Army Headquarters as well as Territorial units looked to the frontier as their main theatre of action. Indeed, while before then units trained for the kind of fighting they might experience overseas in Europe or Mesopotamia, the Army in India's focus remained frontier warfare. The main training pamphlet issued by the Adjutant-General, George Kirkpatrick, affirmed that 'training in open and trench warfare must not be allowed to obscure the necessity for training in mountain warfare'.[19] Terriers detailed to serve on the frontier now had to learn the lessons of decades.

'Concentrated experience': Abbottabad Mountain Warfare School

But what were Territorials to be taught? Indian officers argued continually about the right responses to the problem of the frontier. The 1911 empire-wide manual *Field Service Regulations*, provided a doctrine applicable to all military challenges: it represented, a frontier expert later advised, 'the concentrated experience of about eighty years on the border'.[20] The peculiar conditions of the frontier, however, persuaded some officers that specialised manuals were needed. Some contended that *Field Service Regulations* were 'a source of confusion and danger'

---

13 Diary, 27 July, 21 August 1915, Herbert Ewing, 1/5th Somerset, Doc.15428, 07/8/1, IWM
14 Bacon, *The Wanderings of a Temporary Warrior*, p. 28. They were probably Baluchis, not Pathans.
15 'The East Surrey Regiment in India 1914-19', ESR/10/14/3/1, SHC, Woking
16 Letter, 3 July 1916, Owen Smith, 1/6th Hants, M766, RHRM
17 Fisher, *The History of Somerset Yeomanry, Volunteers and Territorials*, p. 209
18 Pte Frederick Wignall, 2/4th Border, E94/2016, CMML
19 *Memorandum on Army Training in India, 1916-1917*, p. 5
20 Villiers-Stuart, *Letters of a Once Punjab Frontier Force Officer to his Nephew*, , p. 32

because commanders at every level interpreted them differently, and argued for more a detailed handbook. Kitchener's moves to turn the Indian Army into an imperial reservoir left frontier training neglected except by units in the specialist Frontier Force and those posted to the frontier divisions, and the loss of experienced units to the expeditionary forces left the army deficient in the skills needed to meet tribal lashkars in action. The crises of 1915 had made the need for further training clear.

In May 1916 week-long courses began specifically to train 27 Territorial officers and 108 non-commissioned officers, at Abbottabad, Dharmsala, Lansdowne and Wellington, regarded as 'highly successful', possibly because the Territorials were keen to learn and quick to assimilate the lessons offered. Sergeant Fred Mundy joined the first mountain warfare course, held at Lansdowne, in the hills east of Roorkee, spending three weeks attending lectures and watching demonstrations by Gurkha and Garwhalis. He and the other students, all non-commissioned officers from seven Territorial battalions, practised picquetting, retirements and other tactics in mountain warfare under instructors from the King's Liverpool. The accommodation was primitive and insanitary (small tents, often flooded out), food was scanty and the work hard and at times dangerous (a man of the Buffs became lost and tumbled down a nullah).[21] Mundy lost two stone from the exertion, but the students – 'a happy little party' – finished knowing something of what Nigel Woodyatt called the 'dangerous sport' of trans-border warfare'.[22]

The 1916 experiment saw longer courses held at Abbottabad for the next three years, spurred by a series of 'disastrous skirmishes' when inexperienced wartime officers contravened the shibboleths of the art. Under the command of William Villiers-Stuart, a charismatic Gurkha officer already renowned for his skill in both training and operations, the Mountain Warfare School distilled and disseminated common understandings, both in theory and in practice. Its students began with a refresher (or an introduction) to the 'principles of war' expressed in *Field Service Regulations*, and then moved to cover the techniques of what Villiers-Stuart called 'trans-border warfare' and practical demonstrations using Gurkha and Nepalese troops in the scrubby ridges north of Abbottabad.[23]

In 1917 Villiers-Stuart again opened the school (complaining of 'this ridiculous business of continuously opening it and closing it' – he was brilliant but damning in his judgments on those less dedicated to soldiering than himself).[24] This time he demanded, and was given, sufficient 'demonstration' troops. Over 500 officers and non-commissioned officers attended Abbottabad in 1917 alone, many of them Territorials. One of the school's significant achievements was to grapple with how to incorporate the new weapons and technology becoming available in frontier fighting. While it was said that the units remaining in India remained inferior in skills to those now at the front elsewhere, even pre-war Regulars needed to revise their methods to cope with changes both on the British-Indian and especially the tribal-Afghan sides of the hill.

Villiers-Stuart, whose candid memoir is such a useful source, was a dedicated and brilliant trainer. He lectured the courses personally (four times a day) and took them into the surrounding hills to pass on his insights. He also personally wrote reports on all the students, and while training the 8,000-strong Nepalese contingent along the lines he had devised on the

---

21 Mundy, *A Journal of the 1/4th Battalion Wiltshire Regiment*, pp. 79-83
22 Woodyatt, *Under Ten Viceroys*, p. 235
23 Moreman, *The Army in India and the Development of Frontier Warfare*, pp.99-102
24 Maxwell, (ed.), *Villiers-Stuart goes to War*, p. 194

1/5th Gurkhas. In 1918 he noticed that the standard of officers under instruction was falling off: 'the predominant type of wartime officer', he felt, 'had no soldiering instincts whatever'.[25] Villiers-Stuart wrote to Army Headquarters (whose officers nursed a profound dislike for him, tempered by their awareness that they needed him) pressing for his demonstrations to be filmed and shown at every station in India, but was refused.

An East Surrey captain preserved a detailed record of his course at Abbottabad in October 1917. Part of a 'study syndicate' including a titled major and a sergeant-major (itself an indication of the social changes the war brought) his notes reveal Villiers-Stuart's view of mountain warfare.[26] In accordance with *Field Service Regulations*, Villiers-Stuart began with the 'principles of war', recognising that 'the enemy know and use these principles against us'. An iconoclast, Villiers-Stuart had no hesitation in modifying the War Office's text, adding 'self-reliance', 'vigilance' and 'judgment', qualities not marked among British soldiers in 1914. He summarised the culture and society of the tribes the British faced on the frontier, assessing their military strengths and weaknesses. (A tribal fighter 'knows his country', but while he 'goes for our flanks … does not protect his own'.) Perhaps surprisingly for the time, Villiers-Stuart did not emphasise technological superiority, but stressed that the 'chief requisite' was to 'cultivate superior minds'. The students heard stories of success and failure, of jehad and blood feuds, of daring and heroism but also of ineptitude in picquetting hills, in which mistakes meant death. And that was in only the first of a dozen lectures.

Later lectures (the first seven delivered over just three days) were interspersed with demonstrations laid on by Nepalese troops and Villiers-Stuart's beloved 5th Gurkhas. The students dutifully noted his pithy aphorisms, garnered over a couple of decades of frontier expeditions and skirmishes and drawing on the experience of other officers. 'Remember,' he would say (the notes faithfully recording his certainty) 'the enemy knows our signals' (because many tribal fighters had served in the Indian Army); 'leave no higher ground within effective range [1400 yards] open to the enemy'; 'the best possible way to lose a convoy is to keep [the] escort tied to it'. But as well as passing on the conventional wisdom of frontier warfare, Villiers-Stuart incorporated the lessons of recent campaigns. He explained (and his Gurkhas showed) how to use Lewis Guns and heavy Vickers machine-guns, and how aircraft were transforming the fight on hillsides and valleys: 'the last Waziristan affair was really broken up by our air service'. (In early 1916 the transport *Berrima* carried to India, as well as over a thousand reinforcements, six aircraft destined for the frontier.) After an intensive series of lectures and exhausting scrambles over the ridges of Abbottabad keeping up with the nimble Gurkhas, Villiers-Stuart's students were ready to go back to their battalions to 'pass it on' in the approved style of frontier war training. No longer were Territorials regarded as unfit for frontier warfare. As William Villiers-Stuart's brother put it in one of his letters to a supposed nephew, schooling him on frontier war, 'a cockney's vision is usually limited to a street', but he could be trained, as the Territorials were – and they included many London, Middlesex, Kent and Surrey cockneys.[27]

Regardless of the disputes about doctrine, units new to the frontier simply needed to acquire fundamental skills. While the Abbottabad school disseminated tactical doctrine, the Territorials' general military skills improved. After men of the 2/4th Somerset returned from

---

25   *Ibid*, p. 208
26   Notes, 'Mountain Warfare Class of Instruction', ESR/25/ATWO/1, SHC, Woking
27   Villiers-Stuart, *Letters of a Once Punjab Frontier Force Officer to his Nephew*, p. 29

Men of the 1/1st Kent Battalion on active service on the frontier, an armoured car and a motor ambulance signs of how mountain warfare was changing. (Album 5 MNERN: 881, Maidstone Museum)

mountain warfare courses (to flat Lahore cantonment) they set up a 'sandbath' – a sand table – on which to demonstrate tactics in theory. Officers of the 1/9th Hants also returned from Abbottabad imbued with its lessons, and in Ferozepore had a bazaar printer produce a pamphlet on *Mountain Warfare Camp and Bivouac Routine*, enshrining detailed administrative and tactical precepts, including the safe siting of night latrines and how to respond if attackers penetrated the perimeter.[28] Walter Gosling's diary reveals how intensively the 1/1st Kent applied the lessons it had learned. The troops described exercises ('all Brigade Field days ... plenty of hard work') as 'scourges', suggesting how demanding they were.[29] The battalion published its musketry scores. In 1917 (a year after arriving) it boasted 667 men out of 711 qualifying as 1st Class shots or marksmen, with only seven men passing as 3rd Class. In 1918 all but one man qualified in the top two classes.[30] The 1/1st Kent was, however, careless over water discipline, drinking muddy water through which animals had passed, a cause of disabling dysentery.

By 1917 Territorials had proved their value. A company of the 1/9th Middlesex was even sent to Mokspuri, high in the Murree Hills, to act as 'demonstration company' for the senior officers' courses held there. Its men regularly dug trenches in the rocky country, sometimes at 10,000 feet. The rest of the battalion was meanwhile part of the Galis Brigade, patrolling the roads and vital water pipelines between Murree and Abbottabad under the 'cheery command' of Brigadier-General Reginald Dyer.[31] (A close observer, William Villiers-Stuart, dismissed him

28 1/9th Bn. Hampshire Regiment, *Mountain Warfare Camp and Bivouac Routine*
29 Diary, May 1917, Walter Gosling, 1/1st Kent, 8512-29, NAM
30 *The Invicta*, Vol. III, No. 1, June 1918, p. 43
31 Wyrall, *The Die-Hards in the Great War*, Vol. II, p. 340

as 'a lunatic ... insane', but he was to exert a profound and tragic influence on British India.[32]) The 1/9th Middlesex was becoming jaded with the demands of frontier campaigning, in which emergencies or potential crises reported by political officers involved the formation of temporary field forces. From Burhan, in the far western Punjab, the Middlesex's officers complained of 'another dose of manoevres, an absolute dust-heap of a camp and a break in the continuity of training'. The disruption of training became a source of dissatisfaction, since a unit's quality depended upon its performance in periodic inspections by visiting senior officers. The 1/9th Middlesex complained in early 1917 that it had been unable to train as a battalion for almost a year, and for much of that time could sometimes not bring two companies together.[33]

Training increasingly involved new weapons and technological support. When Stanley Goodland took an advance party of the 1/5th Somerset to Burhan early in 1917 he met a staff major who assured him that 'they are equipping this Division regardless of expense ... all the newest Maxim & Lewis Guns'.[34] Goodland assumed that it heralded that the division (the 16th Indian) was to go on active service beyond India, but it indicated only that the frontier demanded a greater intensity of equipment, both in combat and in support. Montagu of Beaulieu had foreseen the need for a 'Mechanical Equipment Department' in India. He advocated introducing caterpillar tractors for guns, artillery-aircraft co-operation and for infantry motor kitchens, motor ambulances, 'a certain number of lorries fitted to take infantry rapidly from one place to another' and even 'travelling ice-making machines; mechanical water filters [and] a travelling bacteriological laboratory'.[35]

Warfare on the frontier involved the see-saw effects of each side countering developments by the other; thus the tribes acquisition of breech-loading weapons following the opening of an arms trade through the Persian Gulf before the war became nullified by the growing British use of automatic weapons during it. By 1916 column commanders had a much greater repertoire of technical aids to draw on, both in weapons and in the supporting services. In addition to the rifles, Maxim machine-guns and mountain artillery already used, weapons developed for trench warfare in France began finding their way to the frontier – grenades, Lewis guns, heavy machine-guns in increasing numbers, and above all aeroplanes.

Technology also supplemented the huge supply service frontier expeditions required, not so much in the columns penetrating tribal territory but in the large bases created on their borders, where lorries and light cars carried supplies and men, and in increasing quantities. A division on the frontier required 100 tons of supplies per day, including not just more and heavier munitions, but the more varied rations and 'greater comforts for wounded'.[36] Montagu of Beaulieu conducted surveys, selecting 'cross-over' points to reduce congestion, 'refuge sidings' and 'reversing bays' to clear jams, secure water points, telephone networks and devised ways to protect convoys from attack, always urging the construction of new roads and the improvement and widening of existing tracks. By 1919 the road through the Khyber Pass was 'fully

32   Maxwell, (ed.), *Villiers-Stuart goes to War*, pp. 196-97
33   Wyrall, *The Die-Hards in the Great War*, Vol. II, p. 340
34   Letter, 25 January 1917, Stanley Goodland, 1/5th Somerset, Noyes, (ed.), *Engaged in War*, p. 73
35   'Report on the mechanical equipment of the army in India', December 1915, Montagu papers 7/16, LHCMA
36   'Transport in the event of mobilisation on the North-West Frontier', January 1917, Montagu papers, 7/25, LHCMA

The 'Joys of the Waziristan Stunt' depicted in the battalion magazine of the 2/6th Royal Sussex. (*Royal Sussex Herald*)

motorable' and in some parts had been 'doubled'.[37] About two hundred military vehicles a day passed through it, so many that a separate lane needed to be created for pack animals.[38] More than three-quarters of the new lorries' drivers were former Territorials.

'A summer campaign': the Mahsud campaign

Frontier operations later in the war focussed on challenges from the Wazirs and Mahsuds. Resistance in Waziristan had called upon them punitive expeditions on nine occasions since 1852, and from 1914 British columns were 'constantly marching into and through their country'.[39] In mid-1917 Northern Army (Monro had reinstituted the two pre-war commands) was obliged to conduct a major but unsuccessful punitive expedition in Waziristan, what historian Brian Robson criticised as 'a severe and unwelcome embarrassment' to the Government of India.[40]

A collection of messages and signals created by Lieutenant-Colonel Frank Johnson's 2/6th Royal Sussex during training operations in January 1917 demonstrates how Territorial units prepared to take part in these frontier operations. The scheme's 'general idea' involved a punitive expedition directed at the 'truculent and unruly' inhabitants of 'Whitelands' under the influence of 'an influential mullah'. The orders Johnson issued reflected a desire to apply the lessons imparted at Abbottabad and other courses, including the destruction of hostile villages ('stores of grain and the principal buildings destroyed') and 'inflicting utmost losses'. Throughout officers were warned to piquet the hills, stay off the skyline, cover their transport, and maintain fire discipline.[41] It was training the Royal Sussex would use later in 1917: in May it was mobilised to fight in Waziristan.

In mid-1917 the 2/6th Royal Sussex and 1/25th London formed part of Major-General William Benyon's South Waziristan Field Force, participating in a 'flying column' sent to relieve a Mahsud siege of the fort at Sawakai. The 2/6th opened a war diary for the first time when it marched from Burhan camp to Tank, the base for operations in Waziristan. The 2/6th served for nearly three months, making hard marches in harsh terrain, often sniped at and making, or rather supporting, attacks on Mahsud positions. Three men were killed (one accidentally) and 18 wounded (one of whom died) during the three-month campaign.[42]

Private James McArthur of the Royal Sussex wrote an account of this frontier campaign – his first encounter with the realities of war. His company spent a month guarding the Gomal Pass, and then, in early June, marched in the heat through the Khirgi Pass, the scene of a fight three days before when 80 Gurkhas held off a Mahsud lashkar five times larger. McArthur saw – and smelled – the Mahsud dead, picked at by vultures, still lying piled around the Gurkhas' sangar. The march ended with baggage animals dropping in the heat and McArthur himself

---

37 Molesworth, *Afghanistan 1919*, p. 33
38 *The Invicta*, Vol. III, No. 4, 1919, p. 19
39 Wylly, *History of the Queen's Royal Regiment*, Vol. VII, p. 128
40 Robson, *Crisis on the Frontier*, p. 161
41 Messages and signals, 2/6th Royal Sussex, 1917, RSRMS 6/11, WSRO
42 War diary, 2/6th Royal Sussex, 1917, WSRO. The Army Headquarters official history gives 2 killed and 22 wounded.

finishing only by hanging onto a camel's loading rope. A couple of days later, at Jandola, a force of 3000 Mahsuds attacked, driven off with heavy losses by rifle, machine-gun and mountain gun fire. Though 'scrapping' on piquet in extreme heat (and tumbling thirty feet down a nullah) McArthur declared that he was 'keeping very fit' and 'really enjoying myself immensely'. A few days on McArthur survived 'a real scrap with the blighters … the most exciting day of my life!' Soon after, McArthur was evacuated sick with malaria.[43]

Reg Howgego gave his mother a similarly grim account of its experience, corroborating McArthur's. He too saw Gurkha dead and wounded, noticing that the Mahsuds used large bullets inflicting 'a very nasty wound'.[44] On the march to Jandola in baking heat the 1/25th London went on 'a little strafe', though 'the Native Troops did the attacking and we covered their retirement'. As novices in frontier warfare the Londoners faced the terror of Mahsud tactics. Advancing against them was straightforward, but 'as soon as you start retiring then the trouble starts and they come you like [hell] … I can tell you we shifted some when we had the order to retire'. If food in cantonments had been scarce, on campaign the commissariat system could produce only basic rations. Reg Howgego recorded that the 1/25th London received only

> 1/2 a rasher of bacon & 8 biscuits (for the day) … we were lucky if we got some bully beef stewed otherwise a tin of bully & the remainder of some biscuits & some tea, that's all we got …

Soon after, at Maimet Khel, the Londons suffered their first casualties:

> Our Lewis Gun Sgt & a pvte. were both shot through the shoulder & another Pvt; was shot clean through the head & killed outright. A Sgt; in D Coy; was wounded in the shoulder & he is up here now [at Murree] convalescent but with no use in his right arm.

Like McArthur, Howgego went sick, 'fairly physically exhausted'. The 1/25th London lost five dead and 13 wounded.[45]

McArthur and Howgego's experiences represented those of their battalions. Within a week of leaving Burhan 100 out of the 2/6th's 795 men were ill, probably with diarrhoea. No fewer than 415 men were evacuated sick, and five died of disease, mostly of dysentery and colitis. By late August only 296 men were 'fit for duty' with a further 105 recorded as 'unfit' – it effectively lost 500 men in 80 days.[46] Most of the serious fighting had been undertaken by experienced Gurkhas, with the Territorials making or repairing roads, but the Territorials were regarded as having performed creditably. Frank Johnson, the Royal Sussex's colonel, received a DSO and was mentioned in despatches.

The Territorials implemented the traditional tactics of the punitive expedition. Ronald Griffiths, a London music librarian, kept a detailed account of the Waziristan operations, in which he described 'our first scrap'. The 1/25th Londons carried out their orders to devastate

---

43 'Account of operations in Waziristan', John McArthur, 2/6th Royal Sussex, MP 1933, WSRO
44 Letter, 11 September 1917, Reg Howgego, 1/25th London, Album C340/9, Mss.Eur.C340/2, BL
45 Army Headquarters, *Operations in Waziristan*, p.157. One man of the 1/4th West Surrey was also wounded, presumably while attached to the force.
46 War diary, 2/6th Royal Sussex, 1917, WSRO

the Mahsud valleys – Griffiths's diary records how they 'burned crops on the way' and 'strafed and burned Manzal village', and returning a week later were 'burning villages all the way' and 'finished by looting village near camp'.[47] The 2/6th Royal Sussex was trusted to take a full part in these punitive operations, leading the column in the advance into the Splitoi valley to destroy the Wazir villages around Nanu in June 1917.[48]

The Waziristan campaign persuaded sceptical British commanders that Territorials were fit to fight on the frontier. Reg Howgego wrote immediately afterwards, while convalescing at Murree how:

> As we were leaving Jandola the commander of the expedition Major-General [William] Benyon, told us how pleased he was with the way we had carried out the work under the very adverse conditions of a summer campaign on the frontier. Of course we had to give him a cheer …[49]

By 1917 Territorials had taken their place besides British and Indian Regulars as active defenders of British India's frontiers. When the 1/6th East Surrey arrived in Rawalpindi early that year, it joined the 5th (Jhelum) Brigade, which comprised also the 1st Duke of Wellington's (Regulars), the 1/9th Middlesex (another Territorial battalion) and the Pasupati Prasad, one of the better Nepalese battalions.

Again the 1/4th West Surrey was mobilised, in May 1917, again in Waziristan. On 15 May, at the hottest part of the year, the battalion went to the Indus by railway, then marched for Tank. Everyone agreed that Tank was 'an appalling spot', with its prevailing heat, bare landscape, perennial dust-storms, inadequate shelter and scanty water supply.[50] So sickly did the Surreys become that only 350 other ranks were well, and they were soon relived by the 1/9th Hants, whose men thought that 'they look about done'.[51] Frontier campaigning demanded stamina, something that not all battalions, called out at the height of the hot weather, were able to demonstrate Indeed, illness proved to be a much more significant danger than Pathan bullets. A hot weather campaign brought sickness as bad as other Territorials found on Gallipoli or in Mesopotamia. In describing Waziristan in 1917 Reg Howgego did not spare his mother the details:

> everything full of flies … quite impossible to eat jam if we were lucky enough to get it. It said in the papers… that the health of the Waziristan Field Force was good but you should have seen some of the poor beggars, they were going into hospital & down the line in dozens every day … fever & dysentery were the worst cases. The majority of us were like skeletons …[52]

---

47 Diary, 15-23 June 1917, Reginald Griffiths, 1/25th London, Doc. 17145, 09/56/1, IWM
48 'Operations of the 45th Brigade, Waziristan Field Force at Nanu', WO106/56, NAUK
49 Letter, 11 September 1917, Reg Howgego, 1/25th London, Album C340/9, Mss.Eur.C340/2, BL
50 Woodyatt, *Under Ten Viceroys*, p. 244
51 Diary, 14 June 1917, Oswald Early, 1/9th Hants, Early, *The Messenger*, p. 46
52 Letter, 11 September 1917, Reg Howgego, 1/25th London, Mss.Eur.C340/2, BL

George MacMunn, a British officer with long Indian experience, grudgingly conceded that operations on the frontier using Territorials had been 'carried out with more or less success', but also 'perhaps with less effect than had the usual seasoned troops been available'.[53]

'Heroes equal': Territorials on the frontier

The involvement of Territorial units in the frontier campaigns of 1917 had a further effect. While for most of the war Terriers in India publicly lamented (but privately were glad of) missing out on more active service, the fighting on the frontier allowed them to feel that they too were doing their bit. At Miran Shah, in Baluchistan, Will Irvin of the 1/1st Kent penned a poem, 'Heroes All', in memory of his comrades who died on the frontier:

> Often you read of the brave, brave lads,
> Fighting in France, 'gainst the German cads …
> But in praising these let us not forget
> Other brave lads to whom we owe a debt.
>
> Up where the sunbaked frontiers wind
> Some of our comrades left behind.
> They fought the good fight bravely and well
> Against the North West horrors till at last they fell
> Heroes equal to those who fight
> On the Western front gainst the German's might.[54]

The 1/1st Kent recorded its service in Baluchistan in *The Invicta* after the Marris, joined by their neighbours the Khetranis, attacked the fort at Gumbaz, believing that the war had denuded British troops in India. In this, 'Our Third Expedition to the Frontier', the battalion mobilised at Ferozepore in March 1918 and joined a column directed at suppressing the rising.[55] Under the direction of political officers they conducted a classic frontier punitive expedition, piquetting the hills overlooking their route as they entered tribal country, gathering forage and destroying villages to coerce the tribes into surrender. The campaign lasted two months until in April the Marris and Khetrans surrendered. The 1/1st Kent had encountered heat, but also wind and snow, sheet lightning, rain, hailstones an inch in diameter and cloying mud underfoot. They re-occupied the ruins of Fort Monro, the hill station for Dera Ghazi Khan which the tribesmen had ransacked, attacking with Lewis Guns supported by mountain guns and aircraft.

In small actions like the fight at Fort Monro Territorial units proved their worth, though they were never as trusted, or proficient, as experienced Regular or Indian units. The reports of the more than thirty campaigns and actions submitted to and by Charles Monro amounts to a sizeable box in WO106/56 in the National Archives. Their titles evoke their character: 'Reports of the Attack by Mahsuds on Tut Narai Post', 'The Action of the Derajat Moveable Column near

---

53   MacMunn, *The Romance of the Indian Frontiers*, p. 257
54   Will Irvin, 'Heroes All', F.J. Barden, Album 5 'India 1916-19', NMERM: 881, MM
55   *The Invicta*, Vol. III, No. 1, June 1918, pp. 2-7

Karab Kot'; 'Action against Baluch Raiders near Fahreh'. The actions, though usually described in the passive prose that came naturally to military officers, and often with admirable modesty and restraint, still convey the drama of small and often isolated detachments operating deep within tribal territory, for whom failure meant death or humiliation. But the abundant reports also disclose how tiny a part Territorial units took in the continuing contest on the frontier, one that remained firmly in the hands of the professional soldiers of the Indian Army and the few over-used Regular British battalions in the 1st and 2nd Divisions.

Despite Territorials' training in mountain warfare, the frontier campaigns of 1917-19 reversed the usual order of expertise in Indian warfare. Hitherto, the Army in India had been (as a 19th century commander-in-chief had put it) 'tipped with steel' – with British troops taking the burden of combat.[56] This remained so for Regular battalions – indeed, they were used over and over during the war. But it became clear that force and column commanders preferred experienced Indian troops to Territorials. As Reg Howgego put it in a letter to his mother describing the 1/25th London in Waziristan, 'the Native Troops did the attacking and we covered their retirement'.[57] Still, as the 1/1st Kent demonstrated, it performed creditably three times, in Waziristan in early 1917, later that year in Bannu and Miran Shah and in Baluchistan early in 1918. The detailed diary of the 2/4th Border shows its transformation from a unit able only to mount routine guards late in 1915 to a battalion on more-or-less constant active service on the frontier from late 1916, adapting to a variety of tasks – holding the blockade line, mounting punitive expeditions and sending companies to isolated frontier posts in all seasons. In many ways the 2/4th Border's published diary reads as if it were a war diary: though the battalion was supposedly not on 'active service' it is a war diary in all but name.[58]

Henry Rawstone Lamplugh, the lance-corporal who edited the 1/1st Kent's magazine, recorded how early in 1918 they had proved their worth. 'From the deck of the Indus ferry we have seen the sun rise', he wrote, describing how they had at last joined the war on the frontier.[59] Crossing the Indus represented a financial boundary as well – units serving to its west received a daily increase in pay of sixpence – a 50% rise. The war years were usually busy on the frontier. The 1/4th West Surrey historian claimed that they were 'crammed with a wider experience of tribal warfare than used to fall in a whole lifetime, to the most hardened warriors of the Punjab Frontier Force'.[60] That was perhaps an exaggeration, but it suggested how some Territorial battalions shared frontier campaigns.

---

56 Stanley, *White Mutiny*, p. 10, quoting a metaphor evidently coined by Colin Campbell, Lord Clyde, Commander-in-Chief in India 1857-60
57 Letter, 11 September 1917, Reg Howgego, 1/25th London, Mss.Eur.C340/2, BL
58 MacGlasson, (ed.), *Diary of the 2/4th Battalion The Border Regiment*
59 *The Invicta*, Vol. III, No. 1, June 1918, p. 20
60 Wylly, *History of the Queen's Royal Regiment*, Vol. VII, p. vi

16

Beyond Mesopotamia, 1918-19

The Territorials' long-expressed desire to see action was at length rewarded. A few Territorial battalions were to serve in France, where they had wanted to go in 1914 There they suffered appalling losses; as they surely would have if they had gone to France in 1915. Others served against the Turks, in Palestine, and in the far reaches of Central Asia, in Persia and Turkestan, where they fought Bolsheviks. Their availability suggested the contribution that Territorials could make to the achievement of Britain's strategic aims in the furthest reaches of the region in ways that could never have been anticipated in 1914.

'Pretty well fagged': field training 1916-17

By the last year of the war virtually all 'Indian' Territorial units were ready for active service abroad or on the frontier. Kitchener Tests continued throughout the war, usually taking place towards the end of the cold weather, the arrival of reinforcements providing a continual challenge to adjutants, company commanders and senior non-commissioned officers. Not that their men necessarily noticed or understood the reason for the exercises. Harry Canham, newly arrived and unfit, recorded after field exercises in January 1917 at Peshawar, that 'pretty well fagged', he had 'not much idea of what we were doing'.[1] More experienced men and their units performed better – when the 2/4th Somerset did its test in camp at Sassaram, in Bihar, only three men fell out on arduous route marches over four days of tests.[2]

Territorial batteries remained the mainstay of the artillery force available. While the number of batteries in India declined during the war (with the despatch of nine batteries to Mesopotamia), the number of gunners per battery actually increased between 1915 and 1917. War Office returns show that while battery strengths averaged about 145 in December 1914, by December 1916 they had increased to an average of about 168.[3] By early 1917, because they had

---

1   Letter, January 1917, Harry Canham, 2/4th Border, CMML
2   Letter, 22 February 1917, Jim Mackie, 2/4th Somerset, Mackie, *Answering the Call*, p. 236
3   'Returns of the Territorial Force Serving Abroad', WO114/52, December 194; WO114/53 December 1916, NAUK

received better guns (and more of them), some batteries were reporting total strengths of around 250 for three Sussex batteries.

Artillery training remained physically taxing – guns and limbers had to be manhandled and drivers cared for their teams whether in barracks or on exercise. As artillery grew to dominate the Great War the demands made on gunners intensified. In the *Memorandum on Army Training in India, 1916-1917*, issued early in 1917, artillery officers were corrected on common mistakes ('quite a number of battery commanders do not understand the methods of dealing with various objectives') and were enjoined to emulate the expertise developed under fire in France. Gunner officers were urged to synchronise their fire with the movement of the infantry they supported, a difficult task to pull off:

> If the battery commander waits until he sees the infantry moving the "rafale" [a rapid burst of fire] will probably not arrive at the enemy position. If, on the other hand, the infantry wait until the burst commences, it will probably be over by the time they are up and in movement …[4]

The reorganisation of Territorial artillery later in the war caused several units to be disbanded. The 1914 men from the 1/1st Wiltshire Battery were dispersed to other units and in January 1918, though it had been hailed as the best in India, the battery 'passed out of existence'.[5]

Rumours persisted that Territorials would see active service. On the way to Bombay and the gulf, Robert Palmer had met 'a Terrier gunner' he knew who told him on the strength of mess gossip at a staff course he had just completed, that the Territorial batteries were to be sent back to Europe to meet the needs of the Western Front – 'in a month's time'.[6] Like all such rumours it was baseless, but in 1917 the second-largest contingent of Territorials did leave India for a major theatre; in the Middle East.

'At last doing our bit': Palestine

By mid-1917 the Egyptian Expeditionary Force was still stuck on the border of Sinai and Palestine, having failed in two battles of Gaza to break the Ottoman line stretching from Gaza on the Mediterranean coast to Beersheba, twenty miles inland. The need for troops for General Sir Edmund Allenby's planned offensive led to troops being sent from India to form the 75th Division, the last British division raised in the war. Commanded by Philip Palin, who had led the 14th Sikhs on Gallipoli, it included nine Territorial battalions, with four Indian battalions (a reversal of the customary proportion of British-to-Indian battalions).[7]

Despite having become enamoured with Baluchistan and its people (and having barely recovered from malaria and rheumatic fever), when the 2/4th Hants was alerted to go to Palestine

---

4   *Memorandum on Army Training in India, 1916-1917*, p. 57
5   Bavin, *Swindon's War Record*, p. 252
6   Palmer, *Letters from Mesopotamia*, pp. 18-19
7   The Territorials, a mixture of units formerly of the 1st and 2nd Wessex divisions, comprised the 2/4th, 1/5th and 2/5th Devon, 2/4th and 2/5th Hants, 1/5th Somerset, 1/4th Cornwall, 2/4th Dorset and 1/4th Wilts.

Two men, probably of the 2/4th Somerset, ticking off another of the wonders of the world before beginning the arduous campaign in Palestine. (DD\SLI 15/7/72, Somerset Heritage Centre)

in April 1917, Victor Manley greeted the news with enthusiasm. He had been a Volunteer and a Territorial on and off since 1906 and was 'determined, come what might, to follow the regiment so long as it was humanly possible'. Remaining as part of the 'garrison mob' was to him 'repugnant'.[8] Men of the 1/5th Somerset welcomed the news in January 1917 that it had been 'chosen for sterner work'.[9] Warning orders for active service brought changes to units – men were detailed as stretcher bearers, runners and Lewis-gunners, jobs not generally been required in garrison duty in India.

The 2/4th Hants, which arrived in Egypt in May 1917, found that 'our Indian equipment was quite suitable for the coming campaign' and as 'the climatic conditions proved to be remarkably similar' their time in India had prepared them well.[10] Or so it seemed, until the rigours of the Palestinian winter caught the Indian units in khaki drill shorts but without greatcoats. Though 2/4th Dorset officers had attended the Mountain Warfare Training School at Abbottabad, early in 1917, in August the battalion was mobilised to go overseas. It was able to be despatched because of the arrival of Garrison battalions, though even then was detained for some months in 1917. At last, in August it steamed from Bombay to Suez. The 1/5th Somerset also joined the 75th Division in mid-1917. It mounted a raid on the Ottoman defenders of the 'Old British Trenches' on the Gaza line in October. Led by Stanley Goodland, it was a complete success, at the cost of one man killed. Drummer Smith of the 2/4th Devon reached the front line at Gaza just before the opening of Allenby's offensive. His diary records the stages of his company's gradual introduction to the war at last: 'wire patrol',

---

8   Victor Manley, 'A Khaki Diary', p. 681, 49M91W/Q3/6, HRO
9   Fisher, *The History of Somerset Yeomanry, Volunteers and Territorials*, p. 225
10 Bacon, *The Wanderings of a Temporary Warrior*, p. 65

'water guard', 'fighting patrol', 'heavy bombardment and 'one of C coy killed by Johnny's shells'.[11]

The 2/4th Somerset also took part in the advance from Gaza and in the fighting on the road to Jerusalem in November and December 1917. In November 1917, when it was called upon to advance through shell-fire, its men 'pressed on without faltering'.[12] The division later adopted as its badge the keys to Jerusalem in token of its contribution to the city's capture. Despite the hardships and losses in Palestine, Jim Mackie found 'no end of satisfaction in feeling we are at last doing our bit with the rest'.[13] The 1/4th Wilts had also left India in September 1917, travelling with the 2/4th Somerset, 'filled with glorious uncertainty', the Wilts especially 'weary and "fed up"' after spending several months in limbo at Poona and Kirkee.[14] (At Poona it had encamped upon the polo ground, an atrocity that Sir William Marshall denounced as 'a Hunnish proceeding'.[15]) In Egypt infantry carried packs – 'a thing unknown to us in India' – but on active service men received better and more varied rations than in India, and free issues of cigarettes and tobacco, which in India they had had to buy individually.[16]

Being sent to fight in Palestine gave men the experience of war for which many had yearned. Spencer Kipling, of the 1/5th Devon, had felt so strongly that Indian service was unworthy that he had refrained from writing to a respected old school-master until after Gaza and the fall of Jerusalem. The fighting in Palestine was indeed sterner work than Indian service. At Nebi Samwil in November 1917 the 1/5th Somerset took part in the taking and holding of the crucial hill. (Historically informed men told their comrades that as Mountjoye it had marked the furthest point of Richard the Lionheart's advance into the Holy Land in 1192.) The 1/5th, attacking with the 1/4th Wilts and 2/4th Somerset, and the 2/3rd Gurkhas, lost 68 dead and 'so many wounded that we could not stop to count them'. Costing some 400 casualties, the action practically destroyed the battalion, which had entered the attack fewer than 700 strong. The large-scale fighting the first Territorials encountered at Gaza brought Territorials to confront the hideous face of modern warfare. Douglas Skinner, the son of a Great Chart blacksmith, who had written of his fears that he might be 'afraid to go to the front', was killed in the advance from Gaza in November 1917. ('Honour!', wrote Mrs Strutts.) Victor Manley helped to identify and bury the dead after the third Gaza offensive (a task palmed off onto late-arriving Terriers). Having 'the most intimate acquaintance with eight-hundred corpses' made him realise 'the vanity of this world' – Indian service having fed his interest in the metaphysical.[17]

Most of the Indian Territorial battalions fought through the 1918 offensive in Palestine which ended in Ottoman defeat and collapse. The 1/8th Hants ended the war at Beirut; the 2/4th Devon and the 2/5th Hants had been disbanded in 1918 in Palestine. (The composing and performing career of 2/5th Hants officer Peter Latham, had ended when he was wounded in the

---

11 Diary, October 1917, D. Smith, 2/4th Dorset, 2014-258, DMM. British troops nicknamed their Ottoman opponents 'Johnny Turk'.
12 Fisher, *The History of Somerset Yeomanry, Volunteers and Territorials*, p, 218
13 Letter, 2 November 1917, Jim Mackie, 2/4th Somerset, *Answering the Call*, p. 303
14 Mundy, *A Journal of the 1/4th Battalion Wilshire Regiment*, p. 137
15 Marshall, *Memories of Four Fronts*, p. 183
16 Mundy, *A Journal of the 1/4th Battalion Wilshire Regiment*, p. 137
17 Preface, Victor Manley, 'A Khaki Diary', 49M91W/Q3/6, HRO

shoulder in 1918. He became a musicologist, an authority on Brahms.) But several of the units sent to Palestine would at last reach France, indirectly fulfilling Kitchener's promise.

'At its fiercest moment': France

The Terriers' dearest wish, so they said sincerely earlier in the war, had been to get to France. As reports of the fighting on the Western Front circulated, even official censorship and cheery communiqués could not conceal the magnitude and cost of the war. (Some men record watching the film *The Battle of the Somme*, in Bangalore, cheering the sight of the King's appearance.) Many battalion and regimental magazines published detailed accounts of men having been killed and wounded, mainly on the Western Front. Men appreciated that 'instead of being in the mud and blood of France' service in India (or Burma, as it happened for Bert Rendall) was 'a picnic'.[18] As they realised what the war entailed, especially on the Western Front, Terriers recognised that however uncomfortable Indian service might be it was nowhere near as dangerous as being at the front. In his letters Harry Canham often referred to the 'safe berth' he enjoyed and noted deaths and wounds among men he had known at home.[19] Reg Bailey confessed to Hilda that he was 'going to speak the truth now, I am more than thankful I am in India, away from all the worry of war'.[20]

Territorial battalions had trained for what Fred Mundy called 'the present day's warfare'. Companies learned to dig trenches on Western Front models (arduous labour even in the cold weather) and gradually were introduced to new weapons; Mills bombs and Lewis guns. But of the 41 Territorial battalions sent to India, only four managed to find their way to France.

The 1/4th Shropshire, which had left Hong Kong in April 1917, did not actually reach Britain; not to land. After a long voyage (including a month-long stay in South Africa, when 200 men went down ill after a sudden winter hailstorm and a week in Sierra Leone) the battalion at last reached Plymouth on 27 July 1917. Not only were the men forbidden from disembarking, but they were not even given any mail. Instead, after tantalisingly lying in sight of land for a day the *Walmer Castle* made for France, and they disembarked at Le Havre on 29 July. The Secretary of State for War, Lord Derby, later apologised for the 'recent trying circumstances', which the men accepted 'without a sign or a murmur of discontent'.[21] After a month of training in new tactics and techniques – wiring, bombing, gas and machine-guns – the battalion became part of the 63rd (Royal Naval) Division. The battalion was given special leave, sending large drafts on home leave later in 1917. They took part in several major actions, at Welch Ridge (where Ben Nicholas was killed) and Bapaume in 1917 and at Messines, Bailleul and Bligny in 1918. Some of the Shropshires killed on the Western Front, however, died without ever seeing their homes again.

In mid-1918 three more Indian Territorial battalions were to see service in France, detached from the 75th Division in Palestine and rushed to meet the manpower crisis afflicting the British Expeditionary Force in the war's climactic campaigns. By this stage of the war any association between battalions in their former Territorial divisions or brigades had long been broken, and

---

18 Interview with Bert Rendall, Mills, *A Strange War*, p. 44
19 Letter, 6 August 1917, Harry Canham, 2/4th Border, CMML
20 Letter, 20 November 1917, Reg Bailey, 1/4th Buffs, 2011-12-3, NAM
21 de Wood, *The History of the King's Shropshire Light Infantry in the Great War*, p. 105

Survivors of the Western Front, a party of the 2/4th Somerset Light Infantry march with the battalion colours through Bath in June 1919, their rifles 'at the trail' in the manner traditional in light infantry regiments. (DD\SLI/15/7/84, Somerset Heritage Centre)

they were moved about in response to requirements in other theatres. The 2/4th Hants, which had spent much of the first two years of the war in Baluchistan, arrived in France in June 1918, joined the 62nd (West Riding) Division, a Kitchener formation. It took part in the attacks of the 'Hundred Days', making its final attack on 6 November 1918, operating in open country virtually untouched by war. In just four months its officers gained three DSOs (and a bar to a fourth officer), 19 MCs (and two bars) and its men 137 Military Medals. In France it had lost 140 men and officers killed, 677 wounded and 181 missing – more than the equivalent of the entire strength of the battalion when it arrived in France.[22]

The 2/4th Somerset arrived in France in May, transformed into the pioneer battalion of the 34th Division. Fighting in the French sector around Soissons, it entered the war 'at its fiercest moment', as the French general Charles Mangin told the British divisions sent to his sector. It saw hard work, performing minor engineering and other labouring tasks, such as digging trenches, repairing roads and interring the dead (some of whom had lain unburied for months). This explains why, as the regimental historian Everard Wyrell wrote, its war diary made 'dull reading'.[23] After their long service overseas, Jim Mackie realised, his men appreciated the green

22 *History of the Hampshire Territorial Force Association*, p. 132
23 Quoted in Mackie, *Answering the Call*, p. 367

French countryside, but tended to speak of the locals as 'natives'.²⁴ In November 1918 it formed part of the Army of Occupation, marching into Cologne with battalion colours sent from Bath.

In July 1918 the 1/5th Devon fought on the Marne, a familiar name from 1914, losing half the battalion in killed and wounded. By the war's end it comprised barely ten officers and under 200 men, a reminder of what would have happened had Kitchener's promise been met in full. It too became part of the occupation army which marched into western Germany later in 1918. Its men were at least demobilised almost a year ahead of their counterparts who remained in India or Mesopotamia.

'Having a rather hard time': after Baghdad's fall

Most Indian Territorials – ten battalions plus many thousands of reinforcements and drafts – served in Mesopotamia, which became their nemesis. Half of the Great Chart men served in Mesopotamia – because most belonged to the 1/5th Buffs – and half of them were killed or wounded. Five were wounded (William Mannering lost a leg) and two died (Charles Byford, killed at Shaik Sa'ad in January 1916 and Harry Brunger dead, probably of disease, in Baghdad in October 1917). All Mesopotamia's sick and wounded ended up back in India.

The 1/4th Hants formed part of Baghdad's British garrison, literally under the eye of Stanley Maude and therefore having to maintain a standard of smartness. Maude wrote to Sir Thomas Sturmy Cave, the Hampshire Regiment's honorary colonel. He had seen the 1/4th many times and he was 'much struck with the smart appearance … and the soldier-like bearing of the men' – his compliment all the more meaningful because both Maude and Cave knew that as citizen soldiers they were not expected to be as soldier-like as Regulars.²⁵ The letter was one of Maude's last – he died of cholera three weeks later. Cave passed Maude's letter on to Claud Matthews, who had commanded the 1/4th since June 1916 and was by then (March 1918) with it in north-west Persia. In his reply, Matthews (a Durham Light Infantry Regular) praised his Hants Territorials, noting that they had been on active service for three years 'which I think is really something of a record' and that only one of their original officers remained, the adjutant, and that he had been wounded three times. He felt unable to reveal where the battalion actually was but described how the men were 'having rather a hard time' with snow, frost and rain. But 'we have got the old Turk out here "stone cold"' and hoped – as they surely all did – that the war would soon be over.²⁶

By this time Indian Territorials were distributed widely across the theatre, many performing specialist jobs, such as Oswald Early, the Hants signaller, who transferred to the newly formed Royal Air Force. As experienced soldiers, wise in how the system worked, many Territorials gained 'comfy billets' – easier jobs than carrying a rifle in their old battalions. Ted Rice, who had endured two years in Mesopotamia with the 1/5th West Surrey, volunteered for a position as paymaster in north-west Persia, as a corporal responsible for up to £5000 in gold (and getting just Rs30 a month extra pay). He provided the wherewithal for the British force in north-west

---

24 Letter, 15 June 1918, Jim Mackie, 2/4th Somerset, Mackie, *Answering the Call*, p. 371
25 Letter, 29 October 1917, Stanley Maude, Mesopotamian Expeditionary Force, War diary, 1/4th Hants, WO95/5177, NAUK
26 Letter, 12 March 1918, Claud Matthews, War diary, 1/4th Hants, WO95/5177, NAUK

Persia (including the long-suffering 1/4th Hants) bolstering resistance to Turkish and Bolshevik penetration of Persia.

Though they knew how unpleasant Mesopotamia was men continued to ask to serve there. Alfred Groucher sought a transfer from the Buffs to the Machine Gun Corps in order to get on a draft for Basra in 1917. He was 'rather anxious to get at it', he told his former neighbours in Great Chart, 'after the idle life we have spent here'.[27] In late 1917 two more battalions went to Mesopotamia (the 1/9th Middlesex and the 1/5th East Surrey). Despite recent calls on the frontier, Charles Monro was content to not seek the return of two Indian divisions from Palestine (which subordinate commanders presumably proposed) and even to release more units for active service.[28] The 1/9th Middlesex, for example, though it had gained considerable skill in frontier warfare, was warned for Mesopotamia, reinforced by 300 fellow Londoners from the 1/10th Middlesex and the 1/25th London. Though malaria prevented 200 men from going with it, the battalion left Ambala in November nearly a thousand men strong.

With Maude's offensive having secured Baghdad the British became the rulers of Mesopotamia's diverse and often dissident ethnic groups, and many units became tied down garrisoning towns and districts far behind the front, now in the north of the country, though active operations continued in 1918. The 1/6th Hants was at Samara and Tikrit on the Tigris and the 2/7th Hants at Mansuriyeh, on the Diyala River, north-east of Baghdad, supervising Ottoman prisoners of war working on bunds. But Territorial battalions remained on active service and at risk. For much of 1918 the 1/4th Somerset became part of a brigade contesting a Shi'a uprising around the holy city of Nejef, in the Euphrates valley. The 1/5th West Kent eroded as a Kent unit. Only one of its four companies comprised Kent Territorials. While another contained the remnants of the Regular 2nd Royal West Kent, the other two companies were of men of the Highland Light Infantry. It was sent on a punitive expedition to Amadia in central Kurdistan after a mutiny among local gendarmerie, giving some of its men a rare 'Kurdistan' bar to their India General Service medal. With the war's end men were posted and transferred to other units. Men of the 1/5th East Surrey, including drafts from the 1/9th Middlesex and 1/5th West Surrey, found themselves serving in northern Mesopotamia, in due course also gaining a 'Kurdistan' clasp.[29]

When the Ottomans sought an armistice late in October 1918 William Marshall's army was within fifty miles of Mosul, in the oil-rich heartland of the Kurds, occupying the city four days after the Armistice. With Ottoman rule in Mesopotamia over, it remained part of the British sphere of influence, in due course incorporated into the empire as a mandate of the League of Nations and in the meantime ruled as an offshoot of British India. Conflict between rival religious and ethnic groups and resentment of British control made the garrison's role difficult, especially as it was reduced under pressure of both financial stress and the desire of wartime soldiers weary of unpleasant service at the fag-end of war.

27 Letter, late 1917, Alfred Groucher, 1/4th Buffs, Great Chart Fund, Book 5, KA&HC
28 Rumbold, *Watershed in India*, p. 28
29 I. Stedman, 'The Kurdistan clasp to the East Surrey Regiment 1919', *Orders and Medals Research Society*, Spring 1986, p. 21

'Menace to the safety of India': Persia 1918

Persia, a nominally independent but actually weak kingdom, imposed upon by both Imperial Russia and by Britain, became the scene of military operations during the war, which accentuated or even caused a prolonged and severe famine. As it had been for a century, Persia seemed to offer a route for Ottoman or even German infiltration toward India, and had seen ineffective espionage by a German mission and more blatant intrusion by British and Russian forces. As the Ottoman regime weakened British officials and statesmen, notably the Cabinet's Eastern Committee, pondered what they naturally called 'The Persian Question'. Should Britain 'clear out of Persia entirely and leave it to stew in its own juice', or should the Government of India to 'induce them to welcome instead of resisting our efforts', Sir Hamilton Grant – effectively the Viceroy's foreign minister – mused in December 1918.[30] Britain continued to treat Persia as the chessboard on which it sought to check-mate Ottoman, German or Bolshevik threats to India.

There is the suggestion in British official responses to the apprehensions and plans of Indian military authorities that Army Headquarters in Delhi or Simla unduly magnified the threat to India. In mid-1918 Sir Michael O'Dwyer, lieutenant-governor of the Punjab, excited comment if not alarm when he told his province's War Conference that a German invasion of India was 'a possibility, no longer a bogey'. O'Dwyer's notoriously pugnacious views were reported to the troops in the West Surrey magazine *The Braganza*.[31] Charles Ellis, the Australian Middlesex captain who volunteered for the British mission to Central Asia, recorded in his 'Notes on operations' how after the Russian collapse 'Turks advance in the Caucasus & SW Persia': but how far would they go?[32]

Charles Monro evidently also believed that control of the Caspian region was necessary to stymy the 'menace to the safety of India'. Indeed, Monro proposed creating a gigantic theatre command spanning from Egypt to India and to co-ordinate responses to the threats Britain faced in the Middle East and Central and West Asia.[33] Henry Wilson, Chief of the Imperial General Staff in 1918, openly derided the view expressed 'in all recent telegrams' from India that 'the security of India is at stake'. 'Nothing emanating from the War Office', Wilson pointed out, 'could possibly have induced India to believe she is going to be attacked by either German or Turkish troops, except in the remote future'.[34] General Sir William Marshall, Maude's successor in Mesopotamia, agreed with Wilson. He deprecated the need for intervention in northern Persia, concluding, rightly, that neither the Turks nor the Germans were capable of exerting effective influence in central Asia. The Cabinet's Eastern Committee did not seek Marshall's advice, but if it had 'I should certainly have advised against the whole project'.[35] The 'general incoherence' of British policy in Persia and Mesopotamia, as the late Keith Jeffery described it, derived from the very different perspectives of London and Delhi or Simla. The idea that India's

---

30 'The Persian Question', WO106/55, NAUK
31 *The Braganza*, 1 June 1918, p. 12
32 'Notes on operations in N.W. Persia, Baku and Transcaspia 1918-1919', Charles Ellis, 1/10th Middlesex, MS Acc13.036 & MS Acc08.093, NLA
33 Telegram, 21 August 1918, Commander-in-Chief to Secretary of State for War, No. 140, Mss. Eur.264/15, BL
34 'Security of India', CAB24/50/1, NAUK
35 Marshall, *Memories of Four Fronts*, p. 282

defence rested on control of the region was to British politicians 'a somewhat fantastic theory' (as Lord Robert Cecil, Under-Secretary of State for Foreign Affairs, told Lloyd George).[36]

But the region was unquestionably in turmoil. At the end of 1917 the Russians held a line running from the southern shore of the Caspian Sea to Khanikan on the Persia-Mesopotamian frontier. Russia's collapse left British forces in northern Mesopotamia exposed to Ottoman and German infiltration, even if without hope of a successful counter-offensive. German and Ottoman intrigue against British India had continued in Persia and Afghanistan throughout the war, and the volatility of central Asia was to draw British troops deep into Persia, Transcaspia and later Turkestan. Early in 1918 'Dunsterforce', a small training mission under Major-General Lionel Dunsterville, was sent into northern Persia to try to mobilise and train local anti-Bolshevik and anti-Turkish forces against any attempt to penetrate British India's north-western flank, traditionally the direction from which incursion had come.

Sir William Marshall, commanding in Mesopotamia, who believed that the entire north Persian venture was a waste of effort, claimed that Dunsterville's mission had been negated when in January 1918 Bolshevik troops had compelled him to remain at Hamadan, a pleasant oasis, though bitterly cold when the wind blew off the Eveland Mountains.[37] In September 1918 Dunsterforce spawned another force, 'North Persia Force', known in staff officers' jargon as 'NORPERFOR', actually larger and more widely distributed than its parent. Comprising mostly British New Army units detached from Mesopotamia, its only Territorial infantry was the hard-worked 1/4th Hants, which had already served for three years in the theatre, but was now to be sent further afield. These, Dunsterville later wrote, comprised 'some real troops', even if the first contingent to reach Baku comprised only a platoon of Hampshire Territorials.[38] It was a far cry from the way British officers and officials had denigrated Territorials joining the campaign in Mesopotamia.

Most of the 1/4th Hants marched north towards the Caspian Sea late in September 1918, passing through barren hills, cold passes and thickly forested country down to the malarial coast. They had neither adequate warm clothing nor bedding, neither mosquito nets nor quinine. Even worse, en route the Territorials fell ill in what became clear was the first bout in the force of the great 'flu epidemic of 1918-19 which had spread from Bombay to Basra and along supply routes to Persia's north-west. Though effective prophylactic measures were wanting, the force's medical officers acted promptly to combat outbreaks of 'flu, malaria, typhus and other contagions, and produced the most detailed medical reports of any such force.

By this time the battalion had been consolidated into two groups, each about 300-strong, separated by over 500 miles and the width of the Caspian Sea, spread between Zinjan in north-west Persia and Krasnovodsk in Turkestan on the eastern Caspian. By the week the war ended a company was at Kaakha, over 400 miles to the east of Krasnovodsk on the Trans-Caspian railway, which was to form the spine of the coming operations.[39] The 300-strong Hants battalion was the only British unit in the 36th Indian Infantry Brigade, which included the 1/2nd and 1/6th Gurkhas and the 36th Sikhs. Soon after joining 'Norperfor' the 1/4th formed part of small British-Indian force confronting Jungali irregulars blocking the road north at

36 Jeffery, *The British army and the crisis of empire 1918-22*, p. 135
37 Marshall, *Memories of Four Fronts*, p. 285
38 Dunsterville, *Stalky's Reminiscences*, p. 278
39 War diary, Mesopotamia North Persia Force, WO95/5045, NAUK

Mianeh. Lieutenant-Colonel Claud Matthews of the 1/4th commanded the British force, in which his men held off a Turkish-Persian force about six times its own size. Matthews's report of the brief action reads exactly like accounts of field days conducted on Salisbury Plain or the South Downs, with the enemy personified as 'he':

> The Gurkhas were on the left, the Hants in the centre ... their centre piquet about 10000 [yards] from the BRICK BRIDGE ... as he was working round my left flank, and I had nothing on my right at all ... I therefore gave the order for retirement, getting the guns away first ...[40]

Operating far in advance of a major force placed great responsibilities on all ranks. By Christmas a Hants company was at Merv [now Mary] in Turkestan, 200 miles north-east from the force's headquarters at Meshed, while 26 men were at Sultanabad, 125 miles east. Not surprisingly, in what was for many their fifth year of active service, many men fell prey to what a medical officer described as 'profound

A column of Ford cars, hundreds of which (often driven by Territorials) supplied British forces operating in Mesopotamia, Persia and Transcaspia at the war's end. (A01441, Australian War Memorial)

depression', with men 'emotional and lachrymose', complaining of bad dreams. It was perhaps surprising that only one transient case of delusional insanity presented, but the Hants men were certainly paying the price of their insouciant volunteering in 1914.[41] In Transcaspia Hants Territorials became part of the final act of the shadowy 'Great Game' played out between rival empires in central Asia.

'Openly opposing the Bolsheviks': Transcaspia

In the wake of the 1917 revolution Bolshevik rule spread across the former Russian empire, by the summer of 1918 reaching what was then called Transcaspia or Turkestan, where native Turkomans and Russian settlers battled over its imposition. The possibility of Bolsheviks

---

40   War diary, 1/4th Hampshire, 15 September 1918, WO95/5047, NAUK
41   'Report on Influenza Epidemic in Kasvin area', 3 October 1918, WO95/5045, NAUK

controlling the northern frontier of Persia, and therefore the north-western approaches to India aroused the concern of both the British government and the Government of India. (As the premier chronicler of this episode, Peter Hopkirk, put it, the Transcaspian railway, running east from Krasnavodsk on the Caspian was seen as 'a dagger pointing toward Afghanistan and India'.[42]) Accordingly, in mid-1918 a small Anglo-Indian force was despatched to central Asia to thwart the revolutionaries' plans and maintain British interests. To the Bolshevik regime, the presence of British-Indian troops in Persia and Turkestan represented an imperialist intervention and an affront. The minor skirmishes in the remote reaches of Turkestan saw the climax of the British and Russian empires' sparring in central Asia over almost a century.

Regional and nationalist groups in Transcaspia resisted the Bolshevik advance, and in towns along the Central Asian Railway, running east from the Caspian Sea into Turkestan on the furthest border of Chinese Sinkiang, opposition coalesced around a fragile anti-Bolshevik regime in Ashkabad. A British mission under Major-General Wilfred Malleson arrived to support the rag-tag army of former Tsarist officers, Armenian conscripts and Turkmen cavalry, like the Bolsheviks fighting from a series of armoured trains. Malleson warned Simla that 'by assisting leaders of the Trans-Caspian movement ... we shall be openly opposing [the] Bolsheviks'. This, he felt, 'may also mean putting our money on the wrong horse' – and so it turned out.[43]

A small body of Territorials, formerly of India, formed part of Malleson's force, though its core were sowars of the 28th Cavalry and sepoys of the 19th Punjabis. One of Malleson's staff officers was Charles Ellis, the Australian violin-and-oboe-playing Middlesex subaltern, who volunteered out of a desire for adventure. Astonishingly, though, the British force included a company of the 1/4th Hants; not only the Territorial unit to have seen long and arduous service in Mesopotamia, but which also formed some of the most advanced troops in the Transcaspian theatre. Separated from the nearest British troops in India by the breadth of northern Afghanistan – about 600 miles – they fought an intermittent campaign, with both sides using armoured trains, moving up and down the Transcaspian railway (which neither would wreck). As Sir William Marshall pointed out, Meshed, Malleson's base, was over 700 miles beyond the nearest railhead in Mesopotamia.[44]

Malleson's mission fought a fluid war across a vast tract of central Asia with a handful of trained troops and with reliable intelligence at a premium. Late in August 1918 at Kaakha, near Dushak, Malleson's men and a motley force fighting for the Transcaspian government held a Bolshevik attack. Soon after a company of the 1/4th Hants, ninety strong (weakened by the influenza epidemic), provided the main British infantry. It is likely that few men who had arrived in Bombay in 1914 remained with it into 1919. Still, it is a demonstration of the strategic reach that the Territorials gave the British government that four years after its arrival the Hampshires were despatched from northern Persia (itself an outpost of a sideshow) to Turkestan. In October Malleson (in defiance of Simla's caution) advanced to Dushak, attacking the Bolsheviks further along the Transcaspian railway. Through the winter of 1918-19 the British force, including the 1/4th Hants, held a position at Bairam Ali, some twenty miles east of of Merv, the ancient and huge oasis in the Karakum, the 'Black Desert' of central Asia. The harsh central Asian winter

---

42 Hopkirk, *On Secret Service East of Constantinople*, p. 369
43 Telegram, 1 August 1918, Foreign and Political Department Secret- War Proceedings, Mss.Eur. E264/54(p), BL
44 Telegram, 28 June 1919 (Marshall to War Office), WO106/55, NAUK

prevented further fighting. Some troops lived in round felt 'kibitkas', familiar to westerners as 'yurts', where British and Indian troops sought refuge from the bitter cold and strong winds. It was among the most exotic (and arduous) service Indian Territorials rendered, comparable in its remote location only to the 1/9th Hants in Siberia. Charles Ellis wrote facetiously to friends in Melbourne that 'the only amusement here is revolution, occasional scraps and a certain amount of game shooting', but complained that they had little time for the third on account of the first.[45]

Malleson's force became part of the British 'Army of the Black Sea', a force of a couple of divisions responsible for a massive and unstable region stretching from the eastern shore of the Black Sea to north-east Persia and Turkestan. The Hants companies were its only Territorial members. As the central Asian spring arrived Malleson began withdrawing his force, beginning with his sick, the last troops crossing the Persian frontier on 1 April 1919. The British had indeed backed the wrong horse, or at least had offered an inadequate stake. In that some officials feared 'if Afghanistan combines with the Bolshevists', as an anonymous War Office staff officer put it then the involvement might have become serious.[46] As it was, it merely reinforced Soviet perceptions (perpetuated in Russian histories) of British imperialist meddling and opposition to the revolution.

Malleson's force (of fewer than a thousand British and Indian troops) had attempted to 'save the whole of Transcaspia from the hateful tyranny of Bolshevism', as an officer of the force put it: or at least to delay the triumph of the commissars. The British evacuation in March 1919 left the Ashkhabad committee to its own devices. Soon after, Soviet troops incorporated Turkestan into the Soviet Union.[47]

As the most recent account of the war in Turkestan and Caspian puts it, the ejection of Bolsheviks in southern Turkestan, along with Allied success on the Western Front and the Ottoman capitulation 'effectively eliminated any real danger of an invasion of Afghanistan and India the western Caspian'; if there ever had been any real danger.[48]

---

45 *Sunday Times* (Sydney), 14 December 1919 [clipping in], Charles Ellis, 1/10th Midlesex, MS Acc 13.036, NLA
46 Telegram, 25 June 1919 (War Office to Marshall), WO106/55
47 'Q.L.', 'The Transcaspian Expedition', *JRUSI*, 1919, p. 488
48 Wright, *Churchill's Secret War with Lenin*, p. 435

17

Armistice, 'flu and Siberia

While in the war's last year the focus of Territorials' service turned elsewhere – to Mesopotamia and Palestine, and beyond – the garrison remained large, serving in their units, in infantry depots, and 'on command' in ancillary transport, supply, signals, training, medical and other administrative postings. Fourteen Territorial artillery batteries remained in India (six others had been disbanded in 1917, their members posted to other batteries). They all continued the routine round of moves between plains and hills, and felt the all-too-familiar feelings of homesickness and separation from their families. Joseph Sturgess, a Hants man, had sent home slippers to his family in Portchester from Darjeeling, hoping that soon 'I shall be home so you can ... get them out for me'. In the meantime, he was happy to see 'the snow clad mountains peeping up above the clouds ... that suits me better than it does on the plains looking at the scorched earth'.[1] But more astute men anticipated that whenever the war ended they would not be home soon. Reg Bailey, though shyly desperate to return to Hilda (it took him over two years to address her as 'Dear Hilda') was clear-sighted enough to realise that 'even when peace is proclaimed ... I reckon we shall have to wait for a long time'.[2]

'Neverendianism': disaffected Terriers

By 1918 many Territorials still in India had found congenial billets. One of the most revealing private sources is the diary and memoir of William Bisset, who joined the 2/4th Hants in 1914 and spent most of 1915 in Quetta. He volunteered for service in Mesopotamia and was wounded in 1916, losing a finger. After convalescing in Poona and Darjeeling he was offered a job as a clerk at Army Headquarters in Simla and Delhi. There he lived an easy life (generally working 9.30 to 4.30), well paid and able to mix with both officers and civilian women, enjoying books, church services, films, classical music and long bicycle rides around Delhi's ancient monuments. His diary is littered with references to a more genteel life than any Territorial might have expected in 1914: 'tea with ladies', 'tennis this morning ... an hour or so with Shakespeare

---

1   Letter, 24 May 1918, Joseph Sturgess, Hampshire Regiment: original letter displayed at the Windamere Hotel, Darjeeling, India
2   Letter, 30 July 1918, Reg Bailey, 1/4th Buffs, 2011-12-3, NAM

Men of the 1/1st Kent in 1918 embody the toughness of Territorials who had spent most of the war in India. Note how several of these men wear wrist watches, a sign of their relative wealth and their initiative. (MNERM: 1990.990, Maidstone Museum)

afterwards'; 'spent the evening with Pickwick and a cigar'. On a trip to Darjeeling Bisset formed a relationship with a young British woman whom in his diary he called 'Chummie' and flirted with a Miss Dobson, one of the 'lady clerks' in the Adjutant-General's office. The diary does not reveal how his romances played out.[3]

Not all Territorials were as contented as William Bisset. The war introduced to British society new ideas, unsettling accepted notions. If British society was not fatally disturbed by war and the stresses it brought, it was seriously challenged. British troops in India were hardly immune from these pressures. In February 1918 Lord Chelmsford wrote to Edwin Montagu advising that 'socialist and republican propaganda' was reaching British troops. Post from Britain was not censored either leaving or arriving, and only the 'accidental opening' of a parcel had revealed that it included twelve different issues of the newspaper *Justice*, which had been proscribed in Britain. Chelmsford acknowledged that Territorials were 'fed up with Indian life and war conditions' and were receptive to 'labour doctrines' and the blandishments of 'Home Rulers' (whether of Ireland or India he did not specify). He asked if there was anything the authorities at home could do to halt the circulation of 'noxious literature' among the troops.[4] Not that troops needed Bolshevik propaganda to feel disaffected. On leaving Cherat, on the frontier,

3 'Dum Spiro Spero', William Bisset, 2/4th Hants and Army Headquarters, M1834, RHRM
4 Telegram, Chelmsford to Montagu, 12 February 1918, No. 30 b, Mss.Eur.E264, BL

Harry Canham bemoaned the monotony of cantonment life, and the 'neverendianism' of the war: and he had only been in India for 21 months.[5]

Dissident literature aside, troops needed no incitement to dissatisfaction and frustration many having spent four years in India and some facing their fourth hot weather on the plains. Some stations were especially uncomfortable, if not unhealthy. Multan, in the barren southern Punjab, was especially hot. Reg Bailey described its ferocious sandstorms and grimly wrote 'this place is slowly murdering me'.[6] Nor were officers immune to disaffection. Montagu of Beaulieu, in a confidential report to Edwin Montagu (no relation) acknowledged that 'a good deal of discontent' existed among other ranks, but also acknowledged 'the difficulties daily experienced in India' by 'junior officers', who had 'told me that they had to give up the struggle against the anna-pinching of the financial Babus'; the latter possibly British as well as Indian.[7]

By this time some Territorial units had spent several summers on the plains. While their equipment and weapons had undergone a revolution, the living conditions of the men using them hardly changed during the war. Even in the big cantonments in the north-west, where troops lived on more-or-less constant alert, conditions had barely improved. Sanitary arrangements, Montagu wrote in 1919, were 'inadequate and poor. There are no fans ... and no electric light for the long evenings of the cold weather', and dim oil lamps made reading impossible. He thought that only the 'devotion of the regimental officers ... in doing everything possible for their comfort' prevented 'serious dissatisfaction among the troops'. Their dissatisfaction was all the greater because 'they were promised all kinds of improvements in the first two years of war' but which were never carried out' – indeed, men arriving from Mesopotamia in 1918 reported that they had amenities (such as fly-screens on hospital windows) unavailable in Peshawar or Nowshera.[8]

The war found stations in a state of transition. Some cantonments did have electricity – Darjeeling's generator became an attraction itself, if not one to rival the view from Observatory Point. The British quarters of Calcutta, Rangoon and other major cities had electric power. Electric fans were installed in some hospital wards and bungalows (and men had to be reminded to turn them off when the rooms were vacant). Electric fans were installed in the troops' bungalows at Lahore, supposedly prompted by Parliamentary debate following the Sind Troop Train Tragedy – even before the station's officers' quarters received them.

Territorials, reading in newspapers and regimental journals of the war they thought they had volunteered to fight remained restive at their isolation. A West Kent man sent to the regiment's magazine a genuine snippet from a circular letter from the Quartermaster-General in India to divisional commanders. It informed them that in future mattresses in hospitals should be made up with 53 buttons, placed in fifteen rows of three or four buttons alternately. 'Even India', he ended sarcastically, 'is getting a move on'.[9] However, the war did bring change – later in the war the pre-war Thursday 'Buckshee day' was abolished, and lectures, courses and training scheduled, at least in the mornings.

5   Letter, 18 April 1918, Harry Canham, 2/4th Border, CMML
6   Letter, 5 October 1918, Reg Bailey, 1/4th Buffs, 2011-12-3, NAM
7   'Army Administration in India', Montagu papers, 7/52, LHCMA
8   *Ibid*
9   *The Queen's Own Gazette*, Vol. XXXVI, No. 12, December 1917, p. 3710

'Absorbed in all sorts of units': Terriers diluted

Territorials, and especially wartime volunteers and later conscripts, failed to observe the rigid discipline expected of Regulars. Though largely compliant, as the complaints on ships or over grievances in 1915 had showed that they suppressed but never lost their civilian demeanour. When the Canadian Sir Charles Dobell (who had directed the disastrous first attack at Gaza in 1917) went to a cinema in Rawalpindi in 1918, he reprimanded Territorials who did not stand up when he entered, and made them stand at attention. As the lights went down, though, a voice from the darkness called 'Where are all the poor fellows you murdered at Gaza?'[10]

Officers remained vigilant toward what they called 'slackness', which could take many forms. In the 2/4th Somerset men were warned at 'the fashion which is becoming prevalent' of reducing the moustache to a line of hairs on the upper lip (wearing a moustache was encouraged). Troops were reminded that 'no portion of the upper lip shall be shaved'. Officers too were prone to deliver a fashionably cursory salute. Sir Charles Monro, the Commander-in-Chief, complained of their 'very slack manner' and reminded them that colonels needed to pull their subalterns up on the matter.[11] The following year a colonel reprimanded his men on their messy hose-tops (three inches; 'no more, no less'), that their hair was too long (imparting an 'unsmart appearance') and that all salutes were offered 'in a very slovenly manner' – the casual wave affected by some officers was spreading.[12]

By the end of 1917 the boundaries between the several categories of British troops in India began to blur. While men were posted to Territorial, Garrison or Regular units, they often came from common sources, especially as conscription took effect. They even lost their distinctive Territorial badges, if they chose to – in 1917 the King 'permitted' Territorial battalions to wear 'the badges with the mottoes and honours worn by the … regiment … of the Regular Force'.[13] This meant that in principle the Somerset Light Infantry could wear the badge bearing the honour 'Jellalabad' or that Royal Artillery badges could bear the honour 'Ubique'. (Whether Territorials accepted this belated compliment 'in recognition of the part played by the Territorial Force in the war', is unknown.) In December 1917, when infantry unit depots were combined into training battalions, with the formation of large 'mixed' depots, especially at Bangalore, regimental distinctions seemed less sustainable. Still, as Gerald Bonham-Carter found, while regimental depots had been abolished, regimental business continued, and he spent many hours patiently sorting out the affairs of West Kent Territorials at Bangalore.[14]

Losses, drafts to Mesopotamia and transfers of all kinds gradually made the 'Territorial' designation less rigid. Geoffrey Burrell was forced by dysentery to farewell his company of the 1/4th Hants in Mesopotamia at the end of 1916. Having looked after them in India and on active service, he now found that 'they became absorbed in all sorts of Units', dispersed 'to various fronts all the world over'.[15] His was an elegy that many Territorial officers could have made. In that men were posted to and from other units rather than being sent home, the

---

10 Maxwell, *Villiers-Stuart goes to War*, p. 209
11 Part 1 orders, 2/4th Somerset Light Infantry, December 1916, DD\SLI/6/36, SHC, Taunton
12 *Ibid*, June & July 1917, DD\SLI/6/36, SHC, Taunton
13 War Office, *Chronology of Events Connected with Army Administration*, 1917, p. 11
14 Letters, Gerald Bonham-Carter, 1/5th West Kent, 1917-18, 94M72/F305, HRO
15 Godfrey Burrell, 'The Diary of a Company Commander', p. 16, M1838, RHRM

Territorial ethos may have permeated India's European military force, in all but the army's eight Regular battalions (and even they received drafts of wartime enlistments). Territorials medically 'boarded' as 'unfit' went to Garrison battalions, but men from other units (such as the Rifle Brigade battalions) were posted to Territorials. Cornelius Scarrott, a 32-year-old carpenter and painter from Small Dole, Sussex, was posted from the 24th Rifle Brigade to the 1/5th West Kent in 1917, because the *Military Service Act* empowered such transfers in wartime. Because they were mostly not posted to Mesopotamia nor quarried for drafts as much as infantry battalions, Territorial artillery units retained a noticeable local composition into 1916. (When George Owers arrived in Ferozepore to join the old 6th Sussex battery – by then C Battery, 221st Brigade, he met many men he knew from Bexhill. Owers had declined 'imperial service' in 1914 but arrived as a reinforcement draft.[16])

While a third of the Territorial battalions sent to India remained there at the beginning of 1918 the question needs to be asked whether the term 'Territorial' had any special meaning by this stage of the war. In September 1917 Jim Mackie reported that only 60 'original men' remained with his battalion, and eight out of thirty officers.[17] The presence in the ranks of both pre-war Territorials or men who had chosen to volunteer for Territorial units in the war's opening eighteen months gave the units serving in India up to the end of 1916 a distinct Territorial character. After the passing of the Military Service Act of 1916 many men posted to India had been conscripted. As the premier historian of the British Army's 'manpower' in the Great War put it, 'by summer 1916, the Territorial Force had lost a significant degree of integrity'.[18] Indeed, Bill Mitchinson closed his authoritative study *The Territorial Force at War* at the end of 1916, because Territorial formations after that became 'indistinguishable from any other division' – but he excepted several Territorial divisions.[19] While battalions remaining in India experienced turbulence in men drafted to Mesopotamia especially, their turnover arguably did not alter their character. In October 1917 a British officer of the Garhwal Rifles who hailed from Surrey was still able to describe the 5th West Surrey as 'a Guildford regiment' while praising its conduct in an action in Mesopotamia.[20] In Palestine, Stanley Goodland described leading 'the old Taunton & Minehead Company' into the trenches at Gaza in August 1917.[21] Albert Bray, who had been orderly room sergeant in the 2/4th Cornwall, estimated that about half of the men who had arrived in 1914 remained with it in 1918 (and it served in India, at Karachi, Multan, Ferozepore and Delhi, throughout the war.)

Territorials certainly became old soldiers, wise to the lurks and perks of Indian service. When men of the 2/4th Border faced musketry tests in 1918 (which passing was worth money to them) men surreptitiously used pencils to make holes in the musketry cards, a practice so common it gained a name – 'cocking on'. Accordingly, the Borders' proficiency was unusually high.[22] It certainly seems that the enthusiasm notable in 1915 had passed. Gerald Bonham-Carter

---

16 Memoir, George Owers, Sussex Battery, Doc.11927, 02/5/1, IWM
17 Letter, 14 September 1917, Jim Mackie, 2/4th Somerset, *Answering the Call*, p. 285
18 Messenger, *Call to Arms*, p. 93
19 Mitchinson, *The Territorial Force at War*, p. 6
20 Letter, October 1917, Nesham, *Socks, Cigarettes and Shipwrecks*, p. 207
21 Letter, 31 August 1917, Stanley Goodland, 1/5th Somerset, Noyes, (ed.), *Engaged in War*, p. 88
22 Letter, 26 September 1918, Harry Canham, 2/4th Border, CMML. 'Cocking on' could explain the 1/1st Kent's very high musketry results, though not the 1/9th Hants' scores at Bangalore in 1916.

lamented the presence of 'muffs' [malingerers] or 'shirkers', even among his fellow Territorial officers, disgustedly detailing instances of 'muffishness' in letters to his sister.[23]

'Most peaceful and happy': the Armistice

After much speculation and anticipation and some false alarms, news of the Armistice on the Western Front reached India on the evening of 11 November. Church bells rang out in some cantonments; in Bangalore Joe Cox watched men go 'crazy with joy'.[24] In Dinapore the 2/5th Somerset behaved so riotously in front of their colonel's bungalow that Edward Ewens declined to describe their antics (silence was 'better for the good name of the battalion').[25] Poona alone learned of the war's end on 12 November – it was said that the general officer commanding the station had a 'strict rule' that telegrams arriving after mid-day were opened only the next morning. A jaundiced Territorial officer explained in the local newspaper that if Poona seemed apathetic about the news 'it must in fairness be remembered that Poona never knew there was a war going on'.[26] The next ten days were declared a holiday for the 2/4th Border, which had been on almost constant alert, and often on active operations, on the frontier since late 1916.

Over the next week many cities and cantonments held parades and church services, though at Patna, with Bihar still suffering from high food prices and communal tensions the Commissioner declined to commit money to fireworks. Bangalore marked the event with Christian services, a 101-gun salute, a huge Hindu procession past portraits of the King and Queen, carrying statues of figures from the *Mahabharata*.[27] Servants received presents and soldiers were treated to teas. The 1/9th Hants received news of the Armistice aboard their transport, the *Dunera* 'without a cheer'. Besides the 200 men who contracted 'flu on the voyage between Bombay and Vladivostok, they knew that they had 'no hope [of] going home', as Bertie Wareham wrote in a memoir.[28] Sick men were left at ports along the way – 17 at Colombo, 14 at Singapore and 12 at Hong Kong. The former Hants cyclists were not only cast down because of the sickness among them. Gerald Bonham-Carter spoke for many in writing to his sister Joan that like her he could not feel '*excessively*' elated' because 'we have lost such dear friends that life cannot be the same again'.[29]

The months between the Armistice and the hot weather of 1919 were the Territorials' 'most peaceful and happy'.[30] The war was over and, they thought, they would soon be repatriated and demobilised. Sadly, that was not to be. The war's end brought relief and the end of conflict overseas, but also, for India, what Algernon Rumbold described as 'distress, unhappiness, uncertainty and tension': and Territorials would face the consequences of what would prove to be British India's most stressful year since 1857.[31]

---

23 Letter, 21 April 1918, Gerald Bonham-Carter, 1/5th West Kent, 94M72/F3005, HRO
24 Cox, *An Ordinary Working Man's Life*, p. 58
25 Edward Ewens, 'A Cook's Tour in Burma and India', DD\SLI/17/1/62, SHC, Taunton
26 Gosse, *Memoirs of a Camp-Follower*, pp. 284-85
27 Diary, 1918-19, Mrs. J.S. Tait, pp. 34-47, Doc 9772, P934, IWM
28 Memoir, Bertie Wareham, 1/9th Hants, M1624, RHRM
29 Letter, 22 December 1918, Gerald Bonham-Carter, 94M72/F304, HRO
30 'The East Surrey Regiment in India 1914-19', ESR/10/14/3/1, SHC, Woking
31 Rumbold, *Watershed in India*, p. 127

The Territorials still in India felt that they had been 'banished', as one told Lieutenant-General Sir Reginald Pole-Carew, a Unionist MP of Cornwall.[32] (Pole-Carew felt he had some responsibility toward Territorials, not only because his constituency included the Duke of Cornwall's Light Infantry depot but because he had helped Kitchener secure Territorials' consent to go to India in 1914.) While in 1916 the War Office's Henry Forster had acknowledged Indian Territorials' 'claim for early demobilisation', by 1918 his successor, Ian Macpherson, frankly admitted in Parliament a week after the Armistice that 'there is no likelihood of these men being considered for early discharge'.[33] Demobilisation, he counselled, would be 'governed primarily by national requirements'. What that meant would become clear to Territorials through 1919.

Punch's Hampshire clerk, whose satirical reports on military life in India had appeared in 1915, had been absolutely accurate when he had foreseen just after Christmas 1914 that he would return after 'several years', 'unhonoured and unsung, with indelible inkstains on my fingers and three vaccination marks on my left forearm as my only mementoes of the Great War'.[34] Army Headquarters hastily issued swathes of demobilisation instructions, so detailed, dogmatic and contradictory that even a general decried them as 'undigested froth'.[35] From the outset, staff officers prudently alerted hopeful men that repatriation and demobilisation could not happen quickly. A circular that Harry Canham included in his papers reminded troops that demobilisation after the South African war had supposedly taken ten months, and after the Franco-Prussian war 28 months, 'and yet none of these wars in any way could compare in magnitude with this, the greatest war the world has ever seen'.[36] Men who had served in India since 1914 became the subject of further questions in Parliament as it became apparent that they would be returning to Britain long after their counterparts in France, Italy, Salonika and even the Middle East. Lord Harris asked the House of Lords to bring back men who had volunteered to go to India in 1914 before the beginning of the 1919 hot weather made the movement of large groups impractical. Viscount Peel, the Under-Secretary of State for War, replied, making clear that the Army Council had considered the case 'very carefully and sympathetically', but he also re-affirmed the absolute necessity of maintaining India's garrison and listed a catalogue of 'difficulties of a technical nature'. Not the least was the explanation that while Territorials who were now in Mesopotamia would be repatriated, those still in India could not be (though as it transpired, events about to unfold would result in many 'Mesopotamian' Territorials remaining in the east). As a final sting, Peel reminded his interlocutor that 'at least the bulk of these men will return to their country and their friends in good health and strength', as one in five of those who served on active fronts could not, of course.[37]

Fifteen Territorial battalions, more than a third of the total, were to remain in India through 1918. They comprised the 1/4th West Surrey, 1/4th Buffs, 2/5th Somerset, 1/1st Brecknock, 1/6th East Surrey, 2/4th Cornwall, 1/4th and 2/4th Border, 1/5th, 1/7th and 1/9th Hants (the latter until November), 1/4th West Kent, 1/10th Middlesex, 2/4th Wilts and 1/1st Kent.

---

32 Dennis, *The Territorial Army 1906-1940*, p. 54
33 Ian Macpherson, House of Commons, *Hansard*, 18 November 1918
34 'A Territorial in India', *Punch*, 17 February 1915, p. 135
35 Woodyatt, *Under Ten Viceroys*, p. 248
36 'Demobilization of the British Service in India', Harry Canham, 2/4th Border, CMML
37 Lord Harris and Viscount Peel, House of Lords, *Hansard*, 13 February 1919

'Germs not Germans': the 'flu

The great influenza pandemic of 1918-19 hit India hard, arguably harder than any other region. Indian medical authorities admitted that 'there is no method by which the deaths actually due to influenza can be calculated', but nevertheless by applying several statistical calculations estimated the death toll as 7,089,694 exactly.[38] It is clear that the waves of epidemics affected India severely, though also selectively. Deaths began to be reported in 'the most terrifying numbers' from western India in June 1918, already in the grip of a widespread drought.[39] Beginning in Bombay, almost certainly arriving via ships' passengers (probably Europeans), influenza soon spread throughout India. It reached as far as Rangoon and Karachi and the Punjab before the first, 'Spring' wave subsided. A second, more severe, wave began in September and reached its height in October. Mortality was heaviest in the large cities (with over a million deaths in Bombay alone, double the death toll of the 1900 bubonic plague outbreak) and the densely populated United Provinces, with some regions barely affected (for example, only 2000 deaths in Coorg, in south-west India), probably because the railway did not reach that far. The number of cases reported continued to climb as the cool weather began: in Delhi 62 cases in two days; in Allahabad 220 in the same time; in Calcutta 389 in a week; in Madras 800 in a week; perhaps 15% of the population of Agra.[40] Supplies of firewood were soon exhausted, with corpses of the poor cast into rivers. As a rough comparison, overall death rates over a few months regarded as 'low' (2%) equated to percentages higher than the losses for Britain's military forces as a result of the *entire* Great War (about 1.7%). Epidemiologists confessed their bafflement at the epidemic's spread and effects, suggesting vaguely that 'the susceptibility ... of the various races in India ... will be investigated'.[41] The global toll was between 50 and 100 million, including up to 17 million in India

Cantonments suffered lower rates of infection than India's crowded and insanitary cities, though the mortality among Indian troops infected was double that of British, at over 21%. The virulence of the 1918 epidemic is demonstrated by comparing the admission rate for influenza in 1915-17 (around 7 per thousand) with that for 1918: 219. Nearly 20,000 British troops became infected, with 775 deaths, Ahmednagar having the highest infection rate (459 per thousand: almost one man in two), though Bangalore had the highest death toll, of 72.[42] The graph for deaths among British troops for 1914-18 shows the cost dramatically: the black bar for influenza is longer than the entire death rate for any other year in total.[43]

Despite concern over dysentery, malaria or cholera, the 'flu constituted the war's most severe threat to British soldiers' lives. In the 2/4th Border exactly half of its 44 fatal casualties in the entire war died in 1918, and half of them in just under a month between late October and mid-November.[44] At Lahore the 1/4th West Surrey lost twenty men to 'flu, at Agra the 1/6th East

---

38 *Annual Report of the Sanitary Commissioner with the Government of India for 1918*, pp. 56-57
39 Barry, *The Great Influenza*, p. 364
40 *Pioneer*, 20 November 1918; Rumbold, *Watershed in India*, p. 129
41 *Annual Report of the Sanitary Commissioner with the Government of India for 1918*, p. 58
42 *Annual Report of the Sanitary Commissioner with the Government of India for 1918*, European Army, pp. 5-7
43 *Ibid*, Graph: 'Death-rate per 1000 Strength'
44 2/4th Border diary, pp. 24-26

Surrey fourteen men, though the station recorded the deaths of 300 'natives' in the same period. At Mhow the number of men dying among the Brecknocks (over a dozen) compelled another donation of a day's pay from every member of the battalion to fund their gravestones. 'Our greatest enemies' now, Harry Canham wrote, had become 'Germs not Germans'.[45] Medical authorities banned gatherings, closed cinemas, soldiers' homes, bazaars and churches and issued orders for preventative measures (irrigations, gargles, smoking) of dubious efficacy. The success of diagnoses and treatments, medical experts noted, 'depends a good deal on the idiosyncrasy of the observer'.[46]

As a Territorial medical officer, Philip Gosse treated 'flu patients at St George's Hospital in Poona. He was distressed to find that 'a large proportion of these cases, all young English soldiers, died, in spite of everything', despite resorting to the conventional remedies, including injections of strychnine and inhalations of oxygen. One man, it seems, recovered because he was a Somerset Territorial. He had been a porter at the Great Western Railway station at Stogumber, a village on the Taunton-Dunster line that Gosse had known as a boy. Recalling how a porter on the line had called out the names of the stations, Gosse recited them in what he hoped was a good 'Zomerzet' accent: '… Crowcombe, Stogumber, Stogursey, Williton, Watchet …' The mention of Stogursey roused the man to whisper 'Stogursey b'aint got no station', but the effect of the catalogue – repeated at the nurses' request at intervals – seems to have helped the man to rally.[47] There is no grave of a Somerset man from Stogumber in the cemetery at St Sepulchre's, Poona, and he perhaps survived to return to his mother's house in that lovely Somerset village.

Reg Bailey described the 1/4th Buffs' ordeal at Multan, where the 'flu caused 'a heap of trouble for everybody'. The Buffs' colonel addressed his men on parade, told them 'he wanted to take us all home' and enjoined them to follow the medical officer's directions. 'We are taking all sorts of precautions, Reg told Hilda, 'have to gargle our throats every day, if anyone feels queer they have to go to hosp[ital] at once'. In spite of these precautions Reg lost one of his platoon (a 1914 man), another soon after celebrating the armistice ('leaving a wife and 2 kiddies) and more within a month.[48] The toll was far lower than in Multan's alleys, though.

'What an extraordinary Battalion': Hampshires in Siberia

While the 'flu raged, a rumour went around the lines of the 1/9th Hants at Ambala late in October 1918 when they received fur hats. Soon the betting men were predicting a posting to Vladivostok. The battalion left Ambala just before the Armistice, embarking from Bombay just over a thousand strong. They carried flu in their kitbags and dropped men off the train on the way to Bombay and lost more men on the voyage leaving others sick on the way to Siberia: at one point a third of the battalion lay prostrate. Arriving in mid-winter, there they were issued Canadian Arctic clothing, including wool-lined overcoats, becoming part of a mixed French, Japanese, Czech and White Russian force. They joined a force intended to demonstrate Allied support for anti-Bolshevik forces in eastern Russia, though the entire effort proved to be futile.

---

45 Letter, 26 October 1918, Harry Canham, 2/4th Border, CMML
46 *Annual Report of the Sanitary Commissioner with the Government of India for 1918*, p. 59
47 Gosse, *Memoirs of a Camp-Follower*, pp. 270-71
48 Letters, 9 November and 1 December 1918, Reg Bailey, 1/4th Buffs, 2011-12-3, NAM

The 1/9th Hants leaving Vladivostok for Omsk, 1918, dressed in Canadian fur hats against the Siberian cold. (M1629, Royal Hampshire Regiment Museum)

Three weeks later they entrained for the three-week, 4,000-mile journey on the Trans-Siberian railway bound for Omsk. In closed wagons, twenty men huddled around stoves 'imperfectly warmed' in temperatures that began at minus 20 and dropped to minus 70 as they travelled through the vast Siberian wilderness. It was a strange Christmas – they ate bully beef, coarse brown bread and tinned fruit – and reached Omsk on 7 January, where they joined the 25th Middlesex, the Kitchener battalion that had arrived (from Hong Kong) in August. The battalion experienced temperatures ranging from 116° to minus 58° below zero within a few months.

The monotony of the Siberian forest, and their exposure hundreds of miles within a land hostile in every sense, frayed the Hampshires' habitual cheerfulness. In March the 'Battalion revolted', Stanley Green wrote, a deputation allegedly giving the colonel, Robert Johnson, twenty minutes to house the battalion's ten prisoners in better quarters, and demanding that he apologise for calling them 'swine'. Perhaps the Bolsheviks' example had rubbed off. The men warned that unless he complied 'we will take the law into our own hands'.[49] The battalion requisitioned a girls' school in Omsk, though performing their ablutions outside with the temperature at 30° below zero. As the Russian Spring began, the Hampshires gave a concert for the White Russian Admiral Alexander Kolchak. As reported in a local newspaper, their eclectic performance captivated its Russian audience. Drawing as it did on the talents the 1/9th's concert parties had displayed in India, the entertainment included British folk songs, Negro spirituals,

49 Diary, 26 March 1919, Stanley Green, 1/9th Hants, M3859, RHRM

some Shakespeare (a scene from *The Merry Wives of Windsor*), a clog dance and the comic turns that had been such a feature of the Territorials' Indian concert parties' repertoires and a female impersonator – ditto. The Russian reporter was entranced: 'what an extraordinary Battalion ... How can they have got all these Singers, Artists, Dancers, imitators, boxers, gymnasts and men who can act Shakespeare [?]'[50] The answer, of course, was that Territorial battalions seemed to have attracted more educated or accomplished men, whose talents the war allowed to shine.

Their families at home were unhappy, in March telling the MP for Aldershot that they had received no letters from Siberia.[51] Other families presented a petition to the War Office calling for the troops return. 'They are coming home', Winston Churchill (now Secretary of State for War) reassured the member for Portsmouth (another Hampshire Parliamentarian) in July. 'They are on the railway now', he said. This turned out to be Churchill economizing with the truth: they would not begin their return journey until autumn.[52] (In Simla, William Bisset had just written to his father, complaining that Churchill was 'all talk and nothing doing'.[53]) Private Stanley Green's diary explained the 'great deal of unrest' simply: 'we want to get home'.[54] Lieutenant-Colonel Johnson seemed to respond to the Bolshevism infecting his men, particularly when he had the chance to leave. Having been offered a job in Britain, possibly with the Royal Mint, he tactfully consulted his sergeants, not wanting to desert his battalion in deepest Siberia. The sergeants, not begrudging him his good fortune, encouraged him to leave.[55]

Rather than coming home, in May 1919 the Hampshires went further into Russia, as far as Ekaterinburg, where the Tsar and his family had been executed in July 1918. William Meads described how the 'Englisky Soldats' visited what had been the Romanovs' place of incarceration and execution. Meads (who claimed to have enjoyed 'My talk with Mr Kerensky') claimed that the Hampshires refused to be involved in the civil war except by training White Russian troops. They drilled a motley band of nominally anti-Bolshevik troops through the humid Siberian summer, assailed only by mosquitos. At Ekaterinburg six Hampshire men were said to have acquired Russian wives, but whether or how they reached Britain is unknown. Reginald Savory, an Indian Army officer who served in intervention force, later admitted that 'I doubt if any of us realised the strength of feeling we aroused', their presence resented even by White Russians.[56]

Exactly how two British battalions could influence a complex and changing political situation remained unclear, and early in August the battalion returned to Vladivostok. They embarked for Vancouver on 1 November 1919, a fortnight before Vladivostok degenerated into fighting between anti-Bolshevik factions until in January 1920 the Bolsheviks seized the port. The battalion steamed across the Pacific to Vancouver. There they boarded trains to journey across Canada, and then crossed the Atlantic, reaching Southampton on 5 December 1919, the only British battalion to circumnavigate the world in the course of the Great War.

---

50 'Translation from the Russian Paper "The Dawn" dated 8/3/19', Adolphus Jupe, M1629, RHRM. The reporter, plainly an Anglophile (and an idealist, given Russian's political situation) ended with a plea to the Hants men to 'teach us your determination, energy, unity of spirit, Calm temper, your Sang-froid expressed in your songs, your sports, your politics.'
51 Viscount Woolmer, House of Commons, *Hansard*, 12 March 1919
52 *Hansard*, 29 July 1919
53 Letter, 7 July 1919, William Bisset, Army Headquarters, M1834, RHRM
54 Diary, 26 March 1919, Stanley Green, 1/9th Hants, M3859, RHRM
55 Adolphus Jupe, 'Round the World with the "P.B.I.", p. 17, M1629, RHRM
56 Savory, 'Vladivostok: 1919-1920', *JSAHR*, p. 12

18

Demobilisation and Amritsar, 1919

The months after the Armistice brought crises to British India. Holding out the promise of political change while maintaining wartime surveillance and repression through the 'Rowlatt Act' prompted unprecedented mass protest. Growing nationalist protests, inspired by Gandhi's philosophy of *Satyagraha* occurred amid dissatisfaction among troops, and especially Territorials. Political protest culminated in the atrocity of the massacre at the Jallianwalla Bagh in Amritsar, an event which changed the direction and character of the nationalist movement and in which Territorials played a minor part. Paradoxically, nationalist activism, which obliged dissatisfied troops to decide which side they were on, temporarily moderated their disquiet over their continuing detention in India.

'This demobilization business': plans and problems

Demobilisation had been planned for a long time: cabinet approved the first plans during the worst of the third Ypres offensive in 1917. At Army Headquarters in Delhi early in 1918, William Bisset was among the clerks re-organised to form a 'Mobilisation and Demobilisation Section': 'sounds hopeful', he wrote in his diary.[1] Within hours of hearing of the Armistice, his fellow Territorials began expressing the hope that they would be brought home promptly. Less than a week later, Harry Canham was writing that 'the chief topic of conversation' in his barrack room was 'the question of demobilization'.[2] Ted Rice, shivering in remote Persia, asked 'When shall we get home' – one of tens of thousands.[3] 'Territorial' wrote to *The Times* to remind readers that 'some of them have been sweltering in the plains ever since [1914], and naturally they long for home'. Having 'done their duty as well as anyone ... it is only fair that they should be brought home as speedily as possible'.[4] 'One of the first' – that is, one of the first Territorials to arrive – asked the *Pioneer* whether the government had 'forgotten that there are troops out here that have been here since 1914?' He refuted the assumption that Territorials had volunteered specifically

---

1   Diary, 15 January 1918, William Bisset, M1834, RHRM
2   Letter, 16 November 1918, Harry Canham, 2/4th Border, CMML
3   Ted Rice, 'All for a Shilling a Day', QRWS/30/RICE/1, SHC, Woking
4   *The Times*, 5 December 1918, p. 3

for India (and that they had been 'too untrained to be sent to the front') and complained that their civilian jobs would be taken by men closer to home and released sooner.[5]

Demobilisation 'hovered in the distance like the silver streaks of dawn', as a writer in *The Invicta* put it, but it proved to be a dawn long in coming.[6] 'This demobilization business', as the Adjutant-General, Sir Neville Macready, called it, was 'enormous'.[7] So severe was the crisis on the Western Front in 1918 especially (with victory by no means certain) that he found it 'quite impossible' to get Lloyd George's cabinet to focus on it. While the War Office appreciated from the outset that it was necessary to make 'arrangements to relieve the British troops in India as soon as possible after peace is declared', Herbert Cox, now Military Secretary at the India Office, knew that realistically, 'India will not be able to dispense with the British Territorial and Garrison troops … until she gets a fresh equivalent of British soldiers – presumably Regulars – in their place'.[8] During 1919 fresh but largely inexperienced Regular battalions would arrive from Britain. (In an ironic reversal of 1914, Territorials, including Joe Cox, were sent on 'conducting duty', meeting newly arrived Regular units 'to show them how to go on'.[9])

Territorial battalions remained in India essentially because Britain could not find a Regular garrison for India in the wake of the war. Though its strength seemed greater than ever – in 1919 the total British strength in India was reported to be 87,000 compared to 75,000 pre-war – the war had hollowed it out. Though the strength returns showed just over forty field batteries, only ten of them had more than a hundred men. The Regular battalions numbered just over 300 men apiece. While in 1919 some seventeen new Regular battalions would arrived, they totalled only 2159 men between them – on average each the strength of a weak company. For now, the mainstay of the force were the Garrison battalions and the remaining fourteen Territorial battalions, all averaging just under 400 men each.[10]

Men's thoughts naturally turned to how – and when – they might return to their pre-war lives and jobs, and many wrote to former employers asking to be made 'pivotal men' – that is, employees vital to economic recovery and justifying early release. Others applied for transfer to other units, speculating on which might be relieved first. Demobilisation regulations were distributed to Territorial units in December 1918, though they would be a long time being implemented. A few men (such as Joseph Gale, a time-expired, married, 1914-man) managed to leave India in March. Gale, who had remained interested in India, its scenery and culture – he had written about seeing Everest at dawn and had been in the middle of the Kumbh Mela – but even he thought that 'the finest sight in the whole of India' would be 'BOMBAY FROM THE STERN OF A STEAMER'.[11]

The first protests arose among troops closest to home, in Britain in January and February 1919 over 'demob delays', and Indian Territorials knew of them. Many occurred in the very counties from which Indian Territorials hailed, from Kent, Sussex, London, Hampshire, Salisbury

5   *Pioneer*, 22 January 1919
6   *The Invicta*, Vol. III, No. 4, 1919, p. 26
7   Telegram, 10 October 1917, Sir Neville Macready, War Office, IOR: L/MIL/7/19183, BL
8   Telegram, 9 October 1917, General Sir Herbert Cox, India Office, 19183
9   Cox, *An Ordinary Working Man's Life's Story*, pp. 56-57
10 *Annual Report of the Sanitary Commissioner with the Government of India for 1918*, Calcutta, Superintendent Government Printing, 1920, Table XI, European Troops 1919
11 Gale, *With the 2/4th Wilts to India*, p. 96

Ridgewell's final cartoon in *Indian Ink* offers a rueful comment on the Territorials' state of mind as they impatiently awaited repatriation in 1919.

Plain and the West Country, because depots and training camps replenishing British forces in France were located in southern England.[12] While the Cabinet handled the protests tactfully, they probably accelerated demobilisation, which in Britain proceeded at an average of 37,000 a week through 1919. By the year's end nearly four million had returned to civilian life. Except for a fortunate few (such as Joseph Gale) none of these men had served in India.[13]

Demobilisation became 'THE subject ... irrespective of rank', but most Territorials were cynical. The schemes, they joked bitterly, applied 'to all men ... excepting those in India'.[14] 'It's no good moaning', one wrote to Reginald Pole-Carew, 'Nobody knows anything about us in England ... and nobody seems to care we were fools in the start and must stand the racket'.[15] Even *Khaki Opinion*, an official magazine, reflected the prevailing cynicism:

12 Rothstein, *The Soldiers' Strikes of 1919*, pp. 37-58
13 'Summaries of Military Events, 1919', WO106/329, NAUK
14 *The Invicta*, Vol. III, No. 4, 1919, pp. 48-49
15 Dennis, *The Territorial Army 1906-1940*, p. 54

> The Statesmen in the quarrels
> Loved all their lands and gold, ...
> And if you think you're coming home,
> We tell you – you've been sold.[16]

Few in Britain besides men's families knew or cared much about those still serving in India, though local representatives lobbied. A Bournemouth councillor urged the War Office to honour 'the Late Lord Kitchener's' 1914 undertaking and bring the Territorials home 'at the earliest practicable date'. His 'gentle reminder' to a War Office oppressed by the burden of garrisoning an expanded empire with an army diminishing literally daily brought no response.[17] Army Headquarters warned that there would be 'little prospect of more than a fraction of the British garrison in India' going home in under six months. The crisis of 1914 – the shortage of trained Regular troops – had sent the Territorials to India in the first place: now a shortage of troops to take up Britain's post-war burdens kept them there. Men serving in India were supposedly to be released 'exactly the same' as men closer to home, but in fact the politics of the Indian empire, both internal and external, was to intervene.[18]

'The volcano': disquiet over demobilisation

Several million men and women in uniform impatiently awaited demobilisation. Shortages of shipping and calls to transport hundreds of thousands of dominion troops home were complicated in India by the impositions of the hot weather. Traditionally, men had not travelled in the hot season to or from Indian ports (and when they had, as in Sind in 1916, look what had happened). By 1 April 1919 just over 20,000 British troops had been repatriated to be demobilised from India. Almost half of them had been sent home as medical cases, but the total included over 3998 coal miners (most probably not Territorials), 2000 men over 41, 1669 pivotal men and 300 students and teachers. Another 2500 men over 41 were hoping to join them.[19]

In the meantime, the India Office recommended that men denied repatriation should be paid a bounty or cash bonus immediately – 'in order to mitigate disappointment'.[20] For Regulars the 'bounty craze' was 'more catching than the flue'.[21] Territorials were less susceptible to payments of £25 for one year or £35 for two. Reg Bailey told Hilda that 'they will have to increase the amounts if they want any of this battalion to stop'.[22] In late February, aware of the impending hot weather, Army Headquarters belatedly sought approval for the creation of 'furlough camps' in the hills which it hoped would 'provide amusements' to distract troops from their disquiet, and at a frugal Rs2 per man. (In doing so Chelmsford's military

---

16 *Khaki Opinion*, quoted in *The Invicta*, Vol. III, No. 4, 1919, p. 47
17 Clipping, Stokes-Roberts papers, M2185, RHRM
18 'Demobilization of the British Service in India', in Harry Canham, 2/4th Border, CMML
19 Telegram, 1 April 1919, IOR: L/MIL/7/19209, 'Demobilisation (War of 1914-1919), BL
20 Telegram, 31 March 1919, *Ibid*
21 *The Roussillon Gazette*, 1 April 1919, p. 67
22 Letter, 1 December 1918, Reg Bailey, 1/4th Buffs, 2011-12-3, NAM

staff conceded that Territorials were right: 'undoubtedly ... some sort of [Kitchener] promise was given'.)[23]

In a confidential report to Edwin Montagu on 'Army Administration', Montagu of Beaulieu specifically referred to 'recent discontent among Territorials' – he was writing at the height of unrest over repatriation. From his frequent contact with men of motor transport units, he knew that many were angry that 'men enlisted in 1916, 1917 and 1918 are being released [from France] ahead of men of 1914 and 1915', all the more galling because 'the 1917 men were conscripts' but who had now 'got away home and secured jobs'. Though most had been in uniform for years, a Territorial was typically still 'a civilian first and a soldier afterwards', he pointed out. Like many commentators, he recognised that 'he is generally of superior social standing to the average regular soldier before the war'. Montagu clearly sympathised with and spoke for men who included some of those he had commanded in the 2/7th Hants in 1914-15.[24]

Early in 1919 members of Parliament from several southern counties raised the Indian Territorials' situation. Percy Hurd, MP for Frome, pointed out that none of the 1/4th Somerset, now in Mesopotamia, had had any home leave. He reminded the House that in 1914 General Colin Donald had promised his men that 'by going to India they would not be the losers', but would be 'brought back home before the end of the War so that men might resume their employment ... before the great rush took place'.[25] Now, of course, men were returning from France. Hurd asked Winston Churchill how he proposed to alleviate 'the sense of hardship which this inequality of treatment has created among the men and in the Somerset community?' Churchill could only answer that demobilisation had to proceed in an orderly way, pointing out that no special consideration could be given to the Indian Territorials, 'since vast numbers of men have also served ... in other theatres where conditions were far more strenuous'.[26] At least by the time most returned the Ministry of Pensions had resolved its initial over-looking of Territorials' eligibility for benefits, an error, Ian Beckett judged, 'not unrepresentative of the thoughtlessness that had characterised attitudes towards the force since 1914'.[27]

Dissatisfaction over delays in demobilisation boiled over into public criticism of the Indian Army's bureaucratic procedures. In 1919 men wrote to the *Bombay Chronicle* decrying the tardy and unhelpful attitude of demobilisation offices and the slowness of military administration generally. Even Territorials who had been seconded to the unfortunately abbreviated Military Accounts Department complained that it was 'in a hopeless muddle'.[28] Men criticised both the 'smooth-faced, wire-pulling puppets' at home who were detaining them in India, but also the officers and officials who were delaying processing applications from men who had been identified as 'pivotal' by former employers wanting them back.[29]

Even men in comfortable jobs at Army Headquarters became openly defiant, a sign both of their familiarity with army life, but also of the social changes the war had wrought, even in

---

23 'Arrangements for Grant of Leave in India to British Troops detained there during the hot weather of 1919', L/MIL/7/13311, BL
24 'Army Administration in India', Montagu papers, 7/52, LHCMA
25 Percy Hurd, House of Commons, *Hansard*, 26 February 1919
26 Winston Churchill, House of Commons, *Hansard*, 18 March 1919
27 Beckett, 'The Territorial Force' in Beckett & Simpson, (eds), *A Nation in Arms*, p. 151
28 '1914 Terrier' in *Bombay Chronicle*, 14 February 1919
29 '1914 Wallah' in *Ibid*, 11 March 1919 and 'Efack', 13 March 1919

Simla. When Monro directed men to attend a thanksgiving service to mark the conclusion of the Versailles treaty many refused – William Bisset thought it 'sauce on the C-in-C's part to order us there when we should be out of uniform and free citizens once again'. Bisset's superiors looked upon him as 'a proper Bolshevik'.[30] Reg Bailey, who also secured an office job, though still in Multan, found that with the war over formality between ranks eased. He found the Brigade Major and Staff Captain 'jolly decent chaps … we talk to them just as we like'. During the war officers were 'far above us … but now, well, they are like the rest of the office staff to us'.[31]

Army Headquarters had not before confronted disaffection on such a scale since the 'White Mutiny' of 1859.[32] Like many other agencies of the British establishment, it was discovering that a mass war ostensibly in defence of democracy (as the war had increasingly been represented) entailed engagement with the feelings and views of the people who had been called on to fight it. The Indian Army's senior officers were ill-equipped to deal with them and after they had failed to honour Kitchener's 'promise' Territorials had lost faith in official undertakings. Reg Bailey summed up its inept approach: 'they keep telling us such awful yarns and altering the tune week after week … we cannot trust them'.[33] In spite of Monro's evident sincerity and desire to do the right thing, he was temperamentally unfitted to communicate with disaffected citizen soldiers serving in dozens of cantonments. He remained sympathetic but firm, in late March issuing a general order to all those 'eligible for demobilization whom it has not been possible to release' in which he affirmed that 'while sympathizing in your natural disappointment, I am confident that the same loyal spirit of devotion to duty will continue to be shown in the future as it has been in the past'.[34]

The role of battalion magazines raising 'legitimate grievances' became crucial in 1919. Men's freedom to vent in the columns of their own journals may have helped defuse potentially explosive feelings. They openly commented upon, and derided, the undertakings men had received. *The Braganza's* editors published a poem from a West Surrey man who described a rumour that 'we're going home next week' as being 'just like Dad at Kempton Park/ I guess we've backed a stumer'.[35] By this time the mood among Territorials in India, and especially '1914 men' had become ugly. The *Bombay Chronicle*, edited by Benjamin Horniman, a Congress sympathiser, printed soldiers' letters through the first quarter of 1919, all anonymous and all airing grievances. They came from 'Fed Up', 'Time Expired', 'Civilian Soldier', '1914 Wallah' and 'Play the Game'.[36] All argued that they had been promised swift repatriation and discharge at the war's end, complained that later enlistments (and especially conscripts) were getting home first, that the reasons they had been given for the delays in leaving were unconvincing and that the process of demobilisation was unduly bureaucratic. 'Civilian Soldier' warned that 'very soon, the volcano

---

30 Letter, 7 July 1919, William Bisset, Army Headquarters, M1834, RHRM
31 Letter, 8 January 1919, Reg Bailey, 1/4th Buffs, 2011-12-3, NAM
32 In 1859-60 10,000 'Bengal Europeans' objected to being transferred from the East India Company's forces to the Crown's army. Their protest, the largest mutiny the British Army has ever faced, saw them granted discharges and bounties; see Stanley *White Mutiny*.
33 Letter, 6 August 1919, Reg Bailey, 1/4th Buffs, 2011-12-3, NAM
34 General Order, 24 March 1919, Monro papers, Mss.Eur.D783/9, BL
35 *The Braganza*, 1 October 1919. Kempton Park is a racecourse in Surrey. 'Stumer' is a slang term meaning sham, worthless or a fraud, as in 'a stumer cheque'.
36 *Bombay Chronicle*, 22 February, 1 March, 10 March, 11 March and 17 March 1919, but virtually every issue contained such letters.

… now brewing will certainly burst'. William Bisset, comfortable at Army Headquarters but keen to go home, felt 'disgusted with the whole business', certain that 'there will be trouble … and there are thousands of more like me who think the same'.[37]

Men in fighting units had a sense of camaraderie and regimental tradition to sustain them. Men in administrative jobs had little sense of loyalty. George Molesworth claimed to have heard that clerks in Poona '"downed pens" and were hardly restrained from more violent action'.[38] Their ire may have been exacerbated by a rumour that although they had secured often more congenial billets than men in their old battalions, the battalions might receive repatriation orders before men 'on command' could be spared from their administrative jobs. (Their former comrades may have circulated this rumour with some relish.) In 1919 experienced Territorials were no longer as patient as they had been. After years in India, and seeing the facilities provided both in Mesopotamia and in more modern cantonments, men became less prepared to tolerate hospitals without fly-screens, smelly drains and ancient punkahs. Montagu of Baillieu observed that 'all these discomforts make for irritation and discontent among the men, especially as they feel it is useless to protest, and that no notice has been taken of reasonable complaints'.[39] Men kicking their heels in transit camps felt even less inclined to obey orders they saw as pointless. Ted Holter, a Territorial gunner who had served in Mesopotamia, was stewing in a transit camp when the rumour spread that men would be sent to the frontier. 'The whole camp refused to parade or do any chores', he recalled, but the camp authorities insisted – he was sent to a howitzer battery in Lahore.[40]

Army Headquarters became increasingly concerned at the temper of 60,000 British troops, many facing their fourth hot season, many in 'concentration camps' such as Deolali at the beginning of summer. George Kirkpatrick, the Indian Army's Chief of the General Staff, was being briefed about the Territorials' temper virtually daily. As soon as staff officers in Bombay read the *Bombay Chronicle* of 27 March 1919 they communicated with Simla, and Kirkpatrick immediately wrote to the Director of Military Intelligence summarising the letters it had published from disgruntled Territorials.[41] On that day the *Chronicle's* editor, Benjamin Horniman, had published another letter, in which a man protested anonymously and somewhat incoherently, at the plight of men awaiting repatriation. The *Chronicle*, Kirkpatrick added, surely redundantly, was a 'local organ of extremist politicians' – Horniman was prominent in Annie Besant's Home Rule League and had supported mass protests against the Rowlatt Acts. He was to be deported on 25 April for distributing gratis copies of the *Bombay Chronicle* among soldiers supposedly 'in the hope of exiting disaffection and insubordination'.[42]

Quoting several soldiers' letters, Kirkpatrick was concerned to note that 'their chief characteristic is their violence'. The previous week an anonymous soldier wrote from Poona asking 'how long civilian soldiers in India are willing to wait'. He urged that if the authorities failed to act, then 'we express our disapproval in [the] only way left … namely strike on May 11th'. In letters published on 27 March, one soldier condemned the military authorities as 'a pack

---

37 Letter, 7 July 1919, William Bisset, Army Headquarters, M1834, RHRM
38 Molesworth, *Afghanistan 1919*, p. 87
39 'Army Administration in India', Montagu papers, 7/52, LHCMA
40 Ted Holter, 'A Terrier in World War I', Doc 4545, 81/9/1, IWM
41 Memo, 27 March 1919, IOR: L/MIL/7/19209, 'Demobilisation (War of 1914-1919), BL
42 Lieutenant-Commander Joseph Kenworthy, House of Commons, *Hansard*, 22 April 1922

of prevaricators' and another criticised retaining men over 35. In the light of the Territorials' frequent complaints at the disdain they had experienced from Anglo-Indian civilians, it was significant that soldiers vilified officials and their wives for their 'attitudes towards civilian soldiers especially to ones who have been used to fairly good homes where standard of conversation and erudition is above [the] usual standard of barrack room stunts'. Clearly, resentment at their treatment – or perceived treatment – became enmeshed in men's frustration over tardy repatriation. A correspondent called upon soldiers to 'assert our rights as Englishmen'. 'The men here', he warned, 'are in a state of ferment and it wants only a match to start a huge conflagration'. The published letters were not, it seems, the only expressions of unease. Horniman reported being unable to publish all the letters he received. A week later Army Headquarters acknowledged 'increasing discontent among British troops in India owing to retarded demobilisation', a concern so serious that it jettisoned decades of accepted Anglo-Indian wisdom. Army Headquarters signalled its acceptance that a further 10,000 men could be repatriated – still only just over half of those who knew they were entitled to be sent home as a 'priority'. They included men over 41, medical cases and others 'as circumstances permit'. Staff officers proposed to make an announcement on 10 April: as it turned out, a fateful date.[43]

'They want us to protect them': the nationalist challenge

The impact of war changed India's relationship with its British rulers. In August 1917 Edwin Montagu, the Secretary of State for India, had risen in the House of Commons to announce that the British government intended to foster 'the gradual development of self-governing institutions', aiming to develop 'responsible government in India as an integral part of the British Empire'.[44] This declaration was as portentous for the sub-continent as, say, Balfour's about the future of the Middle East two months later. The real fruits of Montagu's words would be seen in the decades after 1917, but the realisation that the traditional British response of limited reform and energetic repression was no longer sustainable or effective in an India which during, if not through, the war had become conscious of its identity, aspirations and power. Jim Mackie, who took a livelier interest than most officers in Indian politics, foresaw at Chelmsford's accession as Viceroy in 1916 that 'he will have some serious difficulties to face when the war is over': and so it proved.[45]

With the war over but anxiety over nationalism intensifying, British officials sought to extend the wartime security powers through draconian and unworkable 'Rowlatt Acts', which would render political activism practically impossible. They construed Indian opposition to repression as justification for further repression. The revival of an Indian National Congress seeking reward for its wartime quiescence ensured that the two would clash, as they did in 1919.

Some British officers attributed to the Territorials India's quiescence until the war's end. Brigadier-General Herbert Iggulden, who commanded the infantry depot at Bangalore later in the war, claimed that:

---

43 Telegram, 8 April 1919, IOR: L/MIL/7/19209, 'Demobilisation (War of 1914-1919)', BL
44 Moore, *The Crisis of Indian Unity*, p. 1
45 Letter, 8 April 1916, Jim Mackie, 2/4th Somerset, Mackie, *Answering the Call*, pp. 163-64

it was very largely due to the correct attitude of the Territorials towards the natives and their general demeanour out there that we enjoyed during the whole War … tranquility, peace and quietness in India.[46]

This demonstrated just how little British officers understood the power of the national ideal. Between the provisions of the Defence of India Act, existing repressive legislation and the hope granted by the Montagu declaration, the years 1918-20 saw a reduction in what the police called 'revolutionary crime'. The Bengal Police recorded only one such crime in 1919.[47] It was now not individual terrorism for which they needed to watch, but mass, peaceful protest. But now that British India's 'tranquility, peace and quietness' seemed imperilled, could its rulers rely on the military force they commanded?

The resolution of the disquiet among citizen soldiers came from an unlikely quarter: Mohandas Gandhi (now honoured as the 'Mahatma'). The years of the Great War saw the first large scale upheaval in Indian nationalist politics. Though the Indian National Congress had been founded nearly thirty years before (by a Scotsman) and though the movement had grown, especially among India's largely English-educated, urban middle-class, impelled both by the idealism of European nationalism, but also from disaffection among those English-educated but denied any real opportunity to benefit from their expectations of British India. Over the summer of 1918 the attitude of key nationalist leaders, and notably Gandhi, 'seemed to change almost overnight'. Philip Mason, a reflective civilian official who became one of British India's most authoritative chroniclers, explained simply that 'Indians were no longer prepared to accept the passive role of being ruled'.[48]

Having attempted both sporadic terrorism and ineffectual moderation, under the leadership of Gandhi the nationalist movement in 1919 mobilised India's masses. Using febrile and poorly-controlled tactics of *hartal* (strike) and *satyagraha* (non-co-operation) massive protests in Delhi, Calcutta and especially the Punjab confronted British authorities with the most severe challenge to its legitimacy since 1857. Indeed, many British believed that the events of the summer of 1919 presaged a 'second Mutiny'. Troops were in no doubt, as Oswald Early wrote in his photograph album, that they were facing the 'Indian Rising of 1919'.[49] (Early, who had transferred from the 1/9th Hants and served in Mesopotamia as an air force signaller, commented cynically in his diary that 'I expect the white people will treat us like heroes now that they want us to protect them, but when there is no danger they will treat us [like] dogs'.[50])

In early April 1919 soldiers' letters abruptly ceased appearing in the *Bombay Chronicle*. Did they stop writing or did Horniman stop publishing them? Since he continued to wholeheartedly promote the non-co-operation movement it would seem that troops, aware of growing protest, decided that the British need to maintain order in the face of unrest trumped their concern about repatriation. They overwhelmingly accepted the official view of nationalist 'agitation', They read British-Indian newspapers which in the main (except for Horniman's) presented the

---

46   Comments of Brigadier-General H.A. Iggulden in Woodyatt, 'The Territorials (Infantry) in India, 1914-1920', *RUSIJ*, 1922, p. 727
47   Government of India, *Terrorism in India 1917-1936*, p. 13
48   Woodruff [Mason], *The Men Who Ruled India*, Vol. II *The Guardians*, p. 227; 229
49   Photograph album, Oswald Early, 1/9th Hants and Royal Air Force, M4236, RHRM.
50   Diary, 18 April 1918, Oswald Early, 1/9th Hants, Early, *The Messenger*, p. 119

nationalist cause as a simple, immature defiance of authority. The government later in the war had offered lectures on Indian political movements and ideals by Sir Verney Lovett, a civil servant who in 1917 published *A Short History of Indian Politics* which presented an unsympathetic view of the nationalist cause. He was shortly after to portray nationalist protest in 1919 as 'violent and inflammatory' exploitation of unwitting dupes by 'bullies and ruffians' innocent of ideals or judgment.[51] Though disgruntled to be held in India, Oswald Early wrote that, 'the natives would think … that we shouldn't fire on them … I think they would be unlucky if they thought that', he concluded.[52] The mass protests that developed across India on the cusp of the hot weather of 1919 effectively curtailed a more explicit or aggressive protest among Territorials aggrieved at their being retained in India when the rest of the empire's citizen soldiers were being shipped home and getting jobs.

'400 was overdoing it': Dyer and Amritsar

North India in 1919 was in a condition of 'acute unrest'.[53] The fate of the Ottoman Khalifate, the continuation of the coercive wartime regime and British failure to meet nationalist expectations alienated Hindu, Moslem and Sikh opinion. A united rebellion among India's constituent communities remained the legacy of 1857. The 1/1st Kent saw their task as 'preventing a recurrence of the terrible story of 1857'.[54] The nightmare of 1857, though sixty years before, hung over British India. It was not so long ago: Territorials had met British Mutiny veterans (as they were known). The very composition and structure of the Indian Army was predicated on the need to prevent 'natives' making common cause, and the terror of an uprising lurked just beneath the surface. In March 1915 Duff proposed to Hardinge that 'he would like to see every European woman out of the country' – plainly unreasonably.[55]

The Punjab, which had contributed more men for the Indian Army than any other province, and had made a vastly disproportionate contribution to the war effort, was regarded as the most prosperous and loyal; but it had also experienced the greatest stress and disruption, not least in the return of soldiers who came home with a different conception of the world to the one from which they had left. In the spring of 1919 north India especially saw mass protests and rioting in Delhi, Calcutta, Lahore and other large cities, with official wariness aggravated by false reports that Indian troops had mutinied, threats of a railway strike and the cutting of telegraph lines, (which would have left the authorities militarily helpless).

Amritsar was a city of 150,000 people, many Sikhs – the city's glory is the 'Golden Temple', the spiritual heart of Sikhism. Amritsar was politically aware: Congress 'hartals' on 30 March and 6 April had brought the city to a standstill, though peacefully. Amritsar's garrison at first comprised 180 Somersets (of its 1st Garrison Battalion) and about fifty gunners. The defence plan in the case of riot anticipated the abandonment of the 'native city' to defend the cantonment and civil lines north of the main Delhi-Lahore railway line and the Grand Trunk Road,

51 Lovett, *India*, p. 207
52 Diary, 5 May 1919, Oswald Early, 1/9th Hants, M4236, RHRM
53 Gwynn, *Imperial Policing*, p. 35
54 *The Invicta*, Vol. III, No. 4 1919, p. 1
55 Mesopotamia Commission, p. 125

with some of the Somersets holding pickets along the railway line and others in reserve in the Ram Bagh, a garden near the Amritsar Club.

Two Congress leaders, a Moslem lawyer and a Hindu doctor (who had served in Aden during the war) co-ordinated Amritsar's peaceful protests. Their arrest on 10 April provoked widespread rioting. Crowds gathered opposite the bridges over the railway line, which were held by small groups of British and Indian troops. At a railway crossing ridge Somersets fired on the crowd on the orders of one of the city's Assistant Commissioners, killing or wounding up to thirty people. Territorials heard garbled versions of the incident. Bert Rendall heard that it had been Sussex Territorials, and recorded a vivid account of how a small detachment of troops had faced 'thousands of real bad, rioting murderers', and had fired over its heads until, with 'one soldier after another ... wounded, clouted' their officer had given orders to fire. This, Bert thought, 'settled a mob of hooligans', though it arguably inflamed the confrontation that ended two days later with what is known in India still as the Amritsar massacre.[56]

A British soldier stands by while a sepoy or policemen flogs an Indian civilian, an image published by Benjamin Horniman. (*Amritsar and Our Duty to India*)

Word of this shooting precipitated the riots in the 'native city'. Public buildings (the town hall, post office and churches) were burned and four Europeans were killed, including the cantonment electrician, a Rifle Brigade sergeant (nominally a Territorial) who seems not to have been included on the Commonwealth War Graves Commission list of dead).[57] A British missionary teacher, Miss Marcella Sherwood, was beaten, one of the most serious crimes Indians could commit against Europeans, and the Territorials' outrage explains their actions in the days following the riots.

The following day parties of Indian troops arrived, and a hundred men from both the 1/25th London and the 2/6th Royal Sussex from Jullunder and Lahore respectively, which took over

---

56 Recollections of Bert Rendall, Mills, *A Strange War*, p. 109
57 He is 'Rowland' in some sources and 'Rawlings' in others; neither can be found in the Commonwealth War Graves Commission roll of honour.

the piquets along the railway line protecting the civil lines. A party of 1/9th Gurkhas also arrived by rail – by chance; they were en route to Peshawar – and were detained. On the 11th Brigadier-General Reginald Dyer, in whose area Amritsar fell, arrived to take command. Dyer was a complex man: stubborn but impulsive, implacably wedded to the idea of British superiority but adored by his Indian troops, As a commander Dyer had not been averse to taking initiative despite his superiors' wishes and directions. In Seistan in 1917, on the Persian border, his biographer shows, he had seized opportunities to increase his own reputation, bending truth and evidence to justify his own agenda. In Amritsar in 1919, that headstrong impulse was to end disastrously.

Dyer decided that the disorder presaged a direct threat to the security of the British raj. He issued proclamations in part of the city forbidding 'seditious' gatherings, and when on the afternoon of 13 April he learned of a large gathering in the Jallianwalla Bagh, in the city's east (half a mile or so from the site of the closest proclamation, and many of those assembled had come in from other areas and knew nothing of the ban on assembly). Dyer personally took detachments of 25 Gurkhas and 25 men of two Frontier Force regiments, apparently mostly Muslim. Two sergeants of the 1/25th London, William Anderson and Reg Howgego went with Dyer as his personal escort. The Jallianwalla Bagh, despite its name, 'bagh', was no garden, but was a large patch of waste ground, practically surrounded by houses and reached by only a few narrow lanes, too narrow to admit Dyer's two armoured cars.

Dyer steadfastly maintained that he had acted justifiably, though later made contradictory statements. Still, it is clear that he opened fire without further warning and kept firing not because he feared that his small party might be threatened or overwhelmed (as he later claimed), but because he regarded the gathering as unlawful and, indeed, presaging a widespread rebellion. That no second "57' occurred, he and his supporters believed, including the great majority of Anglo Indians, was attributable to his firmness. Their ammunition practically exhausted, Dyer ordered his troops to leave the Bagh through the only useable exit, leaving some 400 dead and perhaps 1200 wounded on the ground in the sun. William Anderson witnessed the firing from close behind Dyer, later admitting that he felt 'bewildered' by the intensity and duration of troops shooting at unarmed civilians, but that also that he felt 'no fear that the crowd would come at us'.[58]

In the days following the massacre British troops in the Punjab felt incensed at the deaths of Europeans and especially the mistreatment of British women – a heightened fear of rape animated their deepest reactions. Dyer ordered, or endorsed, orders that 'natives' should be forced to crawl on the Kucha Duglan, the street where Miss Sherwood had been attacked, an order which men of the 1/25th London enforced scrupulously and, it seems, with relish. A shopkeeper living on the street testified that 'British soldiers' – and they can only have been Londons – 'eased themselves in our well in the bazaar, so we could not draw water from it'.[59] Reg Howgego, among the 1/25th London detained in Amritsar, took or obtained photographs of Territorials enforcing Dyer's notorious 'crawling' order, an action so offensive and inflammatory that even Sir Michael O'Dwyer, the Punjab's pugnacious lieutenant-governor, repudiated it. Howgego's comrades were unrepentant. One of his photographs is annotated 'Punishment

---

58   Collett, *The Butcher of Amritsar*, p. 260, quoting the *Times Literary Supplement*, 9 April 1964
59   Gandhi, *Report of the Commissioners appointed by the Punjab Sub-Committee appointed by the Indian National Congress*, p. 128

Amritsar City ... An English woman was attacked in this street, as a deterrent Natives who wanted to go down [it] had to crawl'.[60] The 'crawling order' became a symbol to Indians of the brutality of the regime many now regarded as morally repugnant and to be opposed. The Territorials' devotion to photography now served to document their antipathy to India and Indians.

Though it saw the worst retributive violence since the re-conquest of Delhi in 1857, the massacre at Amritsar, the historian Robin Moore wrote, actually became 'the graveyard of government by force'.[61] A military authority on 'Imperial Policing' fifteen years later, undoubtedly reflecting on Dyer's decision in Amritsar, emphasised that the 'military force employed must be the minimum the situation demands'.[62] British India faced another 25 years of nationalist protest, but it never again resorted so nakedly to bullets. But the 'massacre', wrote Nigel Collett, author of a detailed biography of Dyer, 'led directly to the bitterness and bloodshed of Indian independence and partition nearly thirty years later'.[63]

Elsewhere in the Punjab, British troops, including Territorials enforced a punitive regime for a further three weeks. Colonel Frank Johnson of the 2/6th Royal Sussex was in charge of Lahore during the Punjab disturbances. He too acted decisively, adored by Lahore's British community, but without Dyer's brutality. He became one of the most notable of the Indian Territorial colonels. Later in 1919 Johnson was co-opted onto a 'Liaison Committee' which Charles Monro established to improve Army Headquarters officers' understanding of the tensions the troops were feeling as repatriation remained remote.

Largely unnoticed by the British press at the time, within months Dyer's actions became the subject of investigations (by the Government of India and – a sign of its growing strength – the Indian National Congress) precipitating a controversy that would bring down Edwin Montagu as Secretary of State for India and Lloyd George's coalition government. The Hunter Committee, convened by the Government of India only after many months and much pressure, investigated the circumstances of the massacre and found that Dyer had acted with undue force, though its criticism seemed reluctant. The committee split on racial lines on the judgment of whether the disturbances in 1919 constituted a rebellion, and Indian members condemned Dyer for seeking to 'strike terror' among largely innocent civilians.[64] Congress's own investigation raised allegations of misconduct by British soldiers. Dyer's decision to fire on an unarmed crowd polarised the empire. Some condemned his 'frightfulness' (a word recently applied to the excesses of the Kaiser's armies), while in British India he became a hero who had forestalled a second Mutiny, presented with a purse subscribed by those who approved of his decisive actions regardless of its consequences. While many British civilians, in India and in Britain, commended Dyer, others condemned his ineptitude rather than his action. 'Poor old Dyer made a mess of it', Henry Sclater wrote to George MacMunn, '100 dead Indians would have served his purpose [but] 400 was over doing it'.[65]

---

60 Photograph, Mss.Eur.C340/10 (29), BL
61 Moore, *Liberalism and Indian Politics, 1872-1922*, p. 126
62 Gwynn, *Imperial Policing*, p. 14
63 Collett, *The Butcher of Amritsar*, p. ix
64 *Report of the Committee Appointed ... to Investigate the Disturbances in the Punjab*, Parliamentary Papers, 1920, Vol. 14, (Cmd 681), p. 113
65 Letter, 14 June 1921, Major-General Sir Henry Sclater, Indian Medical Service, LHCMA

'Six weeks terror': the Punjab crisis of 1919

There seems to be no doubt that British troops accepted and approved of Dyer's action. One of the consequences of the Territorials' growing familiarity with British rule in India was that almost all seem to have accepted its necessity and inevitability, no more than in 1918. Oswald Early, at Deolali awaiting what he hoped would be repatriation (though he was in fact sent to the Afghan frontier), repeated in his diary his belief that 'if any natives here try any little games they will get a shock'.[66]

The 'Punjab disturbances' disrupted the seasonal pattern to which the Territorials had become accustomed. Despite the onset of the hot weather few parties were sent to the hills. While ordinarily men would be confined indoors between 9 in the morning and 6 in the evening, in 1919 men were on duty outside for weeks at a time. Though actual disturbances were confined to the Punjab and Delhi, the emergency affected units across northern India. The 1/6th East Surrey at Agra reported only 'a certain amount of showing of ill-feeling', but faced the additional duties in a 'right soldierly spirit'.[67]

Troops were called out all over the Punjab. Two days after the Amritsar massacre, in remote Multan (where a Sikh rebellion against the British had begun in 1848) Reg Bailey reported how the Buffs were guarding the railway station and the city. 'The idea is to let the natives hold meetings ... in the city but to keep them from ... the cantonments'. Multan was quiet ('at the sight of a Lewis gun the crowd disappears').[68] 'The populace', as the commander of a column including 1/1st Kent troops reported, 'seemed to be overawed' but 'sullen' – especially the students who over the next twenty years would carry the burden of the struggle for independence.[69] Soldiers especially had trouble understanding the Indian desire for a greater voice in the governance of India. Nigel Woodyatt described them as 'seditionists' and their feelings as 'a kind of mental disorder'.[70]

Elsewhere, unrest occurred in the south, at Bangalore and to the west among the Muslim Moplahs around Cannanore. George MacMunn remained happy to describe the events of the year as the 'Indian rebellion of 1919', as it seemed to many alarmed Europeans.[71] They included Territorials, such as men of the 1/25th London, who saw prolonged exposure in the Punjab: London men bought pamphlets summarising the *Punjab Disturbances* (comprising reprinted articles from the *Civil and Military Gazette*), and the version of 1919 they recorded in their regimental journal and history firmly reflected the official view.[72]

For British troops the crisis meant standing guard, day after day, or serving in an improvised armoured train made of sheet iron, in heat of 115 degrees or over. The troops detained in India because of the 'Punjab disturbances' resented the effects on their lives:

---

66 Diary, 1 May 1919, Oswald Early, 1/9th Hants, Early, *The Messenger*, p. 122
67 'The East Surrey Regiment in India 1914-19', ESR/10/14/3/1, SHC, Woking
68 Letter, 15 April 1919, Reg Bailey, 1/4th Buffs, 2011-12-3, NAM
69 Bristow, 'The Kent Cyclist Battalion', pp. 96-99
70 Woodyatt, *Under Ten Viceroys*, p. 284
71 MacMunn, *Turmoil and Tragedy in India*, p. 155
72 *Punjab Disturbances*, in Reg Howgego, 1/25th London, Mss.Eur.C340/2, BL; 1/25th London website: http://www.25thlondon.com/

It has kept us from home; … it has prevented many from returning to their civilian status; it has kept back our financial and business progress. It has been a real bar to us at the very best time of our lives.[73]

Bert Rendall's motor transport company was ordered to drive overnight on the 14-hour journey from Rawalpindi to Lahore (partly to avoid the summer heat but also responding to the urgency of the call). Its drivers heard rumours – untrue – that 'one white woman and two little kids in a pram' had been killed by rioters, which immediately hardened their attitude toward the protesters. The 1/5th Hants, which had returned to Ambala from Burma in October 1918, faced 'serious riots', escorting trains of civilians, mainly women and children, evacuated from the Punjab to the hills.[74] The 1/1st Kent moved from Kasauli, where they were to have spent the summer, to form a mobile column supported by armoured cars and aircraft to secure the crossing over the River Sutlej, some going to Amritsar, by road. Motor Transport company lorries fitted with Lewis guns patrolled the streets of Lahore, with orders to shoot at groups of more than four 'natives'. Bert Rendall recalled that 'we didn't use the gun, we didn't want to if we could help it', but they continued 'warning the natives that … we … could kick'.[75]

If Territorials had thought favourably about Indian nationalism during the war, then the disturbances of 1919 changed their minds. A writer in *The Invicta* damned the 'rabble of the bazaars and revolutionary and irresponsible youths of the student class'.[76] Evidence from Indian sources suggested that some Territorials took out their frustration on villagers in the Punjab. British soldiers – who can only have been Territorials – are reported to have helped themselves to food and goods from shops, to have mistreated Sikh men by pulling off their pagris, and even to killing a boy who had herded his goats too close to a military cordon (then dragging his body to a nearby pond).[77]

Troops toured the districts about Amritsar, Gujrunwala and Lahore seeking to intimidate villagers who overwhelmingly had committed no disturbance. They acted under the direction of district officials who without doubt exceeded their authority (and the imperatives of humanity) in collectively punishing villagers guilty of no crimes. British troops set up and demonstrated firing machine-guns, at Sangla Hill and Sheikhpura according to named eye-witnesses, to intimidate villagers. Men of the 1/4th West Surrey, who formed a 'flying column' patrolling the Jullunder-Lahore railway in armoured trains went one step further. Evidence collected by Congress's committee alleged that they had fired machine-guns at villages along the track.[78] Benjamin Horniman, the dissident journalist by this time deported from Bombay, published an expose of the martial law imposed in the Punjab, describing the period as 'the six weeks terror'.[79]

Most Territorials, like much of the British community in India, agreed that Dyer had forestalled what appeared to be an incipient rebellion. Bert Rendall believed that Dyer had prevented 'one hell of a big North West mutiny'.[80] The belief that India faced 'rebellion' was common

---

73 *The Invicta*, Vol. III, No. 4, 1919, p. 2
74 Atkinson, *The Royal Hampshire Regiment*, Vol. II, p. 440
75 Recollections of Bert Rendall, Mills, *A Strange War*, p. 108
76 *The Invicta*, Vol. III, No. 4, 1919, p. 26
77 Gandhi, *Report of the Commissioners appointed by the Punjab Sub-Committee appointed by the Indian National Congress*, pp. 121, 137, 115
78 *Ibid*, pp. 124, 143; 135-36
79 Horniman, *Amritsar: Our Duty to India*, p. 107
80 Recollections of Bert Rendall, Mills, *A Strange War*, p. 109

beyond the Punjab: in Bangalore, Joe Cox recalled depot troops deterring a mob 'attacking' its railway station.[81] Oswald Early spoke for many disaffected Territorials. He felt that the Regular garrison (Indian and British) should be 'quite capable of looking after a few mad niggers', and said that 'our fellows' – that is, Territorials denied repatriation because of the unrest – 'would shoot every Indian they see if it were allowed'.[82]

The conduct of other troops in 1919, many of them Terriers, offers a reminder of how differently Amritsar might have been handled. Alfred Bray of the 1/4th Cornwall (which spent the summer of 1919 facing rioters around Delhi) recalled on the voyage home how 'an infuriated and uncontrolled mob' (such as the battalion faced) required 'strong and tactful handling' in 'self-control, dignity and cool courageous endurance'. The 1/4th did not fire a single round, preserving order 'without inflicting loss of life or even suffering on the people'.[83]

Men awaiting repatriation at Karachi and Deolali supposedly 'volunteered [to remain in India] unconditionally'.[84] This, a critic replied was 'mischievous, damaging, and false'. The writer, evidently with a relationship to a Kent Territorial, claimed that the men were paraded and told that 'there was not an earthly hope of their getting away so long as the prevailing disorder continued', and were told that they would have be regarded as having volunteered to remain. The men were naturally 'furious' at the Government of India's 'characteristic shiftiness'. The writer wanted employers (who might be holding jobs open for men) to know that men were not remaining in India voluntarily. The Territorials' defenders sought to counter the impression that they had become 'soldiers of fortune who are hawking their services round the world'.[85] A discharged officer wrote from home that it was 'inconceivable' that these men, who had not seen their families for four-and-a-half years, had volunteered to remain, especially when they knew that men who volunteered after them had been demobilised.[86] 'Detained' wrote from Deolali confirming that reports that they had volunteered were false, and that they had been told that they would remain for one month – which now stretched into three.[87]

'Quite out of touch': the crisis surmounted

Evidence of British apprehension was and remains everywhere in British India. The railways, the arteries enabling troops to be moved around the sub-continent, were heavily defended. Castellated keeps protected each end of the Dufferin Bridge at Benares, with loopholes enabling riflemen to fire down if threatened. The railway station at Lahore, a massive Indo-Saracenic castle, had crenellated walls and great solid gates enabling the tracks to be closed off, turning the entire station into a fortress. At Attock on the Indus a fort protected the railway bridge over the river, permanently protected by a company of infantry.

81 Cox, *An Ordinary Working Man's Life Story*, p. 54
82 Diary, 20 April 1919, Oswald Early, 1/9th Hants, Early, *The Messenger*, p. 120
83 Albert Bray, 'Brief notes on service', p. 4, B.4289, CRM
84 *Bombay Chronicle*, 18 April 1919
85 *The Times*, 12 July 1919, p. 8
86 *Ibid*, 19 July 1919, p. 10
87 *Ibid*, 1 August 1919, p. 8

Sir Algernon Rumbold, whose magisterial book on India 1914-22 dissected India's war as its 'watershed', argued that the Amritsar massacre and its subsequent handling by British ministers and officials represented not just the fulcrum of British rule, but the beginning of the de-colonisation that dominated the next half-century. Critically, Amritsar and its aftermath confirmed what the Indian National Congress's premier historian called 'the twilight of the moderates', a gloom from which they never emerged.[88]

Damned by the Hunter Committee for his use of 'unreasonable force', Dyer returned to Britain ostensibly in disgrace, never to be employed again. The Punjab's bellicose lieutenant-governor, Sir Michael O'Dwyer, condemned him being 'thrown to the wolves'.[89] A campaign by reactionary imperialists in Britain and India ruined Edwin Montagu (who bore the opprobrium for the government's condemnation, withdrew from politics and died prematurely, in 1924), while Dyer's supporters subscribed over £30,000 for his defence and comfort in retirement. They undoubtedly included former Territorials, especially of the 1/25th London, about 50 members of whose Old Comrades' Association attended his funeral in London in 1927, displaying a large wreath of carnations.[90] Several wrote to newspapers in his support – one had been a driver in Amritsar in 1919 – and soon after the Londons' regimental history praised Dyer for having 'saved India for the Empire'.[91]

The Londons, whose members had been more closely involved in the massacre than any other unit, adopted a fiercely protective attitude toward Dyer and his actions. Around 1930, Reg Howgego recalled in 1978, he had attended a unit reunion in London at which one of Dyer's sons had attended as a guest. 'He said his father had died of a broken heart', Reg wrote.[92] Its members maintained this view for decades. In 1978, in anticipation of the sixtieth anniversary of the massacre, Jan Morris's evocation of the end of empire, *Farewell the Trumpets* and a documentary on BBC Radio 4 described the event. One of the few surviving witnesses was Reg Howgego, who wrote indignantly to both the BBC and to the *Sunday Express* (which had reviewed Morris's book). Frugally using the back of old Christmas cards, Reg affirmed that the protestors had been 'killed yes – massacred No'. Dyer, he re-affirmed, had been 'the man who saved India'. But Stanley Chapman, another Londoner, wrote in 1982 reflecting the judgment of posterity that 'General Dyer was unwise to use so much force'.[93]

1919 had seen the Raj's challenges multiply. The release of the 'Montagu-Chelmsford' reforms, which opened the era of 'dyarchy' – a system in which British and Indian interests were balanced in provincial governments – provoked not gratitude and co-operation, but resistance. (Algernon Rumbold, having read his way through the Government of India's archives, judged that it was 'quite out of touch with Indian political feeling'.[94]) In the disorder that followed, 1/1st Kent men noticed among the crowds mobilised by nationalist activists 'constant repetition of

---

88 Mehrota, *A History of the Indian National Congress*, Vol. I, p. 292
89 O'Dwyer, *India as I Knew It*, pp. 318-29
90 Collett, *The Butcher of Amritsar*, pp. 427-33
91 *The London Cyclist Battalion*, p. 178
92 Letter, 1978, Reg Howgego, 1/25th London, Mss.Eur.C340/2, BL
93 Letter, 1982, Stanley Chapman, 1/25th London, 1993-11-87, NAM
94 Rumbold, *Watershed in India*, p. 137

the name "Gandhi"', even though many had little understanding of the demanding, idealistic discipline he tried to impose on them.[95]

The demands of war had run down India's British garrison not so much in the total of troops available, which in 1919 still amounted to over 80,000, but in the number of operational battalions. The 52 Regular battalions of 1914 had dwindled to eight Regular and fifteen Territorial: Garrison units were incapable of taking part in active operations on the frontier. The Indian Army, which had expanded hugely during the war was mostly overseas, and the units available were largely inexperienced.

Indians in favour of any form of home rule – a majority of those literate and able to follow news in any language – asked why the Montagu-Chelmsford reforms (foreshadowed in mid-1917) remained unacted upon, but that the Rowlett Acts, directed at extending repressive wartime measures to suppress unrest, could be speedily enacted. Surely dispensing with juries to intern suspects smacked of the very 'Prussianism' the war had been fought to defeat?

While the troops maintained racial solidarity, as it were, as Kirkpatrick's minutes disclosed, the Indian Army's senior command had been seriously concerned at the temper of the British garrison's largest single component. On 2 May Army Headquarters circulated divisional commanders warning that 'rumours of dissension' among British troops could be used by 'the Indian agitator class' to 'persuade the ignorant and excitable Indian population that they may with impunity defy law and order'.[96] Thus the two great threats facing the Raj might yet coincide. On that very day, the new emir of Afghanistan crossed the border and invaded British India.

---

95 Bristow, 'The Kent Cyclist Battalion', p. 93
96 Telegram, 2 May 1919, L/MIL/17/5/3080, BL, quoted in Cowley, *Loyal to the Empire*, p. 271

19

War with Afghanistan and repatriation

The hot weather of 1919 saw 'India at its worst', as a 1/1st Kent chronicler wrote, a time of 'dust and filth, filth and dust'.[1] With the influenza epidemic barely over, the Punjab and North-West Frontier provinces faced cholera outbreaks and summer temperatures 5-7 degrees hotter than any season for the past twenty years. Inspired by Gandhi's vision, India's cities had experienced huge, unprecedented protests against the Rowlatt Acts and the repression of the Amritsar massacre. What followed was, as Sir Hamilton Grant (the Viceroy's foreign secretary) wrote, 'the most meaningless, crazy and unnecessary war in history', the third conflict between Afghanistan and British India.[2]

'Trouble on the North West Frontier': Afghan invasion

The end of the world war did not mean the end of vigilance, training and readiness on the frontier. No sooner had the 2/4th Border completed its ten-day holiday following the Armistice than it began a brigade tactical training scheme near Jamrud, at the entrance to the Khyber Pass – exactly the terrain in which British India's first major post-war external threat would emerge. The third Anglo-Afghan war erupted three weeks into the crisis summed up by the word 'Amritsar'. Already, routine hot-weather moves to hill stations had been cancelled and headquarters were in a 'state of readiness' against threats to internal security.[3] In the event the threat came from exactly where the Indian Army had foreseen for sixty years, but during the 'Punjab disturbances' and the crisis over the delayed repatriation of wartime volunteers.

As it had since the 1840s, the Government of India sought a quiescent Afghanistan as a buffer between British India and Russia. The pro-British British Amir Habibullah Khan kept Afghanistan out of the war. Wary of German intrigue and influence in Afghanistan (in 1916 Sir George Roos-Keppel, the chief commissioner at Peshawar, had considered an Anglo-Afghan war an even chance) Habibullah had resisted German intrigue. His son, Amanullah Khan, seized power in a squalid coup after his father's murder in February 1919 and soon after

---

1   *The Invicta*, Vol. III, No. 4, 1919, p. 10
2   Robson, *Crisis on the Frontier*, p. xi, quoting *The Times*, 28 July 1919
3   Molesworth, *Afghanistan 1919*, p. 37

A section of the 2/4th Border Regiment on active service on the Baluchistan frontier during the third Anglo-Afghan war of 1919. (Album 18 Acc. Nos 1332-1427, Cumbria's Museum of Military Life)

embarked on a war against British India, seeking to restore Afghanistan's independence in determining its own foreign policy.

Afghan troops crossed the frontier at Landi Kotal, in the Khyber, on 2 May 1919 and occupied Bagh, at the western end of the pass. The Afghan army was neither well equipped nor trained, but if it emboldened the much more numerous border tribes to revolt then the British could be facing a greater danger than ever, at a time when the war had left them weaker than usual. Afghan advances, in the Khyber Pass, the Kurram valley and towards Quetta in Baluchistan prompted a swift and massive British response.

The Government of India declared war on 6 May. On 7 May, Oswald Early wrote portentously in his diary: 'all demob has been stopped as I hear there is trouble on the North West Frontier'. Early immediately foresaw the implications for himself and tens of thousands of disaffected Territorials: 'I am beginning to wonder if we shall ever get home'.[4] Later that day, he was sent to a wireless station at Risalpur, and soon after to the Khyber Pass.

'None of their business': Terriers and the war

As Oswald Early had immediately perceived, the Afghan invasion would further disrupt the repatriation and demobilisation of Territorials and other men who had enlisted in wartime. Regulars of the 2nd Somerset Light Infantry mobilised in Peshawar and were among the first troops to meet the invasion. The Regulars received reinforcement drafts of Territorials (of the 1/4th Devon as well as the 1/4th Somerset), diverted from demobilisation to active service.

---

4   Diary, 7 May 1919, Oswald Early, 1/9th Hants, Early, *The Messenger*, p. 123

Lorries entering the Khyber Pass, showing how by 1919 motor transport was supplanting the camel caravans, one of which can be seen on the road on the upper level in the middle distance. (2/4th Border Album, Cumbria's Museum of Military Life)

From their sangars they peered down at Jellalabad, the Khyber fortress whose name appeared on their cap-badges. The fighting occurred at the height of the hot weather – temperatures in the Khyber averaged 117 degrees in tents, and in June and July in the mid 120s. Senior officers (who, as Montagu of Beaulieu had complained, rarely looked beyond departmental files) now realised how much they now relied upon Montagu's Territorial drivers to carry over 500 tons daily from Peshawar and Jamrud through the Khyber for much of the campaign. Sir John Maffrey, the Chief Political Officer told Chelmsford that in Peshawar 'the burden of everybody's song here is "Motor Transport. More Motor Transport"'.[5] The lorries that Army Headquarters was now glad of were overwhelmingly driven and maintained by Territorials posted from their units.

Though professing to be hard-pressed, Army Headquarters quickly assembled a force of over 300,000 troops to counter the Afghan incursions, supporting it with the logistic resources created during the war. Huge camps housed and sustained the field forces. Bert Rendall's motor transport company's lorries each carried two one-ton blocks of ice to Burhan, the blocks melting as the lorries went, but delivering three-quarters of the load to the hospitals and rest camps in the valleys. All the force's water had to be trucked or pumped in, so heavily chlorinated that an officer claimed that 'sometimes one was nearly "gassed" by the contents of one's water-bottle'.[6]

---

5   Letter, 27 May 1919, John Maffrey (Chief Political Officer, NWF Field Force), 'Correspondence with Persons in India, 1919', Chelmsford papers, Mss.Eur.E264/22, BL
6   Molesworth, *Afghanistan 1919*, p. 83

The crisis of the Afghan invasion, and what it might precipitate, caused the authorities to halt the embarkation of men who were expecting to go home. Monro decided to defer the repatriation of troops from Mesopotamia and India 'with very great reluctance'.[7] The worst off were men who had served in Mesopotamia who had been in transit in India awaiting shipping, who were detained in India and (many) posted to battalions destined for the frontier. So sensitive were the men's feelings that Nigel Woodyatt, commanding the 4th Division on the Baluchistan frontier, felt impelled to both split drafts up between units and to visit them and address them at 'the earliest opportunity'. He 'sympathised with them in their disappointment' and made clear how he admired – but also perhaps expected – 'their stoicism and spirit'.[8]

This, George Molesworth (adjutant of the 2nd Somerset) noted, was 'a most grievous blunder'. He observed that 'feeling among these men ... ran very high'. At Hassan Addal, on the railway east of Rawalpindi, 2000 men, mostly Territorials, refused to do anything but draw rations. 'They were perfectly orderly,' Molesworth said, 'but refused to go further westwards' – to where the campaigns against the Afghans and Wazirs were being fought. They were called 'O'Dowda's Bolshie Brigade', after the officer in nominal charge.[9] Reg Bailey's letters from Multan offer an illuminating commentary on the shifts in official policy and the troops' reactions. By August the authorities were telling them that 'we are indispensible ... and must keep straight and have patience until they can spare us'. Bailey gave Hilda what was surely a bowdlerised version of the men's response: 'Well, they can go down on their hands and knees ...' Realising that men detained on the way back from Mesopotamia had been repatriated (by having 'kicked up rough' in transit camps) 'it makes one think that the best way is to make a nuisance of oneself'.[10]

While Territorials sent to bolster Regular battalions seemed to accept their fate, men of the transport companies and the administrative depots supporting the campaign became, so a Regular officer recalled, 'highly "dissatisfied" over delays in demobilisation'. They said

> ... in effect that they had joined up to fight the Germans but, if India was going to conduct a new war against Afghanistan, it was none of their business and beyond what they had contracted for.

The drivers said they were prepared to maintain the force in the Khyber, 'but no further'.[11]

Unlike when they had been new to the army, when they suppressed the expression of grievances or expressed them through the proper channels, in 1919 many men, now experienced in the army's ways, exercised no such restraint. Charles Monro became well aware of the temper of the Territorials who formed the bulk of his British force. Territorials often formed the guards when Monro toured cantonments, and especially when he visited units on the still uncertain frontier. He entertained men of the 1/25th London to his residence, 'Snowden', near Simla – the London Regiment had formed part of his Territorial division before the war, and may have conveyed their feelings. When he visited Dakka (one of the furthest posts facing the Afghans

---

7   Despatch ... on the Third Afghan War 1919, Despatches to the Secretary of State 1919, Mss.Eur. E264/37, BL
8   Woodyatt, 'The Territorials (Infantry) in India', *JRUSI*, 1922, p. 727
9   Molesworth, *Afghanistan 1919*, p. 87
10   Letter, 6 August 1919, Reg Bailey, 1/4th Buffs, 2011-12-3, NAM
11   Molesworth, *Afghanistan 1919*, p. 80

on the Khyber) and Peshawar in July 1919 a party of four men of the 2/4th Border provided his personal escort. Could these men or their sergeants have conveyed to him or other officers the depth of their feeling about delays in repatriation? They would spend hours on guard and at attention in his presence, but would perhaps chat informally, to staff officers if not Monro himself. Did they or the Londons express their dissatisfaction, however obliquely?

It was said that a deputation of twenty one 'mutineer "delegates"' (as Monro's latest biographer called them) – probably Territorial sergeants – visited Monro and put the troops' case to him: a brave act on their part.[12] He responded prudently with a mixture of 'firmness, tact and understanding', but did not concede.[13] Monro certainly took trouble as the crisis of 1919 continued to attempt to at least discern the men's feelings. In the middle of the trying summer he formed a 'Liaison Committee' on which officers of units advised Army Headquarters of problems. It met at Simla for a week and visited camps and cantonments in the vital areas of the forward divisions between Rawalpindi and the Khyber Pass, ranging as far as the hill station of Murree and the Kurram valley. (At Dakka, Frank Johnson met Albert Falkenstein, formerly one of the Royal Sussex's most enthusiastic boxers and now a lieutenant.)

In transit and holding camps men talked back to strange officers in ways they would never have dared earlier in their service. At Deolali Oswald Early was one of a group who spoke to 'a colonel and staff officers' who had been sent to explain the men's detention. The officers had foolishly given them 'a definite promise' that they would be detained no more than a month. The men suspected the assurance, and asked for it in writing, which the officers declined to provide. Early expressed the men's disgust: 'the white people were not worth fighting for … [Territorials] would fight to defend themselves but not the whites'.[14]

Still, the Territorials remained compliant, if grudgingly. The 1/4th Buffs at Multan was required to provide a draft of men to reinforce units on the Baluchistan front ('my word there is some moaning about it'), Reg Bailey wrote. A draft of 300 Buffs arrived to strengthen the King's Liverpool at Quetta. 'They are a regular crowd', Reg told Hilda, 'and our boys cannot tell them much … except Mountain Warfare', he added cheekily – in four years Territorial units had become proficient in the warfare the Indian Army had made its own.[15] But how would Territorials perform in the ultimate test in combat in India?

Although many units across the north-west had been on alert in response to the Punjab disturbances, within days three field forces had been created (the North-West Frontier Force, Baluchistan Force and – again – Waziristan Force). The British response was to repel the Afghan incursions, but also to divide and deter the Mohmands and Afridis from supporting the Afghans and monitor and repress any attempt to capitalise on the invasion. Territorial battalions in the north-west mobilised, and relieved Regular units to enable them to join the field forces. The 1/4th West Surrey, for instance, took over 'Internal Security' duties in Nowshera to allow the 1st South Lancashire to proceed on service (after a delay because cholera broke out in the Nowshera lines). There is a strong sense in the documents that the Afghan war was the business of experienced India and especially frontier hands. British Regular soldiers and experienced

12 Crowley, *Loyal to Empire*, p. 272
13 Barrow, *The Life of Sir Charles Carmichael Monro*, p. 231
14 Diary, 25 April 1919, Oswald Early, 1/9th Hants, Early, *The Messenger*, p. 121
15 Letters, 6 August and 1 September 1919, Reg Bailey, 1/4th Buffs, 2011-12-3, NAM

Indian units were necessary; Territorials were useful, but not essential.[16] The main theatre, in the Khyber, involved only British Regulars and Indian troops (with Territorials in supporting units) but Territorials took part in operations in Baluchistan (at Spin Baldek), in the relief of Thal and in subsidiary operations, and performed variably.

'Repeatedly ordered to advance': Spin Baldek

Though the main Afghan thrust came in the Khyber, Amir Amanullah also launched columns against garrisons on the Baluchistan frontier, though they were small and widely dispersed. The defending Baluchistan Force included two British battalions, the Regular 1st Duke of Wellington's and the Territorial 1/4th West Kent, with British artillery (some Territorial), but otherwise entirely Indian. The West Kent was sent to the Afghan frontier to join in taking the supposedly impregnable mud fort at Spin Baldak, just inside the Afghan border. Its men marched for Chaman, over the Khojak Pass: the route British troops had followed exactly eighty and forty years before. The lessons of the 1917 frontier campaigns appeared to have been heeded. At Chaman, the force's advanced base, Nigel Woodyatt policed sanitary measures so assiduously ('Sanitation and hygiene being amongst my hobbies') that an inspecting committee supposedly could not find a single fly.[17]

The West Kent was allotted the task of attacking the fort's eastern face when the attack opened on an exceptionally hot day in late May, supported by what had originally been a Devon Territorial battery. Active service would not wait on the conventional responses to Baluchistan's climate: the West Kent at Spin Baldak endured eight hours in the sun at the hottest time of the year. The Territorials do not seem to have performed well. At first pinned down by sniper fire, and then assailed by a sudden Afghan sally from the fort, the Territorials inflicted heavy losses on the defenders. But the official report noted that the battalion was 'somewhat delayed' in attacking the fort. 'Repeatedly ordered to advance' the Territorials 'remained hung up by some hostile riflemen in Sangers'.[18] The Regulars of the Duke of Wellington's made the final successful assault on the fort. Four Territorials were killed or died of wounds and another four were wounded. The West Kent's colonel recommended ten of his men for the Military Cross, Distinguished Conduct Medal or a Mention-in-Despatches, though only two awards resulted. The judgment implied in the report of it being 'repeatedly ordered to advance' seems damning.

The battalion garrisoned the fort in very hot weather, with inadequate water supplies, and joined in June by a draft of West Kents from Mesopotamia who had believed they had been going home, and by Wiltshire gunners originally the 2/1st Wessex Battery.[19] Through July the West Kents alternated with the Duke of Wellington's and Indian battalions, skirmishing with Afghan troops in the surrounding hills. At last early in August the troops learned that the fort was to be handed back as part of the peace terms and they destroyed everything they had built or

16 1919 Government of India Foreign and Political Department Secret – Frontier Proceedings July 1919 Third Afghan War (Part I) 1-19 May 1919, Mss.Eur.E264/55 (f), BL
17 Woodyatt, *Under Ten Viceroys*, p. 251
18 'Report on action at Spin Baldak, 27 May 1919', WO106/56, NAUK
19 War diary, May-July 1919, 1/4th West Kent, WKR/B4/A1, KH&AC; Bavin, *Swindon's War Record*, p. 255

repaired before marching out. Back on a peace-time footing again, the West Kent defeated the Duke of Wellington's at football 2-1, a sign that Territorials were not quite the inexperienced newcomers they had once been.

'In support': Dyer and Thal

Territorial units, some quite new to frontier warfare, became involved in reacting to an Afghan force which advanced into the Kurram Valley to besiege the mud fortress of Thal. They became part of a column under Brigadier-General Reginald Dyer who, not yet sanctioned for using excessive force in Amritsar, was given command of a column ordered to relieve Thal. The Afghan force commanded by Nadir Khan, an officer of unusual skill and initiative, sought to incite tribal insurgency in the Kurram. Local militia wavered and even deserted, and by late May Thal's garrison comprised four Indian battalions and some mountain artillery. Army Headquarters committed a large relief force. It included three Indian battalions but also the 1/25th London (the most heavily employed unit), the 2/6th Royal Sussex, the 1/5th Hants and a company of the 1/4th Border, the largest single group of Territorial units to see active service in India.

The relief column travelled by rail to Togh, near Kohat, 25 miles east of Thal, then marched, in intense heat, suffering from thirst, with Dyer riding with the foremost troops (making good use of the lorries and cars built up by Montagu of Beaulieu). Arriving after two arduous marches, Dyer immediately decided to attack the tribal lashkars and Afghan troops around Thal. Dyer used his experienced Indian battalions for the most significant attacks, using Territorial infantry 'in support'. George Molesworth recorded that he 'wished to avoid British casualties as much as possible', and no British other ranks were killed at all.[20] Dyer made the most of the technological advantages British troops enjoyed. Aircraft supported the attacks, reporting on Afghan dispositions, and Dyer employed a small force including 60 London infantry, with Lewis guns in lorries, accompanied by armoured cars and artillery in an attempt to seize Nadir Khan's camp. Historian Michael Barthorp described the Londons as 'disgruntled', but recognised that they responded well to Dyer's leadership.[21]

Dyer's men, both British and Indian, willingly met his demand that they attack Thal swiftly and aggressively, in very trying conditions. They defeated a tribal lashkar and an Afghan force about 19,000 strong on the very eve of the armistice (with characteristic pugnacity, when the Afghans advised that they were offering an armistice Dyer advised that his guns would give an immediate reply). His decisive actions left the Afghan force in full retreat and the local inhabitants 'most humble'.[22] Dyer had acted callously in the Jallianwallah Bagh six weeks before, but in the relief of Thal he demonstrated qualities of decisive leadership in the best traditions of the Indian Army. The Territorials under his command, all disillusioned with the army and desperately hoping for demobilisation and repatriation, responded impressively to Dyer's demands.

20 Molesworth, *Afghanistan 1919*, pp. 119-21
21 Barthorp, *The North-West Frontier*, p. 157
22 'Operations for the Relief of Thal', WO106/56, NAUK

'A filthy little blockhouse': on the Mohmand line

One of the subsidiary operations the Afghan army launched was an incursion onto the Lower Mohmand country, north-west of Peshawar. There the Mohmand Blockade line ran for some 17 miles between the Swat and Kabul Rivers, seeking to control the Mohmands ('the most inveterate troublemakers on the frontier', as one of the frontier's last British protagonists called them).[23] It comprised a chain of fortified blockhouses between 300 and a thousand yards apart, linked by wire fences intended to prevent Mohmand raiders entering the vale of Peshawar. Even so, isolated raiders got through to harass villages west of the Indus, even firing into Peshawar cantonment, albeit ineffectively. A brigade including the 1/1st Kent from the army's Central Reserve arrived in late May to stop them. Aided by tribal lashkars, the Afghans then switched to infiltrating through the Besai Ridge, south of Jamrud fort. The columns included companies of the 2/4th Border, which had been broken up and used as a reserve in several operations that summer. The Border battalion had previously been regarded as insufficiently trained to be trusted to undertake active operations. In 1918, however, it had been distributed in detachments to garrison the blockhouses of the Mohmand blockade line, relieving Regulars of the Durham Light Infantry for active operations. A young lieutenant of the 2/4th Border lamented how he was in charge of 'a filthy little blockhouse … miles beyond the pale of civilization'.[24] (Fred Wignall's collection of postcards includes one of Ali Musjid fort in the Khyber Pass which he annotated 'a village close by was blown up yesterday, *Some Noise* rather!'[25] This frontier campaign could have been illustrated in postcards produced before hostilities began.)

While the campaign against the Afghans continued, Border, West Surrey and London companies patrolled and responded to reports of 'badmashes' taking advantage of the turmoil to raid the plains.[26] In some ways these duties were no more than Territorials had done since their earliest days in India – the 2/4th Border war diary records it setting guards over artillery lines, the magazine and hospital at Peshawar, just as it always had (though it also mounted guards over wireless, motor transport and aircraft compounds, novelties showing how war had changed the frontier). The atmosphere of 1919 gave point to these seemingly routine duties, with an invasion in progress barely 30 miles to the west and disorder in the Punjab to the south-west. (On 1 June the 2/4th Border recorded 'nothing to report', but the next day 'Armoured Train … attacked and derailed by 40-50 tribesmen'.[27]) Meanwhile the 1/5th Hants, which though prepared for mountain warfare had been sent to Burma, returned and in May 1919 was allotted to the 46th Mobile Brigade at Kohat. Holding Mohammed Zai fort it suffered from bad water and poor rations, twice attacked by Afghans, without loss, but in great discomfort at the height of the hot weather.

23 Elliott, *The Frontier 1833-1947*, p. 162
24 Letter 28 November 1918, H.S. Priestley, 2/4th Border, Doc 16482, 08/96/1, IWM
25 Pte Frederick Wignall, 2/4th Border, E94/2016, CMML
26 War diary, June 1919, 1/4th West Surrey, WO95/5392, NAUK
27 War diary, June 1919, 2/4th Border, WO95/5392, NAUK

A platoon of the 2/4th Border Regiment photographed in a blockhouse on the Mohmand Blockhouse Line, north-west of Peshawar. (Percy Harrison collection, Cumbria's Museum of Military Life)

'Ceased to be on Field Service': the end of the crisis

After protracted negotiations British and Afghan emissaries concluded a treaty at Rawalpindi in August. The Afghans were compelled to accept the existing frontier but British representatives accepted that Afghanistan should follow its own foreign policy, a victory on points for them. The war had cost almost exactly 100 British-Indian dead, two-thirds of them Indian, the British dead 'all 1914-15 men', as an MP put it, men who in November 1918 had hoped and even expected to survive the war.[28] More deaths ensued, however, as British troops returned to their stations in the hills. The 1/5th Hants, which had served through the crisis at Kohat (where six men had died of cholera) lost more men from heatstroke when the troop trains carrying them to Ambala (and on to Solon in the Simla Hills) were delayed. At least one man died at Jhelum, and others were left in hospital along the way. The war's timing was not amenable to the careful lessons reinforced by the Sind Tragedy.[29] Gradually the tension eased – in July leave parties could at last be sent from the plains cantonments to hill stations and on 9 September units recorded 'ceased to be on Field Service'.

28 'Statement by Mr Montagu', House of Commons, *Hansard*, 10 July 1919; Clifton Brown, House of Commons, *Hansard*, 9 July 1919
29 *History of the Hampshire Territorial Force Association*, pp. 142-43

'The conclusion of peace with Afghanistan', Monro reported, though, 'did not bring general peace to our border'.³⁰ Despite the armistice, through the summer of 1919 tribal risings broke out on a 550-mile stretch of the frontier between the Khyber and Chaman, on the Afghan frontier near Quetta. Lashkars of up to 10,000 strong at times closed the Khyber Pass, continuing the conflict of the summer. The most protracted and costly fighting occurred as British-Indian columns once again attempted to penetrate Waziristan and force the Mahsuds to accept British authority. The fighting died down in July as tribesmen returned home to sow crops, but flared up again in the autumn, when the Indian Army faced some of its hardest frontier campaigning, so severe that Major-General Andrew Skeen, regarded as a frontier specialist, panicked and asked to use poison gas.³¹ Despite air support, mainly Indian units lost men and weapons in Waziristan as battle-wise Mahsud tribesmen exploited their opponents' inexperience. The fighting in Waziristan cost more British and Indian lives than any other frontier campaign. Not until May 1920, after a year of intense and costly fighting, were the Mahsuds compelled to come to terms, and it precipitated a major change in frontier strategy, with fortified camps constructed in tribal areas. By then virtually all of the Territorials had gone.

Though they had been sent to India, and retained there, in anticipation of a crisis, in the Afghan war Territorial units had in fact formed a minute proportion of British-Indian military strength; about six out of sixty battalions mobilised. Ironically, while the 1/25th London and 2/6th Royal Sussex responded to Rex Dyer's leadership on the march to Thal, the 1/4th West Kent, disillusioned and disaffected had demonstrated at Spin Baldak that Territorials actually were as undependable as their critics had anticipated in 1914. While willing to fight the Kaiser and other enemies of the King, many were evidently unwilling to risk their lives in a minor clash on the furthest frontier of the Indian Empire.

The war's end had not eased Britain's military burden in the east; if anything it had intensified strain. In briefing notes published as the last Territorials left India, George MacMunn listed the military challenges Britain faced. They included 'unrest' in India, Egypt, Mesopotamia and southern Arabia. Then there were the 'Afghan troubles' (now over, but the possibility of the Bolsheviks making common cause with the Afghans, now responsible for their own foreign policy, remained a nightmare). A peace settlement with Turkey remained elusive. To meet these demands the Indian Army had lost experienced soldiers to 'very necessary' furloughs, and British units were no more than 'cadres'.³² Soon open rebellion would indeed erupt in Mesopotamia. But none of this was now the concern of Territorials. They were at last going home.

---

30 'Minor military operations … May 1919-April 1920', WO106/56, NAUK
31 Robson, *Crisis on the Frontier*, pp. 200-01
32 'Notes on Military Organization in Mesopotamia and North Persia', WO106/55, NAUK

20

Territorials after India

The thread of subordination held just long enough. The Punjab was at last quiescent, the Afghans had signed a treaty, the monsoon had ended, and shipping was available to carry the Territorials (and other 'hostilities-only' men) home. On reaching Britain, most units were demobilised within days of their formal welcome-home. Men returned to families, to jobs and to the possibility of a future. The Indian Territorials passed into history, except that hardly anyone besides themselves wrote their history, and few took any notice of it. The memory of their service lived only among their families; some of them.

'No ships. No hopes': repatriation

At last, drafts were once again allowed to flow through the marshalling camps like Deolali (often spending weeks under canvas). Men endured their final long train journeys. Most of the individuals who appear in this book recorded their journeys to the docks, often frustratingly slow. Oswald Early, now back in Risalpur but no closer to being repatriated, recorded his vexation that his draft's orders had been cancelled once more. His comrades had now been told that they could not be relieved until replacements arrived from Britain. 'If they start those little games', he recorded ominously, 'I can see trouble'. The next day a group of Mesopotamian veterans voiced their rising anger and talked about cabling the Air Ministry (they now belonged to the Royal Air Force) or 'the Labour leader in England'.[1]

Planning and transport staffs were at last able to implement long-dormant plans to start to move men from their stations to holding camps and on to the ports, mainly Bombay. Reg Bailey had left the headquarters that had given him a congenial billet through the summer and received word that he was on a draft due to leave on 15 October. There was 'plenty of telegrams, letters, notes [and] demob papers flying about in all directions'. Then, with his valise packed, the sergeants' mess closed, bedding handed in, Reg and his comrades received a telegram 'concentration camp full'. 'My word there was some blue air', he wrote ruefully.[2] (He left soon after, to

---

1 Diary, 22 & 23 August 1919, Oswald Early, formerly 1/9th Hants, Early, *The Messenger*, p. 157
2 Letter, 8 October 1919, Reg Bailey, 1/4th Buffs, 2011-12-3, NAM

be reunited with Hilda, whom he married.) Morale among troops waiting for orders to board trains for the embarkation ports remained low: 'No ships. No hopes', as a contributor to *The Invicta* put it.[3]

Meanwhile, Territorials continued to die, though in nothing like the numbers in 1918. At least twenty died in the second half of 1919, including Private James Strange, a 1914-man of the 2/6th Royal Sussex, who died of snake-bite at Dalhousie when he 'had already started on the journey home'.[4] Seven died in 1920; the last Private Herbert Evans of the 1/5th Buffs, at Deolali on 10 August 1920, the last of over a thousand Territorials who were destined never to leave India; about one man in fifty of those posted there.

'India might offer a career': staying on

Frustrated by delays in demobilisation, some men 'resolved their own difficulties', as a history of the 1/4th Hants put it, by finding employment in India or Mesopotamia.[5] Throughout the war various British-Indian commentators had pondered possible futures for the Territorials. A few men found jobs in India. Ernest Twin, a lithographer serving with the 1/9th Middlesex, had been courted during the war with offers from the Calcutta *Statesman*, the East Indian railways printing works and a Calcutta 'Fine Art Studio'. (He was unable to leave, but by 1918 was a '2nd Corporal' with the Sappers and Miners, clearing 90 rupees a month and living in 'comparative luxury'.[6]) Other skilled men were discharged or seconded to work in munitions factories in India.

British commercial firms recognised the economic potential of skilled Territorials, and businessmen proposed that the Government of India establish a 'Bureau for the purpose of providing suitable employment after the war' for Territorials, though as the National Archives of India has lost the file the outcome remains tantalizingly opaque. A jute factory, for instance, had sought to entice turners to work on making spindles for its mill – unsuccessfully, so the proposal may have failed.[7] While British-Indian firms seeking workers among British troops at the war's end circulated lists, few men wanted to stay on, not after spending up to five and for a few men who returned in 1920 (such as Joe Cox) even six years away from home. Drafted into an office processing repatriation drafts, Cox had 'long lists of firms offering work' in India, but found few takers. Like him, 'most wanted to get home'.[8]

A few Territorials responded passionately and wholeheartedly to India. Perhaps the most notable instance of a man who remained and, indeed, devoted the rest of his life to India was Olaf Caroe of the 1/5th East Surrey. Caroe, a Liverpool architect, recorded the origins of his life-long infatuation with India in his memoir, subtitled 'A Saga of East and West'. Caroe was

---

3   *The Invicta*, Vol. III, No. 4, 1919, p. 44
4   'Obituary', *The Royal Sussex Herald*, 1 September 1919 [sic], p. 276
5   Anon, 'War-time Wanderings of the 1/4th Battalion, Hampshire Regiment', p. 26, M3910, RHRM
6   Letters, 5 November 1915 and 29 August 1918, Ernest Twin, 1/9th Middlesex, Doc.16077, 08/35/1, IWM
7   'Obtaining of skilled mechanics from Territorial units for industries in India' Indian Munitions Board, Industrial Intelligence Branch, Jan 1918, File No I-306, NAI
8   Cox, *An Ordinary Working Man's Life Story*, p. 58

captivated by India (and especially the Punjab). He had pondered the possibility of staying on early in his service when he had commanded a guard at the Residency in Hyderabad. Its magnificence spawned the thought that 'India might offer a career if it could be lived in such a setting!' He observed in reflecting on his career that the impression given by books that appeared long after 1947 was that 'we British were but aliens who did not understand the values of the people among whom we moved'. Caroe vigorously contested this belief, and in his actions demonstrated the depth of his understanding, but few became as informed and committed as he.[9]

Territorial drivers were offered promotion to sergeant and a bonus if they were to remain to train Indian drivers for a further eighteen months. Bert Rendall volunteered to stay on, but then, changing his mind, had to creep into the orderly room at night to remove the completed form.

'Departure of the 1914 Men': returning home

Finally – not until October 1919 – units learned of the long-expected 'Departure of the 1914 Men'.[10] At last, widespread embarkation orders arrived. Men settled accounts, sold or gave away pets and handed in weapons and stores. Some performed private services. The day before he had embarked from Bombay, the Brecknocks' adjutant, Molyneux Thomas, visited the grave of Sergeant Joseph Hicken, who had died at Colaba of malaria two years before.[11] When the first of the 1/4th Cornwall's '1914 men' left Ambala (but only about a week ahead of the battalion's departure as a whole) they departed to 'quite a modest cheer, no exultant joy'. The main body left soon after in 'dead silence'.[12] Two hundred of the 1914 men of the 2/5th Somerset were sent in a draft to Deolali in October, chagrined to find their train side-lined while trains carrying later volunteers passing them on the line to Bombay. They reached Britain after the remainder of the battalion.[13]

Sheer chance played its part. Edward Read of the 1/6th Hants, who had served in Mesopotamia with a draft and been repatriated sick, later became an instructor. He missed three drafts in 1919, once because a farewell celebration got out of hand, once because he was drafted to security duties in Bombay and then because he had been exposed to cholera. Harry Canham became ill late in 1919, receiving his demob. orders at last while in hospital with colitis. He convinced the medical officer to let him go, spending the four day-journey to Deolali suffering from cramps and bloody diarrhoea and losing two stone in weight. But sick or not, Harry seemed to make the boat at Bombay. Ted Holter, who had arrived on the *Somali* in 1914, found himself posted from Basra to four stations (and a stint supporting the last operations of the 1919 uprisings) before being sent to Deolali for three weeks. After collecting documents and back-pay Ted was stopped on the dockside at Bombay. 'We ranted and raved', he wrote, but

---

9   Caroe, 'The Flames of Enchantment', pp. iii; iv-6, PP/MCR/207, IWM
10 *The Invicta*, Vol. III, No. 4, 1919, p. 59
11 Annotation to letter, 26 August 1918, Correspondence relating to the grave memorials in Aden and India during the Great War, Box 17a, RMRW
12 Albert Bray, 'Brief notes on service', p. 5, B.4289, CRM
13 Anon, *The Book of Remembrance*, pp. 105-06

Family members greet a man of the 1/9th Hants on the battalion's return to Portsmouth on 5 December 1919 after its three-year absence. (M1629, Royal Hampshire Regiment Museum)

despite his frustration had to spend another three weeks in hospital until he was told one day at breakfast 'grab your kit, the gharri's here', and he left Bombay that morning.[14]

Their voyages home presented a contrast to those that took them to India three or even five years before. When the transport *Stephan* left Bombay on 16 September, a band played the National Anthem. Oswald Early, one of its passengers, wrote that they 'simply made cat calls and laughed'.[15] Conditions on the voyage were worse than the journey out. Arthur Bell, who left Deolali at Christmas 1919 described his vessel as 'the 'flu ship', and when the troops learned that it had no canteen the fed-up troops (many Territorials) almost rioted.[16] Christopher Mills, who wrote about Bert Rendall's experience in the 2/5th Somerset and later as a driver, quoted Bert describing his voyage home in late 1919. Aboard the *China* officers commandeered a large area of deck (as they had in the *Ionian* in 1914). This time, with five years' service behind them, Rendall recalled 'we were having none of it'. In the Red Sea a gunner loudly asked 'Will we stand for this, boys?' and they cut the ropes marking the forbidden area. 'Have a care, sir', a gunner warned, 'we're all on our way home'. After 'a stand up hamjam' with men throwing musical instruments overboard, the officers conceded the issue and the ropes were removed.[17]

As some of the returning troops' transports passed through the Suez Canal they encountered ships carrying drafts to form India's post-war garrison. Naturally, 'a lot of chaff' passed between

14 Ted Holter, 'A Terrier in World War I', Doc 4545, 81/9/1, IWM
15 Diary, 16 September 1919, Oswald Early, formerly 1/9th Hants, Early, *The Messenger*, p. 159
16 'RF & MP', 'Scenes of India during the First World War', *Queen's Royal Surrey Regiment Newsletter*, SHC, Woking
17 Recollections of Bert Rendall, Mills, *A Strange War*, pp. 123-24

Mrs Fanny Say laying flowers at Trowbridge's new war memorial in memory of her son John, whose name appears on the plinth above the wreath. (SBYRW25912, Rifles Berkshire and Wiltshire Museum)

the ships. 'One fellow', Oswald Early wrote, perhaps remembering the Regulars' rebuke in 1914 that they were 'going the wrong way', shouted to the newcomers 'they were five years too late'.[18]

Units detailed to join the occupation of Germany were demobilised more swiftly than those in India. The 2/4th Somerset, which served in the Army of Occupation in Germany, was disbanded in May 1919, long before most of the other 'Indian' Territorial units were released. Some Territorial units in Palestine also got home in mid-1919, but the Egyptian rebellion also caused troops to be detailed, and as the 1/4th Wilts even sent a detachment to Gebeit, near Khartoum in the Sudan, the last cadre did not return to Trowbridge until a year after the war's end. Units in Mesopotamia came home even later. The 1/5th West Kent left Mosul on 27 November 1919, travelling by lorry, rail, barge and ship, reaching Bombay on 31 December and returning to Plymouth on 22 January 1920. On the very day the transport arrived its colonel, Lieutenant-Colonel C. Douglas Clark, died of illness.

'Killed, wounded and other': Territorial casualties

Colonel Clark was one of perhaps two thousand Territorials who did not return to Britain out of the more than fifty thousand who had left. Indian service imposed a cost on every unit and, indeed, every individual. Establishing exactly the cost in each case is surprisingly complicated. For individuals, details of the effects on men's health in later decades lies in medical or pension

---

18   Diary, 29 September 1919, Oswald Early, formerly 1/9th Hants, Early, *The Messenger*, p. 165

records, unavailable for this book. For units, it is clear that losses occurred because of transfers and drafts as well as wounds and illness. The figures for 1/7th Hants suggest the Territorial battalions' mobility. It had arrived 800 strong and received 680 men in reinforcement drafts. It had lost 200 men to sister battalions in Mesopotamia, 130 to various transfers (to the Supply and Transport Corps or to signals) and 40 to Garrison battalions (unfit men were posted to sedentary units rather than invalided home). Thirty men had been commissioned and a further hundred had been invalided or had died.[19] When it returned from Aden in 1919 just sixty of its original '1914' men remained.

Indian territorials' total fatal casualties are not easily computed. While battalion histories, casualty returns, cemetery registers and memorial plaques often give precise figures, they remain indicative across the forty-one battalions and twenty-nine batteries. The casualties of units which saw action beyond India are almost impossible to specify, not least because the status of individuals is impossible to establish, especially for members who volunteered for drafts to other battalions. The only reliable conclusion is that casualties among units which saw service were heavy. The 1/4th Hants, which had served in Mesopotamia from April 1915 to beyond the war's end Persia and Transcaspia, lost 20 officers in action and 700 other ranks – virtually the entire strength of the battalion.

The 1/6th East Surrey (which served in India throughout except for eleven months in Aden) seems to be representative. It lost 74 dead:

16 killed or died of wounds (most in Mesopotamia; 5 in Aden)
12 died as prisoners of war of the Turks, most after being captured at Kut
12 died of disease (10 in Mesopotamia, 1 at Tank on the Frontier; 1 at Aden)
1 man accidentally drowned
1 man shot by rifle thieves
1 man accidentally shot
30 died of disease in India.[20]

Establishing exactly how many Territorials died *in India* is relatively straightforward, though complicated by the difficulty of confirming the identity of Territorial gunners transferred to other Royal Artillery units. Totting up the Territorial *infantry* in the Imperial (later Commonwealth) War Graves Commission cemetery registers discloses that just under a thousand Territorial infantry were buried or commemorated in India and Burma, and a further 90 in its satellite campaigns and deployments (to Aden, Siberia and North-West Persia). Counting exactly how many Territorials died in Mesopotamia, Palestine and France is practically impossible, but it must total at least as many again. The battalions and batteries that remained in India for the entire war lost about 600 dead, though the most severe losses occurred in the 2/6th Royal Sussex, which alone lost almost a hundred men killed, and it arrived only in 1916. Even so, after the war, Indian Territorials came to realise that the order to go to India had been 'the equivalent of a reprieve from a very early death for many of us'.[21] How many had Indian service spared? In that a death rate of about 20% prevailed on the Western Front – and a greater rate for 1914

19 Atkinson, *The Royal Hampshire Regiment*, Vol. II, p. 442
20 'The East Surrey Regiment in India 1914-19', ESR/10/14/3/1, SHC, Woking
21 Blick, *The 1/4th Battalion The Wiltshire Regiment*, p. 15

men – it seems reasonable to calculate that had the Territorial divisions gone to France, as their members had wished, then notionally perhaps 10,000 of them might have died. Being ordered to India might have saved the lives of more than eight thousand men.

'Come from India's shore': Territorials return

Reflecting their local origins and connections, many battalions were welcomed at civic receptions. The Surrey battalions were welcomed at Guildford (for the West Surrey) and Kingston (for the East Surrey) when they returned in 1919. Speakers – the lord lieutenant, mayors and other county worthies – made fittingly appreciative speeches ('it was the white men who held [India] for the Empire') and consoled them for having to stay overseas for an extra year ('hard luck') but their return could have passed unnoticed except by men's families.[22] In Portsmouth the 1/6th Hants were welcomed at a reception at the Town Hall on 30 December 1919. Before a rostrum decorated with bunting, greenery and a banner 'Home, Sweet Home', the Earl of Selborne welcomed them back, with mixed feelings, perhaps.[23] Two of his sons had served in the battalion: one, Robert Palmer, had been killed in Mesopotamia.

Former prisoners of war generally returned unobtrusively as individuals, but so many Hants Territorials had been captured at Kut – though so few had survived – that the 1/4th Battalion Comforts Fund welcomed them at a dinner in Winchester's Guildhall in 1919. Hosted by Esme Bowker, their former colonel's widow, the men were treated to dishes including somewhat tactlessly named Steak and Kidney Pie (Busra Flavour), Kut Grass, Roots [vegetables] and 'Plum Pudding and Tigris Water Sauce [custard].[24] The 1/4th Hants had been reunited in Zinjan in 1919 from where '1914' drafts left for home, returning by the exotic route via the Caspian Sea, the Caucasus mountains, the Black Sea and then by ship, through the Dardanelles and the Mediterranean. Not until October 1919 did the rest of the battalion travel by lorry across Persia to Quarib in Mesopotamia, then by train to Kut, by river to Basra, arriving in Bombay by 28 November. It did not reach Plymouth until January 1920. A small cadre of three officers and six non-commissioned officers (and one private) travelled to Winchester to be formally welcomed.

The Territorials returning from India were indeed among the last to be demobilised – by early 1920 over 90% of the wartime army had preceded them.[25] Men stepped out of the 'Dispersal stations' wearing a suit of civilian clothes – jacket, waistcoat and trousers, and a greatcoat (welcome when most Indian Territorials arrived home in the winter of 1919-20). Other ranks, on the assumption that they were working men, were given cloth caps rather than hats, and, until men objected, mufflers, later neckties (a further sign, if it were needed, of the Territorials' complex social composition). Some carried their Indian cotton uniforms home, wrapped in a brown paper parcel, though they were hardly to be used.[26] Not many men showed a profit at the end of four years' service. Lance-Sergeant Charles Clinker, who left the 1/6th Hants after five years in India and Mesopotamia was given £18 at the Fovant demobilisation depot (and a

---

22 *Surrey Advertiser*, 20 May 1919; 15 November 1919
23 *The Hampshire Regimental Journal*, January 1920, p. 8
24 Unidentified clippings, Esme Bowker papers, M1539, RHRM
25 Beckett, 'The Nation in Arms' in Beckett & Simpson, (eds), *A Nation in Arms*, p. 26
26 'Provision of clothing for soldiers on discharge', WO163/22, NAUK

greatcoat worth a pound) and three payments of about £10 each at the post office in his home village in the three months following his return.

For weeks after the battalions' formal return detached men came home from other fronts – Somerset men were recorded as arriving from Persia, China, Mesopotamia and elsewhere in India and Burma. By early in 1920 the remaining office staff in the county Territorial association offices were able to close their books. Though fêted on their return at civic receptions and luncheons, the Territorial battalions soon dispersed. Arriving home in Yeovil, Bert Rendall recalled how he experienced 'mixed feelings, between crying like a baby and being the brave soldier at the prospects of meeting my folks again'.[27]

Sir Charles Monro made sure that he wrote to all departing battalions, thanking them for their 'self-sacrifice', sympathizing with them in the disappointment many felt in missing more active service and that many had endured 'the somewhat dull routine of garrison duty'. He especially acknowledged the stress they had been subjected to in awaiting repatriation. His messages to different battalions were almost word-for-word the same.[28]

Just as the last Territorial units left India, someone in the Government of India belatedly thought of thanking them for their service. On the last day of 1919 Lord Chelmsford and his Council agreed to commend the Territorials who had garrisoned India. The Viceroy approved the printing of an elaborate testimonial to 'place on record his high appreciation of the services which these Units have rendered to the Empire'. Chelmsford paid tribute to their patriotism in joining the Territorial Force before 1914 and for volunteering to serve overseas (as he himself had). He sympathised with their 'disappointment' in being denied the opportunity to serve in Europe, but acknowledged that many had served in Mesopotamia, Egypt, Palestine, Aden and on the North-West Frontier, and thanked all for the 'faithful performance of garrison duties'. He praised the Territorials for having displayed 'soldierly qualities of the highest order' and for the 'efficiency, discipline and exemplary conduct' which had, he wrote, won the 'respect and affection' of British and Indian comrades and of 'the people of India as a whole' – the latter plainly a gross distortion of the truth. Finally, he acknowledged the patience with which they accepted the delays in their repatriation. While the resolution was published in the *Gazette of India*, the actual testimonials were distributed only to commanders of battalions, some now far from India.[29] It seems likely that many if not most of the men Chelmsford had praised did not know of or read his proclamation.

The Territorial Force's contribution to the war, and to ultimate victory, vindicated Haldane's vision for the force a decade before the Armistice. In 1908 Charles à Court Repington, the influential Military Correspondent for *The Times*, had foreseen its value:

> A second-line army of young soldiers under good, young, active officers, the whole recruited from among the intelligent classes of the community, gains in military value and cohesion with every day's training after mobilization.[30]

---

27   Recollections of Bert Rendall, Mills, *A Strange War*, p. 125
28   See, for example, messages to the 1/6th East Surrey on 3 October ('A History of the 1/6th The East Surrey Regiment in India and Aden 1914-1919', ESR/10/14/3/1, SHC, Woking) and the 2/5th Somerset on 27 October (Anon, *The Book of Remembrance*, p. 106)
29   Resolution of the Government of India No. 17406, 31 December 1919, 1994-02-27, NAM
30   [Repington], *The Foundations of Reform*, p. 342

And so it had proved. The Indian Territorials, while they felt disregarded and slighted for much of their first two years in India, did by the end of 1916 possess a 'military value', and demonstrated it on active service in Aden, in Mesopotamia, Palestine and in France and, indeed, on India's North-West Frontier and in the Afghan War. By the war's end all the Territorial battalions had seen either active service or internal security duty: exactly what they had gone to do in 1914.

Even during the war few people in Britain realised what Territorials had done in India. Despite the creation of a massive system of war correspondents and censorship, creating and managing the news allowed to be read, no such propaganda machine extolled the Territorial's part. Henry Brain of the East Surreys copied into his note book a bitter verse imagining a patriotic 'Lady' visiting men in hospital and asking if they had been wounded in France. It expressed the Territorials' sense that they had been overlooked and slighted:

> Oh no Madam was the answer, I have come from India's shore
> I had a lot of sickness there and been invalided from Peshawar
> Oh indeed, the lady answered, as she quickly turned away
> These flowers are for the wounded only, I will wish you good day ...[31]

Territorial service in India had given men experiences, skills and perspectives they could never have gained in contemporary Britain. Owen Smith's line in a letter to his sister 'I went to a most delightful Tennis Party at the vicarage yesterday' sounds incongruous, not just for a corporal in a military cantonment, but also for the 'counter-jumper' he had been at home in Portsmouth before the war: not that he survived the war.[32] But in India men had shared bungalows with comrades of different classes, learned middle-class sports such as tennis, or gained marketable skills. For several hundred men it gave them the experience of becoming commissioned officers, a future none could have imagined as citizen soldiers before the war.

However much men had learned new skills (such as driving or typing), found confidence in leadership or satisfaction in comradeship, the war represented a waste of time, delaying marriage or careers. At 23 years old, Reg Howgego was given a 'Certificate of Employment During the War'. There was little call for the skills of scouting and bombing in Ipswich, though a reference certifying that he had been 'a very excellent NCO and competent instructor' may have helped him find a job in 1920.[33] Because they arrived home long after most wartime troops had been demobilised, many faced, as an Indian Territorial put it, 'endless queuing outside Labour Exchanges' in the post-war slump.[34] Some believed that their Indian service had harmed their prospects. One former officer told a politician that he could '... not help feeling that the fact I am a 'territorial' instead of a 'Kitchener' makes it much more difficult to get a decent job'.[35] Some battalion associations established funds to assist former comrades out of work – the 1/9th Hants used unexpended regimental funds as the basis for a Trust for that purpose.

---

31 Memoir, Henry Brain, 1/6th East Surrey, ESR/25/BRAIN/2, SHC, Woking
32 Letter, 28 September 1916, Owen Smith, 1/6th Hants, M766, RHRM
33 'Certificate of Employment During the War', Reg Howgego, 1/25th London, Mss.Eur.C340/2, BL
34 Anon, 'War-time Wanderings of the 1/4th Battalion, Hampshire Regiment', p. 26, M3910, RHRM
35 Dennis, *The Territorial Army 1906-1940*, p. 53

Ridgewell anticipates one of the difficulties returning Territorials might face. A Territorial veteran asks for 'a Burra Char and Rote Mukun – and Jeldy!' – buttered toast and tea quickly! (*Indian Ink*)

The material and symbolic rewards of the Territorials' service were meagre. Henry Brain, a leather dresser from south-west London, served in the 1/6th East Surrey from November 1915, in Rawalpindi, Aden and Agra. He qualified for a war gratuity of just Rs330 – about £22 in 1919 prices – and one medal, the British War Medal. A 1919 proposal to strike a Territorial Force Medal for men who had embarked in 1914 and 1915 but who did not reach a theatre of war resulted in 1920 in a Territorial War Medal being issued to 33,000 men (and a few Territorial Nurses) who had been in uniform on 3 August 1914 and who volunteered for overseas service. The rules governing eligibility were strictly enforced. The 1/6th Devon appears to have missed out on the 1914-15 Star by arriving in India three days after the cut-off date.[36] Only units that saw active service, such as the 1/1st Brecknock in Aden, received the 1915 Star: volunteering in 1914 or serving overseas was not relevant; service in a war zone was the only criterion. While troops had understood in 1914 that they would share in 'all the Honours of the War', they were disappointed. Several MPs representing constituencies in the southern counties took up the cause in Parliament, quoting Kitchener and listing various battalions' services, but to no avail. Major-General Colin Donald, to whom Kitchener had made his promise, lobbied and Parliament considered the matter, but their claim was rejected. 'I can only say that they are very sore about it', Donald said bitterly in 1922.[37]

At the time service in India was represented, even by government ministers who ought to have been better informed, as a cushy option. Andrew Bonar Law, the Lord Privy Seal, while he had been quoted in the *Bombay Chronicle* affirming that Territorials in India had been the 'worst used', in Cabinet said that they had 'escaped all active duty and had saved their skin'.[38] Some eventually read official thanks. Frank Johnson, who had commanded the 2/6th Royal Sussex, had received a copy of the Government of India's 'Resolution of Thanks' scroll, along with other commanding officers. With demobilisation over, Johnson decided that men of his former battalion might like a copy. He arranged for duplicates to be printed, though owing to an error they sat in a cupboard in his office for three years. At last, early in 1924 he posted them out to addresses provided by the battalion's 'Old Comrades' Association. Three years after the 2/6th at last came home, men received a reminder of their Indian service. 'Wishing you the best of luck through life', Frank Johnson's covering letter ended.[39]

'A shaky start': a new Territorial Army

Worry over what people might think of them after the war exacerbated many Indian Territorials' anxieties over seemingly evading doing their bit during the war. From the *Border Gazette*, 1915:

> Young Willie. What did you do Father?
> Father. I held the outpost at Maymyo.
> Y.W. And which part of Germany is that in Father?
> Father. Off to bed at once ...[40]

---

36 *Ibid*
37 Woodyatt, 'The Territorials (Infantry) in India', *JRUSI*, 1922, p. 731
38 *Bombay Chronicle*, 20 March 1919; Dennis, *The Territorial Army 1906-1940*, p. 53, quoting War Cabinet minutes for 28 January 1919, CAB23/9, NAUK
39 'Certificate of Appreciation', E.L. Lloyd, 2/6th Royal Sussex, Misc 207, 3012, IWM
40 Clipping, Lawrence Hoggarth, 1/4th Border, Album 35 Acc. Nos 3024-3345, CMML

In the aftermath of victory the Territorial Force's future remained in the balance. Its members (and those volunteers – and later conscripts – who joined it) had contributed no fewer than 30 of the 75 infantry divisions which served in the war. As the wartime army demobilised the government and the War Office grappled with the responsibilities of peace it became clear that a part-time citizen force would again be needed. Even before many of the Indian battalions had come home, Churchill announced that a 'Territorial Army' would be raised. He acknowledged the discrimination the Territorials had endured (admitting that Kitchener's by-passing of the Territorials had been an error) and undertook to rectify grievances, such as allowing Territorial officers to command some of the 56 Territorial brigades envisaged. Regular officers, however, disagreed on the way in which Territorials could reinforce or support the Regular army overseas and the wrangling continued into 1920, with Regulars and County Associations rehearsing grievances, fears and slights going back to 1906. In 1921 a renewed Territorial Army at last came into existence, though again only after the King had appealed to the County Associations to overcome the mistrust they felt: as Peter Dennis put it, 'a shaky start'.[41]

In January 1919 Lloyd George's Cabinet decided that Britain needed a force of 900,000 men to resume the burden of defending Britain, occupying the Rhineland, prosecuting a war against Bolshevik Russia and garrisoning a larger empire, including troublesome regions such as Mesopotamia and the Middle East and, as ever, 'the far north of India'.[42] The War Office's failure to affirm that a Territorial Force would be valued depressed the force's members, and recruiting dragged accordingly. The 4th Dorset had reached less than a quarter of its establishment by 1 January 1921; the 5th East Surrey's records show a steady decline through the 1920s, with members in Leatherhead numbering just 27, compared to the strong contingent before the war.[43]

'When the boys come home': memories

'You will never forget your various experiences in India', a friend assured Cornelius Scarrott, a Sussex man serving with the 1/5th West Kent in 1917.[44] She had thrilled at the postcards he had sent to Small Dole, a village on the downs north of Brighton, and had followed his movements on a map. On the voyage home late in 1919 Albert Bray reflected on what he and fellow Cornwalls would *not* miss about India: 'its intense heat, its sweltering plains, its flies, mosquitoes, scorpions and centipedes; its dust storms and monsoons; its bazaar odours; its doubtful dishes; its subtle business systems …' and so on. At the same time, Albert and many others regarded their time in India as 'an invaluable education'. He appreciated having had 'the opportunity of catching a glimpse of the fringe of Indian life', and thought that it was 'bound to widen our respect' with its people.[45]

At the time, Territorials expected Indian service to change them. In *Indian Ink*, a series of annuals published in aid of the Imperial Indian War Fund, the cartoonist Ridgewell, possibly

---

41 Dennis, *The Territorial Army 1906-1940*, pp. 47-52; 56-63
42 *Sydney Morning Herald*, 31 January 1919, p. 7
43 Report, 1930, 5th East Surrey Unidentified clippings, 1984-11-110-2, NAM
44 Letter, 5 July 1917, Cornelius Scarrott, 1/5th West Kent, AM 719/1/4, WSRO
45 Albert Bray, 'Brief notes on service', pp. 5-6, B.4289, CRM

himself a Territorial, contributed a cartoon depicting an Indian Territorial in a 'West End Tea Shop' in London 'when the boys come home again'. In it, a nattily-dressed gentleman addresses a puzzled waitress: 'I say, would you mind getting me a Burra Char and Rote Mukum [a large tea and buttered bread] – and Jeldy [quickly]!'[46] Ridgewell imagined a scene that for most Territorials could not take place for another four years, but he presumed that they would be so imbued with Indian language that they would turn to it once they went home. Owen Smith anticipated that after he came home, he would often use the expression 'It'll do peachy' – 'meaning presently' or 'bye & bye'.[47] (Sadly, Owen did not return.) War service unsettled many men. Even in 1916 Geoffrey Coombs confessed to his pen-friend Lillian how 'I do not think I shall settle down to the hum-drum of the life I lived before the war'.[48]

One of the recruiting posters with which Shropshire men had been confronted in 1915 had pictured an old man sitting disconsolately in 1965, holding his head in hands while be-medalled contemporaries talked animatedly in an adjoining room. 'How will you fare', it asked, 'When you sit by the fire in an old man's chair and your neighbours talk of the fight?'[49] In fact, while from 1964 the fiftieth anniversary of the Great War's outbreak saw an unprecedented outpouring of memoirs, books and television documentaries, the voices of Indian Territorials were practically absent. Except for a couple of officers' memoirs or books based on letters, no Indian Territorials' memories appeared, nor would they for decades.

But memories remained. When former Territorials did speak of their service, as Adolphus Jupe did to a community group in 1959, some were embarrassed to admit, as he did, that 'my 5½ years in uniform were the happiest years of my life'.[50] Those who had served in Mesopotamia had a rather less romantic recollection. Ted Rice of the West Surrey wrote a long memoir in the 1960s, to present 'a view of the campaign as seen through the eye of a private soldier'. Nearly fifty years on, Ted was still outraged by the 'gross negligence, deliberate concealment of the truth, incompetence in high places, [and] total disregard for the treatment of sick and wounded', as exposed by the Mesopotamia Commission.[51] In writing their memoirs (as many did – with several in most regimental collections) men mused on the epic journey on which the war had taken them. Hampshire student Victor Manley, among the most loquacious of the Terriers, described his diary as 'really a travelogue'. It carried him (and his readers, had any the stamina to keep up) 'to the far-off, barren mountain lands of the North West Frontier to the well-watered [Punjab] and Mogul palaces of Delhi …'.[52]

The degree to which service in India became a part of local remembrance largely depended on the proportion of county battalions that carried a memory of it. To take the most extreme example, as only one of the London Regiment's more than forty battalions that saw overseas service, the 1/25th's was hardly going to make an impact against the dominant experience of the Western Front. At the other extreme, as eight out of eighteen Hampshire battalions that served overseas saw service in India, it might have retained a presence in local remembrance.

46 'When the boys come home again', Digby, *Indian Ink* [1915], np
47 Letter, 20 December 1915, Owen Smith, 1/6th Hants, M766, RHRM
48 Letter, 21 March 1916, Geoffrey Coombs, 1/4th Buffs, EK/U127/2, KH&AC
49 Recruiting poster, 1915, 3614/2/166, SA
50 Adolphus Jupe, 'Round the World with the "P.B.I."', M1629, RHRM
51 Ted Rice, 'All for a Shilling a Day', QRWS/30/RICE/1, SHC, Woking
52 Preface, Victor Manley, 'A Khaki Diary', 49M91W/Q3/6, HRO

Against these raw figures needs to be set the fact that fewer than a third of the Territorial battalions remained in India for the entire war, and that service in other theatres caused the losses which were naturally a prime motive for remembrance. Thus it was only in Hampshire (and perhaps Devon, which had 5 out of 14 battalions in India) that it might have figured in local remembrance.[53]

India, however, became a presence in many former Territorials' homes. (Joseph Sturgess, who had missed his children so strongly while staying at Jalapahar, near Darjeeling, in 1918, after the war actually named his house in Portchester 'Darjeeling'.) While a Wiltshire officer declared (early in 1915) that 'he wasn't going to take back any mementoes of the d____d country', almost every other man sent home photographs and souvenirs.[54] Harry Canham sent home a parcel with a sandalwood box, brass ashtrays, lace doilies, elephant charms, packets of postcards and sundry 'curios'.[55] Owen Smith also detailed a shipment in 1916 that cost him over 30 shillings to despatch. It too contained inlaid marble paperweights, brass cups and elephants, a wooden snake, cobra candlesticks and pairs of sandals.[56] Their letters and diaries contained odd souvenirs of India – dried jonquils (from the garden of the Taj Mahal sent home to Trowbridge); the wing of a locust (one of a huge swarm that passed over Alfred Cornell's Somerset comrades at Meerut in July 1916). Arthur Copeland pasted into his diary the centre of a target into which he put four neat holes, and men preserved various badges, flashes and stripes from their uniforms. Bert Rendall, who served in Burma for two years, later spent seven years making a model of the Shwe Dagon Pagoda. The house in which he lived in old age in Yeovil was adorned with photographs of the Khyber Pass, brightly polished Indian brass-work and cobra candlesticks, souvenirs of the five years he spent in India and Burma. Victor Manley brought home not tourist souvenirs, but artefacts such as clay pipes, purchased from potters in the remote villages he visited, often alone: 'my long-delayed wish to ramble freely in the Bolan Pass was at last fulfilled', he had written in September 1916.[57] In 1936 he donated the artefacts he had collected to the Cambridge Archaeological Museum.[58] Those who returned with photograph albums had a means to keep memories alive (and the thousands of images in them today constitute some of the most vivid evidence of the Terriers' time in India).

India lived in family memories, for a time. Keith Solomon described how his father, Francis, a Bodmin coach-painter, had served with the 1/4th Cornwall in India 1914-16 (nicknamed 'Striper', from one of his essential professional skills). 'Striper' Solomon had also served in Aden and Palestine, but it was his Indian service that made the greatest impact on him. After the war, as well as continuing in his trade, he co-ran a pub in Bodmin, The Masons Arms. The pub became the focus of informal gatherings in which Striper and several fellow Indian Territorials met to reminisce. Keith remembered that 'to exclude would be interlopers' they spoke in the Hindustani they had learned in India. Keith recalled that he and his brothers 'became fairly

---

53   The numbers of battalions serving overseas has been established using the battalion summaries on the excellent website The Long, Long Trail: http://www.longlongtrail.co.uk/
54   Gale, *With the 2/4th Wilts to India*, p. 36
55   Letter, nd, Harry Canham, 2/4th Border, CMML
56   Letter, 10 March 1916, Owen Smith, 1/6th Hants, M766, RHRM
57   Diary, 26 September 1916, Victor Manley, 'A Khaki Diary', 49M91W/Q3/6, HRO
58   I am grateful to Dr Mark Elliott of the CAM who responded to an appeal circulated by Ms Emily Gibbs, my research assistant. It resulted in Manley's journal being connected with his artefacts.

proficient in the Bazaar Bat'.[59] Long after the war Ernest Chant, who had served with the 2/5th Somerset, intrigued his grandson, Christopher, by using Indian words ('there was the milk wallah and the bread wallah, the insurance wallah, the post wallah and so on') to the point that Christopher wrote the one of the few books to deal with Territorials' experience. Christopher heard 'mysterious stories of Burma and India, of Gurkhas and ruby mines, rupees, tigers and snake charmers'.[60] The granddaughter of a Cornish veteran remembered that 'he often came out with Hindi [or Arabic] phrases', especially 'imshi' – hurry up.[61]

India lived long in men's memories. Edward Read, who had survived dysentery in Mesopotamia, served in 1919 in an office in Poona. In the last weeks of his life, in 1987, he recalled a day off he was given in 1919 when he caught a train from Poona to spend a day visiting the Karla caves, a Buddhist site about 40 miles north-west of Poona. He spent the day walking in the hills, a sign of how comfortable he had become in being alone in the country, even when unrest gripped India's cities.[62] But even those who revelled in the experience, such as Ted Holter, who wrote a memoir of his Indian service as a Territorial gunner, did not necessarily wish to repeat the experience. Ted married his sweetheart in London (who had waited for him) but refused to travel again: 'call me a coward if you like but I never left my native Sussex again'.[63]

'I wonder where the boys have gone': reunions

Former East Surrey Territorials remembered how one day on the frontier their signallers had practised semaphore by exchanging messages concocting an imaginary menu for a dinner at a London hotel. A decade later, they recalled, they met at a hotel for just such a dinner, recalling their Indian service in 'breezy and reminiscent' tone.[64] Former members of the 1/1st Kent also formed an 'Old Pals' body while still on service. The editor of *The Invicta* anticipated that in years to come men would think, 'Ah! I remember India … I wonder where the boys have gone?'[65] The 1/1st Kent formed no fewer than three 'old comrades' associations, for officers, sergeants and other ranks, which amalgamated in 1929. Two hundred of the 1/9th Hants still met annually in 1959, and the survivors of a company of the 1/4th Hants met in Basingstoke in 1964 to mark the 50th anniversary of their departure from Southampton. With two Duke of Cornwall's Light Infantry battalions having served in India (a quarter its battalions serving overseas) Indian Territorials were a large proportion of the county's Great War veterans, and in the 1920s reunions of up to 500 men were held in Truro.[66]

Likewise, East Surrey veterans held reunions in The Greyhound Hotel in Croydon in the late 1920s and early 1930s, like many 'Indian' Territorial units sustained by the continuation of their battalion in a renewed but often hardly flourishing Territorial Army. In an atmosphere of good

---

59   email from Keith Solomon, 30 May 2017
60   Mills, *A Strange War*, p. 2
61   Email from Liz Hocking, May 2017
62   Edward Read, 'Hampshire to the Himalayas', p. 7, M1798, RHRM
63   Ted Holter, 'A Terrier in World War I', Doc 4545, 81/9/1, IWM
64   *The Herald* [Croydon?], 2 March 1928, in Press cuttings 5th East Surrey, 1984-11-110-2, NAM
65   *The Invicta*, Vol. III, No. 1, June 1918, pp. 30-31
66   email from Mr Keith Solomon, 30 May 2017, quoting *The Cornish Times*, 25 October 1925

cheer, lubricated by drink and wreathed in smoke, men laughed indulgently at speeches by their former officers. But as men aged and became more frail, most associations withered and eventually died. Only the 1/1st Kent survived, by mutating into the Sons of Kent Cyclist Battalions association in 1954, and that was sustained mostly by the sons of members of the two other Kent cyclist battalions, which had served in France and therefore had more members. The fathers' and sons' associations amalgamated in 1979. By 1985 there were just 22 former members of the 1/1st Kent on the association's roll.[67]

One day, though, Adolphus Jupe mused in 1959, 'an aged reveller' would arrive for a reunion of his battalion – in Jupe's case, the 1/9th Hants – only to find the room empty and silent, realising that he was the last survivor of the thousand men who had served in India. That man, Jupe decided, 'will dine in the solitary splendor of the last survivor and drink a melancholy toast to friends, now only too truly, absent'.[68]

'A place in the sun': regimental histories and museums

At a reunion in Croydon in 1928 Lieutenant-Colonel Ralph Harvey, who had commanded the 1/5th East Surrey throughout its service in India, told his men that after they had all died, 'no doubt historians … would write page by page of what the Territorials did in the Great War', but acknowledged that 'it would not interest them very much'.[69] Colonel Harvey was, of course, correct in his modest appreciation of how the Territorials' war would, or rather would not, be recorded, but not about its interest. In a war of such magnitude – a Great War – the Territorials' services gained scant recognition. That they should have been ignored by the nation at large is hardly surprising: the Wiltshire Indian battalions' dead constituted about 1% of the 4767 men killed in its battalions.[70] What is somewhat curious is the extent to which their regimental communities failed to even notice their contribution. On average, the regimental histories of the Indian Terriers' battalions devote about three pages to them. The history of Somerset Territorials devoted just two paragraphs to the first two years the 1/5th Somerset spent in India – it was 'in no way different from those employed on garrison duty in our great Eastern Empire'.[71] The first wartime history of the Duke of Cornwall's Light Infantry lamented that 'too little recognition was given them for their unselfish devotion to duty': but that was the only mention made of it.[72] The omission induced former officers of the Somerset Light Infantry to publish a handsome memorial book in 1930, but they were one of a handful.[73]

The Territorials' units returned with precious few souvenirs of their time in India. Though the 1920s and '30s saw the creation and growth of regimental museums, mainly in their depots, they acquired few Territorial artefacts. The 1/4th West Kent returned with Afghan drums as a reminder of its active service in 1919, and officers' and sergeants' messes of the Border Regiment

---

67 Bristow, 'The Kent Cyclist Battalion', p. 4
68 Adolphus Jupe, 'Round the World with the "P.B.I.", p. 18, M1629, RHRM
69 *The Herald* [Croydon?], 2 March 1928, in Press cuttings 5th East Surrey, 1984-11-110-2, NAM
70 Vernon, *Our Glorious Dead*, p. 84
71 Fisher, *The History of Somerset Yeomanry, Volunteers and Territorials*, p. 224
72 Wyrall, *The History of the Duke of Cornwall's Light Infantry*, p. 80
73 Anon, *The Book of Remembrance*

acquired some regimental silver and ivory items from its battalions' Burma service. In due course several regimental museums obtained sola topees with their coloured flashes and items such as the 'khud' or 'swagger' sticks many men had brought home as souvenirs. As a result, some regimental collections, such as the Shropshire and Hampshire museums, now include small showcases at least alluding to their Territorial battalions' service. Most, however, like their regimental histories, barely refer to the service of several thousand men for several years, focusing on the Western Front, for obvious reasons.

Rawstone Lamplugh of the 1/1st Kent, who had been a mainstay of its magazine *The Invicta*, published in the tedious months between the end of the Afghan campaign and the battalion's eventual repatriation 'A Narrative', which in verse celebrated his comrades' service on the frontier and lamented their lot in awaiting orders for home. Lamplugh admitted that the lion's share of credit would go to those who had fought on the Western and other fronts: 'Good luck to those who did well in the fray', he wrote, 'All honour to them for the work they have done'. But he wanted to ensure that the 1/1st Kent also gained 'a place in the sun':

> The historian, however, can put to their score,
> The marching of one thousand miles, yes, and more,
> Four times on the Frontier, three years in the East,
> And a war when the Great War in Europe had ceased.[74]

This historian is glad to have been able to fulfil Lamplugh's desire.

---

74 Bristow, 'The Kent Cyclist Battalion', p. 112

Epilogue

'Almost impossible to trace'

The Territorials returned under no illusion that their contribution to the war had been or would be noticed. A sceptical 'Retrospect' published by a confessed 'fed up' Kent man in 1919 observed that 'it was our affair to help keep this edge of the Empire intact … The fact that nobody noticed us doesn't count much, after all'.[1] Hardly anyone, besides the men returning from India and their families, knew much of what they had experienced and achieved during the war. Even Nigel Woodyatt, whose 1922 memoir, *Under Ten Viceroys*, devoted a chapter to them, advised his readers that if they found the subject 'dull … I hope they will skip the chapter altogether'.[2]

Finding the Terriers in India today demands some persistence. Because they lived in cantonments mainly still inhabited and used by the notoriously security-conscious and camera-shy Indian army, photographing their former stations can be difficult. But seeing the immense 'bungalows' in which they lived, the churches in which they worshipped (still with their cut-outs in which to place rifles) and the sudder bazaars in which they mingled with Indians remains rewarding. Some of India's major tourist sites are close to cantonments. Agra Fort is accessible, though its barracks are not. Visitors enter Delhi's Red Fort through the Lahore Gate, whose bazaar was, Fred Mundy wrote, 'used a great deal by the soldiers', while the adjacent Selimgargh Fort, where Fred was stationed early in 1915, is virtually as it was in the Great War.[3] British soldiers are also present in India's churches, some of which include memorials to men who died while in garrison (such as the memorial to Captain Fritz Bartelt in St Luke's Dinapore, or the large brass panel Edward Cockcroft arranged for the Brecknock battalion to leave in Mhow). Finding them and gaining entry to them sometimes requires enterprise and persistence, but they are often moving reminders of those who gave their lives in India.

Likewise graves can be found in cantonment cemeteries, now in the custody of the Commonwealth War Graves Commission. The idea for this book occurred to me in October 2012 in the cantonment cemetery of Ferozepore, in the Punjab, when I noticed the graves of Buffs, Surrey, Devon and Cornwall infantrymen, Kent, Surrey and Hants cyclists and Surrey Territorial gunners. Some cemeteries, in New Delhi cantonment, the Khadki cemetery in Pune and Bhowanipore (Kolkata), for example, are beautifully cared for. Less-frequented cemeteries – the majority – as at Dagshaie, Dinapore, Benares and Allahabad, were largely neglected, locked,

---

1 *The Invicta*, Vol. III, No. 4, 1919, p. 62
2 Woodyatt, *Under Ten Viceroys*, p. 256
3 Mundy, *A Journal of the 1/4th Battalion Wiltshire Regiment*, p. 25

choked with vegetation and littered with rubbish respectively. Despite the Commonwealth War Graves Commission's efforts, many Territorial graves are in parlous condition, unvisited from one year to the next. At St Mary's cemetery, in Chennai, where six Territorial graves are cared for amid appalling neglect of those not in the Commission's care, the previous visitors had signed the visitors' book almost a year before me.

In Britain, the Terriers' service in India is commemorated sparsely. Some individuals (such as Fritz Bartelt) are remembered individually (and fully: his family also donated a window and a peal of bells to All Saints, Corston). Some units have individual memorials, such as the 1/25th London in All Saints, Fulham, while most are mentioned or at least covered by memorials in churches or on municipal or county memorials. On the Hampshire war memorial, in front of Winchester Cathedral, a few hundred yards from both the Hampshire Regiment's depot and its present museum, the regiment's Indian Territorials' service is represented by the words 'MESOPOTAMIA', 'PERSIA' and 'INDIA'. (The memorial was commissioned by the Earl of Selborne, who lost his son, Robert Palmer at Hana in Mesopotamia with the 1/4th Hants.)

Many other regiments dedicated memorials in their home counties to their members who died in India, though most combined them with those who died on active service. Most do not include names – as the Honorary Colonel of the 1/7th Hants said at the dedication of its memorial in a drill hall in Bournemouth (then part of Hampshire), it was 'almost impossible to trace every man ... whom we have lost'.[4] Often memorial plaques were affixed to the walls of drill halls, necessarily seen only by members of the Territorial Army (as it formally became) and lost when they closed as the British army contracted after 1945. But remembering their service cannot compare with the greater scale, and certainly the greater losses, of the Western Front, the Dardanelles or Mesopotamia. Though individually tragic, the scale of their losses is negligible. The Brecknocks, one of the battalions losing heavily in India and Aden – 55 men – represent a tiny proportion of the losses of the South Wales Borderers as a whole, which lost 5777 men in the Great War. But families and former comrades were writing to Edward Cockcroft as late as 1929 to obtain copies of the photograph of it he had publicised in Brecon and Hereford newspapers.

In the decades after 1947 many of the cantonment cemeteries became regarded as 'unable to be maintained' and were either consolidated or were essentially abandoned. So the 629 graves (including 75 Terriers) in Sewri cemetery, in Bombay, were re-located to Kirkee (now Khadki, part of Pune), the remains buried en masse in front of the Cross of Sacrifice and the names inscribed on a memorial, including Sergeant Joseph Hicken of the Brecknocks, whose grave Molyneux Thomas visited as his last duty in India. While the Commonwealth War Graves Commission has recently devoted considerable resources to renovating and documenting Indian cemeteries, many smaller cantonment cemeteries remain in disrepair. The difficulty of maintaining cemeteries in Pakistan, which looks askance on overt manifestations of Christian commemoration, and small or remote Indian cemeteries, often with small or poor congregations, makes the large memorials more important. Memorials to those 'who lie buried in civil and cantonment cemeteries' are maintained at Karachi War Cemetery (Pakistan), Madras War Cemetery (Chennai), Khadki War Cemetery (Pune), and on the great India Gate in New Delhi.

---

4 *The Hampshire Regimental Journal*, November 1921, p. 195

'Left no documentary evidence': Territorial sources

As the Bibliography demonstrates, the sources for a study of the Indian Territorials are abundant. Territorials have not been neglected for a century for want of records on which to base a book: indeed, the sheer quantity of material has been practically overwhelming. Still, the vast bulk of Indian Army documentation was destroyed, sooner or later. (Sooner: when William Villiers-Stuart asked at Army Headquarters for the records of his predecessors as Inspectors-General of Infantry he found that they had 'perhaps wisely left no documentary evidence of their activities'.[5] Later: Partition compelled the break-up of the Indian Army's massively detailed records, which were largely destroyed, one of the minor tragedies of 1947. The Headquarters war diaries available today in the National Archives of India represent a fraction of what had been created.) However, the sources are scattered, dispersed across several national archives and about fifteen regimental and county record offices and heritage centres in Britain.

Unlike most military subjects there is no single 'natural' source: Territorial units in India, because they were not at war, were not required to keep war diaries, the framework source for most military studies: only units on active service in Aden, Mesopotamia, Persia, Siberia and in the third Anglo-Afghan war kept war diaries. Routine regimental records exist for only a few battalions – the 1/4th Wilts's order book was simply 'lost after it was brought back to Trowbridge'.[6] Regimental historians varied in the attention they devoted to the Indian service of their Territorial battalions.

Accordingly, this story has had to be pieced together from a great range of sources in a great variety of repositories. Private records – collections of letters, diaries, memoirs and photograph albums – have been much more important than they might sometimes be regarded. Many of the Terriers' private records are relatively slim – sequences of letters; diaries begun and dropped or intermittently completed. But a large minority are substantial: each regimental collection boasted at least one such detailed and sustained primary source, including the diaries, correspondence and memoirs of individuals quoted throughout this book – Joe Cox, Harry Canham, Owen Smith, Arthur Copeland, Gerald Bonham-Carter, and many others, all of whom would repay closer scrutiny and more extensive quotation than has been possible in this book. As is also apparent from this book, one source that has been much more significant for Territorials has been the photographs men took, which are held in many albums and folders in regimental museums and county archives.

Joe Cox towards the end of his life, a photograph that appeared on the cover of his autobiography, *An Ordinary Working Man's Life Story*.

5 Maxwell, (ed.), *Villiers-Stuart goes to War*, p. 213
6 Blick, *The 1/4th Battalion The Wiltshire Regiment*, p. 7

Some periods are well documented – everyone opened diaries on the voyage out, so novel was life at sea. Less amply documented are the wearisome months of summer. A hundred or so collections of individual correspondence or memoirs may seem a tiny proportion of the 50,000 Territorials who served in India, but they present a coherent and overwhelmingly consistent portrait of what Territorials did in India, and how they responded to it. As Chapter 11 reveals, the only inconsistent theme concerns how men reported how Anglo-Indian civilians treated them. For every soldier who recorded an act of consideration or kindness another described an act of coldness or alienation. But the sheer quantity of letters, diaries or memoirs – complemented by dozens of photograph albums – cumulatively presents a compelling body of evidence.

Astonishingly, almost none of the evidence on which this book is based has been used before. Dozens of collections have only ever been read since their acquisition by the curators and archivists who have cared for them, awaiting the arrival of someone interested in them. Even so, almost every aspect of the experiences with which this book deals would justify more detailed investigation: the composition and particular histories of Territorial units, their experiences in Aden, Burma or Mesopotamia, war on the frontier; above all, perhaps, the Indian responses to the very different British citizen soldiers who served among India's people at a crucial time in its history.

Appendix I

Territorial units in India, 1914-19

Infantry

Forty-one Territorial battalions served in India in the course of the Great War. Some remained in India for just a few months – the first, the 1/4th Shropshire, left in February 1915 – while eight battalions served there for the entire war, remaining until late 1919. Those which served in India for the entire war appear in bold.

1/4th, 1/5th Queen's (Royal West Surrey) Regiment
1/4th, 1/5th Buffs (East Kent Regiment)
1/4th, 1/5th, 1/6th, 2/4th, 2/5th Devonshire Regiment
1/4th, 1/5th, 2/4th, **2/5th** Prince Albert's (Somerset Light Infantry)
1/1st Brecknockshire Battalion, South Wales Borderers
1/5th, **1/6th** East Surrey Regiment
1/4th, **2/4th** Duke of Cornwall's Light Infantry
1/4th, **2/4th** Border Regiment
2/6th Royal Sussex Regiment
1/4th, **1/5th**, 1/6th, **1/7th**, 1/9th, 2/4th, 2/5th, 2/6th, 2/7th Hampshire Regiment
1/4th, 2/4th Dorsetshire Regiment
1/4th, 1/5th Queen's Own (Royal West Kent Regiment)
1/4th King's Shropshire Light Infantry
1/9th, **1/10th** Duke of Cambridge's Own (Middlesex Regiment)
1/4th, **2/4th** Wiltshire Regiment (Duke of Edinburgh's)
1/25th London Regiment
1/1st Kent Cyclist Battalion

Artillery

Territorial batteries arrived in 1914 organised in field brigades which (like infantry formations) were immediately dispersed and rarely re-constituted. In 1916 batteries were re-organised and increasingly integrated into non-Territorial Royal Artillery formations, in India and Mesopotamia.

Appendix I

1st Wessex Brigade
1/1st Hampshire Battery became A Battery, 215th Brigade, RA – Served Mesopotamia
1/2nd Hampshire Battery became B Battery, 215th Brigade, RA – Served Mesopotamia
1/3rd Hampshire Battery, became C Battery, 215th Brigade, RA – Served Mesopotamia

2nd Wessex Brigade
1/4th Hampshire Battery became A Battery, 216th Brigade, RA – Remained in India
1/5th Hampshire Battery became B Battery, 216th Brigade, RA – lost at Kut
1/6th Hampshire Battery became A Battery, 217th Brigade, RA – Remained in India

3rd Wessex Brigade
1/1st Dorset Battery became B Battery, 217th Brigade, RA – Remained in India
1/1st Wiltshire Battery became C Battery, 217th Brigade, RA – Remained in India
1/1st Devonshire Battery became A Battery, 218th Brigade, RA – Remained in India

4th Wessex Brigade
1/2nd Devonshire Battery became B Battery, 218th Brigade, RA – Remained in India
1/3rd Devonshire Battery became C Battery, 218th Brigade, RA – Remained in India

1st Home Counties Brigade
1/1st Sussex Battery became A Battery, 220th Brigade, RA – Served Mesopotamia
1/2ns Sussex Battery became B Battery, 220th Brigade, RA – Served Mesopotamia
1/3rd Sussex Battery became C Battery, 220th Brigade, RA – Served Mesopotamia

2nd Home Counties Brigade
1/4th Sussex Battery became A Battery, 221st Brigade, RA – Served Mesopotamia
1/5th Sussex Battery became B Battery, 221st Brigade, RA – Served Mesopotamia
1/6th Sussex Battery became C Battery, 221st Brigade, RA – Served Mesopotamia

3rd Home Counties (Cinque Ports) Brigade
1/1st Kent Battery became A Battery, 222nd Brigade, RA – Remained in India
1/2nd Kent Battery became B Battery, 222nd Brigade, RA – Remained in India
1/3rd Kent Battery became C Battery, 222nd Brigade, RA – Remained in India

2/1st Wessex Brigade
2/1st Hampshire Battery became A Battery, 225th Brigade, RA – Broken up 1917
2/2nd Hampshire Battery became B Battery, 225th Brigade, RA – Broken up 1917
2/3rd Hampshire Battery became C Battery, 225th Brigade, RA – Broken up 1917

2/2nd Wessex Brigade
2/6th Hampshire Battery became A Battery, 227th Brigade, RA – Remained in India
2/1st Dorset Battery became B Battery, 227th Battery, RA – Remained in India
2/1st Wiltshire Battery became C Battery, 227th Brigade, RA – Remained in India

2/3rd Wessex Brigade
2/1st Devonshire Battery became A Battery 228th Brigade, RA – Broken up 1917
2/2nd Devonshire Battery became B Battery, 228th Brigade, RA – Broken up 1917
2/3rd Devonshire Battery became C Battery, 228th Brigade, RA – Broken up 1917

Appendix II

Glossary

The Army in India used a patois of English, Hindi and Urdu all its own, words which vividly evoke the texture of the Territorials' life in their cantonments. While every effort has been made to explain or define these terms in the text, this glossary may be helpful.

Babu	clerk; generalised to mean 'educated Indian', usually derogatory
Backsheesh	a gift; alms; a tip
Backsheesh day	a holiday (usually Thursday); also 'buckshee'
Bagh	garden
Bat	language
Bhisti	water-carrier
Bobaji	cook
Chai/Char	tea
Chakla	brothel
Charpoy	string-cot
Char-wallah	tea-seller; also 'chai'
Connor	food
Cushney	good
Dacoit/dacoity	thieves or bandits; robbery
Daftar/dufter	office
Dekko	to look, see
Dhobi	launderer
Drabbie	cook
Dudh-wallah	milk-seller
Dufter	office
Durzi	tailor
Juldi	'now!'; 'immediately!'
Lashkar	a tribal force
Looswallah	a thief, especially of rifles

Maidan	a parade or exercise ground
Mouchie	boot-maker (or mender)
Mali	gardener
Mehta	sweeper
Munshi	teacher (especially of language)
Nappi-wallah	barber
Nullah	a gully
Peachy	'presently'; 'soon'
Punka	flapping curtain to cool a barrack-room
Ramsammy	Indian religious festival
Sangar	a stone shelter built by troops on the frontier
Tiffin	lunch (what the troops usually called 'dinner')
Wallah	man

Bibliography

ARCHIVAL RECOREDS

Australia

Canberra: National Library of Australia
MS Acc13.036; MS Acc08.093; MS Acc14.037 Charles Ellis, 1/10th Middlesex

Britain

Bodmin: Cornwall's Regimental Museum
B1170, Photograph album, 1/4th DCLI
B.1824, Photograph album, Maj H.J. Hood, 1/4th DCLI
B.4289, Albert Bray 'Brief note on service …' 2/4th DCLI
B.6597, Diary, Thomas Heard, 1/4th DCLI
B.6599, 'Diary since 1914', H. Burt, 1/4th DCLI
D11914, Norman Palmer, Voyage to India
'A Short History of the 1/4th Bn, Duke of Cornwall's Light Infantry, 1914-1919'
War diary, 1/4th DCLI, 1915-19
'Press cuttings 1907-25'

Brecon: Regimental Museum of The Royal Welsh
Box 17 Brecknock Battalion, South Wales Borderers 1911-39
Box 17a Brecknock Battalion, South Wales Borderers. Correspondence relating to the grave memorials in Aden and India during the Great War
Box 18 Brecknock Battalion, South Wales Borderers Pre-1900-39

Carlisle: Cumbria's Museum of Military Life
08/A2a/4/913, Company Order Book, 2/4th Border
Letters, Harry Canham, 2/4th Border
Percy Hamilton, 2/4th Border
E16/2001, Thomas Davidson, 2/4th Border
E94/2016, Frederick Wignall, 2/4th Border
Diary, 2/4th Bn The Border Regiment, 1914-19

Album, 2/4th Border
Part 2 Orders, 2/4th Border, 1914-18
Album 16 Acc. Nos. 1140-1235 (1/4th Border)
Album 17 Acc. Nos 1236-1331 (1/4th Border)
Album 18 Acc. Nos 1332-1427 (Hoggarth)
Album 20 Acc. Nos 1530-1622 (2/4th Border)
Album 21 Acc. Nos 1623-1717 (2/4th Border)
Album 23 Acc. Nos 1784-1828 (1/4th Border)
Album 24 Acc. Nos 1829-1876 (1/4th Border)
Album 25 Acc. Nos 1877-1981 (1/4th Border)
Album 26 Acc. Nos 1982-2052 (1/4th Border)
Album 28 Acc. Nos 2121-2226 1/4th Border)
Album 31 Acc. Nos. 2443-2640 (1/4th Border)
Album 33 Acc. Nos 3644-3701 (Hoggarth)
Album 35 Acc. Nos 3024-3345 (Hoggarth)
Album 42 Acc. Nos 3786-3872 (Martindale)
Album 44 Acc. Nos 4030-4058 (Turner)
Album 56 Acc. Nos 5256-5319 (2/4th Border)
Album 68 Acc. Nos 6973-6991 (1/4th Border)
Albums 88 Acc. Nos. 7945-7988 (2/4th Burma)
Album 89 Acc. Nos 7989-8036 (2/4th Border)

Chichester: West Sussex Record Office
AM 719/1/4, Cornelius Scarrott, West Surrey
MP1933, James McArthur, 2/6th Royal Sussex
RSR/MSS/ Records of the 2/6th Bn, Royal Sussex Regiment
RSR/MSS/ 6/3, 2/6th (Cyclist) Bn Royal Sussex Regiment Policy and Training
RSR/MSS/ 6/4, 'Notes on History of 2/6th Bn'
RSR/MSS/ 6/5, War diary, 2/6th Royal Sussex, 1917
RSR/MSS/ 6/6, Officers' roll, 2/6th Royal Sussex
RSR/MSS 6/7, Battalion orders, 1917
RSR/MSS 6/8, Photographs, 2/6th Royal Sussex
RSR/MSS/ 6/9, Orders and memoranda, 2/6th Royal Sussex, 1916
RSR/MSS/ 6/10, *Royal Sussex Herald*, 1916-18
RSR/MSS/ 6/11, Orders and memoranda, 2/6th Royal Sussex, 1917
RSR/MSS/ 6/12, Battalion orders, 2/6th Royal Sussex, 1917-18
RSR/MSS/ 6/14, Memorial in Lahore
RSR/MSS/ 6/17, Obituary and correspondence, Lt-Col Frank Johnson
RSR/MSS/ 6/17, *Royal Sussex Herald*, 1916-19

Chippenham: Wiltshire and Swindon History Centre
1818/42, 'Parishioners believed to be at the front 28 April 1915'
930/41, Rector's notebook, Bremerton
G15/229/4, Harry Saunders, *Trowbridge Roll of Honour 1914-1918*, Trowbridge, 1924
L/1 Wiltshire Territorial and Auxiliary Association

/110/5, Establishments of Territorial Force, 1909-10
/120/3, Wiltshire Territorial Force Association, Strength returns, 1909-10

Dorchester: Dorset History Centre
D-1235/1, Letters of Pte C. Larcombe
D-414, Dorset Territorial Force Association minutes
D.1373, Bloxworth Roll of Honour
NP.4/MR/1/3, Church manual, Christchurch Congregational Church, 1914

Dorchester: The Keep Museum
1971-71, Captain John Roper, 1/4th Dorset
2004-1286, Lance Corporal Cobb, Dorset Regiment
2005-44, William Inkpen, 2/4th Dorset
2007-331, Fred Pickett, 2/4th Dorset
2007/542-60, Leonard Shapter, 1/4th Devon
2007-589, B. Lynwood, 2/4th Dorset
2007-1474, Sergeant Charles Gibson, 1/4th Devon
2007-1550-3, Captain Charles Lart, 1/4th Devon
2012-518-2 Edwin Davey, 1/4th Devon
DORMM2007-1550-1, Photograph album
EX1219 Orders, 1/6th Devon, 1915
EX1213 Orders, 2/6th Devon, 1916
EX2579, Herbert Chapple, 1/4th Devon
EX2543, Private Hugh Creek, 1/4th Devon

London: British Library (India Office and Oriental Collections)
L/MIL/5/736, Viceroy's fortnightly telegrams, 1917-18
L/MIL/5/744, 'General security of India, 1918'
L/MIL/7/2731, 'Applications for Indian Army commissions from British service, 1917-18'
L/MIL/7/12571, 'War Office decisions likely to affect British soldiers serving in India … 1914-15'
L/MIL/7/13309, 'Returns of re-enlistments, 1918-19'
L/MIL/7/13311, 'Arrangements for the grant of leave for British troops, 1919'
L/MIL/7/13893, 'Contagious Diseases and Cantonment Regulations, 1911-24'
L/MIL/7/19183, 'Scheme for demobilization of the Army, 1918-19'
L/MIL/7/19209, 'Demobilisation (War of 1914-1919)'
L/MIL/17/5/2386, 'Correspondence regarding the deficiency of troops in India, 1915'
L/MIL/17/3/2387, 'Further correspondence regarding the deficiency of troops in India &c., 1915'
L/MIL/17/5/2397, 'Memorandum regarding the provision of a British garrison for India after the war'
L/MIL/17/5/2401, 'Military Department minute on the military situation in India consequent on the war' India Office, June 1915'
L/MIL/17/5/2406, 'Imperial War Cabinet: memorandum on events in India 1917-18'
L/MIL/17/5/2407, 'Demobilisation orders, India, 1919'

Mss.Eur.E264 Papers of Lord Chelmsford
Mss.Eur.C340 Sgt Reginald Howgego, 1/25th London
Mss.Eur.D783 Papers of General Sir Charles Monro

London: Imperial War Museums
Doc. 10461, Misc. 225, Anonymous account of Indian service
Misc. 123, item 1916, Anonymous diary, [1/4th Hants]
Doc. 12642, 03/16/1, Bruce Baily, 5th Wilts
Doc. 15057, 06/68/1, F.E. Banks, 1/25th London
Doc. 8094, 99/15/1, Francis Bowker, 1/4th Hants
Doc. 14551, 67/164/1, Henry Broad, 1/5th Hants
Doc. 6711, 97/26/1, Cyril Burgess, 1/5th Buffs
PP/MCR/207, 'The Flames of Enchantment', Olaf Caroe, 1/5th East Surrey
Doc. 12537, 02/55/1, Richard Cawsey, 2/4th Hants
Doc. 12478, Misc 231, Herbert Cott, Army Service Corps
Doc. 10921, Con. Shelf, Christopher Dawson, 1/5th East Surrey
Doc. 21639, 73/110/1, M. Drew, 1/4th Dorset
Doc. 7435, 75/2/1, Percy Ellis, 1/25th London
Doc. 15428, 07/8/1, Herbert Ewing 1/5th Somerset
Doc. 15015, 06/69/1, William Fox 1/10th Middlesex
Doc. 17145, 09/56/1, Reginald Griffiths, 1/25th London
Doc. 13306, 04/38/1, Ernest Head, 1/6th East Surrey
Doc. 4545, 81/9/1 Ted Holter, 'A Terrier in World War I'
Doc. 7306, 76/111-112/1, Herbert Jones 7th North Stafford
Doc. 17422, 10/3/1, William Jupp, 1/5th West Kent
Misc. 207, 3012, E.L. Lloyd, 2/6th Royal Sussex
Doc. 7758, 74/161/1, Robert Macey, Hampshire Regiment
Doc. 5877, 84/9/1, John Marsh, 1/5th Hants
Doc. 11927, 02/5/1, George Owers, Royal Artillery
Doc. 7435, P331, H. Pearson, 1/25th London
Doc. 7760, 74/163/1, W.E.H. Piper, 2/4th Devon
Doc. 16388, 08/74/1, John Porthouse 2/4th Border
Doc. 16482 08/96/1, H.S. Priestley, 2/4th Border Regiment
Doc. 16335, 08/57/1, Lt James Racine, Hampshire Regiment
Doc 13388, 05/7/1, Gnr Reuben Rusbridge Royal Artillery
Doc. 6571, 79/15/1, Lt Walter Saunders, 10th Middlesex
Doc. 7350, 76/154/1, Pte A.E. Searle, 1/4th Devon
Doc. 8004, 98/28/1, Charles Sprague, 5th Wilts
Doc. 1383, 87/18/1, Don Stevenson, 1/5th Hants
Doc. 9772, P394, Mrs. J.S. Tait, Bangalore
Doc. 8236, 99/37/1, Sister Marjorie Thomas (née Swynnerton) 'Child of the Empire'
Doc. 13590, 05/53/1, F.E, Tipper, Royal Artillery
Doc. 16077, 08/35/1, Ernest Twin, 1/9th Middlesex
Doc. 13205, 13/8/1, H.B. Watson 1/6th Buffs
Doc 13809, 73/66/1, C.R. Willis, 'Gunnery notes and other documents

London: Liddell Hart Centre for Military Archives
Papers, General Sir Ian Hamilton
Papers, Lord Montagu of Beaulieu
Papers, Major-General Robert Montague Poore
Papers, Maj Gen Sir Henry Sclater, Indian Medical Service
Cuthbert Sprawson '37 Years in the I.M.S.'

London: London Metropolitan Archives
12.606/2, City of London Territorial Force Association Minutes, 1913-18
0994/002, Middlesex Territorial Force Association, Minutes 1910-18
LMA/4014, Soldiers & Sailors Families' Association, Uxbridge

London: National Archives, UK
CAB6 Committee of Imperial Defence
CAB6/4, Memoranda on the Defence of India, 1901-39
CAB24 War Cabinet memoranda
CAB24/6/22, 'Additional assistance from India', February 1917
CAB24/9/17, Provision of further troops to India', 28 March 1917
CAB24/29/42, 'Position in India', October 1917
CAB24/50/1, 'Security of India', 30 April 1918
CAB37 Photographic copies of Cabinet papers
CAB37/129/16, 'Military situation in India consequent on the war', 17 June 1915
CAB37/131/12, 'Reinforcements for Aden'
CAB37/131/16, 'Situation in Aden'
CAB37/131/32, 'Reoccupation of Sheik Othman'
CAB37/131/38, 'Military Report from Aden'
CAB42 Cabinet papers
CAB42/3/11, 'Extract from a letter from the Viceroy of India concerning the effect on Indian opinion of Gallipoli a withdrawal from the Dardanelles', 27 July 1915
CAB42/5/21, 'The Military Situation in India and the Middle East'
CAB42/5/22, Minutes of War Committee, 25 November 1915
CAB42/6/5, 'The Military Situation in India', 7 December 1915
CAB42/12/5, War Committee minutes, 7 April 1916
CAB42/12/12, War Committee minutes, 28 April 1916
CAB42/14/6, 'The Reinforcement of the Garrison of India', 20 May 1916
CAB42/15/9, 'Proposal for raising Territorial units in India', 19 June 1916
CAB42/22/15, 'General Review of the War', October 1916
PRO30, Kitchener papers
WO32/9698, Territorial Force Advisory Council
WO33 War Office: Reports, memoranda and papers
WO33/708, General Programme of Moves by Sea 1914
WO33/716, Numbers conveyed by Sea
WO33/736, General Programme of Moves by Sea, 1915
WO33/1021, Index of the Decisions of the Army Council 1914-21
WO95 War diaries, 1916-19

/5045, Mesopotamia-North Persia Force, 1918-19
/5047, North Persia Force/ 1/4th Hampshire Regiment, 1918-19; 36th Brigade
/5433, British Military Mission, Vladivostok /1/9th Hampshire Regiment, 1918
/5438, 1/4th The Buffs, 1915-16; 1/4th Cornwall, 1916-17; 1/7th Hants, 1918-19; 1/1 Brecknock, 1915
/5045, North Persia Force, 1918-19
/5177, 1/4th Hampshire Regiment, 1916-18; 1/6th Devon, 1915-16
/5392, North West Frontier Force; Peshawar Area; 1/4th Queen's Royal West Surrey; 2/4th Border, 1919

WO106 Reports on Military Operations
/55, British Troops in Persia
/56, Military Operations, India, 1916-19
/329 Summaries of Military Events, 1919
/565, The Action at Imad, 16 March 1916
/566, Operations of the Aden Field Force, 1917
/567, Operations of the Aden Field Force, 1917
/568, Operations of the Aden Field Force, 1918
/742, Minor Military Operations … including Aden, 1914-16

WO114 Returns of the Territorial Force Serving Abroad
WO114/52, 1914-15
WO114/53, 1916
WO114/54, 1917
WO162/7 Embarkation of units
WO163/21, Minutes of the Proceedings of the Army Council, 1915 & 1916
WO163/22, Minutes of the Proceedings of the Army Council, 1917

London: National Army Museum
1972-07-19, Scrapbook, Lady Monro
1984-11-110-2, Press cuttings 5th East Surrey
1985-12-29, Pte Walter Gosling, 'Diary of a Territorial in India 1916-17'
1983-05-91, Pte Bennett Young, 1/4th Dorset
1993-11-87, Pte Sydney Chapman, 1/25th London
1994-02-27, Resolution of the Government of India, 31 December 1919
1997-05-87, Military traffic map of India, 1916
2000-10-228, R .T. Whyman, 'A Soldier's Life in India' 1/5th Bn The Buffs
2001-10-91, Sgt Henry Norris, 1/4th The Buffs
2004-05-43, Sgt Harry Oke, 1/25th London
2004-10-189, Pte William Fox, 1/10th Middlesex
2005-06-682, L/Cpl Harold Vincent Yates, 1/25th London
2010-11-2; 2010-12-8, Sgt Henry Iggulden, 1st/10th Middlesex
2011-12-3, Sgt Reginald Bailey, 1/4th The Buffs

Maidstone: Kent Archives and History Centre
Great Chart Soldiers and Sailors Fund
Ch144/C5 'Letters received from men who are in India'

Ch144/C9 Letters received from men in Mesopotamia, India, China'
Ch144/C15 'Letters … 1916-18'
C/A 2/16/39, The Territorial Buffs Comforts Fund
EK/U127/2, Letter, Geoffrey Coombs to Lily Vass
MD/TA, Territorial Force Association of the County of Kent, Minute books
WKR/B4/A1, War diary, 1/4th West Kent, 1919

Maidstone: Queen's Own Royal West Kent Regimental Museum (Maidstone Museum)
Cyril Bristow, 'The Kent Cyclist Battalion: Territorial Force 1908-1920'
E10, Arthur Addison Collection
MNERM Album 17 Album, H.J. Packham, 1/4th West Kent
NMERM: 825 Album 4, 1/5th West Kent; Indian photographs
MNERM.852 a & b, Address Book, 1st Kent Cyclist Battalion, 1919
NMERM: 881, F.J. Barden, Album 5 'India 1916-19'
NMERM: 1980.756, F.W. West Collection
MNERM 1987:934, Album 24, 1/5th West Kent
NMERM: 1990.996, L.H. Allen Collection
NMERM 2008-1640, Bernard Searle Collection

Salisbury: The Rifles Berkshire and Wiltshire Museum
SBYRW 4259, Charles Alberry, 1/4th Wilts
SBYRW 1999, Lionel Bithell, 2/4th Wilts
SBYRW 19762, Bernard Carter, 1/4th Wilts
SBYRW 4367, G.C. Couldry, 1/4th Wilts
SBYRW 25913, John Say, 2/4th Wilts
SBYRW 34954, George Smith, 1/4th Wilts
SBYRW 26535-6, Jack Welch, 1/4th Wilts

Shrewsbury: Shropshire Archives
866/6/75, Captain George Bright, Photograph album
867/6/75, Captain George Bright, Photograph album
3614/2/142-161, Captain Roger Haslewood album
3614/2/166, Recruiting poster, 1915
6005/SHYTA/0928E, Photographs, 4th KSLI
6005/SHYTA/0979a *Scenes in Burma*
6005//SHYTA/09779d, Photographs, 4th KSLI
6005/SHYUS/10/0617, Lord Kitchener's message

Taunton: Somerset Heritage Centre
DD\SLI/1/12, 'Historical record of 2/4th Bn SLI, 1914-1916'
DD\SLI/2/17, War diary, 1/4th Somerset Light Infantry, 1916-19
DD\SLI/2/18, War diary, 1/4th and 2/4th Somerset Light Infantry, 1916-19
DD\SLI/6/29, Battalion orders, 4th and 2/4th Bns, Somerset Light Infantry, 1915-16
DD\SLI/6/32, Battalion orders, 2/4th Bn, Somerset Light Infantry, 1916
DD\SLI/6/36, Battalion orders, 2/4th Bn, Somerset Light Infantry, 1917

DD\SLI/15/6/74, Photograph of football game
DD\SLI/15/6/79, SLI gymnastic team in India
DD\SLI/15/6/94, View of Subathu
DD\SLI/15/6/196, Photograph of B Coy 2/4th Somerset Light Infantry
DD\SLI/15/7/46, Photograph album (unidentified officer)
DD\SLI/15/7/59, Album, Sgt H.G. Maidment, 1/5th Somerset Light Infantry
DD\SLI/15/7/72, Album, Sgt H.G. Maidment, 1/5th Somerset Light Infantry
DD\SLI/15/7/75, Photographs of the Mohmand expedition, 1917
DD\SLI/15/7/84, Album, Major E.W. Farwell, 2/4th Somerset Light Infantry
DD\SLI/15/7/83, Album 'India 1915-16'
DD\SLI/16/1/41, Postcards, William Skinner, Somerset Light Infantry
DD\SLI/17/1/61, Herbert Ewing, 1/5th Bn, Somerset Light Infantry
DD\SLI/17/1/62, [Edward Ewens] 'A Cook's Tour in Burma and India'
DD\SLI/17/1/84, A.J. Connell, 1/5th Bn, Somerset Light Infantry
DD\SLI/17/1/87, Douglas Macmillan, 1/4th Bn, Somerset Light Infantry
DD\SLI/17/3/93, William Jennings, 1/4th Somerset Light Infantry
DD\SLI/17/3/303 Douglas Macmillan, 1/4th Somerset Light Infantry
DD\SLI/19/6/5 Bugle calls, 2/5th Bn Somerset Light Infantry
DD\SLI/20/3/16 George Molesworth, Afghanistan maps, 1919
DD\SLI/20/6/7 List of Somerset Light Infantry graves in India

Winchester: Hampshire Record Office
19M75/FC17, Letters, Robert Palmer, 1/6th Hants, 1914-16
49M91W/Q3/6, 'A Khaki Diary', Victor Manley, 1/5th Hants
49M98W/B3/20, Letters to Harold Warren from a friend in India
94M72/F303-305, Letters, Gerard Bonham-Carter, West Kent, 1917-18
94M72/F238-243, Diaries, Gerard Bonham-Carter, 1914-18
128A08/1-4, Diary and letters, Arthur Copeland, 1/5th Hants

Winchester: Royal Hampshire Regiment Museum
M252 Leonard Adams, 1/4th Hants
M340 Francis Oatley, 1/7th Hants
M757 John Marsh, 'My Service in India', 1/5th Hants
M766 Owen Smith, 1/6th Hants
M830 Percy Wilkinson, 1/5th Hants
M906 William Evans, 1/9th Hants
M1359 Francis Bowker, 1/4th Hants
M1360 Esme Bowker
M1446 Reginald Welch, 1/6th Hants
M1543, Hinton Harris, 1/5th Hants
M1624, Bertie Wareham, 1/9th Hants
M1627, Standing Orders, 1/9th Hants
M1629, Adolphus Jupe, 'Round the World with the "P.B.I." 1/9th Hants
M1630, Bangalore manoeuvre map, 1/9th Hants
M1798, Edward Read, 'Hampshire to the Himalayas', 1/5th and 1/6th Hants

M1830, Esme Bowker
M1834, William Bisset, 'Dum Spiro Spero', 2/4th Hants
M1838, Godfrey Burrell, 'The Diary of a Company Commander', 1/4th Hants
M2011, 'The Territorials. Arrival in India' 1/6th Hants
M2056, John Gosling, 2/4th Hants
M2185, Stokes-Roberts papers, 1/7th Hants
M2338, Bertram Gotobed, 1/7th Hants
M2564, George Alexander, 2/4th & 1/7th Hants
M2565, 'The North-West Frontier of India in Picture' [sic]
M3538, Charles Clinker, 1/6th Hants
M3859, S.A. [probably Stanley] Green, 1/9th Hants
M3910, Harold Wheeler, 'Wartime Wanderings of the 1/4th Battalion, Hampshire Regiment'
M4041, Gordon Neads, 1/9th Hants
M4236, Oswald Early, 1/9th Hants
M4243, Archie Brewer, 1/9th Hants

Woking: Surrey History Centre
ESR/2/13/3, East Surrey Regiment clippings, 1870-1950
ESR/6/5/1, War diary, 1/5th Bn East Surrey Regiment; with details of POWs
ESR/6/9/11 Album, 1/6th East Surrey
ESR/10/4/8, Pay Sergeant's account book, 1/6th East Surrey
ESR/10/10/2/7, Clippings (unidentified) re 1/6th East Surrey in India
ESR/10/12/1, Scrapbook '6 Surreys'
ESR/10/14/3/1, 'A History of the 1/6th The East Surrey Regiment in India and Aden 1914-1919'
ESR/25/ANDR/1, George Andrews 1/5th East Surrey
ESR/25/ATKI/1-12, Ernest Atkinson, 1/6th East Surrey
ESR/25/ATWO/1, C.F. Atwood, 1/5th East Surrey
ESR/25/BELA/1, Arthur Bell, 1/6th East Surrey
ESR/25/BOWERS/1/6th East Surrey
ESR/25/BRAIN/1-5, Henry Brain, 1/6th East Surrey
ESR/25/BROWH/1, Harry Brown, 1/5th East Surrey
ESR/25/BURGHS/1 H.S. Burgess, 1/6th East Surrey
ESR/26/CARP/1, Sgt H. Carpenter, 1/5th East Surrey
ESR/25/GILLH/ Letter from his bearer 1919
ESR/25/LORD/1, R.E. Lord, 1/5th East Surrey
ESR/25/ORR/4-6, Edward Orr, 1/5th East Surrey
ESR/25/SWIF/1 Allan Swift, 1/6th East Surrey
ESR/25/THOMP/1, F.W. Thompson, 1/5th West Surrey
QRWS/1/16/13 Albums 1/5th WestSurrey
QRWS/30/BIRC/1, James Birch, 'The Voyage from Devonport to Bombay'
QRWS/30/CRAV/2 E.W. Craven, 1/5th West Surrey
QRWS/30/EDEN/1, Percy Eden, 1/5th West Surrey
QRWS/30/GIBBH/2, Harold Gibbons, 1/5th West Surrey
QRWS/30/PEAC/3, A. [probably Alfred or Arthur] Peacock, 1/5th West Surrey
QRWS/30/PEAC/1, Herbert Peacock, 1/4th West Surrey

QRWS/30/RICE/1, Ted Rice, 'All for a shilling a day'
QRWS/30/SMITGE/1 G.E. Smith, 1/5th West Surrey
QRWS/30/WHITM/1 Arthur Whitmore 1/5th West Surrey
QRWS/30/WIGA/17 'A Few Hints for Territorials Officers'

India

New Delhi: National Archives of India
Army Department Proceedings
WWI/147-58/H, General war diary, Army Headquarters
WWI/363/H, Synopses of events up to 31 December 1916
WWI/389-92, War diary, General Headquarters, Miscellaneous
WWI/405/H War diary, Army Headquarters
WWI/491-93, Reliefs and Disturbances, 1915
WWI/659-75/H, Army Headquarters, Correspondence relating to the European Crisis
Home Department, Political Branch, June 1916, Deposit 22 & K.W., Part A, 'Question of the grant of special permission to the families of territorial units to sail by the transport Caronia proceeding through danger zones to the United Kingdom'
Reports of Native Newspapers – Punjab
Indian Munitions Board, Industrial Intelligence Branch, Jan 1918, File No I-306, 'Obtaining of skilled mechanics from Territorial units for Industries in India'
Foreign and Political Department Proceedings
    Personal papers
    Lala Lajpat Rai
    Dadabhai Naoroji
    Lord Chelmsford

United States of America

St Paul: Minnesota Historical Society Archives
P1282 Thomas and Carmelite Christie Family Papers

Collections in private hands

'The Diary of Sergeant Ben Nicholas 1914 to 1917', ttps://docs.google.com/viewer?url=http%3A%2F%2Fwulfrunianinlondon.files.wordpress.com%2F2014%2F01%2Fthe-diary-of-ben-nicholas-1915-to-19174.pdf
Diary, Arthur Foster, 1/4th Hants, https://sites.google.com/site/ajcfosterhistory/home/4-diary
Register of Members, Ootacamund Club, Tamilnadu, India

Websites

1/25th London Cycle Battalion website: http://www.25thlondon.com/

Fieldwork, 2012-18

Agra, Bangalore, Barrackpore, Chennai, Delhi, Dagshai, Darjeeling, Dinapore, Hong Kong, Istanbul, Kussowli, Kolkata, Lebong, Meerut, Mumbai, Ootacamund, Patna, Simla, Singapore, Subathoo, Varanasi, Wellington, and all the counties in Britain from where Territorials came.

Regimental journals

2nd/5th Hampshire Battalion Journal
5th East Surrey Magazine (1/5th East Surrey)
The Braganza [West Surrey Regiment]
Hampshire Regiment Journal [Hampshire Regiment]
The Invicta [1/1st Kent Battalion]
The Londoner [1/25th London Regiment]
The Queen's Own Gazette [Queen's Own Royal West Kent]
The Tiger [2/4th Hants]
Middlesex Regiment Magazine
The 1/9th Middlesex
Regimental News [East Surrey Regiment]
The Roussillon Gazette [Royal Sussex Regiment]
The Royal Sussex Herald [2/6th Royal Sussex]
The War Dragon [East Kent Regiment]

Official publications

1st Kent Regiment (1/1st Kent Cyclist Battalion) Provisional Standing Orders, Bangalore, 1916
1/9 Battalion The Hampshire Regiment: List of Members, 1920
1/9th Battalion, The Hampshire Regiment, *Mountain Warfare Camp and Bivouac Routine*, Ferozepore, 1917
5th Battalion The Hampshire Regiment Battalion Standing Orders, Thacker, Spink & Co., Calcutta, 1916
General Staff, Army Headquarters India, *Operations in Waziristan 1919-1920*, Calcutta, 1921
General Staff, *Principal measures taken in India during the War to Maintain Training at the Standard Required in Modern War*, Calcutta, 1919
Memorandum on Army Training in India, 1916-1917, Government Central Press, Simla, 1917
Memorandum on the Musketry Training of the Troops in India 1915-16, Army Headquarters, Simla, 1916

Standing Orders of The Brecknockshire Battalion of the South Wales Borderers, Thacker, Spink & Co., Bombay, 1919

Newspapers and serials

The Argus (Melbourne)
The Bombay Chronicle
The Brecon County Times
Brecon Radnor Express
Bristol and the War
Calcutta Capital
Civil and Military Gazette
Kent Messenger
Punch
Salisbury and Winchester Journal
Shepton Mallet Journal
South-Eastern Gazette Maidstone and Kentish Journal
Sydney Morning Herald
The Pioneer (Allahabad)
The Statesman (Calcutta)
The Times
Wells Journal
West Sussex Gazette
Western Gazette
Westmoreland Gazette
Weston Mercury
Wiltshire Times and Trowbridge Advertiser

Parliamentary Papers and other published official records

House of Commons
1914-15, Vol. 49, (Cmd 8087), *Report on Sanitary Measures in India in 1913-14*
1914-16, Vol. 39 (Cmd 7678), *Statement showing the Financial Position of Territorial Force County Associations on 31 March 1914*
1916, Vol. 7 (Cmd 8375), *Report on Sanitary Measures in India in 1914-1915*
1916, Vol. 19, (Cmd 905), *Colonial Reports – Straits Settlements*
1917-18, Vol. 16, (Cmd 8610), *Mesopotamia Commission Report*
1917-18, Vol. 10, (Cmd 8873), *Report on Sanitary Measures in India 1915-1916*
1917-18, Vol. 10, (Cmd 8672), *Report ... of the Committee Appointed to Consider Measures ... for Settling Within the Empire*
1920, Vol. 14, (Cmd 681), *Report of the Committee Appointed ... to Investigate the Disturbances in the Punjab* [The Hunter Committee]

1921, Vol. 20, (Cmd 1193), *General Annual Reports on the British Army (including the Territorial Force…) for the Period from 1st October, 1913, to 30th September, 1919*
Annual Report of the Sanitary Commissioner with the Government of India for 1918, Calcutta, Superintendent Government Printing, 1920
General Staff Branch, Army Headquarters India, *The Third Afghan War 1919 Official account*, Government of India Calcutta, 1926
General Staff Branch, Army Headquarters India, *The Army in India and its Evolution*, Superintendent Government Printing, Calcutta, 1924
War Office, *Chronology of Events Connected with Army Administration*, 1914-1919

PUBLISHED SOURCES

Contemporary published sources (most pre-1939)
Richard Aldington, *Roads to Glory*, Doubleday, Doran & Company, New York, 1933
Ampthill, 'Fiat Justitia: The Case of a Scapegoat', *National Review*, April 1920, pp. 205-10
Anon, *A Handbook for Travellers in India Burma and Ceylon*, John Murray, London, 1913
Anon, *A Pictorial Souvenir of the Duke of Edinburgh's 2nd Battalion 4th Wiltshire Regiment …*, British Historical and Art Publishing Co., Poona, 1915
Anon, *History of the Hampshire Territorial Force Association and War Records of Units, 1914-1919*, Hampshire Advertiser, Southampton, 1921
Anon, *How India Can Save the Empire*, Ganesh & Co, Madras, 1918
Anon, *The Indian Army A.B.C.*, np, 1915
Anon, *The Book of Remembrance of the 5th Battalion (Prince Albert's) Somerset Light Infantry*, privately published, London, 1930
Anon, *The Coconut Tree – and After*, privately published, Shrewsbury, c. 1922
Anon, *The Sufferings of the Kut Garrison*, The Adjutant's Press, Ludgershall, 1923
Anon, *Loyal India: an Interview with Lord Hardinge of Penshurst*, Sir Joseph Causton & Sons, London, 1916
William Archer, *India and the Future*, Hutchinson & Co., London, 1917
'A Territorial Officer', *Promotion While You Wait, or a month in a Chelsea Barrack Yard*, Foster Groom & Co., London, 1909
Alban Bacon, *The Wanderings of a Temporary Warrior*, H.F. & G. Witherby, London, 1922
Harold Baker, *The Territorial Force: A Manual of its Law Organization and Administration*, John Murray, London, 1909
George Barrow, *The Life of General Sir Charles Carmichael Monro*, Hutchinson, London, 1931
Upendra Nath Banerjee, *Memoirs of a Revolutionary*, Calcutta, nd
W.D. Bavin, *Swindon's War Record*, Swindon Town Council/John Drew, Swindon, 1922
Robert Campbell Begg, *Surgery on Trestles: a Saga of Suffering and Triumph*, Jarrold & Sons, Norwich, 1967
W.D. Bird, *Some Principles of Frontier Mountain Warfare*, Hugh Rees Ltd, London, 1909
George Blick, *The 1/4th Battalion The Wiltshire Regiment 1914-1919*, Butler & Tanner, Frome, 1933
C.D. Bruce, *History of the Duke of Wellington's Regiment, 1st and 2nd Battalions 1881-1923*, Medici Society, London, 1927

Edmund Candler, *The Long Road to Baghdad*, Cassell, London, 1919
Nirad Chaudhuri, *Autobiography of an Unknown Indian*, Macmillan, London, 1951
Winston Churchill, *The World Crisis 1911-1914*, Thoraaanton Butterworth Ltd, London, 1931
Ian Colvin, *The Life of General Dyer*, William Blackwood & Sons, Edinburgh, 1929
Joseph Cox, *An Ordinary Working Man's Life Story*, PP, Alton, 1967
Everard Digby, (ed.), *Indian Ink: Being Splashes from Various Pens in aid of the Imperial India War Fund*, Thacker, Spink & Co., Calcutta, 1914-1918
L.C. Dunsterville, *Stalky's Reminiscences*, Jonathan Cape, London, 1928
Reginald Dyer, *The Raiders of the Sarhad : being the account of a campaign of arms and bluff against the brigands of the Persian-Baluchi border during the Great War*, H.F. & G. Whitherby, London, 1921
Russell Early, (ed.), *The Messenger: the World War 1 Diary of a Wireless Operator*, Mereo, Cirencester, 2014
R. Evans, *A Brief Outline of the Campaign in Mesopotamia 1914-18*, Sifton Praed & Co., London, 1926
Elsie Fisk, *The Great Shikār in Quetta*, Marshall, Morgan & Scott, London [1934?]
C.L. Flick, *A Record of the Actions, Marches, Movements and Stations of the Sixth Battalion Devonshire Regiment in England, India and Mesopotamia during the Great War*, privately published, Barnstaple, 1920
E.M. Forster, *A Passage to India*, [1924], Penguin, 2011
J.W. Gale, *With the 2/4th Wilts to India*, privately published, Marlborough, 1935
Mohandas Gandhi and others, *Report of the Commissioners appointed by the Punjab Sub-Committee appointed by the Indian National Congress*, Vol. I, Report, Indian National Congress, Lahore, 1920
M.K. Gandhi, *The Collected Works of Mahatma Gandhi*, Vols1-74, New Delhi, Ministry of Information and Broadcasting, 1958
Gerald Gibbs, *Survivor's Story*, Hutchinson, London, 1956
Philip Gosse, *Memoirs of a Camp-Follower: a Naturalist Goes to War*, Longmans Green, London, 1934
Robert Graves, *Goodbye to All That*, Jonathan Cape, London, 1929
Charles Gwynn, *Imperial Policing*, Macmillan & Co., London, 1934
Aylmer Haldane, *A Soldier's Saga: the Autobiography of General Sir Aylmer Haldane*, William Blackwood & Sons, Edinburgh, 1948
Richard Haldane, *An Autobiography*, Hodder and Stoughton, London, 1929
Hardinge of Penshurst, *My Indian Years 1910-1916*, John Murray, London, 1948
Aubrey Herbert, *Mons, Anzac and Kut*, Hutchinson & Co., London, [1924?]
Benjamin Horniman, *Amritsar and Our Duty to India*, T. Fisher Unwin, London [1920]
Intelligence Bureau, Government of India, *Terrorism in India 1917-1936*, Government of India Press, Simla, 1937
F.B. Jefferiss, 'Suggestions for removing difficulties encountered by British units arriving in India ...', *Journal of the United Services Institution of India*, Vol. XLVI, No. 207, pp. 159-71
M.A.B. Johnston & K.D. Yersley, *Four-Fifty Miles to Freedom*, William Blackwood, Edinburgh, 1919
William Linton Lewis, *Haunting Years: The Commentaries of a War Territorial*, Hutchinson & Co., London, [1933?]

Verney Lovett, *A History of the Indian Nationalist Movement* [1920], Frank Cass, London, 1968
——, *India*, Hodder and Stoughton, London, 1923
A.C. MacDonnell, *The Outlines of Military Geography*, Hugh Rees Ltd, London, 1911
John Mackie (ed.), *Answering the Call: Letters from the Somerset Light Infantry 1914-19*, Raby Books, Eggleston, 1999
L. MacGlasson, (ed.), *Diary of the 2/4th Battalion The Border Regiment, 1914-19*, [Border Regiment], Carlisle, 1920
George MacMunn, *Behind the Scenes in many Wars being the Military Reminiscences of Lieut.-General Sir George MacMunn*, London, John Murray, 1930
——, *The Romance of the Indian Frontiers*, Jonathan Cape, London, 1931
——, *Turmoil and Tragedy in India 1914 and After*, Jarrolds, London, 1935
William Marshall, *Memories of Four Fronts*, Ernest Benn Ltd, London, 1929
Christopher Mills, *A Strange War: Burma, India & Afghanistan 1914-1919*, Alan Sutton, Gloucester, 1988
Edwin Montagu, *An Indian Diary*, William Heinemann, London, 1930
Richard Moody, *Historical Records of the Buffs, East Kent Regiment (3rd foot) ... 1914-1919*, Medici Trust, London, 1922
Fred Mundy, *A Journal of the 1/4th Battalion Wiltshire Regiment 1914-1918*, The Rifles, Wardrobe and Museum Trust, Salisbury, 2011
R. Muniswamy, *Mysore Administrative Papers*, Vol. IV, *Dewan M. Visesvaraya*, Karnataka State Archives, Bangalore, 1994
Dorina Neave, *Remembering Kut*, Arthur Baker, London, 1937
Jawaharlal Nehru (General Editor: S. Gopal), *Selected Works of Jawaharlal Nehru*, Second Series : Vol.1-28, New Delhi, Jawaharlal Nehru Memorial Fund, c. 1972-1982
Ann Noyes (ed.), *Engaged in War: the Letters of Stanley Goodland 1914-1919*, Twiga Books, Guildford, 1999
Michael O'Dwyer, *India as I Knew It 1885-1925*, Constable & Company Ltd, London, 1925
'One who was in it', 'A Queer War', *Journal of the Royal Artillery*, Vol. LIV, 1927-28, pp. 257-69
[Robert Palmer], *Letters from Mesopotamia in 1915 and January 1916 ...*, privately printed [1916]
'Q.L.', 'The Transcaspian Expedition', *Journal of the Royal United Services Institution*, Vol. 64, No. 455, 1919, pp. 478-89
'The Military Correspondent of *The Times*' [Charles à Court Repington], *The Foundations of Reform*, Simpkin, Marshall and Co., London, 1908
Frank Richards, *Old Soldier Sahib*, Faber & Faber, London, 1986
E.W.C. Sandes, *In Kut and captivity with the Sixth Indian Division*, John Murray, London, 1919
Harry Saunders, *Trowbridge Roll of Honour 1914-1918*, privately published, Trowbridge, 1924
Vinayak Damodar Savarkar, *The Story of My Transportation for Life*, Sadbhakti Publications, Bombay, 1950
A.C.S. Savory, 'Vladivostok: 1919-1920', *Journal of the Society for Army Historical Research*, Vol. LXXI, No. 285, Spring 1993, pp. 8-23
J.J. Sheppard, *Territorials in India: A Souvenir of their Historic Arrival for Military Duty in the 'Land of the Rupee'*, J.J. Sheppard, Bombay, 1916
Roy Simmonds, *Humours of India*, privately published, Bombay, 1914
John Still, *A Prisoner in Turkey*, John Lane, London, 1920

Alexander Sturt, *Our Indian Empire: a Short Review and Some Hints for the Use of Soldiers Proceeding to India*, HMSO, London, 1913

J.P. Villiers-Stuart, *Letters of a Once Punjab Frontier Force Officer to his Nephew*, Sifton Praed & Co., London, 1925

Edgar Wallace, *Kitchener's Army and the Territorial Forces: The Full Story of a Great Achievement*, George Newnes Ltd, London, 1915

War Office, *The Territorial Year Book: A Handbook for the Territorial Soldier and the Citizen, containing an account of the origin, organization and progress of the Territorial Force and its place in National Defence*, London, 1910

F.A.M. Webster, *Britain's Territorials in Peace and War*, Sidgwick & Jackson, London, 1915

H.S. Wood, *Milestones of Memory: A Plain Tale of Service, Sport and Travel in the East and West*, Heath Cranton, London, 1950

Nigel Woodyatt, *Under Ten Viceroys*, Herbert Jenkins Ltd, London, 1922

———, 'The Territorials (Infantry) in India, 1914-1920', *Royal United Services Institution Journal*, Vol. 67, no. 468, 1922, pp. 717-37

George Wright, *Priest and Parish in India: European Congregations*, Society for Promoting Christian Knowledge, London, 1928

Secondary works

Clare Anderson and others, *New Histories of the Andaman Islands: Landscape, Place and Identity in the Bay of Bengal, 1790-2012*, Cambridge University Press, Cambridge, 2016

Anon, ['RF & MP'], 'Scenes of India during the First World War', *Queen's Royal Surrey Regiment Newsletter*, No. 66, November 1999

W.J.P. Aggett, *The Bloody Eleventh: History of the Devonshire Regiment, Vol. III, 1915-1969*, Devonshire and Dorset Regiment, Exeter, 1995

Charles Allen, *Raj: A Scrapbook of British India 1877-1947*, Andre Deutsch, London, 1977

George Arthur, *Life of Lord Kitchener*, 3 Vols, Macmillan & Co., London, 1920

C.T. Atkinson, *The Dorsetshire Regiment*, Vol. II, Oxford University Press, Oxford, 1947

———, *The Royal Hampshire Regiment*, Vol. II 1914-1918, Robert Maclehose & Co. Ltd, Glasgow, 1952

———, *The South Wales Borderers 24th Foot 1689-1937*, Regimental Committee/Cambridge University Press, Cambridge, 1937

Abdul Karim bin Bagoo, 'The Origin and Development of the Malay States Guides', *Journal of the Malayan Branch of the Royal Asiatic Society*, Vol. 35, No. 1 (197) 1962, pp. 75-76

Corelli Barnet, *Britain and Her Army 1509-1970: A Military, Political and Social Survey*, Allen Lane, London, 1970

John Barry, *The Great Influenza: the Story of the Deadliest Pandemic in History*, Penguin, New York, 2005

Michael Barthorp, *The North-West Frontier: British India and Afghanistan*, New Orchard, Poole, 1986

Brian Bates, *Dorchester Remembers the Great War*, Roving Press, Frampton, 2012

Ian Beckett & Keith Simpson, (eds), *A Nation in Arms: A Social Study of the British Army in the First World War*, Manchester University Press, Manchester, 1985

Mark Bence-Jones, *The Viceroys of India*, Constable, London, 1982
Timothy Bowman & Mark Connelly, *The Edwardian Army: Recruiting, Training and Deploying the British Army, 1902-1914*, Oxford University Press, Oxford, 2012
Russell Braddon, *The Siege*, Viking Press, New York, 1969
John Broomfield, 'The Bengal Muslims and September 1918', and 'The Bengal Muslims and September 1918', in Anthony Lowe, (ed.), *Soundings in Modern South Asian History*, University of California Press, Berkeley, 1968
J.J. Burke-Gaffney, *The Story of the King's Regiment (Liverpool)*, Sharpe & Kellet Ltd, London, 1954
Suhash Chakravarty, *Anatomy of the Raj: Russian Consular Reports*, Shubhi Publications, Gurgaon, 2009
Nigel Collett, *The Butcher of Amritsar: General Reginald Dyer*, Hambledon and London, London, 2005
Patrick Crowley, *Kut 1916: Courage and Failure in Iraq*, Spellmount, Stroud, 2009
——, *Loyal to Empire: the Life of General Sir Charles Monro, 1860-1929*, The History Press, Stroud, 2016
Durga Das, *India From Curzon to Nehru & After*, Collins, London, 1969
Peter Dennis, *The Territorial Army 1906-1940*, Royal Historical Society/The Boydell Press, 1987
[Dorsetshire Regiment] Regimental History Committee, *History of the Dorsetshire Regiment, 1914-1919*, Henry Ling Ltd, Dorchester, [1932]
James Elliott, *The Frontier 1839-1947*, Cassell, London, 1968
Charles Ellis, *The Transcaspian Episode 1918-1919*, Hutchinson, London, 1963
John Ellis, *Newton Abbott's Great War: Forgotten Times – Forgotten Men*, privately published, Newton Abbott, 2014
W.G. Fisher, *The History of Somerset Yeomanry, Volunteer and Territorial Units*, Goodman and Son, Taunton, 1924
Roger Ford, *Eden to Armageddon: World War I in the Middle East*, Phoenix, London, 2009
Robert Furneaux, *Massacre at Amritsar*, George Allen & Unwin, London, 1963
David Gilmour, *The Ruling Caste: Imperial Lives in the Victorian Raj*, Farrar, Straus and Giroux, New York, 2005
Alan Harfield, 'A Territorial soldier in India 1914-1917', *Durbar: Indian Military Historical Society*, Vol. 23, No. 1, Spring 2006, pp. 2-9
——, 'A Territorial soldier in India 1914-1917', *Durbar: Indian Military Historical Society*, Vol. 23, No. 2, Summer 2006, pp. 49-66
T.A. Heathcote, *The Military in British India: the Development of British Land Forces in South Asia, 1600-1947*, Manchester University Press, Manchester, 1995
Peter Hopkirk, *On Secret Service East of Constantinople*, Oxford University Press, Oxford, 1995
Keith Jeffery, *The British empire and the crisis of empire 1918-22*, Manchester University Press, Manchester, 1984
Eustace Keogh, *The River in the Desert*, Wilke & Co., Melbourne, 1955
P.K. Kemp, *The History of the 4th Battalion King's Shropshire Light Infantry (TA) 1745-1945*, Wilding & Son, Shrewsbury, 1955
Norman Litchfield, *The Territorial Artillery 1908-1988*, The Sherwood Press, Nottingham, 1992
H.O. Lock & O.C. Vidler, *History of the Dorsetshire Regiment, 1914-1919*, Part II, *The Territorial Units*, Henry Ling, Dorchester, [1932]

Cliff Lord & David Birtles, *The Armed Forces of Aden 1839-1967*, Helion & Co. Solihull, 2000
G.D. Martineau, *A History of the Royal Sussex Regiment*, Moore & Tillyer, Chichester, 1954
Frederick Maurice, *Haldane 1856-1915: The Life of Viscount Haldane of Cloan*, Faber & Faber, London, 1937
Robert Maxwell, *Villiers-Stuart on the Frontier, 1894-1914*, Pentland Press, Edinburgh, 1989
——, *Villiers-Stuart Goes to War*, Pentland Press, Edinburgh, 1990
S.R. Mehrota, *A History of the Indian National Congress*, Vol. I, 1885-1918, Vikas Publishing House, New Delhi, 1995
Charles Messenger, *Call to Arms: the British Army 1914-18*, Wiedenfeld & Nicholson, London, 2005
K.W. Mitchinson, *England's Last Hope: The Territorial Force 1908-14*, Palgrave Macmillan, Basingstoke, 2008
——, *The Territorial Force at War, 1914-1916*, Palgrave Macmillan, Basingstoke, 2014
F.J. Moberly, *The Campaign in Mesopotamia 1914-1918*, Vol. I, HMSO, London, 1923
——, *The Campaign in Mesopotamia 1914-1918*, Vol. II, HMSO, London, 1924
——, *The Campaign in Mesopotamia 1914-1918*, Vol. III, HMSO, London, 1925
——, *The Campaign in Mesopotamia 1914-1918*, Vol. IV, HMSO, London, 1927
George Molesworth, *The Somerset Light Infantry 1919-1945*, Somerset Light Infantry, [Taunton?], 1951
——, *Afghanistan 1919: an Account of Operations in the Third Afghan War*, Asia Publishing House, Bombay, 1962
R.J. Moore, *The Crisis of Indian Unity 1917-1940*, Clarendon Press, Oxford, 1974
——, *Liberalism and Indian Politics 1872-1922*, Edward Arnold, London, 1966
Tim Moreman, *The Army in India and the Development of Frontier Warfare, 1849-1947*, McMillan, Basingstoke, 1998
John Moulsdale, *The History of the Corps of the King's Shropshire Light Infantry*, Vol. 3, *1881-1968*, Leo Cooper, London, 1972
Félicité Nesham, *Socks, Cigarettes and Shipwrecks: A Family's War Letters 1914-1918*, Allan Sutton, Gloucester, 1987
J.A.B. Palmer, *The Mutiny Outbreak at Meerut in 1857*, Cambridge University Press, Cambridge, 1966
H.W. Pearse & H.S. Sloman, *History of the East Surrey Regiment*, Vol. II 1914-1917, The Medici Society, London, 1923; Vol. III 1917-1919, 1924
Karl Pieragostini, *Britain, Aden and South Arabia*, Macmillan, Basingstoke, 1991
Brian Robson, *Crisis on the Frontier: the Third Afghan War and the Campaign in Waziristan 1919-20*, Spellmount, Staplehurst, 2004
Andrew Rothstein, *The Soldiers' Strikes of 1919*, Macmillan, London, 1980
Algernon Rumbold, *Watershed in India 1914-1922*, The Athlone Press, London, 1979
A.V. Sellwood, *The Saturday Night Soldiers: the Stirring Story of the Territorial Army*, White Lion Publishers, London, 1974
Edward Spiers, *Haldane: an Army Reformer*, Edinburgh University Press, Edinburgh, 1980
Laura Spinney, *Pale Rider: The Spanish Flu of 1918 and how it Changed the World*, Jonathan Cape, London, 2017
Peter Stanley, *White Mutiny: British Military Culture in India 1825-75*, Christopher Hurst, London, 1998

——, *Bad Characters: Sex, Crime, Mutiny, Murder and the Australian Imperial Force*, Murdoch/Pier 9, Sydney, 2010
I. Stedman, 'The Kurdistan clasp to the East Surrey Regiment 1919', *Orders and Medals Research Society*, Spring 1986
Arthur Swinson, *Six Minutes to Sunset: the Story of General Dyer and the Amritsar Affair*, Peter Davies, London, 1964
Shashi Tharoor, *Inglorious Empire: What the British did to India*, Scribe Publications, Melbourne, 2017
Raleigh Trevelyan, *The Golden Oriole: Childhood, Family and Friends in India*, Secker & Warburg, London, 1987
Kristian Ulrichsen, *The First World War in the Middle East*, Hurst & Company, London, 2014
Charles Vernon, *Our Glorious Dead: Malmesbury and the Great War 1914-21*, Malmesbury Civic Trust, 2008
H. Whalley-Kelly, *Ich Dien: The Prince of Wales's Volunteers South Lancashire 1914-1934*, Gale & Polden, Aldershot, 1935
Hugo White, *One and All: A History of the Duke of Cornwall's Light Infantry 1702-1959*, Tabb House, Padstow, 2006
W. de B. Wood, *The History of the King's Shropshire Light Infantry in the Great War 1914-1918*, The Medici Society, London, 1925
'Philip Woodruff' [Philip Mason], *The Men Who Ruled India*, Vol. II, *The Guardians*, Jonathan Cape, London, 1965
Damien Wright, *Churchill's Secret War with Lenin: British and Commonwealth Military Intervention in the Russian Civil War, 1918-20*, Helion & Company, Solihull, 2017
Everard Wyrall, *The Die-Hards in the Great War*, 2 vols, Harrison & Sons, London, 1926
——, *The History of the Duke of Cornwall's Light Infantry 1914-1919*, Methuen & Co. Ltd, London, 1932
——, *The History of the King's Regiment*, Vol. I 1914-1915, E. Arnold, London, 1928; Vol. II, 1916-1918, E. Arnold, London, 1931
——, *The History of the Somerset Light Infantry (Prince Albert's) 1914-1919*, Methuen & Co. Ltd, London, 1927
H.C. Wylly, *History of the Queen's Royal Regiment*, Vol. II, Gale & Polden Ltd, Aldershot, [1923?]
——, *The Green Howards in the Great War*, The Yorkshire Regiment, [Richmond?], 1927

Thesis

M. Sundara Raj, 'Studies in the History of Prostitution in Tamilnadu', PhD, University of Madras, 1986

Index

People

Albery, Charles, 90
Aldington, Richard, 189
Allen, Charles, 99
Allen, Private, 76-77
Allenby, Edmund, 254
Ampthill, Lord, 106
Anderson, William, 288
Andrews, George, 31
Andrews, Harry, 31
Archer, William, 98
Armstrong, Allan, 192
Asquith, Herbert, 83
Astor, Waldorf, 105
Atkinson, Christopher, xvii, 44
Atkinson, Ernest, 210
Audrey, Neville, 223
Aylmer, Fenton, 144, 145

Bacon, Alban, xviii, 33, 40, 52, 82, 89, 103, 105, 183, 237
Bailey, Lance, 223
Bailey, Reg, xxii, 106, 152, 178, 187, 219, 228, 231, 257, 266, 267, 274, 280, 282, 290, 298, 299, 305
Bailey, Vivien, 223-24
Banks, Mitchell, 236
Barrett, Oswald, 122, 126
Barnet, Corelli, 55
Barrow, George, 51, 115, 238
Bartelt, Freidrich, 223, 322, 323
Barthorp, Michael, 301
Bathurst, Charles, 218
Beckett, Ian, 30, 281
Bell, Arthur, 123-124, 183, 207, 234
Bence-Jones, Mark, 152
Benyon, William, 248, 250

Beresford, Charles, 147
Berryman, Ted, 174
Besant, Annie, 283
Bethune, Edward, 27, 29, 36, 40, 43, 47
Bhurtpore, Rajah of, 103
Bissett, William, xxiii, 39, 94, 101, 142, 163, 174, 211, 213, 266-67, 277, 282, 283
Bithell, Len, 78, 159, 206, 218
Blick, George, xviii, 209
Board, Fred, 220
Bonar Law, Andrew, 83, 315
Bonham-Carter, Gerald, xxiii, 31, 164, 209, 234, 269, 270-71, 324
Bouverie, Jacob, see Radnor, Lord
Bowker, Esme, 138, 149, 155, 195, 311
Bowker, Francis, xxiii, 137-139, 141, 145, 155, 191, 193, 236
Braddon, Russell, 144
Bradfield, James, 209
Brain, Henry, 65, 92, 163, 199, 214, 313, 315
Bray, Albert, 132, 224, 292, 316
Brewer, Archie, 57, 62, 96
Broad, Henry, 174
Brown, Harry, 225
Brown, Private, 162
Brunger, William, 154, 194, 259
Burrell, Geoffrey, 78, 101, 138, 228, 269
Burt, Lance-Corporal, 213
Burton, Fred, 93
Butler, Harcourt, 229
Byford, Charles, 65, 259

Campbell-Bannerman, Henry, 27
Candler, Edmund, 146, 205
Canham, Harry, xxiii, 57, 63, 75, 76, 86, 94, 97, 101, 120, 132, 161, 176, 180, 190, 191, 205,

210, 226, 228, 253, 257, 267, 272, 274, 277, 307, 318, 324
Caroe, Olaf, xxiii, 89, 101, 118, 155, 180, 187, 306
Cawsey, Richard, 216
Cecil, Robert, 262
Chamberlain, Austen, 105, 142, 143
Chant, Ernest, 319
Chapman, Stanley, 293
Chapple, Herbert, 103, 179, 185, 228
Chaudhuri, Nirad, 169
Chelmsford, Frederick, 203
Chelmsford, Lord, 152-53, 193, 203, 229, 267, 280, 284, 297, 312
Churchill, Winston, 39, 276, 281, 316
Clark, C. Douglas, 309
Clinker, Charles, 40, 95, 311
Clutterbuck, Hugh, 212
Coates, Everard, 84, 191
Cockroft, Edward, 222, 223-24, 322, 323
Collett, Nigel, 289
Collingham, Lizzie, 213
Collins, Fanny, 195
Coombs, Geoffrey, 54, 60, 162, 182, 196, 317
Copeland, Arthur, 37, 47, 48, 70, 72, 85, 87, 92, 94-95, 159, 160, 172, 218, 227, 318, 324
Cornell, Arthur, 70, 178, 216, 318
Cox, Herbert, 278
Cox, Joe, xv-xvi, xix, 32, 62, 90, 132, 142, 163, 165, 271, 278, 292, 306, 324
Craske, Edward, 220
Creek, Hugh, xxiii, 66, 72, 80, 81, 90, 97, 99, 102, 121, 139, 141, 157, 182, 192, 212, 217, 219, 231
Crewe, Marquess of, 51, 55, 77, 79, 80, 110, 135, 137, 170
Crichton, Harry, 193
Cutler, Norman, 236
Curzon, Lord, 55, 134, 196, 229

Dell, Ethel M., 122
Dennis, Peter, 26, 39, 316
Derby, Lord, 257
Diver, Maud, 122
Dobell, Charles, 269
Docker, Arthur, 48
Donald, Colin, 43, 44, 47, 49, 155, 281, 315
Drayson, Alfred, 234-36
Duff, Beauchamp, 41, 51, 140, 147, 152, 153, 156, 227, 240, 241, 286

Duncan, Sarah Jeanette, 84, 191
Dunsterville, Lionel, 240, 262
Dyer, Reginald (Rex), 76-77, 85, 245-46, 288-89, 290, 291, 301, 304

Early, Oswald, xxiii, 95, 132, 173, 175, 182, 188, 220, 259, 285, 286, 290, 292, 296, 299, 305, 308, 309
Edward VIII, King, 25, 27, 29
Ellis, Charles, 97, 126, 261, 264, 265
Ellis, Frederick, 149
Ellis, Percy, 120, 126
Esher, Lord, 54
Evans, Herbert, 306
Ewens, Edward, 42-43, 48, 53, 108, 176, 186, 234, 271
Ewing, Herbert, xxiii, 39, 58, 63, 66, 72, 82, 84, 89, 130, 172, 182, 186, 187, 191, 209, 211, 215, 230, 242

Facey, Albert, 118
Falkenstein, Albert, 118-119, 299
Fiske, Elsie, 131, 178
Folkstone, Viscount, 31
Forster, E.M., 116, 125
Forster, Henry, 106, 149, 272
Foster, Arthur, 203
Fox, William, 131

Gale, Joseph, xix, xxiii, 66, 81, 83, 86, 92, 105, 278, 279
Gandhi, Mohandas, 226, 277, 285, 294, 295
Garrett, Arthur, 40, 112
George V, King, xvii, 36, 41, 68, 86, 226, 257, 271
Gibbs, Gerald, 48, 107, 190, 211
Gibson, Charles, 101, 205, 218
Gilmour, David, 51
Glanusk, Lord, 135, 223
Goodland, Stanley, xix, 38, 43, 47, 62, 102, 137, 204, 227, 246, 255, 270
Gosling, Walter, 130, 180
Gosse, Philip, 92, 101, 106, 182, 183, 225, 274
Gotobed, Bertram, 127, 128
Grant, Hamilton, 261, 295
Graves, Robert, 189-90
Green, Ernie, 136
Green, Stanley, 275, 276
Griffiths, Ronald, 249

Groucher, Alfred, 230, 260

Haldane, Richard, 26-29, 34, 39, 80, 82-83, 158
Hamilton, Ian, 30, 36, 37, 164
'Hampshire *Punch* clerk', 46, 49, 72, 74, 75, 80, 86, 125, 163, 217, 219, 222, 272
Harding, Ernest, 154
Harding, William, 154
Hardinge, Lord, 41, 51, 55, 68, 84, 87-88, 115, 135, 140, 142, 147, 152, 226, 241, 286
Harris, Lord, 272
Harris, Perce, 149, 221
Harrison, Percy, 105, 180
Hartnall, Archibald, 198
Harvey, Ralph, 236, 320
Haslewood, Roger, 32, 36, 46, 109, 110, 112
Hawkes, Gilbert, 136
Head, Ernest, 123, 198, 199, 200, 210
Heard, Thomas, xxiii, 61, 85, 103, 131, 132, 169, 197, 218
Herbert, Aubrey, 143, 144, 145
Hicken, Joseph, 307, 323
Hodge, William, 220
Hoggarth, Lawrence, 108
Holman, William, 113
Holter, Ted, 34, 40, 80, 87, 164, 203, 283, 307, 319
Hopkirk, Peter, 264
Horniman, Benjamin, 282, 283, 284, 285, 291
Howard, Henry, see Suffolk, Lord
Howgego, Reg, 96, 222, 249, 250, 252, 288, 293, 313
Hughes, William, 146
Hurd, Percy, 281

Iggulden, Henry, 175, 213
Iggulden, Herbert, 284
Irwin, Will, 251

Jeffery, Keith, 261
Johnson, Frank, 177, 188, 230, 238, 248, 249, 289, 299, 315
Johnson, Lt-Col (1/9th Hants), 276
Jupe, Adolphus, 188, 317, 320
Jupp, William, 139

Khalil Pasha, 147
Khan, Amir Amanullah, 295

Khan, Amir Habibullah, 295
Khan, Nadir, 301
Kipling, Rudyard, 65, 89, 122, 158, 237
Kipling, Spencer, 256
Kirkpatrick, George, 242, 283, 294
Kitchener, Lord, 36, 38-44, 45, 54, 55, 80, 86, 147, 155, 241, 243, 280, 315, 316
Kolchak, Alexander, 275

Lamplugh, Henry Rawstone, xxiii, 120, 122, 126, 252, 321
Lake, Percy, 140, 144
Latham, Peter, 125, 126, 256-57
Lloyd George, David, 45, 278, 289, 316
Lloyd, William, 136
Lovett, Verney, 286
Lucas, Private, 121, 174
Lutyens, Edwin, 51

Mackie, Jim, xix, xxiii, 33, 58, 59, 68, 74, 85, 93, 99, 115, 119, 158, 159, 168, 181, 207, 218, 228, 233-34, 256, 258, 270, 284
MacMillan, Douglas, 58, 62
MacMunn, George, 37, 168, 171, 289, 290, 304
Macpherson, 272
Macready, Neville, 278
Maffrey, John, 297
Malleson, Wilfred, 264
Mangan, Charles, 258
Manley, Victor, xxiii, 28, 47, 61, 83, 90, 92-93, 98, 100, 106, 123, 172, 180, 186, 255, 256, 317, 318
Mannering, John, 77, 80
Mannering, William, 155, 259
Marsh, John, 174
Marshall, William, 206, 256, 260, 261, 262, 264
Mason, Philip, 285
Matthews, Claud, 259, 263
Maude, Stanley, 201-06, 259, 261
May, Francis, 112
McArthur, James, 248-49
Meads, William, 276
Midleton, Viscount, 106
Mills, Christopher, xviii, xix, 308, 319
Mitchinson, Bill, 27, 270
Molesworth, George, 283, 298
Monro, Charles, 156-57, 167, 201, 203, 210, 248, 251, 260, 261, 269, 289, 298, 299, 304, 312

Monro, Mary, 184
Montagu, Edwin, 229, 267, 268, 281, 284, 285, 289, 293
Montagu of Beaulieu, 38, 59, 75, 246, 268, 281, 283, 297, 301
Moore, Robin, 289
Morris, Jan, 293
Mundy, Fred, xix, xxiii, 30, 39, 42, 43, 47, 85, 90, 99, 100-101, 141, 190, 225, 257, 322

Naish, Walter, 236
Nicholas, Ben, 110, 257
Nickalls, Leslie, 151, 157
Nixon, John, 108, 141
Nodder, Ruth, 220
Nureddin Pasha, 143, 147
Nute, William, 148

O'Dwyer, Michael, 261, 288, 293
Oke, Harry, 158
Owers, George, 92, 230, 270

Palin, Philip, 254
Palmer, George, 149
Palmer, Laura, title page
Palmer, Robert, xviii, xxiii, 31, 72, 84, 103, 130, 135, 140, 142, 143, 145, 146, 170, 173, 213, 216, 218, 221, 254, 311, 323
Paull, James, 234
Peacock, Private, 139
Peake, Herbert, 61, 131, 134, 160, 185, 212
Peel, Viscount, 272
Pinhey, Alexander, 66
Piper, Reginald, 149
Playfair, Frederick, 83
Pole-Carew, Reginald, 272, 279
Poore, Flora, 184
Povey, Henry, 136, 200

Radnor, Lord, 31, 49, 77, 88, 238
Ranjitsinhji, 51
'Rawlings', Sergeant, 287
Read, Edward, 164, 307, 319
Repington, Charles, 28, 42, 312
Rendall, Bert, 46, 47, 66, 95, 108, 131, 163, 185, 186, 257, 287, 291, 297, 307, 308, 312, 318
Rice, Ted, xxiii, 30, 38, 42, 60, 83, 99, 145, 164, 166, 168, 175, 184, 201, 203, 230, 259, 277, 317

Richards, Frank, 189
'Ridgewell' (cartoonist), 279, 314, 316
Ridout, Dudley, 112
Roberts, Lord, 28, 54
Robson, Brian, 248
Roos-Keppel, George, 295
Roper, John, 50, 62
'Rowland', Sergeant 287
Rowley, John, 112
Rumbold, Algernon, 271, 293
Rusbridge, Reuben, 87, 97, 175

Sanders, Harry, 195
Savarkar, Vinayak, 114
Saunders, Walter, 33, 35, 48, 182, 211
Savory, Reginald, 276
Say, Asaph, 223
Say, Fanny, 223, 309
Say, John, 223, 309
Scarrott, Cornelius, 195, 270, 316
Sclater, Henry, 289
Searle, Bernard, 82
Selborne, Earl of, 31, 79, 135, 170, 311, 323
Shaw, David, 106, 135
Shaw, George, 109
Sherwood, Marcella, 287
Skeen, Andrew, 304
Skinner, Douglas, 65, 179, 256
Smith, Drummer, 255
Smith, George, 234
Smith, Owen, xxiii, 53, 59, 62, 63, 84, 85, 89, 96, 97, 121, 126, 127, 132, 143, 145, 150, 155, 194, 202, 212, 213, 227, 242, 313, 317, 318, 324
Solomon, Francis, 98-99, 318
Solomon, Keith, 318
Sprawson, Cuthbert, 163, 166, 219
Stainer, John, 126
St Audries, Lord, 212
Stevenson, Don, 160
Stewart, James, 196, 200
Strange, Brigadier, 233
Strange, James, 306
Strutts, Elizabeth, 194, 256
Sturgess, Joseph, 266, 318
Sturmy-Cave, Thomas, 29, 259
Sturt, Alexander, 50, 65, 172, 215
Suffolk, Lord, 88, 203
Swift, Allan, xxiii, 41, 47, 58, 60, 62, 63, 65, 66, 67, 69, 90, 100, 183, 190

Swynnerton, Marjorie, 219, 222
Syddall, John, 90, 107, 108, 213

Tait, Mrs J.S., 184-85
Tharoor, Shashi, 55
Thomas, Molyneux, 52, 307, 323
Tilak, Bal Gangadhar, 171, 226
Townsend, Charles, 141, 148
Trefusis, John, 234
Twin, Ernest, 306

Villiers-Stuart, William, 191, 243-45, 324
Vyner, Pym, 160

Waddy, John, 236
Wadiyar IV, Krishna Raja, 177
Wallace, Edgar, 42
Wareham, Bertie, 271

Wathan, Gerald, 183
Wedgwood, Josiah, 227, 241
Wheat, Private, 183
Wignall, Fred, 82, 96, 99, 241, 242
Wilkinson, Percy, 154
Williams, E.V., 101
Williams, Rees, 136
Wilson, Henry, 261
Woodville, R. Caton, 172
Woodward, Elizabeth, 223
Woodward, Frank, 223
Woodyatt, Nigel, xviii, 45, 50, 70, 77, 168, 181, 230, 240, 243, 290, 298, 300, 322
Wright, George, 166
Wyrell, Everard, 258

Young, George, 110
Younger, Lord Justice, 147

Places

Abbreviations: Cd, Cumberland; Cl, Cornwall; Dv, Devon; Dt, Dorset; Hts Hampshire; Kt, Kent; L, London; M, Map; Mx, Middlesex; Sh, Shropshire; St, Somerset; Sx, Sussex; Sy, Surrey; W, Wales; Wd, Westmorland; Wts, Wiltshire.

Abadan, M5, 137
Abbottabad, M3, 191, 243-46, 255
Aberdeen (Andamans), 114
Abu Shitab, 129
Aden, M6, M7, 52, 106, 111, 123, 131, 134-37, 162, 174, 196-201, 210, 218, 287, 310, 315
Afghanistan, M7, 262, 294, 295-304
Afion, 148
Agra, M2, M3, M4, 63, 71, 80, 83, 84, 89, 96, 97, 99, 100, 101, 124, 126, 132, 156, 199, 212, 216, 224, 225, 227, 273, 290, 315, 322
Ahmednagar, M2, M3, 50, 62, 71, 166, 273
Aleppo, 148
Allahabad, M2, M3, 52, 68, 70, 80, 85, 87, 92, 168, 218, 227, 232, 273, 322
Alton (Hts), xv
Amara, M5, 221
Ambala, M2, 54, 59, 72, 82, 84, 87, 90, 121, 127, 132, 150, 151, 158, 170, 172, 186, 213, 216, 227, 260, 274, 291, 303, 307
Amritsar, xvii, M2, xvii, 90, 94, 95, 99, 100, 121, 183, 228, 277, 286-89, 291, 293, 295, 301
Andaman Islands, M7, 113-15, 172

Appleby (Wd), 192
Arab Village, 129
Arrah, M3, 231, 232, 233
Ashford (Kt), 32, 37, 96, 117, 192
Ashkabad, 264
Assam, M2, M3, 230
Attock, 209, 216, 292
Australia, 40, 42, 112-13, 152
Avebury (Wts), 93
Axminster (Wts), 192
Ayodyha, M2, 100

Baghdad, M5, 137, 159, 201, 203, 205, 209, 259
Baku, M7, 262
Baluchistan, M2, M7, M8, 81, 89, 90, 92, 93, 103, 123, 251, 252, 296, 298
Bangalore, M2, M3, 44, 59, 60, 92, 95, 96, 97, 104, 115, 119, 121, 123, 125, 126, 130, 131, 132, 175, 177, 178, 180, 183-86, 188, 194, 220, 230, 257, 269, 271, 273, 284
Bannu, M3, M8, 240, 252
Bareilly, M2, M3, 54, 69, 71, 85, 90, 98, 106, 132, 166, 187, 213, 220, 228, 230

Barrackpore, M2, M3, 68
Barry (W), 36
Basra, M5, 138, 139, 140, 143, 146, 201, 260, 307, 311
Bath (St), 93, 195, 258
Battersea (L), 48
Bawi, 203
Bengal, M2, 230
Belgaum, M3
Benares, M2, M7, 68, 91, 99, 100, 101, 232, 292, 322
Bexhill (Sx), 32, 270
Bhurtpur, M2, 103
Bihar, M2, 175, 230, 231-33, 253, 271
Bodmin (Cl), 37, 318
Bolan Pass, M8, 318
Bombay, M2, M3, 46, 49, 50, 52, 103, 104, 106, 116, 141, 161, 164, 165, 166, 170, 184, 191, 216, 226, 254, 271, 273, 274, 278, 305, 308
Bournemouth (Hts), 323
Bovington (Dt), 35
Brampton (Cd), 192
Brecon (W), 136
Bridgnorth (Sh), 36
Brighton (Sx), 209, 316
Burhan, M8, 246, 297
Burma, M2, 82, 103, 107-08, 166, 174, 212, 213, 222, 228, 229, 230, 234, 291, 321
Buxar, M3, 231, 232

Calcutta, M2, M3, M7, 49, 69, 96, 100, 102, 120, 122, 125, 127, 165, 169, 175, 181, 182, 184, 185,186, 212, 223, 234, 268, 273, 286
Calicut, M2, 74, 222, 228
Callington (Cl), 118
Campbellpore, M2, 209
Cannanore, M2, 165, 290
Canterbury (Kt), 46
Carlisle (Ca), 104
Caspian Sea, M7, 261, 262
Cawnpore, M2, 52, 68, 94, 99, 100, 101
Central Asia, 253, 261-62
Ceylon, M7, 205, 224
Chakrata, 83, 187, 198, 228
Chaman, 300, 304
Chasma Tangi, M2, 93, 151
Chaubattia, 90, 123, 225
Cherat, 86, 239, 267

Colaba, M3, 131, 307
Cologne, 259
Colombo, M7, 271
Coonoor, M2, 96, 131
Coorg, 273
Corston (St), 223, 323
Crater, The, M6, 197, 198
Croydon (Sy), 187, 319
Ctesiphon, 139, 143
Cyprus, 149

Dagshai, 83, 172, 241, 322
Dakka, M8, 298, 299
Dalhousie, 83, 102, 126, 179, 306
Dallington (Sx), 118
Darjeeling, 83, 91, 266, 267, 268, 318
Dehra Dun, 83, 228
Delhi, M2, M7, 44, 51, 58, 68, 71, 75, 81, 87, 88, 96, 99, 100, 101, 103, 106, 122, 127, 131, 152, 156, 170, 172, 174, 175, 177, 181, 182, 224, 266, 270, 273, 286, 290, 322
Deolali, M2, 220, 290, 292, 305, 306
Dera Ghazi Khan, M8, 251
Devonport (Dv), 36
Dharmsala, 243
Dinapore, M2, M3, 52, 53, 63, 68, 96, 175, 220, 223, 228, 233, 271, 322
Diyala, River, M5, 206
Dorchester (Dt), 32
Dover (Kt), 54
Dowlish Wake (St), 220
Dujaila, 146
Dum Dum, M2, 222
Dushak, 264

Eastbourne (Sx), 32
Egypt, 254-55, 304
Ekaterinburg, M7, 276
El Orah, 146
Epsom (Sy), 30
Euphrates, River, M5

Ferozepore, M2, M3, 52, 66, 72, 122, 151, 212, 216, 230, 231, 245, 270, 322
Folkestone (Kt), 68
Fort William, M3, 58, 169, 175, 212, 232
France, 257-59
Fyzabad, M2, M3, 52, 54, 58, 63, 65, 69, 71, 79, 100, 129, 151, 166, 227

Gallipoli, 33
Gaza, M7, 254, 256, 269, 270
Gibraltar, 42, 47
Glastonbury (St), 46
Gomal Pass, 248
Great Chart (Kt), M1, 32, 77, 154, 157, 179, 193, 220, 230, 256, 259
Guildford (Sy), 187, 270, 311
Gujrunwala, 291
Gumbaz, 251

Hamadan, 262
Hanna, 145
Hardwar, 228
Hassan Adal, M8, 298
Hatum, M6, 199
Hebbal Camp, 131
Henzada, 220
Hit, M5
Hong Kong, M7, 112, 257, 271, 275
Hyderabad, M2, 66, 307

Imad, M6, 197
Istabulat, 203
Istanbul, 149

Jalaphar, 83
Jamrud, M2, 237, 295, 302
Jandola, 249
Jebel Hamrin, 206
Jellalabad, M8, 29, 44, 269, 297
Jhansi, M2, M3, 163, 173, 184
Jhelum, M3, 303
Jubbulpore, M2, M3, 53, 58, 190, 198
Jullunder, M3, 104, 287
Jutogh, 83, 126, 236

Kaakha, 262
Kabul, M7, M8
Kachin Hills, M2, 108
Kailana, 85, 190, 241
Kamptee, M2, 65, 72, 77, 96, 153, 160
Karachi, M2, M3, M8, 49, 104, 105, 163, 165, 172, 179, 211, 270, 273, 292
Kasauli, 84, 85, 291
Kelantan, M7, 110-12
Kendal (Wd), 107, 128, 192
Keswick (Cd), 192
Khartoum, M7, 309

Khirgi Pass, 248
Khyber Pass, M8, 95, 246, 295-300, 302, 318
Kingston (Sy), 48, 311
Kingsway Camp, 131
Kirkee, M2, 54, 58, 156, 205, 218, 256, 323
Kohat, M3, M8, 301, 302
Kojack Pass, M8, 300
Kola, 184
Kota Bharu, M7, 111
Krasnovodsk, M7, 262
Kuldana, 66, 101, 118, 126
Kurdistan, 260
Kurram, M8, 296, 301
Kut-al-Amara, M5, 31, 129, 138, 139, 141-49, 201, 202, 221, 311

Lahore, M2, M3, M7, M8, 58, 68, 96, 103, 170, 171, 207, 216, 224, 226, 268, 273, 286, 287, 288, 291, 292
Lahej, M6, 106, 135-37, 196
Landi Kotal, 296
Lansdowne, 243
Leatherhead (Sy), 30, 316
Lebong, 83, 91, 105, 119, 131, 233
Lewes (Sx), 27
Liverpool (NSW), 113
Longparish (Hts), 236
Lucknow, M2, M3, 31, 38, 44, 68, 81, 99, 100, 101, 105, 123, 131, 142, 151, 176, 183, 210, 212, 230, 236

Maddur, M2, 177
Madras, M2, M3, M7, 58, 62, 104, 164, 273
Mahabaleshwar, 83
Maidstone (Kt), 96, 160
Maimet Khel, 249
Malappuram, M2, 68, 228, 229
Malling (Kt), 78, 79
Malmesbury (Wts), 223
Malta, 54
Mandalay, M3, 80, 107
Mansur, M6, 200
Mansuriyeh, 260
Margate (Kt), 68
Maymyo, 60, 90, 108, 128, 155, 164, 188, 213, 315
Meerut, M2, M3, 103, 131, 178, 216, 238, 318
Merv, M7, 263, 264
Meshed, M7, 263, 264

Mesopotamia, M5, 75, 132, 137-49, 174, 184, 191, 193, 201-06, 220, 221-22, 225, 234, 259, 269, 272, 283, 298, 304, 310, 311
Mhow, M2, M3, 52, 90, 166, 169, 193, 221, 222, 223, 274, 322
Mianeh, 262
Minehead (St), 38
Miran Shah, 251, 252
Mohammerah, M5
Mohmand Blockade Line, M8, 162, 240, 302-03
Mosul, M5, 148, 149, 206, 260, 309
Moulmein, 107
Mount Abu, 83
Multan, M8, 168, 268, 270, 274, 282, 290, 299
Murree, 83, 96, 187, 245, 249, 250
Mussoorie, 83
Muttra, M2, 63, 225, 226
Myitkyina, M2, 107, 228
Mysore, M2, 44, 177, 185, 230

Nagpur, M2, 143
Naini Tal, 83, 84, 130, 215, 222
Nanu, 250
Nasirabad, M3, 190
Nasiriya, M5, 139, 142, 206
Nebi Samwil, 256
Nejef, 206, 260
Newport (W), 36
Newton Abbott (Dv), 194, 195
Nowshera, M2, 63, 86, 93, 146, 150, 198, 242, 268, 299
Nushki, M2, 77

Omsk, M7, 275
Ootacamund, 83
Orissa, M2, 230

Palestine, 174, 192, 193, 254-57
Pasir Puteh, M7, 111
Pathankote, 151
Patna, M2, M3, 228, 231, 271
Paulton (St), 33
Penzance (Cl), 81
Persia, M7, 174, 206, 253, 259-60, 261-65, 277, 311
Peshawar, M2, 68, 76, 94, 97, 132, 138, 180, 215, 216, 228, 230, 237, 240, 241, 242, 268, 288, 296, 302

Pevensey (Sx), 32
Piro, M3, 231
Plassey, 49
Plymouth (Dv), 39, 43, 311
Pools of Siloam, 146
Poona, M2, M3, 50, 52, 58, 71, 92, 101, 105, 165-66, 171, 177, 189, 205, 216, 256, 266, 271, 274, 283, 319
Portchester (Hts), 266
Portsmouth (Hts), 31, 32, 40, 276, 308, 311, 313
Prome, 107
Punjab, M2, 52, 170, 172, 261, 290-92

Quetta, M2, M3, M8, 52, 76, 81, 82, 94, 100, 102, 104, 118, 130, 131, 161, 174, 178, 188, 266, 296
Qurna, M5, 137, 142

Radstock (St), 33
Rajputana, M2, 101
Ramadi, M5
Rangoon, M2, M3, 49, 58, 107, 109, 131, 163, 171, 188, 268, 273
Ras-al'Ain, 148
Rawalpindi, M2, M3, M8, 54, 66, 85, 87, 95, 101, 123, 127, 150, 156, 175, 185, 188, 190, 195, 215, 216, 220, 230, 240, 241, 250, 269, 298, 299, 315
Risalpur, M2, 296, 305
Robat, M2, 76
Rohri, M2, M8, 105
Roorkee, M2, 97, 243
Ross (Andamans), 119

Sa'na, M7, 200
Salisbury Plain (Wts), 34
Samarra, M5, 206, 260
Sangla Hill, 291
Sanna-i-yat, 129
Sassaram, M3, 232, 253
Sawakai, 248
Secunderabad, M2, M3, 53, 180, 215, 230
Seistan, M7, 76, 77, 288
Shahabad, M3, 231
Shaiba, 139
Shatt-el-Hai, 202, 206
Sheerness (Kt), 36
Sheikh Othman, M6, 136, 197, 198, 200

Sheikhpura, 291
Sheikh Sa'ad, M5, 144, 259
Shepton Mallet (St), 77, 175, 212, 220, 228
Shifnal (Sh), 32
Shrahraban, 209
Shrewsbury (Sh), 34, 36
Shumran, 202
Shwebo, M2, 107, 108, 163
Siberia, M7, 152, 274-76, 310
Simla, M2, 81, 83, 84, 105, 119, 126, 127, 156, 157, 182, 184, 191, 207, 213, 266, 299
Singapore, M7, 109-10, 112, 135, 271
Sinn, 129
Sittingbourne (Kt), 36
Small Dole (Sx), 195, 270, 316
Soissons, 258
Solon, 83, 84, 85, 151, 155, 191, 242, 303
Southampton (Hts), 32, 37, 45, 319
Spin Baldek, M8, 300-01, 304
Steamer Point, M6, 197, 198, 200
Stogumber (St), 274
Stonehenge (Wts), 93
Subathu, M2, 127, 209
Sultanabad, 263
Swansea (W), 221
Swindon (Wts), 32
Sydney (NSW), 113

Taj Mahal, M4, 101, 163, 318
Tank, 248, 250, 310
Taunton (St), 34, 47, 95, 144, 274

Thal, M8, 301, 304
Thayetmayo, M2, 108, 109
Tigris, River, M5, 138-47, 201-06, 211
Tikrit, M5, 206, 260
Totten (Hts), 38
Transcaspia, M7, 206, 263-65
Trowbridge (Wts), 195, 223, 309, 318
Tunbridge Wells (Kt), 117
Turkestan, 253, 263-65

Vladivostok, M7, 224, 271, 274-76

Wadi, The, 144, 145
Waht, M6, 196
Watchet (St), 233
Waziristan, M8, 130, 176, 222, 247, 248-51, 299, 304
Welch Ridge, 257
Wellington, M2, 58, 83, 131, 179, 215, 243
Wells (St), 46
Westbury (Wts), 149
Western Front, 34, 153-55
Widcombe (St), 87, 188
Winchester (Hts), 32, 33, 138, 149, 153, 195, 311, 323
Wye (Kt), 37

Yemen, 200
Yozgad, M7, 149, 221

Zinjan, 262, 311

Formations and units

Divisions, British
  2nd Territorial, 156; 8th, 27th, 28th, 29th, 48; 34th, 258; (42nd) East Lancashire, 29, 42; (43rd) Home Counties, 29, 42, 45; (44th) Wessex, 29, 42, 45, 49, 178, 254; (45th) 2nd Wessex, 29, 45, 54, 254; 62nd (West Riding), 258; 63rd (Royal Naval), 257; 75th, 254-57
Divisions, Indian
  1st, 252; 2nd, 252; 4th, 298; 6th, 137; 7th, 238; 14th, 144, 206; 15th, 201, 206
Baluchis, 130th, 109
Bedfordshire Regiment, 158
Border Regiment, xx, 29, 82, 103, 235, 315, 320; Battalions: 1st, 188; 1/4th, 32, 45, 60, 71, 72, 82-83, 90, 104, 107, 108, 109, 128, 154, 155, 160, 164, 165, 186, 188, 213, 228, 272, 315; 2/4th, xxiii, 32, 45, 52, 57, 75, 76, 86, 94, 96, 97, 99, 105, 120, 126, 132, 143, 161, 162, 176, 177, 180, 191, 204, 205, 210, 224, 226, 228, 237, 240, 242, 252, 253, 257, 268, 270, 272, 273, 274, 274, 280, 295, 296, 299, 302, 303, 318
Brecknockshire Battalion, xx, 29; 1/1st, 45, 52, 120, 135-37, 151, 166, 184, 193, 197, 200, 221, 222-24, 272, 274, 307, 315, 323
Buffs (East Kent), xx, 32, 78, 154, 196; Battalions: 1/4th, xxii, 37, 39, 54, 60, 68, 98, 106, 127, 142, 152, 162, 166, 182, 187, 195, 196-97, 219, 228, 230, 231, 257, 260,

266, 268, 272, 274, 280, 282, 290, 298, 299, 305, 317; 1/5th, 48, 65, 72, 77, 80, 82, 96, 132, 143, 144, 145, 146, 153, 154, 155, 160, 178, 179, 194, 201, 203, 206, 228, 259, 306; 1/6th, 154

Calcutta Scottish, 69, 181
Camceronians, 187
Cavalry (Indian), 8th, 173; 21st, 172; 28th, 264
Cornwall (Duke of Cornwall's Light Infantry), xx, 37, 44, 316, 319, 320; Battalions: 1/4th, xxiii, 44, 61, 118, 131, 149, 160, 176, 187, 197-98, 213, 220, 224, 234, 254, 292, 307, 318; 2/4th, 71, 270, 272
Cossipore Artillery Volunteers, 186

Devonshire Regiment, xx, 41, 44, 318; Battalions: 1/4th, xxiii, 49, 52, 66, 72, 79, 80, 81, 90, 102, 113, 119, 125, 131, 132, 139, 141, 144, 151, 152, 157, 170, 179, 182, 192, 201, 202, 205, 206, 217, 218, 219, 228, 231, 296; 1/5th, 254, 256, 259; 1/6th, 144, 146, 161, 176, 194, 202, 206, 315; 2/4th, 48, 254, 255, 256; 2/5th, 254, 256; 2/6th, 157, 161, 162, 176, 209
Dorsetshire Regiment, xx, 49, 65, 127, 161, 201, 316; Battalions: 1/4th, 32, 36, 49, 50, 62, 70, 129, 201, 206, 210; 2/4th, 48, 50, 54, 77, 157, 161, 213, 254, 255, 256
Duke of Cambridge's Own (Middlesex Regiment), see Middlesex Regiment
Duke of Cornwall's Light Infantry, see Cornwall
Duke of Wellington's Regiment, 1st, 190, 250, 300-01
Durham Light Infantry, 259

East Kent Regiment, see Buffs
East Surrey Regiment, xx, 46, 54, 150, 187, 189, 190, 208, 242, 311, 316, 319; Battalions: 1/5th, xxiii, 30, 31, 48, 63, 89, 118, 119, 127, 160, 163, 166, 191, 225, 236, 260, 306, 316, 319, 320; 1/6th, xxiii, 27, 34, 40, 41, 45, 47, 58, 60, 62, 63, 65, 66, 67, 69, 79, 89, 90, 92, 100, 107, 123, 125, 127, 139, 150, 164, 175, 183, 190, 198-200, 210, 214, 234, 236, 240, 242, 250, 272, 273, 290, 310, 312, 313, 315

Garhwal Rifles, 174, 270

Green Howards, 1st, 240
Gurkhas: 1/5th, 191, 244; 1/9th, 202, 288; 2/2nd, 238

Hampshire Regiment, xx, 29, 33, 35, 76, 104, 168, 190, 201, 259, 266, 291, 311, 318, 321; Battalions: 1/4th, xxiii, 32, 33, 78, 83, 87, 101, 137-49, 155, 179, 188, 191, 195, 201, 202, 203, 204, 206, 213, 221, 228, 236, 259, 260, 262-64, 269, 272, 306, 310, 311, 313, 319; 1/5th, 31, 32, 37, 49, 50, 52, 54, 68, 70, 71, 72, 85, 86, 87, 92, 94, 95, 103, 104, 108, 137, 138, 150, 156, 159, 160, 170, 172, 174, 218, 219, 233, 272, 291, 301, 302, 303; 1/6th, xxiii, 37, 40, 52, 53, 59, 62, 63, 71, 78, 84, 85, 89, 90, 95, 96, 97, 120, 126, 127, 132, 135, 140, 144, 146, 150, 151, 155, 161, 188, 191, 194, 202, 212, 218, 220, 228, 242, 260, 307, 311, 313, 317, 318; 1/7th, 29, 32, 38, 47, 52, 127, 128, 129, 188, 200-01, 237, 272, 310; 1/9th, 33, 57, 62, 94, 96, 101, 127, 129, 132, 152, 156, 158, 159, 174, 175, 178, 182, 188, 220, 224, 245, 265, 271, 272, 274-75, 285, 286, 290, 292, 296, 299, 305, 306, 308, 309, 313, 319; 2/4th, xxiii, 28, 35, 39, 47, 52, 53, 82, 83, 90, 92, 93, 94, 99, 100, 102, 103, 105, 121, 122, 130, 141, 142, 152, 162, 163, 166, 172, 174, 188, 211, 214, 216, 236, 242, 254, 255, 256, 266, 267; 2/5th, 53, 63, 66, 71, 81, 123, 125, 126, 151, 153, 188, 254, 256; 2/6th, 86, 106; 2/7th, 59, 202, 206, 260, 281
Hampshire Yeomanry, 31
Hertfordshire Yeomanry, 226
Highland Light Infantry, 260
'Huffs', 145

Infantry, 17th, 233
Infantry, 97th, 145

Kent Cyclist Battalion
 1/1st, xxiii, 64, 82, 93, 95, 97, 120, 126, 130, 158, 159, 177, 179, 180, 189, 214, 215, 245, 251, 252, 267, 272, 286, 290, 291, 293, 295, 302, 319, 320, 321
King's Liverpool Regiment, 243, 299
King's Shropshire Light Infantry, see Shropshire

Lancers, 21st, 226

Light Infantry, 5th, 109-10, 135
London Regiment, xx
    1/25th, 32, 90, 95, 96, 120, 122, 126, 157, 158, 178, 222, 248-49, 260, 287-89, 290, 293, 298, 301, 304, 313, 317

Mahrattas, 114th, 138
Malay States Guides, 110-11, 135
Middlesex Regiment, xx, 29, 33, 35, 42, 48, 72, 76; Battalions: 1/9th, 36, 41, 47, 72, 104, 115, 127, 129, 150, 183, 206, 228, 245-46, 250, 260, 306; 1/10th, 33, 34, 35, 41, 48, 59, 102, 107, 120, 125, 126, 151, 157, 175, 192, 211, 212, 213, 265, 272; 25th, 112, 275

Nepalese army
    Mahindra Dal, 238
Norfolk, 2nd, 139, 143, 202
North Staffordshire Regiment; Battalions: 2nd, 187, 191, 240; 7th, 163, 165, 214

Oxfordshire & Buckinghamshire Light Infantry, 50; 1st Garrison Bn, 118

Prince Albert's (Somerset Light Infantry), see Somerset Light Infantry
Punjabis
    19th, 264; 84th, 240; 89th, 72, 228

Queen's Own (Royal West Kent Regiment), see West Kent
Queen's (Royal West Surrey) Regiment, see West Surrey

Rajputs, 7th, 172
Rifle Brigade, 287; Battalions: 18th, 115; 24th, 270
Royal Army Medical Corps, 173, 183
Royal Artillery, 28, 87, 111, 203
    Territorial Artillery, 61, 194, 201, 310, 327; Devon, 68, 185, 198, 228; Dorset, 126, 166; Hampshire, 52, 68, 137, 138, 142, 143, 148, 197; Home Counties, 34, 40, 87, 142; Surrey, 87, 97, 175; Sussex, 32, 92, 144, 151, 190, 203, 230, 270; Wessex, 103, 186, 203; 2nd Wessex, 87, 300; Wiltshire, 32, 68, 88, 103, 203, 254
Royal Flying Corps, 211

Royal Sussex Regiment, xx; Battalions: 1st, 53; 2/6th, 95, 44, 101, 118, 120, 122, 127, 158, 159, 161, 171, 172, 175, 177, 179, 183, 188, 213, 230, 234, 239-40, 247, 248-50, 287-89, 299, 301, 304, 306, 310, 315
Royal Welsh Fusiliers, 189-90

Shropshire (King's Shropshire Light Infantry), xx, 157, 321; 1/4th, 32, 34, 36, 40, 45, 46, 49, 71, 107, 109-13, 257-58
Sikhs: 14th, 254; 35th, 240; 36th, 202; 45th, 202
Somerset Light Infantry, xviii, xx, 33, 44, 91, 176, 222, 269, 320; Battalions: 2nd, 296, 297; 1/4th, xviii, 39, 58, 62, 86, 146, 152, 201, 206, 213, 240, 260, 281, 296; 1/5th, xviii, xxiii, 38, 39, 43, 46, 47, 53, 54, 58, 62, 63, 65, 66, 72, 82, 84, 89, 90, 102, 120, 130, 137, 140, 151, 173, 178, 182, 186, 187, 191, 192, 204, 215, 230, 238, 242, 246, 254, 255, 256, 270, 320; 2/4th, 33, 39, 58, 60, 74, 93, 95, 100, 107, 113-15, 119, 140, 157, 158, 162, 168, 175, 181, 195, 205, 207, 209, 212, 218, 223, 228, 229, 233, 234, 236, 244, 253, 255, 256, 258, 259, 269, 270, 309; 2/5th, 39, 42-43, 47, 48, 48, 53, 68, 85, 108, 120, 140, 151, 166, 169, 176, 182, 186, 190, 232-34, 271, 272, 284, 308; 1st Garrison Bn, 286
South Lancashire, 1st, 299
South Wales Borderers, xx, 135, 323
4th, 221
South Wales Borderers, see also Brecknockshire
Supply & Transport Corps, 172

Territorial Force Nursing Service, 220

West Kent (Queen's Own (Royal West Kent Regiment)), xx, xxiii, 44, 103, 184, 186, 187, 234, 268, 269; Battalions: 1st, 134; 2nd, 190, 191, 260; 1/4th, 25, 40, 174, 164, 190, 196, 272, 300-01, 304, 320; 1/5th, 25, 40, 48, 139, 158, 173, 195, 209, 234, 242, 260, 269, 277, 309, 316
West Surrey (Queen's (Royal West Surrey) Regiment, xx, 25, 40, 75, 105, 156, 175, 207, 230, 234, 311
1/4th, 75, 158, 236, 249, 252, 273, 291, 299, 302; 1/5th, xv, xxiii, 30, 32, 38, 42, 51, 52, 60, 61, 63, 83, 129, 131, 134, 139, 142, 145,

147, 166, 168, 184, 185, 201, 203, 206, 212, 230, 242, 259, 260, 270, 316

Wiltshire Regiment (Duke of Edinburgh's), xx, 31, 43, 102, 211; Battalions: 1/4th, xix, xxiii, 30, 31, 34, 35, 39, 42, 43, 44, 47, 49, 50, 54, 61, 68, 75, 81, 82, 85, 88, 90, 100, 101, 106, 117-18, 127, 141, 149, 152, 153, 156, 161, 177, 181, 190, 192, 195, 209, 218, 225, 238, 241, 243, 254, 256, 309, 310, 322, 323, 324; 2/4th, xviii, xxiii, 50, 52, 58, 66, 77, 84, 85, 92, 102, 105, 106, 159, 181, 195, 206, 216, 223, 232-34, 272, 318

General

Abbreviations, xxii
Amritsar massacre, xvii, 286-89
Armistice, 271-72
Art, 123-25
Artillery, 254
Army in India, 54-56,

Badges, regimental, 29, 269
Bazaars, see 'Sudder bazaars'

Campaigns
   Aden, 134-37, 196-201
   Afghanistan, 295-304
   Bihar, 231-34
   Kelantan, 110-112
   Mahsud, 248-51
   Mesopotamia, 75, 132, 137-49, 174, 184, 191, 193, 201-06, 220, 221-22, 225, 234, 259-60, 269, 272, 283, 298, 304, 310, 311 137-49
   Mohmand, 302-03
   Persia, 206, 261-63
   Siberia, 274-76
   Transcaspia, 206, 263-65, 311
   Turkestan, 163-65
   Waziristan, 248-51
Cantonments, structure, M4, 58-59
Cartoons, 98, 173, 314
Casualties, 309-11
Concert parties, 127-29
Cyclist units, 32, 158-59

Demobilisation, 277-84, 305-09, 311-15
Death, 118, 220-24, 309-11

'Flag marches', 230
'flu, see Influenza
Followers, 59-60, 178-80
Food, 67, 125, 211-14
Funerals, 221-22156,

Health, 54, 58, 65, 114-15, 214-17
   Dental, 218-19
   Mental, 219-20
Hill stations, 83-85
Hunting, 101-103

'Internal security', 41, 42, 55-56, 86-88, 113-14, 115-16, 225-34
Indian Army, 68-69, 172-74
   Bureaucracy, 60, 74-75
Indian Mutiny, 28, 44, 99-100, 113, 130-31
Indian National Congress, 226-29, 284-86, 286-94
Indians, relations with
   Barrack servants and followers, 60-65, 178-80
   Brutality toward, 178-80
   Assaults by, 179-80
   Indian civilians, 121, 168-69, 174-80, 230-31
   Indian nationalists, 170-72
   Sepoys, 172-74
   Women, 178
Influenza, 273-74
'Internal Security', 225-34

Jallianwalla Bagh, see Amritsar massacre

Kitchener's 'promise', 43-44, 153-55
Kitchener's Test, 70-74, 150-51, 234

'Loosewallahs', 66-68

Magazines, 120-25
Malaria, see Health
Medals, 43, 300, 315
Military Service Act, 157-58
Memoirs, xviii, 324
Mesopotamia Commission, 143, 204-05, 238, 241, 317
Monro Canteens, 156

Monsoon, 85-86
Mortality, see Death
Mosquitoes, see Health
Motor Transport, 76-77, 246-48, 297
Mountain Warfare Schools, 173, 240-48
Museums, xviii, 222, 320-21
Mutiny, see Indian Mutiny

Nationalism, see Indian National Congress
North-West frontier, 238-52

Palestine, 254-57
Photography, 93-96, 105
Prisoners of War, 147-49
Prostitution, 162-67
Punjab crisis, 290-94

Railways, 52, 103-106
'Rangoon fever', 114
Regimental titles, xx-xxi
Royal Air Force, 259, 285, 305
Royal Army Temperance Association, 79, 128, 131, 162

Sex, 162-67, 178
Ships
  Alaunia, 48; *Almara*, 47; *Alnwick Castle*, 47; *Assaye*, 50; *Caledonia*, 47; *Cawdor Castle*, 47; *China*, 308; *City of Marseille*, 49; *Desado*, 46; *Dilwara*, 47; *Dongola*, 47; *Edavana*, 109; *Grantully Castle*, 47; HMS *Hampshire*, 155; *Ionian*, 48; *Kenilworth Castle*, 47, 49; *Montoro*, 112; *Royal George*, 48; *Stephan*, 308; *Uganda*, 112, *Walmer Castle*, 257
Shwe Dagon pagoda, 107, 318
Sind Troop Train Tragedy, 105-06
Snakes, 65-66
Soldiers' Homes, 59, 131, 150
Spin Baldek, attack on, 300-01
Sudder bazaars, 60, 64

Territorial Army, 315-16
Territorial Force
  arrival in India, 49-50, 51, 52-54
  artillery, 28, 32, 34, 40, 41, 52, 61, 68, 87, 88, 92, 97, 103, 126, 137, 138, 142, 143, 144, 148, 151, 166, 175, 185, 186, 190, 194, 197, 198, 201, 203, 228, 230, 254, 270, 310, 300
  Associations, 26-29, 192-93
  camps, 27, 30
  cemeteries, 310, 322-24
  commemoration of, 309, 317, 323
  composition and character, xv, 29, 30-34, 37-38, 40-41, 50
  changes during war, 39, 269-71
  commissions, 207-11
  concert parties, 127-29, 185,
  British civilians, relations with, 181-86, 192-95
  crafts, 82
  culture, 120-25
  demobilisation, see repatriation
  discipline, 159-62
  drinking, 132, 154, 162
  duties, 57-58
  grievances, 77-80, 213-14, 266-68
  hot weather, 80-83
  Imperial Service, 39-43
  Indian languages, 96-99, 318, 314, 317
  Indians, relations with, 54, 59-61, 80-81, 121, 168-80
  interest in Indian culture, 89-93
  magazines, 120-25
  memories of India, 316-19
  mobilisation (1914), 34-36
  music-making, 125-26, 185
  officers, 30-31, 38, 207-11, 234-37
  origins, 25-30
  pay, 67
  pets, 151-52
  photography, 93-96
  purpose, 29-30,
  reading and writing, 121-25
  Regulars, relations with, 28, 47, 53-54, 59, 82, 187-92, 238
  reinforcements, 225-26
  religion, 59, 129-33, 169
  repatriation, 277-84, 305-09
  re-unions, 319-20
  prisoners of war, 147-49
  purpose in Britain, 26
  purpose in India, see Internal Security
  and sex, 162-67, 178
  and sport, 117-20, 177
  units, relations between, 186-88
  units, titles, xxi
  as tourists in India, 90-91, 94-96, 99-101, 319

training, 70-74, 117, 150-51, 151-52, 234, 238-40, 253-54
  transfers, 75-77, 158
  uniforms, 57, 79, 160
  voyages to India
Thal, battle of, 301
Technology, 244-45, 246, 251
Tourism, 99-101
Tradition, regimental, 29, 43-44

Venereal Disease, 164-67
Volunteer force, 25
Voyages to India, 45-49

Weapons, 29, 71, 87-88, 246
Western Front, 43, 48, 153-55, 257-59

YMCA, 59, 97, 131, 164, 166